UNDERSTANDING THE
FOURTH GOSPEL

UNDERSTANDING THE FOURTH GOSPEL

❋

John Ashton

CLARENDON PRESS · OXFORD

Oxford University Press, Walton Street, Oxford OX2 6DP
Oxford New York Toronto
Delhi Bombay Calcutta Madras Karachi
Kuala Lumpur Singapore Hong Kong Tokyo
Nairobi Dar es Salaam Cape Town
Melbourne Auckland Madrid
and associated companies in
Berlin Ibadan

Oxford is a trade mark of Oxford University Press

Published in the United States
by Oxford University Press Inc., New York

© John Ashton 1991
First published 1991
First issued in paperback 1993

British Library Cataloguing in Publication Data
Ashton, John 1931–
Understanding the Fourth Gospel.
1. Bible. N. T. John — Critical studies
I. Title
226.506
ISBN 0-19-8263538 (pbk)

Library of Congress Cataloging in Publication Data
Ashton, John, 1931–
Understanding the Fourth Gospel
Includes bibliographical references and index.
1. Bible. N. T. John — Criticism, interpretation, etc. I. Title.
BS2615.2.A74   1991   226.5 06—dc20   90-43422
ISBN 0-19-826353-8 (pbk)

Printed in Great Britain
on acid-free paper by
Bookcraft (Bath) Ltd
Midsomer Norton

To my friends
at the Universities of London,
St Andrews, Edinburgh,
and Oxford

Un état dangereux: croire comprendre

Paul Valéry

Begeisterung ohne Verstand
ist unnütz und gefährlich

Novalis

ACKNOWLEDGEMENTS

After my teacher Xavier Léon-Dufour, to whom I owe the dawning realization that there is more in John's Gospel than meets the eye, my first debt is to the many friends who, sometimes without knowing it, encouraged me to embark upon the writing of this book at a time, nearly ten years ago, when I had lost confidence in myself: James Bradley, Robert Butterworth, Dick Caplice, Tom Chetwynd, Peter and Margaret Hebblethwaite, Maurice Keane, Judy Leon, Andrew and Beryl Murray, Rosemary Sharpe, Lois and Donald MacKinnon, Robert Murray. Once the project was under way, some of these, especially the last two, assisted me by offering a variety of shrewd observations on what I had written by the middle of 1981. Not long after that John Bowden, James Crampsey, and Christopher Evans gave me further encouragement, although I am uneasily aware that the last-named disapproves of what he regards as my excessive use of adjectives as well as of sentences beginning with 'But'. At about the same time Douglas Templeton, whose own lapidary style all too successfully masks a keen understanding of the earliest Christian writers, made other helpful comments, and un-mixed some of my metaphors.

In 1984 I joined the Faculty of Theology at Oxford, since when I have benefited from the experience of Wilma Minty at the TFL, who was constantly turning up new books and articles on the Fourth Gospel, and from the generous assistance of Doreen Abrams and Jane Pusey at the Faculty Office. I am especially grateful to Berna-dette O'Reilly, who, in 1988, transcribed on to floppy discs well over half an already bulky manuscript, and to Alicia Gardner, who added another chapter the following year. I should also like to thank the staff of Bodley's Lower Reading Room for their virtually limitless patience, and those members of the Oxford University Press whose collective talents have contributed so much to making this book look as a book should, notably Katy Douglas, who also suggested the design on the cover, and above all Heather Watson, who eliminated innumerable blemishes, and whose skill as a copy-editor has left me lost in admiration. I am indebted to Margaret Barker for many

stimulating telephone conversations, and to John Hyman for his unwavering interest and support.

The extent of my debt to Rudolf Bultmann will be obvious to any
reader, and I am grateful to Basil Blackwell for permission to use and
cite the English translation of his commentary, published in 1971.
J. L. Martyn has also kindly allowed me to quote from his *History and
Theology in the Fourth Gospel.* The extract from *The Apocalypse of
Abraham* printed on pp. 143–4 is taken from *The Old Testament
Pseudepigrapha,* edited by J. H. Charlesworth, published and copy-
right 1983 by Darton, Longman, and Todd Ltd. and Doubleday and
Co., and is used by permission of the publishers.

Finally I should like to thank the friends and colleagues who read
the manuscript when it was nearing completion, and helped me to
improve it in a variety of ways: Mark Goodacre, my severest critic;
Clare Palmer, who thinks that the book should be called *From Points
to Stars*; Robert Morgan, for steering me sternly away from stylistic
aberrations; Peter Coxon, for hunting up some rabbinical references.
My greatest debt is to Robert Murray, whose benign shadow has
been hovering over this book $\dot{a}\pi$’ $\dot{a}\rho\chi\hat{\eta}s$, and whose valuable advice
made it possible for me to introduce a number of last-minute
corrections. Had I been able to follow up all his suggestions this
would have been a better book, and a more interesting one. But this
simply means that there is more work to be done.

Oxford
April, 1990

CONTENTS

ABBREVIATIONS

Standard abbreviations for biblical books and the Dead Sea Scrolls are not included.

ANRW	*Auftstieg und Niedergang der Römischen Welt*
Ant. Bib.	Pseudo-Philo, *Liber Antiquitatum Biblicarum*
Apoc. Abr.	*Apocalypse of Abraham*
b.	Babylonian Talmud
2 Bar.	*Syriac Apocalypse of Baruch*
Barn.	*Letter of Barnabas*
BASOR	*Bulletin of the American Schools of Oriental Research*
Bib	*Biblica*
BJRL	*Bulletin of the John Rylands Library*
BZ	*Biblische Zeitschrift*
CBQ	*Catholic Biblical Quarterly*
CII	*Corpus Inscriptionum Iudaicarum*
1 Clem.	*1 Clement*
1, 2, 3, Enoch	*Ethiopic, Slavonic, Hebrew Enoch*
Ep. Arist.	*Epistle of Aristeas*
ET	English translation
ETL	*Ephemerides theologicae lovanienses*
Eusebius, *HE*	*Historia Ecclesiastica*
EvT	*Evangelische Theologie*
ExpT	*Expository Times*
Gen. Rab.	*Midrash Genesis Rabbah*
Hermas, *Sim.*	Shepherd of Hermas, *Parables*
Vis.	*Visions*
HeyJ	*Heythrop Journal*
Hippolytus, *Ref.*	*Refutatio omnium haeresium*
HTR	*Harvard Theological Review*
HUCA	*Hebrew Union College Annual*
ICC	International Critical Commentary
IGRR	*Inscriptiones Graecae ad Res Romanas Pertinentes*, ed. R. Cagnat *et al.*

Int.	*Interpretation*
JBL	*Journal of Biblical Literature*
J. Eccl. Hist.	*Journal of Ecclesiastical History*
JNES	*Journal of Near Eastern Studies*
Jos. As.	*Joseph and Aseneth*
Josephus, AJ	*Antiquitates Judaicae*
BJ	*De Bello Judaico*
Vita	*Vita Josephi*
JR	*Journal of Religion*
JSJ	*Journal for the Study of Judaism in the Persian, Hellenistic and Roman Period*
JSNT	*Journal for the Study of the New Testament*
JSP	*Journal for the Study of the Pseudepigrapha*
JSS	*Journal of Semitic Studies*
JTS	*Journal of Theological Studies*
Jub.	*Jubilees*
Justin, Apol.	*Apology*
Dial.	*Dialogue with Trypho*
KuD	*Kerygma and Dogma*
m. Ber.	*Mishnah Berakoth*
m. Ḥag.	*Ḥagigah*
m. Sanh.	*Sanhedrin*
m. Yad.	*Yadayim*
Mek.	*Mekilta de-Rabbi Ishmael*
MT	Masoretic Text
NRT	*Nouvelle Revue Théologique*
NT	*Novum Testamentum*
NTS	New Testament Studies
OTPs	Old Testament Pseudepigrapha, ed. J. H. Charlesworth
OTS	*Oudtestamentische Studiën*
PG	*Patrologia Graeca*
Philo, Quod Omn. Prob.	*Quod Omnis Probus Liber Sit*
Spec. Leg.	*De Specialibus Legibus*
PL	*Patrologia Latina*
Pss. Sol.	*Psalms of Solomon*
RB	*Revue biblique*
RGG	*Religion in Geschichte und Gegenwart*

RHE	*Revue d'histoire ecclésiastique*
RHR	*Revue de l'histoire des religions*
RScR	*Recherches de Science Religieuse*
RSR	*Religious Studies Review*
Sib. Or.	*Sibylline Oracles*
Sif. Deut.	*Midrash Sifre on Deuteronomy*
Num.	*on Numbers*
Sifra	*Midrash Sifra on Leviticus*
Str.–B.	Strack–Billerbeck
SuppVT	*Supplements to Vetus Testamentum*
T. Abr.	*Testament of Abraham*
T. Jud.	*Testament of Juda*, etc.
Test. Mos.	*Testament (= Assumption) of Moses*
ThDNT	*Theological Dictionary of the New Testament*
ThDOT	*Theological Dictionary of the Old Testament*
TLS	*Times Literary Supplement*
TLZ	*Theologische Literaturzeitung*
TRu	*Theologische Rundschau*
TU	*Texte und Untersuchungen*
TZ	*Theologische Zeitschrift*
v.l.	*varia lectio*
ZNW	*Zeitschrift für die neutestamentliche Wissenschaft*
ZTK	*Zeitschrift für Theologie und Kirche*

PART I

QUESTIONS AND ANSWERS

INTRODUCTION

Approaches and Perspectives

There are many ways of approaching the Fourth Gospel. One may turn to it for enlightenment, for inspiration, for encouragement or consolation, for theological proofs (the old-fashioned rod-and-line exegesis), for evidence about early Jewish Christianity, for insight into the mind of Jesus, and much more besides. One may approach the work as an historian, a theologian, a simple Christian, or an enquiring unbeliever. What the Gospel reveals of itself will be coloured, even controlled, by the interest one brings to it. There is no disinterested reading.[1] Nor, by the same token, is there any disinterested writing; and anyone picking up a book on the Gospel, especially one that is neither a commentary nor, in the ordinary sense, a monograph, may reasonably expect its author to declare some interest from the outset. This book is academic. But is its approach primarily historical, theological, a mixture of both, or something entirely different? What, in other words, is the nature of its understanding?

In the opening chapter, I want to move into this question by scrutinizing some previous attempts to explain the Gospel, asking in each case from what perspective the explanation is being attempted. One reason why this is a useful method of proceeding is that 'the Johannine problem' is not one but many, and when tackling it commentators are sometimes convinced that they have pinned it down without realizing that in another of its protean shapes it may have eluded them altogether.

If the survey attempted in the first part of this book is to be profitable it must also be methodical, and so it will be helpful before embarking on it to offer a few preliminary methodological observations.

---

[1] With John's Gospel we are also deep in what Hugh Kenner calls 'the whispering forest of all traditional poetries, where the very words to which millions of minds respond have helped to form the minds that respond to them' (*The Pound Era* (London, 1972), p. 521). But to examine this truth any further would involve questions of high hermeneutics beyond the scope of this book.

The range of questions that may be asked concerning any literary composition, fact or fiction, art or science, is virtually limitless. Nevertheless it is possible to describe four circles of enquiry within which all conceivable questions must fall. Provisionally we may name these (1) content; (2) author; (3) readers; (4) the work itself.[2] Put schematically in a diagram, these can be organized in the following way: the *work itself* occupies the centre of the page, with *author* and *readers* on either side. Arrows pointing from both author and readers towards the work indicate that the nature of the work is determined from two directions. The fourth circle, *content*, may be placed anywhere on the periphery of the page. In a three-dimensional model it would probably cover the surface of the sphere, with the work itself at the centre.

Now if we take our stand within each of these four circles in turn and attempt to draw up a preliminary list of questions concerning the Gospel, we immediately find ourselves in difficulties. For of none of the four circles can it be said that there is any consensus, perhaps not even the possibility of one, concerning what or whom we are dealing with.

1. What is the Gospel's *content*? Does it belong in the realm of fact or imagination or even of myth? Have we to do with speculative thinking in a religious vein, as in Philo, say, or even Plato, or is the work closer to mysticism? If it is primarily a speculative or mystical work, then its universe will be light years from history, maybe in a different galaxy. But is it not concerned with a historical personage, Jesus of Nazareth, known by the author to have been a Galilean Jew who 'suffered under Pontius Pilate'? What is the Gospel attempting to reflect or describe, a man, a god, an event, or an idea?

2. Who was its *author*? Is he to be identified in the first place with the apostle John, son of Zebedee and brother of James, as was

---

[2] Early drafts of this chapter began with an outline of four approaches to literary theory that are distinguished in M. H. Abrams's impressive study, *The Mirror and the Lamp*: mimetic, pragmatic, expressive, and objective, each of which is particularly associated with one or other of our four circles. It was pointed out to me, however (by Christopher Evans), that since I was clearly unable to render Abrams's categories serviceable without a good deal of chopping and changing I had best abandon this procrustean bed and start independently afresh. In doing so, however, I wish to signal my indebtedness to Abrams's illuminating account.

traditionally held, and as many people even today continue to believe? If not, was he nevertheless an eyewitness of the events he describes, an old man, perhaps, rummaging in his memories?[3] Or was he another John entirely, John the Presbyter, mentioned by Clement of Alexandria, or John Mark, who figures in Acts as an assistant of Paul?[4] Is he the unnamed 'beloved disciple' of the Gospel, the recipient of Jesus' most intimate confidences, and if so, is it possible to give him a name—if not John, what about Lazarus?[5] It has even been suggested, and argued with great ingenuity, that one of the Gospel's part-authors was the evangelist Luke, not completely satisfied with his own work and anxious to edit the work of another along the right lines.[6] Yet another suggestion is the Alexandrian Apollos, Paul's arch-rival at Corinth.[7] Again, one can ask where the author came from. Was he, if not a Palestinian Jew, a native of Ephesus (there is at least a strong tradition that he died there) or Antioch or Alexandria? Was he Greek or was he Jewish (or perhaps Samaritan), when did he write, and what was his native language, Aramaic or Greek?[8] Was he a churchman, interested in institutions and ritual, especially sacramental, or did he advocate a new kind of worship, one not tied to particular forms or places?

3. What kind of *readers* did the writer have in mind? He seems to have written for people who needed to be told the significance of the

[3] This is the picture that dominates Robert Browning's fascinating poem *A Death in the Desert*, which was in fact quoted by Westcott (p. xxiv, n. 1) 16 years after its publication in 1864, and then by many other commentators since (including Hoskyns and Bultmann). For a 'scholarly' view along the same lines, less imaginative but more far-fetched, see G. Hoffmann, *Das Johannesevangelium ein Alterswerk*.

[4] Perhaps the most implausible of the early attributions is that of the Roman presbyter Gaius, who claimed that the Gospel was the work of the Gnostic Cerinthus.

[5] A surprising number of scholars have maintained this: F. V. Filson, K. A. Eckhardt, J. N. Sanders.

[6] M.-É. Boismard, 'Saint Luc'. An alternative explanation of the sometimes quite striking resemblances between John and Luke has been defended by J. A. Bailey, *Traditions*. Bailey maintains that John borrowed from Luke. I have even heard it argued, in a public lecture by Michael Goulder, that the author was a follower of Paul, subtly suggesting to his readers that the 'beloved disciple' was really his own master and hero. Friedmar Kemper ('Zur literarischen Gestalt') has proposed the equally novel theory that the author was a Roman Jew, working during the reign of Nero and taking advantage of the relaxed atmosphere consequent upon the Empress Poppaea's well-known sympathy for things Jewish.

[7] As has been urged most recently by Simone Pétrement in *Le Dieu séparé*.

[8] It has actually been maintained (by D. D. Runes) that the Gospel as we have it is a Greek translation of a Hebrew original composed by an eyewitness of all he records.

word *Messiah* (1: 41) and of names like *Siloam* (9: 7). On the other
hand, he was prepared to give the 'Hebrew' version of Greek terms
meaning 'pavement' (19: 13) or 'the place of the skull' (19: 17). But
if his audience read and presumably spoke Greek, were they native
Greeks, whatever their city, or Jews of the diaspora, who had lost all
familiarity with Hebrew or Aramaic? These questions rapidly lead to
others that are directly bound up with the purpose of the book. Most
crucially, was it written primarily for the encouragement, edification, or instruction of Christian converts, or was the writer thinking
of non-Christians whom he wished to attract to the new faith, pagan
Greeks, Jews of the diaspora, or (partially at any rate) Samaritans?
Did he have a particular audience in mind, or did he intend his work
to be, like that of Thucydides, a κτῆμα ἐς αἰεί, a possession for all
time?[9] If the book was intended for Christian readers, especially ones
belonging to a particular community (the author's own), were they
acquainted with any or all of the Synoptic Gospels, and if so was the
Gospel designed to supplement these or to supplant them? And in
any case, what kind of Christians were they? What was their
situation?

4. What kind of *work* is it? A gospel, yes (this is the only question
in this long list to which there is but a single, universally agreed
answer). But then what is a gospel? (Informed that Dante's *Commedia* or Milton's *Paradise Lost* was an epic, how much would a person
acquainted only with the *Iliad* or the *Aeneid* then know about it?) In
particular, is a gospel history or theology, neither or both? Does
Martin Kähler's famous definition (description) of a gospel as 'a
passion-narrative with an extended introduction'[10] fit the Fourth
Gospel? Should not rather any genre be defined in terms of aim and
audience? In that case we are returning by another route to some of
the questions already listed under (3). And if we think such
questions pointless without a close examination of the work itself,
how are we to approach it? Are we to proceed as if it were a single,
unified composition, projecting a coherent, easily identified point of
view, or is it a book with a history, which has been subjected to
revisions and reworkings, and has perhaps gone through a number
of different editions which need to be identified if the work is to be
properly understood? Should it be examined in other words (to use

---

[9] As C. K. Barrett expressly affirms: 'John was ... writing theology in a book that
was to be a possession for ever' (*Prologue*, p. 24).

[10] *Historical Jesus*, p. 80 n. 11.

modern jargon) synchronically or diachronically? What can be learned from a study of its structure and/or its style?

Now at least two conclusions can be drawn even before any answers are attempted to this list of questions. The first is that there is a considerable overlap between the questions placed under the four headings, so that any given answer to questions from one group may entail certain answers to questions from another. For instance any definite and single answer to the questions of group 3 (readers) would greatly facilitate answers to some of the questions of group 4 (work). (But then might it not be necessary to answer the questions of the latter group first?) The second conclusion, obvious enough, is that even if it were possible to answer all the questions thoroughly and satisfactorily it would take an even longer book than this one to do so. So for the sake of interest and of brevity (if only relative) one must be selective.

Because of these uncertainties the study of the Fourth Gospel is necessarily beset with more problems than that of the majority of literary compositions. In investigating a play by Sophocles or Shakespeare we already know who the author is, the genre of his work, and its intended audience; we may even be already quite well-informed about its content. Here the four circles offer reasonably secure and familiar starting-points. In the case of the Fourth Gospel, however, we find ourselves in the situation of a dog casting around for a scent or of a cat warily treading down a likely spot before she is prepared to settle. A surprising number of questions on our list are of this kind—what biblical scholars call *Einleitungsfragen*, introductory questions: preliminary chartings or soundings that have to be undertaken before the vessel can get under way.

In the following three chapters I shall explore each of the four circles twice, first in order to see how the various questions were formulated in the early years of the critical study of the Gospel, and the second time with a view to assessing the present state of Johannine studies. The change of nomenclature between Chapters 1 and 3 is intended to indicate the shift in interest which took place within each of the circles as scholarship progressed. It proved convenient, the second time round, to reverse the order in which each of these is examined. For instance, although I begin with

questions about the aims and readership of the Gospel, consideration
of more recent questions concerning the situation and circumstances of the readers is deferred until the concluding section of
Chapter 3.

The central chapter of this first part will be devoted to a
consideration and criticism of the contribution of Rudolf Bultmann.
Those who are familiar with his work are unlikely to need persuad-
ing that it constitutes a watershed in the history of Johannine
scholarship. But it will also be seen that he virtually ignored one
particular area of enquiry. The filling of this gap has marked the
most significant advance in Johannine studies in the latter half of the
twentieth century.

I

BEFORE BULTMANN

I. AIMS AND AUDIENCE

Nowadays students approaching one of the books of the Bible for the first time are expected to ask themselves whilst reading it what were the author's aims, what audience he was addressing, and what was their situation. In the early years of critical scholarship interest in such questions was much less widespread than it is today, but in the case of the Fourth Gospel three additional reasons may be suggested why they were largely ignored. In the first place, the author states his own intentions very firmly and (one might think) unambiguously towards the end of the book: 'these [signs] are written that you may believe that Jesus is the Christ, the Son of God, and that believing you may have life in his name' (20: 31).[1] In the second place, the Gospel conveys a rare impression of self-containedness. 'It seems right', remarks C. K. Barrett, 'to emphasize a certain detachment of the gospel from its immediate surrounding; no book ever was less a party tract than John.'[2] Even if this opinion cannot be accepted unreservedly one can see what Barrett means. The message of the Fourth Gospel is so patently sublime, the writing so calmly self-assured, that it seems almost sacrilegious to take to this 'spiritual Gospel', as Clement of Alexandria called it, the finely meshed net of critical scholarship and then to pin it down for close and scientific examination. And the various explanations offered of this spiritual quality (myth, allegory, mysticism) tended to reinforce the view that its purposes were somehow remote from the everyday cares of mankind. In the third place, the Fourth Gospel is so different from the other three that questions concerning its aim often ran along a single track: what relation did it have to the Synoptic Gospels and in particular was it designed as a supplement or as a replacement? This

---

[1] As late as 1959 C. F. D. Moule, arguing that the Gospel is a missionary work, directed primarily to outsiders, bases his case solely upon an exegesis of this verse: 'Intention', p. 168.　　　　　　　　　　　　　　　　[2] *Gospel*[1] p. 115.

question itself depended upon the dominant consensus that John actually made use of the other Gospels whilst composing his own. Only when this consensus was challenged and the wind shifted to another quarter did scholars feel free to question John's purposes with no reference at all to the Synoptists.[3]

At the same time it must be stressed that these are broad generalizations to which there are many notable exceptions. As early as 1820 Carolus Theophilus (Karl Gottlieb) Bretschneider 'modestly submitted to the judgement of scholars' what he called 'theses concerning the character and origin of the gospel and letters of the apostle John'.[4] Bretschneider explicitly rejected the view that the Gospel was written to supplement and emend the other three; he also cites the opinion of a certain Storrius who had published a book in 1786 arguing that the Gospel was written against the followers of John the Baptist (a view which was to be taken up and defended at some length over a century later by W. Baldensperger)[5] as well as against Cerinthus and Gnostics in general (an opinion borrowed from Irenaeus, Bishop of Lyons in the second century). Bretschneider himself saw a resemblance in the Gospel to the apologetic writings of Justin Martyr, another second-century writer:[6]

The Fourth Gospel appears to have been composed in the same historical context; its apologetic and polemical purpose is plain to see; it seems to have been published partly in order to defend the person and teaching of Jesus from contemporary criticisms, partly with an eye to Greeks (who might be disturbed by such attacks) to convince them of the religion of Jesus and his story and to dispose them favourably towards Christianity. ... It is more an apologia than a work of history, and its author assumed the role of a polemicist rather than of a historian. Hence (1) the frequent clashes between Jesus and the Jewish Scribes, whom he calls Jews (οἱ 'Ιουδαῖοι) to distinguish them from the people (λαός) or the crowd (ὄχλος); (2) all those debates; (3) the foolishness of the Jews, who always misunderstand Jesus' words; a foolishness the author was really using to depict the stubborn objections of Jewish adversaries *of his own day*; (4) the debates and doctrinal

---

[3] This did not occur until the publication, in 1938, of P. Gardner-Smith's *Saint John and the Synoptic Gospels*, whose thesis that John made no direct use of any of the other three Gospels still commands a wide measure of assent. Two years earlier E. C. Colwell was putting forward the contrary view: *John Defends the Gospel*. See too E. K. Lee, 'St. Mark and the Fourth Gospel'; S. Mendner, 'Zum Problem'; J. Blinzler, *Johannes und die Synoptiker*. For a good summary discussion of the various views see D. Moody Smith, 'John and the Synoptics'.

[4] *Probabilia.*   [5] *Prolog.*

[6] An opinion shared by Albert Schweitzer, *Mysticism*, p. 351.

sections (*dogmata*), which concerned controversies not between Jesus and the Pharisees but between Christians and Jews of the second century.[7]

Bretschneider's remarkable little book, containing many insights that were not properly followed up until much later, created a storm of controversy at the time and provoked a series of refutations from theologians anxious to defend the apostolic authorship of the Gospel. When the dust had settled, some four years later, Bretschneider, somewhat disingenuously one suspects, declared himself satisfied with the opposing arguments his book had elicited; indeed, he said, he had written it in the first place precisely in order to stimulate such a response.[8] But the fact is that the Christian world was simply not equipped at the time to cope with his suggestions or to absorb them into its own orthodoxy.

Much later (1861), in the course of a somewhat complex article that set out to reconcile the two most ancient views of the purpose of the Gospel—(*a*) to refute heretics and (*b*) to complement the other Gospels—M. von Aberle introduced into his argument (for the first time, as far as I am aware) a discussion of the famous 'Blessing against Heretics' (ברכת המינים), long thought to have been inserted by the rabbinic academy of Yavneh (Jamnia) into the prayer of the Eighteen Benedictions with Christians in mind. This little passage was to be a crucial element over a century later in the important work of J. L. Martyn, *History and Theology in the Fourth Gospel* (1968). In general one is surprised to see the extent to which the ideas and arguments of subsequent scholarship were anticipated by nineteenth-century exegetes and theologians. Aberle concludes his article with these words: 'John's Gospel is the letter of repudiation (*Absagebrief*) addressed to restored [i.e. post AD 70] Judaism, which was already beginning to direct against the young Church all the weapons with which it was later to attempt to arrest her victorious march through the centuries.[9]

Of those commentators who have been struck by the anti-Jewish strain in the Gospel one of the most interesting is Carl von Weizsäcker. To him John's hostility appeared so pervasive and intense that he believed it had to be taken into account in any interpretation of the *meaning* of the Gospel. Writing in 1864 under

---

[7] *Probabilia*, pp. 118 f.
[8] *Tschirners Magazin für chr. Prediger*, 2 (1824), p. 153. Quoted by M. Goguel, *Introduction*, ii. 23.
[9] 'Zweck', p. 94.

the liberating influence of F. C. Baur, he had already abandoned the
idea of apostolic authorship. None the less the evangelist was a
disciple of the apostle and his work was written under his aegis if not
under his direction. But his soul had been seared by his treatment at
the hands of the Jews, which had left him convinced that 'of all the
enemies of Christianity the Jews are the most malevolent'. This deep-
seated conviction could not but colour his own version of the story of
Jesus. Consequently the motif of 'the guilt and blindness, the
incredulity and selfishness of the Jews dominates the gospel narratives so powerfully that one can only conclude either that this was
written directly against the Jews or else that the author's account
was controlled by personal recollections'.[10]

The same theme was taken up at the beginning of this century by
William Wrede, who when writing on John showed a characteristically robust disregard of prevailing pieties. He specifically rejects the
thesis that the Gospel was written to complement the other three,
pointing out that it contains a great deal of the same material. The
view that its purpose is purely didactic (teaching about Christ) also
falls short of the truth: 'rather any historical understanding depends
upon taking the Gospel as arising out of and written for a polemical
situation.'[11] Who then is the enemy? Why, Judaism, of course. Far
from being the cloudy visionary he appears to many, the evangelist
is a tough-minded apologist, the forerunner of Justin Martyr; though
Wrede admits that formally speaking (*formell*) he addresses his
Gospel not to his adversaries or to the public at large, but to the
Christian community—as can be seen above all from the farewell
discourse. Read in this way, suggests Wrede, the Gospel takes on a
completely fresh look. No doubt one's understanding is helped by
some insight into its doctrinal concerns: 'but in the midst of all these
dogmatic propositions and formulae what really allows us to discern
the true fulcrum (*Hebel*) of the Gospel is an acknowledgement of its
polemical thrust. In a word, from being a timeless meditation, the
Gospel becomes a writing that belongs to a particular period, has a
particular situation in view and is written for a particular purpose.'[12]

It is to be noted that both Weizsäcker and Wrede address
themselves more directly to the question of personality and experience of the evangelist than to that of the situation of the community

[10] *Untersuchungen*, p. 187.   [11] *Charakter*, p. 40.   [12] Ibid., p. 67.

for which he was writing. Even so what they have to say about the Gospel's aims and intentions cannot be lightly dismissed: they rank among the most intelligent and perspicacious commentators of their age. Yet their thesis, at any rate Wrede's version of it, is difficult to swallow whole because of its peculiarly bitter flavour. Wrede allows that the Gospel was written with a Christian readership in mind; but his almost totally negative view of the evangelist's purposes scarcely does justice to the text—especially when one thinks of the four chapters that comprise the farewell discourse and prayer.

Rather less than thirty years later a completely different interpretation of the same evidence was propounded by Karl Bornhäuser in a book whose title sufficiently indicates its thesis: *Das Johannesevangelium: Eine Missionsschrift für Israel* (1928). At first blush the suggestion that the Gospel was written to attract Jewish converts is just as one-sided and even less plausible than Wrede's; but Bornhäuser does at least attempt to distinguish between different senses of the word Ἰουδαῖοι, recognizing in particular that the Jews of the diaspora cannot be identified *tout court* with the Jews of Judaea. Out of six possible meanings (he really means references) of Ἰουδαῖοι he finds five in the Fourth Gospel. One of these, which he regards as especially characteristic, is close to a view that I shall myself be defending later. According to this they are 'Torah fanatics who are at the same time *inquisitors* whose job it is to watch over the law [*das Recht*] and to rectify and punish any infringement'.[13] Bornhäuser's thesis is not fully worked out, but it does at least approach an explanation of the curious fact that John's Gospel is at once the most Jewish and the most anti-Jewish of the four. There is already a suggestion that the origins of the Johannine community are to be sought in the milieu of Jewish sectarianism and that important clues towards an understanding of the Gospel may be found in the context of internal dissensions within contemporary Judaism. This is a question that will engage our attention in Chapter 4.

But is the Gospel actually directed to Jews, of whatever colour or persuasion? Does it not have a certain universalistic ring ('other sheep I have that are not of this fold'), which points to an even more far-flung audience than the Jewish communities scattered around the Eastern Mediterranean could provide? Wilhelm Oehler thought so, and defended his position in a book whose title is once again self-

[13] *Johannesevangelium*, p. 141.

explanatory: *Das Johannesevangelium: Eine Missionsschrift für die Welt* (1936). Anticipating to some extent the views of C. H. Dodd, he argued that the novelty of the Gospel's phraseology and conceptual apparatus must be put down to a desire to make the new religion accessible to readers of a Hellenistic cast of mind. In a second book with a very similar title, published five years later, he reinforces this argument. 'Either', he says, 'the Gospel has been so strongly influenced by foreign thinking that the best of it grew upon foreign soil; or else the close convergence of its language and style with the world around it serves more or less consciously a missionary purpose. The preaching of the gospel has adopted this form so as to win Greeks and Hellenists, that is the world in general, over to Christ, in such a way that its content is neither diminished nor impaired.'[14]

To maintain this view Oehler has somehow to account for the farewell discourse (in which he includes chapters 15–17 but not chapter 14), because this was clearly written for Christian converts. He takes it to be 'an extract from the apostle's preaching to the community'; the rest of the Gospel, which he sees as essentially self-contained, can only be properly understood, he says, as a missionary work.

Reading (or reading of) these early attempts to assess why and for whom the Fourth Gospel was composed, one may be pardoned for feeling somewhat confused. Each of the various theories has a certain plausibility, yet none is entirely convincing. In particular, none gives a satisfactory explanation of the farewell discourse— manifestly composed with the situation of the writer's own community in mind.[15] The problem is how to give full weight to this circumstance without abandoning the insights of scholars such as Wrede and Oehler who for one reason or another feel it necessary to exclude this important section from their total explanation. We shall see that Bultmann's way of treating this problem is to transcend it altogether. But this may seem more of an evasion than a solution.

In general it may be said that the search for what some writers, following Willi Marxsen, have called the *Sitz-im-Leben-des-Evangeliums*

---

[14] *Missionscharakter*, pp. 11 f.

[15] The 3rd edition of H. J. Holtzmann's commentary (1908) is the first to include a section on the purpose of the Gospel. It is not primarily a polemical work but is addressed to Christians with a view to strengthening their faith: the rebuttal of Jewish criticisms is a secondary aim.

did not begin in earnest until the advent of redaction criticism in the 1950s. Directed primarily towards determining the 'life-situation' of the Synoptic Gospels, this new exegetical style certainly helped to inaugurate another phase of Johannine studies also.

2. AUTHORSHIP AND ORIGINS

The question of authorship was the Johannine question *par excellence* throughout most of the period under discussion. As late as 1973, introducing a collection of essays of various periods on *Johannes und sein Evangelium*, K. H. Rengstorf is still prepared to define the Johannine question as 'the question concerning the real author of John's Gospel'.[16] Why then did this question dominate Johannine scholarship for so long? For surely the Gospel poses many more interesting and important problems than the puzzle of its authorship. The reason is simple: if the author of the Gospel should turn out to be someone other than the apostle John or the beloved disciple (the two were generally identified), then the credibility of his testimony, on which the Gospel itself insists so strongly ('He who saw it has borne witness—his testimony is true, and he knows that he tells the truth' (19: 35)), must be severely reduced, if not destroyed completely.[17] Of course those who held that the Gospel was neither history nor biography but something utterly different were for the most part unperturbed by the suggestion that the author was not after all an eyewitness of the events he describes. In fact the so-called 'liberal' or 'radical' theologians felt more at ease when they could dismiss as non-Johannine fabrications stories such as the marriage-feast of Cana and the raising of Lazarus.

One of the earliest to contest the Johannine authorship of the

---

[16] p. xiv.

[17] From the vantage-point of later scholarship it may be hard to see how two questions that appear to us so evidently distinct, and whose distinctness had been argued by F. C. Baur as long ago as 1847, could ever have been thought joined together by an indissoluble bond. But even in 1925 the Dominican M.-J. Lagrange insisted that whereas it would make little difference if the second Gospel were suddenly discovered to have been written not by Mark but by Silas, 'the Fourth Gospel would lose all its authority if it were proved not to have been the work of an eyewitness' (p. xi). Two years later, perhaps a little prematurely, Vincent Taylor, not a radical scholar by any means, found seven points on which there was general agreement concerning the Gospel, the last of which was 'that the authorship is not apostolic' ('Fourth Gospel', p. 728).

Gospel was the Unitarian Edward Evanson, sometime Vicar of Tewkesbury, whose aggressive little book (1792) opens with the affirmation that 'after all that has been said and written upon the subject, those Evangelical histories contain such gross, irreconcileable contradictions that no close reasoning, unprejudiced mind can admit the truth and authenticity of them all', and continues by rejecting as spurious all the Gospels except that of Luke. Evanson huffs and puffs a good deal over the marriage-feast of Cana: whoever, he says,

has observed how utterly incompatible every degree of sensual excess is with the Gospel precepts of sobriety, temperance, moderation, and the subjection of our bodily appetites to reason and religious duty, will find such a miracle as this incredible, though it had been recorded in all the four histories, and coming in so very exceptionable a form, upon the single, unsupported testimony of so very exceptionable an historian, it is altogether as unworthy of belief as the fabulous Roman Catholic legend of St. Nicholas's Chickens, of later times. To St. Luke's credit ... he does not tell us of our Lord's changing so much as one firkin of water into wine on that charitable occasion, though, here, he is said to transmute eighteen firkins for the use of those jovial topers of Cana.[18]

A little earlier, referring to the passage in which Jesus is said to have baptized in greater numbers than John (4: 1), Evanson comments: 'This passage is so replete with the most palpable falsehood, that it is astonishing how any kind of delusion should have induced creatures endowed with reason so long to have received it as the word of truth and the work of an apostle of Jesus Christ.'[19]

But for all Evanson's solemn strictures it was a long time before 'creatures endowed with reason' arrived at even the broadest consensus concerning the non-apostolic authorship of the Gospel, and when they did so it was not because of the arguments advanced with such portentous pedantry by the ex-Vicar of Tewkesbury.

The German rationalists soon joined in the hunt; and so we have works by Vogel (1801–4), Horst (1808), and of course Bretschneider (1820), all contesting apostolic authorship. The great theologian Schleiermacher resisted this trend, arguing that John's

---

[18] *Dissonance*, p. 241.

[19] Ibid., p. 226. In the fourth of his *Four Discourses on the Miracles of our Saviour* (London, 1728) Thomas Woolston had suggested that both Jesus and his mother probably got drunk at the Cana wedding-party. (Woolston was convicted of blasphemy the following year and died in gaol in 1733.)

portrait of Jesus was no less credible than the Socrates of Plato or Xenophon. But then came the powerful challenges of David Friedrich Strauss (1835) and Ferdinand Christian Baur (1844/7), whose arguments in the long run were to win the day.[20] (Since, however, both of these writers were more concerned with the nature and content of the Gospel than with the question of authorship as such, we may postpone our consideration of them until later.)

For over two decades the only German scholars continuing to deny the apostolic authorship of the Gospel were, like Weizsäcker, disciples of Baur. Gradually, however, the question of authenticity was detached from that of historical reliability. Some of Baur's more extreme views (especially his very late dating of the Gospel) were abandoned, whilst the defenders of apostolic authorship came to acknowledge the evangelist's responsibility for a certain reorganization (*Umbildung*) of his historical material. In a survey lecture delivered in 1889, Emil Schürer concluded that 'the mark of present-day scholarship is the gradual convergence of opposing positions'.[21]

Had this lecture been given much later, Schürer would have been forced to take into account the advent of a new school of radical historical criticism which would eventually focus attention upon a different and much more important question than authorship—that of the *origins* of the Gospel. But it would be a long time before this, the so-called 'history-of-religions school' (*religionsgeschichtliche Schule*) was to make any headway at all outside Germany.

It is true that Alfred Loisy, in France, formally acknowledged the shift of interest at the very beginning of his great commentary (1903). He notes that the question of authorship is of less significance than that of the origins of the Gospel, 'one of the most serious problems to have been raised by modern criticism'.[22] Nevertheless in the course of his long (150-page) introduction he says disappointingly little on the question of origins: in point of fact he confuses it with the question of authorship and spends a lot of time arguing that the beloved disciple is not a historical personage but a *type*. Eventually he defines the problem as one of establishing 'the relationship

---

[20] In fact Strauss wavered somewhat in his views on the inauthenticity of the Gospel. See his preface to the 3rd edition of his *Leben Jesu* (Tübingen, 1838): 'Not that I have been convinced of its authenticity; it is just that I am no longer convinced of its inauthenticity' (p. v).

[21] E. Schürer, 'Über den gegenwärtigen Stand', p. 10. For the information in the last two paragraphs I am also indebted to W. G. Kümmel, *The New Testament: History*, Part III, ch. 2. [22] p. 1.

between the witness of the book itself and that borne by the tradition';[23] and then he concludes rather hastily by conjecturing that the author was a Hellenistic Jew acquainted before his conversion with the ideas of Philo.

Meanwhile scholars shy and bold, radical and conservative, continued to play the same old game, knocking the familiar texts back and forth as if across an invisible net.[24] Symptomatic of this general trend is one of a series of survey articles written by A. Meyer for a new German periodical, *Theologische Rundschau*, between 1899 and 1906. In his contribution for 1902 he canvasses the views of more than a dozen authors who had expressed their opinions in print, some more than once, in the previous two years on the question of the authenticity and authorship of the Gospel.[25]

In Britain and America it was a similar story. B. F. Westcott opens his famous commentary (1880) with a chapter on 'the authorship of the Gospel', in which he undertakes to prove successively that the author was (*a*) a Jew, (*b*) a Jew of Palestine, (*c*) an eyewitness, (*d*) an Apostle, and finally (*e*) St John. A quarter of a century later, in a work entitled *The Fourth Gospel, its Purpose and Theology* (1906) E. F. Scott managed to move away from the question of authorship so as to focus, as Baur had advised long before, upon the spiritual content of the book; but a few years later the great American scholar B. W. Bacon, far from conservative in his general outlook, could say: 'Since the problem of the Fourth Gospel *is no longer a problem of date, but of authorship*, the main question to be determined by the indirect internal evidence will be that of the personality reflected in the work, and with this is inextricably bound up that of the figure, elsewhere unknown, of "the disciple whom Jesus loved".'[26]

Again, on opening H. Latimer Jackson's *The Problem of the Fourth Gospel* (1918) we soon learn that for him too the Johannine problem

[23] p. 130.

[24] Even today these old shuttlecocks are still fetched out, as commentaries on the Fourth Gospel continue to appear, and hit somewhat dispiritedly from one side of the court to the other. Small wonder that, used unchanged for so long, they have a somewhat ragged appearance.

[25] 'Johanneische Literatur', pp. 316–33.

[26] *The Fourth Gospel*, p. 301 (my italics). Bacon concludes, following Scholten (and of course Loisy), that the beloved disciple is 'a purely ideal figure' (p. 320). Yet as late as 1986 S. S. Smalley asserts that he has 'found no convincing reason to deny that the beloved disciple was John the son of Zebedee, one of the twelve, and that his initial witness brought the Fourth Gospel to birth' ('St. John's Gospel', p. 103).

comprises first of all 'questions relating to the authorship and historicity of the book'.[27]

Now it may seem that the shift of interest from authorship to origins is not, after all, particularly momentous. For in both cases we are concerned to enquire when and where the Gospel had its beginnings. In fact, however, the two questions belong to different worlds of discourse. In the first place, a decision for apostolic authorship could be seen as a sufficient explanation in itself of the *content* of the Gospel ('he has seen—and his testimony is true'); however strange and sublime the teaching of the Gospel, its truth was guaranteed by its source—the personal testimony of an eyewitness, the best loved of Jesus' disciples and the one most privy to his secrets. Some writers, notably Lagrange, felt it necessary to hold fast to this opinion at all costs: to abandon it was equivalent to destroying the Gospel's authority and thus entailed the loss of a most precious witness to the life and teaching of Jesus. But not all scholars, even those of a conservative bent, felt obliged to cling so tenaciously to apostolic authorship: a certain flexibility was still possible. Suppose for instance one were to maintain, with Weizsäcker, that the author wrote under the watchful eye of the apostle John but adjusted the story slightly in order to accommodate his own bitter feelings towards the Jews who had maltreated him. Or suppose that the author was incorporating into his account his own vision of what the message of Jesus had come to mean, a vision simply not accessible to Jesus' own contemporaries. Such suggestions as these could be assimilated fairly easily by traditional theology. First, however, it had to relinquish the theory of the direct verbal inspiration of the four evangelists and accept instead the idea of a gradually unfolding revelation under the guidance of the Holy Spirit[28]—who, according to the Gospel itself was to lead the disciples into all truth after Jesus' departure to the Father (16: 13).

So Lagrange notwithstanding[29] all these new ideas could flourish

---

[27] *Problem*, p. 2.

[28] It is worth noting that one of Bultmann's strongest reasons for abandoning the approach of traditional (which for him would mean 'liberal') theology in favour of that of the history-of-religions school was his detestation of this concept of unfolding revelation. He was himself a pupil of Johannes Weiss, Hermann Gunkel, and Wilhelm Heitmüller, all leading members of the school.

[29] Without questioning Lagrange's integrity, one may wonder how far his views were influenced by the pronouncements of the Biblical Commission set up by Pius X in 1904 as a bastion against the encroachments of modernism. In a reply dated 29 May

[*cont. on p. 20*]

quietly within the ambit of traditional Christian teaching. That is to say, they could be readily assimilated by anyone who saw the Christ-event and all that surrounds it, especially the writings of the New Testament, as the result of the direct intervention of God in human history. In other words, it was still possible to contain the new ideas within a theology of salvation-history, whether this was conceived as existing somehow alongside ordinary human history or as an epiphenomenon floating upon it.[30] In this way the exegete or theologian could still operate from within the very tradition whose finest flowering he was investigating.

The history-of-religions school, on the other hand, consciously and deliberately took up a position outside the tradition and outside the Church. Christianity, like any other religion, was a historical phenomenon that could be examined without prejudice or presup-position. Historical study was an independent discipline that could not permit any prior commitment, be it to Christ himself, to influence its judgement of the evidence in front of it.

Already in 1788, J. D. Michaelis had suggested that in giving to the divine person of Jesus the name of *Logos* (Word), John was borrowing a term from the Gnostics, from a source, that is, outside and even opposed to the traditional locus of revelation.[31] By the middle of the next century Adolf Hilgenfeld had come to regard the whole Gospel as a Gnostic tract.[32] F. C. Baur, by consistently advocating and practising the scientific study of Christianity, had already fallen foul of more conservative exegetes and theologians. But in certain respects Baur himself remained a traditional theolo-gian, in that he was content with the concept of a Christian 'idea' that developed dialectically in the first two centuries and culminated in the Fourth Gospel. So it was not Baur but one of his pupils, Otto Pfleiderer, who was regarded as the founder-father of the history-of-

1907 it declared that 'the historical reasons for maintaining that the author of the Fourth Gospel is none other than the apostle John are so sound that this tradition is not in the least weakened by any opposing arguments': *Enchiridion Biblicum* (Rome, 1927), p. 67. A few months later, brandishing threats of excommunication, Pius ordained that the replies and decrees of this Commission were to have the force of Papal pronouncements, an edict that applied to statements it had already issued. This was the substance of the Motu Proprio *Praestantia Scripturae Sacrae* of 8 Nov. (ibid., pp. 86–9).

[30] Once again, Bultmann was a relentless critic of the concept of salvation-history, which he regarded as woolly and incoherent.

[31] Cf. Kümmel, *NT: History*, p. 69.

[32] *Evangelium.*

religions school, though Pfleiderer declared that it was to Baur, his revered teacher, that he owed his own unwavering conviction 'that Christianity as a historical phenomenon is to be investigated by the same methods as all other history, and that in particular its origin is to be studied as the normal outcome of the manifold factors in the religious and ethical life of the time'.[33]

Here in a nutshell we have the aims and methods of the *Religionsgeschichtliche Schule*, which was actually founded in the late 1880s by a group of young scholars in Göttingen, among them William Wrede, Hermann Gunkel, and Wilhelm Bousset. As far as the New Testament is concerned the one chiefly responsible for seeing Pfleiderer's programme through was Bousset, whose epoch-making work *Kyrios Christos* (how few are the books of which this can truly be said) was published in 1913. So while Loisy, in 1903, was still able to say that anyone with a proper appreciation of the Gospels can see that the content of the Fourth Gospel is derived from the Synoptic tradition,[34] there was building up in Germany an impressive body of critical opinion which would say, 'No, many of the ideas found in the New Testament, and especially those of its two greatest thinkers, Paul and John, come from elsewhere.'

Now it is important to see, I believe, that to a conservative Christian this opinion could seem not just shocking but frightening. With its roots buried deep in German rationalism (some of the early advocates of the methods of comparative religion, notably Franz Overbeck, had no Christian faith) it should not perhaps be surprising that the mature plant too should seem to some both sickly and sinister, threatening as it did to get a stranglehold upon all biblical study with scholarly pretensions.[35] The strange and exotic flowers of the *Hermetica* (Bousset) or, later, of Mandaism (Bultmann) must not be allowed to enter the tidy garden of Christianity or be thought to have fertilized one of its most precious plants.

This is a rhetorical way of putting the matter but not, I think, a

---

[33] *Urchristentum*. Quoted by Kümmel, *NT: History*, p. 210.

[34] p. 61.

[35] Anger as well as irritation is manifest in the response of William Sanday to what he calls 'the younger [German] theologians' (among whom he numbers the fifty-three-year-old Schmiedel): 'They all start', he says, 'with the "reduced" conception of Christianity current in so many quarters' and 'if a writer starts with a conception of Christianity that is "semi-Ebionite" or "semi-Arian", he is bound at all costs to rule out the Fourth Gospel, not only as a dogmatic authority but as a record of historical fact': *Criticism*, p. 29.

fundamentally mistaken one. One has only to read Wrede's programmatic lectures on 'The Task and Methods of "New Testament Theology"',[36] first delivered in 1897, to see how little theology is left if the principles of historical criticism are allowed to hold undisputed sway. It is scarcely surprising that scholars of a different persuasion reacted angrily and disdainfully to what seemed to them an arrogant iconoclasm.

A more nuanced response came from Adolf Schlatter[37] and also from Rudolf Bultmann. Looking back more than half a century later, in an introduction he wrote in 1964 to the fifth edition of Bousset's *Kyrios Christos*, Bultmann briefly enumerates the advantages of the new school:

> Finally a word should be said about the history-of-religions school's aim of expounding the *religion* of primitive Christianity and of using the New Testament as a source for this purpose. We may well ask today whether we should not rather revert to the old question concerning the *theology* of the New Testament. But here it must be recalled that the aim of investigating the religion of primitive Christianity instead of the theology of the New Testament was grounded upon the opposition of the history-of-religions school to what, with the solitary exception of Schlatter, was currently the dominant approach, i.e. one chiefly interested in so-called doctrinal concepts. In this respect the history-of-religions school took a decisive step towards a better understanding of the New Testament. For the question concerning the religion of the New Testament was basically a question concerning the existential (*existentiell*) meaning of its theological expressions, a fact which also comes to light in the choice of the term 'devotion' (*Frömmigkeit*)[38] in preference to that of 'religion' and in the interpretation of christology as 'devotion to Christ' (*Christusfrömmigkeit*).[39]

This decidedly ambivalent paragraph (is Bultmann opting for history or theology?) well illustrates the dialectic between the twin concerns that dominated his own scholarship.

Whatever one may think about the speculative issues involved, the search for the origins of the Fourth Gospel ultimately promises much more than the quest for its historical author. All that is to be known of the evangelist's identity, character, personality, and

---

[36] This may now be found, along with an equally important lecture by Adolf Schlatter, in Robert Morgan's *The Nature of New Testament Theology*. Morgan himself provides an interesting and informative introduction.

[37] See previous note.

[38] This rendering seems to me less misleading than the standard 'piety'.

[39] *Kyrios Christos*[6], p. vi.

experiences (little enough in all conscience)[40] must ultimately be derived from the pages of the Gospel itself, and in consequence can tell us nothing more about the nature of the Gospel than what we will have learnt in the course of our enquiry. Wayne Meeks remarks that 'if only we knew with comparable certainty one-tenth as much about the Gospel's author and the setting of his community as we know about Philo and the Alexandrian Jews, then our task would be much simpler'.[41] But this comment, far from implying any wish to revive the old 'quest for the historical John' is really an endorsement of the principles of Bousset and Wrede.

The first to give the Johannine problem its classic formulation was Adolf Harnack, in his huge *History of Dogma*, first published in 1886: 'The origin of the Johannine writings is, from the stand-point of a history of literature and dogma, the most marvellous enigma which the early history of Christianity presents.'[42] Literature and dogma: what has to be explained is the *conceptual world* of the Fourth Gospel and its incarnation in language. There are roughly speaking six different but partially overlapping areas in which such an explanation may be sought: (1) first one may look, as Loisy did, to the Synoptic tradition; but however many beliefs and traditions the fourth evangelist shares with the other three, neither his ideas nor his style are to be accounted for by appealing to this tradition alone; (2) in the second place, one may turn to Paul, the only other New Testament writer to match the fourth evangelist in profundity and power. Most of the critics of the period we are discussing believed that John was indebted to Paul. Harnack actually speaks of John's Christ as 'Pauline',[43] and Bousset says of him that he 'stands on Paul's shoulders'.[44] Wrede, it is true, voices a certain uneasiness when he writes: 'reference to Paul explains very little here, though it is certain that Paulinism is one of the presuppositions of Johannine theology'.[45] But Maurice Goguel (1924) has no such reservations. In response to the question 'How does the problem of the Fourth Gospel present itself nowadays?' he lists five areas of study (significantly, the question of the Gospel's origins is not among them). On the second of these, 'the analysis of Johannine thought', he simply

---

[40] The evangelist actually hides behind his work and addresses his readers, as Hoskyns put it (p. 86), 'with impersonal, almost hieratic, unapproachability'.

[41] 'Divine Agent', p. 60.   [42] A. Harnack, *History of Dogma*, i. 96 f.

[43] Ibid.   [44] 'Johannesevangelium', col. 620; *Kyrios Christos*, p. 180.

[45] 'Task and Methods', p. 88 n. 38.

remarks: 'There is no longer very much to be expected from this ... .
All, it would seem, that can be said with certainty is that the
dependence of Johannine thought (le johannisme) upon Pauline
thought shows that the Gospel cannot be dated earlier than the
second generation of Christians.'[46] For the moment one might just
remark that it is hard to see how such assurance can be justified; a
fuller discussion of this topic must be deferred till later.

Although there is nothing in principle about the aims and
methods of the history-of-religions school to prevent its practitioners
from seeking to explain the later writings of the New Testament on
the basis of the earlier, in point of fact they mostly looked elsewhere.
One area where one might have expected them to look was (3)
Judaism, but it seems to have been largely left to Adolf Schlatter to
hunt for parallels to Johannine thought and phraseology in rabbinical sources, especially those of the earliest, so-called tannaitic
period.[47] Schlatter himself, for all his learning and theological
acumen, remained outside the mainstream of German scholarship.
Methodologically he was close to the history-of-religions school
(though never a member) but theologically he was on a different
planet. Perhaps that is why his important little work Die Sprache und
Heimat des vierten Evangelisten (1902) made so little impact.[48]

---

[46] Introduction, pp. 73 ff. Even more remarkable is J. Moffat's conclusion that
'apart from the Old Testament the main currents that flow through the gospel are
those of (a) Paulinism, (b) the Jewish Alexandrian philosophy, and (c) Stoicism'
(Introduction, p. 522). A more recent defence of the view that John learned from Paul
is to be found in A. E. Barnett, Paul Becomes a Literary Influence, pp. 104–42.

[47] This is all the more surprising when one remembers that Bousset himself made
one of the most important contributions to the study of early Judaism in his Die
Religion des Judentums im spälhellenistischen Zeitalter (1903). Bousset does in fact
remark that the Johannine 'Son of man' is of Palestinian origin (Kyrios Christos,
p. 156) but then he goes on to argue that the typically Johannine 'Son of God' is not
Palestinian but Hellenistic.

[48] A. Meyer, in his regular survey of Johannine studies, comments dismissively
that Schlatter's linguistic researches would have some general bearing on the origins
of the Gospel if only they were watertight: TRu 7 (1904), pp. 475 f. More than a quarter
of a century later Schlatter published a full commentary, Der Evangelist Johannes (1930)
in which he expanded his original work without altering its perspective. The English
scholar G. H. Box cannot have known of Schlatter's early work when he asserted
apropos of Jewish midrashic literature that 'it would not be difficult ... to derive from
this literature a good deal of illustrative material which would form a remarkably
suggestive Jewish background for the Fourth Gospel. The Johannine Gospel is indeed
Jewish through and through, and it is much to be desired that a commentary on it,
written from this point of view, could be produced' ('Jewish Environment', pp. 24 f.).
See now S. Brown, 'From Burney to Black'; W. Meeks, '"Am I a Jew?"'.

Working along similar lines, but pushing his researches far into the cloudy realms of Jewish mysticism, Hugo Odeberg published in 1929 the first volume of a projected commentary entitled *The Fourth Gospel interpreted in its relation to contemporaneous religious currents in Palestine and the Hellenistic-Oriental world*. As this title indicates, Odeberg's work is broader than Schlatter's and instead of confining himself as Schlatter had done, to quoting parallels, he comments, often quite extensively, on their significance. His method is to quote a short passage from the Gospel and then to intermingle citation and discussion in a wide-ranging fashion. One peculiarity of his work is its selectivity: from the first twelve chapters of the Gospel (which is as far as he got) less than a score of passages are singled out for comment; but some of these (e.g. 3: 13–21) receive very detailed treatment indeed. Some idea of the unique flavour of Odeberg's commentary may be obtained from its opening paragraph. First he quotes (in Greek) 1: 51: 'Truly, truly I say to you, you will see heaven opened, and the angels of God ascending and descending upon the Son of man.' Without further ado (not a word of literary or contextual analysis) the commentary begins:

The allusion in this utterance to Gen. 28: 12 is immediately apparent and generally recognized. The OT passage in question had been the subject of much speculations in Jewish circles, both Palestinian and those of the Diaspora, long before Jn. It has been especially adaptable for mystical notions, and has indeed remained a favourite source of similes for mystical doctrines up to the present day. The picture of 'Jacob's-ladder' immediately appeals to a mystic mind as echoing a certain inner experience or conviction. The question here arises whether the Jn-ine passage links up consciously not merely with the OT-passage but with some particular or generally current speculations on or interpretations of Gen. 28: 12. A hint of the wide range of speculations attached by the Rabbinical teachers to Gen. 28: 12 may be found in *Gen R* 68, 18 (*Yalq* nr. 119) which runs as follows: ...[49]

This midrash is then quoted (in Hebrew) and translated. Then come a further nine pages of comment and further parallels (from Philo and the Mandaean texts). And that is all. The next verse discussed is 2: 25. (One sometimes wishes that other commentators on the Gospel would follow Odeberg's self-denying ordinance in restricting

---

[49] It is interesting to note that Schlatter has nothing whatever to say on this verse.

themselves to those sections of the Gospel on which they have something fresh to say.)

Among the 'Jewish' sources could be included the Old Testament Apocrypha and Pseudepigrapha, the Targumim, the *Odes of Solomon*, the Samaritan writings, the Dead Sea Scrolls (which Odeberg of course did not know), as well as the rabbinical material and various works of Jewish mysticism. Together, these constitute a vein not likely to be exhausted for many years.

Among the Jewish writings one might also wish to include those of the Alexandrian Jew Philo. But it is perhaps better to put (4) Hellenistic Judaism (which would also include Josephus) in a separate compartment. Adjoining this would be (5) a group of writings relating to what C. H. Dodd calls 'the higher religion of Hellenism: the Hermetic literature'. For the preliminary study of both these areas (at least in so far as they bear upon the Fourth Gospel) we owe most to Reitzenstein and Bousset, and subsequently to Dodd himself. Nowadays one is inclined to wonder how deep the resemblances reach. Probably a majority of scholars would be inclined to echo the cautionary note sounded by Harnack long ago: 'the reference to Philo does not satisfactorily explain even one of the external aspects of the problem [of the origin of the Johannine writings]' and 'even the Logos has little more in common with Philo than the name'.[50] Again, Bousset devotes a whole section of his chapter on John in *Kyrios Christos* to the theme of light and darkness,[51] offering abundant evidence, notably from the *Corpus Hermeticum*, of its popularity throughout the Hellenistic world. But the force of this parallel dwindled to nothingness when the same theme was later found to be equally characteristic of the thought-world of the completely Jewish community of Qumran. Nor is it as obvious as Bousset maintained that the best possible summary of the essence of Johannine mysticism was the phrase 'divinization through the vision of God' (*Vergottung* [*sic!*] *durch Gottesschau*); he may be right in thinking that 'the intense mysticism' (*die hochgespannte Mystik*) expressed in this phrase flourished on the soil of Hellenistic belief and practice.[52] But is it truly Johannine?

Finally (6) there is Gnosticism and most especially, because of Bultmann, Mandaism. Writing in 1903, Wrede remarks that the question regarding the origins of the fourth evangelist's character-

---

[50] *History*, i. 98.   [51] pp. 172–7.   [52] Ibid., p. 164.

istic ideas 'has not yet been solved' but acknowledges that he himself tends to think that at the basis of the Gospel lie intuitions of a Gnostic kind (*gnostisch geartete Anschauungen*), adding tantalizingly, 'but here I must content myself with briefly drawing attention to this feature'.[53] In fact Johannes Kreyenbühl, in a book of which the first volume appeared in 1900,[54] had been stretching this idea as far as it would go. But it was not until the three main Mandaean texts, the Book of John, the Liturgies, and the *Ginza* or Treasury, were all available in the German translations of Mark Lidzbarski (the *Ginza* was published in 1925) that biblical scholars became aware of the full extent of the conceptual parallels. In the same year, 1925, came the second edition of Walter Bauer's commentary on the Gospel,[55] the first to make use of Mandaean texts, and a seminal article of Bultmann which we shall be considering in due course.

Harnack and Wrede had left the Johannine problem where they found it, offering only hints and guesses for other scholars to follow up. The early years of this century saw a lot of praiseworthy but preliminary spadework. But as long as John was believed to 'stand on Paul's shoulders' the problem could neither be seen nor set in all its acuteness. We shall see shortly how Bultmann put the question and offered his own strikingly coherent solution.

3. COMPOSITION AND SOURCES

'The major literary problem of John is its combination of remarkable stylistic unity and thematic coherence with glaringly bad transitions between episodes at many points.'[56] This is Wayne Meeks's admirable summing-up of a problem which, like the puppets in a Punch and Judy show, has often been flattened but still stubbornly refuses to lie down. Yet the strongest impression the Fourth Gospel must make upon a reader coming to it for the first time, especially if he happens to be acquainted with the other three, is one of extraordinary self-containedness. D. F. Strauss suggested that the Gospel is to be equated with 'that seamless garment (*jener ungenähte Leibrock*) of

---

[53] *Charakter und Tendenz*, p. 30.

[54] *Das Evangelium der Wahrheit.*

[55] In a foreword (p. iii) Bauer acknowledges his debt to Lidzbarski for allowing him to make use of the translation of the *Ginza* before it was actually published. He also respected Kreyenbühl as one of the pioneers of this approach.

[56] 'Man from Heaven', p. 144.

which it speaks':[57] pick at any one thread and the whole thing will unravel. Only on much closer inspection is any stitching revealed, some of it quite clumsy.

The first attempts to pull the Gospel apart and to distinguish between the authentic bits and the inauthentic bits were made on theological rather than literary grounds. The motive-force behind these was German rationalism, which was anxious to explain away the prodigious elements of the Gospel and thus to leave its sublime teaching untainted by anything likely to cause offence to minds operating exclusively with what Pascal calls 'the spirit of geometry'. So in 1838 Chr. H. Weisse, arguing that the narrative sections of the Gospel are of scant importance when compared with the discourses (to which they are in any case only loosely connected), separated out the earlier, genuine, discourse material from the narrative material which, according to him, had been added on later.[58] (It was in protesting against the slashes of Weisse's scissors that Strauss used the famous metaphor I have just quoted.) Alexander Schweizer (1841) and H. H. Wendt, whose commentary on the Gospel appeared at the turn of the century, employed much the same procedures.[59] Commenting upon these dogmatically inspired theories, from Weisse to Wendt, Bousset remarks that for all their shortcomings, they led to 'a whole series of good, purely literary observations, which deserved better than the summary dismissal they often received later at the hands of the majority of scholars'.[60] They are also the remote ancestors of all subsequent source theories.

An example of the kind of important observation to which Bousset refers is to be found in a later work of Weisse (1856).[61] This

[57] The paragraph in which this phrase occurs is quoted *in extenso* (but not translated) by W. F. Howard in *The Fourth Gospel*, p. 258.

[58] *Evangelische Geschichte*, i. 102–38; ii. 183–304. In fact 'partitionist' theories began with J. Chr. Eckerman (1796). Cf. S. Schulz, *Untersuchungen*, p. 48 n. 3. In 1803 G. K. Horst was prepared to divide the Gospel up into 'kernel and husk'. Note too the title of a book by Christoph Friedrich von Ammon, published in 1811: *Johannem auctorem ab editore huius libri fuisse diversum*.

[59] Meanwhile Ernest Renan had reached the opposite conclusion. He describes the Fourth Gospel as 'valueless if it is a question of knowing how Jesus spoke, but superior to the Synoptic Gospels wherever it is a matter of the order of the facts', *Origines*, vi. 58.

[60] Following the appearance of the works of Wellhausen and Schwartz to be discussed presently, Bousset wrote a two-part article: 'literarische Einheit', in which he assessed the achievements of 19th-century scholarship in the light of the new theories. (This quotation is from p. 2.)

[61] *Evangelienfrage*, p. 116, quoted by Bousset, 'literarische Einheit', p. 4.

concerns the conclusion of chapter 14 of the Gospel, which offers an impossible transition to the beginning of chapter 15, since after pronouncing the words 'Arise, let us go from this place' (ἐγείρεσθε, ἄγωμεν ἐντεῦθεν), Jesus carries on talking for a further three chapters. Weisse's solution was to excise the last three words of chapter 14, but the problem was not to be solved so easily.[62]

The first general solution offered by those not content with an uneasy acceptance of the present order of the transmitted text was the so-called 'displacement' theory, first put forward, according to Kümmel,[63] as early as 1871. What makes this theory different from earlier ones is that it supposes the present order to be the result of a mistake: the sheets of the original manuscript (presumably papyrus) were somehow scattered, only to be subsequently reassembled in the wrong order. B. H. Streeter, rather later, offers a typical defence of this type of theory:

Everyone who has ever sent manuscript to be copied on a large scale knows that either through his own inadvertence or that of the copyist, sheets often get transposed, and paragraphs added by way of correction get inserted in the wrong place. The same kind of thing is frequently to be observed in ancient MSS of classical authors; and there is not the slightest improbability in its having happened in one of the earliest, or even in the earliest, copy of this Gospel. At any rate there are certain places where the connection is immensely improved if we suppose there has been an accidental transposition of paragraphs or sections. Thus it is difficult to believe that Jn. xiv. 25–31, which reads like a concluding summary, leading up to the words 'Arise, let us depart hence', was intended by the author to be followed by chap. xv.–xvi. But move these seven verses to the end of ch. 16, and they make a magnificent close to the discourse, xiv. 1–24, xv., xvi.[64]

Here, however, we come across one of the major difficulties with this theory, which is to estimate a page-length (in this case apparently one covering a mere seven verses) that would account for the

---

[62] The ingenious suggestion that Jesus delivered the remainder of his address *en route* for the garden (adopted by, among others, Westcott and Haenchen) fails to reckon with the virtual impossibility, despite Chaucer, of communicating with more than two or three fellow wayfarers at the same time. Cf. J. Beutler, *Habt keine Angst*, p. 9 n. 4.

[63] *Introduction*, p. 198.

[64] *The Four Gospels*, pp. 380 f. Archbishop Bernard in his ICC commentary of 1928 still maintained a version of this theory, and yet another was proposed by F. R. Hoare in *The Original Order*. It seems to hold a particular fascination for British scholars, as can be seen from a glance through the relevant chapters of W. F. Howard, *Recent Criticism*.

reshuffling.[65] Besides, generally speaking one would expect an author to have spotted the confusion on the return of his manuscript from the copyist, especially if the text was one that was going to be used regularly within his own community.[66]

In 1907 two scholars working along the same lines—independently, but aware of each other's interests[67]—advanced reasons for holding that the displacements were not accidental but deliberate.[68] Julius Wellhausen's earlier triumphs in Old Testament studies (though not the first, he is the most famous pioneer of Pentateuchal source theories) evidently stimulated him to look for evidence of similar restitching elsewhere. It is worth examining the most extended of his arguments in some detail. It too concerns the end of chapter 14.

The nub of the difficulty, as Weisse had noticed long before, lies in the transition between chapter 14 and chapter 15. But excising the last three words does not solve very much. For in 14: 30 Jesus announces firmly, 'I will not converse with you much longer.' Yet he does, for three more chapters!

Wellhausen reinforces the difficulty by pointing out that a Syriac manuscript (known as the Sinaiticus since its recent—1892—discovery at St Catherine's monastery on Mount Sinai) omits the 'much' (πολλά). He infers from this that the reading of the Sinaiticus Syriac (to which he has frequent recourse in his opusculum) must be accepted as original. The word πολλά will have been added by a later editor to the Greek text to make the contradiction less blatant. Chapters 15–16, he concludes, did not belong to the original Gospel but were added by a later hand.

The next step is to observe that in chapter 14 Jesus says that the *Father* will send the Paraclete (14: 16–26), in words that became the corner-stone of Greek Orthodox teaching on the Trinity. In chapters 15–16, on the other hand, it is *Jesus himself* who will send

---

[65] For a more extended discussion, with especial reference to Bultmann's commentary, see D. Moody Smith, *Composition and Order*, pp. 175 ff.

[66] G. Hoffman actually regards the displacements and gaps as the consequence of a doddery old age, and expounds this thesis at some length in *Alterswerk*. Renan too speaks of John's 'vanité de vieillard' and thinks it possible that he eventually became weak in the head; cf. *Origines*, v. 429 f.

[67] Or rather, according to Bousset, Schwartz was stimulated by Wellhausen's observations to proceed further in the same direction.

[68] Stylistically their work is quite distinct. In stark contrast to Wellhausen's elegant prose, the arguments of Eduard Schwartz are heaped together higgledy-piggledy in a series of four 'articles' entitled 'Aporien im vierten Evangelium'.

the Paraclete (15: 26; 16: 7), and it is on these sayings that the Latin Church rested its case. 'The difference is clear,' says Wellhausen.

A more important disagreement concerns the parousia or Second Coming.[69] The whole point of chapter 14 is to demonstrate that this is superfluous—because the disciples can now find their own way to the Father; meanwhile Jesus himself will be ably and adequately represented on earth by the Paraclete, who is to stay with them indefinitely. But this broadly consistent picture is spoiled at two points. In the first place there is the hypothetical clause at the beginning of the chapter (v. 3): ἐὰν πορευθῶ καὶ ἑτοιμάσω τόπον ὑμῖν (literally, '*if* I go and prepare a place for you'). This verse, Wellhausen continues, consorts ill with the context and is omitted by one or two of the early versions. If this clause is left out the result is a natural sequence: 'otherwise I would have told you [*hypothetical affirmative*] that I was going to prepare a place for you and that [   ] I would come again and take you to myself.' Read in this way the sentence becomes a denial of the parousia, not an assertion of it.[70] (Wellhausen does not explain why the grafting operation should have been performed so unskilfully.) For similar reasons the conclusion of v. 18 ('I will come to you') must be reckoned as a later addition, made in order to adjust the theological perspective of the chapter to include a belief in the parousia. So if we were to strip chapter 14 down to its original form it would be seen to have contested belief in the parousia.

A different picture emerges, however, as soon as we turn to chapters 15–17. There is a whole section (16: 16–24) devoted to the parousia, affirming very clearly that Jesus will return: 'a little while and you will see me no more; again a little while, and you will see me' (v. 16). This sentence, says Wellhausen, introduces a new twist into a familiar saying that simply asserted Jesus' imminent departure. (If compared with 14: 19—on which this section was probably modelled—that verse can be seen to make no suggestion whatever that Jesus would actually return to earth.)

---

[69] John does not use the word παρουσία: Matthew is the only one of the four evangelists to do so. Like 'apocalyptic' and 'eschatology' it is a slippery word, and has been responsible for many an exegetical pratfall. None the less, Wellhausen was right to detect in the farewell discourse some trace of an expectation of Jesus' personal return after his death. (See Ch. 12.)

[70] Wellhausen was wrong to build upon the hypothetical nature of the ἐάν clause, since this word may be used in contexts where it has to be translated 'when'; e.g. 12: 32.

Wellhausen adds other minor arguments along the same lines. What is important is to see how, starting from discrepancies within the text, he lays bare (admittedly after some juggling) a sinister theological plot to alter, or at any rate water down, the evangelist's strong but—from a traditional point of view—unorthodox opinions of the parousia.[71] The ecclesiastical redactor is born![72] One is not surprised that Bousset, commenting a couple of years later on the twin contributions of Wellhausen and Schwartz, saw momentous implications in their work. They have shown, he concludes, 'that a large question-mark must be placed beside previous assumptions of the absolute integrity of John's Gospel. The composition of this Gospel has become a serious problem, one which is unlikely to receive a simple solution. [*How right he was!*] It must have been the work of several successive writers.'[73]

There is no doubt that Wellhausen's observations and his methods are of more significance than his rather precipitate conclusions. But among modern commentators Schnackenburg accepts the hypothesis that chapters 15–17 were a later insertion, whilst Barrett, Brown, Sanders, and Lindars all believe that chapter 14 and (parts of) chapters 15–16 represent alternative forms of a single discourse. Bousset was right: the work of Wellhausen and Schwartz in 1907 was of seminal importance.

The year before Bousset's article appeared, Wellhausen published his short commentary *Das Evangelium Johannis* (1908). Basing his case chiefly on his earlier observations, he argued that the Gospel was built round or upon an original early document, which he called the *Grundschrift* and which he introduced as follows:

The confusion of the Fourth Gospel is all the more striking in that, unlike Mark, it is not an ordered collection of traditional material gathered together according to one particular perspective. The narrative shows insertions, the discourses have neither structure nor easily remembered arguments; they swarm with variants and frequently burst out of their setting, so that one no longer knows where one is. Nevertheless a few passages stick up like stepping-stones amid the disorder, indicating a definite though not unbroken line. They stand out in relief from the rest of the Gospel but also mark

---

[71] *Erweiterungen*, pp. 7–15.

[72] This is the name Bultmann was to confer upon the unknown personage who among other things did exactly what Wellhausen claimed by reinserting a futuristic eschatology in the (theologically much more acceptable) realized eschatology of the evangelist himself.

[73] 'Literarische Einheit', p. 63.

its backbone and can be designated its *Grundschrift*. This forms the warp of the Gospel, but since its compass is far exceeded by what is woven over it, it cannot be considered the Gospel proper—simply one of its ingredients. The *Grundschrift* has not been preserved fully intact, and neither it nor the other various layers can be discerned with any certainty. Yet whatever the risks, some attempt must be made at this. If this proves only partially successful, that is no good reason for ignoring the data that make it necessary.[74]

Soon afterwards W. Soltau, partly anticipating the theories of Bultmann, argued that the Gospel was composed from two separate *Grundschriften*, the first a collection of discourses upon the person of Jesus, the second a collection of Synoptic and other stories. Each of these had its own independent origin and must be treated apart from the other.[75]

It is not necessary to discuss the work of Wellhausen and Soltau in detail, nor that of F. Spitta, which was published in 1910.[76] But they undoubtedly blazed a trail for others to follow. Bousset, in his *RGG* article, expressed the view that there is no possibility of getting back to the original text by applying the methods of source criticism; but he agreed that the Gospel was probably the work of several hands and wondered gloomily whether any agreement would ever be reached about where the lines should be drawn.[77]

The next important contribution came from Alexander Faure, in 1922, the first to suggest that the *Grundschrift* was in fact a miracle source, as Bultmann was later to name it.[78] Faure notes (not quite accurately) that even Bousset, despite certain reservations, continued to maintain the literary unity of the Gospel; and he claims to have discovered new data which make this position no longer tenable. He starts by observing that there are two different ways of citing the Old Testament in the Gospel. One, which sees Scripture as a collection of proof-texts (e.g. 5: 39—'Search the Scripture'), contains no special citation formula, the other regards Scripture as a kind of Logos that has to be incarnated in history, an Idea that demands expression ('eine Idee, die Gestalt gewinnen will und muss'). Here there *is* a special formula, 'that the Scripture may be fulfilled', and

---

[74] pp. 6 f.   [75] *Das vierte Evangelium.*

[76] *Das Johannes-Evangelium als Quelle.* Spitta had already argued for considerable changes in the order of the Gospel in an earlier book, *Zur Geschichte*, in a section entitled 'Unordnungen im Text des vierten Evangeliums' (pp. 155–204).

[77] 'Johannesevangelium', col. 618.

[78] 'Die alttestamentlichen Zitate'. And note the similar suggestion, even earlier (1915), of J. M. Thompson: 'Structure'.

Faure remarks that even those who cannot accept his theoretical observations must admit that a break occurs in the Gospel between 12: 15 (the last example of the first type of reference) and 12: 38 (the first example of the second type): 'On each side of this divide different hands have been at work.'[79]

Faure admits that this theory requires further support and he attempts to show differences in style and vocabulary that point to the same conclusion. He observes in particular that the conclusion of chapter 20 ('Jesus did many other signs ... which are not written in this book') cannot refer to the second half of the Gospel, where there are no signs at all: they really belong to the first half, which is not in any case satisfactorily concluded at 12: 37: 'Rather they point, in my opinion, to a self-contained literary unity, a source-document (*Quellenschrift*) used in the first half of the Gospel, whose traces have not been entirely obliterated by subsequent reworkings.'[80] This must be the book ($\beta\iota\beta\lambda\iota\sigma\nu$) mentioned in 20: 30: 'The verse clearly indicates the content and general tendency of the *Grundschrift*: it is a collection of miracle-stories assembled for an apologetic or missionary purpose.'[81] (It is worth remarking that Faure does not bother to decide which.)

This conclusion leads Faure on to consider whether the link between faith and miracle might represent a different theological viewpoint from that of the evangelist himself. He admits his own uncertainty on this point: 'But it seems to me beyond question that there existed a source-document whose aim was to establish Jesus' messianic dignity by appealing to his miracles, perhaps in order to counter objections from two sides, the Jews or the disciples of John the Baptist.[82] This, he says, is the lowest stratum, one that occupies a relatively small place in the variegated thinking of the Gospel, and is perhaps the least representative of the Gospel as a whole. There is also present in the Gospel a very different idea of the ground of faith, namely the word of Jesus. The two conceptions are incompatible: 'One cannot put the emphasis both on the visibly prodigious *and* on the interior life.'[83]

Besides the author of the *Grundschrift* and the evangelist proper, Faure detects the hand of a redactor. The presence of the contradictions and doublets suggests an *unfinished* work, one which has been pieced together by someone else. This view is supported by the

---

[79] 'Die alttestamentlichen Zitate', p. 101.
[80] Ibid., p. 109.
[81] Ibid.
[82] Ibid., p. 111.
[83] Ibid., p. 112.

presence of 'churchy' (e.g. sacramental) bits and other insertions indicating a futuristic eschatology very different from the 'eternal life' of the body of the Gospel: 'In the last instance the Gospel has been worked over by a dogmatically inclined redactor, ill-informed and ill-equipped.'[84] Faure concludes his article by observing that one's appreciation of a cathedral is not spoilt by knowing where its stones have been quarried.

Faure's work has received quite a mauling at the hands of later critics: the foundation of his theory (the distinction between two ways of citing the Old Testament) is, it has been said, extremely insecure; and his stylistic distinctions have been shown to be unreliable touchstones of authorial difference. What is more, standing as he does in the shadow of Bultmann, who was impressed by his work and absorbed much of it into his great commentary, he is seldom accorded his rightful place in the history of Johannine studies. Yet his observations are fresh, his insights keen, his theological sense acute: in the period under discussion his article constitutes an outstanding attempt to *understand* the composition of the Gospel.

Nevertheless by no means all scholars were (or are) convinced of the superiority of source theories over displacement theories. Streeter who, as we have seen, himself favoured a type of displacement theory, comments sardonically on the approach and the prospects of source criticism: 'If the sources have undergone anything like the amount of amplification, excision, rearrangement and adaptation which the theory postulates, then the critic's pretence that he can unravel the procedure is grotesque. As well hope to start with a string of sausages and reconstruct the pig.'[85] It is a clever remark. But what if one wants to *explain* a sausage? Athene, we are told, sprang fully armed from the the head of Zeus, a myth no doubt partly designed, like Streeter's sausage simile, to discourage further speculation about her origins. But should we capitulate so easily? And are we, anyway, quite in the same situation as that of the savage with the sausage? Provided that testable criteria can be offered then we are surely entitled to proceed as far as the evidence will take us. Moreover, as Wellhausen pointed out when introducing the concept of the *Grundschrift* for the first time, the hazards of the enterprise do not obliterate the data that made it necessary in the first place. We have not heard the last of source theories.

[84] Ibid., p. 120.   [85] *The Four Gospels*, p. 377.

4. HISTORY OR THEOLOGY?

When Evanson launched his attack upon the authenticity of the Fourth Gospel in 1792, he was of course at the same time impugning its veracity. In fact most of his argument was based upon what he considered to be the incredible nature of the events recorded: how, he asked, could such a farrago of nonsense have been written by an apostle of Jesus Christ? Less crudely Bretschneider, in 1820, regarded the evidently apologetic and polemical aims of the work as sufficient proof that it must have been composed after the apostolic age. And although Schleiermacher felt able to defend the position that the author was an eyewitness of the events he describes, and to do so precisely on the basis of the spiritual content of the work, this quixotic view could not hold the field for long. A powerfully persuasive alternative was put forward by D. F. Strauss in his notorious *Das Leben Jesu* (1835),[86] and Schleiermacher's view, subtle and in its way quite perceptive, proved unable to withstand the onslaught.

What primarily interested Strauss and, after him, Baur, was the *content* of the Gospel, to much of which Strauss had no hesitation in applying the term 'myth'. John, he maintained, was offering a more highly developed version of the Christian myth already adumbrated by the Synoptists. So there emerged clearly for the first time the alternative that was to dominate subsequent discussion: history versus myth. 'Myth' of course did not hold its side of the field to itself for very long; it was replaced first by 'Idea' (Baur); then by 'philosophy' (Jülicher), 'allegory' (Loisy, von Hügel), 'mysticism' (Bousset, Albert Schweitzer), 'meaning' (Hoskyns), and finally by 'theology'. But it was Strauss who first laid down the lines of future debate by his unwearying insistence upon the *mythological* character of much of the material in this Gospel.

How Strauss argued may be illustrated by a passage in which he is discussing the scene in Gethsemane. (This is not found as such in the Fourth Gospel, but 12: 27 ff. clearly depends upon the same tradition.) Strauss has stated earlier his criterion of verisimilitude: 'where, in narratives having a tendency to aggrandize a person or fact ... two contradictory statements are found, that which best

---

[86] The printed edition of the second volume of this work is dated 1836. But my colleague Robert Morgan informs me that it was actually published in 1835, the same year as the first volume.

corresponds to this aim is the least historical'[87]—a criterion which is obviously bound to tell against John in every case. But the Synoptists too are open to the suspicion of heightening what must have been a natural presentiment on Jesus' part into a clear prescience. So

we must pronounce unhistorical not only one of the two but both representations of the last hours of Jesus before his arrest. The only degree of distinction between the historical value of the synoptical account and that of John is, that the former is a mythical product of the first era of traditional formation, the latter of the second,—or more correctly, the one is a product of the second order, the other of the third. The representation common to the synoptists and to John, that Jesus foreknew his sufferings even to the day and hour of their arrival, is the first modification which the pious legend gave to the real history of Jesus; the statement of the synoptists, that he even had an antecedent experience of his sufferings, is the second step of the mythical; while, that although he foreknew them, and also in one instance had a foretaste of them (John 12: 27 ff.), he had yet long beforehand completely triumphed over them, and when they stood immediately before him, looked them in the face with unperturbed serenity—this representation of the fourth gospel is the third and highest grade of devotional, but unhistorical embellishment.[88]

'In order to understand Strauss', wrote Albert Schweitzer, 'one must love him.'[89] Not an easy assignment! Because of his shockingly unorthodox views Strauss was dismissed from his tutorial post at the famous Tübingen *Stift* and not allowed to occupy the professorial chair he had been promised at Zurich, with the result that he remained embittered and aggrieved for the rest of his life. But his first *Life of Jesus*, unlike the second, written 'for the German people',[90] was a relatively youthful work (he was twenty-seven when it appeared) and it is not personal affection but an appreciation of the heady idealism in which he was nurtured[91] that is required for understanding this most radical of theologians.

'Myth' as Strauss employed it was far from being a totally

---

[87] *Life*, p. 229.   [88] Ibid., p. 649.   [89] *Quest*, p. 68.
[90] *Das Leben Jesu für das deutsche Volk bearbeitet*, 1864.
[91] Strauss himself claimed that his philosophical studies resulted in his case in an early 'liberation of the feelings and intellect from certain religious and dogmatical presuppositions' (*Life*, p. iii), a liberation which he regarded as the necessary basis of any scientific theology. Strauss was introduced to the philosophy of Schelling by his teacher F. C. Baur whilst still a schoolboy at Blaubeuren. It may have been from Schelling that Strauss derived his notion of myth. Cf. Kümmel, *History*, p. 426 n. 166.

dismissive or pejorative term.[92] It is true that he was jousting against the champions of the historicity of the Gospels; but for him the history of events was less important than the history of ideas. All the same it is scarcely surprising that his work was greeted with fear, obloquy, and derision by traditionally minded Christians, or even that it cost him his job.[93] Some historical core, however slight, is indispensable for a faith that rests on a historical revelation. Strauss did not in fact set out to deny *all* historicity ('it is not by any means meant that the whole history of Jesus is to be represented as mythical'),[94] but the general impression he conveys is that the little history that was left had neither value nor significance. As far as he was concerned, 'The supernatural birth of Christ, his miracles, his resurrection and ascension, remain eternal truths, whatever doubts may be cast on their reality as historical facts.'[95] At which comment his orthodox readers must surely have spluttered indignantly— though Bultmann was to say much the same a century later without losing the esteem of his less radical colleagues.

Baur, who had been Strauss's teacher at two separate establishments, carried his criticism of the Fourth Gospel even further by denying it any historicity at all: 'If John's Gospel, unlike the others, is not a historical account, if it has unquestionably an ideological thrust, then it can no longer be set over against the Synoptic Gospels as a rival source.'[96] Baur naturally concluded that the historian should leave the Fourth Gospel aside and cease to measure it against the other three, as Strauss had done[97] when he asked in each instance which presented the more plausible account.

[92] 'The term "myths"', he says, 'will give an intelligent man no more offence than a mere word should give such a person at any time, for everything of double meaning that clings to that word because of the recollection of pagan mythology disappears as a result of the argument to this point, viz., that by New Testament myths is to be understood nothing else than the expression of primitive Christian ideas formulated in unintentionally poeticizing sagas and looking very like history' (*Das Leben Jesu* I[1], pp. 74 f.). (This passage is omitted from the English translation, which follows the subsequent editions at this point.)

[93] Archdeacon Hare spoke of it as 'a book which a person can hardly read without being more or less hurt by it. If we walk through mire, some of it will stick to us, even when we have no other aim than to make our way through it, much more when we dabble about in it and sift it.' Quoted by Rosemary Ashton, *The German Idea* (London, 1980), p. 148.

[94] *Life*, p. li.   [95] Ibid., p. lii.   [96] 'Einleitung'.

[97] In fact Baur accused Strauss of offering a criticism of the gospel history without any criticism of the Gospels themselves (*Kritische Untersuchungen*, p. 41); and he had already written to Strauss in 1838 denying that the Fourth Gospel was of any value as a historical source. Cf. Kümmel, *History*, p. 428 n. 190.

With one or two exceptions (e.g. Ernest Renan)[98] the more radical scholars followed Strauss and Baur to form what Hoskyns was later to call 'the critical orthodoxy',[99] whilst more conservative scholars continued to fight on the terrain where the original challenge had been issued (from English Deists in the seventeenth century and Enlightened Germans in the eighteenth). That is to say, they continued to defend the primitive tradition that the Gospel was composed by John the Apostle, the son of Zebedee, and to insist that as an eyewitness he deserved full credence.[100] These scholars (they include such names as Bleek, de Wette, Zahn, Knabenbauer, Grandmaison, Lightfoot, and Lagrange) are lined up together by Hoskyns under the standard of 'traditional orthodoxy'.[101]

From our privileged vantage-point so many years later, we may be surprised at the stubbornness with which more conservative scholars continued to dig themselves into positions which one would have imagined to have been long since overrun by their adversaries. But as late as 1910 we find the American critic B. W. Bacon once again underlining the necessity, when making a historical judgement, of deciding between the Synoptists and John:

Either the former are right in their complete silence regarding pre-existence and incarnation, and their subordination of the doctrine of Jesus' person, in presenting his work and teaching as concerned with the Kingdom of God, with repentance and a filial disposition and life, as the requirement made by the common Father for that inheritance; or else John is right in making Jesus' work and message supremely a manifestation of his own glory as the incarnate Logos, effecting an atonement for the world, which has otherwise no access to God. Both views cannot be true, and to a very large extent it is the science of literary and historical criticism which must decide between them.[102]

---

[98] Who, as Hoskyns says (p. 32), 'refused to acquiesce in the current opinion that a document written from a theological view was altogether suspect and could contain no valuable historical material'.

[99] p. 21. One great English scholar Hoskyns omits from his list (all his names are either French or German) is F. C. Burkitt, who roundly declared in 1906: 'The evangelist was no historian. Ideas, not events, were to him the true realities and if we go to his work to learn the course of events we shall only be disappointed' (*Gospel History*, p. 256).

[100] A novel way of defending the credibility of the Fourth Gospel was adopted by Bernhard Weiss (*Lehrbuch*, 1868), who considered that John relied upon his own reminiscences (greatly modified and expanded) and that his work cannot be judged alongside the Synoptic Gospels, for he is completely independent of them. Thus Weiss foreshadowed the position so powerfully defended by C. H. Dodd in his *Historical Tradition*.   [101] p. 23.   [102] *The Fourth Gospel*, pp. 12 f.

In fact the year before Bacon's work was published there had appeared a collection of essays in which one author (A. E. Brooke) had, in the words of W. F. Howard, 'refused to be impaled on either horn of this fashionable dilemma—either Synoptic or Johannine, either historical or allegorical'.[103] But undoubtedly the most urgent and sustained attempt to overcome this dilemma is that made by Sir Edwyn Hoskyns in the introduction to an uncompleted commentary that appeared in 1940, three years after his death.

The kernel of Hoskyns's argument is that to opt for either history on the one hand or theology on the other in reading this Gospel is *totally to misconstrue the intentions of the evangelist*. Though still preoccupied by the now ancient challenge and obviously aware of the need to square up to it, Hoskyns realizes that the traditional positions are indefensible and so moves on to an easier terrain, at the same time deliberately blocking any access back to the old one. The purpose of his commentary, he states at the end of his long introduction, is

to hear and set forth the Meaning which the author of the gospel has himself heard and seen in the concrete, historical life and death of Jesus of Nazareth, in his separate actions and in His audible words. The purpose of this commentary is to barricade the roads which seek to solve the problem either by regarding this Meaning as an idea of the author or as something which itself belongs to the mere hearing or sight of an eyewitness, regarded as historian, for in that case his faith would be not merely irrelevant, but actually suspect, since the eyewitness who believed could not be accepted as an impartial witness. The purpose of this commentary is also to barricade the roads which lead to a disentangling of history and interpretation. This triple barricading does not, however, originate in some perversity of the author of this commentary, but because these barricades have been erected by the original author of the book, and the meaning of his book must remain closed to those who tear down the barricades which he has so carefully erected. Did we say that he had 'erected' these barricades? No, we must not say this. He found the barricades there already, for he is persuaded that the meaning which he has heard does veritably lie in the history. Without it the history is meaningless. Take away the meaning and we should have merely the record of an eyewitness. Take away the history and we should be left only with a human notion or idea.[104]

Many years earlier E. F. Scott had similarly insisted that 'in this narrative we are to recognize the work of one who identified the

---

[103] *Recent Criticism*, p. 28.   [104] p. 132.

eternal Christ of inward religious experience with the Jesus of history'[105]—approaching close to Hoskyns's insight. More significantly, Bousset, in his *Kyrios Christos*, noticed that the evangelist had conceived the grand idea of 'putting myth and dogma back into the history'[106] and that consequently he 'reconciled myth with history, in so far as this was possible'[107] (and equally *the* myth with *the* history). Hoskyns's key idea had evidently ocurred to Bousset too; but he was so disinclined to attempt the same *kind* of explanation that he spoke instead of this 'great thought' (*großer Gedanke*), quite paradoxically, as conceived 'unconsciously and instinctively'. What interested him was a *religionsgeschichtlich* ('history-of-religions') explanation, that is to say an explanation *from the outside*. He thought that the evangelist was responding to the mounting threat of docetism, and at the same time yielding to the refinements of an age that could no longer be content with the 'much too earthy and concrete' Christ of the Synoptists. Asking a different question about the Gospel, he consequently understood it in a different way from Hoskyns, and would certainly have seemed to the latter to have altogether misunderstood it. It is perhaps significant that Hoskyns, who knew the older school of German criticism extremely well, ignores Bousset completely.[108]

In a section devoted to questions of *content* and not of *origin* Bousset seems something of an intruder—like an atheist at a prayer-meeting. Naturally the question arises whether there is any possibility of integrating the two questions or of transcending their opposition; for it looks as if Hoskyns, in claiming to overcome the old antithesis of meaning versus history, has himself chosen to occupy one side of the divide, choosing to ask a *theological* question in contrast to the *historical* question of Bousset. But this is not the place to enter into this important problem in detail—for the present we must return to Hoskyns and his 'insider's' view of the Gospel.

The essential feature of Hoskyns's interpretation (one he has in common with Bultmann, writing about the same time) is that he

---

[105] *The Fourth Gospel, its Purpose and Theology* (1906), as paraphrased by Howard, *Recent Criticism*, p. 38.
[106] 'Der große Gedanke, den er, natürlich nicht mit Bewußtsein, sondern instinktiv erfaßte, war der, Mythos und Dogma in die Geschichte ganz zurückzutragen' (p. 159).
[107] 'Er hat den Mythos mit der Geschichte ausgesöhnt, soweit das überhaupt noch möglich war' (p. 162).
[108] See the discussion by Wayne Meeks, *The Prophet-King*, pp. 2–6.

identifies his own perspective with that of the author of the Gospel. In doing so he is deliberately barring the path to anyone who might wish to study it from outside the magic circle in which 'meaning' and 'history' are bound together in an inextricable whole. Neither the historian, asking 'Did Lazarus rise from the dead?' nor the philosopher, asking 'What is the central *idea* of the book?' is to be admitted to this hallowed spot, which is reserved for initiates—for those prepared to make the act of faith which according to John, Jesus himself required.

This is a persuasive view of the Gospel, and Hoskyns in some ways gets closer to the heart of the matter than Bultmann. But is the old problem to be resolved so easily, by flatly refusing to acknowledge that it was a two-horned dilemma and making it impossible to tell the two horns apart? In fact the problem has not really been disposed of: it exists transposed on to a higher register: it lies, says Hoskyns, in the Gospel's 'steady refusal to come to rest in any solution which conservative or radical scholars have propounded'.[109] Commenting on Renan's *Vie de Jésus*, he says,

No later critic has been able to draw the line between history and interpretation with any greater success than Renan. Many have, of course, attempted to do so, but they have failed because the gospel moves inexorably on as one great whole. Its author's major purpose was to maintain and to insist upon this unity. The commentator is therefore continually brought back to respect this deep-seated interlocking of history and interpretation. Separate the two, and the extremity of violence is done to the text. What Jesus *is* to the faith of the true Christian believer, He *was* in the flesh: this is the theme of the Fourth Gospel, and it is precisely this unity that constitutes the Problem of the Gospel.[110]

Now one may think it odd that Hoskyns should have hit upon 'the Problem of the Gospel', as he obviously did, whilst wrestling with the work of earlier scholars and being forced to acknowledge the pressure they put upon him to find an alternative solution to the dilemma they presented. One may well feel that he has invented a new problem for the purpose of camouflaging an old one—or rather that he has spirited the old problem away, like a conjuror announcing to his audience that the handkerchief which has just vanished before their eyes now exists no longer, if indeed it ever

---

[109] *The Fourth Gospel*, p. 131.
[110] Ibid., p. 35.

did.[111] One rubs one's eyes: was the problem that so preoccupied earlier generations of scholars really no problem at all?

Hoskyns's editor, F. N. Davey, who wrote the all-important seventh chapter ('The Fourth Gospel and the Meaning of History'), piecing it together from scraps and fragments Hoskyns had left behind, certainly sounds very evasive when pretending to tackle the question (which he himself admits to be crucial), 'Did Lazarus rise from the dead?' The answer', he says, 'cannot be either a simple "Yes" or a simple "No".'[112] This reply should scarcely surprise us, for we may well feel that according to his own principles Hoskyns should have disallowed the question—ruling it out of order straight away. Small wonder then that Davey, having committed himself to tackling this 'crucial' question, sets about doing so very gingerly indeed and ends up still sitting, resolutely if uneasily, on the fence erected by his mentor.[113]

In my view Hoskyns is undoubtedly right to insist that the evangelist systematically fuses history and interpretation into an indissoluble whole. But why does he call this procedure a *problem*? If he is right to do so then the problem is one that he expounds rather than resolves, evidently feeling the need to preserve some mystery to present to his own readers. But the fusion of history and theology (if we may call it that) seems to me less a problem than a programme, less an enigma than a key, and one which the evangelist has discovered for himself after a very profound reflection upon the implications of the genre he has taken over. For all that, Hoskyns has penetrated as deeply as anyone into the meaning of the Gospel and we shall be compelled to give his insights due weight in the third part of this book.

---

[111] Hoskyns appears to sense that there is some kind of prestidigitation going on here, but he attributes it to the evangelist: 'Explain the "But" which the Gospel sets against our solutions and which pulls away the cup just when it is on our lips, and we shall have solved the riddle of the book' (p. 131). [112] p. 109.

[113] Such answer as he does give (too long to quote here) is reserved for the concluding paragraphs of the chapter, pp. 127 f.

2

BULTMANN

The Fourth Gospel has been well served by its commentators, especially this century. In Germany there is the pioneering work of Walter Bauer ([1]1912/[2]1925/[3]1933), still outstanding for its uncompromising adherence to the tenets of the history-of-religions school; the radical and stimulating commentary of Jürgen Becker (1979–81) is a recent addition to the long line of Protestant commentaries;[1] whilst on the Catholic side the huge three-volume commentary of Rudolf Schnackenburg (1972–5) must be given pride of place. In France can be seen the two opposing figures of Loisy (1903) and Lagrange (1925), with the squat shadow of Pius X falling between them; more recently the huge and idiosyncratic work of Marie-Émile Boismard (1977) testifies to the vigour of the French scholarly tradition. From Ireland comes Archbishop Bernard's ICC commentary, old-fashioned in its approach, in the tradition of Westcott, but still useful; in England Sir Edwyn Hoskyns (1950) and C. H. Dodd—though strictly speaking his *Interpretation* (1953) is not a commentary—offer innumerable insights of enduring value; in addition there is the careful work of C. K. Barrett ([1]1955/[2]1978); of those commentaries that have appeared after Dodd, Barnabas Lindars's volume in the New Century Bible series (1972) is one of the best, offering an independent view and adapting itself very successfully to the awkward format.

---

[1] The unfinished work of Ernst Haenchen (1980), pieced together with admirable *pietas* by his pupil Ulrich Busse, is a sadly uneven patchwork that scarcely merits the extravagant encomium it receives from James M. Robinson, who speaks of it in a foreword to the German edition as one of the two most promising commentaries on John in the second half of the 20th century. (The other author named by Robinson is Georg Richter, who, like Haenchen, did not live to see his work to completion.) This observation, with its slighting disregard of the major commentaries of Schnackenburg and Brown, is wisely omitted from the English edition (1984), but it is still a matter for regret that Haenchen's work was selected for the Hermeneia series of commentaries in preference to that of Jürgen Becker, the finished work of a single hand.

Finally from America we have the important Anchor Bible commentary of Raymond Brown (1966–70), the first to make extensive use of the recently discovered Dead Sea Scrolls. All men of
no small stature then, each occupying his own position in a far
from narrow world; yet over them all Rudolf Bultmann, un-
matched in learning, breadth, and understanding, towers like a
colossus. Nevertheless, in spite of his pre-eminence, every answer
Bultmann gives to the really important questions he raises—is
wrong.

Where then does his greatness lie? First in the clarity with which
he sees the problems, and his tenacious refusal to allow them to be
buried under his or others' learning or to be swept out of sight in the
interests of tidiness or conformity; secondly in the sheer elegance of
his solutions, in which are contained coherent and consistent
answers to questions of three kinds, literary, historical, and theological; thirdly in the industry and energy with which, not content
with half-answers, he has designed and constructed his splendid
commentary brick by brick, so that it stands as an enduring
challenge to find alternative answers, answers as consistent and as
thorough. But if one were to try to distil the essence of Bultmann's
achievement into a single word by isolating the quality that sets his
commentary above all others, the choice should not fall upon
learning, vast though Bultmann's learning is, nor upon *integrity*,
though Bultmann's single-minded honesty cannot be called into
question, nor upon that combination of thoroughness and consistency the Germans call *Konsequenz*: the best word, I think, would be
penetration—the peculiar ability to see John clearly and to see him
whole.

I.   LITERARY QUESTIONS

Bultmann's grasp of all (save one) of the questions that go to make
up 'the Johannine problem' is one of two factors that enable him to
achieve a view of the Gospel unrivalled in depth and completeness
(the other, as we shall see, is his refusal to dissociate theology and
exegesis). There is a roundedness in his work that makes it
unusually difficult of access, exemplifying as it does the so-called
'hermeneutical circle' which fascinated his friend Heidegger. But
since we must cut into the circle somewhere the best place to do so is

undoubtedly the segment devoted to questions of structure and composition.[2]

This is in fact where Bultmann himself begins in his review of two books by Emanuel Hirsch, whose explanation of the way the Gospel came to be constructed is not dissimilar to his own. Both begin with Schwartz's 'aporias', the rough sutures that disfigure the apparently seamless garment the Gospel was held to be by Strauss. In the previous chapter discussion of these was restricted to a single example, the intolerably awkward transition at the end of chapter 14. But of course there are other places too in which the stitches are readily observable to the critical eye, and Bultmann lists the main ones:

I agree with Hirsch that there are certain points that establish the necessity of [this kind of] analysis and indicate the direction to be followed. It seems to me, as to him, incontestable that chapter 21 is the work of a second hand, added later; incontestable too that the farewell discourse has not been transmitted in its original form—rather, 14: 31 must have been the original conclusion; incontestable that 7: 19–24 is in an impossible position as it stands and must originally have belonged to chapter 5; incontestable that chapter 10 is in the wrong order; much else too is incontestable—and I go further than Hirsch.[3]

Most of what Bultmann regards as incontestable continues of course to be contested (wrongly, in my opinion), but now he goes on to make another important point. There are, he says, two questions which must be carefully distinguished: first, whether scholars are justified in changing the order of the transmitted text; and secondly, how if so the original displacements are to be explained: what accounted for them in the first place? Accordingly, he insists that 'the right to make critical observations and the attempt to discover

---

[2] Bultmann does not deign to lend his readers a guiding hand through his great commentary, leaving them instead to work out his literary theory for themselves from occasional indications in text and footnotes. Indeed a reader anxious to find out what Bultmann has to say on a particular passage may spend some time searching through the German original, which, unlike the English translation, does not even provide a list of page references for chapter and verse of the Gospel. The only places where Bultmann sets out his own theory in any detail are (1) his review-article, 'Hirsch's Auslegung'; and (2) his article 'Johannesevangelium'. But readers of English are fortunate to have a comprehensive guide in the full-scale study of D. Moody Smith, *Composition and Order*. Besides a detailed analysis of Bultmann's own work, this contains an assessment of scholarly reactions appearing in the twenty years or so after the publication of the commentary in 1941.

[3] 'Hirsch's Auslegung', p. 117.

the original order does not depend upon answering this [second] question successfully'.[4] In point of fact Bultmann's own hypothetical restoration is astonishingly bold. For instance, the order he follows in the section of his commentary headed 'The Light of the World' is as follows: 9: 1–41; 8: 12; 12: 44–50; 8: 21–9; 12: 34–6; 10: 19–21. Other bits of chapter 8 are scattered even further afield: 8: 13–20 is treated along with chapter 5 ('The Judge') and 8: 30–40 much later, under the heading 'The Way to the Cross'. One may blink or one may smile, but the uncomfortable fact is that once one has accepted the accuracy of the original observations there is no proper way of evading the challenge to which Bultmann himself responds so whole-heartedly. The likelihood, the inevitability even, that scholars will continue to wrangle over any proposed solution does not mean that there is no point in offering one. All it means is that such solutions as are put forward by those brave enough to take up the challenge must in the nature of the case be both speculative and tentative.

All the same it is reasonable to ask whether Bultmann is right to hold the two questions so firmly apart. In theory it is at least possible that the nature of one's speculative reconstruction might be determined to some extent by the answer one has given to the second question. For if we could explain how and why the original text suffered such severe dislocations we *might* have already taken the first step towards restoring the original order. And we may wonder too whether to speak of an 'original text' and an 'original order' is not somehow begging the question. Let us suppose that the 'original' text underwent a series of revisions and that these involved a number of accretions and (perhaps) excisions. In that case not merely is the desire to establish an *Urtext* doomed to frustration from the outset, but even if *per impossibile* it were to be granted, then the elusive object of desire might prove on inspection so small and unimpressive that any satisfaction would be short-lived. (Which does not mean that the search itself would be uninteresting or unenlightening.)

What then of the second question: how to account for the dislocations? Wellhausen, it will be remembered, had argued that some of these at least were the result of deliberate decisions. Faure had christened the unknown operator 'the ecclesiastical redactor',

[4] Ibid., pp. 118 f.

and this personage reappears in the pages of Hirsch's study, as
indeed in those of Bultmann's. But does his interfering hand
constitute a totally satisfactory explanation of the present state of the
Gospel text, not just in the sense that he may have put the pieces
together for some ascertainable reason of his own but also in the
sense that he will have been responsible for their original excision—
in other words that he applied the scissors as well as the paste? Hirsch
answers yes to this question, but Bultmann has his doubts:

I too tried for a long time to explain the displacements in this way; and such
an attempt can be supported by the fact that only very rarely does the
present order make no sense at all—which is why many exegetes want to
hold fast to the transmitted order. But all this circumstance proves is that
the redactor did not proceed unreflectively. There remain some cases in
which the transmitted order really makes no sense at all, for instance the
order of the farewell discourse, which can only be understood as resulting
from a counsel of despair (*eine Verlegenheitsordnung*)—also the position of
12: 44–50.[5]

Consequently Bultmann feels unable to dispense altogether with
the 'displacement' theory: after looking very hard he has failed to
find any controlling purpose behind the present arrangement of the
text: 'There is in my view only one answer left: the redactor was
faced with a text that had fallen into considerable disorder, and tried
his best to bring it into order.'[6] As a typical example Bultmann cites
3: 31–6 (a passage that even a casual reader might find rather
baffling, since in spite of its high christology, it seems to have been
spoken by John the Baptist). 'The passage certainly fits in with the
train of thought of the Nicodemus episode (probably at the end, after
3: 21). The redactor found it on its own (as a loose sheet) and put it
into its present place after the speech of the Baptist, 3: 27–30—
seduced by the same considerations that prompt modern exegetes
even now when they try to explain 3: 31–6 as a speech of the
Baptist. With a little good will some kind of train of thought can
always be constructed.'[7] Rather hesitantly Bultmann suggests the
kind of hypothesis we have already seen defended by Streeter:
separate sheets assembled in the wrong order. But he sees that this
will not work in every case: 'the devastation must, at least in some
places, have been more extensive, as I believe is shown by the
present disorder of chapters 6 and 10.'[8]

---

[5] 'Hirsch's Auslegung', p. 119.   [6] Ibid.   [7] Ibid.   [8] Ibid.

So Bultmann wheels in the 'displacement' theory to account for the odd stitchings he is unable to explain in any other way, much as Newton brought God in as a kind of addendum to his planetary theory, to make the minor adjustments he saw to be necessary if his theory was to work properly. How nice it would be if one could say, as Laplace did when asked how God fitted into the theory in which he had finally ironed out the few wrinkles Newton had not managed to eliminate: 'Je n'ai pas besoin de cette hypothèse-là!'

The 'displacement' theory and the 'ecclesiastical redactor', therefore, are two factors that help to explain the present state of the Gospel text. Bultmann, however, assigns to the latter a much smaller role than does Hirsch. Apart from the appendix (chapter 21) the redactor does not add much of importance to the body of the Gospel. What Bultmann questions is not the accuracy of Hirsch's observations but the conclusions he draws from them: 'There are indeed in the Fourth Gospel a large number of passages which give the impression that they are interrupting an original [continuous] text—some because of their form and terminology, others because they are clearly glosses. But these passages are not (or seldom at any rate) to be attributed to a redactor but to the evangelist himself.'[9] Hirsch fails to recognize

that *throughout the Fourth Gospel three layers must be distinguished*: 1. the *redaction*, which has played a great part in the ordering of the text but a very small one in the fashioning of its content; 2. the *evangelist* himself, who has constructed his work from the tradition (both oral and written) available to him; 3. this *tradition* itself, which means to a great extent written *sources*. Among these I believe I can single out two with some certainty: a) a collection of Jesus' miracles ($\sigma\eta\mu\epsilon\hat{\iota}a$), the $\sigma\eta\mu\epsilon\hat{\iota}a$-source, b) a collection of Jesus' discourses, in which he speaks as revealer, speeches whose form is to be thought of as related to that of the *Odes of Solomon*. These 'revelation-discourses' are completely different from the sayings (logia) of the synoptic tradition.[10]

By the time he had completed his own commentary, Bultmann had added a third source (the 'Passion and Easter stories') to the other two. In other respects he gives in his review of Hirsch a complete, though rough, outline of his theory of the composition of the Gospel. He reproaches Hirsch for failing to use the kind of stylistic criteria which would have enabled him to detect the 'revelation-

---

[9] Ibid., p. 120.   [10] Ibid.

discourse source'. Even in those discourses in which the work of the evangelist himself takes up the largest place the source, thinks Bultmann, can be seen to run through them 'like a red thread'.[11] But in fact the thesis of the revelation-discourse source has proved the most fragile of all Bultmann's suggestions; it is certainly the one which has received least support from later critics.[12] The stylistic criteria he employed to distinguish the work of the evangelist from that of his source have not stood up to examination. Now this particular source has, as we shall see, an important part to play in the next segment of Bultmann's theory of the Gospel, that of the 'history-of-religions', in which he looks back behind and beyond the text of the Gospel itself. And since as Bultmann himself acknowledges any *literary* analysis must have some bearing upon one's understanding of the Gospel as a whole, we need to approach the next section with some caution. Even before we start there is a big question-mark hanging over it.

2. HISTORICAL QUESTIONS[13]

As an exegete Bultmann shared the concerns of the history-of-religions school in which he was nurtured. In particular he fully agreed with its refusal to admit any dogmatic presuppositions into the study of the origins of Christianity—which, from the historian's point of view, is just another religion. One of his most enduring contributions to Johannine studies was to locate with fine precision the problem which Harnack, Wrede, and finally Bousset had attempted to formulate many years earlier: he defines this problem as '*the riddle of where John's Gospel stands in relation to the development of early Christianity*',[14] and he explains this by saying that it cannot be

---

[11] 'Hirsch's Auslegung', p. 121.

[12] It is subjected to a detailed criticism by E. Ruckstuhl, *Die literarische Einheit*. See also D. Moody Smith, *Composition and Order*, ch. 2 ('The Discussion of Bultmann's Theory of Sources').

[13] Apart from his commentary and a paragraph in the *RGG* article already cited, by far the most important contribution Bultmann made to the questions discussed in this section was his article 'Bedeutung'. This seminal piece is not available in English (although part of it is usefully summarized by Wayne Meeks in his *Prophet-King*, pp. 6–10), which is why I have chosen to quote from it very extensively. Bultmann's reconstruction of the Gnostic myth may also be found in his *Primitive Christianity*, pp. 193–204.

[14] 'Bedeutung', p. 55 (italics in the original).

considered to belong to any of the three main branches of doctrinal development that can be distinguished in the early Church, namely Hellenistic Christianity (Paul), Jewish–Hellenistic Christianity (*1 Clement*, the *Shepherd of Hermas*, Hebrews, the *Letter of Barnabas*), or Palestinian Christianity (the Synoptic Gospels).[15] On the face of it one might think that the most likely influence on John in these three groups must be Paul, as most earlier scholars had tended somewhat unreflectingly to assume. But this will not bear scrutiny. Bousset had already observed the virtual absence of the title κύριος (Lord) in John, the dwindling importance of the Pauline concept of πνεῦμα (spirit), and the substitution of a cosmological dualism for the ethical or anthropological dualism of Paul's characteristic opposition between πνεῦμα (spirit) and σάρξ (flesh).[16] But since Bousset maintained none the less that John was indebted to Paul he was unable to see the problem in all its acuteness. If it be said that both writers are preoccupied with the relation between Christianity and Judaism, the answer must be that the focus is completely different in the two cases. John shares none of Paul's obsession with the Law; he never speaks of the righteousness of God, or sees human history in terms of God's plan for the world. Such resemblances as there are lend no plausibility whatsoever to the thesis that John 'stood on Paul's shoulders'. This means that an alternative source has to be sought for John's central ideas, especially his high christology (e.g. the notion of pre-existence), which far transcends anything in the Synoptic Gospels. Martin Dibelius once wrote that the main problem of christology is this: 'How did knowledge of the historical Jesus change so quickly into faith in the heavenly Son of God?'[17] But one answer will no longer suffice: to see how Paul reached this position does not help us with John.[18] Dibelius's problem has to be solved not once but twice.[19]

[15] This triple division, which formed the framework of Bultmann's earlier work on the Synoptic Gospels, would be rejected by most scholars nowadays as over-simple. For the English reader a useful book based on this division (whose very simplicity is still something of a commendation from a heuristic point of view) is R. H. Fuller's *The Foundations of New Testament Christology*.

[16] Cf. *Kyrios Christos*, pp. 162 ff.; Bultmann, 'Johannesevangelium', col. 846.

[17] 'Christologie', col. 1593. This article is also available in English in *Twentieth Century Theology in the Making*, ed. J. Pelikan (London, 1970), 62–90.

[18] Consequently C. F. D. Moule's *The Origin of Christology* and Martin Hengel's brilliantly concise *The Son of God* are of no help to us here.

[19] If not three or even four times; for the christology of the Synoptic Gospels (especially that of Matthew and Mark) is 'higher' than is often supposed.

In the case of the Fourth Gospel the problem is exacerbated by its self-containedness and self-allusiveness. Wellhausen, who certainly had no motive for grinding this particular axe, insisted that 'in spite of its different layers, from a historical perspective the Gospel may be considered as essentially a unity. It is to be assumed that the expansions mostly stem from the same circle as that within which the *Grundschrift* took its rise and found its first readers.'[20] Bousset is no less convinced than Wellhausen of the existence of numerous aporias, and agrees that 'considered from a history-of-religions perspective, the Johannine literature remains a unity';[21] but this does not prevent him from recognizing that it was the work of several hands. Strauss may have been mistaken in thinking the Gospel a seamless garment, but he was right in one respect: the central themes are so tightly interlocked and intertwined that they are hardly likely to have been developed independently before being woven together into the fabric of the Gospel.

Bultmann makes the same point in reviewing a book by E. Percy that is highly critical of his own position. It is no use trying to explain the central concepts of the Gospel piecemeal, as Percy attempts to do:

Why does John use a different language from that of the Synoptics? ... Why is Jesus' quarrel with the law so unlike that in the Synoptics? Why is his eschatology completely different? ... If the problem is to be seen clearly, John must be recognizable as a unified and individual whole (*als ganze Gestalt in seiner Eigenart sichtbar*). There is no point in adducing a synoptic or Pauline analogue for this or that expression of John, or in comparing one term taken in isolation from the rest (such as 'light' or 'life') with expressions drawn from the Old Testament or Judaism; for John's language is a whole and it is in this whole that each individual term finds its meaning (*seine feste Bestimmung*).[22]

Bousset of course had attempted to tackle the problem as a whole, much as Bultmann demands; but his explanation is unsatisfactory—not because his parallels are unconvincing or badly chosen, but because the concepts he discusses are like the spokes of a wheel with the hub missing. There is another reason too why Bousset's search for the origins of the Fourth Gospel is doomed to failure: he is looking in the wrong place, in what Dodd calls 'the higher religion of

[20] p. 119.   [21] 'Johannesevangelium', col. 618.
[22] 'Johanneische Schriften', p. 154.

Hellenism'. 'What separates the Gospel from Paul', argues Bultmann, 'also separates it in part from Hellenistic mysticism: its picture
of man is very different, it has no πνεῦμα/σάρξ (i.e. anthropological)
dualism, no asceticism, no leanings towards a theory of the passage
of the soul or to a devotion based on experience (*Seelenleitung und
Erlebnisfrömmigkeit*). By contrast, John's Gospel has a dogmatic
character. Its christology is not determined by any cosmic catastrophe nor by the dying and rising of a cult-divinity, but by the
concept of revelation. And Jesus does not reveal the mysteries of God
or man or the cosmos, but one thing and one thing only: that he is
the Revealer.'[23]

Here for the first time Bultmann enunciates the formula which
marks his interpretation out from any other. 'So this', he continues,
'is the second great riddle of John's Gospel: taking the Gospel as it
sees itself (*für sich*), *what is its central intuition, its basic idea?*'
'Doubtless', he answers, 'it must lie in the constantly repeated
proposition that Jesus is the emissary of God (e.g. 17: 3, 23, 25),
who through his words and deeds brings revelation. He performs the
works given him by the Father, he speaks what he has heard from
the Father or what he has seen in his presence. The man who
believes is saved, he who does not is lost. But there lies the riddle.
Precisely what does the Jesus of John's Gospel reveal? One thing
only, though put in different ways: *that* he has been sent as
Revealer.'[24] So here, for Bultmann, is the hub of the wheel—the *fact*
of revelation, or rather Jesus' revelation of himself *as Revealer*. And it
is this, the answer the Gospel itself offers (*für sich*) to the second great
riddle, that furnishes the object of the first riddle: what (*an sich*) is the
historical origin of this extraordinary conception—how is it to be
explained?

Having expounded the riddle to his safisfaction, Bultmann next
proceeds to consider and dismiss various solutions that might
conceivably be suggested:

1. Should the answer be that the intuition of John's Gospel is purely
dogmatic, so that what is revealed is the *dogma* of Jesus' divine mission, and
whoever believes in this is saved, even without being able to understand it?
No, that is clearly not the intention of the Gospel, in which 'faith',
'knowledge' and 'vision' [*Bultmann uses the infinitive of the verb in all three
cases*] are synonymous, and whose Prologue declares that δόξα [glory] is

[23] 'Bedeutung', p. 57.   [24] Ibid.

seen in Jesus, and that this vision leads to the gift of χάρις [grace/favour] in exchange for χάρις.

2. Or instead of asking the question, should one not rather simply admit that the real centre of gravity of Johannine religious practice (*Frömmigkeit*) may lie outside the express statements of the Gospel, so that it is to be understood only in connection with a communal practice with the *cult* of Christ at its centre, forming its main source of strength? But in that case why are there no specifically cultic characteristics? Why is the title κύριος missing?

3. Or is the author a mystic? Not of course of the contemplative kind that becomes absorbed in the vision of the Crucified One, crowned with thorns, wounded and bleeding. The 'ecce homo' of 19: 5 is obviously not mystical. Possibly then a mystic to whom the miracle-man walking the earth would be a symbol of ineffable divinity? In fact the Farewell Discourse does contain some well-known mystical terminology: the formula of mutual mystical immanence—we in Jesus—Jesus in us; he dwelling in us and God too in us along with him; all one in one, the Father, the Son and those who belong to him. But are these anything more than mere formulae? Is their purpose to describe an *experience* as distinct from faith? For apart from them there is no other trace of mysticism; no mystical names for God, no anthropological dualism, no doctrine of the passage of souls, no devotion based on experience.[25]

None of these answers, concluded Bultmann, is satisfactory. Rather the solution must lie somewhere in the reiterated proposition that 'Jesus is sent by God, is one with the Father and as such is the bearer of revelation. There must be more in this proposition than meets the eye. And in fact what lies behind it is a powerful *myth*, and the recognition of this myth is the first step in the correct understanding of the Gospel.[26]

The use of the word 'understanding' (*Verständnis*) at this point is probably intended to recall the title of his article, which promises to show how the Mandaean and Manichaean texts can help towards the understanding of the Gospel. This then is where Bultmann finds his answer to the first great riddle; and the next forty-odd pages of this long article are devoted to a detailed comparison of selected themes from the Gospel (twenty-eight in all) with a variety of texts picked not only from the Mandaean and Manichaean literature mentioned in the title but also from more familiar sources such as the *Odes of Solomon* and the *Acts of Thomas*. The Gospel themes, it

---

[25] 'Bedeutung', pp. 57 f.   [26] Ibid., p. 58.

should be observed, are listed in an order which has evidently been carefully worked out *so as in itself to constitute a coherent story*:

1. The Revealer is the eternal divine being who was in the beginning; 2. He has been sent by the Father into the world; 3. He has come into the world; 4. He is at the same time one with the Father; 5. The Father has endowed him with authority; 6. He possesses life and bestows it; 7. He leads out of darkness into light; 8. In the Fourth Gospel, as in the literature cited for comparison, the twin concepts *truth* and *falsehood* correspond to the other pairs of concepts, life/death, light/darkness; 9. In the Emissary there is neither fault nor falsehood; 10. He does the works his Father has commissioned him to do; 11. He speaks of his own person in revelatory discourses (ἐγώ εἰμι); 12. He knows his own and they know him; 13. He gathers them, or rather chooses them. They belong to him, or will do so; 14. To the powers of this world the Emissary appears like a stranger—they do not know where he comes from since his origin is different from theirs; 15. Those who hear the Emissary's preaching have hardened hearts; 16. The Emissary is abandoned in the world, and hated; 17. As he has come, so will he go; as he has descended, so will he ascend; 18. Then he will be sought but not found; 19. He is 'justified' in his ascent; 20. At his departure the Emissary prays for his own; 21. As the Redeemed One,[27] the Emissary leads the redeemed with him; 22. He prepares a dwelling for his own; 23. He has shown his own the way, or rather prepared it for them; 24. He is the door; 25. He sets all prisoners free; 26. His ascension is the downfall of the cosmos; 27. He is the Judge; 28. He is the Son of man.[28]

Now if Bultmann's argument is not to remain completely incomprehensible (especially to the more traditionally minded Christian) one must allow oneself to fall under his spell, to be intellectually seduced by him. He himself was convinced that he had found the answer to the riddle, the explanation which makes all things clear. And it is particularly important to stress that, right or wrong, he does actually offer a solution—that is to say he meets the difficulties head on and does not attempt to camouflage them or to spirit them

---

[27] Wayne Meeks remarks that *Erlöster* (Redeemed) must be a misprint for *Erlöser* (Redeemer) 'since the passages Bultmann quotes do not contain the notion of "the redeemed redeemer"' (*Prophet-King*. p. 7 n. 3). If so, the mistake remained uncorrected when the article was reprinted for *Exegetica*.

[28] 'Bedeutung', pp. 60–97 *passim*.

away. For though many of his twenty-eight propositions are traditional enough, and could be explained fairly easily by appealing either to the Synoptic tradition or to the Old Testament, this is not true of them all; and Bultmann would of course insist that it is the composite picture that has to be explained—one cannot hope to understand a cake simply by knowing the origins of its ingredients—the cow and the cornfield. So Bultmann would be totally unimpressed if one were to point out, for instance, that the idea of the prophet as a divine emissary is a familiar one in the Old Testament. He knows this perfectly well; and he counters by observing, in his commentary, that 'the Old Testament nowhere speaks of the equality of the prophet with God', adding 'It is not only that Jesus' equality with God is asserted of his actions as well as his words, it is also that Jesus' words of authority are not interpreted in terms of election, vocation and inspiration, but *in terms of the Gnostic myth.*'[29]

Bultmann is equally unimpressed by the argument that the Mandaean texts are much later (seventh century) than John; the myth itself, he says, is certainly older. Besides, there are many more elements in the myth than are actually found in the Gospel; in fact the main point of interest in the myth is the passage of the soul after death into the realm of light. If this (and much else) is not found in John, this is because the evangelist has selected what interests him most: 'It is evident that we must see the ideas and images of this myth as the material out of which John has formed his own picture.'[30] In his 1925 article Bultmann does not attempt to settle the question ('which needs further discussion')[31] whether there was a direct literary influence on the Gospel from a particular religious community; but he inclines towards this solution, and adopts it in his commentary. He even suggests (and finds the suggestion 'extraordinarily likely')[32] that the Mandaeans themselves might be this very community, arguing that the correspondences between these texts and those of Marcionite and Valentinian Gnosticism show that the sect must have existed long before these second-century Christian Gnostics. Perhaps they could actually be identified with the followers of John the Baptist who appear to be a target of attack in the early chapters of the Gospel. In an article published two years earlier in 1923, Bultmann had suggested that the present Prologue

[29] pp. 250 f.   [30] 'Bedeutung', p. 98.   [31] Ibid., p. 99.
[32] Ibid., p. 100.

was originally a hymn composed by a member of this sect in praise of its founder.[33]

In his 1925 article Bultmann does not claim to have answered his first riddle completely: the puzzle, he says 'has not been solved but it has been brought closer to a solution'.[34] The full solution, in his eyes, was reached when he was finally in a position to isolate his revelation-discourse source. I have no doubt that the inspiration to seek for this came not only from his study of the Mandaean texts but also from the fact that the Prologue at least had an independent existence (as was already widely recognized) before 'the evangelist' took it over to serve as the introduction of his Gospel. It is worth stressing then that unlike the signs source, which was originally put forward as a hypothetical solution of textual aporias, the *Offen-barungsreden* source was 'discovered' by following up a clue located *elsewhere in the Gospel*. One may doubt if textual and stylistic criteria alone, however minutely observed, would have led to the discovery of this source, which is therefore epistemically of a different order from the signs source. On the other hand, Bultmann's Mandaean theory does not stand or fall by the existence or non-existence of this second source. Certainly it offers a *tidier* solution to the problem of the Gospel's origins, but in exegesis, as in life, a tidy solution is not always available.

Besides its obvious exegetical advantages the hypothesis of revelation-discourse source (or indeed the Mandaean hypothesis in its earlier, more primitive form) has considerable *theological* advantages also; and it is convenient to discuss these now (because they are still relevant to the answer to the first riddle) before going on to consider Bultmann's general theological interpretation (which is the answer to his second riddle).

Bultmann was both an outstanding biblical scholar and an outstanding theologian. Most British and American theologians are amateur exegetes and some exegetes are amateur theologians, but

---

[33] 'Der religionsgeschichtliche Hintergrund.' (A slightly abbreviated translation of this is available in *Interpretation*, ed. J. Ashton, pp. 18–35.) Bultmann concludes that Bousset's old distinction between Palestinian and Hellenistic Christianity within the early Church is inadequate, for two strata have to be distinguished within Palestinian Christianity itself: 'To formulate the problem as sharply as possible, I might say this: we must reckon with the possibility that type for type Johannine Christianity is older than Synoptic Christianity', by which he means that 'Jesus' public life and preaching may have been much more closely related to the Gnostic-Baptist movement than the Synoptic tradition allows us to recognize' ('Bedeutung', p. 102).

[34] 'Bedeutung', p. 103.

since few are competent to cover both fields together the majority, when discussing Bultmann's work, elect to restrict themselves to one or other aspect of it. Bultmann himself saw things differently. In a foreword to a collection of some of his major scholarly articles published in 1967 under the title *Exegetica*, Bultmann comments approvingly on the editor's preface: 'He rightly stresses as the dominant characteristic of my work that I have been resolutely concerned to effect a unity between exegesis and theology, but in such a way that exegesis in fact takes precedence.'[35] This is repeated in a later, more general collection, *Gesammelte Aufsätze* (1973): 'from first to last I strove to be an exegete and in doing so I was concerned with the unity of exegesis and theology.'[36]

One may hazard the guess that the main reason why Bultmann selected the Fourth Gospel as the object of his major contribution to New Testament studies is that the Gospel itself exemplifies, uniquely and excitingly, both his exegetical methods and his theological beliefs. Evidence for what may seem on the face of it an absurd claim is already to be found at the conclusion of his 1925 article. How, according to Bultmann, did the evangelist proceed in what after all was the most characteristic and original part of his work? He took over a non-Christian source, one steeped in Gnostic mythology, and adapted it to his own purposes, so as to convey a message which is neither myth, nor dogma, nor mystery, but radical challenge. Since the other hypotheses have to be excluded, 'there is only one possibility left, that the concept of revelation is conceived radically, which means renouncing any attempt to describe its *content*, whether in terms of speculative propositions or in terms of spiritual circumstantialities,[37] because either of these would drag [divine] revelation down to the level of the merely human.' And Bultmann ends his article with these words: 'The only way of presenting revelation is as the annihilation of everything human, the refusal of all human questions, the rejection of all human answers—in short, as the putting of man into question',[38] a Kierkegaardian conclusion

---

[35] *Exegetica*, p. vii.
[36] *Gesammelte Aufsätze*, p. v. Bultmann's foreword was written in 1970. But this is not just hindsight on his part, or wishful thinking at the end of a long life. He makes basically the same point in an article entitled 'Das Problem einer theologischen Exegese des Neuen Testaments', written as early as 1925 and reprinted in this very collection, pp. 353–78.
[37] *Seelische Zuständlichkeiten*: the German is as difficult as the English translation.
[38] 'Bedeutung', p. 104.

that some may find disquieting or even distasteful, but whose vigour can scarcely be denied.[39]

The uncompromising starkness of Bultmann's theology may cause one to miss the sheer elegance of his total solution. For by assigning the mythical elements of the Gospel to a source, *he allows the evangelist himself to do his own demythologizing.*[40] All the interpreter has to do is to *understand*, to understand, that is, how the evangelist is operating and his motives for doing so, so that his own interpretation can be simply the obverse, the public side, so to speak, of his private understanding. The exegete who rejects Bultmann's solution assumes in so doing the burden of interpretation and splits understanding into two distinct functions, a split that is the price modern exegesis has had to play for claiming the status of a science. Before the critical question was posed—before, that is, the gap between the old text and the modern reader became too wide to be ignored—no distinction was needed, no distinction could be *seen* between finding the meaning *of* a text and finding the meaning *for* its readers. The interpreter simply got on with the job of interpreting and that was that. In his interpretation of the Fourth Gospel, Bultmann succeeds in recovering an ancient innocence, and he does so *in the process of* offering a scientific solution and without in any way having to compromise the standards of scholarly exegesis he himself regarded as taking precedence over theology. To put the matter in another way: if the Gospel is to make its full and proper impact it must be stripped of the strange exotic clothing which the evangelist has borrowed from his Gnostic source. The exegete's task, as he assists with the stripping, is simply to ensure that flesh is not confused with fabric, or the myth mistaken for the message. And this is to conform very precisely to the intentions of the evangelist himself, for this is one case in which most decidedly the medium is *not* the message.

All this helps to explain why Bultmann's commentary is so much more urgent and exciting than run-of-the-mill commentaries that have followed it. He is, as it were, getting inside the evangelist's head

---

[39] It should also give pause to those who accuse Bultmann, somewhat unfairly, of constructing an *anthropology* instead of a *theology*.

[40] Bultmann says as much in his response to Percy: 'That John's language is mythological and is taken from Gnosticism I do not deny: in fact I assert it; that this language is demythologized, that is to say loses its mythical meaning, in John I do not deny either—this too I assert' ('Johanneische Schriften', p. 152). Cf. Commentary pp. 143 n. 1; 251; *Jesus Christ and Mythology*, p. 52.

and speaking with his voice—and for the exegete such a move is equivalent, as I said, to recovering an ancient innocence. Other commentators, having paid the price of eating of the fruit of the tree of knowledge, are forced to remain outside. Bultmann alone has found the key to unlock the gates barring the entrance to the garden.

It must be conceded that Bultmann's solution to his first riddle is, if not simple, breathtakingly bold—a mission impossible executed with flair and daring. But his sweeping synthesis could not pass unchallenged, and a full study of all the responses it elicited would itself be a major undertaking. Because of its size and scope his work is vulnerable at many points. A few of these, arising directly out of the article under discussion, deserve particular attention.

1. In the first place, there is no consensus among the students of Gnosticism concerning either the origins of this movement (was it hatched in Iran or was there perhaps another nest somewhere in Palestine?) or the date by which the fledgeling could fly (was there in fact a pre-Christian Gnosticism in the proper sense, or is mature Gnosticism simply a second-century Christian heresy—a view which was not challenged until as late as 1897?). Biblical scholars are scarcely noted for marching in step, but compared with gnoseologists they are a brigade of guards.[41] Here I simply want to make the point that whether we speak of Gnosticism in general or of Mandaean Gnosticism in particular, we do not really know whether it was sufficiently fully-formed by the end of the first century AD to have exercised the kind of influence (as a coherent redeemer-myth) called for by Bultmann's theory. That there were ideas in the air which were at some time incorporated into the full myth (e.g. the dualism of the Qumran texts) is certain; but much more is required if Bultmann's theory is to work.

2. In the second place, Bultmann has *extracted* from the Mandaean texts those elements that present points of similarity with the

---

[41] In his book *Pre-Christian Gnosticism* (London, 1973) E. Yamauchi mentions a work called *Haran Gawaita*, a Mandaean source unavailable to Bultmann, since it was not published until 1953. Confronted with the objection that this is thoroughly confused (it places Jerusalem in Babylonia!), one eminent scholar, R. Macuch replies: 'All Mandaean traditions are confused, but they are clear for one who is able to read them.' Quoted by Yamauchi, p. 134. Henry Chadwick similarly remarks: 'the blessed word "gnostic" has become so overloaded today that it is hardly more than a generous wave of the hand in an uncertain direction, and has come to lack any precise significance'. 'Reflections', p. 267.

Fourth Gospel and placed them in an order which is itself an interpretation of the Gnostic doctrine. Jumbled up once more and regarded in context, they would look very different. With two documents in front of one, the *Ginza*, say, and the Fourth Gospel, it is not too hard to draw up a list of parallels because both works are already fully composed—even if one is infinitely more readable than the other.[42] But Bultmann's final theory postulates a document occupying a position somewhere between the *Ginza* and the Gospel. One might, I suppose, think of this as a rather more compact version of the former, avoiding all its sprawling excesses. But this is not apparently how Bultmann conceived it. He himself suggested something more along the lines of the *Odes of Solomon*—no miracle stories, no passion or resurrection narrative, but simply a collection of discourses differing from John's version chiefly by the absence of any reference to Jesus:[43] it will have been the evangelist who identified the redeemer-figure of his source with the Christ of his faith. But this theory loses most of its plausibility once the stylistic and other differences Bultmann claims to discern in the Gospel text have been proved wanting. For these constitute the only tangible evidence for the existence of such a document in the first place.

3. We should also reckon with the possibility that the influence worked the other way round; if so, then the Mandaeans will have taken over some of their key ideas from Christian sources, much as Marcion and Valentinus did. When E. Percy put forward this suggestion Bultmann rejected it on the grounds that the Mandaeans, on this account, make so little use of the possibilities: in particular, they do not recognize any definite *event* of revelation.[44] But as an *argumentum ad hominem* one might just raise the question why if the

---

[42] Mark Lidzbarski's translation of the *Ginza* (Göttingen, 1925) covers very nearly 600 large pages. It is an *extremely* messy and involved piece of work. Bultmann plays the Ariadne in offering to guide the reader through this maze, but one suspects that he himself found the 'red thread' in the Fourth Gospel.

[43] I know only one extended comparison between the Gospel and the *Odes*, an unpublished dissertation for the University of Durham by A. T. Morrison (1980). Morrison concludes that with one striking exception (a parallel between Ode 31 and John 17) there are no significant links between the two writings but that they probably share a common background in early Gnosticism. James Brownson reaches the very different conclusion that 'The Odes represent a theological perspective similar to those who separated from the Johannine community as represented in 1 John' ('The Odes of Solomon', p. 52).

[44] 'Johanneische Schriften', pp. 166 f.

evangelist is allowed to have left so much out, the Mandaeans should not have left much out also.

4. Finally one may ask whether Bultmann has given sufficiently serious attention to the alternative hypotheses that he mentions —and so rapidly dismisses—at the beginning of his article. Summonsed and sentenced within the space of a single page, they do not stand much chance against the big theory that follows. Given that chance, one or other might prove stronger and more attractive than Bultmann's curt and somewhat contemptuous treatment of them allows. Or there might be another solution, as yet unglimpsed and unrecognized, lurking somewhere in one of the areas that neither Bousset nor Bultmann has properly explored. What is certain is that it is easier to reject Bultmann's solutions than to find a viable alternative. Few of his critics have had as keen an appreciation of the very real problems he set out to solve.

3. THEOLOGICAL QUESTIONS[45]

We have seen that in his 1925 article Bultmann discerned two great 'riddles' or puzzles (*Rätsel*) set by the Fourth Gospel, the first historical, the second exegetical or theological. In that article he was mainly concerned with the first of these, and attempted to answer from the outside, as it were, without deviating from the principles of the history-of-religions school, the puzzle concerning the place or positioning (*Stellung*) of the Fourth Gospel in what are sometimes called the 'trajectories' of early Christianity. In tackling this question (which I have called the question of *origins*) he found it necessary to wrestle briefly with the second riddle also. This is more an insider's question: what is the central conception (*Grundbegriff*) of the evangelist—in current idiom, what is the Gospel all about? The first of these questions was that of Bousset, the Christian historian, the second that of Hoskyns, the Christian exegete. And it may be argued that the second question is primary. For what is the point of

[45] For a full appreciation of the force and cogency of Bultmann's theological interpretation of the Fourth Gospel, it is necessary to turn to his commentary. For the sake of convenience I make more use in what follows of his more schematic account in his *Theology of the New Testament*, ii. An even more compact version is to be found in his *RGG*³ article, 'Johannesevangelium'. What is offered here is not a comprehensive survey of these various writings, but simply a criticism of a single theme, the one Bultmann himself regarded as the most central.

attempting an explanation of something until you have a clear grasp of what it is you are trying to explain?

We shall return to this objection later. Our present concern is with Bultmann's answer to his second great riddle. His fundamental insight, from which he never wavered, was that the central theme of the Gospel is *revelation*. Yet there is something paradoxical about this revelation as Bultmann conceived it. The Revealer came to earth to say one thing and one thing only—*that* he is the Revealer. In this particular parcel there is nothing to unpack: it is empty.

If one were to protest that the Jesus of the Gospel does in fact reveal more about himself than Bultmann allows (for instance that he is the *Son* of God and has been *sent* by him) Bultmann would no doubt reply that 'mission' and 'sonship' are mythological concepts taken over by the evangelist from his Gnostic source. It is true that he clothes his message in these concepts, but they no more belong to the essence of what he has to say than figurative expressions like 'living water', 'bread of life', 'the Shepherd', and 'the Vine'. Stripped of these superfluous images the message is 'revealed' for what it truly is, a bare, a naked 'that' (*ein bloßes Daß*).[46]

In trying to understand Bultmann's position it is helpful to realize that he makes a very clear distinction in his own mind between *faith* and *religion*. Religion is tethered to earth; faith floats free. Religion is the proper object of historical study: faith is the affair of the theologian. And although Bultmann was anxious, as we have seen, to hold the two together (like Schlatter, he reproaches Wrede with tearing apart the act of living from the act of thinking),[47] it may be doubted whether his own synthesis carries total conviction.

Be that as it may, it is evident that Bultmann sees the central message of the Fourth Gospel (and indeed of the New Testament as a whole) as a call to faith, and he does not wish to permit this message to remain encumbered by its grosser Gnostic accoutrements. Moreover one can detect behind his insistent refusal to state what the Christian revelation consists in a passionate detestation not just of *myth* but of *dogma*. Christian faith means to believe in Jesus Christ, and to reduce this act of faith (Luther's *fides qua creditur*) to a proposition or a series of propositions (*fides quae creditur*) is to disfigure it beyond recognition. For after all, 'Jesus' words are not didactic propositions but an invitation or a call to a decision.'[48]

---

[46] *Theology*, ii. 66.   [47] Ibid., ii. 246.   [48] Ibid., ii. 21.

Now the implications of this very Kierkegaardian view for Bult-mann's picture of Jesus are profound, but not at all easy to grasp, especially for Christians not afflicted with a similar discomfort in the presence of dogma and tradition. It is here perhaps more than anywhere else in Bultmann's exegesis that one can detect a theological *parti pris*, an option the exegete makes before even opening the book he is to expound, what one might call, to use a term Bultmann employs in a different connection, a pre-understanding (*Vorverständnis*). A very important element in Bultmann's own pre-understanding in the sense I am using the word in is his conviction that 'the quest for the historical Jesus' is not just futile but misguided, resting upon a monumental *mis*understanding of Christian faith. In a famous passage in one of his shorter writings Bultmann says that he would be happy to consign all the fanciful portraits contained in the nineteenth-century lives of Jesus to the flames, for what would be lost thereby would be 'nothing other than "Christ after the flesh" (Χριστὸς κατὰ σάρκα)'[49] This is clearly more than a theological opinion: it is for Bultmann, to put the matter somewhat ironically, an article of faith. What C. H. Dodd undertakes in his second big book on the Fourth Gospel, a meticulous sifting of all the evidence in a search for little gold nuggets of historical fact or eyewitness tradition, would no doubt earn from Bultmann the kind of grudging respect a historian might accord to a scholar working with un-flagging energy and careful methodology at a project he him-self considered valueless. But whatever Dodd's results, they will certainly have seemed to Bultmann hugely irrelevant to true Christianity. At all costs the strong, pure, living water of Christian faith must be kept unsullied by the murky but somehow assimilable silt of history.

The fundamental conviction of Bultmann leads him to treat the historical elements in the Gospel, such as they are, as mere platforms from which to ascend into the world of the spirit, rather than as the matter in which the divine can find concrete expression. And in fact Bultmann is closer philosophically to Plato and Kant than to Aristotle and Hegel. When he asks of the Johannine Christ, 'Is his human figure a translucent figure through which his divinity gleams?',[50] there is no need for him to answer his own question. But what does he mean by restricting Jesus' revelation to a mere *that*

---

[49] *Faith and Understanding*, p. 132.　　[50] *Theology*, ii. 42.

(curiously close to Aquinas' position concerning the natural know-ledge of God)?

Bultmann's concept of revelation may be compared to a fire or burglar alarm, whose entire *raison d'être* is to *warn*. To pause to identify its pitch or tone would be to deflect one's attention from its one essential function. Similarly the sole purpose of Jesus' coming on earth is to *reveal*, to signal the presence of God to the world and to trigger off an appropriate human response. Although he demands faith in his own person he is not so much the object of faith as its mere occasion. What he was like as a man, his character or temperament cannot possibly have any bearing upon the message he has come to bring. To ask of him, 'Why this specific man?' 'is to put a question that must not, may not, be answered—for to do so would be to destroy the offense [*sic*] which belongs ineradicably to the Revealer'.[51]

For all that, the warning has to *sound*: to reduce it to an electric impulse or to a sequence of jarring notes scribbled on a page would be to eliminate its single most important feature. For no one can *hear* the flicker of a needle or be startled into attention by a musical score. In the same way the Word had to become flesh if it was to sound in human ears; an emissary had to be sent to deliver the message. There is no getting round the Incarnation, and Bultmann set his face resolutely against any attempt to water it down: 'The Revealer appears not as *man-in-general*, i.e. not simply as a bearer of human *nature*, but as a *definite human being in history*: Jesus of Nazareth. His humanity is genuine humanity: "the word became flesh".'[52] But for all his vaunted anti-docetism, Bultmann presents a Christ in whom all salient individual characteristics have been flattened out: the splendid 'I am' sayings in which so much of his revelation is contained have but a single message: 'All that I say is I.'[53] The incarnate Christ is no more than a voice, his particular and contingent human qualities all drawn off, volatilized, until there is nothing left but a smear on a slide—the ultimate essence of a Word.

The truth is that Bultmann's severely uncompromising christo-logy is not substantial enough to stand up to the attacks to which

[51] Ibid., ii. 69.   [52] Ibid., ii. 41.

[53] Ibid., ii. 65. This is what Bultmann says on this subject much later: 'John gives all due emphasis to the humanity of Jesus, but presents none of the characteristics of Jesus' humanity which could be gleaned, for example, from the Synoptic Gospels. The decisive thing is simply the "that"' ('Primitive Christian Kerygma', p. 20 [= *Exegetica*, p. 450]).

Käsemann would later subject it. The humanity of his Jesus is itself altogether too scrawny and spindly to stand a fighting chance against the power and the glory of Käsemann's 'über die Erde schreitender Gott'. But before we can take our leave of Bultmann there is one further point to be added. His answer to his second great puzzle, we recall, lies in the reduction of the Revealer's revelation to a bare *that*. But is this right? Is it not at least possible that Sir Edwyn Hoskyns catches the evangelist's central conception more successfully than Bultmann? And if so, then some important consequences follow. It was Bultmann's own very special interpretation of the evangelist's christology that, as he saw, required a special kind of explanation, one which he himself sought in Mandaean Gnosticism. But if he is wrong about the christology, and John's central conception is not what he says it is, then perhaps a different *kind* of explanation must be sought. As Käsemann says, 'the theological problems [of the Fourth Gospel] must, after all, point to a specific sector of primitive Christian belief, and, conversely, we must be able to deduce it from them'.[54] Once again, this is a question that cannot be pursued here, though it must be stressed that any particular answer to Bultmann's second riddle will leave the first intact. That is to say, John's developed christology, however interpreted, is different enough from the Synoptic tradition (and from Paul) to require a new account, and an especially strong and coherent one, of how it arose. And if we dismantle the fantastic apparatus of Mandaean Gnosticism, reminiscent to an English eye of one of Heath Robinson's more extravagantly constructed machines, then we must replace it by something sufficiently powerful to have generated the extraordinary, indeed the unique vision of John the Evangelist.

[54] *Testament*, p. 3.

3

AFTER BULTMANN

Johannine studies burgeoned after the war. To keep pace with them would be a full-time occupation.[1] Some of the monographs on single words and/or themes are themselves major contributions towards the understanding of the Gospel. Clearly any comprehensive survey is out of the question, and this section will be restricted to the discussion of a number of works which, in different ways, have a particular bearing upon Bultmann's second great puzzle: what is the central concept of the Gospel, its *Grundbegriff*?

Hoskyns and Bultmann are agreed upon the answer to this question: revelation. Where they differ—very profoundly—is in their view of the content and nature of this revelation, and of the faith that gives it welcome.

Under one of its aspects the coming of Christ is seen as God's judgement upon the world, a judgement in which human beings are necessarily implicated in so far as they are obliged to take some stand, negative or positive as the case may be, towards the revelation with which they are confronted. Those who reject Christ are siding with darkness against light, preferring falsehood to truth, and in so doing are imposing upon themselves their own sentence of condemnation. Those who 'believe' in him, embracing the truth and aligning themselves with the light, win eternal life. We have to do then with a series of interlocking themes: light and darkness, truth and falsehood, faith and life, and finally judgement and condemnation (for which Greek has the one

---

[1] H. Thyen, surveying work done on the Gospel in the course of less than a decade (1966–74), takes 37 pages simply to list the titles: 'Aus der Literatur'. The next two surveys, by J. Becker, cover a mere 5 years apiece (1975–9; 1980–4): 'Aus der Literatur'; 'Im Streit der Methoden'. See too the more discursive surveys of R. Kysar: *The Fourth Evangelist* and 'The Fourth Gospel'.

word: κρίσις).[2] These are all grouped together by Bultmann under the general term 'eschatology'. From Bultmann's point of view one of the advantages of stressing eschatology is that it can be discussed at considerable length without paying any direct attention to the *content* of the all-important revelation of Christ.

How is it possible to use the term 'eschatology' in this way? In the Synoptic Gospels Jesus' preaching is focused upon the kingdom of God; and the urgency of this is largely explained by the belief that this expression was associated with an imminent cataclysm involving the end (ἔσχατον) of the world as we know it (the present age). So Jesus' message was thought to be essentially eschatological in the proper sense. For a long time after his death Christians looked forward to his return in a Second Coming (parousia) which once again was expected to take place soon after the close of the present age. This too is an eschatological belief. But in the Fourth Gospel, although traces remain of this futuristic element, it is on the whole replaced by the immediate promise of a new kind of life in the here and now. Similarly the heavenly figure of the Son of Man, whose eventual appearance on the clouds of heaven is prophesied in the Synoptic Gospels, is no longer distinguished at all in the Fourth Gospel from the person of Jesus the man from Nazareth. '"Do you believe in the Son of Man?"' he says to the blind man, who responds by asking in his turn who this is: 'Jesus said to him, "You have seen him, and it is he who speaks to you"' (9: 35 ff.). Any judgement once thought to be exercised by the Son of Man in a remote and inaccessible realm is pulled down into the world we know. It might be objected that this to all intents and purposes de-eschatologizes the message; but writers on the Fourth Gospel generally follow Bultmann's lead in using the term 'eschatology' to cover the same set of themes, so that faith, for instance, is identified as 'eschatological existence'.[3]

---

[2] The verb κρίνειν also has overtones of discrimination and discernment, to which words it is etymologically related. One of the subtleties of the Gospel, though not one that is difficult to master, is its insistence that to refuse faith is to judge and condemn oneself.

[3] *Theology*, ii, Part II, ch. IV, § 50 (pp. 75–92). This illustrates the extent to which Bultmann employs 'eschatological' in contexts where traditional Catholic theology would use 'supernatural' or perhaps 'transcendent' instead. But for Bultmann 'eschatological' came to have a markedly existential ring, with overtones of challenge and commitment and the need for authenticity. Of course the beliefs which first justified the use of the term were as saturated in myth as any Bultmann was to

[*cont. on p. 69*]

If it is asked what part the facts of salvation in the traditional sense—incarnation, death, resurrection, Pentecost, parousia—play in the Fourth Gospel, Bultmann answers that they are all subsumed under the single event of 'the revelation of God's reality in the earthly activity of the man Jesus combined with the overcoming of the "offense" in it by man's accepting it in faith'.[4] The fourth evangelist has his own vocabulary for many of these 'events'—coming, going, mission, lifting-up, glorification—these are all key terms that mesh into the rich pattern of John's full theology. It would not be difficult to draw up a series of quotations through which the Gospel would be allowed to make all its points without aid of commentary (although of course the *selection* of these would itself be a form of exegesis).[5]

Some later scholars, by stressing the eschatology of the Gospel at the expense of its christology, upset the delicate balance of John's essentially simple argument. As a consequence of this imbalance, the work of Jacques Dupont and Oscar Cullman is of less significance than it otherwise might have been.

In a study appearing in 1951 the Belgian Benedictine Jacques Dupont argues that what he calls a 'théologie des essences' or an *incarnational* theology as we might nowadays understand the term did not enter within the purview of the Fourth Evangelist. Rather it is appropriate to speak of a 'théologie fonctionelle'.[6] John is not interested in expounding what Christ was in himself but what he achieved on behalf of mankind. 'Consequently', says Dupont, agreeing here with Bultmann, 'Jesus' ministry is placed in its entirety in an eschatological light (*sous un éclairage eschatologique*): what was originally expected from the parousia is already partially realized in the historical coming of the Son of God.'[7] Unlike Bultmann Dupont does not go so far as positively to exclude all 'doctrinal' content. But such statements as are to be found concerning the person of Christ are subordinated to his function as the bringer of life; the title

combat under the banner of demythologization. Cf. Paul Ricœur, 'Preface to Bultmann'. Josef Blank, though no Bultmannian, retains and defends, however lamely and uneasily, Bultmann's use of 'eschatology' to refer to the Johannine concept of judgement. See his excursus, 'Zum Sprachgebrauch von "Eschatologisch"' (*Krisis*, pp. 65 f.). This question will receive further attention in Ch. 6.

[4] *Theology*, ii. 58.
[5] I have attempted an exercise of this kind in Ch. 14.
[6] *Essais sur la Christologie de Saint Jean*, pp. 7 f.
[7] Ibid., p. 8.

'Logos', for instance, 'does not designate Jesus in the manner of a proper name: it is in his relationship to the world and to mankind that Jesus is the Word of God.'[8]

To one interested primarily in what the Gospel has to say about Christ Dupont's work may appear rather evasive. He cleverly dodges the challenge to consider 'what manner of man is this' that John is presenting to his readers. Similarly Oscar Cullman, in his *Christology of the New Testament*, maintains that John, like the other writers of the New Testament, never speaks of the *person* of Christ without at the same time speaking of his *work*.[9] So although we are naturally inclined to enquire what was the nature of Christ's relationship to God, this is not a question the New Testament is concerned to answer directly. Like Dupont, Cullman offers a purely functional christology.

From the perspective of the history of dogma there is certainly much to be said for this approach. In general the doctrinal debates of the early Church proceeded from a conviction of what Christ had achieved (soteriology) to an affirmation of what he was (christology). 'Agere sequitur esse', runs the medieval tag, and the metaphysically minded argued from the activity (*agere*) of whatever happened to be the particular object of attention to its essence (*esse*), from ἐξουσία (power), as manifested in action, to οὐσία (essence). But once a wedge has been driven between eschatology and christology there is at least a prima-facie case for arguing that the Fourth Gospel itself had directly christological interests, or, in the terms we are using, that the eschatology of the Gospel arises out of and is therefore secondary to its christology. And this is the position of Josef Blank, who is conscious of moving in the shadow of Bultmann's arguments. 'Christology', he says, 'is not a function of the Gospel's eschatology but vice versa: Johannine eschatology is a function of christology.'[10] And in conclusion he states: 'The eschatological Christ-event is founded upon the person of its bearer, upon the divine Logos, who became man, upon the person of the Son, one with the Father and yet distinct from him. We found that if they were to be taken precisely all the Gospel's propositions had to be referred back to this christological foundation, because without it

---

[8] *Essais sur la Christologie de Saint Jean*, p. 58.   [9] p. 3.

[10] *Krisis*, p. 38. Whatever reservations one may have about this work, it remains an enduring contribution to the subject; many of Blank's detailed analyses of individual passages have not been bettered.

the Christ-revelation cannot appear as an eschatological salvation-event, nor as divine revelation in the precise, classic, theological sense. There is nothing to be gained here from a universal and global concept of revelation.'[11] One sees here that Blank's position, in so far as he wants his conclusions to fit in with 'the precise, classic, theological sense' of revelation, is just as 'prejudiced' as that of Bultmann.

Ernst Käsemann, who, like Blank, makes a frontal attack upon Bultmann's views, is also caught up in the same problems, but unlike Bultmann he believes that in John's Gospel, as he puts it: 'eschatology has turned into protology'.[12] Bultmann, by his subtle adjustment of the theme of eschatology, had put all the weight of the Gospel's message upon the individual choices of human beings confronted with the kerygma. Käsemann, however, denies the appropriateness of Bultmann's phrase 'dualism of decision' and argues that the real crisis occurs not at the end but at the beginning: 'The Johannine dualism marks the effect of the Word in that world in which the light has always shone into the darkness. As specific decisions of individual men, faith and unbelief confirm the separation which already exists.'[13] But you cannot redress the balance of a see-saw by jumping on the other end of the plank. In totally opposite ways both Bultmann and Käsemann succeed in reducing the importance of the career and teaching of Jesus (which is after all what the Gospel is about), the one by making the incarnation a function of what he calls eschatology, the other by seeing it simply as a particularly significant illustration of the primary act of creation that separated the light from the darkness: 'John understands the incarnation as a projection of the glory of Jesus' pre-existence and the passion as a return to "that glory which was his before the world began".'[14]

When Käsemann launched his first full-scale attack upon Bultmann's picture of the Johannine Christ, in 1957, he did so by proposing an alternative reading of the Prologue, which laid all the emphasis upon the second half of the crucial verse 14.[15] Whereas Bultmann had seen the central message of this text to consist in the

---

[11] Ibid., p. 346.   [12] *Testament*, p. 51; cf. pp. 21, 53 ff.   [13] Ibid., p. 63.
[14] Ibid., p. 20. See too Käsemann's earlier criticisms in his review of Bultmann's commentary, 'Rudolf Bultmann'.
[15] 'The Evangelist allows the weight of his propositions to fall not on 14a but on 14c' ('Structure', p. 164).

affirmation of incarnation, 'And the Word was made flesh', Käsemann brushed this aside in favour of what follows: 'and we beheld
his glory, the glory as of the only-begotten Son.' His objection to
Bultmann's view is summed up in his short book *The Testament of
Jesus*: 'Does the statement "The Word became flesh" really mean
more than that he descended into the world of man and there came
into contact with earthly existence, so that an encounter with him
became possible? Is not the statement totally overshadowed by the
confession "We beheld his glory", so that it receives its meaning
from it?'[16]

Now there may seem something quixotic, not to say perverse, in
arguing for a docetic interpretation of the Gospel from the very verse
which has always been at the heart of the Church's confession of
faith in the incarnation. And there are undoubtedly serious flaws in
Käsemann's argument.[17] Even so that famous phrase 'der über die
Erde schreitende Gott' (God striding over the earth), derived, with
acknowledgements, from F. C. Baur and others, conveys fairly
accurately the impression that an unbiased reader would get from a
first reading of the Gospel. Jesus' 'death, to be sure, takes place on the
cross, as tradition demands. But this cross is no longer the pillory,
the tree of shame, on which hangs the one who had become the
companion of thieves. His death is rather the manifestation of divine
self-giving love and his victorious return from the alien realm below
to the Father who had sent him.'[18] Or again, 'Lowliness in John is
the nature of the situation, of the earthly realm which Jesus entered.
In entering it, he himself is not being humbled. He retains the glory
and majesty of the Son until the cross. There once more he judges
his judges as he has always done before. When he is given up by the
Father, he demonstrates more clearly than ever that the earth has
no power over him.'[19] This is surely true. But is it also true, as
Käsemann asserts, that John is 'the first Christian to use the earthly
life of Jesus merely as a backdrop for the Son of God proceeding
through the world of man and as the scene of the inbreaking of the
heavenly glory'?[20]

Käsemann's book is hard to assess, not just because of the
difficulty of his style, but because it is so riddled with rhetoric. Reading

---

[16] *Testament*, pp. 9 f.
[17] In particular his contention that v. 14 did not form part of the original hymn is,
I think, wrong, and in any case far from certain.
[18] *Testament*, p. 10.   [19] Ibid., p. 18.   [20] Ibid., p. 13.

it, one has to proceed slowly, with constant backward glances, to make sure of grasping all the connections. (One wonders how much the first audience of these lectures made of them, listening to Käsemann's accented English somewhere on the campus of Yale University.) Furthermore, Käsemann appears preoccupied with categories of orthodoxy and heterodoxy that are scarcely appropriate to a period when Christian doctrine was still forming in its shell.

One major weakness of the book is that its platform, chapter 17 (which he calls his 'basis and guidepost'),[21] is too flimsy to bear all the weight Käsemann wishes to put upon it. He remarks, rightly I think, that this chapter is the counterpart of the Prologue, but also states with disconcerting assurance that 'it is unmistakable that this chapter is a summary of the Johannine discourses'. Yet it contains no mention of the Paraclete, no final commandment, no promise of return, not even any formal adieu. Are all these elements, together with many others belonging to the earlier discourses, somehow concealed in what is actually (unlike the previous three chapters) a prayer? Käsemann does not answer this question since his categorical affirmation is the only strut he provides to keep his 'guidepost' steady. No doubt the three themes he chose for the subject of his lectures are all there. But are they as central as he implies? I do not think so.

The reason why Käsemann's docetic interpretation is ultimately unsatisfactory can be put very simply. It emerges vividly from a comparison with 1 John, by general consent a horse out of the same stable as the Gospel, whether or not it had a common sire. 1 John is firmly, even angrily, anti-docetic. How likely is it that the very same school should produce writings of such glaringly contrary views as are postulated by Käsemann's thesis? The peculiar relationship between the two writings is easily understood once one has seen that the writer of 1 John is setting his face against what he regards as *misinterpretations* of the Gospel.[22] And this hypothesis accounts at the same time for the initial plausibility of Käsemann's thesis. The unusual flavour of John's Gospel, so much richer than the relatively plain fare of the Synoptists, is partly to be accounted for by the fact that the evangelist was so anxious to get his spiritual message across

---

[21] Ibid., p. 3. The German is *Basis und Richtung*.

[22] As is overwhelmingly demonstrated in Raymond Brown's commentary on the Epistles (New York, 1982), pp. 69–115. Cf. J. L. Houlden, *A Commentary on the Johannine Epistles* (London, 1973).

that he neglected (though not completely) to put in the provisos which a later age, under the direct threat of Gnosticism, would have inserted. It was not that he wished to deny Jesus' humanity but that he was not interested in deriving from it the kind of inferences that a modern theologian might wish to underline (above all intimations of ignorance and uncertainty). Of course this lack of interest has itself to be explained. Bultmann, Käsemann, and Bornkamm agree in attributing it to the influence of Gnosticism—a point that must await later discussion. But it is to be observed that Käsemann, arguing against Bultmann the desirability and possibility of a 'new quest for the historical Jesus', remarks that John couched his theology in the form of a Gospel, that is to say a form which of its very nature seeks to justify the identification of Jesus of Nazareth with the Risen Lord.[23]

The point is that the two essential elements of the gospel form are necessarily held in tension. On the one hand, there are the traditions (whether eyewitness or not) of Jesus of Nazareth, on the other, belief in the Risen Jesus Christ. And to evacuate the historical Jesus of all his humanity would make nonsense of John's decision to write a Gospel.

Perhaps the evangelist was insufficiently on his guard against the possibility that his high christology, culminating in the affirmation of the divinity of Christ, might be taken in a docetic sense. But the suggestion that he himself would have denied the full humanity of Jesus is absurd: if it be true that he neglects to protect his Gospel adequately against such a misinterpretation, this must be because he was not aware of the extent of the danger.[24]

Of the surveys of Johannine theology since Bultmann, none is totally satisfactory. Käsemann's is interesting but tendentious, and has too narrow a base. Kümmel, in his *Theology of the New Testament*, adds nothing to the argument. Of the myriad monographs, one that deserves special mention is Franz Mussner's short study *Die johanne-ische Sehweise und die Frage nach dem historischen Jesus*.[25] Mussner

---

[23] 'Blind Alleys', p. 40; cf. 'Problem', pp. 31 f.

[24] Georg Richter ('Fleischwerdung') maintains that 1: 14–18, as well as certain other passages in the Gospel, is an insertion made by an *anti-docetic* redactor, anxious to dispel the generally docetic impression left by the remainder of the Gospel. I am left unconvinced by his arguments and also by those of U. Schnelle, *Antidoketische Christologie im Johannesevangelium*.

[25] The English translation, *The Historical Jesus in the Gospel of St. John* omits the crucial term *Sehweise*, 'mode of vision' or 'way of seeing'.

takes a line not dissimilar to that of Hoskyns (with whose commentary he was apparently unacquainted), but approaches the task
differently by an examination of what he calls John's 'gnoseological
terminology'. This consists entirely of familiar terms: see, hear, come
to know, know, testify, and remember. There follows a series of short
chapters on other themes including, notably, the Paraclete. Mussner
is refreshingly aware of modern hermeneutics: Heidegger and
Gadamer hold no fears for him. But he does not allow them to
distract him from his main purpose. If the English version still
sounds rather foreign, what is said comes close to the heart of the
matter:

In the act of vision the time-horizons merge, but this of course must not be
misunderstood. In this merging, the past is not annulled; in its actualization
for the present and in the present, it entirely preserves its importance,
supplying the material by which the act of vision can perpetually enkindle
anew. But the act of vision takes its bearings not only from the past, but also
from the present, in this case from the present time of composition with its
questions. Precisely these questions, the situation in theological history,
contribute to determining the direction of the act of vision; they provide the
angles from which the historical material (to which tradition also belongs) is
focused. To put it concretely, Jesus of Nazareth is so expressed by John in his
act of vision that the history of Christ projected and presented by him
simultaneously gives an answer to the Christological questions of the time of
its composition. This answer is not, however, obtained by speculation about
the mystery of Jesus, but precisely by that retrospective gaze which the act of
vision makes possible, as has been seen by the analysis of gnoseological
terms. Retrospection is not a mechanical reproduction of the history of
Jesus, and in the act of vision there occurs the exposition effected by the
Spirit, and so the historical Jesus becomes the Christ of the kerygma, who
precisely as such is also the Jesus of history. For 'history' in the proper sense
is of course 'history as operative influence'.[26]

Mussner's work, valuable and perceptive as it is, does not answer
all our questions. John's *Sehweise*, his way of looking at things, is in
fact a conscious appropriation of the implications of the gospel genre
and is shared in a more immediate and less reflective fashion by the
other evangelists, especially Mark. Mussner's evident reluctance to
indulge in or enquire into 'speculation about the mystery of Jesus'

---

[26] *Historical Jesus*, pp. 46 f. The phrase 'history as operative influence' is an
allusion to Gadamer's 'wirkungsgeschichtliches Bewußtsein', which appears in the
English translation of Gadamer's work as 'effective-historical consciousness'. Cf. *Truth
and Method*, pp. 305–41.

suggests that he is inclined to shirk the task of tracing the origins of John's highly idiosyncratic picture of Jesus, which is more peculiar to him than is implied by Mussner's phrase 'his actualization of the past for the present and in the present'.

Another study which, like Mussner's, derives inspiration from the philosophical hermeneutics of H.-G. Gadamer, is Takashi Onuki's *Gemeinde und Welt im Johannesevangelium* (1984). Although its ostensible subject is Johannine dualism, this book is remarkably wide-ranging. It puts forward the view that the Gospel cannot be understood one-sidedly either from the perspective of Jesus' situation *vis-à-vis* his disciples or from that of the post-Easter community. For a satisfactory interpretation both must be included.

This thesis is established in two ways: first by a rapid survey of the whole Gospel and then by a detailed analysis of chapters 15–17. The exegesis is bracketed by penetrating observations upon the theological interpretations of Bultmann and Käsemann on the one hand and Günther Bornkamm on the other.[27] The double imbalance of Bultmann's exaggerated emphasis upon 'eschatology' and Käsemann's reversion to what he calls 'protology' is partly redressed by Bornkamm's insistence upon the role of the Spirit in the post-Easter community. But this too requires to be offset by highlighting the role of Jesus in his own concrete historical situation. Onuki's thesis has some striking affinities with X. Léon-Dufour's theory of the 'deux temps de lecture'.[28] The theological argument is underpinned by the sociological insights of Wayne Meeks and J. L. Martyn, to be discussed in the concluding section of this chapter.

2. COMPOSITION: SOURCES AND EDITIONS

'So exhaustive was Bultmann's source theory, but at the same time so unacceptable in parts, that a kind of tacit moratorium was declared with the result that since the Second World War there has been on the whole only a discussion of the problems raised by his work, and (since Ruckstuhl's study in 1951) a dwindling one at

---

[27] Basing himself in Bornkamm's case mainly upon 'Interpretation', his extended review of Käsemann's *Testament*.

[28] As he himself points out in his generally favourable review of Onuki's book in *RScR* 73 (1985), 253–6. Onuki's work, and especially his use of Gadamer, will be considered further in Ch. 11.

that.'[29] With these words Robert Fortna introduces his own power-fully argued attempt to restate and reinstate one part (the signs source) of Bultmann's multiple-source theory. It is an attempt to which we shall have to return.

The 'tacit moratorium' of which Fortna speaks is not hard to comprehend. For one thing, the sheer complexity of Bultmann's literary analysis exposed it to detailed criticism on many fronts. To some no doubt it seemed like a house of cards, ready to tumble down at the slightest nudge; but after its great fall few have shown any eagerness to put the theory together again. It is obvious that any alternative theory of comparable weight and density will receive the same sort of treatment as Bultmann's has done; so it is no wonder that the majority of subsequent commentators have either stuck rigidly to the order of the received text or else confined their suggestions regarding structure to a few passages that have seemed to them especially awkward and intransigent.[30] But such desultory tinkering is a world apart from Bultmann's grand design.

Among those who, since Bultmann, have proposed variations on the 'displacement' theory, F. H. Hoare deserves special mention for the ingenuity and completeness of his proposals.[31] But his and other similar attempts are unsuccessful for two reasons. The first is that they depend on the false premiss that individual papyrus sheets will have generally terminated at the end of a period or sentence. (Other theories depend on the more defensible theory that ancient scribes wrote pages containing an equal number of lines and lines con-taining an equal number of letters.)[32] The second reason is that they offer, I am convinced, the wrong *kind* of explanation of the phenomena.

Nevertheless such theories, however untenable, do at least square up to the literary puzzles presented by the Gospel. Those who

---

[29] *The Gospel of Signs*, p. 1 n. 1.

[30] Though this is true of most commentaries (Boismard and Becker being notable exceptions), there has been no dearth of suggestions dealing with one aspect or another of the question and appearing in various journals, as well as a number of monographs. Once again this survey is necessarily very selective. For the period up to 1965 it would be hard to match D. Moody Smith's lucid and judicious appraisal in his *Composition and Order*, ch. 2.

[31] *The Original Order and Chapters of St. John's Gospel.*

[32] Ernst Haenchen, in a few succinct pages of his commentary headed 'Unordnung und Umordnung', puts forward cogent arguments effectively disposing of all such theories; 'the time of displacement theories', he concludes, 'is past' (*Johannesevangel-ium*, pp. 48–57; ET, pp. 44–51).

continue to treat it as if it were a unified composition generally do so
for one of two motives, conviction or convenience. The first of these
is rationalized along theoretical, the second along practical lines.

The practical case was put as long ago as 1924 by B. H. Streeter,
commenting sardonically, as we have seen, upon the earliest efforts
at reconstruction.[33] Raymond Brown, who has himself put forward
one of the most plausible theories so far of how the Gospel was
composed, refrains, unlike Bultmann, from building his theory of
composition into his interpretation. And in general most commentators shrink for obvious reasons from too radical a recasting. Brown
fully recognizes the objection that in restricting his observations to
the received text he is perhaps dealing only with the work of a
secondary redactor. 'Yet', he answers, 'if one thinks of the final
editor as someone loyal to the evangelist's thought, there will be
very few times when editing has completely changed the original
meaning of a passage. We prefer rather to run this risk than—by
ingenious rearrangement—run the much greater risk of imposing
on passages a meaning they never had.'[34]

The second kind of argument against attempting to alter the order
of the Gospel is based on principle. The exegete's job, it is argued, is
to interpret the text before him, not to burrow underneath it. What
is proposed for his analysis is not the lost work of some hypothetical
evangelist—*Das Evangelium des Johannes*—but *Das Johannesevangelium*, the Fourth Gospel as we have it.[35]

This argument is well exemplified in C. H. Dodd's introduction to
the third part of his *Interpretation*, and partly because his case,
expressed with Dodd's customary grace and plausibility, would still
command a wide measure of assent,[36] partly because my own
approach is so different, it deserves to be set out and examined in
some detail:

[33] Cf. *Supra*, Ch. 1, p. 35.

[34] p. xxxiv.

[35] Brown (p. xxvii) thinks it unfair to read so much into Bultmann's title. But in
fact for Bultmann the *real* Gospel is the one he attempts to reconstruct.

[36] See, for instance, F. J. Moloney, who quotes this passage approvingly in *The
Johannine Son of Man*, p. 44; G. C. Nicholson: 'we are assuming that despite what
seems to us to be tensions and doublets within John 1–20 ... this text made sense to
someone. We call this person the evangelist': *Death as Departure*, p. 13. See too Ulrich
Wilckens's review of G. Richter's collected essays in *TLZ* 106 (1981), 815–17, where
he characterizes attempts to reconstruct the history of the community on the basis of
source-analysis as a 'gigantic error' (*horrender Irrweg*) (p. 817). For a good counter-
statement see J. Becker in *TRu* 51 (1986), pp. 7–21.

Many attempts have been made to improve the work by rearrangement of its material ... It is of course impossible to deny that the work may have suffered dislocation, and plausible grounds may be alleged for lifting certain passages out of their setting, where there seems to be some *prima facie* breach of continuity. Unfortunately, when once the gospel has been taken to pieces, its reassemblage is likely to be affected by individual preferences, preconceptions and even prejudices. Meanwhile the work lies before us in an order which (apart from insignificant details) does not vary in the textual tradition, traceable to an early period. I conceive it to be the duty of an interpreter at least to see what can be done with the document as it has come down to us before attempting to improve upon it. This is what I shall try to do. I shall assume as a provisional working hypothesis that the present order is not fortuitous, but deliberately devised by somebody—even if he were only a scribe doing his best—and that the person in question (whether the author or another) had some design in mind, and was not necessarily irresponsible or unintelligent. If the attempt to discover any intelligible thread of argument should fail, then we may be compelled to confess that we do not know how the work was originally intended to run. If on the other hand it should appear that the structure of the gospel as we have it has been shaped in most of its details by the ideas which seem to dominate the author's thought, then it would appear not improbable that we have his work before us substantially in the form which he designed.[37]

There are seven salient points in Dodd's argument:

1. There are indeed prima-facie breaches of continuity in the Gospel, and it may have suffered dislocation.
2. However, attempts at rearrangement are attempts to improve the work.
3. It is difficult in any case to carry these through with any objectivity.
4. It is the interpreter's duty to deal with the text in the order in which it has been transmitted 'before attempting to improve upon it'.
5. A useful 'provisional working hypothesis' is that the present order is not fortuitous but planned.
6. If no intelligible thread to the argument can be found then (and then only) this hypothesis must be abandoned.
7. But if the structure seems to have been largely shaped by the author's central ideas, then we probably have his work 'in the form which he designed'.

[37] *Interpretation*, pp. 289 f.

Let us take these points in order:

1. The difficulty is much understated. The data on which Wellhausen and his successors base their case are incontrovertably there and hard to reconcile with any theory of unified composition. But there are other possible explanations of these data besides the displacement theory, which is the only one that Dodd appears to envisage.

2. The insinuation here is that in changing the order of the received text the exegete is trying to do a better job than the evangelist. But this is rather begging the question. If the work of the religious genius whom we think of as the evangelist has been distorted by the well-intentioned efforts of a secondary redactor, then the exegete is surely performing a service by attempting to recover this work as far as it is possible to do so.

3. Objectivity is always difficult, but as Wellhausen pointed out when introducing his little commentary, the difficulty of the enterprise does not diminish the significance of the data that make it necessary. And is not Dodd himself guilty of a certain prejudice in this matter?

4. The same insinuation as in 2. One counter-argument is that some attempt at reconstruction (at least in certain cases) might be a necessary preliminary step before tackling the received order.

5 and 6. It is only because this 'provisional working hypothesis' fails to stand up to examination that it has to be discarded. Bultmann, in his review of Hirsch, makes this very point. Clearly there has been some attempt to order the material in a way that will preserve some continuity. But this attempt sometimes breaks down and the impression of uninterrupted continuity is lost. Besides, is it not important to know whether the mind responsible for the final plan (however intelligent) is that of the genius whose ideas are bodied forth in the Gospel, or that of a secondary redactor (a possibility Dodd specifically allows for)?

7. This crucial phase in Dodd's argument is altogether unclear. In what sense can the leading ideas of the Gospel (light, life, judgement, etc.) be said to shape its structure? Surely these are not structural ideas? Dodd himself devotes the whole of the second part of his book (well over 100 pages) to a fruitful discussion of these, one which has a value quite independent of his conception of the Gospel's overall

design. If, then, the structure is not shaped by the ideas, it is open to us to speculate that the final redaction of the Gospel may not be the work of the evangelist after all.

Taken as a whole, Dodd's arguments are extremely weak and leave one wondering whether his decision to ignore questions of redaction was not motivated to some extent by convenience as well as conviction. A priori it would seem at least possible that the study of the awkward transitions in the Gospel could prove a useful tool for determining how it was composed. It is a matter of some regret that an exegete of Dodd's learning and insight should have thrown this tool away without ever attempting to apply it.

Strongly individual as it is, Dodd's work neither flows from nor feeds into the mainstream of Johannine studies—at any rate in regard to questions of composition. And as Fortna implies, it was in response to Bultmann rather than to Dodd that scholars began once again to try to account for the literary puzzles of the Gospel without resorting to the rather desperate expedient of the displacement theory. There were three possible directions open to them. The first was to revive the theory of John's dependence upon one or more of the Synoptists (a theory for the most part abandoned since the appearance of Gardner-Smith's book[38] in 1938). Still it is held today by a number of experts, including J. Blinzler, C. K. Barrett, and F. Neirynck.[39] But although John almost certainly knew Mark, and possibly Matthew and Luke as well, his differences from the Synoptists are so great that they cannot be satisfactorily explained by a simple theory of literary dependence.

The essence of the second approach, called the multiple-stage theory, is that it postulates two or more editions of the Gospel. The third possibility is a return to the signs-source theory of Bultmann and Faure. These last two possibilities may be combined. Bultmann's suggestion of a revelation-discourse source has received much less support.[40]

---

[38] *Saint John and the Synoptic Gospels.*

[39] J. Blinzler, *Johannes und die Synoptiker*; C. K. Barrett, 'John and the Synoptic Gospels' (also his commentary); F. Neirynck, 'John and the Synoptics'. A good assessment of the state of the question is to be found in an article of D. Moody Smith, 'John and the Synoptics'. Smith concludes that the balance of probabilities is in favour of non-dependence. For a more recent assessment, see Robert Kysar in *RSR* 9 (1983), 315 f.

[40] For one example see H. Becker, *Die Reden des Johannesevangeliums.*

(a) Multiple-stage theories

There are basically two kinds of multiple-stage theory. According to the first (Wilkens, Boismard), the earliest draft of the Gospel (*Grund-schrift*) is more or less recoverable from the Gospel as we have it. Lying behind this are Synoptic-type traditions, usually thought of as oral. According to the second (Brown, Lindars), the first edition of the Gospel will have been compiled from a number of documents already composed along Johannine lines within a Johannine school. We may point to some of these in the present Gospel, but the idea of a *Grundschrift* is misleading.

The possible permutations of these theories are endless and this survey will be confined to the work of the four scholars already mentioned.[41]

W. Wilkens[42] differs from the other three in postulating a single author (whom he thinks of as an eyewitness) who twice revised and expanded an original document of his own composition. This is a conscious reversion to the early suggestion of Wellhausen. The *Grundschrift* consisted of an account of Jesus' signs in Galilee, his entry into Jerusalem, the events leading up to the passion, and the passion itself. In his first revision the evangelist introduced much of the discourse material; but it is his second revision that gave the Gospel the 'paschal' character it now has by transferring to the first half certain episodes originally associated with the passion, namely the cleansing of the temple (2: 13–22, the anointing at Bethany (12: 1–11), and that part of chapter 6 (vv. 51c–58) which alludes most directly to the sacrament of the Eucharist. At the same time he expanded the passion narrative in order to give it an overtly paschal character. Subsequently a final redactor (not John himself) made some further additions, notably chapter 21.

Brown, in his commentary,[43] postulates at least five stages,

---

[41] Two other theories require a brief mention. Georg Richter has set out his ideas in a monograph, *Die Fußwaschung im Johannesevangelium*, and a series of articles, *Studien zum Johannesevangelium*. Richter believes that the inconsistencies within the Gospel are the consequence of a series of bitter struggles within the community. As a general explanation of the growth either of the Gospel or of the community, this theory seems to me in the highest degree implausible. It is shared, however, by W. Langbrandtner, except that Langbrandtner thinks that the Gospel *started* as Gnostic apologia and was subsequently transformed into a Christian Gospel by an anti-Gnostic group that appealed to the authority of the beloved disciple: see *Weltferner Gott*.

[42] *Entstehungsgeschichte*.   [43] pp. xxxiv–xxxix.

suspecting that 'the full details of the Gospel's prehistory are far too complicated to reconstruct': (1) a body of Synoptic-type traditions of Jesus' words and works; (2) the development of this material, 'over a period lasting perhaps several decades' in Johannine patterns. As an example of the work done during this important period Brown cites the 'superb drama' of chapter 9; (3) 'The organization of this material from Stage 2 into a consecutive work. This would be the first edition of the Fourth Gospel as a distinct work.' At this point Brown is conscious of parting company with Wilkens, who 'would see in the first edition only a collection of signs'; (4) the evangelist's second edition of this work. Brown thinks that although he may have re-edited his Gospel several times, 'most of the features that seem to require a secondary editing can be explained in terms of one re-editing'. As an instance, Brown cites the parenthetical verses 9: 22 f., which seem to represent 'an adaptation of the story of the blind man to the new situation in the late 80s or early 90s which involved excommunication from the Synagogue of Jews who believed in Jesus as the Messiah'; (5) 'A final editing by someone other than the evangelist and whom we shall call the redactor.' This personage was probably 'a close friend or disciple of the evangelist and certainly part of the general school of thought to which we referred in Stage 2'.

Lindars[44] does not think it possible to account for John's narrative sections without some source theory. He rejects the idea of a single signs source, and thinks that the evangelist drew upon 'a mass of unrelated traditions or from several short collections (or perhaps both: some short collections and some individual items)'. And 'as there is evidence that short collections lie behind the Synoptic Gospels, it is reasonable to suppose that the same holds good of John'.

From these sources, John 'dresses up the individual pericopae as ghosts of himself, before presenting himself in more substantial form in his more creative writing which follows them. ... John himself retells the miracles in the manner of an epiphany in order to lead into the crisis of decision which really interests him.' 'Only strictly narrative details', he concludes, 'can be attributed to the sources, and the element of dialogue in them is always coloured by John's rewriting.' At the same time, 'John is also probably himself responsible

---

[44] *Behind the Fourth Gospel*, chs. 2 ('The Sources of the Fourth Gospel') and 3 ('The Making of the Fourth Gospel'), pp. 27–60. See too his commentary, pp. 46–54.

for some degree of fusion of similar but originally distinct stories which were available to him. These may have been in different collections, from which he has selected only what he found needful.' One example of this process is the anointing at Bethany (12: 1–8), which is 'a fusion of the Bethany story of the anointing of Jesus' head ... with a Galilean story of the washing of Jesus' feet with the woman's tears, found only in Luke 7'. Besides his narrative sources 'John also had at his disposal a number of sayings and parables of Jesus, which may have belonged to one or more short collections, or have been included in some of the collections from which he has drawn his narratives, or have existed independently as floating items of tradition.' This makes it unnecessary to postulate an independent discourse source; and Lindars adds that the intertwining of discourse and narrative in the account of the raising of Lazarus in chapter 11 shows how the evangelist blends the two types of material, without himself distinguishing them, into a satisfying whole.

Lindars does not imagine, however, that all this work of composition was carried out at the same time. Rather, arguing from the case of chapter 8, where the writer uses the techniques of a preacher, he remarks that there is 'a prima facie case for the supposition that the Fourth Gospel began life as separate homilies, which John subsequently used as the basis for a continuous Gospel'. In particular, starting from the story of the feeding of the multitude, the evangelist has used the manna tradition to compose a long homily whose connection with the preceding sign 'is really very thin'. Another such homily is the discourse in chapter 5, whose relation to the healing miracle it follows is equally slight. The account of the witness of the Baptist and call of the disciples in 1: 19–51 exhibits a similar technique, as does the story of the raising of Lazarus in chapter 11. This chapter, as well as chapter 6, is sufficiently detachable from the body of the Gospel to make it reasonable to think that they belong to a second edition (as do the Prologue, the second supper discourse in chapters 15–16, and the prayer of Jesus in chapter 17).

What, though, of the first edition? How did that come about? It was the answer, thinks Lindars, to a request on the part of John's audience 'to put his homilies into some permanent form'. The form he selected, naturally enough, was that of a Gospel: 'the Gospel has a plan and a plot of its own, and is not merely a matter of stitching together the existing homilies. We must assume that much of it is new matter, composed specifically for the Gospel as it now stands. On the other hand, certain sections stand so much apart from the main course of the narrative, that it is reasonable to suppose that John has done the work in more than one stage. He has revised and considerably expanded his work for a second edition.'

Lindars's overall view resembles that of Brown, involving as it does a pre-Gospel group of Synoptic-type traditions, an indefinite period in which John composed a number of independent homilies, mostly on the basis of these (Brown at this point allows for a number of different 'preachers', all of the same school), a first attempt to incorporate these into a Gospel, and a second edition in which the Gospel is expanded by the addition of other 'homilies'. (Lindars also assigns most of chapter 21 to a later redactor.) In his emphasis upon the homiletic techniques discernible throughout the Gospel, Lindars's work marks an advance upon Brown's,[45] and in general he is rather more successful in using his compositional theories as an interpretative aid.

Boismard, whose commentary rivals Bultmann's in intricacy and ingenuity,[46] also thinks in terms of two separate editions both attributed to the same author (whom he names, somewhat confusingly, Jean II) and of a final redaction by another hand (Jean III). But unlike Brown and Lindars, he thinks that the first draft of the Gospel (which he calls the 'Document C') can be reconstructed from the present text. Like Wilkens, he combines the multiple-stage theory with a version of the *Grundschrift* theory.

Boismard's analysis, conducted with a deft and dazzling panache and carried through with consistency and determination, cannot be fairly assessed in a single paragraph. (In my second Excursus, I probe into his reconstruction of Document C in John 1 and conclude that his argument is circular.) Where Boismard scores, and scores

[45] It should be said, however, that Lindars has benefited considerably, as he acknowledges, from the work of P. Borgen, *Bread from Heaven*. In the preface to the 2nd edition of his commentary (1978, pp. 25 f.) C. K. Barrett expresses guarded approval of Lindars's views.

[46] This is a huge book, almost 11" × 9", comprising 562 pages set out in double columns. As an example of Boismard's results, one may point to the order he gives, on p. 43, for a section of the hypothetical first edition of the Gospel. Starting with the story of the royal official's son (4: 46 ff.) he continues with the multiplication of loaves (ch. 6), the parables of ch. 10, the ascent to Jerusalem and the healing of the cripple (first part of ch. 5), the reference to signs at Jerusalem (2: 23), and the dialogue with Nicodemus (ch. 3), and concludes with the discourses on witness and judgement (second part of ch. 5).

heavily, over his predecessors, is in his realization that in studying the successive stages of the Gospel's development one must at the same time consider the growth of the Johannine community. Changes in the composition and circumstances of this group are likely to be reflected in its literary products. (We can see this to be true of the Letters; in the nature of the case it will be less obviously true of the Gospel.) Lindars's picture of the Johannine preacher composing his homilies for an attentive audience must be fleshed out by a consideration of the differing situations to which these were addressed. But though Boismard's reconstruction is unconvincing, his approach marks a significant advance in Johannine scholarship.

(b) Signs-source theories

The importance of Robert Fortna's *The Gospel of Signs* is such that it continues to this day to be the object of lively discussion, and the discussion has been animated still more by the appearance of a second book on the same topic.[47] In his first book Fortna combined Bultmann's two narrative sources (signs and passion) into one, and spoke of a Signs *Gospel* (SG), 'hypothetical and perhaps incomplete as it may be',[48] rather than a signs *source*. But by including so much material in which there is no mention of signs he removed much of the justification for the name 'Signs Gospel'. In his second book Fortna reverts to the more familiar theory of a signs source, but argues that this was soon combined with an early version of the passion narrative.

There are two great merits in Fortna's work—his clear enunciation of his methodological principles, and his readiness to carry through his programme of reconstruction in detail. This makes him more vulnerable to criticism, but such vulnerability is not itself a fault.

Fortna states what he believes to be the first principle of source criticism as follows: 'A source analysis of the narratives in Jn presupposes, so long as it is feasible to do so, that *(a) the gospel is the work of one principal author* ('John'), *(b) whose work substantially we have, and (c) who in the course of editing earlier material produced some or all of the aporias which the present text displays.*[49] He argues in defence of what might appear an unjustifiable presupposition that 'it

---

[47] *The Fourth Gospel and its Predecessor.*   [48] *Gospel of Signs*, p. 221.
[49] Ibid., p. 8.

is invalid to begin by treating an obscurity as secondary', since it might be 'a valuable clue to the evangelist's meaning as that can be perceived through *his* handling of *earlier* material.'[50] What such a principle amounts to is simply an option to call the final redactor the evangelist, so that the work as we have it is to be assigned to him and the aporias regarded as ensuing from the intractable nature of the material he is working with. Exit the ecclesiastical redactor! (We shall return to the question of nomenclature at the end of this section.) This is in itself of course a perfectly permissible option. After all, we do not think of Mark or Q as the 'authors' of Matthew and Luke: in the case of the Synoptic Gospels the 'redactors' are readily conceded to be authors in the full sense. And if Fortna's hypothetical Signs Gospel were the only material the final redactor (John) had to handle, this initial stance of Fortna's would require no special defence. But one of the inbuilt weaknesses of his work is that it leaves out of account the discourse material. Even if the simple picture of source and redaction adequately accounted for the composition of the narrative sections (and I agree with Boismard and Lindars that it does not) it clearly breaks down if applied to the discourses—in particular the notorious puzzle of the conclusion of chapter 14.

Another reservation regarding Fortna's work concerns a different kind of presupposition, the assumption that in adapting his source the evangelist proceeded by a simple method of addition and subtraction. In trying to reconstruct John's narrative source we are in much the same position as we would be if we were faced with the task of reconstructing the Gospel of Mark from, say, that of Luke. There is no reason to suppose that John (or the other preachers of his community) was any more anxious to preserve the precise wording of his source than Luke was. But a reconstruction of a hypothetical Mark along the same lines as Fortna's hypothetical Signs Gospel would leave us not with Mark, or anything approaching it, but with a woefully attenuated Luke.[51]

---

[50] Ibid., pp. 5 f.

[51] Accordingly I have some doubts concerning Fortna's attempt to reapply the stylistic criteria elaborated—and discredited—by Ruckstuhl. To take one small example, Fortna divides Ruckstuhl's 'partitive ἐκ', not uncommon in the rest of the New Testament, into four sub-categories, one of which is τις, τινές, πολλοί, or οὐδείς followed by ἐκ, another the use of the partitive ἐκ with a numeral (εἷς or δύο). The former usage occurs frequently in John (i.e. the redactor of the source), never in the

[cont. on p. 88]

That is not to say that the hypothesis of a signs source is to be discarded altogether. On the contrary, many of Faure's arguments are still valid.[52] Nor is the effort involved in such reconstructions as Fortna's without value.[53] Even so, once the verses and half-verses added by the evangelist have been sifted out from the postulated source, the residue is likely to retain a Johannine colouring and flavour that no amount of analysis, however fine, will eliminate completely.

(c) Conclusion

Two further remarks may be added. The first concerns the question of nomenclature, the second prospects for future work.

One methodological principle adopted by Fortna is that the exegete should start by regarding the Gospel's formation 'as involving only two principal stages, *basic document* and *redaction*'.[54] And we have seen that in addition he elects to consider the redaction as Johannine, the basic document as pre-Johannine. This is acceptable enough as it stands, but introduce a single complication and the question is transformed. For suppose that instead of two stages there are actually three: basic document, adaptation into the Gospel form, subsequent redaction. This is more or less Bultmann's position, except that he postulates not one basic document but three. He has no doubt about where to look for the evangelist: he is the writer responsible for Stage 2. Stage 3 is assigned to the 'ecclesiastical redactor' (although of course Bultmann thinks that many of the additional comments—or glosses—in the Gospel are to be accredited to the hand of 'the evangelist' himself).

Now if this is our picture of the Gospel we may be inclined to dismiss as somehow non-Johannine (*a*) the sources—such as the Gnostic document supposedly taken over and adapted by the evangelist, and (*b*) the contributions of the redactor, such as, in Bultmann's theory, the sacramental passages and the bits of futur-

source itself; the latter is common in the source, but is found only twice in John. It is hard to agree with Fortna that we have here 'a telling state of affairs' (p. 209). Lindars asserts that in Fortna's reconstructed text of the source he sees features characteristic of John assigned to the source 'again and again' (*Behind the Fourth Gospel*, p. 33).

[52] They have been repeated in an interesting article by J. Becker, 'Wunder und Christologie'.

[53] I have myself attempted a partial reconstruction of two episodes of the source: cf. Excursus II.   [54] *Gospel of Signs*, p. 4.

istic eschatology inserted as sops for the reactionary. Some parts of the Gospel, such as the final chapter ('the appendix'), will naturally receive less attention than the rest. 'John' on this understanding is a religious genius who has made use of sources and traditions and whose own work has suffered dislocation and/or adulteration at the hands of a less gifted redactor. The truly inspired writing, according to this rather romantic conception, occupies the middle ground between source and redaction.

This is clearly not the only possible view of the matter. What we can now see as a subtly invidious decision is smartly evaded by Wilkens when he postulates a single author constantly revising his own work. Dodd adopts the rather conservative position that the inspired text is the one that has come down to us: this a priori conviction is clear and, from the commentator's point of view, convenient. It also brings the Fourth Gospel into line with recent work done on the other three, for redaction criticism, as we have seen, attributes the present theological thrust of each of these to the final 'redactor'. But it would be equally possible to locate the true source of inspiration wherever the earliest traditions can be detected, on the grounds that these are closest to the historical Jesus, the fountain-head of all inspiration; and it is probably this kind of conviction, paradoxically enough, that lies behind the later of Dodd's two books, *Historical Tradition in the Fourth Gospel*.

In view of this small but tricky problem it might be asked to what extent it is necessary to pin the name 'John' upon any one of the three or more writers who are thought of as having played an important role in the construction of the Gospel as we know it. The answer to this is probably that the name itself carries with it the attribution of inspiration. Moreover it is easier to imagine one religious genius than many, which is no doubt why Brown envisages 'the principal preacher' as the one mainly responsible for shaping the source material into Johannine patterns. A provisional answer to the problem, once we have been alerted to it, may be to allow the name to float free. Certainly the ascription of the name John to any particular passage or any particular idea must continue to be not just an exegetical judgement but an accolade.[55]

[55] The problem of nomenclature, like much else in biblical criticism, is highly reminiscent of the Homeric question. F. A. Wolf, whose *Prolegomena ad Homerum*, i (1795) triggered off the modern debate, is unusual in placing 'Homer' at the *beginning*

[*cont. on p.* 90]

Finally, it may be asked, where does one go from here? Certain blind alleys—the dislocation theory, the revelation source—have been sealed off. Certain advances have been made. Whatever one may think of their detailed proposals, Brown and Lindars are surely on the right lines. And Boismard, wilful as he is in many respects, has travelled further on the same road, or at least pointed in the direction that others must follow. If the Gospel was indeed composed over a period of years, years in which the situation of the Johannine group was never altogether stable, then it seems certain that the Gospel must have grown *pari passu* with the community whose faith it expressed. It is no longer possible to confine oneself to an examination of the purely literary data from which all these various theories of composition took their rise. To progress any further, the literary critic must don the mantle of the historian and the theologian. A start has been made by Raymond Brown in his little book *The Community of the Beloved Disciple*, which has as its subtitle, *The Life, Loves and Hates of an Individual Church in New Testament Times*. But any detailed consideration of this book and other suggestions along similar lines must be deferred until the whole issue is discussed at length in Chapter 5.

3.   ORIGINS: INFLUENCES, BACKGROUND, TRADITIONS

The area of Johannine scholarship occupied by what I have called the question of origins saw a number of changes in the early years of

of a period of development which lasted some four centuries (as opposed to possibly four decades for the Fourth Gospel) yet at the same time praising the literary merits of the finished composition. Had Wolf written further on into the Romantic era, when belief in the inerrancy of great poets had been erected into a principle, he might well have expressed his views differently. It is even less likely that the same person composed the original Catalogue of Ships in Book II of the *Iliad* and the brilliant dramatic dialogue in Book IX than that the same person composed both the signs source alluded to in John 2 and the brilliant dramatic dialogue of John 9. And in the discussion of the Homeric question there are some critics (e.g. Lachmann) whose views make it meaningless to speak of 'Homer'; just as there are critics whose dissection of the Fourth Gospel leaves little room for an evangelist. But lovers of Homer are more impressed by the unity of the poem than by what Josephus called its διαφονίαι (disharmonies); and the same is true of lovers of the Fourth Gospel. At the end of the day these may feel like G. S. Kirk, who, in a chapter entitled 'The search for the real Homer', insists that 'there was someone called Homer, who was primarily responsible for the creation of the Iliad at least'—*Homer and the Oral Tradition* (Cambridge 1976), p. 201. Cf. J. A. Davison, 'The Homeric Question' in A *Companion to Homer*, ed. A. J. B. Wace and F. H. Stubbings (London, 1982), 234–65, esp. pp. 246 ff.

the present century. Scholarship had already been shunted on to a different track by the history-of-religions school and had passed from questions of authorship to questions of origins. (While this shift was taking place the two questions were sometimes confused, as they were for example by Loisy.) This change was certainly an advance, for it meant that attention was deflected from a tedious and ultimately unanswerable question to an interesting and important one. The only major issue in the authorship question, as came to be acknowledged, was whether the author was an eyewitness or not. Once it had been proved, to the satisfaction of all but a stalwart few, that the answer to this question was negative, there was not much to be gained by continuing to speculate upon the author's identity.[56]

Meanwhile the history-of-religions school was directing its powerful searchlight upon hitherto obscure regions of Hellenistic thought, above all the *Hermetica*. Bousset in particular had given a new impetus to Johannine studies with his proposal that John was a child of his time, dissatisfied with the crude earth-bound portrait of Jesus found in the Synoptic Gospels and eager to replace it with a new one of his own, better calculated to appeal to the contemporary taste for the mysterious and esoteric.[57]

Bousset and his colleagues, however, fascinated as they were by the *Zeitgeist* of the New Testament, had a more rigorous programme in mind. Bousset pointed to parallels in Hellenistic literature which could throw light on the genesis of the Gospel. For these parallels were more than curious resemblances. To Bousset they suggested a shared culture. The currents of thought swirling round the evangelist were conceived as flowing into his Gospel, providing as it were an additional source of inspiration independent of the Christian revelation. We have seen that to accept this view would mean admitting that the Fourth Gospel had a strong pagan streak, one that was part of the very fabric of the Gospel and therefore could not be baptized away.

Rudolf Bultmann gave the question of origins a new precision by speaking not just of influences but of sources. By 'sources' he meant literary sources, in exactly the same sense that Mark and Q had come to be regarded as sources for Matthew and Luke. Not that Bultmann had in any way renounced the methods or presuppositions

---

[56] This should not be taken to mean that no attention should be paid to the role of the beloved disciple.

[57] Cf. *Kyrios Christos*, pp. 158–62.

of the history-of-religions school, but he was so convinced of the unity of the fourth evangelist's theology of the Divine Emissary that a general and necessarily somewhat vague appeal to origins seemed to him an unsatisfactory explanation. In fact he would have been keenly critical of any suggestion that the myth taken over and purified by the evangelist could have been anything less than a unified composition available for study and adaptation. His own alternative solution may be wrong, but it was neither lazy nor incomplete.

Ernst Käsemann did not share Bultmann's conviction that the evangelist made very extensive use of written sources, but he was equally clear that the theological problems of the Gospel 'must, after all, point to a specific sector of primitive Christianity and, conversely, we must be able to deduce it from them'.[58]

Käsemann declares that this is the question that interests him most,[59] but his treatment of it is oddly perfunctory. In his opinion, which represents a partial return to the views of Bousset, the origins of the Gospel are to be sought in the heady atmosphere of first-century Christian 'enthusiasm'.[60] This movement, if it can be called that, has often been thought to be the main target of Paul's criticisms in his first letter to the Corinthians. But where, one might legitimately wonder, is its connection with the Fourth Gospel. Käsemann's answer centres upon the idea of 'eternal life'. This, the invariable Gospel, means sharing in the new mode of existence which is that of the Risen Christ. Consequently the term 'eternal life'

---

[58] *Testament*, p. 3.

[59] He professes himself more interested in the first of Bultmann's puzzles than in the second: 'A theological interpretation of the Fourth Gospel is not our ultimate aim. Rather, I shall unfold the complex of theological problems only in so far as it can serve as a key for the historical question of the historical situation out of which this Gospel grew' (ibid.).

[60] This is how Käsemann himself expresses the matter: 'We have already stated that John was dependent on an enthusiastic piety which affirmed a sacramentally realized resurrection of the dead in the present. To be sure, John unfolded his own proclamation of the resurrection not from the sacrament but from his christology. Beginnings for this perspective can be found in the primitive Christian tradition. Already, prior to John, hymns that had developed within the same enthusiastic piety described Jesus as a pre-existent heavenly being whose earthly existence was but a stage of a journey to take him back to heaven' (*Testament*, pp. 20 f.). What might be true of the Prologue should not be assumed without further proof to hold good for the rest of the Gospel also. Cf. pp. 14 ff.; p. 75. Modern English readers sometimes have trouble with 'enthusiasm' used in this sense, though it is a respectable and ancient usage. Ronald Knox adopted it as the title of a major book (in which he devotes a chapter to the study of the 'enthusiasts' of Corinth).

implies that to believe is to partake in the resurrection, or at least to share in all its fruits, an implication that Paul always hastened to guard against, no doubt because of the dubious moral inferences which the Corinthians in particular drew from what they believed to be their own privileged situation. But Käsemann is scarcely justified in extrapolating on such slender evidence from Paul's 'babes in Christ' to the members of the Johannine community.

In any case eternal life is only one of the leading ideas in the Gospel. What of the rest? Käsemann has surprisingly little to add. He makes the strange suggestion that the Johannine concept of the obedience of Christ must be linked somehow with the humiliation theme of the Philippians hymn.[61] It is hard to see why, since, as Käsemann himself insists, John's theology has nothing in common with the self-emptying ($\kappa\acute{\epsilon}\nu\omega\sigma\iota\varsigma$) referred to in that passage.

Altogether Käsemann's attempt to substitute the rather obscure world of pre-Pauline christological hymns for Bultmann's Gnostic revelation source must be pronounced a failure. But though insufficiently worked out and poorly argued, his suggestions are consistent and coherent, and nowhere does he call into question Bultmann's central contention that all the key ideas of the Gospel demand a common explanation; in fact he too insists upon an integral solution.[62]

The unspoken consensus between Bultmann and Käsemann was breached in two ways and for two reasons. The first breach marks an abandonment, at least in certain circles, of Bultmann's problematic in favour of a less precise and less threatening kind of question. This move is signalled by the substitution of the term 'background' for that of 'origins'. Wayne Meeks commences his outstanding dissertation, *The Prophet-King* (1967), with a critical account of the theories of Hoskyns and Bultmann. He concludes: 'It is no exaggeration to say that Bultmann has carried the field in Johannine studies, at least in the sense that the question of the extra-biblical background for the christology of John has become unavoidable. Even C. H. Dodd, who stands closest to Hoskyns in his approach to John, nevertheless devotes more than one-fourth of his study of the Fourth Gospel to "the background".'[63] The qualification, 'at least in the sense ...' is important—and revealing. It marks a shift in perspective that blurs the focus instead of sharpening it, as Bultmann had done, and has as a consequence allowed much subsequent scholarship to evade the

---

[61] Ibid., p. 18.   [62] Ibid., p. 73.   [63] W. Meeks, *The Prophet-King*, p. 10.

questions he raised. A knowledge of the 'background' of the Gospel can never contain the answer to the question of its origins, if only because the term is a neutral one and does not in itself imply either source or influence.

Early on in the book Meeks was referring to, C. H. Dodd says this:

The fact is that the thought of this gospel is so original and creative that a search for its 'sources', or even for the 'influences' by which it may have been affected, may easily lead us astray. Whatever influences may have been present have been masterfully controlled by a powerful and independent mind. There is no book, either in the New Testament or outside it, which is really *like* the Fourth Gospel. Nevertheless, its thought implies a certain background of ideas with which the author could assume his readers to be familiar. How far are we able to reconstruct that background?[64]

What follows (in the next 124 pages) is not offered as an explanation of the Gospel, for 'the powerful and independent mind' of the evangelist may have produced something rich and strange, bearing no more essential resemblance to his 'sources' or 'influences' than coral to old bones. Of course knowledge of the background will facilitate understanding: not just individual passages but large and complex themes will be illuminated; but understanding here entails knowing what the work means, and that is all. Dodd declines to offer the kind of explanation demanded by Bultmann, that is to say an explanation of where the Gospel stands in history, and he deliberately avoids what for Bultmann was its main puzzle—*das erste Rätsel*. Even if his refutation of Bultmann's Mandaean theories is successful, as it may well be, this does not in any way imply that Bultmann's question has been answered: it simply removes the only answer available. The huge gap between what we may suppose the evangelist inherited from his Synoptic (or Synoptic-type) sources and his own remarkably new and elaborate christology is far too great for any mind, however powerful, however independent, to have traversed alone.

Now Meeks is fully aware of this difference between Dodd and Bultmann. In fact he devotes an important and especially perceptive section of his introductory chapter to a comparison between Bultmann and Hoskyns (whose general perspective is, as he says, very close to Dodd's). In particular he enlarges upon Hoskyns's reluctance to allow that non-biblical sources 'may have contributed

---

[64] *Interpretation*, p. 3.

important ideas to the evangelist's "workshop"'—'By what criterion', he asks, 'does Hoskyns decide?'—'Is the criterion dogmatic,
as the statement quoted above seems to imply ('Such parallels belong
to ... comparative religion rather than to ... exegesis ...')? Or is it a
historical criterion, which concludes that the circles represented by
the other extant sources could not have impinged upon that
represented by John? The question is not discussed. Instead Hoskyns
appears to regard it as axiomatic that only the Old Testament and
(orthodox) Christian literature are of primary importance in illuminating the Fourth Gospel.'[65] Yet the question is a highly pertinent
one and Meeks is fully justified in underlining it.

Nevertheless Meeks's picture of the evangelist in his 'workshop',
with a large selection of different woods at his disposal, probably
hewn from different forests, deserves some scrutiny. For it brings us
up against another concept which, like background, has played and
continues to play an important role in many modern treatments of
the Johannine question. This is the concept of syncretism, a maid-of-
all-work who is asked to cover a remarkable amount of ground. The
comment of Rudolf Schnackenburg is typical:

Granted the importance of recognizing the dominant themes in the parallels
discovered by the history-of-religions approach, this does not change the
fact that the Gospel of John is clearly a syncretistic work. The Hellenistic and
Gnostic components cannot be eliminated.

It thus becomes extremely difficult to pin down the Gospel of John with
certainty to a definite area and to a clearly recognizable environment. For
the entire contemporary culture was syncretistic, and the eastern half of the
Roman Empire, the only half which comes in question as the place of origin
of the Fourth Gospel, contains several likely regions and cities: Syria with
Antioch, Asia Minor with Ephesus, Egypt with Alexandria. The problem is
further complicated when we start distinguishing the background of the
author, the intellectual milieu of the place of origin, and perhaps also the
stages of development of the work itself. Only at one point do scholars
interested in the history-of-religions approach appear to agree: the work in
its present form cannot be dated too early, but must be located at the end of
the first Christian century. For more exact information, the history-of-
religions method can provide very little help.[66]

---

[65] *The Prophet-King*, p. 5. In view of his shrewd assessment of all the issues
involved it is surprising that Meeks excludes from his own survey of possible sources
of the prophet-king motif in John precisely those materials to which Hoskyns, as he
observes, unjustifiably restricts himself.

[66] 'Origin', p. 225.

As far as it goes this observation cannot be faulted. But one must be on one's guard against offering as a kind of blanket-explanation a term that is properly employed as an excuse for failing to explain. Indeed, in some of the suggestions put forward by George MacRae the blanket becomes a patchwork quilt. Commenting on the number of different solutions proposed to the problem of the Johannine background, he remarks:

I have not yet read anyone who argues that John's background was Indian or Far Eastern, but I should not be greatly surprised to do so. The least one can conclude is that it is a remarkable biblical book indeed that is capable of eliciting such a variety of theories about its milieu or origin. But one can pose the question in a slightly different manner: since the age of the Fourth Gospel was the age of Roman Hellenism, characterized in many respects by a kind of religious universalism or syncretism, is it not possible that the Fourth Gospel may have tried deliberately to incorporate a diversity of backgrounds into the one gospel message precisely to emphasize the universality of Jesus.[67]

MacRae's article affords a good example of a common modern vice—a confusing disregard of the important differences in meaning between words like 'source', 'influence', and 'background', e.g. 'John deliberately uses [*sic!*] whatever religious background he knows'[68] —but how does one *use* a background? MacRae even introduces a term of his own ('analogy'), when comparing the Johannine 'I am' sayings with the Isis-aretalogy of the Kyme inscription (where Isis' claim to be 'all things to all men' is 'expressed particularly in the form of "I-am" sayings which identify Isis with all manner of universal power').[69] This is interesting, no doubt, but since MacRae carefully refrains from any suggestion that John is even aware of the Isis-cult, let alone influenced by it, it is hard to see where his

---

[67] 'The Fourth Gospel and *Religionsgeschichte*', p. 14. The gap left by MacRae has subsequently been filled by H. C. Kee, 'Myth and Miracle': 'Both the religious needs of the Greco-Roman world and the popular modes of meeting those needs have clearly and deeply affected the author of the Gospel of John. The miracle stories are reminiscent of the Isis aretalogies. The self-pronouncements recall her self-revelatory utterances. The location of the entire redemptive scheme in the context of a creation myth—in which the same agent comes from God, is the instrument both for creating and sustaining the world, and also approaches humanity with an invitation to mystical communion—is a basic feature shared by all three of these literatures' (p. 160). This is a good example of one of the fallacies of what Samuel Sandmel has named 'parallelomania': the assumption that any resemblance must imply a debt. See *JBL* 81 (1962), 1–13.

[68] 'The Fourth Gospel and *Religionsgeschichte*', p. 22.   [69] Ibid., p. 24.

'analogy' gets him. John's universalism (which seems to me rather more problematic than it does to MacRae) bears some resemblance to that of Paul; but here again there can be no question of direct influence. All in all, what MacRae, with an engaging Teutonism, calls 'the genial work of Bultmann' is much easier to assess, with its sharpness and clarity, than any woolly suggestions of syncretism can ever be. Moreover since all Jews, even to some extent Palestinian Jews, had long been exposed to Hellenistic influences there seems no need to search outside the world of first-century Judaism for such Greek traits as are exhibited by the Fourth Gospel.

A further question is whether it is legitimate to pass from the syncretism said to be characteristic of an age to the syncretism of a writer? For in the first case one has to do with the *Zeitgeist*, a kind of all-pervasive miasma affecting every human being within its orbit; in the second case we are faced with two distinct alternatives: either the atmosphere penetrates a writer's bones without his realizing it—in which case it is wrong to speak of his 'workshop' (a term that implies the selection of materials and the application of tools)—or else the writer has a conscious choice. In that case we must reckon with a *source* or *influence*, and it may be important to decide which. Just because we do not know exactly where John 'came from' it does not follow that we should picture him flitting round Asia Minor like a jackdaw, picking up a bright idea whenever one catches his eye and inserting it into the stuff of his Gospel. Such evidence as we have suggests that the activity of the fourth evangelist was confined to a single region. So great is the stylistic and thematic unity of both Gospel and Letters (far greater than in, say, the authentic letters of Paul) that it was only relatively recently that the arguments against a totally unified composition became too strong to ignore.

Provisionally we may postulate that John was from a Greek-speaking area containing a sizeable Jewish community. (The Greek of the Gospel is coloured with Aramaisms, and cannot have been out of the range of Aramaic influence.) One thinks naturally, like Schnackenburg, of the Jewish diaspora in the eastern half of the Roman Empire, but the particular place could be very close to Palestine, where Hellenistic culture had been actively present for centuries. In other words, whilst we can say with some confidence that the origins of the Gospel were 'Jewish' in some broad sense yet to be defined, we are not yet in a position to arbitrate between the claims of Hellenistic versus Palestinian Judaism, if indeed there is any meaningful way of pursuing this distinction.[70] But whatever the home of the Johannine community it was set in one individual spot, rooted in one dear, perpetual place, as Yeats would have his daughter be, and while the author was consequently open to many diverse cultural influences he was relatively immune from others. Why was it, for instance, that despite Paul's remarkably wide-ranging activities in the Greek-speaking world on both sides of the Aegean, John seems to have been virtually unaffected by *his* central ideas? Surely any self-respecting Christian syncretist of the period would have shown *some* Pauline influence?[71]

At this point it is necessary to keep in mind two very different and contrasting facts about the Gospel. On the one hand there is its striking thematic unity and sustained self-allusiveness, the homogeneity which made Strauss think of it as a seamless garment, convinced Wellhausen that it was composed within a single recognizable circle and above all led Bultmann to insist that there must be a single explanation for the Gospel's pattern of themes. On the other hand there is the fact that intertwined as they are, the themes of the Gospel can be distinguished; and it is a mistake to assume a priori that the explanation for their interconnectedness lies behind and outside the Gospel itself. In other words, while it is wrong to presuppose that the essence of the Gospel is entirely attributable to a single mind, there may well have been one mind chiefly responsible for organizing the materials of the Gospel into their present shape.

Accordingly we are led by a natural route to consider the question of traditions. Could the Fourth Gospel resemble a broad river that many different sources have helped to swell? If so, then 'sources' here is a metaphor for 'traditions', and each one of these must be established by a separate argument.

[70] The distinction has come under increasingly heavy fire since Martin Hengel's *Judentum und Hellenismus*. Cf. I. H. Marshall, 'Palestinian and Hellenistic Christianity'; L. H. Feldman, 'Hengel's Judaism and Hellenism in Retrospect'; S. Sandmel, 'Palestinian and Hellenistic Judaism and Christianity'. Sandmel argues against any over-easy or 'comfortable' rejection of the distinction between Palestinian and Hellenistic, whether applied to Judaism or to Christianity. He asks in particular, 'Why must one feel that he must deny that there was a hellenistic Christianity different from Palestinian Jewish Christianity?' (p. 147)

[71] For this reason, despite a well-attested tradition, I believe that Ephesus must be excluded from the list of candidates. 'It is one of the odd and almost comical features of the history of Johannine interpretation', remarks Käsemann, 'that the writing should have been connected with the Ephesian presbyter who as a very old man could only speak about love' (*Testament*, p. 63).

We saw earlier that the consensus between Bultmann and Käsemann concerning the need to find a single overriding explanation for all the Gospel's theological ideas had been weakened in two ways. One way has just emerged: it involves the twin notions of background and syncretism. The other way, resulting directly from a sense of unsatisfactoriness of Bultmann's sweeping synthesis, is characterized by the careful study of individual traditions.

An early advocate of this method was Siegfried Schulz, who devotes the first half of an important study[72] to tracing the history of the various methods that have been employed in elucidating the Fourth Gospel. He discusses thirteen of these and then comes up with a fourteenth: *Themageschichte*, the history of themes. How is this to be distinguished from earlier methods such as the history of religions (*Religionsgeschichte*), the history of traditions (*Traditionsgeschichte*), and the history of concepts (*Begriffsgeschichte*)? It appears to be a less ambitious offshoot of the history-of-religions school, in so far as, without sacrificing the principles and aims of that school, it makes no attempt to account for the whole complex of Johannine thought at one swoop, but rather concerns itself with individual passages of the Gospel that have a clear thematic relationship. What Schulz calls *Traditionsgeschichte* (its first important practitioner was C. Clemen, before the First World War) was originally put forward as an alternative to the attempt to find a written source or *Grundschrift*. A modern representative of this approach is Barnabas Lindars. And what Schulz calls *Begriffsgeschichte* is focused on ideas (usually on words too) without paying much attention to the text itself.

Schulz himself says that *Themageschichte* typically begins by analysing 'small units of tradition on the basis of their thematic content'.[73] The theme in question thus forms the starting-point of an enquiry into the whole fund of traditions (*Traditionsgut*). The method is therefore a type of *Überlieferungsgeschichte*, an attempt, that is to say, to get back to the pre-literary stage of the tradition or traditions embodied in a particular text and to see how these have been adapted by a writer for insertion into his or her own composition. Thus there are two other methods to which *Themageschichte* is clearly related—form criticism (*Formgeschichte*) and redaction criticism (*Redaktionsgeschichte*), though the latter term had yet to be coined.

---

[72] S. Schulz, *Menschensohn-Christologie*.   [73] Ibid., p. 91.

Schulz's proposals are important less for the novelty of his approach than for his attempt to be clear about what he is doing and what he is trying to achieve. And in fact there is much to be said for the method he advocates. If source analysis (at least for the discourse material) is no longer practicable, then close examination of individual passages linked thematically with one another might prove fruitful, always provided that it is possible to distinguish with a fair measure of probability between what the evangelist has taken over and what he has contributed himself. In that case one would at last be in a position to understand—partially at any rate—how the extraordinary message of the Fourth Gospel originated and at the same time to accord due weight and importance to what Dodd calls 'the powerful and independent mind' of the evangelist. For it must be conceded that Dodd has a genuine insight here, one whose importance, once all the necessary provisos have been made, can be properly acknowledged.

Seemingly independently from Schulz, Wayne Meeks arrived at similar conclusions concerning the need for a fresh approach. For him this would consist in the investigation of 'a narrow aspect of the Johannine christology in the face of Bultmann's elaborate theory that had seemed to account so cogently for the *total* christological picture in John'.[74] It is only by close attention to a single phenomenon or group of closely related phenomena that 'scholarship can move from Bultmann's great synthesis, now made problematical, toward the possibility of a new synthesis which may account more adequately for the additional facts and insights that have come to light'.[75] (By this Meeks seems to mean chiefly the work done upon the Mandaean texts by scholars such as Rudolph and Colpe.)

Unfortunately the theme Meeks himself selected for investigation, the figure described by the merging of the functions and titles of 'prophet' and 'king', rests near the periphery of the Gospel's web of concern, which explains why his meticulously conducted enquiry is in some respects so inconclusive.[76]

The themes selected by Schulz (Son of Man, Paraclete, the Return of Jesus) are more central, but they are examined with less care and

---

[74] *The Prophet-King*, p. 16.   [75] Ibid.

[76] In this respect I agree with the conclusions of Marinus de Jonge: 'Jesus is prophet and king because he is the Son sent by the Father, and only as Son of the Father' ('Jesus as Prophet and King', p. 69).

thoroughness. One of the most important and influential scholars working along the same lines is Peder Borgen, whose work on the manna theme, *Bread from Heaven*, gave a fresh impetus to attempts to discern Jewish influences in the Gospel over and above the Old Testament itself.

Probably the most valuable contribution to date in this general area has been that of J.-A. Bühner. In his study of the theme of the Divine Emissary, *Der Gesandte und sein Weg im vierten Evangelium* (1977), he not only singled out what is beyond all question one of the central themes of the Gospel, but brought to bear upon it very considerable learning and insight. He shows an awareness of the Johannine problem similar to that of Bultmann: 'It is a matter of the correct placing (*Einordnung*) of the Johannine community in the history of early Christianity, the placing of its literary work in the genesis of the New Testament, the question concerning the origin of the christological outline of the journey (*Weg*) of the Son of God who is sent into the world and then returns to his heavenly home.'[77] The reference to the Johannine *community* introduces a further dimension of the problem, one to which Bultmann never adverts. It is to this aspect that we must now turn.

4. AUDIENCE: SITUATION AND CIRCUMSTANCES

One of the general weaknesses of Bultmann's theology is that its austere challenge is issued directly to each individual, poor, bare, forked, human animal in isolation from all the rest. It has, in other words, virtually no social dimension. What is more, it is curiously timeless. Bultmann never subjected his own existential categories to the relentless scrutiny with which he probed the 'mythological' language of the Bible.[78] And if he was able to present his understanding of the Fourth Gospel as a message addressed directly to his own contemporaries, with no need of modification or adaptation, this is because he was convinced that this message had lost none of its urgency or validity. The situation in which the message was first proclaimed had consequently no importance for

---

[77] *Gesandte*, p. 1.
[78] See P. Ricœur, 'Preface to Bultmann'. This essay was originally composed as a preface to the French edition (1968) of Bultmann's *Jesus* (1926).

Bultmann.[79] 'Unlike the prophets' words,' he says, apropos of the Fourth Gospel, 'Jesus' words do not thrust the concrete historical situation of the People into the light of God's demand with its promise or threat; they do not open men's eyes to what some present moment demands. Rather, the encounter with Jesus' words and person casts man into decision in his bare, undifferentiated situation of being human.'[80] Accordingly, his solution to Lessing's fundamental dilemma ('contingent truths of history can never serve as the demonstration of eternal truths of reason') was to lop off one of its horns: history does not count.

Hence whereas in each of the other areas of interest (book, content, origins) Bultmann's great commentary had made an indelible mark, there was one area in which he left a gap. Slowly this gap began to be filled; not just because in a field as well-trodden as the Fourth Gospel it was encouraging to come across a relatively green patch, but also no doubt because of the growing influence of redaction criticism.

The possibilities are not infinite, and it may be useful to categorize them schematically. There are, broadly speaking, three questions that may be asked concerning John's audience or readership: was it (*a*) universal or particular; (*b*) Jewish or Gentile (or possibly Samaritan—somewhere in between the two); (*c*) Christian or non-Christian? If a non-Christian audience is intended then the writer's aim could be either polemic (attack) or apologetic (defence) or kerygmatic (missionary); if, on the other hand, the audience is Christian then the purpose could be either hortatory (to warn or encourage) or catechetic (to teach or remind). These possibilities are not all mutually exclusive, since a writer may have more than one purpose in writing and more than one audience in mind. Besides, if it is allowed that the work may have gone through successive stages, then it must also be allowed that the purpose of each may be different. A document that was directed in the first place, say, to refuting the claims of the followers of the Baptist could be taken over and adapted as a missionary tract by a disciple of Jesus. And so on.

[79] The nearest Bultmann gets to defining the purpose of the Gospel is in his *RGG*[3] article, 'Johannesevangelium', col. 847, where he says that the evangelist was responding to the Gnostic understanding of man and the world. Yet certain asides in his commentary, e.g. on the historical background against which chs. 5 and 9 are to be understood (p. 239) show that he could have pursued this line of investigation if he had chosen to do so. Cf. also p. 335 n. 5.

[80] *Theology*, ii 62 f.

The situation is complex, but provided that the key questions are borne in mind it is possible to shape the enquiry fairly straight-forwardly.

Bultmann nowhere spells out his universalistic presuppositions. C. K. Barrett, who in his commentary, as we have seen, avows himself impressed by 'a certain detachment of the gospel from its immediate surroundings',[81] held a similar view and expressed it unequivocally: 'John was not engaging in a pamphlet war, either with Judaism or with the disciples of John the Baptist, but writing theology in a book that was to be a possession for ever.'[82] The reasons for thinking this view mistaken will emerge in the discussion that follows.

Concerning the original conclusion of the Gospel,[83] C. H. Dodd has this to say: 'If ... we try to enter into the author's intention, it must surely appear that he is thinking, in the first place, not so much of Christians who need a deeper theology, as of non-Christians who are concerned about eternal life and the way to it, and may be ready to follow the Christian way if this is presented to them in terms that are intelligibly related to their previous religious interests and experience.'[84] Anyone who reads this with some knowledge of what follows will realize straight away that it affords more insight into Dodd's own intentions than into those of the fourth evangelist. For his whole book rests upon the assumption that the Gospel is to be explained in the way he suggests. In this one respect he resembles Bultmann, for he justifies his own procedures in advance by aligning them with the alleged intentions of the author. What he calls 'background', for instance, he thinks of not as intrinsically bound up with the beliefs of the evangelist but as an external stimulus prompting him to find a new language in which to couch a message

---

[81] *Gospel*[1], p. 115.

[82] *The Prologue of St. John's Gospel*, p. 24. In *The Gospel of John and Judaism* Barrett asserts, 'John wrote not for pagans, not for Jews, but for Christians' (p. 17). But in the concluding paragraph of this short book he reaffirms that 'in the final reckoning this gospel is to be explained not historically, but theologically' (pp. 75 f.).

[83] 'This has been written in order that you may hold the faith that Jesus is the Christ, the Son of God, and that, holding this faith, you may possess life by his name' (20: 31). In this translation the words 'hold the faith' show that the reading of Sinaiticus and Vaticanus is being followed, where the present tense ($\pi\iota\sigma\tau\epsilon\acute{u}\eta\tau\epsilon$) is thought by some to imply that the purpose of the Gospel is not to induce belief but to preserve it. Yet such an implication would appear to conflict directly with the interpretation of the passage Dodd is defending. (Other manuscripts read $\pi\iota\sigma\tau\epsilon\acute{u}\sigma\eta\tau\epsilon$, which could be translated 'come to believe'.)

[84] *Interpretation*, p. 9. It will be seen that Dodd's view is very close to that of Wilhelm Oehler. Cf. *supra*, Ch. 1, p. 14.

that does not differ in any essential respect from the kerygma he has inherited. It is hard to avoid the impression that Dodd is reading his own interpretation into the conclusion of the Gospel, which is just not clear enough to allow us to make any direct inference concerning John's projected readership.

As for the particular reader envisaged by Dodd, a devout and thoughtful citizen of Ephesus tolerably well acquainted with Hellenistic ideas, he is too Greek and insufficiently Jewish. Dodd does admittedly devote a short section of his 'Background' chapters to a consideration of rabbinic Judaism; but because his often brilliant analyses of the Gospel's leading ideas were worked out long before the discovery of the Dead Sea Scrolls[85] it is perhaps not surprising that they are based largely on the Hellenistic material already studied, though less thoroughly, by Bousset and others.

In 1957, Dr W. C. van Unnik of Utrecht read a paper at a New Testament congress in Oxford designed to draw attention once again to the essential Jewishness of the Gospel.[86] He specifically dissociates himself from the views expressed by members of the history-of-religions school from Wrede to Bauer, who considered that the evangelist's attitude towards the Jews was completely hostile. Against these, van Unnik first remarks upon the emphasis the Gospel places upon exclusively Jewish titles like 'Messiah' and 'Son of God' and then goes on to ask who would be most likely to respond positively to this emphasis. After adducing further evidence from Acts and extra-biblical Jewish-Christian literature, he concludes that 'the purpose of the Fourth Gospel was to bring the visitors [he presumably means congregation] of a synagogue in the Diaspora (Jews and Godfearers) to belief in Jesus as the Messiah of Israel'.[87] Elsewhere he correctly asserts that the Johannine phrase 'Jesus is the Christ' 'is a formula which has its roots in the Christian mission among the Jews'.[88] None the less, the scholar from Utrecht exhibits in this paper a certain short-sightedness, or rather strabismus, for with both eyes turned inwards on the messianism undoubtedly

---

[85] Professor Donald MacKinnon, in a personal communication, tells me that he heard Dodd give six lectures in Oxford in 1935–6 on key concepts in the Gospel: κρίσις, λόγος, ἀλήθεια, κτλ.: 'The audience', he says, 'was pitifully small, the lectures superb.' But had the lecturer had the benefit of access to the Qumran texts he might have been more hesitant about giving, to take one instance, a Platonizing view of the Johannine concept of truth. Cf. I. de la Potterie, *La Vérité dans Saint Jean*, p. 8.

[86] 'The Purpose of St. John's Gospel'.   [87] Ibid., p. 410.
[88] Ibid., p. 397.

present in the Gospel, he misses (like others before him) the broader implications of the evangelist's developed christology. Moreover, if this Gospel, as van Unnik says, 'was not an apology to defend the Christian church, but a mission-book which sought to win [*sic!*]',[89] then the evangelist must be adjudged to have set about his task in a singularly ham-fisted way. Interestingly enough, Karl Bornhäuser, whose arguments van Unnik declares himself unable to accept, had pointed the way he should have taken if his views were to gain ground.[90] What is required is the possibility of distinguishing different senses of the word Ἰουδαῖοι, or rather of finding another name for the 'Jews' of the diaspora. For how could anyone believe that the evangelist was setting out to plead his cause with those he calls Ἰουδαῖοι when he excoriates their perversity and obstinacy on almost every page?

J. A. T. Robinson[91] takes up a position very similar to van Unnik's, stating that it is the title 'Messiah' rather than 'Logos' 'which controls John's Christology in the body of the Gospel'. And he adds, astonishingly, 'This is obvious from a concordance.'[92] If, leafing through his concordance, he had paused at υἱός, he would have found that the occurrences of 'Son' as a special title—quite apart from the title 'Son of God' that is arguably to be linked with 'Messiah'—considerably outnumber all the rest. It is true that the Gospel does furnish some arguments for the view that it was originally designed as a missionary-tract, even one specifically directed to Jews of the diaspora, but like van Unnik, to whom he appeals, Robinson fails to consider the ground and nature of the Gospel's *opposition* to οἱ Ἰουδαῖοι. This question cannot be satisfactorily countered by observing that the Gospel is not 'anti-Semitic, that is, racially anti-Jewish' or that 'the world of the Gospel narrative is wholly a Jewish world'.[93] Rather, the question of the identity of οἱ Ἰουδαῖοι becomes even more acute. Robinson slips easily from 'Jews' to 'Judaism', and says that 'to John the only true Judaism is one that acknowledges Jesus as its Messiah. Becoming a true Jew and becoming a Christian are one and the same thing.'[94] But where in the Gospel is there any invitation to 'become a true Jew' or any advocacy of 'true Judaism'? Certainly, as Robinson points out, '"the Jews" for the Gospel are not merely the Jews of Palestine, but with

---

[89] Ibid., p. 410.   [90] *Johannesevangelium*.   [91] 'Destination and Purpose'.
[92] Ibid., p. 198.   [93] Ibid., p. 193.   [94] Ibid., p. 197.

two exceptions only (vi. 41 and 52) the Jews of Judea'.[95] (In fact, as Bornhäuser had shown, the term frequently has an even narrower extension—the Jewish authorities in Jerusalem.) But if one translates οἱ Ἰουδαῖοι by 'the Jews' and then goes on to employ *the same term* for those to whom the Gospel is addressed, then the result can only be thoroughly confusing. Robinson actually believes that in its earliest period the milieu of the Johannine tradition was 'the Christian mission among the Jews of Judea'.[96] But this multiplies the difficulties. As for the phrase 'the children of God who are scattered abroad' (11: 52), Robinson may once again be right in asserting that it does not refer to Gentiles.[97] But that is not to say that it must refer to the Jews of Judaea: it could just as well refer to other Christian Jewish groups.

Robinson does not consider sufficiently seriously the suggestion that the Gospel was not only composed within a Christian community (which he concedes) but primarily addressed to that community.[98]

The articles of Robinson and van Unnik both appeared in 1959, some six years after the earlier of Dodd's two books. Meanwhile the impact of the Dead Sea Scrolls had begun to make itself felt; and there was an increasing readiness in the scholarly world to accept that the origins of the Gospel were in some sense Jewish, though there was not then (and is not now) any agreement about where precisely to locate the Johannine community. As yet there had not been published any major commentary that made use of the new finds, though except for a handful of German scholars who still leaned towards Bultmann's Gnostic theories the tide of opinion was beginning to flow away from both Bultmann and Dodd. In 1966 came the first volume of Raymond Brown's important commentary, and his sensible and balanced advocacy of a Jewish setting for the Gospel established this case beyond reasonable doubt. Moreover his theory that the Gospel had gone through a number of different editions, none the worse for a certain imprecision, was, as we have seen, very definitely along the right lines, so that Schnackenburg, assessing the results of what he called the 'traditio-historical' method a few years later, could speak of an almost universal

---

[95] 'Destination and Purpose', p. 201.   [96] Ibid., p. 202.   [97] Ibid., p. 203.
[98] The arguments of Robinson and van Unnik are examined by R. Schnackenburg in a characteristically thorough article in which, having sifted carefully through all the available evidence, he concludes that their views, in spite of some positive merits, are one-sided and misleading. See 'Messiasfrage'.

consensus 'that we are actually faced with a somewhat lengthy process of composition, with levels of composition leading up to a final redaction'.[99]

This double agreement, first on origins, secondly on composition, paved the way for J. L. Martyn's *History and Theology in the Fourth Gospel*, which for all its brevity is probably the most important single work on the Gospel since Bultmann's commentary. From the first section of his introductory chapter (headed 'The Problem') a new note is sounded:

Our first task ... is to say something as specific as possible about the actual circumstances in which John wrote his Gospel. How are we to picture daily life in John's church? Have elements of its peculiar daily experiences left their stamp on the Gospel penned by one of its members? May one sense even in its exalted cadences the voice of a Christian theologian who writes *in response to contemporary events and issues* which concern, or should concern, all members of the Christian community in which he lives?[100]

It is not simply that the old problem of the Gospel's origins is being presented with a new sharpness and clarity. *The problem itself has changed.* Harnack's 'greatest riddle', cited by Martyn on the preceding page, clearly belongs very definitely to the area of questions I have grouped under the term 'origins'. Martyn is equally clearly concerned with the *situation* of the Gospel, and he obviously expects to find an answer to his question largely within the pages of the Gospel itself. No doubt he is enabled to put this new slant on the 'Johannine problem' by his conviction that the evangelist and his readers spring from the same milieu, and that this milieu is essentially Jewish—though we have already seen how tricky and elusive this description can be. But in doing so he finds the right order; this is where one should begin; this is indeed, as he says, 'our first task'.

How then does Martyn's approach differ from those of the authors we have just been considering? For their questions (and some of their answers too) are often very close to his: To whom is the evangelist addressing his work? Is his audience Gentile or Jewish? What is their situation and where is their location? These are all questions that require answering if we are to be in a position to define the *intention* of the Gospel. Martyn, unlike most of his predecessors, realizes that not all these questions have a single answer, because the Gospel is

---

[99] 'Origin', p. 224.   [100] *History and Theology*[1], p. xviii.

not a unified composition, but spans a long period of time in the course of which the situation of the Johannine community altered, and quite dramatically so. Within this period of development Martyn selects a particular point at which to insert his probe. This is the point of rupture between the Christian group that was to form the community and its Jewish matrix.

In the second place Martyn makes fresh use of an old insight. Hoskyns had long ago argued that the evangelist's main concern was to show the theological significance of the story (or history) of Jesus. That this entailed reading the Gospel on two levels, first as story, making sense of Jesus' struggle with the Jewish authorities during his own lifetime, and secondly as theology, having a direct spiritual relevance to the concerns of the evangelist's own community, was an inference Hoskyns did not draw. The first to do so (to the best of my knowledge) was Xavier Léon-Dufour, in an illuminating but little-noticed article[101] based on 2: 19–22, the only passage in the Gospel in which the evangelist provides an explicit key to one of his riddles.

Where Martyn proceeds beyond Léon-Dufour is in his suggestion that (at least in certain passages) the Gospel tells the story of *an actual event in the life of the community* in such a way that it may be seen to re-enact an episode in the career of Jesus. He begins with chapter 9 (the healing of the blind beggar), which he plausibly construes as a drama. All the main characters, including Jesus himself, have their counterparts in the experience of the community: the beggar is a Christian convert, the Sanhedrin the local Jewish city council (for which Martyn employs the Greek term 'Gerousia'), Jesus a latter-day prophet speaking in his name. When the beggar's parents deny all knowledge of his healing they do so because, we are told, 'the Jews' had decided that anyone who confessed Jesus to be the Messiah was to be ejected from the synagogue (9: 22). Now the Greek word used here, ἀποσυνάγωγος, occurs again in 16: 2, in a context in which, as Martyn says, 'the word clearly gives a *characteristic* of persons now members of the Johannine church'.[102]

---

[101] 'Le Signe du Temple'. See Ch. 11.

[102] *History*[1], p. 20. Martyn argues strongly that this excommunication is to be linked with the famous insertion into the Eighteen Benedictions of the clause expelling 'Heretics' (c. A.D. 85–90). As we saw, this suggestion had been made more than a century earlier by Aberle and it had been put forward again relatively recently by K. L. Carroll, 'The Fourth Gospel and the Exclusion of Christians'. Martyn's argument

[*cont. on p. 109*]

Starting from this conjunction, Martyn goes on to build a most impressive case, which carries conviction because of the wealth of illumination it sheds upon the Gospel itself and the satisfactory way it accounts for one of its most puzzling features: why is the Gospel at once so Jewish and yet so anti-Jewish?

At the same time Martyn postulates a series of stages in the developing relationship between the Christian group and the parent community. These must form the object of our investigation in a later chapter (Chapter 5).[103]

Martyn has developed and expanded his thesis in a number of masterly articles,[104] the details of which need not detain us at present. They make entertaining, even exciting, reading for anyone caught in the grip of 'the Johannine problem'; and the ideas, always fresh and stimulating, are attractively presented. It is still, no doubt, possible and permissible to cavil at a few small points, but one is scarcely surprised to be told, in the preface to the second edition of Martyn's book (1979), of numerous indications 'that its major theses have won a rather wide following'.[105] It is largely because of his work that one can say that this area of Johannine research (that is, the one concerned with audience and situation) has been roughly mapped out. What remains is a matter of adjusting a few details and filling in some gaps.

Apart from Raymond Brown there are two other scholars who have made significant contributions towards the better understanding of the questions tackled with such signal success by Martyn. The first is Herbert Leroy, who has written one of the relatively rare

is severely criticized by J. A. T. Robinson, *Redating the New Testament*. It is true that the connection is not *proved*. But the plausibility of the hypothesis depends upon the light it sheds on the Gospel; and, in any case, Martyn's reading of ch. 9 is not *built upon* his interpretation of the Eighteen Benedictions; at most it is buttressed by it. This means that even if Barnabas Lindars ('Persecution') and William Horbury ('Benediction') are right in suggesting that the Jamnian ordinance simply reinforced an earlier and more drastic action on the part of the Jews in John's region, Martyn's main case still stands firm.

[103] Also to be considered in this connection is Raymond Brown's fascinating little book, *The Community of the Beloved Disciple*, an appetizer for his Anchor Bible commentary on the Johannine Letters that appeared shortly afterwards.

[104] Three of these (one slightly adapted) are now available in book form: *The Gospel of John in Christian History*. Also worth consulting is a rather earlier essay, 'Source Criticism and *Religionsgeschichte* in the Fourth Gospel'.

[105] *History*[2], p. 13. The latest and best of the many attempts to follow up Martyn's insights by combining theological and sociological analysis is David Rensberger's *Overcoming the World*, first published in 1988.

properly form-critical studies on the Fourth Gospel. His chosen topic
is the Johannine riddle, and he suggests as its first *Sitz-im-Leben*
Christian catechesis, specifically the initiation of new disciples into
the separate (and separating) mysteries of their faith.[106] We shall see
that there is something in the Johannine community of the mood
and nature of what Peter Berger calls 'cognitive minorities', em-
battled in-groups fighting for survival in a predominantly hostile
environment. Ritual too can play an important part in helping the
group to establish a sense of its own identity, a fact which allows
Leroy to integrate into his interpretation many of the 'sacramental'
elements in the Gospel that Bultmann had assigned to the 'ecclesiastical redactor'.

The same kind of insight has been briefly developed by Wayne A.
Meeks in 'The Man from Heaven in Johannine Sectarianism'.
Starting from the earlier realization of Bultmann and his pupil Hans
Jonas that myth in general and the Gnostic myth in particular
represents the objectivation of religious people's sense of themselves
and their relation to the world, he attempts 'to discern the function
which the motif "ascent and descent" serves, first within the literary
structure of the Fourth Gospel, then, by analogy, within the
structure of the Johannine community and its relationship to its
environment'.[107]

After giving an answer to the former question, he rephrases the
latter: 'What functions did this particular system of metaphors have
for the group that developed it?' Looked at from this new perspective,
'even its self-contradictions and its disjunctures may be seen to be
means of communication'. His answer to the reformulated question,
italicized in the original, is that 'the book functions for its readers in
precisely the same way that the epiphany of its hero functions
within its narratives and dialogues'. What this means in practice
cannot be appreciated until the life of the Johannine group is set over
against its Jewish parent community: 'coming to faith in Jesus is for
the Johannine group a change in social location. Mere belief without
joining the Johannine community, without making the decisive
break with "the world", particularly the world of Judaism, is a
diabolic "lie". ' Accordingly, 'the book defines and vindicates the
existence of the community that evidently sees itself as unique, alien

---

[106] *Rätsel und Missverständnis.* This conclusion is based directly upon a study of the
temple prophecy in John 2, which will be discussed in Ch. 11.
[107] 'Man from Heaven', p. 145.

from its world, under attack, misunderstood, but living in unity with Christ and through him with God'; and one of its primary functions 'must have been to provide a reinforcement for the community's social identity, which appears to have been largely negative. It provided a symbolic universe which gave religious legitimacy, a theodicy, to the group's actual isolation from the larger society.' Finally, 'the Fourth Gospel not only describes, in etiological fashion, the birth of that community; it also provides reinforcement of the community's isolation. The language patterns we have been describing have the effect, for the insider who accepts them, of demolishing the logic of the world, particularly the world of Judaism, and progressively emphasizing the sectarian consciousness. If one 'believes' what is said in this book, he is quite literally taken out of the ordinary world of social reality. Contrariwise, this can hardly happen unless one stands already within the counter-cultural group or at least in some ambivalent relationship between it and the larger society.' Meeks sums this up by saying: 'It is a case of continual, harmonic reinforcement between social experience and ideology.'[108]

This series of extracts from the concluding pages of Meeks's very condensed article cannot do justice to its richness, but from it as well as from the work of Martyn, Leroy, and Brown, certain conclusions can be drawn. The Fourth Gospel was neither a missionary tract destined for Jews or Gentiles nor a work of theology intended as 'a possession for ever'. In its present form, and in any recognizable earlier version or edition, it was written for the encouragement and edification of a group of 'Jewish' Christians who needed to assert their identity over against the local synagogue, which was almost certainly where the Christian group had taken its rise.

These findings, thus far, seem to me assured. But Martyn's book, however strong on history, is, unlike much of his later work, rather short on theology. What remains is to direct the light that has been generated by the work of these outstanding scholars into areas of study that are still, for all that has been achieved, relatively obscure.

[108] Ibid., pp. 161–5.

CONCLUSION

Looking back and looking forward

Aristotle held the view that in order properly to know or understand an individual thing you have first to know how it is (or has been) caused. For a long time he was also believed to have held that there are four kinds of causes—material, formal, efficient, and final. Now since only one term in this list (efficient) seems to denote what *we* mean by causality, it is easy to consign such an apparently nonsensical view to the dustbin of 'mere' metaphysical speculation. If, however, one translates αἰτία not as 'cause' but as 'explanation', then what Aristotle wrote immediately begins to make sense. For we can look at a bronze statue (Aristotle's most famous example), from different points of view; from the point of view of the bronze from which it is made, the sculptor who fashioned it, the purpose for which he did so, and finally from the point of view of its formal characteristics—τὸ εἶδος καὶ τὸ παράδειγμα.

Having started the first, historical, part of this book with a consideration of four types of literary criticism, I wish to conclude it by comparing Abrams with Aristotle. Out of this comparison will emerge a structure for the remaining two parts of the book.

The first type of explanation, that of *efficient cause*, is obviously covered, in the case of literature, by the concept of authorship. But this concept is not always appropriate for works composed over a long period, especially if they derive wholly or partly from an oral tradition. And in fact where the authorship of such works has been traditionally ascribed to a single figure, such as Homer or Moses, this has proved an obstacle in the path of understanding—whereas in other cases, the Chansons de Geste for example, for which any attribution that exists is very much looser, the way is immediately clear for a different and more comprehensive reading. The majority of modern readers probably still share the deference of the Romantics towards artistic genius, and would consequently deprecate any attempt to 'explain' *Hamlet*, say, or *Lear*, in terms of the particular influences and sources that helped to shape the mind of the dramatist. But if, in the search for efficient causes, it seems reasonable to attribute the Shakespearian magic to his individual genius, this is less true of his 'ideas' than of the peculiarly poetic delicacy and vividness with which he expressed his wonderfully sympathetic understanding of the human condition, and created living human beings for future generations to marvel at. But whereas Shakespeare's 'ideas', like those of Chaucer or Dante (at least in his poetic works), were mostly commonplace and derivative, it is the distinctiveness of the *ideas* of the Fourth Gospel that justifies the search for their origins; if one discounts a theory of direct verbal inspiration, there is a need to explain the elaborate conceptual web that is such a remarkable feature of this work. So without altogether discarding the hypothesis of an individual religious genius, it is legitimate to confine the space reserved for 'efficient causality' to a study of the Gospel's origins—understood in terms of background, sources, influences, and traditions. This is how I construe Bultmann's 'first great puzzle'—*das erste Rätsel*.

Bultmann, as we have seen, tends to assume that the 'final' explanation of the Gospel, its τέλος in the Aristotelian sense, is to be sought in the answers it gives to timeless questions regarding the human condition, the nature and destiny of man. This lofty stance excuses him from asking less wide-ranging questions concerning John's intended readership. But anyone taking a more pragmatic view of the immediate purpose of the Gospel is justified in narrowing the search for a 'final' explanation in order to focus upon the handful of people whom the author or authors had in mind when composing it. I have named these the work's *readers*; and although Aristotle's terminology allows a more extrinsic view of a writer's purpose (e.g. to earn money or to stave off boredom) the intended impact on the readers is the only kind of aim or purpose which is really integral to a full understanding of the work as such. *Pace* Bultmann, it must be included in any complete account of *das erste Rätsel*: the problem of locating the Fourth Gospel within the history of early Christianity.

My discussion of the fourth and central category, *the work itself*, was deliberately limited to a single aspect of this: *the history of the Gospel's composition*. It was helpful to proceed in this manner because the Fourth Gospel is one of those awkward artefacts, like a medieval cathedral, which cannot properly be understood if regarded as the expression of a single overarching design. Winchester Cathedral, for all its beauty and, indeed, coherence, is not properly understood or appreciated unless one is fully aware—to take the most obvious example—that its transepts are Norman and its nave Gothic. All the same, the study of the differing styles and strata of a cathedral really belongs to the story of its construction, the work of designers and builders, masons and craftsmen. As a kind of explanation, it is not fully distinguishable from that of causality in the first sense.[1] Accordingly, the study of the history of the composition of the Gospel is to be directly associated both with the causal explanation and with the 'final' explanation: it, too, must be included in any answer that one can give to Bultmann's first puzzle.

That is why in the second part of this book, entitled 'Genesis', questions concerning the nature and history of the Johannine community must be handled alongside questions of composition. In addition to this, another old question must be tackled afresh: where did the evangelist get his central ideas, above all his christology? How can this strange new portrait of Christ be best accounted for? Chapter 4 begins by attempting to locate the broad cultural context of the Johannine community and finds it in religious dissent.

---

[1] This is also the reason why I have said nothing in this survey about what some may regard as the most significant shift of direction that Johannine scholarship has undergone since the work of Bultmann—the attempt to apply to the Gospel the tools and insights of modern literary criticism, especially of what has come to be known as 'Reader Response Criticism'. Before this term had become common coinage Birger Olsson had already offered 'a text-linguistic analysis' of John 2: 1–11 and 4: 1–42 in a work entitled *Structure and Meaning in the Fourth Gospel* (1974). Then came the work of R. Alan Culpepper, *The Anatomy of the Fourth Gospel* (1983). Since then Jeffrey Lloyd Staley, in *The Print's First Kiss* (1988), has attempted to improve upon Culpepper's work by emphasizing the inherent temporality and linearity of narrative. Despite its whimsical title this is an incisive work, containing a number of good insights. Staley's exegesis of the wedding-feast at Cana, especially the conclusion, is a brilliant piece of exegesis that powerfully vindicates the use of the new methods. It too, however, is vitiated by a neglect of any diachronic perspective, so necessary if one is to make any real progress in the study of a many-layered text like the Fourth Gospel: 'to understand the implied author in the Fourth Gospel means that we must begin by assuming the book's unity (p. 29), for 'the assumption of unity endows the entire text with intentionality' (p. 30). But unless this assumption can be justified (and it is hard to see how it could be) this is a spurious intentionality. However many incidental insights such an approach may produce, it can offer no help in answering the real riddles of the text. Similarly flawed are more traditional attempts to discern the plan or pattern of the Gospel as a whole, e.g. Peter F. Ellis, *The Genius of John* (1984); George Mlakuzhyil, *The Christocentric Literary Structure of the Fourth Gospel* (1987), even though the latter work in particular is distinguished by a refined analytic technique that goes beyond all earlier attempts of the same sort. In spite of these reservations, the literary and structural study of the Gospel merits a more extended discussion than it can be given here. I hope to return to this question elsewhere. Cf. Ch. 14, n. 53.

Chapter 5 gives an outline of the history of the Johannine community and its book. Chapter 6 is devoted to a study of one of the most distinctive and pervasive features of the Gospel, its dualism. It offers a suggestion about the provenance of the evangelist. What follows in the last three chapters of Part II (Messiah, Son of God, Son of Man) is an attempt to penetrate the history of the Gospel's developing christology.

Turning back to Aristotle's bronze statue, and asking what could count as the *material explanation* of a play or poem, we find that some adjustment is necessary. For whereas part of one's understanding of a statue depends upon knowing the material from which it is made (in that bronze is different from marble and marble from wood), the 'matter' out of which a play or poem is constructed will be of a very different kind. (We can exclude any banal definition of the 'matter' of a poem as the ink with which it is written.)

Part of the material of a play or a poem might be lifted bodily from elsewhere. Shakespeare's Enobarbus takes his description of Cleopatra's barge from North's Plutarch and himself furnishes T. S. Eliot with the starting-point for a description of a Chair. But on the whole we might wish to say that a play's matter or material is that aspect of human existence (whether it be the mores of the court of Charles II or those of the kitchen-sink) which its author has selected to represent. And this corresponds fairly closely to what I have called *content*. Similarly the 'material' explanation of the Fourth Gospel must cover its content in two senses of the word: both the traditions the evangelist has inherited and the thought-world he projects.

But whereas in the case of the statue it is easy enough to distinguish, mentally at any rate, the bronze from the shape the sculptor gives it, there is no such tidy division available when we are considering works of literature. If you ask what makes a statue like Rodin's Age of Bronze a masterpiece your answer must be along formal lines. But in order to make the transition from sculpture to literature it may be expedient to introduce Clive Bell's term 'significant form'. This term, though more valuable for its suggestiveness than its precision, has the advantage of indicating that man-made beauty cannot be fully assessed without bringing in the notion of *meaning*. This is certainly true of works of literature. But the meaning of any written composition fuses content and form into an indissoluble whole.

There is, however, another sense in which the notion of *'formal' explanation* is relevant. Aristotle himself often spoke of questions concerning the form of a thing as equivalent to asking simply what it was, or rather what kind of thing it was. And in literature this means asking about the genre of a piece of writing. This question might be thought to differ only slightly from questions concerning the aim or purpose of a writing, as can easily be seen when we reflect on the nature of an epic or a play. But though the difference is slight, it is none the less crucial. Questions concerning genre resemble those the form critics put concerning individual forms or *Gattungen*; that is to say, the answers they seek are general rather than particular: they relate to the kind of situation, the kind of audience to which a work is addressed. In so far as such answers necessarily reach out beyond the work of art itself, they are the sort of general answer implied in terms like 'apologetic', 'catechetic', and 'kerygmatic', not the sort that involve mentioning a particular historical situation, except in so far as this too needs to be described in order to specify the genre or *Gattung* in question. Taken together, these two senses of 'formal' explanation pretty well cover what I have called *the work itself*.

The third part of this book (Revelation) is an extended attempt to answer Bultmann's second great puzzle: what is the Gospel's central conception, its *Grundkonzeption*? This is really the problem of the meaning of the Gospel: what did the evangelist make of the traditions he inherited, and what is the significance of his choice of the gospel form? Questions, then, of matter and form.

The third part opens with a chapter (Intimations of Apocalyptic) that harks back to the conclusion of the second part. Since the Fourth Gospel is a self-conscious appropriation of the gospel genre, the next chapter (11) is devoted to an answer to the question of the Gospel genre. Chapter 12, 'Departure and Return', is an extended exegesis of John 14. The title of Chapter 13, 'Passion and Resurrection', is self-explanatory. The last chapter, 'The Medium and the Message', concludes the study of the Johannine concept of revelation. As it happens, most of the material used in the second part of this book comes from the first half of the Gospel, whilst the third part focuses mainly on the second half.

The body of this book is intentionally more discursive than an ordinary commentary, of its nature, is allowed to be. But since any interpretation of the Gospel must depend ultimately upon a close study of the text, I have inserted at intervals five technical excursuses intended for readers already acquainted with the Greek text and the rudiments of exegesis. This is a deliberate reversal of the procedure of the standard commentaries, which concentrate upon a line-by-line exegesis and reserve for appendices the extended treatment often demanded by the conceptual world of this richest of Gospels. I do not pretend to have plumbed its riches. My aim has been to further their understanding.

PART II

GENESIS

INTRODUCTION

As we prepare to embark upon the search for the origins of the Gospel a few more words of methodological explanation are in order. Of the many questions one may have in mind when perusing a work of literature two are especially important. The first is that of someone interested in literature for its own sake. We may call this person the exegete, whose central concern, as we saw at the beginning of this book, is *the work itself*. The exegete is prepared to use a variety of different tools—whatever comes to hand—in determining the *meaning* of the work, and this requires some understanding of its content.

The second question is that of the historian: how may this particular writing help us to understand the period in which it was composed? The historian may be interested in a variety of different subjects: politics, trade, social change, botany, agriculture, and many other things besides. What generally characterizes the historical approach, however, is that it does not tackle the writing for its own sake but for what it can tell us about something else. E. P. Sanders, for example, in his *Jesus and Judaism* explores and exploits a large number of literary works, including the Synoptic Gospels. But what he seeks to reconstruct and explain in that book is not the origins of the Gospels but the career of Jesus. He writes as a biographer.

There remains, however, one kind of historian with a *direct* interest in the literary works that furnish other historians with much of their source-material. This is the literary historian, who, unlike the exegete, is less concerned with *interpreting* the works in question than in situating them in their historical context, either by relating them to contemporary culture and society or by accounting for their genesis in terms of sources and influences. This involves flinging the net far and wide, for the explanation sought here encompasses much more than a single text or group of texts: it depends upon an understanding of the circumstances in which a particular work or series of works was composed and may, as Lucien Goldmann has argued,[1] necessitate the discernment of deep structures of which the actual writer may be unaware.

The distinction between the historian and the exegete is not impermeable. This is especially so when, as in the case of all four Gospels, the work in question is neither pure fantasy (although this too may come within the historian's purview) nor pure history (although the works of major historians from Herodotus onwards may be treated simply as literature) but a mixture of the two.[2] That is why any study of the Gospels that neglects their 'factual' content can offer at best a partial understanding of their meaning.

In accounting for the genesis of the Fourth Gospel one must focus primarily upon its ideas. These, after all, are what singles it out from the other Gospels and makes it so hard to explain. Hence the importance of Bultmann's first riddle. But clearly the ideas of the Gospel must also engage our attention when our primary aim is to elucidate its *meaning*. Some might think the overlap so great as to make the distinction unworkable. In Chapter 6, for example, I investigate the dualism of the Gospel by examining certain key concepts that are also important strands in the fabric of its meaning. Should not that chapter belong to Part III rather than to Part II? Well, my main concern at that point will be *to account for* the dualism of the Gospel and not to see how it is deployed and articulated, in other words to find an answer to Bultmann's first riddle. For him too, it will be remembered, the dualism of the Gospel cannot be explained from within. Provided then that the distinction between history (*explanation* in Goldmann's sense) and exegesis

---

[1] See 'Structuralisme génétique et création littéraire'. Goldmann argues that literary analysis comprises two quite distinct procedures. The first of these, *compréhension*, involves the attempt to understand the text from the inside without adding to it or venturing outside it. This is roughly equivalent to what I call exegesis. The second procedure, *explication*, cannot be carried out without taking into account factors and forces outside the text itself: it addresses itself to the question how the text came to be written, its genesis, and can be directed equally well to any human artefact or activity that can be read as a structured text. As examples Goldmann takes Racine and Pascal (two writers he had studied in depth in his best-known work, *Le Dieu caché*). The tragic vision of Racine's theatre and Pascal's *Pensées* may be grasped from the inside, but to explain them in Goldmann's sense it is necessary among other things to analyse the structure of Jansenism. A *comprehension* of this will enable one to *explain* Racine and Pascal. To *explain* Jansenism, which itself may be read as a structured text, would involve, he says, an analysis of the structure of *la noblesse de la robe* in 17th-century French society.

[2] The nature of the mixture may vary from Shakespeare's historical plays and the novels of Walter Scott to more modern writings as diverse as *War and Peace*, *Les Mémoires d'Hadrien*, *The White Hotel*, and *Flaubert's Parrot*.

(what Goldmann calls *comprehension*) is flexibly employed and not hardened or exaggerated, it can be of some service.

In Part II, therefore, which comprises my answer to Bultmann's first riddle, I approach the Gospel as a historian, attempting to explain its genesis from without. In Part III, where my answer to Bultmann's second riddle, revelation, is basically the same as his own, my purpose will be more straightforwardly exegetical.

4

RELIGIOUS DISSENT

In the beginning of any historical enquiry some account may be expected of the questions to which answers are being sought. Of course, without any knowledge of the problems or opinions about possible solutions one could not even put the questions in the first place. And when Bultmann poses (or proposes) his two Johannine riddles he is keenly aware of the *kind* of answer he is looking for. His first riddle, the position of the Gospel in early Christianity, implies that the fundamental difficulty is to explain the momentous shift from the message of the earliest Christian preachers to that of the fourth evangelist. His solution, which places a hypothetical Gnostic source *between* early and late, virtually isolates John's distinctive teaching from other sources and influences. In any case, if we are to avoid being trapped inside Bultmann's personal problematic we must change or rather expand his question: I believe it is necessary to ask instead what is the position of the Gospel in the history of *Jewish thought* (leaving the term 'Jewish' provisionally vague, since any closer definition would prejudice the issue of our enquiry). Evidently such a reformulation of the question carries its own presuppositions, and part of the purpose of the present chapter is to justify these.

The Gospel itself has a number of different doors through which we may enter: one might, for instance, choose to begin with some of its central themes, especially the titles of Jesus and the claims made for him. For if the question being asked is the position of the Gospel in Jewish *thought* it might seem best to start with ideas or symbols (Messiah, prophet, Son of Man, etc.) of unquestionably Jewish provenance, and to consider how they have been transformed so as to serve the fresh purposes of the fourth evangelist. And that is, in fact, what will be attempted in subsequent chapters. But first it is worth trying to specify as closely as possible the nature of the community within which the Fourth Gospel was conceived and brought to birth. There are two possible perspectives on this question, one close and the other distant. The next chapter will take a closer look at the community's origins and the immediate circumstances of the composition of the Gospel. In the present chapter the more distant perspective is preferred, and this involves an attempt to locate the origins of the Johannine community in the period of the Second Temple—what scholars used to call, confusingly, late Judaism.[1]

First, though, it is necessary to be clear about the terms of our question. In asking about the origins of the Gospel are we looking for sources, influences, or merely background? All three, certainly,[2] but we often need to look in different places.

(a) Sources

One apparent merit of Bultmann's commentary is the precision with which he delineates the Gospel's sources: signs source, revelation-discourse source, passion narrative. The work of the evangelist in organizing and adapting these various materials is laid open to inspection and the otherwise seemingly inexplicable readily explained. But, with the exception of the Prologue and possibly the passion narrative, Bultmann's suggested sources have not won widespread acceptance. And even if we include the signs source and an indefinite number of Synoptic-type narratives and sayings, we are still left with the material Bultmann assigned to the revelation source; and it is this, along with the evangelist's own contribution, that gives the Fourth Gospel its distinctive flavour. No source theory hitherto advanced is of any help here. And even supposing another Arab shepherd-boy were lucky enough to stumble upon a document closely resembling Bultmann's revelation-discourse source, future scholars would still be left with the task of explaining how this marvellous new discovery had come to be written. In general no source theory offers more than a very partial entry into a work of literature (Aristotle's 'material' explanation). How much does one

[1] 'Second Temple' denotes the long period (more than half a millennium) between the rebuilding of the Temple after the Babylonian exile towards the end of the 6th century BC and its destruction in AD 70. The term fails to take into account the important restoration work undertaken by Herod the Great. This lasted over 80 years, and was completed less than a decade before the fateful date of AD 70.

[2] See the discussion in the previous chapter, § 3.

understand of *Macbeth* or *Cymbeline* from knowing Holinshed's *Chronicles*, or of *King Lear* from knowing *King Leir*? It seems preferable to remain with the Gospel itself at this juncture instead of shifting the problem further back to the work of an unknown religious genius.

That there was a religious genius behind and beneath the work of the fourth evangelist is a truth whose significance is often neglected. But the contribution of Jesus to his thought is not easily demarcated, and in any case is better characterized as an influence than as a source.

(b) Influences

The preaching and teaching of Jesus, his work as a teacher and exorcist, his impact on his disciples, his trial and crucifixion, and the beliefs that arose about him after his death—all these must be included, and remembered, in any discussion of the influences on the Fourth Gospel. But these same influences worked upon the Synoptic Gospels also, with vastly different results; so it is necessary to cast our net wider.

How much wider? Wide enough, certainly, to cover the whole religious scene in contemporary Palestine. But to do this satisfactorily we are forced to look back—perhaps as far back as the sectarian squabbles in post-exilic Israel, and forward—perhaps as far forward as the Dark Ages.

That we must look back will be readily conceded. Like any other historical events, the religious movements in first-century Palestine are partly to be explained as responses to contemporary events and situations (like the increasingly oppressive burden of taxation), partly as the legacy of the past. The multifarious writings testifying to the religious turmoils of the Second Temple period must all be scanned for traces of ideas that may plausibly be thought to have influenced the first Christian thinkers. To these we must add the Hebrew Bible, the most obvious influence of all, whether or not this was exercised directly or through the mediation of the Septuagint.

If it were possible to account for the genesis of the Gospel by appealing to sources and influences anterior to or roughly contemporary with it, then our task would be the relatively simple one of assembling and correlating these materials. Unfortunately, however, this is not the case. We are forced to extend our survey to include writings composed later, some of them much later, than the Gospel itself.

In doing so we are liable to find ourselves taking long journeys both in time and space. For the most striking fact about the proposed sources and influences is their range and diversity. The sophisticated allegories of Philo may well have been composed about the same time as some of the Qumran documents, but conceptually they are worlds apart. The same is true of the *Hermetica*, that strange blend of Stoicism and Platonism upon which Dodd drew so extensively. Some of these are roughly contemporary with parts of the Talmud, but there the resemblance ends. Geographically, the locations of the different writings range from Egypt to Iraq, chronologically from the third century BC (the date of the earliest sections of *1 Enoch*) to the eighth or ninth century AD.

If we look at a single theme, that of 'prophet-king' in Meeks's book of that name,[3] we find that in hunting for the origins of this relatively peripheral motif he examines a large number of different bodies of literature—rabbinic, Samaritan, and Mandaean writings, Philo, Josephus, and the Dead Sea Scrolls. None of these is altogether discounted, although Meeks puts more weight on some than on others. There is no suggestion that John actually drew upon any of these sources, most of which are too late for him to have known; but it is implied that in each case the *origin* of the tradition, e.g. the Jewish source of Philo's concept of Moses as a prophet-king, may have had some influence on the writer of the Gospel.

There is, I suggest, an image or model discernible in Meeks's work and in other studies which, like his, work with 'background' as a key concept. This model is nowhere explicitly delineated: it has to be inferred from what he says: the materials he examines may be compared to a number of broad rivers, each very different from the rest, whose sources have been lost sight of and can only be guessed. If we were able to trace them back we would find innumerable rivulets, which we might call traditions, feeding into streams or sources which in turn feed into the big rivers, the only ones for

---

[3] I single out Meeks's *Prophet-King* not because it is particularly bad but because it is particularly good. Indeed, it is a model of the monograph genre, meticulously planned and executed and never drawing exaggerated conclusions from the evidence. If we had a library of such works, all devoted to a single motif or theme, we should be in a position to draw all the threads together. My point is that in order to avoid an inextricable tangle it would then be necessary to trace the threads back to a common origin—a task Meeks deliberately declines.

which we have names. Some of the rivulets at the origins of the rivers will also have fed into the Fourth Gospel. This explains both why the Gospel has points of resemblance to many divergent bodies of literature and also why the rivers are so different from one another.

Now this is a very complex model, and it is worth observing that the only point where the big rivers actually coalesce is Meeks's book (and other works conducted along the same lines) just as the only point where the rivulets coalesce, according to the theory, is the Fourth Gospel. What alternative can be offered?

There are four factors that need to be taken into account by any theory of the origins of the Gospel. Three of them are uncontentious; these are the Jesus-tradition, the situation of the Johannine community, and the creative power of the author or authors of the Gospel. The fourth, I suggest, the one we are looking for, is the unorthodox or dissenting Jewish tradition within which the seeds of the Gospel were first planted. To say this is to replace the fluid image of flowing waters with the static image of soil or earth. If the concept of syncretism is required to explain the origins of the Gospel, it should be applied, I believe, not to the conscious eclecticism of the author but to the rich loam in which the message concerning Jesus was planted and in which it continued to thrive. It is unnecessary to picture the evangelist flitting from one background to another or pottering about his workshop making a selection from the various woods at his disposal: rather, the place of origin of the Gospel was one where ideas foreign to 'orthodox' Judaism and less obviously present in the other early manifestations of Christianity were already strongly and deeply rooted.

To accept this model it is necessary to discard the view that the dominant religion of the Jewish world in the centuries preceding the composition of the Gospel can be reconstructed simply from a close examination of rabbinic, Pharisaic, and deuteronomic orthodoxy; we shall see that such a reconstruction, or something like it, is probably what is being rejected by the evangelist when he speaks of 'the Jews'. What is not included in this term is the world of religious discourse, equally Jewish, which we find in the so-called Apocrypha and Pseudepigrapha, in Qumran, and indeed anywhere broadly 'Jewish' outside what G. F. Moore called 'normal' Judaism.[4]

---

[4] *Judaism*. i. 128. Nowadays few scholars would accept as legitimate any such implied distinction between 'normal' and 'abnormal' Judaism.

Throughout the Second Temple period, and especially in the work of the deuteronomists and the Chronicler, one can see deliberate attempts to suppress alternative religious positions such as that represented, say, in 1 *Enoch*. These attempts continued into rabbinical times, as is well demonstrated in Alan Segal's fine study, *Two Powers*: eventually they proved successful, though perhaps never completely.

The idea of 'normal' Judaism was derived from later rabbinical Judaism, and is nowadays seen to be inapplicable to the period of the Second Temple, during which the views of those who would subsequently seem unorthodox had more space and air. They flourished in ways conditioned by the varied circumstances of different groups scattered throughout the Near East. In any of these we may expect to find patterns of thought retained from ancient times, family resemblances to be explained by their ultimate derivation from a single, variegated tradition.

This means that we should be very wary of thinking of, say, Samaritanism or Jewish Gnosticism in terms of sources and influence. Nobody supposes that documents composed, in some cases, centuries later than the Gospel itself were accessible to the fourth evangelist in precisely the form in which we have them now. But it is often impossible to say precisely when a developed doctrine like the Gnostic redeemer myth received its definitive shape. Hence the precariousness of Bultmann's Mandaean hypothesis and of arguments like those contained in Klaus Haacker's *Stiftung des Heils* that rely too indiscriminately upon the fourth-century *Memar Marqah*.[5]

Broadly speaking the influences on the Fourth Gospel are all Jewish, provided this term is used widely and vaguely enough to cover ideas emanating from the circle of Jesus. Christianity began life as a Jewish sect.

(c) Background

The somewhat nebulous concept of background, whose explanatory power is very limited, needs to be introduced to account for the relevance of such writers as Philo and Josephus, as well as of post-Mishnaic Judaism. The light shed by these may be quite strong, but

[5] See R. Bergmeier, 'Frühdatierung'. Bergmeier criticizes Haacker on similar grounds, pp. 124f.; 130-3. For a useful survey see R. Pummer, 'The Present State of Samaritan Studies'. Pummer, though cautious, is less sceptical than Bergmeier.

for the most part it is too indirect to justify speaking of sources or even influences. A reading of Philo, as Borgen has shown, helps us to understand what is going on in the Bread of Life discourse in John 6, not because John knew Philo, but because they shared a common exegetical technique. Josephus can help us because, as a historian writing at the same time as the evangelist, he can give us relevant historical information (filtered though it may be through his own ideological grid); but also because his opinions and attitudes are representative of certain current ways of thinking and speaking. The rabbinical writings can help us because they have some common ancestry with Christianity (though not as much as is often assumed) and because many of their principles, above all legal and exegetical, can be seen to be at work in Christian writings also. We are thus enabled to understand the gist of otherwise puzzling lines of argument. Borgen's well-known article 'God's Agent in the Fourth Gospel' carries conviction because of the light shed by the Jewish law of agency upon John's christology. The same can be said of some of the central arguments in the important monograph of J.-A. Bühner. These suggestions will be more fully elaborated later, but we may say at once that while these writings are helpful for elucidating many otherwise cryptic passages in the Gospel, they afford little or no assistance in the understanding of the ideas and impulses that precipitated the central teaching of the Gospel—Jesus' revelation concerning his mission and person and his relationship with the Father.

(d) Conclusion

While the distinction between sources and influences is virtually self-justifying, that between influences and background must be viewed more as a heuristic device than as an a priori principle. Only after careful inspection can a particular document or corpus of writings such as those of Philo or Josephus be ranged on one side or the other. And one must allow for the possibility that the light shed may be direct in some cases and indirect in others. None the less, any failure to distinguish between the two kinds of illumination, one from below, the other from behind, not only generates confusion but allows certain writers, notably Dodd, to employ the term 'background' as a way of evading the central issues of influences and origins.[6]

[6] See *supra*, Ch. 3, p. 94.

2. THE JOHANNINE JEWS[7]

My discussion up to this point may have seemed to imply that the only problem in investigating the origins of the Fourth Gospel is to locate and identify its sources, influences, and background within the Jewish tradition and to distinguish these from one another. But there is an obvious objection against such a procedure. If one is to attempt to situate the Fourth Gospel in the history of Jewish thought, how is one to explain the attitude of the Gospel itself to those it calls 'the Jews'?

(a) The problem

'Among the unsolved riddles of the Fourth Gospel is to be numbered its attitude to Judaism, which was one of profound ambivalence, a strange love–hate relationship, prompting C. K. Barrett to remark that "John is both Jewish and anti-Jewish".' So opens one of the most recent attempts[8] to state and solve the unsolved riddle. But the terms in which Hartwig Thyen poses the problem are misleading, and this augurs ill for a full solution. Even if we ignore the easy substitution of the ambiguous word *Judentum* ('Judaism'/'Jewry') for John's specific οἱ Ἰουδαῖοι, there remains the clear implication that the evangelist was somehow torn between love and hatred (*Haß-Liebe*) in his feelings towards those he thus names; whereas in fact there is no love and little sympathy, only hostility tinged with fear. The 'Jewish' in Barrett's dictum refers to customs and ceremonies, turns of phrase and ways of thought: the 'anti-Jewish' applies to a people or a nation.

Of course, this distinction does not solve the riddle: it only sharpens it. Why *does* the evangelist, who never attempts to disguise the Jewishness of his hero, evince such hostility to his hero's people? Surely it is hard to rest content with the apparently obvious answer that he is merely putting on record the sad story of the consistent vindictiveness shown towards Jesus by those of his own race and nation? There *are* mysteries here, and it is into these dark waters, the

---

[7] For a more detailed treatment of the problems raised in this section see my article, 'Identity and Function'.

[8] 'Das Heil kommt von den Juden'. The English version of the Barrett citation is in *The Gospel of John and Judaism*, p. 71. See too the fine article of Wayne Meeks, '"Am I a Jew?"', which sharpens Barrett's paradox by asserting that 'the Fourth Gospel is most anti-Jewish at the points where it is most Jewish' (p. 163).

source, horrifyingly, of so much Christian anti-Semitism, that we must venture in our search for the origins of this extraordinary book. In fact, the term 'origins' conveys only part of the problem, for the Gospel as we know it was largely inspired by the traumatic experience of the community's expulsion from the synagogue. It tells, with graphic symbolism, of the birth, the very painful birth, of a new sect, or, to slant the matter differently, of a new religion. What was once a group of Jews owning allegiance to the Jewish Messiah, was to become an important branch of the young Christian Church, bringing into it principles and convictions which were themselves the germ of some of the strange ideas that would intrigue thinkers and theologians for centuries—including the twin doctrines of Trinity and Incarnation, the most puzzling as well as the most distinctive of all Christian beliefs.

When tackling this problem it is necessary to begin by distinguishing two questions: identity and role. Both of these questions are primarily *exegetical*—that is to say, they concern the interpretation of the Gospel text—but they lead on to the *historical* question which is our present concern: how to explain the Gospel's anti-Jewish bias.

(b) Identity

The question 'Who are the Ἰουδαῖοι?' has been answered in roughly two different ways. In the first place, they are identified as the Jewish (or Judaean) authorities—not the people of Jerusalem or Judaea, still less the Jewish nation as a whole, but simply the men with the power and influence that entitle them to speak on behalf of everybody else.[9] Such a solution would effectively clear John of the charge of anti-Semitism, but is open to the objection that the word he uses, whatever its immediate reference, is not for the most part 'rulers' (ἄρχοντες) nor even 'chief priests' or 'Pharisees' (though these words are familiar to him and he does use them from time to time)[10] but οἱ Ἰουδαῖοι,[11] the entire nation, or seemingly so.

There is an important distinction to be made here between the

[9] See U. C. von Wahlde, 'The Johannine Jews'. Von Wahlde, who himself espouses this solution, gives a useful summary of earlier treatments of the problem.

[10] There are 3 instances of ἄρχοντες in the Gospel, 10 of ἀρχιερεῖς, and 19 of Φαρισαῖοι, as against 66 of Ἰουδαῖοι, roughly half of which are examples of the typically Johannine, hostile use of the word.

[11] In what follows it is necessary to retain the Greek word, since either of the alternative English renderings, 'Jews' or 'Judaeans', would beg the question.

denotation of a word (the individual or group to which it refers in any given context) and its *connotation* (the range of sense or meaning which its use evokes in the reader or listener—this may, of course, differ from one person to another). Applied to the Johannine Jews, this distinction, crude though it is, and capable of much greater elaboration, suffices to demonstrate that in order to free the Jews as a whole from the blame of rejecting the message of Jesus and causing his death it is not enough to show that in most instances in the Gospel the word denotes the religious authorities in Jerusalem. When the Argentinians invaded the Falkland Islands the actual forces involved were no more than a few thousand military and naval personnel. And the number of people who determined upon the invasion was smaller still. But unfortunately, as in all such cases, the use of the word 'Argentinians' implies that the whole nation was somehow involved. And is this not so? (The Argentinians themselves described the operation as 'la liberación de las Malvinas'—a good instance of how two terms can have the same denotation but very different connotations.)

The second solution, on the face of it even more attractive, has been forcefully argued by Malcolm Lowe.[12] It consists of the proposal to translate Ἰουδαῖοι by 'Judaeans'. This would root the extraordinary hostility evinced by the Gospel in the kind of local or tribal enmity all too familiar in the war-torn history of the human race. Ranged against the Judeans would be Galileans and/or Samaritans, both of them groups that figure noticeably if rarely in the pages of the Gospel. Unfortunately, however, although there is plenty of evidence in contemporary writing (above all Josephus) for the use of the term Ἰουδαῖοι to refer to the people of Judaea, it is nowhere used to *distinguish* them from Jews of the diaspora or of other parts of Palestine. Indeed, the Ἰουδαῖοι who debate with Jesus on the shore of Lake Tiberias in John 6 can scarcely be anything other than Galileans.[13] And the term οἱ Ἰουδαῖοι is just as proper a designation for the people of Galilee as it is for the Jewish communities of, say, Antioch or Alexandria.

A further drawback to Lowe's solution is that it offers no satisfactory answer to the puzzling question of the source of John's hostility towards the Ἰουδαῖοι. Even if some degree of local

---

[12] 'Who were the ΙΟΥΔΑΙΟΙ?'

[13] They also resist inclusion among the Jewish authorities, a fact which leads von Wahlde to make a special case of the two verses in question, 6: 41, 52.

antipathy between Galileans and Judaeans may be said to have crept
into the Gospel, it has done so only fleetingly;[14] it is certainly not
sufficiently pervasive to account for the continual enmity and
distrust of the evangelist towards those he calls οἱ Ἰουδαῖοι.

But if these two solutions are rejected, and we conclude that the
Ἰουδαῖοι cannot be straightforwardly identified either with the
Jewish authorities or with the people of Judaea, what is the
alternative? Though for the moment the answer to this question
must be deferred, it is possible to state one condition that any answer
must satisfy: it must take account of the specifically *religious* nature
of the antagonism between Jesus and the Jews in the Fourth Gospel.
(Having rejected the rendering 'Judaeans', we may now return to
the more generally accepted 'Jews'.) Jesus himself, of course, was a
Jew and in giving him the title 'King of the Jews' the Gospel is
appealing to one of the best-attested stories in the whole tradition.
But when, as happens time and time again, he explicitly or implicitly
dissociates himself from the Jews whom he is addressing,[15] he speaks
as the representative, it is fair to say, of the community which
acknowledges him as its founder and head. And the opposition of
this community to the Jews, that sense of total alienation which
permeates the pages of the Gospel, has quite clearly a religious
inspiration. Whatever the influence of local rivalries (and obviously
the mistrust and hostility of the Samaritans at least has a long
history) the essentially religious character of the Gospel's anti-Jewish
bias is inescapable.

(c) Role

This means that the question of the *role* of the Jews, their function
within the book, can be answered with relative ease. No one has
answered this question more brilliantly or tellingly than Rudolf
Bultmann:

The term οἱ Ἰουδαῖοι, characteristic of the Evangelist, gives an overall
portrayal of the Jews, viewed from the standpoint of Christian faith, as the
representatives of unbelief (and thereby, as will appear, of the unbelieving
'world' in general). The Jews are spoken of as an alien people, not merely
from the point of view of the Greek readers, but also, and indeed only

---

[14] Most obviously in the little episode in 7: 45–52. See *infra*, Ch. 8.
[15] As in the phrase 'in your law', 8: 17; 10: 34 (*v.l.* 'the law'); 'for fear of the Jews'
(7: 13; 19: 38; 20: 19; cf. 9: 22).

properly, from the standpoint of faith; for Jesus himself speaks to them as a stranger and correspondingly, those in whom the stirrings of faith or of the search for Jesus are to be found are distinguished from the 'Jews' even if they are themselves Jews. In this connection therefore even the Baptist does not appear to belong to the 'Jews'. This usage leads to the recession or to the complete disappearance of the distinctions made in the Synoptics between different elements in the Jewish people; Jesus stands over against the Jews. Only the distinction between the mass of the people and its spokesmen occasionally proves to be necessary for the Evangelist's presentation of his theme; but this, characteristically, is often drawn in such a way that the Ἰουδαῖοι, who are distinguished from the ὄχλος [crowd], appear as an authoritative body set over the Jewish people, Οἱ Ἰουδαῖοι does not relate to the empirical state of the Jewish people, but to its very nature.[16]

To its nature, yes, or rather essence (*Wesen*), since the essential role of the Jews in the Fourth Gospel is to represent and symbolize human obduracy and incomprehension when confronted with the revelation of Jesus. That the role of the Jews is as Bultmann describes it is surely beyond serious dispute.

(d) The question rephrased

Yet over this elegant exegesis hovers a historical question of some importance, which Bultmann does not even begin to tackle. Why does the evangelist pick on the Jews to play this part?[17] Who can these Jews be that he loathes them so intensely? For it is not just the Jewish authorities who attract his ire. If he had wished to do so he could have followed Synoptic usage in putting most of the blame upon the Scribes and Pharisees or the chief priests, or alternatively have made more use of the colourless word ὄχλος ('crowd')—which he does in fact employ a score of times. It is a surprising fact that the only overlap between the Johannine and the Synoptic use of the word 'Jews' is to be found in the title 'King of the Jews' in the passion narrative. Only once, moreover, in Matt. 28: 15, does the word correspond to the typical Johannine usage. Bornhäuser, speaking of what he calls 'the innermost circle of the Johannine Jews', says that it is composed of the leading Jews in Jerusalem: 'they are the men

---

[16] pp. 86 f.
[17] Nils Dahl, who agrees with Bultmann's general thesis that the Jews are the representatives of the world in its hostility to God, adds: 'it is, however, equally important that the *Jews* are those who represent the world', 'Johannine Church', p. 126.

whom the Synoptists call Φαρισαῖοι καὶ γραμματεῖς.'[18] But why then does not John simply take over this terminology and speak himself of Scribes and Pharisees? Bornhäuser does not answer this question, or even ask it.

Who, then, *are* the Jews of the Fourth Gospel? Must we identify them with the Jewish nation as a whole, in Judaea and the diaspora? In view of the essentially religious nature of the dispute this would seem to be too drastic a solution; besides, it overlooks the peculiarly Jewish character of the evangelist's own ideas. It is doubtful whether a fully satisfactory answer to this puzzle can be found within the pages of the Gospel itself. What is required, it seems, is evidence of the use of the word 'Jews' to refer to a particular religious group— not to be identified *tout court* with the Pharisees—which might plausibly be regarded as the chief target of the evangelist's resentment.

It should be observed that when he comes to treat specifically of the enemies of the *community*, as he does in the farewell discourses, chapters 14–17, he avoids the word 'Jews' altogether, substituting the word κόσμος (world), which has obviously a very different resonance. Certainly there is no rigid distinction between the denotation of the two terms. In John 16: 2 those who threaten to expel the disciples from the synagogue can be no other than the Jewish authorities. But the characteristic object of Jewish venom in the Gospel is not the community as such but Jesus himself, always in connection with his special revelation. In order to determine more precisely the issues in dispute between Jesus and the Jews, and thereby possibly to find further clues to their identity, we need to look in some detail at the passages in which the specifically religious argument between the two parties is most fully deployed.

There are three passages in the first half of the Gospel in which the antagonism of the Jews reaches murderous proportions;[19] and our next task is to examine these in the hope of sharpening our

---

[18] *Missionsschrift*, pp. 140 ff.

[19] I leave out of account the allusions to the Jews' determination to kill Jesus in ch. 7 (vv. 1, 19 f., 25), as well as the various attempts to arrest him (πιάζειν: 7: 30, 32, 44; 8: 20 [?]; 10: 39; 11: 57). 11: 57 speaks of the final, successful plan of arrest, and the other instances, with the exception of 10: 39, are found within the context of less portentous debates. Broadly speaking, the controversies with the Pharisees stem from a period when the Jewish and Christian groups were still in active dialogue with one another. This is not true of the passages in question here. See E. Bammel, '"John did no miracle"', p. 197. The difference between the two kinds of debate will be given more extended treatment in the next chapter.

understanding of what caused the final breakdown in communication between the followers of Jesus and those they call the Jews. These passages occur in chapters 5, 8, and 10, and a disinterested bystander witnessing any one of these debates might well feel that he had dropped in on one of those fierce family rows (family, as it happens, is a central issue in the second of these confrontations) which so astonish the outsider by their vehemence and bitterness. Only the reflection that the real reasons for this bewildering virulence must lie buried in a past known only to the participants allows him a glimmer of understanding.

3. FAMILY QUARRELS

(a) *'Equal with God'*

But Jesus answered them, 'My Father is working still, and I am working.' This was why the Jews sought all the more to kill him, because he not only broke the sabbath but also called God his father, making himself equal with God. (5: 17–18)

Anyone familiar with the Fourth Gospel knows that the discourse following the healing of the cripple in chapter 5 is one of its high points. But its very familiarity is liable to obscure the fact that nothing in the first four chapters (except perhaps the Prologue) has prepared the reader either for the staggering boldness of Jesus' claim or the murderous hostility with which it is greeted: 'This was why the Jews sought *all the more* (μᾶλλον) to kill him'—yet this is *the first time* in the Gospel that they are reported to seek his death.[20]

Why then the μᾶλλον? And why, indeed, is Jesus thought to be claiming equality with God simply because he calls him father? It is true that the evangelist has already commented, in two closely related passages, upon the role of 'the only Son of God' (ὁ [μονογενής] υἱός, 3: 16–21, 31–6); but these are the comments of a voice off-stage, and are no more integrated into the story of Jesus' dealings with the Jews than the Prologue is. Moreover, in the preceding chapter (ch. 4) 'Father' is simply an alternative name for God. That God was indeed the father of his people is a commonplace in the

[20] On this difference between chs. 1–4 and what follows, see C. J. A. Hickling, 'Attitudes to Judaism'.

Jewish tradition; 'sons of God' is a regular way of speaking of Israel,[21] and a little further on the Jews themselves will assert that God and God alone is their father (8: 41). Why, then, should this seemingly innocent remark, 'My father is working still, and I am working', precipitate such implacable rage?

To answer this question we must first examine how this link passage (5: 17 f.) is related to what comes before and after it. Closely connected as it is with the miracle story, we can easily see that it has been grafted on to this subsequently by the evangelist.[22] The first quarrel of the Jews is with the cripple himself, who breaks the law by carrying his pallet on the sabbath (v. 10). This complaint is then transferred to Jesus, who is tracked down[23] for having performed an act of healing on the sabbath (v. 16). In his reply, however, Jesus shows no interest in this charge: he simply declares, 'My father is working still, and I am working' (v. 17); and it is this declaration which the Jews see as a claim to equality with God and consequently as a reason for having him killed. The literary welding is particularly clever, because these transitional verses also serve as an anticipatory summary of the argument that is about to follow—a profound and detailed justification of Jesus' claim. His seemingly simple words are thus loaded with meaning, and his hearers respond to all they imply. One might almost say that on Jesus' lips the name 'Father' contains *in nuce* the whole of the evangelist's christology.[24] Thus the proper

---

[21] e.g., 'Beloved are Israel, that they are called sons of God', *Pirke Aboth* 3: 19. The key text in the Old Testament itself is Deut. 14: 1—'You are the sons of the Lord your God.' G. Delling cites these and dozens of other instances in his article, 'Die Bezeichnung "Söhne Gottes"'.

[22] J. L. Martyn thinks that the evangelist's expansion of the original story begins at 5: 9 (*History and Theology*[1], p. 49); and it is true that a controversy dialogue has been appended to the miracle story, as in Mark 2: 1–12 (cf. Bultmann, p. 239 n. 2). But both the content (sabbath) and the tone of 5: 10–16 are uncharacteristic of the evangelist—especially the injunction to 'stop sinning, in case something worse happens to you' (cf. Bultmann, p. 243). At the same time John is the only evangelist to call Jesus' adversaries Jews. Perhaps this is a secondary modification designed to pave the way for the key statement, v. 18. In all probability the original ending of the story is to be found in 7: 19–24, which, as it stands, contradicts the suggestion (in 7: 3) that Jesus had not yet worked any miracles in Judaea. See Excursus III. For an alternative exegesis of this passage, based upon the improbable supposition that the evangelist was deeply concerned about the sabbath legislation, see S. Pancaro, *Law*, pp. 9–16; 54–6.

[23] 'Persecute' (RSV) is certainly the wrong translation of διώκειν in v. 16. A. E. Harvey argues that the phrase ἐδίωκον αὐτόν should be rendered, 'they sought to bring a charge against him' (*Jesus on Trial*, pp. 50 ff. and nn. 11 f.). This may be right but 'they started to track him down' is equally possible.

[24] More so than the 'Amen-sayings', *pace* Heinrich Schlier, *ThDNT.* i. 338.

context of this first report of the Jews' determination to see Jesus dead, the only one that gives it any real intelligibility, is the whole of the debate, now started in earnest, between the two warring sections within the Jewish community: the disciples of Jesus and his enemies.

Especially noteworthy is the skilful use made by the evangelist of the theme of healing on the sabbath. In a well-known Synoptic saying (Mark 3: 4 par.) Jesus asks, 'Is it lawful to heal on the sabbath?', but receives no reply. Another story, associated with this, concludes with his assertion, 'The sabbath was made for man, not man for the sabbath' (Mark 2: 27 par.). But John, unlike his source, is no longer interested in this kind of legal debate. Questions of halakah that still occupy the Synoptists, worry Paul, and absorb the rabbis, are totally remote from his concern. For him the sabbath healing is just a stepping-stone to the affirmation of Jesus' divinity.

In making the transition from one theme to the other he calls attention, Odeberg points out, to the accepted truth that, whereas God himself observes the sabbath in respect of the physical creation, he never relaxes at all from his work of judgement.[25] Accordingly, the conclusion of v. 17 suggests 'that Jesus stands in the same relation to the Sabbath as God and is continually active in the same work ... of judgement'.[26] This, of course, is one of the two kinds of work reserved for the creator alone (the other being the bestowal of life) that are singled out in the discourse that follows. Implicitly, then, Jesus is asserting that he has performed a healing miracle on the sabbath because God, as his Father, is associating him with a work that is properly divine. Consequently his words constitute a claim to equality with God, and the enraged reaction of the Jews is fully comprehensible.

The question that now arises is how Jesus' claim is to be explained against the background of first-century Jewish religious beliefs. How could a man, and a Jew at that, possibly claim divine status? It will

---

[25] Most of the relevant material has been assembled by Strack–Billerbeck, ad loc., and other commentators for the most part realign this in the way that best suits them. Bultmann (p. 246 n. 3) adds a valuable reference to *Ep. Arist.* 210. In my opinion the two commentators that shed most light on this passage, each from his own perspective, are Dodd and Odeberg. There is a late medieval midrash upon Exod. 7: 1, where Moses is told that he is to be God to Pharaoh. According to this (*Midr. Tanḥuma* B וארא 11b, § 7 (Buber, pp. 22 ff.)) four kings in history blasphemously claimed divine status: Hiran, Nebuchadnezzar, Pharaoh, and Joash (2 Chron. 24: 17). Each paid the penalty for his effrontery by being sodomized!

[26] p. 202.

not do to appeal to Paul, even though he makes similar claims for Christ, for there is no trace of his influence here. As for the Synoptic tradition, it too makes strong claims for Jesus (some of the strongest put in the mouths of devils: Mark 1: 24; 3: 11; 5: 7), but not in ways that have discernibly affected John. And certainly there is no help to be found in the picture of pure and unsullied monotheism painted for us in all the 'orthodox' Jewish sources. Rather, what we have here is something akin to a family row, in which any hope of reconciliation has already vanished and the situation is one of total deadlock. Jesus' subsequent expansion of his remarks contains no hint that he might be prepared to modify his claims, to couch them in less offensive terms, or even to explain his apparent blasphemy in the face of the Jews' understandable outrage.[27] For their part, instead of requesting an explanation, the Jews have already determined that Jesus must die. The dispute is conducted close to the borders of a shared faith in which both parties had laid claim to the exclusive possession of the truth—a classic instance of *odium theologicum*, though not one that the evangelist's absolute partiality allows him to acknowledge. But by this time Jesus and his followers had already crossed the frontier of the faith they once shared with the Jews, and they would never return. The irrevocable step had been taken, the ultimate blasphemy uttered.[28] On the story level, the Jews' determination to see Jesus dead has the effect of drawing up the battle lines, not merely for all that follows (cf. Mark 3: 6), but also retrospectively (by the $\mu\hat{a}\lambda\lambda o\nu$) for all that precedes. Symbolically, the separation of the Johannine community (and, more generally, of Christianity from Judaism) is already assured.

The explanation, then, for the abruptness of the death threat is that it reflects the anger of the Jewish establishment at the effrontery of the Johannine group within its ranks. John's earliest readers will have readily detected the reference to a hatred whose effects they had recently endured themselves; but the nature of the gospel form is such that this experience can only be alluded to obliquely by the evangelist.

---

[27] For this reason I cannot agree with M. de Jonge when he says that 'in 5: 17–30 it also becomes evident that, in the opinion of the evangelist, according to Jewish views, anyone who calls God his Father makes himself equal to God' ('The Son of God', p. 148).

[28] It is the one singled out by Jesus' accusers in the passion: 'We have a law; and by that law he ought to die, because he has claimed to be the Son of God' (19: 7). Cf. W. Meeks, 'The Divine Agent', p. 59.

(b) 'Greater than Abraham'

Jesus said to them, 'Truly, truly, I say to you, before Abraham was, I am.' So they took up stones to throw at him. (8: 58–9)

In some respects chapter 8 is a rag-bag. Even after excluding the inauthentic story of the woman taken in adultery, Bultmann splits it into ten fragments, a couple of them no longer than one verse apiece, and scatters them liberally around 250 pages of his commentary. The short saying that concerns us here concludes a long section (8: 31–59) lumped together by Brown under the unpromising title 'Miscellaneous discourses'—though later he changes his mind and speaks of 'a rather homogeneous discourse'.[29] Homogeneous it is not, although much of it is loosely tied together by a single string—the name of Abraham (which does not figure elsewhere in the Gospel).

This exceptionally bitter debate ends in violence. After exchanging angry words for some time the Jews turn from insults to injury, and start to pick up stones to hurl at Jesus. To his final declaration this is the only reply they have left: as commentators agree, it is their response to blasphemy.

Once again it is right to underline the peculiarly Jewish character of Jesus' claim: 'Before Abraham was, I am.' In every case, the strongest and clearest of Jesus' self-revelatory utterances, those which immediately elicit the standard response to blasphemy, have an unmistakably Jewish ring: they are made from within the Jewish tradition and *cannot be explained in any other way*.

Bultmann fails to give this saying of Jesus due weight: he treats it as a simple assertion of pre-existence.[30] Of course it is that, but it is

---

[29] p. 361. For Dodd it is the seventh and last of the series of dialogues which make up chs. 7–8 of the Gospel. Commentators like Dodd, whose only concern is with the final state of the text, are entitled to ignore the dislocations in the interests of an integral exegesis. (Cf. H. E. Lona, *Abraham in Johannes 8*.) Martyn, *Gospel of John*, pp. 109 ff., is too hasty in assuming that 'the Jews who had believed' (8: 31) are involved in the whole of the subsequent dialogue. This was surely not true of the prehistory of the text. (On this see de Jonge, *Stranger*, p. 101 and notes.) For a study of the composition of the whole passage see now B. Lindars, 'Discourse and Tradition'.

[30] 'The ἐγώ εἰμι in 8: 24, 28', he claims, 'is of a completely different character from the ἐγώ εἰμι in 8: 58. ... For if the ἐγώ εἰμι was intended as a paraphrase of the divine name the Jews could not ask, "Who are you?" but would have to take offense at what in their ears would be a gross blasphemy' (p. 349 n. 3). This is in fact what happens at 8: 59, but Bultmann's exegesis of that passage does not account for the reaction of the Jews. For an extended discussion of the absolute 'I am' sayings see P. B. Harner, *The 'I Am' of the Fourth Gospel*.

much more besides. Jesus is aligning himself with God at this point,
laying a claim to divinity *alongside* that of the Father. But if so, how is
the claim being pressed? 'The general consensus', according to
Odeberg, favours an intentional allusion to the divine oracle, 'I am
he' (אני הוא). On the face of it this is a straightforward equivalent of
'I am Yahweh'. Odeberg objects to this solution that 'אני הוא as a
solemn declaration by Jesus would equal "I am God" or "I am the
Father", a declaration that is clearly out of keeping with the general
bearing of Jesus' self-predicative utterances'.[31]

Rather than in the אני הוא, suggests Odeberg, the link is to be
found 'on the side of אהיה אשר אהיה ['I am who am'], i.e. in the
speculations evolved from Exod. 3: 14'.[32] Bultmann counters this by
saying that Jesus' statement would then mean 'I am the "I-am"', the
ἐγώ being both subject and predicate. But this is not necessary,
provided that the ἐγώ εἰμι be taken simply as an *echo* of the divine
revelation. Odeberg cites as a parallel the enigmatic figure of
Metatron, of whom it is said, 'He (God) called me the little (lesser)
Yahweh' (3 *Enoch* 12: 5). This text is closely paralleled by a passage
from another important pseudepigraphical writing, *The Apocalypse of
Abraham*, roughly contemporary with the Fourth Gospel. This
document merits careful consideration.[33]

The passage that concerns us (chs. 9–10) follows an introductory
section where we are told how Abraham first sees a number of idols
destroyed in the house of his father Terah, and then watches as the
house is struck by lightning and burnt to the ground. Abraham
himself is saved from destruction by the direct intervention of God.
Knowing that Abraham is genuinely seeking for the true God, 'the
God of gods, the Creator', he calls down from the heavens in a
stream of fire, and says 'I am he' (8: 3). Then he tells him to leave the
house so as to avoid being killed.

After this God speaks to Abraham again: 'Behold, it is I. Fear not,
for I am Before-the-World and Mighty, the God who created
previously, before the light of the age. I am the protector for you, and
your helper' (9: 2–3). In all these introductory declarations the
characteristic self-proclamations of God ('I am ...') come through

---

[31] p. 310.

[32] p. 309. The Hebrew equivalent of the phrase πρὶν Ἀβραὰμ γενέσθαι, ἐγώ εἰμι
would be, as he says, לפני אברהם אנכי (p. 308).

[33] *The OT Pseudepigrapha*. i. 681–705: a new translation and introduction by
R. Rubinkiewicz. Cf. G. Quispel, 'L'Évangile de Jean et la Gnose', pp. 201 f.

strongly. In what follows, Abraham is promised great revelations: 'I will announce to you guarded things, and you will see great things which you have not seen ... I will show you the things which were made by the ages and by my word, and affirmed, created and reserved' (9: 6, 9).

At this point another important character puts in an appearance. His name, Yaoel, appears to be a conflation of the two divine names, Yahweh and El (יהוה אל). Subsequently this personage will act as a heavenly guide to Abraham, leading him almost to the point of a Merkavah vision (ch. 18) before silently disappearing from the scene and allowing God himself once again to speak to Abraham directly. At one point (17: 13) the very same name, Yaoel, is given to God.

It is worth quoting the whole of the passage in which Yaoel introduces himself to Abraham. From it we can see that, in spite of obvious differences, Yaoel's role closely resembles that of Jesus. He too proclaims himself as sent by God and shares in the authority of his name (5: 43; and 10: 25). God has made him a gift of this name (17: 11) and he has manifested it (17: 1: ἐφανέρωσά σου τὸ ὄνομα) and made it known to his disciples (17: 26).[34] More generally, he introduces them to heavenly things, and offers them the same sort of protection and guidance that Yaoel here promises to Abraham. (I italicize some of the most suggestive parallels.) Abraham is speaking:

And it came to pass that when I heard the voice pronouncing such words to me that I looked this way and that. And behold there was no breath of man. And my spirit was amazed, and my soul fled from me. And I became like a stone, and fell face down upon the earth, for there was no longer strength in me to stand up on the earth. And while I was still face down on the ground, I heard the voice speaking, 'Go, *Yaoel of the same name, through the mediation of my ineffable name*, consecrate this man for me and strengthen him against his trembling.' The angel he sent to me *in the likeness of a man* [cf. Dan. 7: 13] came, and he took me by my right hand and stood me on my feet. And he said to me, 'Stand up, Abraham, friend of God who has loved you, let human trembling not enfold you! For lo! I am sent to you to strengthen you and to bless you in the name of God, creator of heavenly and earthly things, who has loved you. Be bold and hasten to him, *I am Yaoel*, and I was called so by him who causes those with me on the seventh expanse, on the firmament, to shake, *a power through the medium of his ineffable name in me*. I am the one who has been charged according to his

---

[34] Cf. *The Gospel of Truth*, 38: 'the name of the Father is the Son'; *Hermas, Sim.* IX. 14: 5.

commandment, to restrain the threats of the living creatures of the cherubim against one another, and I teach those who carry the song through the medium of man's night of the seventh hour. I am appointed to hold the Leviathans, because through me is subjugated the attack and menace of every reptile, I am ordered to loosen Hades and to destroy those who wondered at the dead. I am the one who ordered your father's house to be burned with him, for he honoured the dead. *I am sent to you* now to bless you and the land which he whom you have called the Eternal One has prepared for you. *For your sake I have indicated the way of the land* [cf. Exod. 23: 20 ff.]. Stand up, Abraham, go boldly, *be very joyful and rejoice.* And I (also rejoice) with you, for a venerable honour has been prepared for you by the Eternal One. Go, complete the sacrifice of the command. Behold, *I am assigned* (to be) *with you* and with the generation which is destined (to be) born) from you. And with me Michael blesses you forever. Be bold, go!' (*Apoc. Abr.* 10)

Now even if we could be sure that this text was composed before the Fourth Gospel (and this is not certain), there is no question of arguing to a direct debt. But the parallels are none the less highly suggestive.

Two further pieces of evidence tend to support the view that the fourth evangelist was influenced by the idea of a revealer-figure sent by God and endowed with the authority of his name.

The first is in a passage from the Babylonian Talmud quoted by Alan Segal:

R. Nahman said: 'He who is as skilled in refuting the *Minim* as is R. Idi, let him do so; but not otherwise.' Once a *Min* said to R. Idi: 'It is written, *And unto Moses He said: Come up to the Lord* (Ex. 24: 1). But surely it should have stated, *Come up to me!*' — 'It was Metatron' he replied, whose name is similar to that of his Master, for it is written, *For My name is in Him* (Ex. 23: 21). 'But if so, we should worship him!'[35]

Exodus 24: 1 is a notorious crux: why should God say to Moses, 'Come up to Yahweh' rather than 'Come up to me'? It is one a Christian or Gnostic might well seize on. In his reply R. Idi sails very close to the wind by alluding to Metatron, whose possession of the divine name seems to the heretic, not surprisingly, a sufficient reason for worshipping him. R. Idi goes on to refute this conclusion with further arguments based on the same text; but it is not difficult to detect in this controversy a claim remarkably similar to the one

---

[35] *Two Powers in Heaven*, p. 68, citing Sanhedrin 38b. See too Segal's collection of essays, 'Judaism, Christianity and Gnosticism'.

rejected as blasphemous in John 8: 59. Segal himself concludes that in spite of the comparatively late date of this talmudic passage (third century) 'the tradition must be based on older traditions in apocalyptic or proto-Merkabah or proto-gnostic texts where the principal angel has a theophoric name' (such as the one from the *Apocalypse of Abraham* we have just been considering).

The scriptural passage taken by R. Idi to indicate Metatron ('My name is in him,'—Exod. 23: 21) may also lie behind John 17: 11 f.: 'Keep them (*or* I kept them) in the name which you gave me,' that name which belongs of right to God alone and is in itself the essence of his revelation. It is also employed in another late pseudepigraphon (the second piece of evidence) to explain and justify Metatron's other name, 'the lesser Yahweh'. This is *3 Enoch*, dated the fifth or sixth century by Philip Alexander and the only pseudepigraphon to have been transmitted by the rabbis. *3 Enoch* 12: 5, the text quoted by Odeberg, testifies to the persistence of a strange tradition surviving on the fringes of Judaism, according to which the hallowed name of Yahweh was bestowed on an angelic being, Yahweh-El or the lesser Yahweh, sent by God to reveal hidden mysteries to mankind—or at least to certain chosen souls.

This slightly more extended speculation on the name suggests that there may be a link between these sectarian writings and what was condemned by the Jewish rabbis as the heresy of the 'two powers'.

Alan Segal has shown that the exegetical root of this heresy was the repetition of the name of God in Exod. 15: 3 'Yahweh is a warrior, Yahweh is his name' (יהוה איש מלחמה יהוה שמו). Upon this text was constructed the notion that there were two different self-revelations of God, one as a young man, appearing at the Sea (the context of Exodus 15), the other as an old man, appearing at Sinai.

Whether or not there was any direct connection between the two groups of texts, one belonging to a sectarian tradition that can be traced back to *1 Enoch*, the other evidence of a heresy within the ranks of Judaism, it seems likely that one or both of the ideas behind them may have made it easier to believe that Jesus the Messiah was also the special emissary of God, bearing the authority of his name to reveal to men certain hidden truths.

Perhaps, however, we should be even bolder in our interpretation of this passage, less preoccupied with defending at all costs the thesis that the fourth evangelist, like all good Jews, was a die-hard monotheist.[36] After all, the easiest and most straighforward explanation of 8: 58, whether the allusion is to Exod. 3: 14 (Odeberg, Schnackenburg, etc.) or to the divine oracle in Deut. 32: 39 and Second Isaiah (Barrett, Harner, etc.), is that Jesus is actually claiming the name of Yahweh for himself. Such a claim is not, as Odeberg argues, tantamount to saying 'I am the Father'. Rather it is an implicit assertion that the protector or redeemer God, Israel's tribal deity, is not after all to be identified with the creator God, El Elyon, but has revisited his people in a new guise.[37] For the fact is that despite many resemblances, the Fourth Gospel differs markedly from the *Apocalypse of Abraham* and *3 Enoch*. Some of its most important teaching is unashamedly controversial. It lies at the cusp between the twin curves of Jewish tradition, one destined to emerge in rabbinic Judaism, the other branching off in a different direction. It is here that the two curves meet—and part. The role of the 'angel interpreter', structurally very similar, has been simplified and streamlined to fit into the story of the earthly career of Jesus: this is after all a Gospel. But his claim to divine status, the terms in which it is couched, and the circumstances in which it is uttered, all indicate that this is not a strange foreign myth breaking into the Jewish religious tradition for the first time, but a dangerously novel manifestation of an old and familiar theme. It is one thing to speculate upon an angelic figure bearing the name and authority of God when his only purpose in visiting men here below is to transport them back to heaven in an apocalyptic dream. It is quite another to

---

[36] The initial assumption that the author and first readers of the Gospel were monotheists spoils Lars Hartman's otherwise perceptive article, 'Johannine Jesus-Belief'.

[37] Robert Murray has suggested to me (and the suggestion has been confirmed by the anthropologist Godfrey Lienhardt) that religious people regularly require two types of deity. Following A. Stolz, *Strukturen*, he calls these 'Far' and 'Near': 'the "Far" as creator and supreme guarantor of cosmic and earthly order, fertility etc., but hardly offering intimate comfort, and the latter, often more anthropomorphically conceived, as being involved with humans and caring for their needs. 'El 'Elyon was a "Far" conceptualization of deity, while YHWH was a "Near" one.' He goes on to suggest 'that the post-exilic absolute monotheism, by insisting on the total identity of YHWH with 'El 'Elyon, left people with one (far) God and a doctrinaire insistence that all pluralistic conceptualizations of deity were unreal. But the need for a near God abhors a vacuum and the gap had to be filled.' This idea, as Murray points out, fits in well with the the theories of political and religious suppression argued in Margaret Barker's *The Older Testament*. It also has a bearing upon the history of Christian doctrine and belief.

allow this figure to coalesce with an individual human being who has already won a wide following as the Jewish Messiah.

Obviously this is not the whole story. A precisely analogous move (and one which is much better attested) is made in regard to the figure of the Son of Man.[38] And had not Jesus already been regarded as a divine emissary exalted to heaven after his death, then it is most improbable that he would have been credited with the authority to echo God's revelation of his own name. When he did so, through the mouth, as we may surmise, of one of his followers in the Johannine camp, it is scarcely surprising that more conservative Jews felt threatened and outraged by the apparent blasphemy that was being uttered in their midst.

(c) 'Son of God'

The Jews answered him, 'We stone you for blasphemy; because you, being a man, make yourself God.' Jesus answered them, 'Is it not written in your law, "I said, you are gods"? If he called them gods to whom the word of God came (and scripture cannot be broken) do you say of him whom the Father consecrated and sent into the world, "You are blaspheming," because I said, "I am the Son of God"?' (10: 34–6)

On a superficial reading this passage appears quite innocuous: other men are called gods in Scripture; and since this is so, argues Jesus, why should not I, sanctified and sent, claim the title of Son of God? But if there were nothing more to his reply than this then it would be simply and solely a clever but otherwise undistinguished *argumentum ad hominem*, seemingly designed more to reassure his audience than to establish his own credentials as a messenger from heaven with a genuine claim to divinity.

Much depends on the identification of those whom God is conceived to be addressing in the psalm that is being quoted (Ps. 82: 6). There are three candidates: (1) unjust judges; (2) Israel; (3) angels. The first two both have rabbinical support;[39] but neither is really satisfactory, for it is hard to see in either case how Jesus could be making a strong enough claim to warrant the response he receives. One recent commentator, Jürgen Becker, points out that such a reading would make Jesus out to be a *primus inter pares*, a

---

[38] This important topic will be discussed in Ch. 9.
[39] See J. S. Ackermann, 'The Rabbinical Interpretation of Ps 82'.

special case in relation to other men similarly addressed by God. This anticipation of Arius is not a theological position found elsewhere in the Gospel, and so Becker is inclined to regard the passage as an editorial intrusion,[40] though he fails to explain why an editor should attempt to draw the teeth of John's argument in this way. Surely it is preferable to look first for a reading strong enough to suit the context: another fierce and trenchant debate with the Jews that actually starts this time (10: 31) with an allusion to their determination to see him dead.

The suggestion that the θεοί in this passage might really be angels was first made in 1960 by J. A. Emerton,[41] who pointed out that in the Peshitta (Syriac) version of the psalm 'gods' (אלהים) in vv. 1b and 6 is rendered 'angels' (ܡܠܐܟ̈ܐ). This gives the translation:

> God stands in the congregation of God
> He judges among the angels
>
> . . . . . .
>
> I said, 'You are angels
> And all of you sons of the most High.'

In a subsequent article[42] Emerton backs this suggestion up with further evidence from the Peshitta and a number of targumim that אלהים is sometimes translated 'angels' or '(sons of) angels'. He also repeats his point that angels are called אלים in various documents from Qumran, and mentions 'the possibility, according to Mr J. Strugnell, that angels are even described as אלהים in one text'.

The text in question is part of a series of manuscript fragments subsequently grouped together, carefully edited (by Carol Newsom), and published (in 1985) under the title of 'Songs of the Sabbath Sacrifice.' What Emerton calls the 'angelological vocabulary' is indeed remarkable. It includes angels, spirits, holy ones, ministers, princes (נשיאי רוש etc.), chiefs (ראשי דבירו etc.), and a number of other titles. Prominent among these are אלים and אלהים. In his translation of these texts (*Dead Sea Scrolls*[3]) Geza Vermes rightly renders the last two titles as 'gods' (usually with scare quotes). They are not merely angelic messengers but truly divine beings who surround the throne of the 'King' or 'God' of gods and pay him continuous homage.

Accordingly, although Strugnell speaks of an 'angelic' liturgy, it would be just as accurate to speak of a 'divine' liturgy. No doubt the great diversity of the terms employed indicates a strong distinction

---

[40] p. 336   [41] 'The Interpretation of Psalm 82'.
[42] 'Melchizedek and the Gods'.

between God and the heavenly court; even so, we are a long way from the austere monotheism of Deuteronomy or Second Isaiah. It is against this background that Jesus' citation of Psalm 82 begins to make sense, especially if we bear in mind the whole of v. 6: 'I say you are gods (אלהים, θεοί), all of you sons of the Most High (בני עליון, υἱοὶ ὑψίστου)'. The big difference is that in the Fourth Gospel the whole heavenly court is encapsulated in the person of Jesus; apart from the Father he alone is given the title (cf. 1: 1; 1: 18, reading μονογενὴς θεός; 20: 28). The enormity of his claim understandably infuriates his hearers.

Emerton discusses yet another document from Qumran;[43] in this the Hebrew אלהים of Psalm 82 is identified with Melchizedek, who is later called אלהיך (thy God). Here we have evidence of a theological leap parallel to that made in the Gospel, since Melchizedek, who once appeared on earth as a man (Gen. 14) is now given what is unquestionably a divine title. J. A. Fitzmyer, in his careful analysis of this text,[44] acknowledges the difficulty by rendering Ps. 82: 1 as 'Elohim has taken his stand in the assembly of El', but like Emerton he follows van der Woude, the original editor, in identifying this *Elohim* not with God (which is what the term denotes at this point in the original psalm) but with Melchizedek. The *Elohim* of v. 2 ('in the midst of Elohim he gives judgement') is taken by van der Woude and Fitzmyer to refer to Melchizedek's supporting team of angels, by Emerton to refer to the opposing team, led by Belial.[45] Whoever is right (and there is obviously much uncertainty in the interpretation of this fragmentary text), there seems little doubt that we have here

---

[43] First published by A. S. van der Woude: 'Melchisedek'.

[44] 'Further Light on Melchizedek'.

[45] Criticizing Emerton's use of this text to elucidate John 10: 34, M. de Jonge and A. S. van der Woude comment: 'In the Johannine context there is no reason to think of angels; v. 33 even makes a clear contrast between god and men. Moreover, nowhere else in the gospel do heavenly beings like those portrayed in 11Q Melch play a role of any importance. Emerton finds the *tertium comparationis* in the commission received by the angels and by Jesus. Jesus' commission is indeed mentioned in vv. 36 f., but the commission received by the θεοί is not even hinted at' ('11Q Melchizedek and the New Testament', p. 314). But neither does the Melchizedek text speak of angels *as such*; and if the other heavenly beings alluded to scarcely figure in the Fourth Gospel, the fact remain that Jesus himself plays a part not unlike the one assigned here to Melchizedek. The Syriac rendering of אלהים in Ps. 82 as 'angels', the datum which first alerted Emerton to the nature of Jesus' affirmation in John 10: 34–6, may well be a kind of bowdlerization, a deliberate weakening of an otherwise disquietingly ambiguous psalm. The fragmentary targum of Job similarly alters 'sons of God' to 'angels' at Job 38: 7. See too the various versions of Deut. 32: 8.

further proof of the existence of a world of religious discourse a long way from the strict monotheism of the Jews who are Jesus' adversaries in the Fourth Gospel. No doubt the Gospel is faithful to its Jewish heritage in continuing to distinguish between God and men, but it also sees Jesus (and specifically in the passage we have been discussing) as both ἄνθρωπος and θεός. The Qumran fragments and the Gospel testify to a boldly speculative alternative theology that orthodox Judaism could not absorb—or even acknowledge.

(d) Conclusion

In the Fourth Gospel there are numerous passages in which Jesus claims divine status. It is no coincidence that some of the strongest and most explicit of these occur in angry confrontations with the Jews: the Gospel has as one of its aims to confirm its readers in their stand against 'normative' Judaism. The debates it records are not readily classifiable as controversy stories, but like the Synoptic pericopes they in some way resemble, they reflect a period of acrimonious argument between Christians and Jews. What is singular in the Fourth Gospel is that so many of these controversies turn upon Jesus' claim to be divine.

The farewell discourses teach us that the Gospel in its finished form was intended for a Christian readership. But this is only part of the evidence. The polemical tone of much of the first half of the Gospel, especially in chapters 5–10, cannot be explained except against a background of Jewish–Christian debate. If the passages we have been considering are catechesis, they are catechesis with a bite— not Sunday-school lessons, but sharp reminders of the dangerous obduracy of the community's Jewish adversaries.

It must be stressed too that Jesus' arguments in these debates are drawn from a tradition with which his hearers are familiar. He is not burrowing into the *Hermetica* or chasing Gnostic hares with a view to demanding from his uncomprehending audience a blind adhesion to alien truths. On the contrary, the truth which can set them free, however novel, is one that springs from a well buried deep in their own soil.[46] Had he gone off to teach Greeks, as it is suggested he

---

[46] This was a well from which Judaism continued to draw, but cautiously and sparingly. To the fastidious it will have seemed a 'religion of the multitude' in Newman's sense—'ever vulgar and abnormal; it will ever be tinctured with fanaticism and superstition, while men are what they are. A people's religion is ever a corrupt religion', J. H. Newman, *Difficulties of Anglicans* (London, 1876), p. 81.

might (7: 35) he could not have expected from them the kind of ready acceptance he blames the Jews for withholding. Only by abstracting altogether from the circumstances of the Gospel's composition and treating it as nothing but a repository of revealed doctrine or as a timeless call to faith, as Bultmann does, can one fail to recognize in these hot-tempered exchanges the type of family row in which the participants face one another across the room of a house which all have shared and all call home.

If this is so, the question which we have postponed is still knocking at the door. Why does the author picture Jesus, Jew though he is, as dissociating himself so categorically from the Jews? What is the significance of the name he gives them? We are now perhaps in a position to go beyond the obvious truth that it is a religious designation, indicating a religious differentiation. It now seems that it refers to a conservative segment within the broad band of a common religious tradition. Is there any other evidence to support this suggestion?

4. THE RISE OF JUDAISM

The argument up to this point has comprised two theses. The first is that the origins of the Gospel lie in what may loosely be called heterodox Judaism. 'Loosely', because notions of orthodoxy and heterodoxy are not entirely appropriate to the period under discussion, when Judaism as we know it was still in its infancy. This thesis has been satisfactorily established as a plausible working hypothesis.[47] Moreover, this part of the argument could also appeal for support to recent work on the Dead Sea Scrolls[48] and to excellent

---

[47] Cf. Robert Murray, 'Jews, Hebrews and Christians'. In a later article ('Disaffected Judaism') he summarizes his argument: 'that Jewish Christianity could never be understood unless "Jewish" is differentiated so as to allow for at least the following two kinds of background: the first is "Jewish" in the proper sense, that is accepting the Jerusalem establishment and terms of reference; the second inherits old quarrels with Jerusalem—either that going back to the early opposition to the new calendar and temple, or the later quarrel which led to the secession to Qumran' (p. 265). He goes on to admit that this rough division suggests too great an assimilation of known dissident movements and perhaps exaggerates their incidence. Nevertheless the first sense of 'Jewish' tallies exactly with what I believe to be the characteristic reference of Ἰουδαῖοι in the Fourth Gospel.

[48] Cf. Otto Böcher, *Der Johanneische Dualismus*, who also compares the Testaments of the Twelve Patriarchs; H. Braun, *Qumran und das Neue Testament*. i. 96–138; ii. 118–44; *John and Qumran*, ed. J. H. Charlesworth (with a full bibliography up to 1970).

detailed studies such as that of Alan Segal on the phrase 'ruler of this world'.[49] And it will receive further confirmation in the remainder of Part II. Finally and conclusively, Chapter 10 will be devoted to showing how the roots of the Gospel reach down into the soil of Jewish apocalyptic—from the point of view of its total meaning the most significant debt of all. There is, then, no need to search outside the Jewish tradition for the kind of historical (exterior) explanation of the Gospel that will emerge from a detailed enquiry into its genesis.

The second thesis, which concerns the community's Jewish adversaries, is much more tentative. Here the main problem is to identify those whom the Gospel calls the Jews. I suggest that this is the name given to the powerful party that took advantage of the disarray following the fall of Jerusalem in AD 70 and gradually assumed authority over the Jewish people. This party, not to be identified absolutely with the Pharisees, laid the foundations of what we know as Judaism. If the Pharisees had a hand in this, as they surely did, they will have been anxious to rid themselves of the isolationist and indeed sectarian implications of their name:[50] what better chance would they ever have of establishing their claim to be the true descendants of Abraham?

(a) The story of a name

The Gospel uses the term 'Jews' more extensively than any other to refer to a *religious* group which is defined and characterized by its hostility to the revelation of Jesus. Only occasionally does the term have a national connotation, as when Pilate asks Jesus, 'Am I a Jew?', or writes on a placard he has affixed to the cross the words, 'The King of the Jews' (historically one of the best attested elements in the whole tradition). As time went on the national sense ('Judaean') would be lost—the decisive moment coming in AD 135 when the Emperor Hadrian, after brutally suppressing the latest Jewish rebellion, drove all Jews out of Jerusalem. From then on the term 'Jew' on the lips of a Gentile would refer to someone who was Jewish by religion or race. The meaning 'Judaean' no longer had any application.[51]

---

[49] A. F. Segal, 'Ruler of This World'.   [50] See n. 66.

[51] One of the last contemporary examples of the local reference might be the term of οἵ ποτε Ἰουδαῖοι that occurs in a 2nd-century inscription from Smyrna (*IGRR* iv 1431. 29 = *CII* 742). This is probably an allusion to Judaean émigrés, not, as used to be thought, to Anatolian converts from Judaism.

At the time the fourth evangelist was completing his Gospel, this cataclysmic event was a long way off. His contemporary Josephus employs the word 'Jews' or 'Jewish' (adjective and substantive are the same word in Greek) to refer indiscriminately to Judaeans and Jews of the diaspora, as well as to the (predominantly religious) laws and practices associated with both. He himself never underlines the distinction, but it is usually possible to determine the reference from the context. Meanwhile Jews continued to refer to themselves as 'Israel', confining their use of the term 'Jew' to dealings with foreigners.[52] Josephus, writing for foreigners, uses 'Israel' sparingly except in connection with the old northern kingdom. But there is some evidence of a more specialized usage, to denote an inner ring, as it were, within the Jewish (or Judaean) nation, a religious party that emerged immediately after Cyrus' decree had put an end to the Babylonian exile.

The first hint comes from Josephus himself, in one of his rare animadversions on the origin of the word Ἰουδαῖοι. It derives, he tells us, from the tribe of Juda, and dates from the time of their return from Babylon (*AJ* xi. 173). This suggests that the name properly belongs to the returning exiles rather than to those who were left behind, and supplements an earlier passage where he says that these (i.e. the returned exiles) were the people who were responsible for the reconstruction of the Temple (*AJ* xi. 84; cf. 22). They are also obviously the men mentioned in a letter to Artaxerxes from some Babylonian officials as 'the Jews who came up from you to us' and 'have gone to Jerusalem', where they 'are rebuilding that rebellious and wicked city' (Ezra 4: 12; cf. Ezra 4: 17–22; Neh. 2: 17 ff.; 3: 35 (Heb.)). This group also presumably includes the 'Jewish brethren' (אחיהם היהדים) who were soon afterwards accused of breaking the law (Deut. 23: 19) by lending money at interest (Neh. 5: 1 ff.).

---

[52] A good example of this discrimination is 1 Maccabees, where, with a single exception (4: 2), the use of the term 'Jews' is reserved in the Greek either for letters to and from foreigners or else for public decrees. (The episode in 11: 45–51, written from the point of view of the Antiocheans, is not a counter-example.) The name 'Israel' may be used for what is only part of the whole, in this case the Maccabean party. Cf. O. Plöger, *Theology and Eschatology*, p. 37; also Schlatter: ''Ιουδαῖος and Ἰσραήλ ... have the same extension and refer to every member of the (Jewish) race. When a Greek speaks of a Jew with his religious practice in mind he calls him Ἰουδαῖος, for this is how the Jew too characterizes his religious position. When a Jew speaks of a Jew with his relationship to God in mind, he calls him Ἰσραήλ,' (p. 59). This thesis has been established beyond all doubt in a pair of articles by Peter J. Jonson: 'The Names Israel and Jew'.

Another story in Josephus, based this time on a non-biblical source, relates how a group of Samaritans were initially prepared to identify themselves as Jews in a face-to-face confrontation with the Emperor Alexander, in the hope of being accorded the same privileges as had already been granted to other Jews. But when challenged on religious grounds they backed down and repudiated the name Jews. This suggests that the term had a religious significance distinct from the racial meaning which, as descendants of Joseph, they were ready to accept. To this story (*AJ* xi. 340–5) Josephus adds a rider concerning Shechem (the main town in Samaria—modern Nablus). Shechem, he says, afforded refuge for escapees from Jerusalem expelled, despite their protestations of innocence, for violating the dietary laws or the sabbath regulations or for 'any other such sin' (xi. 346).

The picture of Shechem as a centre of religious dissidence inhabited by renegade Jews (xi. 340) can be held up against the very different-looking picture of a Jerusalem reserved for the good and the pure. The Passover kept to celebrate the termination of the long exile was reserved for 'the people of Israel who had returned from exile, and also by every one who had joined them and separated himself from the pollutions of the peoples of the land to worship the Lord, the God of Israel' (Ezra 6: 21).

In speaking of those hostile to the Temple as the 'people of the land' (עם הארץ : Ezra 4: 4), the Chronicler makes no distinction between them and 'the adversaries of Juda and Benjamin' (4: 2); and Josephus, who has Ezra as a source at this point, bluntly identifies this group as Samaritans (or Chuthaeans—*AJ* xi. 19–30; 84–8). Whatever the precise relationship between 'the people of the land' and the Samaritans, there must have been some links between the northerners (not, after all, so very far away) and those southerners who had remained behind at the exile and subsequently earned the disapproval of the powerful group (*the* Jews?) of which Ezra, the *bête noire* of the Samaritans, came to be a leading representative.[53] (The rabbis themselves saw Judaism as originating with Ezra, who inaugurated the age of the scribes.) So it may be no coincidence that Jesus, besides being associated with the people of the land (those

---

[53] So R. J. Coggins, with reference to Second Isaiah, concludes of 'the northerners and ... those who had remained in Judah during the exile' that 'these two groups came to be identified with one another, and both would be dismissed as no true part of the people of God' (*Samaritans and Jews*, p. 37).

'ignorant of the law' in John 7: 49), treated the Jews as aliens and failed to rebut the charge that he himself was a Samaritan (8: 48).

Whether or not the Samaritans were actually those who opposed the rebuilding of the Temple in the late sixth century is less important for our purposes than the fact that Josephus thought they were. Since the identification in the source (Ezra) is unclear, it may be that Josephus was reading back into the past conditions and attitudes obtaining in his own day.

The books of Ezra and Nehemiah, representing the official position of the powerful party I have hesitantly identified with 'the Jews', evince (as do the books of Chronicles) an overriding concern with the Temple and its appurtenances. Much later, various pieces of evidence testify to the abiding importance of the Temple and the hostility provoked by what was seen as the endemic corruption of its administrators. On the positive side, a second-century author speaks of 'those who live round Solomon's great temple' in a passage which singles them out as pious (εὐσεβεῖς) and their ancestors as just (δίκαιοι).[54]

On the negative side, various sectarian documents point to a deep distrust, if not of the Temple itself, at least of the rites enacted there: *I Enoch*, the *Testament of Moses*, the *Damascus Rule*.[55] One is led to reflect how little would be known of the alternative religious

---

[54] *Sib. Or.* iii. 213 ff.; cf. 702–4 and 573–9, where the sacrifices offered in the Temple are listed, including λοιβῇ τε κνίσσῃ τ᾽ἠδ᾽ αὖθ᾽ ἱεραῖς ἑκατόμβαις (a conflation of Homer, *Il.* ix. 500 and xxiii. 146). A fragment of Polybius also mentions 'those of the Jews who inhabit the so-called holy place of Jerusalem' (τῶν Ἰουδαίων οἳ περὶ τὸ ἱερὸν τὸ προσαγορευόμενον Ἱεροσόλυμα κατοικοῦντες, Polyb. xvi. 39. 5). Josephus, who quotes this (*AJ* xii. 136) reads ἱερὸν as a reference to the Temple, not as an adjective qualifying Ἱεροσόλυμα.

[55] *I Enoch* 89: 73; *Test. Mos.* 5: 1–6 ('They will pollute the house of their worship with the customs of the Gentiles; and ... their city and the bounds of their habitation will be filled with crimes and iniquities'); CD 4. 16–18; 5. 6–7. Some criticisms of the temple cult are also to be found in the *Psalms of Solomon*, usually regarded as stemming from Pharisaic circles: *Pss. Sol.* 1. 8; 2. 2, etc. G. W. E. Nickelsburg thinks that such passages simply reflect 'halakhic discussion between Pharisees and Sadducees' (*Jewish Literature*, p. 212). There is a hint of a similar attitude in Jesus' conversation with the Samaritan woman, John 4: 20–4; and more than a hint in Stephen's militantly challenging speech in Acts 7. But Jesus himself, for all his anger with the buyers and sellers within the Temple precincts (if the Gospels are right about this), continued to worship there, as did his earliest followers. Some indication of the (increasing) disaffection of the Johannine group from the official religion of the central Jewish party may be seen in the Gospel's heavy-sounding insistence on the Jewishness of Jewish feasts and customs (2: 6, 13; 5: 1; 6: 4; 7: 2; 11: 55; 19: 42). Even Greek converts, surely, would hardly need reminding that the Passover was 'a feast of the Jews'.

groups outside the Judaean establishment if we had to rely on writings sanctioned or canonized by the rabbinical schools started by the Scribe, according to tradition, during the Second Temple era. Both inside and outside Palestine there is abundant evidence—the best known and most impressive being the Elephantine papyri[56]—of continual and flagrant violations of the deuteronomic code.[57] Within Palestine there is perhaps a distinction to be drawn between the rigid conservatism of Judaea itself and the greater flexibility of other regions, more receptive to Hellenistic influences of a recognizably non-Jewish kind (such as public gymnasia).[58] This may be a further argument in favour of a firmly orthodox temple-party with considerable authority over a fairly small area.

Two centuries later there is no likelihood of any greater uniformity. If the Judaism we know today is a single tree (albeit with a number of branches), at the time of Jesus it was a jungle. Josephus speaks of three religious sects ($\alpha\acute{\iota}\rho\epsilon\sigma\epsilon\iota\varsigma$) or philosophies ($\phi\iota\lambda\sigma\sigma\phi\acute{\iota}\alpha\iota$) —Pharisees, Sadducees, and Essenes—plus a fourth, generally identified with the Zealots, not so much a religious sect as a liberation movement. He tells us that there were roughly 6,000 Pharisees and 4,000 Essenes[59] (among whom, as is now generally agreed, were the Qumran group). If the other two sects were comparable in size, the four between them would account for only a small proportion of the country's inhabitants, probably several hundred thousand at this time.[60] As with a badly damaged fresco, our confidence that the original picture was much bigger than the surviving fragments gives us no real hope of being able to restore it with any accuracy.

That there must have been many more sects than those named by Josephus is now widely held: 'the number of types and varieties

[56] See *Aramaic Papyri*, ed. A. Cowley.

[57] The evidence is conveniently gathered together by Morton Smith in ch. 4 (headed 'The Survival of the Syncretistic Cult of Yahweh') of his brilliant, if controversial, book *Palestinian Parties and Politics*, pp. 82–98. Smith explains the spread of what he calls 'the Yahweh-alone party' in the diaspora as consequent upon the syncretistic cult, and instances the letters from the Jerusalem community to the Jews in Egypt urging them to observe Hanukah in 2 Macc. 1: 1 ff. (p. 96 n. 89).

[58] Cf. J. Goldstein, 'Jewish Acceptance and Rejection of Hellenism', pp. 64–87.

[59] *AJ* xvii. 42; xviii. 20; cf. Philo *Quod Omn. Prob.* 75.

[60] Cf. M. Broshi, 'The Population of Western Palestine'. His article is intended to demonstrate 'that the population of Palestine in antiquity did not exceed a million persons' (p. 7). But he makes it clear that it was probably not far short of this number at peak periods.

could probably be reckoned in dozens'.[61] Two somewhat later (second-century) lists give some indication of the extent of our ignorance. They have three names in common: Pharisees, Sadducees, and Galileans. Then they diverge. Hegesippus[62] names in addition Essenians, Samaritans, Hemerobaptists, and Masbotheans; Justin (himself hailing from Samaria) makes no mention of Samaritans but names instead Genists, Merists, Baptists, and Hellenians.[63] What he says of them is worth noting: although they would all call themselves 'Jews and children of Abraham' and profess their belief in God, in reality they are not properly speaking Jews at all, let alone Christians. Here there seems to be one final use of the term 'Jews' to refer to a particular religious tradition distinct from all others.

(b) The late first century

The effect upon Judaea of the catastrophic rebellion against Rome is hard to imagine. With the destruction of the Temple, the powerful priestly caste referred to in the Gospels as 'the chief priests' had lost its *raison d'être*. It seems likely that the priests regrouped along with the very influential Pharisees in an attempt to regain control and to preserve what they could of their traditions. The extraordinary amount of legislation in the Mishnah relating to a defunct temple-cult testifies to their success.[64] At the same time the Pharisees may have seized their opportunity to divest themselves of a name with isolationist and sectarian connotations. This can be surmised from the surprising infrequency of the name in the pages of the Mishnah

---

[61] M. E. Stone, *Scriptures, Sects and Visions*, p. 58.

[62] Cited by Eusebius, *HE* iv. 22. 7.

[63] *Dial.* 80. 4. Hippolytus (3rd century), in a rather obscure passage relating to the Pharisees, says that they are all called Jews but also have personal (*v.l.* appropriate) names because of the singular views they hold: πάντων μὲν Ἰουδαίων καλουμένων, διὰ δὲ τὰς ἰδίως δοξαζομένας γνώμας ὀνόμασι κυρίοις (*v.l.* καιρίοις) ἐπικαλουμένων (*Ref.* ix. 28). The so-called Tripartite Tractate from Nag Hammadi also speaks of 'many heresies which have existed to the present among the Jews' (*The Nag Hammadi Library*, ed. J. M. Robinson, p. 86).

[64] 'More than half of the Mishnah', remarks Shaye J. D. Cohen, 'is devoted to one aspect or another of the temple and its cult, either because the Mishnah is confidently awaiting the time of their restoration, or because the temple cult has been ordained by God and the study of its regulations was now the equivalent of their implementation, or because the rabbis were attempting to create in their minds an ideal and perfect world to which they could escape from the imperfect world around them': *From the Maccabees to the Mishnah*, p. 219.

(it occurs in only three places).[65] As A. J. Baumgarten observes, 'the rabbis seem to have been reluctant to call their predecessors "Pharisees". … They seem to have preferred other names and when the name Pharisees occurs it is usually in the mouth of their opponents.'[66]

This alliance of chief priests and Pharisees was evidently determined to establish its authority and to take what advantage it could of the further fragmentation of the populace that must have followed the Roman triumph. In trying to stamp out views it regarded as subversive it will eventually have come into conflict with the Johannine group: one of the chief targets of the rabbis, as A. Segal has shown, was the heresy of 'the Two Powers in Heaven', a doctrine nowhere more clearly exemplified, in the Christian world at least, than in the Fourth Gospel.[67]

Those who incurred the hostility of the fourth evangelist, we may conclude, were not all or any of the many dissenters still on the fringe of what was turning into orthodox Judaism, still less the Jewish race and nation as a whole, but those who, after the débâcle of AD 70, had succeeded once again in gathering the reins of power into their own hands. Karl Bornhäuser, writing in 1928, was not after all so wide of the mark: 'Torah-fanatics'[68] may not be the best way of describing the Jews of the Fourth Gospel; but no doubt they were also in fact sticklers for the Law.

In the Gospel itself the *only* clear synonym for Jews is 'the chief priests and Pharisees' (*not* 'Pharisees' alone).[69] Perhaps we are now

[65] *m. Ḥag.* 2: 7; *m. Soṭa* 3: 4; *m. Yad.* 4: 6–8. It has even been questioned whether the *perushim* in these passages should be translated 'Pharisees' at all. Cf. E. Rivkin, 'Defining the Pharisees'. But if Rivkin is right, the relationship between Pharisees and rabbis becomes even more obscure.

[66] 'The Name of the Pharisees', p. 425. Baumgarten argues that there are two plausible derivations of 'Pharisees', one meaning 'separatists' (פְּרוּשִׁים), the other 'specifiers' (פְּרוֹשִׁים), which is the interpretation the Pharisees themselves probably preferred.

[67] There is some doubt about whether the line between the pre-70 Pharisees and the post-70 rabbis is as straight and uninterrupted as is commonly supposed. Cf. P. S. Alexander, 'Rabbinic Judaism and the New Testament', esp. pp. 244 f.; E. P. Sanders, *Paul and Palestinian Judaism*, pp. 60–2. The relatively restricted use of the term 'Pharisees' in the Fourth Gospel may go some way towards reinforcing this doubt. But that the Pharisees played *some* part in the proceedings of the academy at Yavneh is virtually certain. Cf. E. Schürer: 'It can scarcely be a coincidence that once a Pharisaic party as such came into existence, most of the more memorable Torah Scholars proceeded from its ranks' (*History*, ii. 389). Cf. ibid., pp. 381 f. for further references.

[68] *Missionsschrift*, p. 141.

[69] In John 18: 3 and 12. This assertion will be defended in the next chapter.

better placed to understand why this should be so. These were the two groups whose successful alliance in the late first century enabled them to establish their own traditions as the basis of a new Judaism.

(c)   Conclusion

Some of the arguments used here to give a plausible identity to the Jews of the Fourth Gospel may appear somewhat tenuous. They are certainly far from conclusive. But their weakness does not affect the main point of this chapter, which is to locate the Johannine Christians themselves somewhere among the religious dissenters who proliferated in Palestine in the first century. The hostility between the followers of Jesus and the Jews is at its most intense at precisely those points where Jesus is unambiguously claiming divine status. And we have seen too that the rows that break out over these claims are family rows: they concern what are in the first place internal disagreements within the broad spectrum of the faith of Israel.

It cannot be overstressed that this kind of doctrinal debate would be inconceivable within a tradition as unswervingly monotheistic as the Judaism we know today (which in this respect has persisted unchanged since the second century). Even if there were no evidence at all to prove the existence of dissenting groups at the turn of the era, and it is no accident that the bulk of such evidence has been transmitted by Christians rather than Jews,[70] we should still have to posit their existence in order to explain the origins of Christianity. The smooth, rounded monotheism of Jewish orthodoxy afforded as little purchase then as it would today for the claims that came to be made for Jesus. The most startling of these, and none are more startling than those examined within this chapter, were made within a religious tradition which in the first place made them possible and continues to give them intelligibility.

[70] 'By the strangest quirk of fate respecting literature that I know of, large numbers of writings by Jews were completely lost from the transmitted Jewish heritage ... Not only the so-called Pseudepigrapha, but even such important writings as those by Philo and Josephus have not been part of the Jewish inheritance from its past; these were preserved and transmitted by Christians.' So Samuel Sandmel in a foreword to Charlesworth, *The Old Testament Pseudepigrapha*, vol. i, p. xi. A quirk of fate?

5

THE COMMUNITY AND ITS BOOK

I. THE BOOK

All we know about the Johannine community is what can be inferred from its writings. Such external guides as we have are at best unreliable, at worst misleading.[1] But within the pages of the Gospel and Letters is buried a surprising amount of positive data enabling us to piece together a picture of the nature and history of the community. Of course the piecing-together cannot be done without conjecture. As in all historical study it is important to hold apart the factual evidence and the shaping hypothesis. At the same time Collingwood's point concerning the correlativity of the two must not be forgotten.[2] Without some hypothesis to inform the material facts with intelligibility there would, properly speaking, be no evidence either.

(a) Some theories surveyed

As always we must begin with the text, in this case with a book of such consistent intricacy that it could impress Strauss as a seamless garment, yet turns out on closer inspection to be full of the awkward conjunctions and disclocations that have come to be known as *aporias* or problem spots. No one theory can satisfactorily account for all of these; and it has to be said that there is still no general agreement among scholars as to the best explanation.

Perhaps the least satisfactory of all the theories, although still advocated by some, is (1) the displacement theory. No rearrangement yields an order completely free from the bumps and blemishes exposed by the careful sifting of Schwartz and Wellhausen. Even Bultmann, who adopted a refined version of this theory, was forced

---

[1] M. Hengel's *The Johannine Question* (London, 1989) reached me too late for me to be able to take account of his arguments in support of the basic reliability of the 2nd-century witnesses.   [2] *The Idea of History*, pp. 278–82.

to conclude that some of the missing fragments were never recovered. Most fragile of all is the assumption that the Gospel did at one time exist as a perfectly composed unity, the work of one man writing at one time and in one place.

The *Grundschrift* theory (2) according to which the Gospel began as a relatively simple single document which subsequently underwent enlargements, alterations, and revisions, has more to be said for it. But it obviously requires further specification. And even if it were possible to reconstruct this document (Fortna's Signs Gospel, say, or—more adventurously—Boismard's C) with any degree of probability, there would still be a lot more work left to do.

The multiple-source theory (3), of which Bultmann is the most famous exponent, is really a variation of the *Grundschrift* theory: if, as is generally assumed, the signs document was a *source*, then it is conceivable that the evangelist had access to other sources too. Bultmann's idea of a revelation-discourse source, the keystone of his whole theory, will not bear the weight he put on it. On the other hand, it is now widely admitted that there was a written source for the passion narrative; though it is still not clear whether this was originally attached to the signs source, as Fortna thought, to form a Signs *Gospel*, or whether it was an independent unity. Lindars, who accepts the latter suggestion, has also proposed that the other sources of the Gospel consisted of a mass of unrelated traditions or several short collections ('or perhaps both').[3] This alternative view merits serious consideration. A more recent advocate of the multiple-source theory is Jürgen Becker.[4] He believes that the evangelist had two sources, a signs source and a passion narrative. He differs from Bultmann not only in his rejection of a discourse source but also in the much more important role that he assigns to the ecclesiastical redactor. Much of the material that Lindars thinks belonged to a second edition is attributed by Becker to this later writer.

Finally (4) there is the multiple-stage theory of the kind advocated by Brown, Lindars, and, most recently, Boismard. Like the *Grundschrift* theory, with which it is easily combined, this requires further specification if it is to work properly. In general, the more elaborate and detailed a theory is, the more useful it is to the interpreter, but at the same time the more vulnerable it is to critical scrutiny. We may

---

[3] *Behind the Fourth Gospel*, p. 38.
[4] Besides his commentary, see his discussion of his own and other compositional theories in *TRu* 47 (1982), pp. 294–301; 51 (1986), pp. 28–39.

think either in terms of small and gradual reworkings, minor revisions, and piecemeal alterations or, as Lindars prefers, of at least two major editions of the Gospel. These are not mutually exclusive alternatives. An interesting suggestion of Brown's that may be taken on board at this point is that at one vital stage in its history the Gospel consisted of independent homilies, subsequently cobbled on to already existing material. Lastly we should remember the possibility of a final redactor, ecclesiastical or other, whose contribution might be quite extensive, as Brown thinks, or relatively insignificant, like that of a sub-editor. But it is widely agreed that at least chapter 21 must have been added on after the body of the Gospel was completed.

One of the weaknesses of Bultmann's theory was its assumption that the evangelist introduced drastic modifications into a document with which he was in radical disagreement. Why did he not simply discard this and start afresh on his own account? Other theories that rely upon a similar hypothesis, such as those of Wolfgang Langbrandtner[5] and, more recently, Udo Schnelle,[6] are open to the same objection. They must also assume that the evangelist botched the job badly; otherwise he would have removed all traces of the views that he found offensive. Altogether this type of theory is probably the weakest and least plausible of the many that have been advanced.

(b) A theory adopted

A fully rounded theory concerning 'the Johannine community and its book' must integrate the study of both of these into a comprehensive account of the Gospel's growth, the successive stages of composition corresponding to the changing situation of those for whom it was being written. I say 'written', but the oral stage of the Gospels may have extended much further, lasted much longer than the application of source and form criticism might lead us to suppose. The evangelists themselves may have been active preachers before their work was finally committed to writing. It is known that Matthew and Luke (and probably John too) made use of written sources; but they may have done so in the first place for the benefit of a listening rather than a reading audience. Certainly the great revelation discourses, which set the Fourth Gospel so strikingly apart

[5] *Weltferner Gott.* See the criticisms of Raymond Brown in *The Community of the Beloved Disciple*, pp. 180–2.   [6] *Antidoketische Christologie.*

from the rest, are best thought of as built upon the words of a preacher addressing a responsive audience and not simply the work of a writer toiling away with calamus and papyrus.

Any theory in which the main arguments all lean on one another runs the risk of circularity. But we can to some degree circumvent this risk by making our excisions into the text at the points indicated by Schwartz's problem spots. The pericopes thus disclosed can then be examined along literary and form-critical lines: in searching for a *Sitz-im-Leben* we must bear in mind that the 'life-situation' sought out in such imaginative reconstructions is already satisfactorily located within the bounds of the Johannine group. Since the publication of Brown's commentary there has been a great upsurge of interest in the Johannine community; consequently one might wonder why there have been so few properly form-critical studies of the Gospel. (Dodd's *Historical Tradition* and Herbert Leroy's *Rätsel und Missverständnis*, to be discussed below, are honourable exceptions.) The reason for this neglect lies partly in the relatively advanced state of the various materials that go to make up the Gospel: it is a long way from the *Kleinliteratur* of classical form criticism. But is also true that the enterprise bristles with difficulties: it can only stand up if supported by theories of compositional development which themselves seem to rest on very shaky foundations. Since Bultmann the only commentaries actually *controlled* by the compositional theories of their authors are the dense and detailed study of Jürgen Becker and the splendidly idiosyncratic work of Boismard, whose very explicitness lays it open to the brutal assaults of critical knives and hatchets. Though Boismard is right in principle to marry his compositional theory to the story of the community's birth and development, there are far too many weak links in his long and elaborate chain. We must rest content with a more flexible theory.

1. The signs source. Faure's suggestion, dating back to 1922, has undergone various revisions and withstood various attacks. The signs source was probably a missionary document, designed to promote belief in Jesus as Israel's promised Messiah. Even if Fortna was right to regard it as a Signs *Gospel*, it must have been composed—presumably in Palestine—before the formation of the Johannine group as this is generally conceived nowadays. It contained none of the high christology characteristic of the finished Gospel. Its extent remains uncertain, but is unlikely to have been as

considerable as Fortna supposed. This source and its nature will be discussed in more detail in Chapter 7.

2. Alongside the signs source are to be postulated (*a*) a passion source (which may or may not have been combined with the signs source in the first place) and (*b*) an indefinite number of Synoptic-type traditions, which certainly included sayings and may have included short narratives.

3. The synagogue which gave a welcome to the signs source and its message was made up of people of differing views. The religious dissenters who championed the gospel had traditional beliefs of their own which affected their understanding of the message concerning Jesus. This in turn led them to reappraise their own faith.

4. If many proved sympathetic to the gospel, others were sceptical, even hostile. The radical questioning of this group prompted Jesus' followers to reflect upon their new faith and to develop it in unexpected ways.

5. Consequently the leader or leaders of the Christian group performed two roles, acting both as apologists and as preachers (or prophets). In what Brown calls the second stage of the Gospel's composition the themes now regarded as distinctive of this Gospel were woven into an impressively cohesive conceptual pattern. Meanwhile certain of the group's new insights were embodied in narratives and discourses that reflected the contrasting situations, of controversy and prophecy, in which they arose. Some of these will have been attached to episodes of the signs source or constructed round traditional sayings available from elsewhere. 'Since the general traits of Johannine thought are so clear, even in the units that betray minor differences of style, we should probably think of a close-knit school of thought and expession. In this school the principal preacher was the one responsible for the main body of the Gospel material.'[7] Moreover, in spite of the obvious cracks and joins in both narrative and discourse it is virtually impossible to find a passage free from all elements of the typically Johannine vocabulary and style. This can be seen from even a cursory examination of the work of any scholar (e.g. Bultmann, Fortna, Boismard) who has attempted a detailed reconstruction of the prehistory of the Gospel. The perplexity such an examination may induce should not lead us to abandon our efforts to trace these earlier stages, still less to

---

[7] Brown, p. xxxv.

conclude that they never existed; but it does help to vindicate Brown's view that for the actual writing-down of the Gospel one man was responsible. To achieve the stylistic unity that is such a marked feature of the Gospel he made numerous adjustments throughout, some quite minor, others involving considerable displacements. Only in the case of really major breaks, such as those at the end of chapters 5 and 14, is it reasonable to speak of separate editions. At the same time, we cannot suppose that the evangelist was anxious to avoid inconsistencies at all costs—otherwise the ingenious suggestions of Bultmann and Boismard would have no plausibility whatever. It seems that between the signs source that preceded the birth of the community and its expulsion from the synagogue not one of the dialogues or discourses in the Gospel was originally composed in precisely the form that we now have it.

6. Towards the end of this second stage the Johannine group was expelled from the synagogue. The first edition of the Gospel included reminders of this experience, now built into dialogue (chs. 5, 8, and 10) and narrative (ch. 9). But it certainly did not contain all the material at the disposal of the evangelist. The narrative section of chapter 6, for instance, was not in the first edition, and the public ministry terminated at the end of chapter 10. Chapters 15–17 were also missing (cf. Lindars, *Behind the Fourth Gospel*).

7. The second edition incorporated more material: it shows evidence of tension within the Johannine community itself (ch. 6) and perhaps a slackening of hostility towards 'the Jews' (ch. 11). The community devotes more attention to its own internal affairs. The allegories of the vine (ch. 15) and those of the door and the shepherd (10: 1–18) belong here. The cleansing of the Temple, which originally led into the passion narrative, is now displaced to its present position in chapter 2. Brown, for whom the second edition involved a relatively minor reworking, assigns most of the major changes to a final redaction. Nevertheless he agrees that 'the adaptation of the Gospel to different goals meant the introduction of new material designed to meet new problems'.[8] Clearly much depends upon one's view of what these problems were. The most important question is how far the evangelist himself was responsible for the various editions. Commentators differ on the extent to which he would have tolerated the dislocations and doublets in the present

[8] p. xxxvi.

text. Brown, for instance, believes that quite a substantial part of the farewell discourse was inserted by the redactor: 'That this ... was the work of the redactor and not of the evangelist seems likely from the fact that the original ending of the Last Discourse in 14: 31 was not tampered with or adapted to the new insertion.'[9] But even such a bad transition as this is not proof that the evangelist himself had no hand in it. Certainly, there are no stylistic differences to support such a hypothesis. Once his work existed in some recognizable shape he may have been reluctant to make more alterations than he was compelled to.

8. Even so it is hard to dispense completely with the theory of a final redactor, responsible at the very least for the addition of the last chapter. Brown, who attaches considerable importance to the redactor's work, insists that 'the fact that this material was added at the last stage does not mean that it is any less ancient than material that found its way into earlier editions'.[10] In assessing the redactor's contribution to the Gospel as we have it we should be particularly on our guard against theological *parti pris*. In addition to chapter 21 he may have added little more than a few touches intended to make the Gospel more intelligible to non-Jewish readers. Thus the only major sections of the Gospel that cannot be directly accredited to the evangelist are (*a*) the signs source which he took over and adapted and (*b*) the concluding chapter in its present form.

2. THE COMMUNITY

Martyn begins one of his programmatic essays by comparing the Gospel to an archaeologist's tell. It contains, as he says, 'numerous strata, and to some extent these strata may be differentiated from one another'.[11] The cracks and joins known as aporias indicate the presence of such strata, but to decide which is the earlier information of a different kind is required. Unlike the tell, the Gospel does not display its strata one on top of the other in a given order. Consequently it is not always easy to relate the different strata to the successive stages of the Gospel's composition. Sometimes these are so intricately connected that there is no discernible *literary* seam, but even if for the sake of argument one were to grant the presence of

---

[9] p. xxxvii.   [10] Ibid.   [11] *Gospel of John*, p. 90.

separate strata there is nothing in the text itself to tell us which came first. Perhaps only the signs source can be located with any assurance as the foundation charter of the community and the earliest written expression of its faith.

Martyn distinguishes three periods in the history of the community, early, middle, and late. The early period involves 'the conception of a messianic group within the community of the synagogue'.[12] In the middle period 'part of the group [*part only?*] is born as a separate community by experiencing two major traumas: excommunication from the synagogue and martyrdom'.[13] The late period is characterized for Martyn by a 'movement towards firm social and theological configurations'.[14] Here Martyn diverges from Brown in assigning to this late period the writing of the Gospel 'in its first and second editions'.[15]

In what follows, whilst retaining Martyn's division of the history into three periods, I have categorized these somewhat differently. In particular, I believe that the charge of ditheism is likely to have preceded (and indeed precipitated) the expulsion from the synagogue. Martyn speaks of this charge and the persecution that accompanied it as 'the Second Trauma' that followed upon the initial expulsion.

(a) The early period

Before the foundation of the community, even before the composition of the signs source, there was a dispute between the disciples of Jesus and those of John the Baptist. Since, however, John already figures as a witness to Jesus in the signs source itself, the earliest discernible stratum of the Gospel, we must relegate this dispute to the prehistory of the community. Accordingly, I follow Martyn in beginning with the foundation of 'a messianic group within the community of the synagogue'. But what kind of synagogue are we speaking of here? And what was the gospel which it first heard?

The second of these questions I defer until Chapter 7 ('Messiah'). The first presents us with considerable difficulties. The evidence

---

[12] Ibid., p. 93. In the foregoing discussion I have retained the term 'synagogue' because it is the word used in the Gospel itself. If the Johannine community was located just outside Palestine, it may well have attended a local synagogue. But the word may equally well refer to a local Jewish religious assembly, and this is how it should be understood in the present chapter; a Jewish community viewed from a religious perspective.   [13] Ibid., p. 102.   [14] Ibid., p. 107.   [15] Ibid.

is scanty and ill-defined, and we must proceed with some caution.

In discussing the origins and background of the community in the last chapter I avoided the term 'Jewish sectarianism' for two reasons, one connected with the adjective, the other with the noun. To speak of the Johannine group as Jews is to fail to take seriously the deliberate alienation-effect of the use of this term in the Gospel. Such is the negative valency the term has acquired within the Gospel that it can hardly be applied to the followers of Jesus without confusion. When, to take only the most obvious instance, the evangelist says of the disciples that they kept the doors shut after Jesus' death 'for fear of the Jews' (20: 19), then he is *ipso facto* distancing them (and himself) from those he calls by that name. In commenting upon the Gospel one should respect this deliberate dissociation. We know that the Samaritans, descendants of Jacob, repudiated the name Jews (as attested in chapter 4); and although there are no strong reasons for identifying the Johannine group directly with the Samaritans,[16] it is obvious that they too, for the most part, thought of themselves as non-Jews. We need to acknowledge that in almost all the contexts in which the Jews play an active role in the Gospel they are the object of fear, anger, or hatred.

The objections to the term 'sectarianism' are of a different order. The fact is that we are sure of the names of only three sects in contemporary Palestine: Pharisees, Sadducees, and Essenes. Of these only the Essenes, who included in their ranks, as nearly all scholars now believe, the members of the Qumran community, exhibited all the features of what modern sociologists would call a sect, in their isolationism and their uncompromising rejection of all other claims to be the rightful heirs of the promises of Israel. The vast numbers of people who, as we must suppose, neither belonged to one of these groups nor supported the Judaean establishment were men and women without a name and, more significantly, without an organ-ization—rather like the fringe members of a political party who feel dissatisfied with the party line but who, for the moment, have nowhere else to go. This is the phenomenon of political (or religious) dissent. It represents a groundswell of opinion that can remain undetected until it has pushed to the surface and the wave crumbles and falls. Without it there would be no breakaway groups

[16] This question is discussed in Ch. 8.

either in religion or in politics: it is a condition of their (future) possibility.

The presence of such dissenters among a Jewish community in Palestine or the diaspora, not presumably, in Judaea itself, where the temple party was too strong, helps to explain (*a*) why the gospel concerning Jesus could receive a welcome in the first place and (*b*) why those who did so welcome it ultimately fell foul of the powerful representatives of the Judaean establishment: 'He came to his own home, and his own people received him not. But to all who did receive him, who believed in his name, he gave power to become children of God' (1: 11 f.).

The original message proclaiming Jesus as Messiah was certainly much weaker than the one later rejected as blasphemous by the Jews. Otherwise it would never have gained a footing among them in the first place. To make sense of what evidence there is we have therefore to postulate a period of development in which the followers of Jesus moved from a low to a high christology. But that came later. For the present, as Martyn suggests apropos of the homiletic material in John 1: 35–49, 'the preacher takes for granted that his hearers already held certain well-formed messianic expectations, and these expectations constitute in his view a sort of launching pad for the *heilsgeschichtliche* christological trajectory which has its fulfilment in Jesus of Nazareth. He is the Mosaic prophet, the eschatological Elijah, the expected Messiah. The preacher of the sermon, therefore, like John the Baptist, points to Jesus, so that those who have been brought up on the traditional Jewish expectations may now *find* the one so long expected.'[17] I agree with this summary, with the caveat that the preacher is unlikely to have had any clear idea of the christological trajectory ahead of him.

The foundation document of the Johannine community was roughly equivalent to what we have called the signs source. I shall argue in Chapter 7 that this was mainly designed to promote belief in the messiahship of Jesus, a relatively modest claim, neither unprecedented nor blasphemous. Though unlikely to make much headway among the die-hards of the Judaean establishment, this claim was put forward within a broadly based context of religious expectation. There were many varieties of messianic hope, but their very diversity testifies to an eager readiness, in large sections of the

[17] *Gospel of John*, p. 96.

populace of first-century Palestine, to embrace any claim that had a measure of plausibility and could somehow be corroborated. Much of the progress of the new faith would be conditioned by the kind of corroboration that was sought and the way in which challenges from non-believers were actually met.

(b) The middle period

If we compare Martyn's version of the history of the community with Brown's version (in his commentary) of the history of its book, we shall find that they diverge at one important point. Only at Stage 4 (the second edition of the Gospel) does Brown speak of 'an adaptation of the story of the blind man to the new situation in the late 80s or early 90s which involved the excommunication from the Synagogue of the Jews who believed in Jesus as the Messiah'.[18] For Martyn the *first* edition of the Gospel was not published until after this traumatic event. Here, though I think Brown is right to suggest that there was an earlier version of the story of the blind man (see *infra*, p. 179), we must side with Martyn. Any version of the Gospel written *before* the split with the Jews must have looked completely different from the one we have now and it would be hazardous even to attempt to reconstruct it.

However this may be, it is evident that Martyn's middle period covers many years of hidden history. Brown speaks of his second stage as 'lasting perhaps several decades'.[19] Throughout this time we must suppose that the Johannine Christians were not only in contact with the synagogue but belonged to it and took part in its worship. This middle period ended abruptly. Its dramatic close has been impressively charted in Martyn's book. But on what happened in the intervening years he has rather less to say.

In the last chapter three short passages of the Gospel were selected for close scrutiny, all exemplifying the blazing 'family rows' that presaged the final severance of relations between the Johannine Christians and 'the Jews'. The ultimate flare-up was one from which neither side could back down, but it was preceded presumably by a longish period of more or less acrimonious debate. The claims put forward on behalf of Jesus were naturally probed and prodded by suspicious Pharisees, but at the same time they were seized upon by

[18] p. xxxvi.   [19] p. xxxiv.

the religious dissenters and excitedly assessed in the light of their own ancient traditions and beliefs. There were then two distinct impulses towards a fresh and creative formulation of the traditions concerning Jesus: first the need to defend the faith against challenges from within the synagogue; secondly the growing awareness that Jesus was in his own person the fulfilment of much more than the messianic claims that had originally been made on his behalf. Comprising as it did at least two groups with differing religious traditions, *the synagogue itself furnished the crucible within which old beliefs and new loyalties were fused into the glowing affirmations of the Fourth Gospel.* To be sure, this was more than a simple chemical reaction. Bearing as it does so many signs of a gradual and complex coming-together, the shining silver of the finished product also carries the hallmark of genius, most probably of an individual genius who may or may not have drawn upon the work of other, less gifted preachers than himself.[20]

Several otherwise puzzling features of the Gospel, especially the 'Jewish and anti-Jewish' paradox that has baffled so many commentators, are explained by the presence within the same congregation of two different groups. We can see how on the one hand Bretschneider, Weizsäcker, and Wrede could conclude that the Gospel was dominated by an anti-Jewish polemic, and why on the other hand modern scholars are convinced that it was primarily intended for the edification and consolation of a Christian community. Finally, the theory espoused by Bornhäuser, J. A. T. Robinson, and van Unnik—that the Gospel was a missionary document compiled to further belief in Jesus' messiahship among the Jewish community— receives much support from the signs source. This theory works well for the early years of the Johannine group—though not otherwise. For a considerable time Jews and Christians lived and worshipped alongside one another. The Christian group was forced to rethink

---

[20] *Pace* D. E. Aune, there is no conflict between the idea of a single creative genius and the belief that the Gospel's theology, as he puts it, 'is the forthright expression of the Johannine community developed in response to its internal and external situations, experiences, values and beliefs' (*Cultic Setting*, p. 65). Individual genius emerges out of a particular culture and society and expresses beliefs and attitudes held in common, for the most part, with that society, It is because of their exceptional ability to portray the ideas and aspirations of their own culture that historians rely on creative artists to tell them about the spirit and temper of the age. Compare what T. S. Eliot says of the artist's relation to the past in 'Tradition and the Individual Talent', *Selected Essays*[3] (London, 1951), 13–22: 'No poet, no artist of any art, has his complete meaning alone.'

and reformulate those beliefs for which the Pharisees, suspicious and hostile, wanted proofs and guarantees. Martyn expresses the challenge with characteristic verve under the heading 'To the Bet ha-Midrash!':

Some of the persons exposed to the Signs Gospel, specifically some of the potential Jewish converts for whom, at least in part, it was written, reacted quite reasonably by saying, in effect, 'Very well, if your claim that Jesus was the Messiah is to be sustained, it must stand up under careful and intensive midrashic examination, carried out by those whose training equips them for such work.'[21]

Martyn is right, as we shall see, to draw our attention to the element of 'challenge and response' in the development of the Christian group's religious convictions. But at the same time there was, it seems, a prophet in their midst, speaking in the name of Jesus and offering new insights into who he was and what he represented. So we find, as we should expect, both controversy and revelation, polemic and exhortation, apologia and homily, the two kinds of discourse held together in the text of the Gospel, where they were united by the writer we think of as the evangelist (who may also have played a double role as prophet/preacher and spokesman/advocate).

(c) *The late period*

In the second edition of *History and Theology* Martyn inserts a clause briefly summarizing the consequences of the break between Christians and Jews: 'what had been an inner-synagogue *group of Christian Jews* now became—against its will—a separated *community of Jewish Christians*'.[22] The traumatic experience of excommunication put a seal on what must have been a growing sense of alienation and, no doubt, isolation. If Martyn is also right in supposing that the rupture was followed by a period of persecution ('the hour is coming when whoever kills you will think he is offering service to God': 16: 2), then the community will have taken even longer to come to terms with its new situation. There is some evidence of a change of focus in its concerns, of splits within its

---

[21] 'Source Criticism', p. 104. Martyn invites us to consider in particular John 5: 39; 6: 30 ff.; 7: 17.   [22] p. 66.

ranks,[23] and of efforts to establish closer ties with other Christian groups.

During its long association with the synagogue the Johannine group continued to hope for converts. Finding itself alone and confronting persecution it had two choices. It could either look for support elsewhere or huddle self-protectively in a small knot. Perhaps it did both these things, but the evidence is stronger for the latter. The community's concern for its own survival found expression in a series of allegories (door, shepherd, vine) which are eloquent testimony of the sustenance it continued to derive from its total commitment to Jesus.

Martyn offers a strong reading of the allegories in 10: 1–18: the sheep stand for the Johannine community; the strangers, thieves, robbers, and wolf represent the Jewish authorities (a really dedicated allegorist would be even bolder at this point); the hireling's cowardice reflects that of the crypto-Christians, the secret sympathizers among the 'rulers' of 12: 42; while the shepherd, of course, is Jesus.[24] Verse 16, which Bultmann rejects as a gloss, opens new vistas for the community by speaking of 'other sheep', not of this fold, which are to be gathered together to form a single flock.

Now at this stage the Johannine community was shut off not just from the synagogue but from the world at large. This is clear from the very negative use of κόσμος throughout the farewell discourses, with chapter 17 affording only a partial exception. Were it not for the single verse (10: 16) on which Martyn builds so much, one might be tempted to think now in terms of a Christian ghetto. But we

---

[23] In his later contributions to Johannine studies Raymond Brown has adopted a similar approach to Martyn's, and in one article, '"Other Sheep Not of this Fold"', he distinguishes no fewer than six groups in what he calls 'the Johannine religious purview'. What he has to say concerning the apostates of John 6: 60–6 is of great interest but does not radically alter our picture of the community itself. The same is true of the 'crypto-Christians', for which the evidence is very slight: 12: 42 f. and *perhaps* ch. 9. Brown's main difference of opinion from Martyn is his view that the community included Gentiles. Cf. 'Johannine Ecclesiology', pp. 391 ff.

[24] *Gospel of John*, pp. 115–21. Contrast Bultmann, who stubbornly resists all efforts to allegorize the passage. For him the παροιμία of 10: 6 is neither allegory nor riddle, but simply parable (p. 358) or comparison (p. 371; cf. p. 370 n. 4 and *passim* throughout his exegesis of this passage). This accords with his view that the Gospel gives general answers to the human predicament, not a response to a particular historical situation. The parable/allegory is probably a secondary expansion of the metaphorical use of the shepherd theme in 10: 26 f. Bultmann compares 'the way in which the theme of the discourse on the bread of life is introduced by a metaphorical expression in 6: 27, and similarly the theme of the discourse on the light in 9: 39–41 (p. 358 n. 3).

shall see that in this Gospel universalism and isolationism go hand in hand: the Jesus worshipped by John and his community is still the light of the world even when the world is blind.

3. THE COMMUNITY IN ITS BOOK

In demonstrating how the nature of the Johannine community is exhibited in the Gospel I shall confine my illustrations to the middle period, in particular the period of growth and development preceding the final rupture with the synagogue. Throughout this time the Johannine group had two preoccupations and faced in two directions. On the one hand, it was forced to respond to challenges from the establishment party in the synagogue (the Pharisees). Hence the controversial tone of so much of the Gospel material. Some of these challenges will be discussed in Chapter 8 ('Son of God'). Others will be given some consideration in what follows.

On the other hand, the group held many ancient beliefs of its own and, more important still, was inspired by new stories about Jesus and collections of his sayings. Partly in response to the external stimulus afforded by the uneasy scepticism of the Pharisees, the community welded these into a new faith. I attempt some analysis of this process in Chapters 8 ('Son of God') and 9 ('Son of Man'). The present discussion is limited to two small but easily detachable groups of sayings, the 'Amen' and the 'I am' sayings.

Altogether three aspects of the life and teaching of the Johannine group will be considered: universalism, particularism, and polemicism. To these correspond three different literary styles or modes of discourse: revelation, riddle, and debate. If we wish to avoid taking a one-sided view of the Gospel and to do justice to all its rich variety, we should begin by recognizing that the community looks both outwards and inwards, sometimes addressing itself to the world which God loves and wishes to save (3: 16 f.), at others hiding itself away from a world it has come to regard as alien and threatening. The Gospel itself acknowledges the potential paradox of a distinction between open and closed, even while freely availing itself of it. So on the one hand Jesus is advised by his brothers that 'no man works in secret (ἐν κρυπτῷ) whilst seeking to be in the open (ἐν παρρησίᾳ). If you do these things, manifest yourself to the world (φανέρωσον σεαυτὸν τῷ κόσμῳ)' (7: 4). On the other hand it indicates the importance of the distinction by introducing it into its own structure. Not for nothing does Bultmann have two main sections in his commentary: there are strong reasons, especially the solemn introduction of chapter 13, for making a break between chapters 2–12, 'the revelation of the δόξα (glory) to the world', and chapters 13–20, 'the revelation of the δόξα before the community'. At least the farewell discourse was composed after the rupture with the synagogue; but even before this there are signs of a marked esotericism which may be reasonably linked with the growing estrangement between the Johannine group and the establishment. Even so, it is unlikely that the community will have lost all sense of the universality of its message as soon as it became preoccupied with its internal affairs.

(a) Controversy

The presence of controversy material is often enough signalled directly and unambiguously: 'You enquire of (ἐρευνᾶν = דָּרַשׁ\דְּרַשׁ) the scriptures ... but their witness is of me' (5: 39). Here, however, I want to examine some less obvious passages, whose controversial nature is indicated first simply by the presence of the Pharisees. 'The Pharisee-passages', writes Ernst Bammel, 'reflect controversies between the Christian community and shades of opinion within the Jewish world. They represent old, valuable tradition.'[25] Part of this material (7: 32, 45–52) is discussed in Chapter 8. Putting this to one side, we are left with two passages of particular significance: 8: 13–20 and 9: 1–41. To these must be added a third, 5: 31–40, thematically linked with the first and responding to the same objection.[26]

(i) 8: 12–20[27]
Reduced to its bare essentials, the challenge to Jesus' authority reads like this 'So the Pharisees said to him, "You are testifying on your

---

[25] 'John did no miracle', p. 197. From this generalization we must except the conjunction 'chief priests and Pharisees' (7: 32, 45; 11: 47; 18: 3). This is always employed in the context of a resolve to arrest Jesus and to put him to death; it belongs to a different redaction from the passages under consideration here.

[26] The theme is *witness*. Cf. especially J. Blank, *Krisis*, pp. 109–230; J. Beutler, *Martyria*, pp. 254–71.

[27] This short passage has been combined with what follows (8: 21–30) to make a recognizable unit. But it too is already composite, comprising at least three different elements: (a) v. 12, 'a fragment of a revelation-discourse, comparable to 7: 37. It is related to the feast of Tabernacles by the illumination ceremony, and it appears to

[cont. on p. 176]

own behalf; your testimony is invalid." Jesus answered, "Even if I do testify on my own behalf, my testimony is valid[28] .... In your law it is written that the testimony of two men is valid; I testify on my own behalf, and the Father who sent me[29] testifies on my behalf as well" (8: 13–14a, 17–18).

It should be observed straight away that the Pharisees' challenge has no *particular* bearing on Jesus' claim to be the light of the world (8: 12). It is directed not to the content of his prophetic utterance but to its form. The Pharisees want proof that Jesus has a right to speak

belong with the theme of chapter 9' (Lindars, p. 313)—or perhaps it was an independent prophetic saying (see *infra*); (b) vv. 13–14a, 17–18, a debate on Jesus' credentials and the validity of his self-witness; (c) 14b–16, the question of Jesus' origins and destiny and his role as judge. What interests us here is the second element (b). The question of Jesus' origins and destiny (c) may seem to arise naturally out of a reflection upon the source of his authority: 'I know whence I have come and whither I am going' (8: 14b). But these two questions are themselves distinct and their eventual association is a matter of great theological significance. Bultmann, p. 280, appeals to Gnostic influences at this point; but the conceptual assistance needed for the move from origin to destiny was ready to hand in the tradition of Jesus' exaltation/resurrection. The sharp distinction Bultmann makes between Jesus' origin and his knowledge of that origin, justified though it may appear from a literal reading of 8: 14, is not really Johannine. In the passage under consideration the various themes have been woven together very skilfully. In particular, the reference to Jesus' destiny (ποῦ ὑπάγω) is fully expanded in the next section, 8: 21–30. That this was originally an independent pericope is clear from 8: 20, an obvious conclusion (note too the shift from 'Pharisees' to 'Jews'). It shows that the theme of Jesus' dying into glory, the special meaning of ὑπάγειν, was itself a subject of controversy. This theme is first sounded in 7: 32–6, where it is clearly out of place. Its presence there, as in 8: 14, can be attributed to the conceptual transition effected *by the evangelist* from the question of Jesus' origins to that of his destiny. For the extent to which the two themes can be understood as a simple extension—mission and return—of the role of the *messenger*, see Ch. 8, pp. 308–28; cf. J.-A. Bühner, *Der Gesandte*, pp. 123–37, under the heading 'Der Weg des Boten'.

[28] The valid or admissible testimony (μαρτυρία ἀληθής) is distinguished from the true judgement (κρίσις ἀληθινή, v. 16). That 'valid' is the correct translation here is shown by the parallel passage in 5: 31, where it is evidently absurd to say, 'If I give testimony on my own behalf, my testimony is *not true*'. The point is not that the evidence is false, but that it is inadmissible or invalid. See J. Beutler, *Martyria*, p. 256, with references to earlier commentators; A. E. Harvey, *Jesus on Trial*, pp. 20, 56 f. Nevertheless, ἀληθής must be allowed to retain a smidgeon of its usual meaning. English, unfortunately, cannot carry the ironic ambiguity.

[29] The name given to God here, 'the Father who sent me', is thoroughly Johannine, and conflates, as will be argued in Chapter 8, the two originally distinct motifs of mission and sonship. But though probably introduced at the compositional stage, it is unquestionably appropriate at this point, as a profound theological reflection upon the source of Jesus' authority, which is at the same time the source of his being. The whole paragraph is a copy-book example of the way in which a theological development can be aided by an external stimulus, in this case, as Martyn puts it, the summons to the Bet ha-Midrash.

as a prophet. This is in itself a perfectly reasonable request; it corresponds moreover to a well-attested tradition: 'As Jesus was walking in the temple, the chief priests and the scribes and the elders came to him, and they said to him, "By what authority are you doing these things, or who gave you this authority to do them?"' (Mark 11: 27 f.) Elsewhere in the Fourth Gospel the same word, 'authority' (ἐξουσία) is employed in the same sense (5: 27). According to the Synoptic version Jesus dodges the question by posing an unanswerable question of his own; the Fourth Gospel exhibits a profound understanding of *why* the question cannot be answered directly. And by the same token the Pharisees exhibit their *misunderstanding* by challenging the validity of Jesus' self-witness. Jesus himself spells out the juridical basis of their challenge, repudiating it as he does so: 'in *your law* it is written that the testimony of two men is valid;' but then he goes on, 'I testify on my own behalf, and the Father who sent me testifies on my behalf also' (8: 18). Thus he ironically undermines the apparently solidly based position of the Pharisees: of the 'two men' to whom he appeals, he himself is one (so that *de jure* his testimony has no validity)[30] and the other is no man at all, but God. Accordingly, as Bultmann remarks, 'What we are taught by this law, with its rule about the two witnesses, is that God's revelation does not have to answer for itself before men, may not be subjected to man's demand for witnesses to support it; for otherwise the rule about two witnesses would have to be applied, and that is sheerly absurd (*eine Absurdität*).'[31]

(ii) 5: 31–40
This episode, like the preceding one, is predominantly concerned with the theme of witness and records an alternative reply to the same challenge.[32] It must have existed independently before being

---

[30] Cf. Num. 35: 30; Deut. 17: 6; 19: 15.

[31] p. 282. It is characteristic of Bultmann to draw a highly general theological inference from a single passage making a contextually determined point.

[32] Bultmann too links these two episodes, but for him the link-word is not 'witness' but 'judge'. In his commentary 8: 13–20 rounds off an important section headed simply, 'The Judge' (pp. 247–84), which also includes 5: 19–47 and 7: 15–24. That these passages are closely connected thematically is certain—though it is less clear that the resemblances entitle the commentator to detach them from their present context. But in ch. 5 the theme of judgement is abandoned after 5: 30 and is only briefly touched on in ch. 8 (v. 16). There are strong reasons for believing that the discourse in ch. 5 was composed of at least three distinct elements: vv. 19–29, 31–40 (joined by v. 30), 41–7. Even Dodd, *Interpretation*, p. 387, sees these verses as an appendix.

placed where it is now. Jesus' adversaries are nowhere named in the
long discourse 5: 19–47; and although this is formally addressed to
the Jews (cf. 5: 18) this datum is irrelevant to the prehistory of the
passage.[33]

There is a formal contradiction, noted by many commentators,
between 5: 31 ('if I give testimony on my own behalf, my testimony
is not valid') and 8: 14 ('even if I do give testimony on my own
behalf, my testimony is valid'). And even though there is no *material*
contradiction (Bultmann is clearly right about this), the difference is
sufficiently marked to make it improbable that the two passages ever
stood side by side in a continuously composed text. 5: 31–40, where
the defence is much fuller, seems to be slightly the earlier of the two,
originating at a time when there was still some dependence on the
testimony of John the Baptist.[34] As the argument progresses, the
significance of this testimony comes to be discounted: 'I do not
receive testimony from (any) man' (v. 34). What testimony Jesus
does allow comes from (*a*) his works (v. 36), (*b*) the Father (v. 37),
and (*c*) the Scriptures (v. 39),[35] though these are not really three
witnesses, but two, Jesus and the Father, as in chapter 8. For just as
there is no real distinction between the testimony of God and that of
the Scriptures he inspired, so there is no real distinction between the
testimony of Jesus and that of his works. Alternatively the witness
may be seen as just one—the witness of the Father, inseparably
associated not only with the Scriptures that he prompted Moses to
write but also with the works he gave Jesus to do.[36]

For the community's theology the most relevant development is
the move from the avowed dependence upon John's testimony so
prominent in the signs source (especially ch. 1) to a formal dis-
avowal of any evidence outside the actual revelation of Jesus. Clearly
this marks a new, deeper understanding of that revelation. In the
final analysis all truth is self-justifying. However many witnesses

[33] Conversely, the allegories of the shepherd and the door (10: 1–18) appear in
their present context to be spoken to the Pharisees, since there is no change of
addressee between 9: 40 and 10: 19. But at their close it is the *Jews* who are divided in
their response. The evangelist was evidently unperturbed by such minor inconsistencies.

[34] *Contra* L. Schenke, who thinks that the author of 5: 30–37a used 8: 13–19 as a
Vorlage: 'Der "Dialog Jesu mit den Juden"', pp. 574–7.

[35] On this verse see Str.–B. ii, p. 467 and any commentary (especially Schlatter,
Dodd, or Boismard).

[36] On the difference between the plural ἔργα in 5: 36 and the singular ἔργον in
17: 4, see A. Vanhoye, 'L'Œuvre du Christ'.

swear to have seen the Loch Ness monster, ultimately only 'Nessie' herself can prove them right. But in religious matters questions of testimony and evidence are especially delicate, and challenges to established authorities especially threatening. 'You search the Scriptures.' Jesus tells the Jews/Pharisees, 'because you think that in them you have the new life; yet it is to me that they bear witness' (5: 39). The Johannine Christians have accepted the invitation to the Bet ha-Midrash and in so doing acknowledged the authority of the Scriptures. But they surprise their opponents by whisking the book out of their hands. Implicitly the whole point and purpose of the appeal to midrash is being challenged and denied. Perhaps the most important lesson they have learned from this brush with rabbinism is that they must go their own way, taking the Scriptures with them.

(iii) 9: 1–41

Along with most modern commentators, Bultmann treats chapter 9 as a unity; but it was not always so.[37] The sardonic query, 'Surely you are not eager to become disciples of his?' (9: 27) originally belonged to an old debate, focused upon a division within the synagogue between the followers of Jesus and the establishment, who declared themselves disciples of Moses (9: 28; cf. 5: 46 f.).

The first step towards reconstructing the earlier form of the debate is to bracket out the central section, 9: 18–23, which is a detachable scene between the blind man's parents and *the Jews*. We are then left with 9: 13–17 and 9: 24–34.[38] Together, these constitute a long dialogue between the blind man himself and the *Pharisees*. In the conclusion, 9: 35–41, the moral of the story is drawn with great art and dexterity.

The central section, in which the Jews interrogate the blind man's parents on their son's cure, recalls their crucial decision to expel from the synagogue anyone confessing Jesus to be the

---

[37] Martyn refers in a note (*History*[2], p. 32 n. 33) to the theory of Wellhausen and Spitta that the evangelist added vv. 18–23 to his source. This view seems to me correct (cf. p. 170 *supra*). Nevertheless *at the level of the final redaction* Martyn's theory may be basically right. Our concern here is with the significance of the story at an earlier stage of the community's history, at a time when the expulsion of the man born blind (ἐξέβαλον, v. 34) did not necessarily imply excommunication.

[38] The introductory words in v. 24 have been added to effect a transition back to the dialogue between the blind man and the Pharisees, but the demand 'Give God the praise,' follows naturally upon the argument broken off at v. 17.

Messiah.[39] Behind this laconic aside, interjected by the evangelist as an explanation of the Jews' intransigence, lies hidden the story of a lengthy debate between Jews and Christians which has now been definitively broken off. But in the earliest form of the story, contained in the exchange between the Pharisees and the blind man himself, the debate is still very much alive.

There are several indications of the primitive nature of this debate. First of all there is an allusion to the infringement of the sabbath rest (9: 16; cf. 5: 16 ff.; 7: 22 ff.), though the writer is clearly impatient with the legalistic simplicity that would end the matter there. Secondly there is the continuing interest in the probative value of Jesus' *signs* (9: 16; cf. 10: 21). Thirdly the blind man's own declaration of faith, 'He is a prophet' (9: 17) is perfectly consistent with the simple creed contained in the signs source. Finally the passage includes what may well have been the earliest formulation of the affirmation of Jesus' divine origin. Subsequently this would be asserted quite categorically and be based on Jesus' exclusive knowledge of heavenly things. Here it figures in an argument of unmistakably rabbinic flavour: '"We know that God has spoken to Moses, but as for this man, we do not know where he comes from." The man answered, "Why, this is a marvel! You do not know where he comes from, and yet he opened my eyes"' (9: 29 f.).

It is important to recognize that the distinctively Johannine (high) christology is absent from this debate. It utilizes simple arguments of the kind that did in fact carry weight with some of the Pharisees: 'How can a man who is a sinner do such signs?' (9: 16.) On reading the story for the first time one might conclude that it was designed to show no more than that Jesus was (*a*) a prophet and (*b*) from God—claims with little difference of meaning. Only in the very last scene, the encounter between Jesus and the man he has cured, is the much stronger title of Son of Man introduced, abruptly and unexpectedly. And this may well be an addition to the original

---

[39] It may seem odd that this anathema should have been provoked by a simple profession of faith in Jesus' messiahship. For we have to suppose that it was as Messiah, and perhaps prophet, that Jesus had won adherents within the synagogue in the first place. This is argued at length in Ch. 7. The answer to the puzzle is that by this time the simple term 'Messiah' had collected larger and more threatening connotations—which may themselves, ironically, have come about as a result of attempts to satisfy questioners from the Jewish establishment. The extent of the accretions to the notion of Jesus' messiahship may be gauged from the exchange in ch. 10, where the Jews ask Jesus to tell them plainly if he is the Messiah and receive a reply culminating in the statement, 'I and the Father are one' (10: 30).

story.[40] Basically what we have here is a straightforward argument based on a miraculous cure and designed to demonstrate to Pharisees of good will the truth of the earliest claims made on Jesus' behalf by his champions within the synagogue.

(b) Revelation

Most recent discussions of early Christian prophecy tend to steer clear of the Fourth Gospel. In an important article attacking Bultmann's assumption that a great deal of spirit-inspired prophecy has found its way into the Synoptic Gospels, J. D. G. Dunn avoids any close examination of the Fourth: 'It must suffice to point out that the discourses in the Fourth Gospel have more of the character of midrashim or meditations on original Jesus-tradition (such as the words of the Last Supper or the parable of the lost sheep) than of prophetic utterances.'[41] David Hill is equally sceptical, insisting on the clear differences between the Gospel and the Book of Revelation:

In the first place the author of Revelation identifies himself as a prophet; the composer of the Johannine discourses does not. Secondly, in the 'I'-words of Revelation the exalted Lord speaks, whereas the discourses of the Fourth Gospel are presented as the sayings of Jesus. ... The view that the homilies or discourses in John's Gospel derive from a Christian prophet, presumably within the Johannine school or circle, remains at best a hypothesis and a hypothesis dogged by some difficult questions.[42]

David Aune, in an even more comprehensive survey,[43] omits the Fourth Gospel altogether.

Those scholars who do accept the thesis that prophets operated

[40] As M. de Jonge says, 'Titles like "prophet", "king" or even "Messiah" do not correspond completely with the real status and authority of Him to whom they point. The terms are not wrong but insufficient; they may be used in a wrong context and are, therefore, in need of further definition' (*Stranger*, p. 83). On three separate occasions the title 'Messiah' is supplemented by that of 'Son of Man': 1: 51; 9: 35; and 12: 34. (Like 1: 51, the section 9: 35–41 may be a subsequent addition.)

[41] 'Prophetic "I"-sayings and the Jesus tradition', p. 196.

[42] *New Testament Prophecy*, p. 149.

[43] *Prophecy in Early Christianity*. Aune's omission is particularly surprising in view of his earlier observation that 'if the "I am" sayings are regarded as a thoroughly Christian product, then their origin can only be adequately accounted for by considering them the products of Christian prophecy, whereby the risen Lord speaks in the first person singular through inspired Christian prophecy within a cultic setting' (*The Cultic Setting*), p. 72; cf. pp. 88 f. Moreover, all the sayings attributed to Jesus in the Fourth Gospel match the first of the five criteria Aune outlines in his later book (p. 317) and many fulfil one or more of the other criteria as well.

within the Johannine community usually confine themselves to
establishing the principle without seeking examples of the practice
within the text of the Gospel itself.[44]

There is something strange about this reticence. Perhaps it stems
from a proper awareness of the very complex *literary* character of
most of the dialogues and discourses. For obviously the Gospel had
to be written down. But a reader's overwhelming impression is not of
writing (which may be taken for granted and ignored) but of speech.
The Gospel itself does not mention writing until the very end. Of
course this is satisfactorily explained on one level as a response to
the demands of the gospel form, which in the nature of the case must
assign most of the spoken words to Jesus. Still, if Jesus did not
actually pronounce more than a small fraction of the words
attributed to him in the Gospel, it seems reasonable to ask who did.
Were they all *written* words, right from the start? And if not, in what
circumstances would they have been spoken? What kind of man
would consciously imitate the few 'Amen' sayings that he found in
the tradition or deliberately utter any or all of the great 'I am'
sayings? Or are we to suppose that a phrase like 'I am the light of the
world' was a secondary invention of the evangelist, recalling a
sermon in which he had pronounced (or heard pronounced) the
words, '*He is* the light of the world'?

The Fourth Gospel is full of individual sayings and extended
discourses that deserve to be called prophetic in a broad sense of the
term. But when it comes to detecting particular logia that might
qualify as charismatic prophecy in the strict sense, uttered within a
context of Christian worship, this very richness is a source of
embarrassment. Some of the prime candidates may have been
inserted into lengthy and carefully constructed discourses that are
most unlikely to have been delivered as impromptu declamations in
a charismatic gathering.

(i) 'Amen' sayings[45]

One possible clue is the use of the word 'declaim' ($\kappa\rho\acute{\alpha}\zeta\epsilon\iota\nu$) to introduce
what have all the appearances of being prophetic sayings.[46] The

---

[44] e.g. G. Johnston, *The Spirit-Paraclete*; D. M. Smith, *Johannine Christianity*,
pp. 15 f.; 244; M. E. Boring, 'The Influence of Christian Prophecy'; M. E. Isaacs, 'The
Prophetic Spirit'.

[45] See especially K. Berger, *Amen-Worte*, pp. 95–117.

[46] There are 4 occurrences of this word in John: 1: 15 (of John the Baptist); 7: 28;
7: 37; 12: 44.

most famous of these is Jesus' proclamation on 'the great day' of the Feast of Tabernacles: 'If any one thirst let him come to me, and let him who believes in me drink. As the scriptures said, "Out of his heart shall flow rivers of living water"' (7: 38).[47]

Another such saying affords an additional clue: 'He who believes in me, believes not in me, but in him who sent me. And he who sees me sees him who sent me' (12: 44 f.). For here, as P. Borgen argues, we have a saying of Jesus with a firm place in the tradition, occurring in one form or another no less than seven times in the Fourth Gospel.[48] This is not the place to discuss this important text in detail. It could easily have been appropriated from the tradition by a Christian prophet in a cultic setting in order to claim, indirectly but unmistakably, the same authority to speak on behalf of Jesus as Jesus claimed when he spoke on behalf of the Father. Elsewhere a different form of the same logion is used to underline this lesson directly: 'Amen, amen I say to you, whoever receives anyone whom I send receives me; and whoever receives me receives the one who sent me' (13: 20). In both cases the sending is a prophetic mission and its reception a listening with faith. And so in a saying that employs an additional device (the introductory 'Amen') to invoke the personal authority of Jesus, the prophet establishes his claim to be heard in terms even closer to the Synoptic tradition. For anyone bold enough to apply it this tradition affords an explicit justification of a practice attested not just in the Johannine group but throughout the early Christian churches.

Closely connected with this saying, and fitted into the same context, is another saying, with a clear formal resemblance to the first: 'Amen, amen I say to you, a slave is not greater than his master, nor is an agent (ἀπόστολος) greater than the one who sent him' (13: 16; cf. Matt. 10: 24 f.).

Of the other 'Amen' sayings in the Fourth Gospel (they total no fewer than 25) two (3: 3, 5) look like Johannine adaptations of

---

[47] The punctuation of this verse is notoriously uncertain. Besides the commentaries, see K. Haacker, *Stiftung*, pp. 50 f.

[48] John 5: 23; 8: 19; 12: 44 f.; 13: 20; 14: 7,9; 15: 23. Cf. Matt. 10: 40; Mark 9: 37; Luke 9: 48; 10: 16; plus further parallels in rabbinic writings, e.g. *Mek.* on Exod. 14: 31 (Lauterbach, i. 252) and *Sif. Num*, 103 on 12: 8. See P. Borgen, 'The Use of Tradition'. J.-A. Bühner offers a different analysis of John 12: 44 ff. in *Der Gesandte*, p. 173.

Synoptic sayings,[49] whilst the rest have apparently been furnished with this solemn introduction by the Johannine prophet himself. Most figure in contexts of major christological affirmations; indeed, they form the nuclei of a whole series of discourses, small and large.

Consequently, while it might be going too far to assert that all the revelatory discourses in the Gospel originated in sayings of the Johannine prophet, most of them appear to have been built round such sayings. Here the authentic logia, with close parallels in the Synoptic tradition, will have furnished the charismatic prophet with valuable models of the form, enabling and inviting him to construct similar sayings on his own—similar, that is, in both form and content. And if this account suggests too much deliberation, it must be remembered that all human speech, even the most inspired, draws instinctively upon a huge stock of models lodged in the individual's memory and immediately available to him in the appropriate circumstances. In this case the Synoptic parallels give us clear examples of a quite distinctive type of saying, and these may be thought to have generated many other similar sayings within the sort of cultic setting that would call them forth.

(ii) 'I am' sayings[50]

To appreciate the force of the 'I am' sayings we must first of all understand their deep structure and the social context which

---

[49] Matt. 18: 3; Mark 10: 15; Luke 18: 17. Lindars ('John and the Synoptic Gospels') argues that this was an authentic saying which the fourth evangelist received in a tradition independent of the Synoptic Gospels.

[50] Here I confine myself to the predicative sayings; 6: 35, 41, 48, 51; 8: 12; 10: 7, 9, 11, 14; 11: 25; 14: 6; 15: 1, 5. The absolute sayings (8: 24, 28, 58; 13: 19) are in a different category; so are the apparently straightforward cases of self-identification. Bultmann (p. 225 n. 3) distinguished four classes of sayings: (*a*) the 'presentation formula', which answers the question 'Who are you?'; (*b*) the 'qualificatory formula', which answers the question 'What are you?'; (*c*) the 'identification formula', in which the speaker identifies himself with another person or object; (*d*) the 'recognition formula', in which the ἐγώ is not subject but predicate, and answers the question, 'Who is the one who is expected, asked for, spoken to?' By classing most of the 'I am' sayings as 'recognition formulae' (he excepts only 11: 25 'and perhaps 14: 6', both 'identification formulae') he empties most of them of any real content. 'In the context of the Gospel', he says, 'the ἐγώ is strongly stressed and is always contrasted with false or pretended revelation.' This is a good illustration of how Bultmann's theological programme works. 'In the source', he admits, 'they were perhaps intended as presentation or qualificatory formulae' (which would mean that they were saying something positive about the revealer). But as it is, they assert nothing more than the bare *that*: they are simply affirmations of the event of revelation that takes place in Jesus. Even if this were right, would it not alter our appreciation of these sayings if we thought that their true 'source' was the Johannine prophet himself, i.e. the evangelist?

originally gave them point. In other words, we need to enlist the services of form criticism. Of the many scholars who have pored over these sayings only J. A. Bühner has succeeded in discovering their true origin. The *Sitz-im-Leben* is prophecy and in particular the prophet as messenger. The broader background is not properly religious but political and social—the convention obtaining throughout the Ancient Near East whereby one man was entrusted by another with a task to perform or a message to deliver in a different place. The messenger first received his errand, then carried it out, and finally returned to report on it.

In presenting himself to the recipient of the message the messenger could begin by announcing the purpose of his mission: 'I have come (to perform such and such a task).' Alternatively he might start by identifying himself: 'I am (so-and-so).' Abraham's servant, for instance ('the oldest of his house, who had charge of all that he had'), informs Laban that he will not eat until he has told his errand, and then opens by saying simply, 'I am Abraham's servant' (Gen. 24: 34). These two formulae correspond, Bühner suggests, to the two basic forms of prophetic speech in the Fourth Gospel: the 'I have come' sayings (ἦλθον-*Sprüche*) and the 'I am' sayings.[51]

Sometimes the name itself can be significant. The angel Raphael says to Tobit in the aprocryphal book of that name, 'God sent me to heal you and your daughter-in-law Sarah,' and continues, 'I am Raphael, one of the seven holy angels who present the prayers of the saints and enter into the presence of the glory of the Holy One'

---

[51] Bühner's discussion of the 'I am' sayings (*Der Gesandte*, pp. 166–80) comes in a chapter of his work headed, 'The cultural–historical presuppositons of messenger-traffic in the Ancient Near East', and builds upon the form-critical work of the first part, 'the human messenger as the exemplar of the divine'. Earlier studies of the 'I am' sayings, suggesting a Gnostic background, are less convincing. See E. Schweizer, *EGO EIMI*, also offered as 'a contribution to the problem of the sources of the Fourth Gospel'; H. Becker, *Reden* (1956). Becker, and to some extent Schweizer also, remains enmeshed in the toils of Bultmann's Mandaean hypothesis. G. MacRae, 'The Ego-Proclamation', uses documents from the Nag Hammadi Library, much closer in time to the Gospel. But for him the most convincing parallel comes in the Egyptian hymns to Isis, where 'the purpose of the many "I am" sayings is to state the *universality* of the goddess Isis; she is known by many names, she is the source and origin of the manifold religious aspirations of men' (p. 153). The Gnostic texts adduced also belong to revelation discourses and resemble the Gospel's 'I am' sayings in form; but they are very different in mood and tone. For revelation speeches closer in mood to those of the Gospel we have to turn to the *Odes of Solomon*. Becker in discussing Ode 33 (pp. 16–18), simply assumes its Gnostic provenance. But the relatively sober language of the Gospel 'I am' sayings contrasts strongly with the lush exuberance of the Odes.

(Tob. 12: 14 f.). The point here is that the name Raphael means 'God heals', so that the errand is actually contained in the name.

Now there is an important *formal* characteristic of the 'I am' sayings: like the beatitudes, they are followed (or in one or two cases preceded) by an explanation or justification.[52] This states the purpose of what is really a divine commission, e.g. 'I am the bread of life; whoever comes to me shall not hunger, and whoever believes in me shall never thirst' (6: 35). In the course of the same dialogue Jesus has already affirmed: 'This is the work of God, that you believe in him whom he has sent' (6: 29)—and the reader already knows that belief in Jesus is what ensures life (cf. 3: 15, 36, etc.).

If, turning from form to content, we enquire *what* it is that the 'I am' sayings affirm, we find further surprising resemblances. All of them, directly or indirectly, contain a promise of *life* (the Gospel's central metaphor for the attendant benefits of faith). Consequently they are all *miniature Gospels*; they affirm simply and graphically the purpose for which the Gospel was written, 'that you may believe, and believing, have life in his name' (20: 31). What is more, they do this by compressing the affirmation into a statement that identifies Jesus with the purpose of his coming ('that they may have life'—10: 10). The supreme examples of this compression ('I am the resurrection and the life', 'I am the way, the truth and the life') are not different in *kind* from the rest, as Bultmann holds, but expressions of an insight common to them all, especially concise in that the purpose and consequence of the reception of Jesus' message (life) is drawn back into his self-proclamation.

[52] In ch. 6, where four sayings in quick succession have been built into an elaborate dialogue, only one (the internal citation of v. 41) omits the explanation altogether. In ch. 10 there are two sayings, each repeated ('I am the door' in 10: 7, 9; 'I am the model ($\kappa\alpha\lambda\delta s$) shepherd' in 10: 11, 14). The explanation of the door-saying is regular, but only given once (v. 9); the shepherd-saying has three explanations, one preceding (v. 10), the others following, with two significant departures from the basic form: 'the model shepherd lays down his life for his sheep' (v. 11) and 'I know my own and my own know me ... and I lay down my life for my sheep' (v. 14). Similarly the explanation of the vine-saying in 15: 2 ('Every branch, etc.') is the starting-point and key of another vivid allegory. Finally, not only is the 'light of the world' saying in 8: 12 apparently quoted in 9: 5 (though its precise relationship to the whole story is hard to determine) but it appears to inform the important development in 3: 16–21, where the light/darkness antithesis symbolizes the nature of judgement. These observations are merely the beginnings of a proper analysis of these complex passages, but they perhaps suggest how an 'I am' saying constituted a natural core round which a full revelation discourse could grow. A major weakness of E. Schweizer's treatment (*EGO EIMI*) is its failure even to mention the justifying explanations that are an essential element of the form.

One further feature of the 'I am' sayings makes them all but unique in the New Testament[53] and distinctive enough in religious literature generally. This is their strikingly bold use of symbolic imagery. Here is where the Gnostic parallels have seemed to some so convincing, especially in contexts which imply a self-revelation of a divine being. But the actual symbols used in the Fourth Gospel are, with one exception,[54] abundantly attested in the Old Testament, and the form, as we have seen, is simply an extension of the messenger formula. It seems likely that the Gnostic texts are mostly independent variants upon the same tradition. For instance, one of the longest and most impressive of these (*The Thunder, Perfect Mind*) commences with an announcement of mission ('I was sent forth from the power'), followed by an 'I came' saying ('I have come to those who reflect on me'), before embarking on a long series of 'I am' sayings chiefly remarkable for polarity and paradox (e.g. 'I am the whore and the holy one').[55] Few of these are as colourfully evocative as the 'I am' sayings of the Gospel: extraordinary as these symbolic affirmations are, it was perhaps not beyond the powers of the Johannine prophet to invent them. But it must be admitted that if he did he was veering as close as he ever got to a typically Gnostic style.

However that may be, the content of the sayings puts them at the heart of the Gospel's teaching. All of them represent a distillation of one of its main themes. Just as in the case of Raphael what is asserted of the messenger (the predicate) anticipates and includes the content of the message. And that content is life.

Such pregnant formulae as these are not likely to have been hit on all at once. Like the Gospel itself, which is both an instance of the gospel form and a comment upon it, the 'I am' sayings sum up and express insights which can only have been reached through a profound reflection on the essence of Jesus' message, a reflection culminating in the realization that what Jesus came to bring was nothing other than himself. (So Bultmann was not after all very wide of the mark.)

The majority of these sayings are now embedded in discourses and dialogues which, however prophetic in tone, are clearly the product

[53] The nearest parallel is Rev. 22: 16—'I am the root and offspring (γένος) of David.'

[54] 'I am the door' (10: 7, 9). Lindars, p. 358, comments that this saying 'does not have the rich overtones of a revelation-formula, but is a pointer to the interpretation of the parable'.

[55] *The Nag Hammadi Library*, pp. 271-7; cf. n. 44.

of deliberate composition. Even so, given the formal background of
the sayings, it is likely that before being incorporated into one or
other of the Gospel's set pieces they were first uttered in a properly
prophetic milieu. This is probable not just because of the history of
the form, its origins as a messenger-formula, but also because it
remained peculiarly adapted to the circumstances of prophetic
speech: it both identifies the speaker and contains, in a remarkably
succinct form, the kernel of his message.

It is not possible to locate each individual saying precisely within
the history of the community. But one may observe that for all their
formal and material similarities they do not all make the same point
in the same way. Some seem wholly positive: the invitation is open
to all. 'I am the light of the world; he who follows me will not walk in
darkness, but will have the light of life' (8: 12). Later on, when the
community had become more inward-looking and isolationist, what
is basically the same invitation ('I am the door') has a condition
attached to it—one must come into the fold: 'whoever enters by me
will be saved' (10: 7–9). This slightly ungenerous interpretation
really depends on the Gospel's own exegesis of the passage in v. 16.
It could nevertheless be wrong, but even if it is, a door of its very
nature is a less universal symbol than a light. For a door can be shut
as well as opened, whereas a light shines out its welcome for all to
see, without any hint in this context that the world is naturally dark
and unreceptive.

In chapter 6 the 'bread of life' saying (a paradoxical example of the
coincidence of revelation and riddle) is the occasion of division and
misunderstanding. As for the vine, 'every branch that bears no fruit
he [the Father] removes ($a\check{i}\rho\epsilon\iota$), and every branch that does bear fruit
he prunes ($\kappa a\theta a\acute{i}\rho\epsilon\iota$)', or *cleanses* so that it becomes clean ($\kappa\acute{a}\theta a\rho\sigma$)
(15: 2). We are reminded that Jesus has already told his disciples,
'You are not all clean' (13: 11): the vine passage belongs in a setting
of potential and actual apostasy.

Finally, while the 'I am' sayings are all revelatory in the full sense,
whether addressed to the world at large, to contemporary Judaism,
or to the Christian community, they all contain an implicit answer
to the repeated requests for some evidence of Jesus' prophetic status.
That his message should be a source of life is the best possible proof
of an authorization from above—no longer an appeal to an external
sign, but testimony to the essential nature of the message itself: 'You
have the words of new life' (6: 68). Despite the distinction between

controversy and revelation (a distinction still worth making), in the experience of the Johannine group the two went hand in hand: the challenge of the Pharisees prompted reflection on the meaning of belief in Jesus, whilst the group's living-out of its faith found expression in prophetic utterances that were in themselves an irrefutable answer to demands for corroboration of the claims which that faith implies.

(c) Riddle

The aim of the riddle may appear to be diametrically opposed to that of the revelatory sayings we have just been considering: 'To you has been given the secret ($\mu\upsilon\sigma\tau\acute{\eta}\rho\iota\upsilon\nu$) of the kingdom of God, but *for those outside* the whole universe comes in riddles ($\dot{\epsilon}\nu$ $\pi\alpha\rho\alpha\beta\upolambda\alpha\hat{\iota}\varsigma$) so that they may indeed see but not perceive, and may indeed hear but not understand; lest they should turn again and be forgiven' (Mark 4: 11 f.). In the strange dictum that follows the parable of the sower in Mark's Gospel the essentially divisive function of the riddle is clearly underlined: it separates out the outsiders from the insiders, the ignorant and foolish from the *cognoscenti*. And although Mark and John differ in the place they assign to the riddle in their Gospels, they agree not only on its function but upon its central importance; for what is Jesus' self-revelation in the Fourth Gospel but the Johannine version of the kingdom of God? So the *content* of the riddle is the same as that of the prophetic sayings; the riddle encloses, as in a box, what is to be revealed. It is thus the quintessence of apocalyptic. Some have the key to this box; others are kept permanently in the dark.

The paradoxical association between riddle and revelation is so close that in one case, as we have seen, the two are combined in a single saying: 'I am the bread of life; whoever comes to me shall not hunger, and whoever believes in me shall never thirst' (6: 35). Here we have an 'I am' saying—a prophetic logion that gathers up the preceding midrash on the manna into a phrase formally indistinguishable from all the other 'I am' sayings that we have just been looking at. But the context is now one of challenge and debate. The bread of life is a variant for the bread of heaven, a consciously ambiguous expression that to Jesus' interlocutors, the Jews, can only mean the manna given in the desert ($\check{\alpha}\rho\tau\upsilon\varsigma$ $\dot{\epsilon}\kappa$ $\tau\upsilon\hat{\upsilon}$ $\upsilon\dot{\upsilon}\rho\alpha\upsilon\upsilon\hat{\upsilon}$—Exod. 16: 4; $\check{\alpha}\rho\tau\upsilon\varsigma$ $\upsilon\dot{\upsilon}\rho\alpha\upsilon\upsilon\hat{\upsilon}$—(LXX) Ps. 77: 24). Only in its hidden esoteric sense can it refer to Jesus' self-revelation—a paradox strongly reminiscent of the purpose assigned to the parables by Mark. The saying is consciously and deliberately divisive, and the consequent incomprehension expected and allowed for.

The best and most thorough treatment of the riddle is in H. Leroy's *Rätsel und Missverständnis*.[56] Leroy is not the first to have noted the deliberate ambiguity of certain expressions in the Gospel; but no one before him had attempted an explanation of the ensuing pattern of misunderstanding along form-critical lines.

All riddles are designed to throw people off the scent, but this can be done in a number of different ways. In its Johannine form the riddle is a statement in which one word or phrase bears two meanings, one surface meaning and one hidden meaning which is concealed from all but the speaker and those who are also 'in the know'. In the everyday form of the riddle the solution rarely depends upon access to a special source of information, though the wit and ingenuity of the audience may indeed be taxed beyond reasonable bounds. But in many societies (the Druids are a good example) the possibility of a correct interpretation depends entirely upon a special revelation that is reserved to a select group of initiates. In this kind of social setting the in-group is distinguished from outsiders by the possession of a key which is jealously guarded. The same pattern operates in numerous myths and fairy-tales.

It is easy to see that many of Jesus' utterances in the Fourth Gospel have the flavour of a riddle. 'Destroy this temple,' said Jesus (2: 19), whereupon the evangelist remarks that he was referring to the temple of his own body. But how could his hearers, standing as they were within the Temple precincts, possibly know this? 'If you knew ... who it is that is saying to you, "Give me a drink," you would have asked him, and he would have given you living water' (4: 10). Living water—ὕδωρ ζῶν—the first meaning of this phrase is *running* or *flowing* water. How could the Samaritan woman be expected to know that Jesus was going to understand the word literally (*living* water) and apply it to his own revelation? Or how could the bewildered Nicodemus, confronted with a remark about being born

---

[56] Leroy is often criticized for taking too narrow a view of Johannine irony. Cf. F. Vouga, *Le Cadre historique*, p. 32 n. 58, who regards his conclusions as 'trivial'; R. A. Culpepper, 'too rigid a definition' (*Anatomy*, p. 154). But Leroy does not pretend to offer a complete survey of *all* John's ironical devices. R. Brown's review in *Bib* 51 (1970), 152–4 misses the point of Leroy's form-critical enquiry.

ἄνωθεν (which he took to mean 'a second time') be expected to take it straight away to mean 'from on high'?

We should be careful not to assume that the function of the riddle is everywhere the same. Leroy, possibly influenced by earlier form-critical studies on the New Testament, suggests two different life-settings: preaching and catechesis. Thus when Jesus tells his disciples, 'I have food to eat which you do not know' (4: 31–4), their natural misunderstanding is immediately corrected. For Leroy this is an instance of how a teacher, when instructing catechumens, could bolster his own authority by appealing directly to the preaching of Jesus. He points out that although this riddle is formally identical with the rest, the fact that Jesus' hearers are now his own disciples indicates a different *Sitz-im-Leben*.[57]

However this may be (and some of Leroy's detailed conclusions are certainly open to question), there is one riddle in the Gospel, the commonest but perhaps the least noticed, that does fulfil two quite distinct functions. This is the term ὑπάγειν. In ordinary speech this means to retire or withdraw. In John's special language it denotes the Easter-event, comprising Jesus' passion, death, and resurrection—his departure from this world and his return to the Father. Out of thirty-two instances of the word in the Gospel, seventeen have the special meaning. There is some precedent for using the term to refer to the passion (Matt. 26: 24; Mark 14: 21) but none for the mystery with which it is surrounded in the Fourth Gospel.

The special meaning is found in two series of texts: (*a*) where Jesus is talking with the Jews, a series confined to chapters 7 and 8; (*b*) where Jesus is talking with his disciples, a series confined to the farewell discourse, chapters 13–16. The word also occurs once in a comment of the evangelist, 13: 33, where, as we should expect, he uses it in its special sense.

Now it is important to recognize that these two series of texts are distinguished from one another not merely by their relative positions in the Gospel and by the fact that in one case Jesus is conversing with his enemies and in the other with his friends, but also by the *kind* of misunderstanding that is exhibited in the two cases. In the first series of texts the misunderstanding is total. Jesus is using the word in its special sense, of his impending departure from the world, and his listeners, initially at any rate, take him to be using it in its

[57] *Rätsel*, p. 154.

ordinary everyday sense. In the second series the disciples realize that Jesus is speaking of his departure from the world but they have not yet grasped what this entails. When they ask, 'Where are you going?' (13: 36) or say that they do not know where he is going (14: 5), they are at least on the same wavelength: unlike the questions of the Jews in chapters 7–8, their remarks are really directed to what Jesus has said. Finally, whereas Jesus tells the Jews emphatically that where he is going they cannot follow him (8: 21; cf. 13: 33), the disciples' inability to follow is only temporary: 'you cannot follow me now, but you shall follow afterwards' (13: 36).

The differences between the two series of texts are significant. In the second series the evangelist has adapted the traditional theme of the misunderstanding of the disciples to make the point (also found in Mark) that there can be no full comprehension of Jesus' message as long as he is still in the world. The implied division is one of time: before versus after. In the first series of texts the division is moral—between Jesus and the Jews. The readers of the Gospel are naturally presumed to share the evangelist's privileged understanding throughout, but in the one case they do so because they have the benefit of hindsight, or rather because of the unseeing faith that has been blessed by Jesus; in the other case they are enabled to look down scornfully on the ignorant Jews from their citadel of knowledge high above.

In the second series of texts, then, the evangelist has used the *riddle* form to illustrate an essential apect of the *gospel* form. In the first series, more typical of his general practice, he exploits the riddle to expose the yawning gulf that separates the knowledge and wisdom of Jesus (and therefore of his disciples also) from the ignorance of his Jewish audience: over against the assured omniscience of Jesus his interlocutors seem a dull, even a stupid lot. The riddle triggers off an immediate misunderstanding, and this persists.

Certain of Jesus' interlocutors, notably Nicodemus and the Samaritan woman, get off more lightly than the Jews *en masse*. Jesus continues to converse with them and their misunderstanding may be partially dispelled. In the structure of the Gospel, moreover, these two characters appear before the disputes with Jesus erupt into violence. No doubt the readers of the Gospel, already in the know, are intended to smile over the bewilderment of Nicodemus and the Samaritan woman as they grope around for the hidden key. But we know even so that Jesus is in fact offering the key to anyone who wishes to take it.

In the next chapter (5: 18) the mood changes dramatically, and in chapter 8 debate degenerates into abuse. Here the effect of the series of riddles is not merely to widen the gulf between the two sides but also to range the readers among the happy few capable of grasping the meaning of all Jesus is saying. Besides reassuring them of their privileged status, their ability to interpret what baffled the Jews increased their sense of isolation.

(d) Conclusion

No attempt has been made in the preceding pages to present a fully rounded portrait of the Johannine community. Nothing has been said of its sacramental life[58] and little enough of the nature of its eschatological expectations. The alternative challenge to Jesus' authority presented by the Moses tradition has been largely ignored. Even Wayne Meeks's suggestive theory of harmonic reinforcement between theology and social experience has been left untouched. Were this chapter primarily concerned with the community as such these would be serious gaps. As it is, they will be partially filled in later chapters. What I have aimed to do here is to give some impression of how and why the community's teaching was shaped in the way we know it. More detailed and intensive form-critical study would, I believe, serve to nourish and strengthen this impression. This should centre upon the *words* of Jesus, in discourse and debate. It was in these, after all, that the fourth evangelist and his community sought and found 'spirit and life'.

4. A LOCAL HABITATION AND A NAME

Nineteenth-century Christian commentators had nothing to say on the problems raised so far in this chapter. They were much more interested in the name of the evangelist and the place where he wrote his Gospel, questions which might seem to afford a welcome respite from windy theory, with answers fabricated from something more substantial than airy nothings. But is this so? Calling the

[58] See now the excellent discussion of David Rensberger, *Overcoming the World*, ch. 4.

evangelist John will not help us to understand his work, and the site of his home is of interest only in so far as it can indicate something about the nature of his community.

(a) Foundation or school?

Die Stiftung des Heils; *The Johannine School*. These are the titles of books by two modern scholars who have searched outside the Johannine tradition itself for ways of getting the community into sharper focus. But are the conceptual tools they hit upon the right ones for the job?

The title of the first of these two books, by Klaus Haacker, means the institution of salvation. 'Founding' is in some respects a better rendering, but fails to catch the ambiguity of a term that can signify not only the act of establishing something but also the result of that act. The foundation or institution in question is the Johannine group; the founder, though, is not the evangelist but Jesus. Haacker seeks to show that the community regarded Jesus as its founder and, what is more, that the relation of founder and founded is central to the understanding of the Gospel. In the course of his demonstration Haacker relies heavily on material drawn from the fourth-century Samaritan document called the *Memar Marqah*, in which Moses figures as the founder-father of the Samaritan community and the one chiefly responsible for its faith.

The importance of a Moses-typology within the Gospel is beyond question,[59] nor can it be contested that the mythological apparatus of the community involved the perception of Jesus himself as its head—the shepherd and the vine. But much more central, in fact quite determinative of the Gospel's vision of Jesus, are the twin concepts of revelation and mediation: he came to reveal the truth and to convey life: by transmitting the truth that bestows life he reveals himself as the way to the Father. Haacker objects to the concept of revealer that it fails to bring out the historical nature of Jesus' mission: it lends itself to a gnosticizing or mythical interpretation; 'the founder', by contrast, 'is a historical human being'.[60] But if the concept of Jesus as revealer is defective in this respect this is a weakness shared by the Gospel itself, which, as time would soon show, was readily susceptible of a docetic reading. In dismissing this

[59] Cf. W. Meeks, *Prophet-King*; J. L. Martyn, *History*[2], pp. 102–28.
[60] *Stiftung*, p. 163.

key concept and replacing it with a much more marginal one of his own, Haacker blurs our understanding of the Gospel instead of sharpening it.

Even more unhelpful, in my view, is Culpepper's argument that the community is to be seen as a *school*. Earlier scholars, he observes, had employed the term rather loosely.[61] When used precisely it compels a *rapprochement* with the great Greek schools that had flourished in the central and eastern Mediterranean since the time of Plato. But this move has two big disadvantages. In the first place it obscures the differences between the two institutions. The great Greek schools were *academies* (the word 'academic' is in fact derived from one of them) and their purpose was properly intellectual. The Johannine group, though it did not neglect study, was primarily a religious body: it looked not for learning but for life. (In this respect it was undoubtedly closer to what Culpepper has no hesitation in calling 'the school of Jesus'.) Of course there were similarities too. If the members of the Johannine group had a favourite designation for themselves, this was 'disciples'. But here we come to the second objection against Culpepper's thesis. For as disciples at whose feet did they sit? Culpepper answers (and his argument demands the physical presence of a living man) that their first teacher and mentor, indeed the one who was probably the actual founder of their 'school', was none other than the evangelist himself, whom they knew as 'the Beloved Disciple'. But this personage, whether we think of him as a symbolic figure or as a flesh-and-blood follower of Jesus, was not in the first place a teacher but a listener: he too sat at Jesus' feet or, rather, close by his side (ἐν τῷ κόλπῳ) and learned from him. Culpepper is surely mistaken in believing that 'the community regarded the Beloved Disciple as its head in much the same way as ancient schools regarded their founder'.[62] If they thought in those terms at all I believe Haacker is nearer the mark in holding that the group saw Jesus as its founder.

That the community shared some features with, say, the schools of Plato and Epicurus is true but unenlightening. All three, for instance, laid stress on friendship (φιλία) and fellowship (κοινωνία)—though neither of these terms is actually found in the Gospel.[63] But such comparisons are valuable only in so far as they enable us to trace lines of influence and raise the question of how

[61] *Johannine School*, p. 1.   [62] Ibid., p. 265.
[63] Κοινωνία, which can also mean 'communion', occurs in 1 Jn. 1: 3 *bis*; 6: 7.

and why these lines diverge. And here Culpepper has nothing to say apart from generalities: 'the influence of the schools is extremely difficult to measure'.[64] No doubt he is right to observe that 'the community engaged in study and interpretation of the teaching of Jesus and the scriptures' and that it was eager to preserve and transmit Jesus' words and commandments and to abide in him, his works, and his love. These are all aspects of the community's self-understanding that deserve consideration. But they are not completely covered by the term 'school', which in any case does nothing to help us to understand the particular modalities which make *this* community unique.

(b) Place

For Culpepper the location of the community remains an unsolved problem: 'it is not possible to move beyond the present impasse (Ephesus, Antioch or Alexandria?).' One has only to reflect on the distances involved to see what a staggering admission of ignorance this is. Ephesus is some 500 miles from Antioch as the crow flies (considerably further by the route Paul had to travel) and about the same distance from Alexandria, on the other side of the Mediterranean. Roughly the distance between London and John o'Groat's, and only a little less than that between Paris and Berlin. Yet all these places were covered by the great net of the Koine, which is why it is so difficult to extract from the fact that the Gospels were written in Greek anything more than a truism.

There is one modern scholar, however, who claims to have found the way out of Culpepper's impasse. This is Klaus Wengst. According to him the community's home was not in Ephesus nor in Antioch nor in Alexandria, but in what used to be the tetrarchy of Herod's son Philip, specifically the region of Batanea and Gaulanitis— roughly the area of Syria known as the Golan heights, occupied by Israel since 1967. In the second half of the first century this formed part of the kingdom of Philip's nephew, Agrippa II.

After disposing of the traditional siting of the Gospel at Ephesus, Wengst summarizes his own case as follows:

—The language of the community is Greek.
—It consists mostly of Jewish Christians.

[64] *Johannine School*, p. 258

—It lives in an environment of mixed nationalities, but one that is Jewish dominated; in fact official power appears to be vested in the Jews.

—It is exposed to measures taken by a Judaism that after 70 is once again consolidating itself under Pharisaic leadership and extirpating all non-Pharisaic tendencies; with the new centre of Yavneh (Jamnia) as a base it is beginning to have some success in Palestine and its immediate neighbourhood.[65]

Now it would be easy to dismiss Wengst's confidently stated conclusions as going far beyond the evidence; to some indeed he may appear bold to the point of brashness. But he argues his case tightly and persuasively. In particular he is able to reconcile two pieces of evidence that at first sight appear to point in opposite directions: the language of the Gospel and its Jewishness.

By the time the Gospels were written the use of Greek was so widespread that it had extended even into Palestine. In the following century, Bar Kosiba was obliged to proclaim his message in Greek, Hebrew, and Aramaic. So it looks as if the Gospel was composed somewhere on the periphery of Aramaic-speaking Jewry. On the periphery, because the Greek is simple and coloured with Semitisms—a world apart from the elaborate language of Philo of Alexandria but equally far from the pidgin Greek of the Book of Revelation.[66]

That the matrix of the community was Jewish has already been proved. Equally important for Wengst's argument is the nature of

[65] *Bedrängte Gemeinde*, p. 80. Wengst relies too heavily on the alleged causal link between the *Birkat ha-Minim* and the expulsion of the Johannine community from the synagogue; moreover his insistence upon interpreting the Gospel as a unified whole prevents him from distinguishing between the situation presupposed by 16: 2 and the earlier conflict to be seen in 9: 22. Nevertheless his suggestion about the geographical location of the community may well be right. It has received strong support from Günter Reim, in a wide-ranging article that also proposes a thesis (very different from my own) concerning the changing fortunes of the Johannine community and the growth of the Gospel: 'Zur Lokalisierung der johanneischen Gemeinde'. There are several weak points in Reim's argument, particularly his assumption that the evangelist was familiar with the Aramaic targumim, for which see 'Targum and Johannesevangelium'.

[66] The debate on the language of the Gospel still goes on. Some scholars, notably C. K. Barrett, are still suspicious of suggestions of Aramaic influence. See *The Gospel of John and Judaism*, pp. 20–39. Wayne Meeks is also cautious, but rather more disposed to allow some Semitic influence: 'it cannot be doubted that some elements of tradition that were originally formulated in a Semitic language are present in John' ('Am I a Jew?', p. 166). See too the judicious assessment of Schuyler Brown, 'From Burney to Black'.

the authority vested in the leaders of the synagogue, who evidently had the power to harass and persecute the Christians in their midst, even to the extent of putting them to death (cf. John 16: 2). Such a power could only have been exercised with the collusion of the Roman government or its local representatives; and after the suppression of the Jewish rebellion the man who best fits this bill is Agrippa II, whose Jewish sympathies are well documented.

Plausible and attractive as Wengst's hypothesis may appear, we must remind ourselves that we are moving in an area where virtually nothing is known. At the beginning of one of his essays, wisely disclaiming certainty, Martyn suggests that 'it would be a valuable practice for the historian to rise each morning saying to himself three times slowly and with emphasis, "I do not know".'[67] Nevertheless a 'may be', even one masquerading as an 'is', often promotes understanding and when it does is to be preferred to a prudent 'don't know'.

[67] *Gospel of John*, p. 92.

Excursus I: The First Edition

Anyone who is convinced (*a*) that the awkward transitions in the Gospel require some explanation and (*b*) that the displacement theory is unsatisfactory must choose between two alternatives: either the evangelist has produced different editions of the Gospel (Brown, Martyn, Lindars) or somebody else, an editor or redactor, has made substantial additions to his work (Schnackenburg, Becker). These two hypotheses are not mutually exclusive, since a final redaction may have been made after extensive revisions on the part of the evangelist himself. This is in fact my own view: I agree with Brown and Martyn, against Lindars, that the appendix, chapter 21, is unlikely to have been composed by the evangelist. In this excursus, however, I am interested only in what, following Lindars, I conceive to be the *first edition* of the Gospel and I shall not concern myself with the problem of how and when the later material was composed or redacted.

If Lindars's theory that there were (at least) two editions of the Fourth Gospel is basically correct, as I believe it to be, it should be possible in principle to suggest what the first edition looked like, to determine, that is to say, its scope and nature. It is important for me to try to do this because the main purpose of the present book is to explain the genesis and elucidate the message of the Gospel when it was first presented to the Johannine group as an authentic record of its faith.

I shall consider Lindars's proposals in turn, starting from what is widely agreed and moving to what is more contentious.

1. *Chapter 21.* Two modern scholars who defend the authenticity of chapter 21 are Minear and Thyen.[1] The great majority, however, continue with good reason to regard it as an appendix and it is unnecessary to repeat the arguments for this view yet again.

2. *Chapters 15–17.* Wellhausen (1910) has won increasing support for his opinion that the farewell discourse originally terminated at the end of chapter 14.[2] His arguments have been tightened

---

[1] H. Thyen, 'Aus der Literatur', *TRu* 42 (1977), 211–70; 'Entwicklungen innerhalb der johanneischen Theologie'; P. S. Minear, 'The Original Function of John 21'.

[2] *Das Evangelium Johannes.*

and improved by subsequent commentators: they do not require further discussion here. Suffice it to say that chapters 15–16 presuppose a very different situation; the community has become a ghetto, and the commandment of faith in chapter 14 (see *infra*, Chapter 12) has been replaced by a love commandment that is markedly less universal than the 'love your enemies' of the Sermon on the Mount.

3. *Chapter 6.* The present position of this chapter is a notorious crux, difficult not only because of the clear allusion in 7: 23 to the miracle of chapter 5, but also because it supposes improbably rapid and frequent journeys between Galilee and Judaea. Suggestions that rely upon the dislocation hypothesis (such as that of Schnackenburg, who places chapter 6 before chapter 5) all present problems of their own. Lindars's solution, elegant and economic, offers a way out of the impasse. Chapter 6 is a later insertion, placed here, he suggests, because it affords such a good illustration of the concluding assertion of chapter 5, Jesus' claim that Moses 'wrote of me' (5: 46).[3] This view can be supported from internal evidence. A new situation has arisen, where some at least of the disputants appear to come from the ranks of the Christian group itself.

As happens so often, internal dissension is accompanied by a slackening of hostility towards enemies from without. The implacably resentful persecutors of the previous chapter have given way to groups of people divided among themselves. (The word ὄχλος occurs 4 times in this chapter, 8 times in chapter 7, where the controversies belong, as I shall argue in Chapter 8, to an earlier stage in the history of the Johannine group, 7 times in chapters 11–12, and only once elsewhere in the Gospel (5: 13).) They continue to be called οἱ Ἰουδαῖοι (6: 4, 41, 52), but their 'murmuring' (γογγυσμός, v. 41) is prompted more by bewilderment than by a real antagonism. Even if, along with many commentators, we regard vv. 51c–58 as a later insertion attributable to the ecclesiastical redactor, the debate really belongs to inter-church discussion. This is certainly how it appears in the concluding paragraphs of the chapter, where the questions addressed to Jesus come from certain of his disciples (v. 60), who, dissatisfied with his response, proceed to part company with him (v. 66). Raymond Brown has proffered the plausible suggestion 'that here John refers to Jewish Christians who

[3] p. 50.

are no longer to be considered true believers because they do not share John's view of the eucharist'.[4]

4. *Chapter 11.*[5] Compared with what precedes and what follows, the attitude of 'the Jews' in chapter 11 is relatively relaxed and unthreatening, a fact that Lindars recognizes when he alludes to Brown's telling observation that here and in 12: 9, 11 'the Jews' are 'the people of Jerusalem who are favourably disposed to Jesus'.[6] This feature is an additional argument in support of Lindars's proposal that chapter 11 too should be classed among the supplementary material that did not figure in the first edition. Here the argument is more intricate, since Lindars also suggests that the evangelist rearranged some of his material in order to accommodate the new episodes (to which the sequel to the Lazarus story in 11: 54–7 and the comment in 12: 9–11 also belong). The original order, he believes, following upon chapter 10, was this: the triumphal entry (12: 12–19); the cleansing of the Temple (2: 13–22); and the priests' plot (11: 47–53). The story of the Greeks (12: 20–6), the sayings grouped round the last passion prediction (12: 27–36a), and the first of the two epilogues (12: 37–43), immediately preceded by the anointing at Bethany (12: 1–8), are left in place, but Lindars is inclined to think that the second epilogue (12: 44–50) is a subsequent addition.

Lindars's case is a persuasive one. The suggestion that the temple episode has been displaced is not new. W. Wilkens,[7] like Lindars, combined it with the hypothesis of a second edition, and if the Lazarus episode is omitted some suggestion of this kind is required to account for the priests' hurried consultation, followed as it is by an immediate decision to secure Jesus' execution. This decision is much easier to understand if the Synoptic order is preferred, since the raising of Lazarus, unlike the cleansing in the Temple, has no overtly political overtones that might account for the sudden urgency to get Jesus out of the way. Thus, although the present position of the temple episode suits John's purposes quite well, one can scarcely believe that this is where he found it in his source.

---

[4] *Community,* p. 74.

[5] Brown (pp. xxxvii, 427) holds that chs. 11–12 as a whole belong to the second edition, but the arguments with which he supports this view hold for the Lazarus episode only, plus a few verses in ch. 12. It is improbable that any edition of the Gospel was published without some form of transition between the public ministry and the passion narrative.

[6] p. 381; cf. Brown, p. 428.   [7] *Entstehungsgeschichte.*

Lindars remarks concerning the end of chapter 11 that '11: 54 is similar to 7: 1 just as 11: 55–57 corresponds with 7: 2–13, implying that the comparatively independent story of 11: 1–44 has been inserted subsequently, just like the story of chapter 6; in fact, 11: 54 makes a suitable continuation from 10: 42.'[8] Actually, 11: 54 follows on much more naturally from 10: 39. The strange little comment concerning John the Baptist in 10: 40–2 ('John did no signs') is probably another editorial insertion,[9] made easier by the gap that now separates the natural ending to the account of Jesus' public career ('Again they tried to arrest him, but he escaped from their hands') from the transition passage, 11: 54–7, which moves the story on to the passion narrative. The very last verse of the chapter, 11: 57, implying as it does that the decision to have Jesus killed had already been taken, belongs to the second edition. In the first edition, 11: 56 may have been followed by 12: 12, which also alludes to 'the feast'. It is possible, however, that the last three verses of chapter 11 all belong to the later edition, because the connotation of 'the Jews' in 11: 55 is the relatively favourable one that we have seen to be typical of the Lazarus episode.

There is also much to be said for the suggestion that the anointing at Bethany originally belonged more or less where Mark places it, immediately before the Last Supper. The end of chapter 11 finds Jesus in 'a town called Ephraim' not far from the desert (11: 54). From the Ephraim we know, near Bethel, there is no need to pass through Bethany, the location of the anointing, in order to get to Jerusalem. Traditionally, however, Jesus started his final journey to Jerusalem from Bethany (Mark 11: 1; Luke 19: 29), which may help to account for the present position of the story in the Fourth Gospel. Read immediately before John's account of the Last Supper, the anointing of Jesus' feet reflects and anticipates Jesus' action in washing the feet of his disciples. Here again John probably knew the

---

[8] p. 381.

[9] See E. Bammel, "John did no miracle", pp. 181–202. Bammel plausibly regards 10: 40–2 as a fragment of ancient tradition stemming from the period in which the Christian group was being challenged about its credentials by the Pharisees within the community: 'Its contents, based on a Jewish scheme, reflect the Christian–Jewish discussion rather than the Christian–Baptist one' (p. 200). He adds that the passage gives the evangelist 'the opportunity to move Christ to a place where he is to receive the call to set out for Bethany and the events of the passion story' (p. 201)—referring, of course, to the anguished plea of Martha and Mary on behalf of their sick brother (11: 1–3). Thus 10: 40–2 belongs, by editorial decision, to what follows rather than to what precedes.

sequence of events found in Mark, where the anointing is seen as a symbolic anticipation of Jesus' burial (14: 8). 'Verbal links between 12: 4–6 and 13: 29,' adds Lindars, 'indicate that John intends the reader to gain an insight into the character of Judas, which will help to account for the theme of his treachery which dominates the last supper.'[10] If the two episodes were originally contiguous these verbal links would have been more striking and effective. As for the verbal reminiscences of the other versions, especially the νάρδος πιστική (12: 3) that John shares with Mark 14: 3 and the πολύτιμος, reminiscent of the βαρύτιμος in Matt. 26: 7, we may explain them along with Lindars as the result of subsequent contamination of the text.[11]

What about the editorial comments, 11: 45 f.; 12: 1b, 2b, 9–11, 17 f., which, according to Lindars, 'can easily be removed without damage to the rest of the material'?[12] In Mark's version the woman who does the anointing has no name, quite paradoxically in view of the prophecy that 'what she has done will be told in memory of her' (14: 9). It is likely, therefore, that the name, along with other modifications identifying her as Mary, the sister of Lazarus, was added by John. The comment in 11: 45 f. is puzzling inasmuch as it alludes to the Pharisees alone. This, I think, is a slip, for without the active collaboration of the priests mentioned in the following verse, 11: 47, the Pharisees had no power to take decisions involving life and death. Elsewhere 'the chief priests and Pharisees' act in collusion, and it may be that the three verses that now conclude the first epilogue (12: 41–3) are a late insertion as well.

The half-verse that immediately precedes the first epilogue, 'With these words Jesus went out and hid from them' (12: 36b), must be retained. It provides an explicit and formal conclusion to the story of Jesus' public career, but would be equally appropriate following upon the anointing scene, where it would reinforce the allusions to the Last Supper by providing a dramatically effective counterpart to the departure of Judas.

5. *Further problem sayings.* Certain passages ascribed by Becker[13]

---

[10] p. 415.

[11] p. 414. But it is just as likely that these phrases simply stuck in the evangelist's memory. Not long ago I saw Boucicault's play, *The Shaughraun*. All that I can remember of it is a rough outline of the plot and a single line: the eponymous hero, 'the vagabond', urged to give up drinking, stipulates that he be allowed 'a thimbleful [of whiskey] a day—to take the cruelty out of the water'.

[12] p. 381.   [13] p. 35.

to the ecclesiastical redactor (3: 31–6; 10: 1–18) may also proceed from a later, more reflective stage of the evangelist's own composition. Like other sections of the Gospel for which Becker invokes this hypothesis, notably chapters 15–16, the peculiarities of these passages are better accounted for by the changing circumstances of the community. Both stylistically and theologically they are characteristic of the fourth evangelist. One has only to compare them in both respects with the First Letter to see how much greater the differences have to be before one can confidently speak of a different writer. Chapter 17 is much harder to categorize; here there are strong arguments in support of both positions, and I prefer to leave this question open.

6

DUALISM

In the previous chapter the enquiry into the nature and circumstances of the Johannine community illuminated, as was to be expected, our understanding of its book. In the present chapter we shall again be considering certain aspects and themes of the book at some depth, but focusing now less upon the community for which it was written than upon the ideas of the man who wrote it. Furthermore, whereas hitherto we have been reconstructing the genesis of the Gospel by speculating upon the relations between the community and the synagogue, especially their disagreements, we shall now be investigating patterns of thought that the evangelist shared with many of his contemporaries—if not with the leaders of the synagogue, then with the circles in which he lived and moved before deciding to become a follower of Jesus.

All early Christians were converts and John was no exception. Bultmann thought that he was a Gnostic; I believe he is more likely to have been an Essene, simply because this is the easiest and most convenient explanation of the dualism that is such a notable characteristic of his thought and marks off his Gospel from the other three. This suggestion is not new, but we shall see that many of its early advocates put it forward rather half-heartedly.[1]

Like the Gospel itself, Johannine dualism had a history. We may distinguish three phases: (1) the signs source, virtually free of dualistic influence; (2) the first edition, full of all kinds of dualistic oppositions; (3) the late period, characterized by what Jürgen Becker calls a 'churchified dualism' (*verkirchlichter Dualismus*).[2] In this chapter I shall be chiefly concerned with the first edition, whose

---

[1] E.g. Brown, Charlesworth, Schnackenburg.

[2] p. 151. Becker is surely right about this, as he is about the first, pre-Gospel stage. Ch. 15, at least from v. 18 on, marks an escalation of the antagonism between the community and the world: 'If you were of the world, the world would love its own; but because you are not of the world, but I chose you out of the world, therefore the world hates you' (15: 19). In the next verse there is an unobtrusive shift from singular

[*cont. on p. 206*]

distinctive dualism we may reasonably ascribe to the Johannine prophet. Although the Prologue may conceivably have been added later it will be included in this survey because its ideas, corresponding so closely to those of the evangelist himself, accord better with this period than with the one following.

In searching for illustrations of dualism in contemporary Jewish thought I have ranged quite widely but put special emphasis upon the Dead Sea Scrolls. Such a procedure calls for no particular justification. It has the great advantage that we know ourselves to be dealing with documents that were certainly composed before the Gospel itself. Just how widely available these documents were we have no means of knowing. At least some of them must have been in the libraries of other Essenian communities besides that of Qumran, and for the hypothesis that I shall be putting forward this is all that is required.[3]

I. THE WORLD

The easiest point of entry into the subject of this chapter is a concept peculiar to the Fourth Gospel—that of the world. This is not a simple concept. On the contrary, there are two quite distinct oppositions implied by the term κόσμος, and although these may coincide they

to plural: 'If *they* persecuted me they will persecute you' (15: 20), a persecution, as we learn in the next chapter, that will take the form of expulsion from the synagogues and of a threat of assassination (16: 2). The opposition of 'the Jews', Jesus' adversaries in the first half of the Gospel, and implicitly the community's adversaries too, has now been hardened into what looks suspiciously like an essential, metaphysical dualism. This, however, is something new, and is to be explained by the changed situation of the Johannine group, no longer part of the Jewish community but a small enclave in a predominantly hostile environment. The weakest part of Becker's thesis concerns the passage from a non-dualistic signs source to a Qumran-type dualism that preceded the arrival of the evangelist in the community. It is not possible to argue convincingly for a separate phase of ethical determinism on the basis of three verses, 3: 19–21. Both in his commentary and in his earlier article, 'Beobachtungen zum Dualismus', Becker relies too heavily on the exegesis of a few carefully selected passages and pays no attention at all to the important motif of judgement. See also *infra*, n. 19.

[3] It would have been possible to have made much more extensive use of *The Testaments of the Twelve Patriarchs*, as O. Böcher does in his excellent book *Der Johanneische Dualismus im Zusammenhang des nachbiblischen Judentums*. In spite of M.de Jonge's contention that these have to be regarded as essentially Christian documents, many of their leading ideas, including the all-pervasive doctrine of the two spirits, are certainly Jewish. Nevertheless, Böcher's contention that the *Testaments* are 'the oldest set of texts after the Old Testament itself' (p. 14) is unwarranted.

also differ significantly. Sometimes ὁ κόσμος appears to mean earth as opposed to heaven, down below as opposed to up above. Thus Jesus can say of his disciples: 'they are not of the world, even as I am not of the world' (17: 16) and inform Pilate that his kingdom is 'not of this world' (18: 36). In these two instances ἐκ of ἐκ τοῦ κόσμου indicates the nature of what Jesus confronts; often it expresses origin as well: 'He who is of the earth belongs to the earth ... he who comes from heaven is above all' (3: 31).[4]

This meaning, which implies what one may call a vertical opposition, is also present in the numerous allusions to Jesus' entry into the world: he does not come into the world like the rest of mankind; he arrives *from another place*.[5] But it is to be stressed that the world he enters is, as Bultmann remarks, 'the world of men'[6] or simply 'mankind'.[7] Only in two instances (17: 5, 24) does κόσμος bear the meaning 'cosmos'. The immediate source of this vertical opposition is the relative location of heaven and earth, respectively above and below, something we are in danger of forgetting because it is always simply assumed. We must conclude that without further specification the contrast between heaven and earth or above and below is not, properly speaking, dualistic at all. The gap between heaven and earth is constantly being bridged, sometimes by theophanies, sometimes by angelic or human messengers, prophets, conceived as sent directly from the heavenly court. Jesus himself was the last of these divine emissaries, entering the world with the God-given task of bringing life (3: 16; 10: 10), light (8: 12; 12: 46) and salvation (3: 17; 4: 42; 12: 47). Clearest of all, and surprisingly unequivocal, is the assertion that 'God so loved the world that he gave his only son ...' (3: 16).

Contrasted with this there is a horizontal opposition, which is played out on earth. This is genuinely dualistic, but the dualism is moral or ethical, not cosmological or metaphysical, what Bultmann calls a dualism of decision (*Entscheidungsdualismus*).[8] The Prologue

---

[4] See Bultmann, p. 138 n. 1.

[5] J. A. T. Robinson affirms that as applied to Jesus the expression 'to come into the world' is the equivalent of being 'born' or 'born into the world' (16: 21), 'which is applied to Jesus [*where?*] and to any woman's child' (1985, p. 370). This is surely either obtuse or perverse.   [6] p. 54.   [7] 'Eschatology', p. 166.

[8] *Theology*, ii. p. 21. Luise Schottroff, who otherwise offers an uncompromisingly Gnostic interpretation of the Fourth Gospel, endorses Bultmann's view here: *Der Glaubende und die feindliche Welt*, p. 231 n. 3. Many scholars rightly emphasize the incompatibility of Judaism with true Gnosticism: 'We have always to keep in mind
[*cont. on p. 208*]

appears to identify the world with darkness (1: 5, 10) and those who did receive the Logos (1: 12) may be conceived as not belonging to the world at all. Later, in the earliest version of the farewell discourse the unreceptivity of the world towards the spirit of truth (14: 17) follows and matches its response to the Logos (1: 10).[9] One might expect a third opposition also—the temporal opposition between the present world and the world to come. But in fact John nowhere employs the term οὗτος ὁ αἰών, the most usual rendering of the Hebrew הָעוֹלָם הַזֶּה , quite common elsewhere in the New Testament especially in Paul.[10] Its absence in the Fourth Gospel may be due to a resistance on John's part to the temporal implications of the term. Whatever the reason, there is no hint of any temporal connotation in the way he uses it. We cannot add the contrast between the two ages to the two spatial oppositions we have already noted.

2. LIGHT AND DARKNESS

There can be few societies if any in the course of history that have *not* seized upon the contrast between light and dark, night and day, to signify the contrast between good and evil or misery and content. This is an archetypal symbol, rooted in the deepest instinct of the human race. No doubt the firm monotheism of Israel's official faith means that the contrast has less *religious* significance than in some

that gnosticism was a religious phenomenon diametrically opposed to everything Jewish; in fact the God of the Jews was considered by the gnostics as an evil deity' (I. Gruenwald, *Apocalyptic and Merkavah Mysticism*, p. 111); 'What distinguishes a gnostic dualism from all other types (e.g. Platonic or Indian) is that it is essentially *anti-cosmic*: that is, its conception includes an unequivocally negative evaluation of the visible world, together with its creator; it ranks as a kingdom of evil and darkness' (K. Rudolph, *Gnosis*, p. 60). Finally, see S. Pétrement, *Le Dieu séparé, passim*.

[9] Many commentators, including Bultmann, see the term 'his own' (οἱ ἴδιοι) in the following verse as alluding to the whole human race. I side with those who think it refers to the Jews. If this is right, and 1: 11 is designed to narrow the focus from mankind in general to the Jews in particular, then in the Gospel as we have it the focus is enlarged once again in the second version of the farewell discourse. This has the effect of reversing the movement of the Prologue, which is one of descent.

[10] See Matt. 12: 32, where it is explicitly distinguished from ὁ αἰών ὁ μέλλων, the age to come; Mark 10: 30; Luke 16: 8; 20: 34; Rom. 12: 2; 1 Cor. 1: 20; 2: 6, 8; 3: 18; 2 Cor. 4: 4; Eph. 1: 21; the Pastorals prefer ὁ νῦν αἰών (the present age): 1 Tim. 6: 14; 2 Tim. 4: 10; Tit. 2: 12. For John's preferred expression ὁ κόσμος οὗτος, see 8: 23; 9: 39; 11: 9; 12: 25, 31; 13: 1; 16: 11; 18: 36; 1 John 4: 17. Cf. Bultmann, p. 340 n. 1.

other cultures, for after all God created darkness as well as light, evil
as well as good (Isa. 45: 7). Nevertheless Amos' question retains its
anguish: 'Is not the day of the Lord darkness and not light, and
gloom with no brightness in it?' (Amos 5: 20).

The symbolism is found occasionally in the Synoptic tradition,[11]
not surprisingly in view of its universality; but in John its importance
is evident from the outset. In the Prologue (which surely emanates
from the Johannine school even if it is not the work of the evangelist
himself) the Logos is identified with the light of revelation that shines
in the darkness: 'but the darkness did not overcome it' (1: 5). It is an
amazing statement, setting out the fundamental opposition to God's
revelatory plan in the starkest possible terms. And the sense of
conflict is heightened a few verses later, where the brooding hostility
of darkness is taken up by the world: 'and the world did not
recognize him' (1: 10). Darkness is virtually identified with the world
(the human adversaries of the Logos) and this identification is what
establishes the basic symbolic pattern of the Gospel. The opposition
therefore does have a certain cosmic dimension—the light is
encompassed by darkness—but the light is the light of revelation
and is not distinct from the Logos even in his human form. There is
no question of light *succeeding* darkness here. The light of revelation
accompanies the existence of the human race; indeed it *is* 'the life of
men' (1: 4) and the present tense in v. 5 ($\varphi\alpha\acute{\iota}\nu\epsilon\iota$), 'shines', which has
puzzled many commentators, does not indicate the bright start of a
new age, but a continuous illumination that finally flames out in the
incarnation of the Logos.[12]

Later in the Gospel the same idea is taken up in one of the famous 'I
am' sayings: 'I am the light of the world; he who follows me will not
walk in darkness, but will have the light of life' (8: 12). Bultmann

---

[11] Cf. Mark 13: 24 and parallels: one sign of the coming of the end will be the
darkening of the sun. Even where there is a deliberate reversal of the natural
symbolism the new meaning rises as a descant over a basso ostinato heard strongly by
the inner ear. The reversal is surprisingly widespread. A good instance is Ps. 139:11,
where the paradox is particularly vivid in the rendering of the Vulgate, *nox illuminatio
mea*, a phrase that made a profound impression upon John of the Cross; similar are
Ruysbroek's *doncker claer* ('dark radiance') and Henry Vaughan's 'deep but dazzling
darkness'. Literary examples range from *Romeo and Juliet* and Wagner's *Tristan und
Isolde* to titles of books by Arthur Koestler and William Golding, *Darkness at Noon* and
Darkness Visible (see too the 'black lightning' that is such an important symbol in
Pincher Martin). Bultmann (p. 43 n. 2) draws attention to Denys the Areopagite (*de
myst. theol.* 1 and 2); also to Novalis and Rilke.

[12] For a fuller version of this reading of the Prologue see Ashton, 'Transformation'.

comments on this verse: 'The decisive feature is not the universality but the dualism; for without the revelation the world is in darkness.'[13] This is true up to a point, for as we have seen, John's view of the world is often negative and pessimistic. On the other hand, the entry of light into the world must at least partially dispel the darkness: the dualism is not absolute. The picture offered by the Gospel is one of a light shining in the darkness and attracting men by its radiance. Drawn to the source of light they come to attach themselves to it, extending and magnifying it and thereby limiting still further the domain of darkness: 'While you have the light,' Jesus tells his followers, 'believe in the light, that you may become sons of the light' (12: 36). The community becomes conscious that in assuming Jesus' mission, sent into the world as he was, it takes on both his pains and his responsibilities.

The ambivalence of John's view of the world is to be explained by the fact that though in darkness it is potentially lightsome. The members of the Johannine group originally belonged to a Jewish community whose leaders' initial indifference to Jesus' message had developed into open hostility. The elliptical brevity of the Prologue can be misleading: 'his own people received him not ... But to all who did receive him ...' (1: 12). What this verse alludes to, however obliquely, is conversion, the kind of conversion found in the ninth chapter of the Gospel, which tells how one man's eyes are opened to the truth. The sad consequence of this conversion, as the evangelist sees it, is further hostility on the part of the Jews, who become increasingly entrenched in their blindness. In his rearrangement of the sequence of the Gospel Bultmann underlines the significance of Jesus' claim to be the light of the world by placing it immediately *after* this episode. But whatever its rightful place the meaning is unaltered.

Accordingly, what looks like and has often been interpreted as a cosmological dualism close to Gnosticism is really a moral dualism: the good (in this case those who accept the revelation of Jesus) versus the wicked (those who reject that revelation—'the Jews' or 'the world'). This polarization (regularly accompanied and supported by the light/darkness symbolism) is very common in the sectarian literature of the period. Just how easy it is to pass from an apparently cosmic dualism to a moral dualism may be seen from a rabbinic

---

[13] p. 343.

comment on the first page of Genesis: 'and God divided the light from the darkness, i.e. the works of the righteous from the works of the wicked, "and God called the light Day" this refers to the works of the righteous; "and darkness he called Night"; this is the works of the wicked' (*Gen. Rab.* 3: 8).[14] This a late passage, but a similar moral dualism pervades virtually the whole of the Old Testament, especially the Psalms.

Nevertheless the division of mankind into good and bad becomes more noticeable and more extreme in the writings of the Second Temple era that emanate from circles outside the establishment. Characteristic is the separation of the wicked from the righteous at the end of time (something to be discussed in a subsequent section under the heading 'Judgement'). In view of Israel's profound and pervasive sense of divine election we might expect the wicked to be identified with the Gentiles. This happens quite frequently, the Qumran War Scroll being a particularly clear example (cf. also *Pss. Sol.* 3: 3–8; 15: 4–13; *1 Enoch* 90: 18). The appellation 'righteous' is also quite commonly reserved for the members of the writer's own sect; in that case the wicked are either their special enemies or even conceivably the rest of the human race. The so-called Epistle of Enoch (*1 Enoch* 91–108), written probably towards the beginning of the second century, labours the point with wearisome insistence from beginning to end: 'And the righteous man will rise from sleep ... and he will live in goodness and righteousness and will walk in eternal light. And sins will be destroyed in darkness for ever and from that day will never be seen' (92: 3–5). The conclusion is similar: 'And they will see those who were born in darkness thrown into darkness, while the righteous shine. And the sinners will cry out as they see them shining, but they themselves will go where the days and times have been written down for them' (108: 14–15).[15] An isolated passage from Qumran exhibits very clearly the rich blend of eschatological and moral dualism that makes it so difficult to insist

---

[14] Cited by Odeberg, p. 140. cf. *2 Enoch* 30: 14 f.; *Barn.* 18: 1–2.

[15] D. Hill, 'Dikaioi', traces the use of the term δικαίοι in Matthew back to *1 Enoch*, e.g. 11: 1; 82: 4, and Qumran. He suggests reading the meaning 'sons of righteousness' into the phrase 'sons of Zadok' in CD 4: 2 f., a midrashic exposition of Ezek. 44: 15; and proposes that the same term in 1QS 5: 2 and 1QSa 1: 2, 24; 2: 3 refers to a leading group within the community, priests as distinct from laity. Many of the passages he cites from *1 Enoch* are from the Parables section, which is probably the latest part of the collection. It is surprising that he does not refer to the *Epistle of Enoch*. To his list could be added 1: 7–8; 5: 6–9; 27: 2–3; 41: 8; 45: 6; 48: 6; 50: 2; 53: 2–7; 81: 7–9. See too *Apoc. Abr.* 13: 10 f.; 29: 18 f.; *T. Abr.* 11; 13: 5; 17: 11.

upon the kind of distinction that was later to become so important in Western philosophy:

And this shall be the sign for you that these things should come to pass. When the breed of iniquity is imprisoned, wickedness shall then be banished by righteousness as darkness is banished by the light. As smoke clears and is no more, so shall wickedness perish for ever and righteousness be revealed like a sun governing the world. All who cleave to the mysteries of sin shall be no more; knowledge shall fill the world and folly shall exist no longer. (1Q 27. 1: 5–7)[16]

One senses in these passages vindictiveness as well as hope; the writers already know who the righteous are and who the impious. The threat of divine punishment is not employed here, as it would be later in certain Christian circles (splendidly satirized in Joyce's *Portrait of the Artist*), to terrorize the faithful into subservient rectitude. Nor is the judgement preceded by an arbitrary decision on the part of God to single out certain chosen souls, whatever their subsequent behaviour, for final salvation (a doctrine savagely lampooned in James Hogg's *Confessions of a Justified Sinner*). Rather what we have here is a way of assuring the members of the writer's own sect that in spite of all appearances they are really on the winning side. The struggle between the forces of good and the forces of evil can have only one outcome: the good will prevail. So Jesus too says of the evil 'ruler of this world' that 'he has no power over me' (14: 30).

Less picturesque than the opposition between light and darkness, but closely associated with it, is the contrast between truth and falsehood. This is to be expected. The writings under discussion are the work of *sects*, groups who have either broken away from the religious establishment like the covenanters at Qumran, or else remain centres of dissent within it. They are therefore what Peter Berger[17] calls cognitive minorities: their discontent finds expression in the burning conviction that they and they alone possess the truth. They may have good reasons for their dissatisfaction; in any event they need to justify it to themselves and if possible to others also on rational grounds. Inevitably too their benefits will reinforce and be

---

[16] This passage shows how easily the ostensibly sapiential distinction between knowledge and folly coheres with the moral distinction between good and bad. The Book of Wisdom itself evinces a clear moral dualism; and many apocalyptic writings, e.g. Daniel and 4 *Ezra*, attest to the pervasive influence of wisdom motifs.

[17] *A Rumour of Angels*, p. 18.

reinforced by their sense of isolation. Given the right conditions they may eventually become strong and numerous enough to go it alone; if so, their fear of being swamped or engulfed by the establishment is likely to fade, and with it the strength of their beliefs. This is a familiar pattern. If, on the other hand, the conditions are *not* right, or if the group somehow needs enemies for its faith to survive, then the outcome may be different, for its sense of identity is buttressed by its fears and may well collapse without them. A group of this kind, seeing itself in the nature of the case as a persecuted minority, will require some assurance that things will come right in the end. At the same time it will retain a powerful conviction of being on the side of truth as well as on that of righteousness.

What would eventually have become of the Qumran sectarians had they not fallen victim to the war against Rome we do not know; they themselves certainly looked forward to victory rather than to integration or compromise.

Their dualism is nowhere more fully expressed than in the long passage of the Community Rule (1QS 3: 13–4: 26) which sets out the basic theological beliefs of the group. Since the parallels between this passage and the Fourth Gospel have been fully explored by James H. Charlesworth[18] and are alluded to in every recent commentary, there is no need to re-examine them here. The covenanters are 'the sons of light' (1QS 1: 9; 2: 16; 3: 13 etc.; 1QM 1: 9 etc.), guided by 'the prince of lights' (1QS 3: 20) in their struggle against 'the sons of darkness' (1QS 1: 10 etc.; 1QM 1: 7 etc.), who are in their turn supported by 'the angel of darkness' (1QS 3: 20 f.). The curious phrase 'do the truth' is also found at Qumran (1QS 1: 5; 5: 3; 8: 2). More eloquent than any comment is the text itself. Here are two short samples:

He, the God of Knowledge (אל הדעות) has created man to govern the world (תבל) and has appointed for him two spirits in which to walk until the time of his visitation: the spirits of truth and the spirit of falsehood (עול). Those born of truth (תולדות האמת) spring from a fountain of light, but those born of falsehood spring from a source of darkness. All the children of righteousness (בני צדק) are ruled by the Prince of Light [or Lights: שר אורים] and walk in the ways of light; but all the children of falsehood are ruled by the Angel of Darkness and walk in the ways of darkness. (1QS 3: 17–21)

---

[18] 'A Critical Comparison of the Dualism in 1QS 3: 13–4: 26 and the "Dualism" Contained in the Gospel of John.' The version of this article published in *John and Qumran* (1972) differs slightly from the original version in *NTS* 10.

Truth abhors the works of falsehood, and falsehood hates all the ways of truth. And their struggle is fierce for they do not walk together. But in the mysteries of his understanding, and in his glorious wisdom, God has ordained an end for falsehood, and at the time of his visitation he will destroy it for ever. (4: 17–19)[19]

‾In John the struggle between truth and falsehood is equally bitter and the upshot equally certain. The symbolism of light and truth is exploited to greater effect than at Qumran, for Jesus is identified not only as the light of the world (8: 12) but also as the truth (14: 6). For John the main task of the 'spirit of truth' will be to recall to his disciples' minds the words of Jesus and to lead them into all truth (14: 26; 16: 13). But if there is both a depth and a deftness in the Fourth Gospel that surpasses anything in the Dead Sea Scrolls, we are none the less forced to recognize an affinity of thought and feeling.

3. LIFE

The Synoptic Gospels have been left on one side thus far because the polar opposites that we have been considering up to now have relatively little place in them. But life (and implicitly death) is different. The richness of this concept in the Johannine writings is due to the complexity of the traditions it reflects. To begin with it virtually replaces the proclamation of the kingdom as the object of the gospel promise; and in the single context in which this does occur, the dialogue with Nicodemus, the real topic of discussion is rebirth from on high, soon to be reinterpreted in John's character-

---

[19] Becker compares this extract from the Community Rule with John 3: 19–21: 'and men loved darkness rather than light because their deeds were evil. For everyone who does evil hates the light, and does not come into the light, lest his deeds be exposed . . .'. He qualifies the dualism of this passage, quite wrongly, as 'prädestinationisch-ethisch' ('Beobachtungen', p. 79). In his commentary he emends this to 'deterministisch-ethisch' (p. 149). But whatever determinism is present here is *self*-determinism. This sharply differentiates it from the Community Rule, which does indeed suggest that mankind is divided into good and bad by the prevenient will of its creator. Both passages, however, are embedded in contexts that appear to contradict them. The varied instructions that constitute the bulk of the Community Rule imply the possibility of free, i.e. undetermined, human decisions. As for the Gospel, the good are generally distinguished from the bad not by their earlier moral choices but by their response to the message of Jesus. To argue, as Becker does, that 3: 19–21 is representative of one particular stage of the Johannine community's dualistic thinking is to build a rather tall theory on a very narrow base.

istic fashion as ζωὴ αἰώνιος, a term usually translated as 'eternal life'. So where does this term come from and why does John select it to denote the fruits of the gospel message?

Its immediate source is the Synoptic tradition. Jesus speaks of entering into life and entering into the kingdom in a passage where the two expressions are clearly equivalent: 'it is better for you to *enter life* maimed than with two hands to go to hell ... it is better for you to *enter the kingdom of God* with one eye than with two eyes to be thrown into hell' (Mark 9: 43, 47). Just how close the two concepts are may be seen from Matthew's adaptation of this passage, for he actually replaces Mark's 'kingdom of God' with 'life' (18: 9). There is also the story of the man anxious to know what to do in order to '*inherit eternal life*' (Mark 10: 17). To his disappointment he is told to get rid of his wealth; whereupon 'he went away sorrowful, for he had great possessions'. At this Jesus drove the lesson home to his disciples: 'How hard it will be for those who have riches to *enter the kingdom of God*' (Mark 10: 22 f.; cf. Matt. 19: 24; Luke 18: 24).

The passage that points most strongly to John's dependence upon the Synoptic tradition is this: 'He who loves his soul (τὴν ψυχὴν αὐτοῦ) loses it and he who hates his soul in this world (ἐν τῷ κόσμῳ τουτῷ) will keep it for eternal life (εἰς ζωὴν αἰώνιον)' (John 12: 25).[20] Now this is an adaptation of a saying found, with slight variations, in all three Synoptic Gospels: Mark 8: 35; Matt. 10: 39; 16: 25; Luke 9: 24; 17: 33. But John has made a significant advance by introducing his own special term, ζωὴ αἰώνιος, into the saying. As Dodd remarks, he alone 'has given it a form which obviously alludes to the Jewish antithesis of the two ages: he who hates his soul בָּעוֹלָם הַזֶּה (in this world/age) will keep it לְעוֹלָם הַבָּא (for the world/age to come) and consequently will possess חַיֵּי הָעוֹלָם הַבָּא (the life of the age to come).'[21] If Dodd is right then John has made two changes, first in distinguishing between ψυχή and ζωή and secondly in selecting the term κόσμος, in which the spatial or local sense predominates, rather than αἰών (age), which preserves the temporal meaning of the classical Hebrew עוֹלם.[22] Nevertheless John continues to attach an

---

[20] Unfortunately English is unable to preserve the distinction between natural and supernatural life. In this context ψυχή means 'self', as its Syriac equivalent ܢܦܫ regularly does.   [21] p. 146.

[22] Schnackenburg (ii, p. 521 n. 5) says of Dodd's suggestion that ζωὴ αἰώνιος in John is connected with the Jewish idea of the life of the age to come that 'it can hardly be right', but he offers no argument. In fact the suggestion that the Aramaic לְעָלַם

[cont. on p. 216]

eschatological dimension to 'life', as is proved by the way in which he opposes it to the traditionally eschatological 'wrath of God': 'He who believes in the Son has ζωὴ αἰώνιος; he who does not obey the Son shall not see life, but the wrath of God rests upon him' (John 3: 36). (Paul establishes an even starker contrast between righteousness (δικαιοσύνη) and the wrath of God when he summarizes his gospel at the beginning of Romans (1: 17).)

John sees ζωὴ αἰώνιος, then, as a present possession. In the *Psalms of Solomon* (a work in which, incidentally, the eschatological force of the term 'kingdom of God' is especially evident) the meaning is different: 'But they that fear the Lord shall rise to eternal life (εἰς ζωὴν αἰώνιον) and their life (ζωή) shall be in the light of the Lord and shall never again fail' (*Pss. Sol.* 3: 12). The 'sons of truth' at Qumran are promised both 'abundant peace with long life' and 'eternal joy with life for ever' (בחיי נצח), plus 'a crown of glory and a robe of majesty in eternal light' (באור עולמים) (1QS 4: 6–8).[23] The elect in *1 Enoch* are to have 'light, joy and peace, and inherit the earth'; once wisdom is given to them 'they will all live' (*1 Enoch* 5: 7–8; cf. Matt. 5: 5). In the Parables section too we are told that 'the righteous will be in the light of the sun, and the chosen in the light of eternal life; and there will be no end to the days of their life' (*1 Enoch* 58: 3).

In these passages eternity undoubtedly includes the notion of endlessness, but also (particularly at Qumran) a special quality of life peculiar to the new age. It is this special quality—not endlessness—that is suggested by John's term ζωὴ αἰώνιος, which might therefore be translated 'the life of the new age'. In none of the passages quoted,

---

might be an abbreviation of לְעָלְמָא דְאָתֵי was made as long ago as 1898 by G. Dalman in *Die Worte Jesu*, pp. 121 f. The first occurrence of the Hebrew equivalent of ζωὴ αἰώνιος is in Dan. 12: 2. 'And many of those who sleep in the ground of dust shall awake, some to everlasting life (לְחַיֵּי עוֹלָם), and some to reproach, to everlasting abhorrence (לְדִרְאוֹן עוֹלָם).' The word עולם is a noun. There are relatively few adjectives in classical Hebrew, and nouns are often employed to qualify a preceding noun. ('Holy Spirit', literally translated from Hebrew, is 'the spirit of holiness, πνεῦμα ἁγιωσύνης (cf. Rom. 1: 4).) עוֹלָם signifies either the remote past or the distant future; but it can also mean 'perpetuity'. In the latter case it is often hard to know whether this is thought of as never-ending, i.e. eternal, or simply as of indefinite duration. One must let oneself be guided by the context. The Daniel passage appears to imply both *another age* and *forever*.

[23] The traditional biblical promise of *long* life is combined remarkably easily with the seemingly very different promise of *eternal* life. The transition is assisted by the ambiguity of עוֹלָם, as the notion of indefinite duration slips into that of perpetuity. Did God really, as the RSV translation of Ps. 21: 5 implies, promise the king 'length of days for ever and ever'? (See previous note.)

including those from the Synoptic Gospels, is there any difficulty in thinking of a life that, in the words of *Pss. Sol.* 3: 12, 'will never fail' (οὐκ ἐκλείψει ἔτι). But once transferred to this world (and the present age) life has become a *symbol*, and if one insists on retaining the rendering 'eternal', which is what αἰώνιος always means in secular Greek, then 'eternal life' can only be a *metaphor*. The new life enjoyed by the faithful is more than ordinary physical existence: it is the life of faith. Christians are no more immune from physical death than other folk.[24] But the benefits that accrue to them from their acceptance of the message of Jesus are, for this evangelist, best symbolized by *life* and all that is associated with it; the term αἰώνιος indicates its radical difference from natural life. Once this is understood it matters little whether the word is taken metaphorically and translated as 'eternal' or given an alternative rendering (this after all is where the logic of Dodd's argument leads) so as to suggest a different *kind* of life—'the life of the new age'.[25] Used as a complementary adjective attached to ζωή, the term αἰώνιος does not *describe* life, nor does it indicate that this new life differs from ordinary human life in extent, not, at any rate, *merely* in extent. Another term that serves equally well to convey the same idea and found frequently in the Odes of Solomon is 'immortal' or 'deathless' life (ܚܝܐ ܕܠܐ ܡܝܬܐ): 'Immortal life rose up in the land of the Lord, and it became known to his faithful ones, and was given unsparingly to those who trust in him' (15: 10; cf. 28: 6; 31: 7; 38: 3; 40: 5). A life that is not subject to death differs from natural life in essence, not just in duration. Conceptually the *Odes* and the Gospel are nowhere closer than in the way they envisage the believer's participation in

---

[24] It just might occur to an attentive reader of the words οὐ μὴ ἀποθάνῃ εἰς τὸν αἰῶνα (John 11: 26) that αἰών, like αἰώνιος, is used metaphorically. But the English ('shall never die') is harder than the Greek. One must sympathize with the correspondent in the pages of *Theology*, 89 (1986), pp. 383 f., who suggests substituting 'shall not die eternally' as a way of alleviating the perplexity of the bereaved when they hear the words 'shall never die' read out over the coffin of a loved one. But 'eternally' too must be construed as a metaphor.

[25] It has been suggested that there is something of the same idea at Qumran, especially in the hymnic conclusion of the Community Rule (1QS 10: 9–11: 22) and in parts of the Thanksgiving Scroll: 1QH 3: 19, 36; 11: 13–14, 15–35; 15. The first to argue this was H.-W. Kuhn in *Enderwartung und gegenwärtiges Heil*. He has been followed by G. W. E. Nickelsburg, *Resurrection, Immortality and Eternal Life*, 152–6; J. J. Collins, 'Apocalyptic Eschatology'; D. Aune, *Cultic Setting*, 29–44. All are guilty, it seems to me, of misapplying theological categories that simply have no place in the Qumran community. Earlier and better than all these is J. Licht, 'The Doctrine of the Thanksgiving Scroll'.

the life of faith: 'All his children will praise the Lord, and they will receive the truth of his faith. ... We live in the Lord by his grace, and we receive life through his Messiah' (41: 1, 3).

Lying behind the eternal life of the Fourth Gospel, therefore, and the immortal life of the *Odes of Solomon* is not just a profound faith in God as the author of life but the very different belief that God would ultimately 'swallow up death for ever' (Isa. 25: 8), a belief that would later find orthodox expression in the prayer of the Eighteen Benedictions: 'may you be praised, Lord, you who give life to the dead'. (Eventually this prayer came to be recited three time a day: *m. Ber.* 3: 3; 4: 1.)[26]

All the eschatological and dualistic implications that could be drawn from such a faith are prominent in a passage from the *Testament of Asher*: 'Death succeeds to life, dishonour to glory, night to day, and darkness to light; but the universe is subject to the day, and darkness to light; and so death is confronted by eternal life (τὸν θάνατον ἡ αἰώνιος ζωὴ ἀναμένει)' (*T. Asher* 5: 2).[27] The same idea occurs in Joseph's beautiful prayer for Aseneth:

> Lord God of my father Israel
> the Most High, the Powerful One of Jacob,
> who gave life to all (things)
> and called (them) from the darkness to the light,
> and from the error to the truth,
> You, Lord, bless this virgin,
> and renew her by your spirit
> and make her alive again by your life.   (*Jos. As.* 8: 9)

By now it should be clear that John has two sources for his notion of ζωὴ αἰώνιος: first Jewish eschatology, from which he derives his concept of a life that transcends human life as we know it; and secondly the Synoptic tradition, which allows him to replace the preaching of the kingdom by a term more suggestive of the benefits that follow upon the acceptance of the gospel. In the symbolic

---

[26] Paul says in his speech before Felix in Acts 24 that he shared his belief in a general resurrection with the Pharisees. The view of Josephus is a good deal less clear (*AJ* xviii. 14; *BJ* ii. 163). According to G. F. Moore it was 'the primary eschatological doctrine of Judaism' (*Judaism*, ii, p. 379). For extended discussions see Str.–B. iv. 2: 1166–98; Schürer², ii. 539–44, with bibliography.

[27] The meaning of the concluding part of this passage is not entirely clear. De Jonge translates: 'that is why eternal life has to wait for death' (*The Apocryphal Old Testament*, (p. 580). If that is correct, then this conception of eternal life is diametrically opposed to John's insistence that it *precedes* physical death.

structure of the Fourth Gospel, for the most part strikingly interlocking and consistent, the concept of life occupies a central place.[28] Applied to the water that represents revelation (4: 10 f.; 7: 38), the word ζῶν, 'living', has a riddling quality, but like 'bread of life' (6: 35, 48) or 'living bread' (6: 51), which have an identical reference, 'living water' is a particularly appropriate term for what the evangelist sees to be the true source of life—'a spring of water welling up to eternal life' (4: 14). We have already seen how in the prophetic 'I am' sayings Jesus is offering life to all prepared to listen to his message. Bread and water, the staple necessities of life, are natural symbols of supernatural life. Wine, in the context of the fruitfulness hoped and prayed for at a wedding-feast (2: 1–11), fits easily into the same broad symbolic field, as does the suggestion of rebirth attendant upon baptism (3: 1–8). In fact all Jesus' great healing miracles carry with them something of the same idea. In the first of them Jesus promises the royal official at Capernaum, 'Your son will live' (4: 50), whilst the second, the healing of the cripple at the pool (ch. 5), is seen as a fitting occasion for a discourse in which Jesus claims to have been given the power to bestow life. The cure of the blind man symbolizes his allegiance to the life that is light; and the most important sign of all, the raising of Lazarus, is the occasion of Jesus' extraordinary claim that he is in person 'the resurrection and the life' (11: 25).

It should be added that life is conceptually very close to salvation, and the proximity both assists and enriches its symbolic significance in the gospel tradition. In Syriac the same word, ܚܝܐ, means both life and salvation,[29] and a similar ambiguity is not uncommon in the Synoptic Gospels, where σῴζειν, which in classical Greek simply means 'to save', is often used of a physical cure: 'your faith has made you well' (Mark 5: 34; 10: 52; cf. 5: 23, 28; 6: 56). In the Fourth Gospel, told by Jesus that Lazarus is asleep, the disciples reply, 'Lord, if he has fallen asleep he will recover (εἰ κεκοίμηται σωθήσεται)' (John 11: 12): Lazarus will be cured, he will recover, he will live.

Here, in the Lazarus episode, late as it is, lies the clearest indication of the likely origins of John's conception of life. Rising

---

[28] In an otherwise exhaustive discussion of Johannine symbolism R. A. Culpepper (*Anatomy*, pp. 180–98) fails to include life. It is a notable omission, for life is the symbol round which all the others cluster.

[29] This root should be distinguished from ܦܪܩ, which means redemption, saving from.

from the dead, Lazarus symbolizes—though he does not exemplify—the new life that Jesus has come to bring. The link between this life and resurrection had already been noticed in the great discourse of chapter 5: 'For as the Father raises the dead, and gives them life, so also the Son gives life to whom he will' (5: 21). Certainly John evinces little interest in the futuristic eschatology implicit in the doctrine of the resurrection of the dead; nevertheless this is most probably the origin of his own concept of the life of the new age.

The occasion of the fusion of these two ideas is doubtless the resurrection of Jesus. This had had a similar impact upon the thinking of Paul. But Paul never quite existentializes or internalizes the concept of resurrection as he does that of death (Romans 6). This task is left to John.

4. JUDGEMENT

If life is what is promised to those who accept the revelation of Jesus, judgement is what is promised to those who do not. So in this respect the theme of judgement (κρίσις) is simply the obverse of that of life. Judgement is also, however, the process of separating the sheep from the goats, the actual sorting-out whereby believers and unbelievers are placed on opposite sides of the divide. The Greek verb κρίνειν means both 'judge', with the additional connotations of separation and discrimination, and 'condemn'. No English translation can do full justice to this ambiguity, as can be easily perceived by comparing the following two quotations. The first is the most complete statement of the theme found in the Gospel:

For God so loved the world that he gave his only Son, that whoever believes in him should not perish but have eternal life. For God sent the Son into the world, not to condemn the world, but that the world might be saved through him. He who believes in him is not condemned; he who does not believe is condemned already because he has not believed in the name of the only Son of God. And this is the judgement, that the light has come into the world, and men loved darkness rather than the light. (3: 16–19)

In the second, English is forced to use 'judge' instead of 'condemn', but the Greek word is the same:

The Father judges no one, but has given all judgement to the Son, that all may honour the Son, even as they honour the Father. He who does not honour the Son does not honour the Father who sent him. Truly, truly, I say to you, he who hears my word and believes him who sent me, has eternal life; he does not come into judgement but has passed from death to life. (5: 22–4)

Just as eternal life is anticipated in the present existence of the believer, so eternal punishment is anticipated in the present of the unbeliever. John nowhere uses this phrase: unlike the Synoptists, especially Matthew (18: 8; 25: 41, 46), he reserves the term αἰώνιος for the bright side of the divide. Nevertheless the absolute gulf between the two groups is nowhere more emphatically or eloquently conveyed than in passages dominated by the judgement motif:

I have come as light into the world, that whoever believes in me may not remain in darkness. If anyone hears my sayings, and does not keep them, I do not judge him; for I did not come to judge the world but to save the world. He who rejects me and does not receive my sayings has a judge; the word that I have spoken will be his judge on the last day. (12: 46–8)

For John, then, darkness is revealed to be darkness by the coming of the light; men are discovered to belong to the darkness only when they refuse the light or insist, in spite of their blindness, that they are actually sighted: 'If you were blind you would have no guilt; but now that you say, "we see", your guilt remains' (9: 41; cf. 15: 22). So from one perspective the shining of the light *is* a judgement, in so far as it discloses the true nature of darkness; from the other it is left to the men of darkness to condemn themselves.

The theme of judgement is the most important single vehicle of John's ethical dualism and the one where all the others culminate and coincide. Despite its subtlety and profundity it is not hard to grasp—except for one point: the extent to which the evangelist retained a properly eschatological belief in the idea of a final judgement on the last day.[30] Certain passages, including 12: 48, quoted above, suggest that in spite of his conviction that the crucial decision for or against Jesus is made in this world he has not altogether abandoned the belief that there will be a *future* judgement as well.

At this point it is necessary to insert a parenthesis on the meaning of that slippery word 'eschatological', often used, like much jargon,

---

[30] The secondary literature on this vexed question is vast, but does not require to be assessed here since there is virtual unanimity that John's *primary* understanding of judgement is that it attends acceptance or rejection of the message of Jesus.

as a substitute for thought. It was coined as a shorter way of saying 'pertaining to the last days', and this is the sense I wish to retain. In a lucid and penetrating discussion on the modes of prophecy in *Oracles of God*, John Barton allows two main meanings of 'eschatology'; one in which it refers to the belief that the world as we know it will soon come to an end, the other in which it refers to belief in 'an end or goal which will one day arrive and the path towards which passes through various distinct phases or epochs'.[31] He is concerned to stress 'a really crucial difference in mentality between what we may call "imminent" and "non-imminent" eschatology'.[32] Most of the texts with which I am concerned are eschatological in the first sense, but what I want to emphasize is that the word properly refers to the *future*, 'the last days', whether or not the end is expected very soon—within the lifetime, say, of the writer and his readers. In fact it is often very difficult to tell from any particular description of the events of the last days just how soon the writer expects them to occur. The opening of *1 Enoch* furnishes us with a good example of this unclarity:

Concerning the chosen I spoke and uttered a parable concerning them. The Holy and Great One will come out from his dwelling, and the Eternal God will tread from there upon mount Sinai, and he will appear with his host, and will appear in the strength of his power from heaven. And all will be afraid, and the Watchers will shake, and fear and great trembling will seize them unto the ends of the earth. And the high mountains will be shaken, and the high hills will be made low, and will melt like wax before the flame. And the earth will sink and everything that is on the earth will be destroyed, and there will be judgement upon all and upon all the righteous. But for the righteous he will make peace, and he will keep safe the chosen, and mercy will be upon them. They will all belong to God and will prosper and be blessed, and the light of God will shine upon them. And behold! He comes with ten thousand holy ones to execute judgement upon them, and to destroy the impious, and to contend with all flesh concerning everything which the sinners and the impious have done and wrought against him. (*1 Enoch* 1: 3–9)[33]

[31] p. 218.
[32] p. 219.
[33] For a commentary on this text, picking up all the biblical allusions, see L. Hartman, *Prophecy Interpreted*, pp. 112–18. He finds the same basic structure in a selection of some 65 apocalyptic texts, 'which covers the following situation: against the background of a sinful and/or otherwise abnormal period there occurs a divine intervention, which is accompanied by judgement and punishment for the wicked and by joy for the faithful' (p. 54).

The most obvious way of reading this text is to assume that 'the chosen' and 'the righteous' are the members of the writer's own community, and that he looks forward to an imminent judgement. But we cannot be sure of this. On the other hand, the Qumran War Scroll, which identifies the enemies of the community as the Kittim, i.e. the Romans, is obviously alluding to a battle that is about to be joined.[34] In the sense in which I am using the term, however, both texts are concerned with the last days. It follows that judgement is essentially an eschatological concept: *of its very nature it is God's last act, his ultimate verdict upon the human race.* Judgement can be anticipated; but to place the act of judgement in the present dispensation is to *de-eschatologize* it. This is why the expression 'realized eschatology' is virtually a contradiction in terms: theoretically it would be possible for God, surveying the scene after he had passed his final verdict, to speak of a 'realized eschatology': 'this is the end and that is my judgement'; but if one wishes to retain the reference to the last days there is no other context that would allow any meaningful use of the expression, *unless it is understood metaphorically,* much as the term 'eternal life', I believe, should be understood in the Fourth Gospel. This, I take it, is what Bultmann means when he speaks of 'eschatological existence':[35] it is an alternative way of saying 'eternal life' but no more to be taken literally than the term 'eternal' which it replaces. The reason why Bultmann's usage is so confusing is his apparent failure to recognize that he is using 'eschatological' *metaphorically* throughout. The advantage of substituting 'the life of the new age' for both these expressions is that one can see straight away the source of this idea and so run less risk of misunderstanding it.

Be that as it may, John's idea of judgement is unmistakably rooted in traditional Jewish eschatology, specifically in the idea that the righteous and the wicked are to be definitively separated on the last day. For the most part John effectively *de-eschatologizes* judgement by making it the immediate consequence of an option for or against Christ in the lifetime of each individual. Naturally even those writers most committed to the inevitability of a final judgement have their

---

[34] This is true of the first and the concluding five columns (15–19), less obviously so of the rest of the work, which may have been inserted later. Cf. G. Vermes, *The Dead Sea Scrolls*[3], pp. 103 f.

[35] *Theology,* ii (1955), 75–92. It is odd, not to say astonishing, that in this long section, devoted exclusively to the Johannine understanding of 'eschatological existence', Bultmann totally ignores the concept of life.

own views about the respective identity of the wicked and the righteous. Although the judgement affects all mankind, it is the circumstances and behaviour of the writer's own contemporaries that provide him with a paradigm of the moral gulf dividing the wicked from the good. This is illustrated with striking clarity in Matthew's parable of the sheep and the goats (ch. 25). The place that people will occupy in the life to come is entirely determined by moral decisions made in the present life. John differs from Matthew in two important respects: in the first place he pulls the actual act of judgement back into the present; in the second place he reduces Matthew's rich variety of moral options (feeding the hungry, clothing the naked, etc.) to one: the act of faith. The latter modification is not without precedent: 'For whoever is ashamed of me and my words in this adulterous and sinful generation, of him will the Son of man also be ashamed, when he comes in the glory of his Father with the holy angels' (Mark 8: 38). Indeed the idea is so fundamental to the faith of the early Christians that it comes as no surprise to find it in a wide variety of New Testament authors: cf. Matt. 10: 33; Luke 19: 26; 12: 9; Rom. 10: 9–11; 2 Tim. 2: 12; 1 John 2: 28. Cyprian's uncompromising slogan '*nulla salus extra ecclesiam*' ('no salvation outside the church') is simply an especially succinct version of the spurious ending of Mark: 'He who believes and is baptized will be saved; but he who does not believe will be condemned' (Mark 16: 16).

In spite of these parallels—and conceivably debts—to other New Testament writings, the central position of the judgement motif in the Fourth Gospel marks it out as the most dualistic of the four Gospels, and the closest in spirit to numerous sectarian works, composed in roughly the same period, that are dominated by a sense of the moral division between the good and the wicked. Since these are Jewish it may be that the opposition between Jew and Gentile underlies them all: it is easy to see how Israel's overwhelming conviction of divine election might be carried over into the beliefs of individual sects. Every Jewish writing of the period that I can think of is permeated with the sense of the divine election of Israel. When John places 'the Jews' among the enemies of God ('You are of your father, the devil' (8: 44)), he is being profoundly ironical; from a Jewish perspective his is a topsy-turvy world: white is now black, and black white—but the basic pattern is the same.

According to Bultmann, as is well known, the remnants of

futuristic belief that persist in the Fourth Gospel are the work of 'the ecclesiastical redactor'. But at least one of the passages in question (11: 25 f.) resists source analysis[36] and there is a simpler explanation available. John may have been converted from what Barton calls an 'imminent' eschatological belief to a 'non-imminent' one. In other words, he may have continued to pay lip-service to the idea of a future judgement, as many Christians do today, but no longer with any sense of urgency. In fact the nature of Christian belief entails some reduction in the importance attached to eschatological expectation of any kind. For by far the most crucial revolution in man's relationship with God has been achieved by Christ; without some conviction of this kind the gospel would be relatively small beer. The decisive event, the divine intervention that occupies the gap between 'before' and 'after' has already taken place. The point of rupture along the line of human history has been displaced, shifted back to the time occupied by the Gospel narratives.

Consequently, alongside unmistakable traces of futuristic eschatology, we should expect to find in the New Testament evidence of its demise (and not just of the kind of conceptual adaptation observable in the Book of Revelation and elsewhere). Which of course is what we do find. Just how far Jesus' own preaching was eschatologically coloured is still disputed. But even if, as I am inclined to believe, the kingdom of God was for him an eschatological concept,[37] it is obvious that it gradually gave way, in the preaching of the early Church, to the good news about Jesus—the Christian gospel. Thus by virtually abandoning the term 'kingdom of God' in favour of the term 'eternal life', and by insisting that the divine judgement is effectively enacted in the earthly life of every individual, John is simply drawing out the most important implications of the Christian message. But he does so in a way that, paradoxically, remains verbally and conceptually very close to contemporary Jewish sectarian writings, in spite of the fact that he had more thoroughly

[36] In his careful study of the relevant passages (*Interpretation*, pp. 144 ff.; 320–8; 364 ff.), C. H. Dodd suggests that the evangelist is deliberately juxtaposing two contrasting eschatologies: 'whether the gift of life is conceived as a present and continuing possession ('he who is alive and has faith in me will never die') or as a recovery of life after death of the body and the end of the world ('even if he dies he will come to life'), the thing that matters is that life is the gift of God—and Christ's gift to men, we know, is Himself (6: 51)' (p. 364).

[37] This is yet another issue on which there is no scholarly consensus. It will be plain that I agree with Christopher Rowland (*The Open Heaven*, pp. 133–6) against Bruce Chilton (*Kingdom of God*). The latter has a good bibliography.

divested himself than any other New Testament writer of the
futuristic eschatology they contain.

5. TRIAL

Starting from the first major confrontation in chapter 5, Jesus' public
career takes the form of a prolonged and bitter dispute with the Jews.
From one perspective this may be seen as a *trial*[38]—a trial whose
eventual outcome, never really in doubt, is the sentence of crucifixion passed by Pilate. But the trial motif in the Fourth Gospel is not
just another theological theme, distinct and separable from that of
judgement. It is judgement in action, judgement *as story* or *drama*. In
two great sequences, the first extending from chapter 5 to chapter
10, the second from chapter 18 (the arrest) to chapter 19 (the
crucifixion), John shows how Jesus successfully refutes his accusers:
in bringing him to trial and eventually sentencing him to death, they
are actually passing judgement on themselves. Judgement ($\kappa\rho\ell\sigma\iota\varsigma$),
which we have so far regarded as a theme or motif, is embodied in a
narrative. Theology, in other words, is fleshed out as gospel. This
enables the evangelist to turn the experience of Jesus into an effective
symbol of the experience of the Christian community. They too will
be challenged by the Jews and the world. They too will see
themselves pitted against the forces of darkness. They too will see life
emerging out of death.

To trace in detail the story of Jesus' trials would take us too far
from the subject of the present chapter. But it is worth remarking
upon the skill with which John moulds together fragments of
tradition and infuses them with his own special brand of dualism.
The traditions are of three kinds: (1) accusations of breaking the
sabbath; (2) accusations of claiming to be king (Messiah) and Son of
God; (3) the trial sequences themselves, first Jewish and then
Roman.

Comparing John's sabbath episodes (5: 1–9; 9: 1–7, 14) with
those in the Synoptic Gospels, A. E. Harvey comments upon the
manifest discrepancy between the two: 'The fourth evangelist pre-

---

[38] A. E. Harvey devotes a whole book to substantiating his claim that 'it is possible
to understand the Fourth Gospel as a presentation of the claims of Jesus in the form of
an extended "trial" ' (*Jesus on Trial*, p. 17). In spite of this he unaccountably ignores
the Roman trial.

sents two sabbath episodes in a form which makes it quite clear that Jesus was running the risk of immediate prosecution; whereas, in the Synoptic Gospels, no illegality is proved and the discussion involves, not the defence by Jesus of a specific action, but a criticism of the existing sabbath customs and legislation.'[39] In fact in the first of the episodes it is not Jesus but the healed cripple who breaks the law, by carrying his bed on the sabbath, and in neither case is the evangelist deeply interested in this particular accusation. In chapter 5, he uses it, as we have seen,[40] as a way of introducing the charge of blasphemy (for claiming equality with God, 5: 18); in chapter 9 the healing miracle is the occasion of the expulsion of the blind man from the synagogue on the grounds that, implicitly at least, he confessed Jesus to be the Messiah (cf. 9: 22). Thus although still observable in the Gospel text, the traditional charge of breaking the sabbath simply opens the way to more serious controversy.

The charge of aspiring to be king, like that of breaking the sabbath, was found by John in his signs source. It too belongs to the prehistory of the Johannine community and of its Gospel, to the time when the message addressed to the synagogue was simply, 'We have found the Messiah' (1: 41). The title 'King of the Jews' marks the only point at which John's usage of the term 'Jews' converges with that of the Synoptists. Seizing hold of this nugget of tradition, he turns it to good account in his version of the Roman trial. Uninterested in any fragment of historical truth the tradition might comprise, he composes a scenario to illustrate how Jesus' claim to kingship, such as it is, proceeds from his revelation, for his sole claim to authority is that he speaks 'the truth'. Listening to Jesus' voice, but not hearing his words, Pilate shows that he is not 'of the truth' (18: 37). Failing to recognize that truth in person is standing in front of him, he ranges himself alongside the imperceptive Jews, and stands as self-condemned in the eyes of the evangelist and his readers.

Even now the irony is not over. Having had Jesus scourged, Pilate has ordered him to be brought out, and in the presence of the Jews, the evangelist records, ἐκάθισεν ἐπὶ βήματος (19: 13). The verb καθίζειν, like 'sit' or, in some English dialects, 'lay', can have a transitive as well as an intransitive sense. This fact has prompted some exegetes to follow Loisy in arguing that Pilate did not himself sit on the judgement-seat but seated Jesus upon it, thereby implicitly

---

[39] *Trial*, p. 76.   [40] *Supra*, p. 139.

acknowledging his authority. Much more probable, in my view, though it has received less attention, is Lightfoot's suggestion of a deliberate ambiguity.[41]

Of greatest interest to the evangelist himself is the tradition that Jesus claimed to be the Son of God. Mark highlights this claim in his version of Jesus' reply to the high priest's question: 'Are you the Messiah, the son of the Blessed?'—'I am' (14: 62). In the other two Synoptic Gospels the reply is more guarded, but Matthew and Luke were no less convinced than Mark that Jesus was truly the Son of God. Whatever the meaning of this title for the Synoptists, John undoubtedly understood it as a claim to divine status; as we have seen when discussing the debate in Chapter 4, he has no interest in rebutting this charge; on the contrary he devotes much of his Gospel to establishing its truth.

In *Jesus on Trial*, A. E. Harvey observes that 'the underlying pattern [of the Fourth Gospel] is of two parties in dispute, Jesus and "the Jews"; and the dispute has to be presented in such a way that the reader is persuaded of the justice of Jesus' case'.[42] He backs this suggestion up with arguments based upon the proceedings in Jewish criminal trials, where, for instance, the function of witness is not distinct from that of judge. There is no obvious support for this thesis in the first four chapters (where there is only one witness, John the Baptist, whose role is simply to point to Jesus from afar); but from chapter 5 onwards, where the dispute with the Jews really gets under way, Harvey has a strong case. Jesus' protracted farewell to his disciples in chapters 13–17 interrupts the trial sequence.

---

[41] Loisy's suggestion is supported by Harnack, Bonsirven, Meeks, de la Potterie, and Haenchen; but as it stands can scarcely be right. The linguistic evidence is inconclusive, and the evangelist's sense of story (not necessarily history) is strong enough to prevent him from bluntly asserting that Pilate deliberately placed the accused man on the judge's seat. Justin, writing some years later (in an apologia, not a Gospel!) recounts how the Roman soldiers seat Jesus upon a tribunal with the demand, 'Judge us!' (*Apol.* 35: 6; cf. *Gospel of Peter* 5: 7), but this is no argument for attributing the same idea to John. On what I call the story level of understanding the straightforward reading 'Pilate sat down' is the natural one. Nevertheless, Lightfoot's suggestion of an intentional ambiguity is attractive and may well be right, since, as I shall show in Ch. 11, the Fourth Evangelist regularly employs the device of two levels of understanding. (C. K. Barrett is the only other commentator, to the best of my knowledge, to favour this suggestion.) Whatever one may think of it, the general point—that any judgement upon Jesus is really a judgement upon the judge—is abundantly clear. Pilate himself, for all his obtuseness, refuses to alter the superscription upon the cross ('What I have written, I have written', 19: 22); so that Jesus' title to kingship is vindicated after all.   [42] *Trial*, p. 15.

Not surprisingly, judgement is by far the most important theological motif in the trial sequence. But the evangelist weaves a whole series of other motifs into the story as well. Indeed the individual episodes give him the opportunity of reinforcing his message by inserting at appropriate points many of the dualistic oppositions that we have been studying in this chapter. Taken together they provide a powerfully sustained argument for the divisive effect of Jesus' revelation and the self-condemnation of his adversaries. Thus in the story of the cripple the main contrast is between life and death; in the debate in chapter 8 truth is set against falsehood and freedom against slavery; in the healing of the blind man, as we should expect, light is opposed to darkness; whilst in the Roman trial Jesus' rebuttal of the charge of pretending to a worldly throne introduces the idea of an opposition between the world above and the world below. Only in chapter 10 is the debate left uncoloured by any of John's symbolic contrasts; here the point is made by the sheer violence of the Jews' hostility to Jesus as they first accuse him of blasphemy and then attempt to stone him.

6. DIVISION

'Do not think that I have come to bring peace on earth: I have not come to bring peace but a sword' (Matt. 10: 34). The divisiveness typical of the fourth evangelist was not invented by him: it is an integral element of the gospel tradition. Matthew too knew that Jesus had come 'to set a man against his father and a daughter against her mother', and that a man's enemies would be those of his own household (10: 35 f.). Prophecy is divisive of its very nature; prophets cause dissension and Jesus was no exception: any religion with a cutting edge starts by severing believers from unbelievers. It was to be expected that Jesus' followers should experience rejection just as he did and project their own experience back on to his. In itself the motif is interesting but unsurprising. What is remarkable and distinctive about the Fourth Gospel is the extent to which the present and past experience of rejection is built into a narrative whose conceptual content is reinforced by a wide variety of literary devices.

So far we have considered Johannine dualism in terms of content: polar opposites like light and darkness, life and death, truth and falsehood, plus the dominant theme of judgement, with its narrative counterpart, equally rooted in the tradition, of trial. But the dualism is also conveyed, sometimes almost subliminally, in many other ways. Form cannot be separated from content, and sometimes the two are so fused as to be scarcely distinguishable. Nevertheless the subject is worth considering from a strictly formal point of view.

From a form-critical perspective the trial sequences are best regarded as an extension of the controversy form. The nature of this is easily seen by looking at the series of controversies in Mark 2: 1–3: 6. In each of these Jesus is taken to task by his adversaries, but ends up by discomfiting them with a sharp rejoinder. In Chapter 8 I shall be examining one such episode in John 7, where Nicodemus defends the uneducated populace against the sneers of the Pharisees in a way that highlights the superiority of Galilee over Judaea (7: 45–52). Earlier in the same chapter the divisive effect of Jesus' message is encapsulated in two words: γογγυσμός (7: 12) and σχίσμα (7: 43; cf. 9: 16; 10: 19). The first of these words is traditional: it recalls the 'murmuring' (תְּלוּנָה) of the Israelites in the desert, and is a powerful reminder of the divisiveness of revelation. John is the only evangelist to use the noun; the verb, γογγύζειν (6: 41, 43, 61), is also found in Matt. 20: 11 and Luke 5: 30. It well conveys the uneasy opposition aroused by Jesus' message: 'There was much murmuring about him among the people. While some said, "He is a good man", others said, "No, he is leading the people astray"' (7: 12). If, as is quite likely, John found this story in the tradition, he took its lesson to heart. One can hardly imagine a simpler or more effective summary of what he saw to be the general impact of Jesus' message upon the people of Judaea. The second word, σχίσμα, was to have a fateful future in Christendom. It does not occur in the LXX but is used by Mark to mean a tear or rent (2: 21). John employs it to refer to dissension among the Jews (cf. 9: 16; 10: 19), but when he speaks of them fighting among themselves in 6: 52 it may well be *Christian* dissension that he has in mind.[43] However that may be, the repeated allusions to squabbling, murmuring, and schisms all help to deepen the readers sense of the uncomprehending hostility surrounding Jesus and his disciples.

Since the importance and significance of the *riddle* in the Gospel

---

[43] See Excursus I for arguments in favour of Lindars's hypothesis that chs. 6 and 11, as well as part of ch. 12, did not belong to the first edition of the Gospel.

has already received sufficient emphasis,[44] it may be enough here simply to reaffirm what an effective instrument it is for convincing John's readers that, being 'in the know', they enjoy an essential superiority over those who, like Nicodemus and the Samaritan woman, are compelled to grope around in the dark as they search in vain for the true significance of Jesus' words. More subtly, the hidden contrasts in chapters 3 and 4, between man and woman, night and day, inside and outside, ensure that the fundamental bipolarity of John's vision of the world is conveyed to his readers with means of which they may not always be aware.

Even the simple fact that the Gospel is divided into two halves has its significance. In the first half, at any rate after the introductory section that terminates with the wedding-feast of Cana, Jesus' interlocutors are for the most part either openly hostile or else puzzled sympathizers who do not yet belong to his circle of friends. But from chapter 13 onwards he begins to address himself to the disciples apart. He tells the high priest, 'I have spoken openly (παρρησίᾳ) to the world; I have always taught in synagogues and in the temple, where all Jews come together; I have said nothing secretly (ἐν κρυπτῷ)' (18: 20); but we know that throughout the preceding four chapters he was conversing with his disciples in private. Bultmann remarks that whereas in the Synoptic Gospels Jesus is continually instructing his disciples at every stage in his ministry, in John this teaching 'is transferred in its entirety to the last night. The result is the radical division of the Gospel into two, illustrating a fundamental Johannine idea; the work of Jesus is the division between light and darkness.' He adds that in the second part of the Gospel 'the darkness, the κόσμος, remains the background to the teaching of the disciples, and as such it is not to be forgotten. ... It is of symbolic significance that the scene takes place at night.'[45]

Less frequently observed is John's constant use of short proverbial or proverbial-type expressions, usually couched as oppositions or contrasts, which serve to enhance the reader's sense of a divided world. Sometimes this is achieved by the use of one of the evangelist's favourite contrasts, for instance the little proverb that introduces the story of the blind man: 'We must work the works of him who sent me while it is day: night comes when no one can work' (9: 4; cf. 11: 9 f.; 12: 35 f.). At other times, if the context of a saying is relatively trivial, the same effect may be achieved without any conscious advertence on the part of the reader. The significance, for instance, of the remark made to Jesus by his brothers as they urge him to leave Galilee for Judaea does not fully emerge until he addresses the high priest much later: 'No man works in secret (ἐν κρυπτῷ) if he seeks to be known openly (ἐν παρρησίᾳ)' (7: 4; cf. 7: 10). Similarly the comment that follows Jesus' exchange with Nicodemus, though difficult to relate to what has just been said, is clearly central to the evangelist's conception of his book: 'If I have told you earthly things (τὰ ἐπίγεια) and you do not believe, how can you believe if I tell you heavenly things (τὰ ἐπουράνια)?' (3: 12.) Occasionally the force of a fairly simple contrast comes from the recollection of an earlier saying: 'You are his disciple, but we are disciples of Moses' (9: 28; cf. 1: 17; 5: 46). Elsewhere the contrasts are meaningful only within the contexts in which they occur, e.g. 10: 1–2, 4–5, 10, 12; 15: 5–6. John can also take over and adapt a well-known proverb and combine it with a traditional saying: 'Unless a grain of wheat falls into the earth and dies, it remains alone; but if it dies it bears much fruit (cf. 1 Cor. 15: 36 f.). He who loves his life loses it' (John 12: 24 f.). For further examples of pithy oppositions see 3: 19 f. (light/dark); 8: 23 (above/below); 8: 35 (slave/son); 9: 39, 41 (sight/blindness); 16: 20 f. (sorrow/joy); 17: 9, 15, 25. Even the most innocuous-sounding proverb such as 'One sows and another reaps' (4: 37) can make a small contribution to the general effect. Sometimes the intended contrast is left to be inferred: 'They hated me without cause' (15: 25).

Following the evangelist, I have left to the last the most significant saying of all: 'Blessed are those who have not seen and yet believe' (20: 29).

CONCLUSION

The foregoing enquiry has been an attempt to understand the Gospel from within rather than to explain it from without. By way of conclusion we may turn back to the question with which we began and ask if it is possible to make any inferences from the nature of John's dualism about *the origins of his Gospel*. Or must it be acknowledged that dualistic thinking was so widespread in the Eastern Mediterranean at the turn of the era that we cannot go beyond the vague, general assertion that it came from somewhere in this region? If we were simply to stop there we would surely be failing to do justice to the distinctive nature of the dualism of the Fourth Gospel, which requires, as Bultmann realized, a much more *coherent* explanation than is generally given. Indeed the great merit of Bultmann's own explanation is its sheer comprehensiveness. It is a pity he was wrong!

Shortly after the discovery of the Dead Sea Scrolls, when many of the most important documents were still unpublished, K. G. Kuhn wrote excitedly that the background of the Fourth Gospel had been recovered at last. He was impressed by the fact that the understanding exhibited by the Scrolls of existence and the world 'is based on a new "knowledge" (ידע), a revelation (נגלה = ἀποκαλύπτεσθαι), a communication (הידיע) of God'.[46] In his conclusion he speaks of a 'profound connection (*tiefgehende Verwandschaft*) with John's Gospel', and also of:

the far-reaching dualism of φῶς and σκότος (light and darkness) in John's Gospel, which is also a dualism of ἀλήθεια and ψεῦδος (truth and falsehood); the existence (*Sein*) of the community of believers, seeing themselves as υἱοὶ φωτὸς (sons of light) over against the rest of men who are ἐκ τοῦ κόσμου, ἐκ τοῦ διαβόλου (of the world, of the devil); this existence seen as eschatological existence, as the νῦν (now) of salvation as well as the νῦν of λύπη (grief) and the hatred of the world; and finally the νικᾶν τοῦ κόσμου, the victory over the world, which is both the goal and the basis of the existence of the community—in all essentials respects, Johannine thought shares this basic structure with the new Palestinian texts. Crucial here (something that Gnosticism cannot properly account for) is the fact that the cosmic dualism of John's Gospel leads neither to asceticism nor to licence, but is indissolubly bound up with an ethic that is obviously rooted in the Jewish tradition. In this ἀλήθεια means ποιεῖν ἀλήθειαν (to do the truth), corresponding to עשה האמת; being ἐκ τοῦ φωτός (of the light) is manifested and has its centre of gravity in ἀγαπᾶν τοὺς ἀδελφοὺς (loving the brethren) and consequently in τηρεῖν τὰς ἐντολάς (keeping the commandments); conversely men love darkness rather than light *because their works are evil*. All these specific connections are anticipated in the Palestinian texts, sometimes verbally.[47]

When he wrote these lines, Kuhn thought that the texts betrayed Gnostic influences. Later, on the publication of the Community Rule (1QS), with its clear rejection of any metaphysical, absolute or

---

[46] 'Die in Palästina gefundenen hebraischen Texte', p. 203.
[47] Ibid., pp. 209 f.

cosmic dualism, he was to revise this view, but he continued to believe that this was where the Fourth Gospel took its rise. Subsequently there has been a wide divergence of scholarly opinion, ranging from enthusiastic acceptance of Kuhn's views (Charlesworth) to contemptuous dismissal (Teeple).

One scholar who took an early interest in the Scrolls was Raymond Brown, but from the outset he showed himself much more cautious than Kuhn. Whilst admitting that 'the argument for interrelatedness between the Johannine writings and the Qumran Library is indeed strong, the resemblances,' he continues, 'do *not* seem to indicate immediate relationship—as if St. John were himself a sectarian or were personally familiar with the Qumran Library. Rather they indicate a more general acquaintance with the thought and style of expression which we have found in the Qumran Library. The ideas of Qumran must have been fairly widespread in certain Jewish circles in the early first century AD. Probably it is only through such sources that Qumran had its indirect effect on the Johannine literature.'[48]

Brown goes on to note that almost every detail of the life and teaching of John the Baptist has an affinity with some aspect of the life and teaching of the Qumran community. He concludes: 'From this it would seem likely that the Baptist, before his contact with Christ, was in relationship with Qumran or other Essenes (perhaps he was raised by the community, or in contact with the community, or the head of a quasi-Essene group). If this is true, and if John the Evangelist was his disciple, we can explain very well the Qumran impact on the Fourth Gospel.'[49]

In his commentary Brown does not repeat the suggestion concerning the Baptist but is still inclined to favour the hypothesis of an indirect influence: the parallels simply suggest 'Johannine familiarity with the type of thought exhibited in the scrolls'.[50] He goes on to consider the objection of H. M. Teeple 'that there are theological concepts and terms that are found often in the Qumran literature but not in John, and vice versa'.[51] As Brown rightly rejoins, 'This means nothing unless one is trying to show that the Qumran literature was the only and direct source of John's thought.'[52]

A very similar point of view was put forward by Rudolf Schnacken-

---

[48] 'The Qumran Scrolls', p. 571.   [49] Ibid., p. 573.   [50] p. lxiii.
[51] 'Qumran and the Origin of the Fourth Gospel'.   [52] p. lxiii.

burg in the first volume of his commentary (published in German in
1965, the year before Brown's):

Though there are close contacts between John and Qumran on important
points, it can scarcely be proved that the evangelist took over Qumran
concepts directly. But that there were some associations must be seriously
considered, however they were set up: by means of the disciples who
came to Jesus from the school of John the Baptist (cf. 1: 35–51), or by
Qumran Essenes who later entered Christian, Johannine communities, or
through the author's meeting such circles, which influenced his theological
thinking.[53]

Writing much later (1979) in yet another two-volume commentary, Jürgen Becker has an alternative suggestion. He too is very
aware of the affinities between the dualism of the Scrolls and the
Testaments of the Twelve Patriarchs on the one hand and of the Fourth
Gospel on the other, but he accounts for these rather differently. He
believes that the Johannine community was thinking along dualistic
lines before being joined by the evangelist himself, but that it was
originally non-dualistic: 'After a non-dualistic phase the Johannine
community must have come under the influence of a dualism close
to that of Qumran. In any case we must presuppose a receptivity for
such a dualism on the part of the community.'[54] Yes indeed, but
where did these ideas come from if not from the evangelist himself?

J. H. Charlesworth, in what is probably the most thorough
examination to date of the parallels between the Fourth Gospel and
the 'theological' section of the Community Rule, concludes that
'John probably borrowed some of his dualistic terminology and
mythology from 1QS 3: 13–4: 26.'[55]

What are we to make of all these suggestions? There is no obvious
advantage, it seems to me, in any theory of indirect influence. The
pervasive and deep-lying dualistic structures so finely perceived by
Kuhn are scarcely to be accounted for by the suggestion that the
evangelist was a disciple of John the Baptist, unless the latter was
himself so deeply soaked in Qumranian ideas as to be virtually
indistinguishable from one of the community's own teachers. And in
that case there is no reason for seeing him as a middleman or
intermediary between Qumran and the evangelist. Again, Becker's
proposal that the community was receptive to dualistic ideas may

[53] pp. 134 ff.   [54] p. 149.
[55] 'A Critical Comparison', *John and Qumran*, p. 104.

seem plausible enough, but really explains nothing. What we need to know is *why* either the community in general or the evangelist in particular was so receptive. The case of Josephus (who actually refers to Essenism as 'a philosophy') is instructive in this regard. Simply to spend a few months in an Essene community[56] whilst, presumably, browsing in its library and dabbling in its teaching was clearly not enough to imbue him with its spirit. Maybe the leaders of the community were right to insist, like the Jesuits, upon a two-year novitiate. Despite his total shift of political allegiance, Josephus' writings testify to his enduring respect and love for the laws and customs in which, as a Pharisee born into a priestly family, he had been brought up. Nor is it a counter-argument to point to his suggestion that the emperor Vespasian was somehow the fulfilment of Jewish messianic expectation (*BJ* vi. 312 f.). For this is precisely the kind of drastic switch that we *should* expect—comparable to the transference all Jewish converts to the new faith made perforce once they had come to believe that the Messiah they hoped for was no other than Jesus. It is one thing to attribute a person's sudden conversion to the visit, short or long, of a charismatic teacher or preacher like Jesus or Paul. But what we know of Paul's converts suggests that they were slow to begin to *think* as he did, or rather to share his deepest and most instinctive responses and attitudes. We have to do, I suggest, with what in modern parlance is sometimes called a mind-set. Just as Paul's underlying convictions concerning the provident dispensations of a beneficent deity remained unaltered when he became a Christian, so, I believe, the author of the Fourth Gospel retained the pattern of thinking with which he was probably familiar from an early age, maybe from childhood.[57]

Accordingly it makes little sense to speak, as Charlesworth does, in terms of 'borrowing', however right he may be, against Brown and Schnackenburg, to adopt a theory of direct influence. For what *kind* of borrowing is he thinking of? Does he picture John visiting the

[56] See *Vita*, 10–11, where Josephus says that he wished to gain experience of all three schools of thought (αἱρέσεις) available to him: Pharisees, Sadducees, and Essenes. He steeled himself, he informs us, and passed through all three, though not without a great deal of trouble. Perhaps we should not lend too much credence to these boastful claims, but my general point retains its validity whether or not Josephus had any experience of Essenism at close range.

[57] In relation to the resemblances and differences in messianic expectations in early Christianity and at Qumran, see the important observations of N. A. Dahl, 'Eschatology and History'.

Qumran Library, as Brown calls it, and taking the Community Rule out of the repository, scrolling through it, taking notes perhaps, and then making use of its ideas when he came to compose his own work? This is surely the sort of question that we need to ask ourselves before settling somewhat timidly, either, like Brown and Schnackenburg, for a theory of indirect dependence, or for the sort of literary indebtedness hinted at by Charlesworth. Here I believe that Bultmann was closer to the truth with his suggestion that the evangelist was a convert from Gnosticism. Such a hypothesis, unsubstantiated as it is, accounts for the depth and pervasiveness of John's dualism much better than any of the rather half-hearted alternatives we have just been considering. Its improbability stems from the fact that there is no proof and little likelihood that a fully fledged Gnostic sect of the kind it postulates was already flourishing in Palestine by the middle of the first century. But the evangelist had dualism in his bones. I have said that the great merit of Bultmann's hypothesis is its elegance and economy: it accounts both for the dualism of the Gospel and for its strange new christology. But it is not necessary, it seems to me, to offer the same explanation for both. The evangelist may well have started life as one of those Essenes who were to be found, according to Josephus, 'in large numbers in every town': ἐν ἑκάστῃ [πόλει] μετοικοῦσιν πολλοί (*BJ* ii. 124). Such a suggestion may appear to some almost as improbable as that of Bultmann. I admit that it cannot be proved. But its apparent improbability is a consequence of its specificity. Unlike all other theories except Bultmann's it offers the right *kind* of explanation of the profoundly dualistic nature of the evangelist's thinking—in terms not of his receptiveness to new ideas but of his own gut reactions.

7

MESSIAH

1. THE NOTION OF MESSIAH

(a) John and the Synoptists

As soon as we turn to a close study of the christology of the Fourth Gospel, we come face to face with one of its greatest puzzles. Looking back over the long Christian centuries, we may be astonished to see how quickly Paul and John, who surely never met in life, came to be joined together after death in other people's writings. And we may be surprised too at the extent to which this comfortable yoking has dominated Christian theology ever since. No doubt the Synoptic Gospels held their place; but for them Christianity might well have rapidly vaporized into some form of speculative Gnosticism. It did not; the parables of the kingdom and the Sermon on the Mount continued to be regarded as indispensable elements of the Christian message, and—more importantly–the Jesus who preached them remained ever present to the Christian consciousness. And if the air-space of theology and the floor-space of worship were both largely occupied by a pre-existent divine being unimagined by the Synoptists, this did not really matter until the tensions and inconsistencies between the two figures were explicitly acknowledged and began to cause an increasing discomfort among the faithful, a discomfort which persists to this day.

Following up the arguments of Bretschneider (1820) and D. F. Strauss (1835), numerous authors, led by F. C. Baur (1847), have been at pains to stress the differences between John and the Synoptists, and in particular the transformation of the portrait of Jesus.[1] To most modern eyes the portrait painted by the Synoptists

---

[1] One of the latest and most brilliant examples is in Käsemann's *Testament of Jesus* (pp. 8–10). Besides Baur, Käsemann refers to G. A. P. Wetter (1916) and E. Hirsch (1936). See also W. Bousset, *Kyrios Christos* (1913), whose phrase 'der auf Erden
[*cont. on p. 239*]

(there are of course three, but the divergences are not felt as intolerably great) is both simpler and more attractive. It is the portrait of a man with a special relationship with God, whom he addresses by the intimate name of Abba, Father. He is the promised Messiah, and he has been appointed by God to preach the kingdom, and thereby to fulfil the promise of the Old Testament. His birth was miraculous and his resurrection from the dead, after appalling suffering, unique. But for all that, he was a man of his time; his teaching and preaching, even his healing miracles, can be readily placed in the context of first-century Palestinian Judaism. If he were suddenly to reappear as he really was he would no doubt seem to us, in Albert Schweitzer's phrase, 'a stranger and an enigma', but a recognizable human being none the less.

Not so the Johannine Christ. He does not belong to this world at all: it is almost true to say that he enters it with the purpose of leaving it, or descends in order to ascend. He is a pre-existent divine being, whose real home is in heaven. He enters an alien world with an unprecedented confidence and assurance, knowing precisely who he is, where he comes from and where he is going. And this too is his message, that he knows both his origin and his destiny, and because of this knowledge he enjoys a special relationship with the Father that verges upon total identification. No doubt he is portrayed as subject to human weaknesses, hunger, fatigue, grief; but these in no way diminish the extraordinary control he exercises upon his own fate. He even orchestrates his own passion; condemned to death, he appears as the judge of the one who condemns him: he can read Pilate's heart, just as he can read the hearts of other men and women. There is in him no trace of that uncertainty, that helpless sense of being flung into the world which Heidegger, with pictur-esque concision, calls *Geworfensein*, that incomprehension and bewilderment which ordinary human beings can never entirely escape. Master of his fate, captain of his soul to an extent even W. E. Henley never dreamed of, his head bloody but unbowed, he never had to confront either the fell clutch of circumstance or the bludgeonings of chance.

wandelnde Gottessohn oder Gott' (p. 159) strikingly anticipates Käsemann's better-known 'der über die Erde schreitende Gott'. But the idea goes back at least as far as Bretschneider, who heads the first section of his book with the words: 'Jesus, quem depinxit quartum evangelium, valde diversus est a Jesu in prioribus evangeliis descripto.'

In the light of these differences a number of questions arise. In the previous chapter we went some way towards explaining how and why the original object of Jesus' preaching, the kingdom of God, was replaced by the promise of eternal life. But a more important question, how the Synoptic portrait of Jesus developed into the Johannine portrait, cannot be answered without a close study of Johannine christology. This will take up the next three chapters, each focused on a particular title: Messiah, Son of God, Son of Man. Around these, as we shall see, are clustered a number of other titles and motifs.

(b) Messiah: a promise fulfilled

It is not customary to distinguish cleanly between the twin titles of Messiah and Son of God, if only because the evangelist himself held them together so closely. Just as Mark places the two titles at the beginning of his Gospel, and uses them at climatic moments in his story,[2] so John places them at the end of his, to sum up the content of the faith he wishes to promulgate and foster: 'that you may believe that Jesus is the Messiah, the Son of God, and that, believing, you may have life in his name' (20: 31).

Roughly, and perhaps a little schematically, one may say that the first of these titles looks back: to a glory achieved and a prophecy fulfilled. It is exclusively Jewish in conception, unintelligible except when viewed against the background of a long religious tradition that is generally summed up in the New Testament as αἱ γραφαί—the Scriptures (literally 'the Writings'), a term covering more or less the book Christians now know as the Old Testament. The second title, Son of God, is very different. Although once closely associated with Messiah (an association which can be confusing), it does not look back to the Jewish past but forward to the Christian

---

[2] The first climax in the Gospel occurs at Caesarea Philippi, when Peter confesses Jesus to be the Messiah (8: 29); the second at the crucifixion, when the title 'Son of God' (surely not just a son of God) is pronounced by the centurion (15: 39). The customary rendering of the opening of the Gospel obscures the programmatic significance of 'the gospel of Jesus, Messiah, Son of God'. The words υἱὸς θεοῦ are missing from some MSS. But some of the better MSS have them, and if they were actually inserted by a later editor he must have known his Mark thoroughly. N. Perrin rightly comments: 'In view of the importance of this title for Mark one is tempted to say that if it was not part of the original superscription it should have been, and the scribe who first added it was Markan in purpose if not in name!' ('The Christology of Mark', p. 182 n. 22).

future.[3] In the strong sense it comes to assume in the Fourth Gospel it constitutes (unlike Messiah) a claim to divinity; and it is scarcely surprising that this claim was rejected by the parent Jewish community as totally unacceptable—blasphemous in fact. Even among Christians themselves the title proved increasingly contentious, until eventually the weak interpretation defended by Arius was condemned by the Council of Nicaea. So behind each of these two simple-sounding titles, Messiah and Son of God, lies a rich and complex range of meaning. The study of the first of them, its background and significance, will take up the remainder of this chapter.

It is necessary to insist from the outset that there is nothing inherently blasphemous in a claim to be the Messiah. Some Christian readers, thinking possibly of the words and actions attributed to the high priest during the trial before the Sanhedrin, have erroneously supposed that he was provoked simply by Jesus' refusal to disown this title.[4] But we are surely meant to understand that Caiaphas was reacting against Jesus' whole reply: '"Are you the Messiah, the Son of the Blessed?" And Jesus said, "I am; and you will see the Son of man sitting at the right hand of Power, and coming with the clouds of heaven"' (Mark 14: 61 f.). There were other messianic pretenders roughly contemporary with Jesus, none of them, as far as we know, accused of blasphemy.[5] So it is a mistake to lump together all the

---

[3] This distinction is not of course made by the evangelist himself. An alternative way of indicating the difference between two christologies running throughout the Gospel is to distinguish the 'vertical' connection between heaven and earth from the 'horizontal' messianic line. This is done by J. Willemse, *Het vierde evangelie* (Hüversum/Antwerp, 1965), 264–71. (I owe this reference to de Jonge, 'Jesus as prophet', p. 71 n. 6.)

[4] On this point see P. Lamarche, 'La Déclaration de Jésus devant le Sanhédrin'.

[5] See R. A. Horsley, 'Popular Messianic Movements', pointing out that leaders such as Athronges, Judas son of Ezekias (both 4 BC), and Menahem (AD 66) 'claimed the kingship', 'were acclaimed as king', or 'set the diadem on their heads' (*BJ* ii. 55, 57; *AJ* xvii. 272 f., 278 f.; cf. Tacitus, *Hist.* 5. 9). Horsley also discusses the messianic movement focused on Simon bar Giora, who dressed himself in royal robes when he eventually surrendered to the Romans, and was tortured before his execution (*BJ* vii. 26–36; 154). In a later article, '"Like One of the Prophets of Old"', he contrasts these with prophetic figures such as Theudas (*AJ* xx. 97 ff., mentioned in Acts 5: 36 f. along with Judas the Galilean), the Samaritan pseudo-prophet (xviii. 85 ff.), and the Egyptian (xx. 167 ff.), none of whom is said to have claimed messianic status. No doubt this distinction is important for the historian, but as Horsley himself acknowledges, the expectation of messianic deliverance exhibited in literary circles, *Ps. Sol.* 17 and Qumran, as well as the New Testament, is rather different. Besides, Theudas and 'the Egyptian' at any rate showed that they believed they had a part to play in an approaching liberation that could be loosely qualified as messianic. Cf. D. Hill, 'Jesus and Josephus' "messianic prophets"'.

claims made by the early Christians on Jesus' behalf as 'messianic' without further ado or distinction.[6] Certainly there came a stage in the history of the Johannine group when the status it accorded to Jesus began to be felt as intolerable by the parent community, who consequently decided to expel the Christian Jews from their midst. But if these claims had been associated with the charge of ditheism right from the beginning, the group would hardly have been allowed to remain within the synagogue in the first place.[7] Precisely at what point in the group's history it came to insist upon Jesus' divine status may be impossible to determine. But had it done so from the outset it would not have lived any part of its history as a group of Christian Jews still revolving within the orbit of the faith of Israel.

In the second place we need to recognize the broader significance of the confidence exhibited throughout the Fourth Gospel that the evangelist and his readers are the rightful inheritors of the whole biblical tradition. Of course this conviction was not confined to the Johannine circle; it was and is shared by all Christians from the beginning; and apart perhaps from the strange letter of James it pervades the whole of the New Testament. But it is of particular importance in the Fourth Gospel, for there the dominant impression is of an alien Christ moving among Jews as a stranger. In overemphasizing this impression or in isolating it from the data within the Gospel that confirm Jesus' essential Jewishness, one can cut the ties which keep the Johannine Christ pinned down to the ground and allow him to drift off in the direction of docetism. Some members of the community appear to have done precisely this, so provoking the alarm and hostility of the author of the Johannine letters.[8] Yet much of the Fourth Gospel is concerned to vindicate messianic claims, and if, as I believe, most of this material stems from a signs source, taken over by the evangelist, it was nevertheless assumed into his Gospel and, although modified, never repudiated. So if one is to preserve a proper balance, this material must be accorded its due weight.

One of the most illuminating stories told in the Acts of the Apostles concerns a visit by Paul and Barnabas to the remote Lycaonian town of Lystra. Paul healed a cripple, in full view of the populace, and won

---

[6] This is one of the major flaws in W. Wrede's *Messiasgeheimnis*.

[7] On the humanity of the Messiah, in the Old Testament at least, see for instance S. Mowinckel, *He that Cometh*, pp. 162, 284 f.; F. Hahn *Titles*, p. 147. Gradually, however, Christians came to attach divine prerogatives to the title Χριστός; John 9: 22 shows how far this process had gone by the time the two communities split.

[8] See Ch. 3.

an immediate response: the crowds, Luke tells us, 'lifted up their voices, saying in Lycaonian, "The gods have come down to us in the likeness of men".' Barnabas they called Zeus, and Paul because he was the chief speaker, they called Hermes (Acts 14: 11 f.). Deeply conscious of the *religious* importance of what they had just witnessed, they had only one way of making the scene intelligible to themselves, and that was to set it in the context of their own religious traditions, which, as it happens, are familiar to us from Greek mythology. Convinced then that they were dealing with gods, the people were on the point of decorating their two visitors with garlands and offering sacrifices—oxen, no less—on their behalf. Paul was horrified and made a little speech, which, remarkably, contains not a single element of the Christian kerygma. The 'good news' Paul proffered was simply that of the creator-God, and the 'witness' to which he appealed God's beneficent providence. A little later, in the famous discourse on the Areopagus (Acts 17: 22–31) Paul did include the central affirmation of the Christian faith, the resurrection, and, as a poor substitute for the Jewish Scriptures, a phrase from the obscure Greek poet Aratus. But mention of the resurrection elicited no other response from his audience than a grumpy bewilderment from some and a puzzled curiosity from others.

The point is that the *intelligibility* of the Christian gospel depended from the first upon the framework in which it was set, that is, the framework of contemporary Judaism.[9] Without this, 'the Son of God' must have appeared to the Gentile world either, like Paul and Barnabas, as a member of the Greek pantheon, or as a magician like the unfortunate Elymas (Acts 13: 6–11), or as a healer or exorcist, or even as a foreign deity coming, as Dionysus did to Thebes, to initiate a new cult whose chief appeal lay in its very strangeness. But cults like these (which may be compared with that of Hare Krishna in the capitals of the West) are essentially 'mystery'-cults: they

[9] Intelligibility here means *historical* intelligibility. This is very different from the philosophical and specifically *existential* intelligibility required by Bultmann, for whom nothing in the Christian message can be understood except in so far as it gives some answer to the universal questions human beings are continually asking about their own lives and destinies. Given this, according to Bultmann, no other sort of intelligibility is required. Indeed, as we have seen (Ch. 2), he is uneasy with any attempt to 'explain' the Christian message along historical lines. 'The scandal of particularity' is just as much a stumbling-block to him as it was, say, to Kant or Lessing.

require no language except the ravings of maenads on the hills or the mutterings of devotees in incense-filled rooms.

The Christian religion is different. Even the tongues of fire at Pentecost were, we are told, 'articulated', διαμεριζόμεναι (Acts 2: 3), and certainly the whole point of the discourse that followed was that it could be *understood* by its differently tongued hearers. So it is important to insist that the Fourth Gospel shares this intelligibility, this rootedness in a rich cultural heritage. This is where the study of Jesus' messianic titles belongs, since with their necessary emphasis upon fulfilment they balance out the ideas of strangeness, alienation, and unbridgeable distance that have to be included in any complete account of Johannine christology.

(c) Messianic claims in the Fourth Gospel[10]

The major commentaries on the Fourth Gospel contain little discussion of the messianic titles. They are absent from Brown's key words, and also from his appendices. Schnackenburg, who had earlier written a long article on 'the messianic question in John's Gospel', no more than grazes the topic in his massive three-volume commentary (although the third of his 18 excursuses, 'The Titles of Jesus in John 1', partly covers the ground). Bultmann, it is true, discusses briefly a few of the subsidiary titles, but he barely glances at 'Messiah'. (Neither Χριστός nor Μεσσίας figures in the useful index of Greek words in the English edition of his commentary.) In view of his bias against the Old Testament, this may not be surprising, but what of Dodd, whom Bultmann takes to task for exaggerating the importance of Old Testament influences on John?[11] One of the sections of his earlier work is actually headed 'Messiah',[12] but it is

---

[10] The titular use of 'the Anointed One' is rare in contemporary Jewish literature. Cf. M de Jonge, 'The Use of the Word "Anointed"', and more generally *Judaisms and Their Messiahs at the Turn of the Christian Era*, ed. J. Neusner *et al.* Instead of limiting myself to this title, however, I shall explore the other titles used of Jesus in the Fourth Gospel to portray him as the fulfilment of Jewish expectation. Justification for this procedure comes from a remarkable document from Qumran (4Q 175), entitled by Vermes 'A Messianic Anthology or Testimonia', which groups together five different passages from Numbers and Deuteronomy that refer in turn to prophet, king, and (by implication) priest. The signs source was not alone in drawing upon biblical passages with a variety of different provenances to construct a cumulative argument.

[11] In his review of *The Interpretation of the Fourth Gospel* in *NTS* 1 (1954/5), 77–91, esp. pp. 78 f., 82.

[12] pp. 228–40.

mostly given over to a discussion of one relatively insignificant title, that of 'Lamb of God'.

This apparent neglect may well arise from a feeling (not always expressed) that Jesus' messianic claims are not after all very important to the evangelist. If this is so, how far is such a feeling justified? Well, these claims lie at the heart of the confrontation with the Samaritan woman in chapter 4, and of the great debate with the Pharisees in chapter 7; they are, apparently, the occasion of the expulsion from the synagogue of the man born blind (ch. 9), and they figure importantly not only in the great confessions of Peter (6: 69) and Martha (11: 27) but also in the summary statement of the purpose of the Gospel (20: 31). Finally, after the Prologue, messianic claims and titles take up virtually the whole of chapter 1. Quite an imposing list, and by no means an exhaustive one.[13] Nevertheless, with the partial exceptions of chapters 4 and 7, the theme of Jesus' messiahship is not really one that excites the evangelist's interest or stimulates his theological imagination.[14] His main *speculative* developments centre upon the nature of Jesus' relationship to God, on judgement and revelation, on the nature and purpose of the Gospel genre. Important as it is, the messianic status of Jesus prompts John's theological creativity much less than the title of Son of Man or the notion of Jesus' divine mission. No doubt John is not alone in this. Paul, too, appears to have had little interest in messiahship as such. The title of Messiah has been so devalued in his writings that it appears there mostly as part of a proper name, 'Jesus Christ'.[15] But if all the ideas of *fulfilment of promise* are to be included under the general rubric 'messianic', then Paul is clearly absorbed by this question in a way that John is not. Fulfilment themes do have some place in his Gospel but they are not at the heart of his theological concerns.

To explain why this should be so we must return to the question of the successive stages of the Gospel's redaction. For all its

[13] The title 'King of the Jews' for instance is the key to some significant developments in the trial before Pilate.

[14] Cf. M. de Jonge, 'Jewish Expectations': 'Titles like "Prophet", "teacher sent by God", "king" or even Messiah', he concludes, 'do not correspond with the real status or authority of them to whom they point. The terms are not wrong but insufficient' (p. 83).

[15] This is also partly true of the Johannine Epistles, and even of the Gospel itself in two instances (1: 17; 17: 3). De Jonge argues (*Jesus*, ch. 7) that the titles 'Messiah' and 'Son of God' are used synonymously in the Epistles. 'Interchangeably' would be better.

compactness and self-allusiveness the Gospel is neither a unified and seamless composition, as Dodd and other conservative commentators would have us believe, nor, as Bultmann suggests, a patchwork pieced together by an intelligent compiler. Rather, we have to think in terms of successive editions and reworkings. At every stage there will have been additions and (more difficult to spot) omissions, some very short, others quite lengthy. It is obviously impossible to produce a totally convincing reconstruction, and the graveyards of New Testament scholarship are littered with discarded skeletons. Nevertheless I am convinced that this is the right *kind* of solution, and that the continual reworkings are best explained as practical responses to the changing conditions of the community and the pressures, from both within and without, to search for answers to the problems to which the new situations had given rise.

In this chapter we shall be concerned with what Martyn calls 'the early period', in which the Johannine Christians, still very much associated with the local synagogue, are distinguished from their fellow-Jews by their profound belief that, in Andrew's words, 'We have found the Messiah' (1: 41).[16] This early stage is represented roughly by what remains of the so-called signs source, in which there are no high christological affirmations, but stories portraying Jesus as a wonder-worker fulfilling the traditional Jewish expectations of a Messiah.[17] Whether this source was a source in the proper sense of the term or whether it was in effect the first draft of what was later to become the Fourth Gospel does not matter for our purposes. What counts is to see that its interests are really very far from those represented by the final version, with its resounding affirmation, on the lips of Thomas, of Jesus' divinity: 'My Lord and my God' (20: 28). 'Can anything good come out of Nazareth?' asked the guileless Nathaniel (1: 46). 'Yes indeed' is the response, a response addressed, presumably, to all those members of the local Jewish community who were genuinely ready to receive and welcome the invitation to 'come and see'.

(d) Early messianic communities?

Is it reasonable to hold that even at the earliest stage of the Johannine community faith in Jesus involved nothing more than an

---

[16] See especially *The Gospel of John*, pp. 93–102.
[17] Robert Fortna argues for this position in *The Fourth Gospel and its Predecessor*. His early article 'Source and Redaction' is less satisfactory.

affirmation of his messiahship? I have already emphasized the a priori unlikelihood of any firm belief in Jesus' divinity making immediate headway within a community dominated by the 'Jewish' establishment. But there are more positive arguments available:

1. In the first place, some evidence in the Acts of the Apostles seems to point in this direction. This evidence is hard to isolate from other, stronger theological motifs, especially those of the 'kerygmatic' discourses. Luke insists as an undeviating principle that Paul must preach *first* in the synagogues and *only then* to the Gentiles. Paul's speech at Pisidian Antioch concludes with a clear programme: 'It was necessary that the word of God should be spoken first to you. Since you thrust it from you, and judge yourselves unworthy of eternal life, behold we turn to the Gentiles' (Acts 13: 46). Luke says that immediately after his conversion Paul began to proclaim in the synagogues of Damascus that Jesus was the Son of God; this is much the same as 'arguing' (συμβιβάζων) that Jesus was the Messiah (9: 20, 22). This conjunction may be purely coincidental but it perhaps suggests that the two titles spring from the same source. Much later we are told how Paul, having, 'as was his custom', gone into the synagogue at Thessalonica, spent three successive sabbaths explaining the Scriptures to the Jewish worshippers and citing texts (διανοίγων καὶ παρατιθέμενος) to show that the Messiah had to die and then rise from the dead (17: 3; cf. Luke 24: 26). Later still, Silas and Timothy arrive at Corinth from Macedonia to find Paul 'testifying that Jesus was the Messiah' (18: 5). At Ephesus too he debated vigorously with the Jews and proved from the Scriptures that Jesus was the Messiah (18: 28). The clear programme of Paul's preaching in Acts, Jews before Gentiles, may well be theologically inspired. Nevertheless the *content* of the preaching affords us a glimpse of a bedrock belief that is usually ignored because it is for the most part effectively concealed by the thick overlay of Luke's developed theology.

One particularly jagged peak rears up in the middle of the range of discourses in Acts: this is Stephen's speech in chapter 7. Sounding hostile, even vindictive, Stephen, who starts very evidently from a Jewish-Christian position, directs a scathing attack upon the Temple and its cult. More positively, he lays enormous stress upon the role of Moses, whose story occupies the whole of the central part of his speech (7: 17–44). This is the Moses who said to the Israelites, 'God will raise up for you a prophet from your brethren as he raised me up' (7: 37), an allusion to Deuteronomy 18: 15, a text whose significance will soon emerge. Jesus is the promised prophet, and Stephen's faith is built upon the fulfilment of this promise. Further-more, the title of Righteous One (ὁ δίκαιος), used only here and in Acts 3: 14 as a title of Jesus, is without question a messianic one:[18] Jeremiah ironically plays upon the word צדקה (righteousness) in order to goad King Zedekiah to live up to his name (Jer. 23: 5 f.; cf. 33: 15). Yet in other respects Stephen's theological position, a kind of reformed Judaism, is somewhat jejune, and Marcel Simon rightly comments, 'His criticism and rejection of some aspects of the ritual Law could provide the starting-point for Christian universalism, by disjoining the Christian message very clearly from Judaism. But something more was needed to make actual that universalism than what he, to judge from Acts, was teaching. And his criticism could quite as well have made the Church just one more sect among many others within Judaism.'[19]

Moreover, if the same author is right in his contention that the Hellenists whom Stephen represents are to be identified as Greek-speaking Jews of the diaspora, advocating 'a renewed Judaism based on the authentic revelation to Moses, rather than a fully new religion',[20] then they cannot have been very far away from the purely messianic faith in Jesus whose possibility I am here concerned to establish. Stephen's dying vision of the Son of Man need not unduly disturb us; for there is no hint here of the conflation of the two figures of Messiah and Son of Man that we find, for instance, in 4 *Ezra* and (embryonically) in the trial-scenes of the Synoptic Gospels.

2. Clearly deriving from Luke's account of Stephen's death, and reflecting a similar strain of Jewish Christianity, is Hegesippus' account of the martyrdom of James, Bishop of Jerusalem, the brother of the Lord.[21] Eusebius tells us that Hegesippus belonged to the first generation after the apostles, and although his account depends not

---

[18] Cf. *ThDNT* s.v. δίκαιος, ii. 186 f.
[19] *St. Stephen and the Hellenists in the Primitive Church* (London, 1958), p. 115.
[20] Ibid., p. 111.
[21] Eusebius, *HE* ii. 23: 8–10. James the Just, whose 'knees grew hard like a camel's from his continually bending them in worship of God', is portrayed here as a *nazir*, belonging to an ascetic tradition that flourished long before Symeon climbed his pillar. But he must have rivalled him in perseverance and pungency, for not only was he a vegetarian and a teetotaller, but he never had a haircut, never took a bath, and never made use of the ancient equivalent of male deodorants.

just on Luke–Acts (and Matthew) but also, probably, on John, nevertheless it may be taken as fairly representative of one element (and that an influential one) within the early Church. The Jewish flavour of the writing is unmistakable:

Representatives of the seven popular sects (αἱρέσεις) already described by me asked him what was meant by 'the door of Jesus', and he replied that Jesus was the Saviour. Some of them came to believe that Jesus was the Messiah: the sects mentioned above did not believe either in a resurrection or in One who is coming to give every man what his deeds deserve, but those who did come to believe did so because of James. Since therefore many even of the ruling class believed, there was an uproar among the Jews and scribes and Pharisees, who said there was a danger that the entire people would expect Jesus as the Messiah. So they collected and said to James: 'Be good enough to restrain the people, for they have gone astray (ἐπλανήθη) after Jesus in the belief that he is the Messiah. Be good enough to make the facts clear to all who come for Passover Day. ... So make it clear to the crowd that they must not go astray as regards Jesus (περὶ Ἰησοῦ μὴ πλανᾶσθαι).[22]

In response, James affirmed his belief in Jesus as the Son of Man who will come on the clouds of heaven—to the dismay of the scribes and Pharisees, who shouted out that 'even the Righteous One has gone astray' (καὶ ὁ δίκαιος ἐπλανήθη), and proceeded to stone him. What is striking about this passage is that the indignation of the Jews could be excited simply and solely by James' teaching that Jesus was the Messiah. The affirmation of belief in the coming of the Son of Man added to their anger but was not what triggered it off in the first place.

3. The most impressive evidence, however, comes from a curious document known to scholars as the *Pseudo-Clementines*. This comprises two versions of a kind of primitive *Bildungsroman*, in which a young man in pursuit of truth eventually arrives at the Christian faith, having discarded on the way a number of less satisfactory answers to his quest. The relevant portion of this long and often tedious narrative is to be found in the first book of the so-called *Recognitions*, chapters 33–71.[23] This roughly follows the course of Stephen's speech in Acts 7, emphasizing in particular the promise of

---

[22] We shall see in the following chapter the significance of the verb πλανᾶν (lead astray). The translation is taken from the edition of Eusebius' *History of the Church* published by Penguin Books (Harmondsworth, 1965), pp. 100 f.

[23] An English translation of these chapters may now be found in J. L. Martyn, *The Gospel of John*, pp. 122–47. He himself takes it from Thomas Smith's version made from the Latin in the 1880s. (The Greek original of the *Recognitions* is not extant.)

another prophet modelled upon Moses (ch. 36: 2). At one point, referring to the fear of the Jewish priests that 'the whole of the people should come over to our faith', the author says that they frequently requested the apostles to tell them of Jesus, 'whether he was the Prophet foretold by Moses, who is the eternal Messiah. *For on this point only does there seem to be any difference between us who believe in Jesus, and the unbelieving Jews*' (ch. 43: 1–2, my italics). The Jews' rejection of Jesus clearly puzzles the writer, since 'it was to be expected that Christ should be received by the Jews, to whom he came, and that they should believe in him' (ch. 50: 1). He resolves the difficulty by appealing to the prophecy 'which said that he was the expectation of the Gentiles'. Thus the natural expectation is reversed, and the Gentiles (just as in Acts) become the true heirs of the Jewish promise. Even so, the picture presented is of a predominantly Jewish community, which has replaced the Temple sacrificial ritual with Christian baptism but is otherwise theologically conservative and (specifically) non-Pauline. It conducts its debates with Jewish or quasi-Jewish groups (the Samaritans are included here) and locates itself with reference to them. The use it makes of the Gospels (Matthew and Luke, but probably not John) is surprisingly discreet, and the occasional allusions to higher christological views appear only in what seem to be later insertions.[24] This 'Clementine' group (a second-century Jewish-Christian church possibly to be located at Pella in Trans-Jordania) endured considerable opposition, amounting to persecution, from the Jewish community, and as J. L. Martyn has brilliantly shown,[25] the document exhibits many motifs that clearly derive from a *Sitz-im-Leben* in Jewish hostility resembling that experienced by the Johannine community. Nevertheless, the implacable resentment towards the Jews that is so marked a feature of the Fourth Gospel is missing here. Apparently persecution has not yet totally alienated this author from his own people.

It is uncertain whether the document contains any actual reminiscences of the Fourth Gospel. Martyn does not entirely reject this hypothesis, although he admits that the arguments in its favour are weak. But what is especially noticeable is that the author betrays no

[24] As is argued by G. Strecker, *Judenchristentum*, pp. 42 f. Shorn of these insertions, the passage indicates a purely messianic faith.

[25] *The Gospel of John*, 55–89. Martyn is less interested in the theology of the group than in establishing this common *Sitz-im-Leben* for the two writings.

conviction of any special relationship between Jesus and God. Jesus appears throughout as the Prophet foretold by Moses (ch. 39: 3);[26] and although the writer makes use of both Matthew and Luke, he does not repeat the special claims they make in their accounts of Jesus' infancy; furthermore, he either does not know or does not want to know of the implicit affirmations of Jesus' divinity discernible in Mark. So if he speaks on behalf of a second-century Christian group, it is one which, from the point of view of later orthodoxy, must be adjudged to be theologically stunted, its growth having stopped well short of the position represented by any of the canonical Gospels, not to mention Paul. All of these start, as Jesus himself did, from a recognizably Jewish faith: but all of them—even Matthew, the most Jewish—end with a belief that is ultimately irreconcilable with establishment Judaism, because all, though with differing emphases, preach a Christ who is very much more than a Messiah. The Johannine group in particular, though its original beliefs were curiously close to those of the Clementine group, branched off in a startlingly different direction, one which brings us back to Bultmann's first and greatest puzzle, to explain how and why the belief of the community developed as it did.

2. THE DISCOVERY OF THE MESSIAH

Answers to this question must be deferred to a later chapter. Meanwhile we must consider an important passage that occurs early in the Gospel. Besides a straightforward account of how Jesus' first disciples came to follow him, this gives a picture of the origins of the Johannine group and an apologia for its early faith. Even at the beginning of the group's history we have to do with a text that must be read on two levels, that of the history of Jesus on the one hand and that of the life of the community on the other. This early use of the principle of two-level interpretation (see Chapter 11) may suggest that we are not dealing with a mere source here but part of a primitive Gospel; for as we shall see, this principle is later seen by the

---

[26] Jesus is also identified as the Mosaic prophet in the other part of the *Pseudo-Clementines*, the *Homilies*. The key text from Deut. 18 is quoted, but not verbatim, and the passage in question (3. 53) might conceivably be a reminiscence of Acts 3: 22. In 11: 26 a quotation from John 3: 5 is attributed to 'the Prophet'; cf. 3: 11, 21; 11: 19; 12: 29; 13: 14.

fourth evangelist as the key to his whole work. However that may be, the passage in question (1: 19–2: 11) shows how the good news of Jesus' messiahship first established itself in our community.

In what follows I make use of a reconstruction of part of the early document known generally, since Bultmann, as the signs source. (Exegetical justification may be found in Excursus II.)[27]

[6]There was a man sent from God whose name was John. [7]He came to bear witness ... so that all might believe through him. [19]And [this was the witness John bore] when priests and Levites sent to ask him, 'Who are you', [20]without evasion he avowed, 'I am not the Messiah.' [21]So they asked him, 'Well then, are you Elijah?' And he said, 'I am not.' 'Are you the Prophet?' And he answered, 'No. [25]So they asked him a further question, 'Why then are you baptizing if you are neither the Messiah, nor Elijah, nor the Prophet?' [26]John answered, 'There stands among you someone whom you do not know ... [31]and I did not know him either, but his manifestation to Israel was the purpose of my coming to baptize. [32]And John bore witness, saying, 'I have seen the Spirit coming down [like a dove] from heaven, and it remained on him: [34]this is the Chosen One of God.' [28]All this took place in Bethany beyond the Jordan where John was baptizing.

[35]The next day John was standing once again with two of his disciples, [36]and as he watched Jesus walking by, he said, 'This is the Lamb of God.' [37]And the two disciples heard what he said, and followed Jesus. [38]Jesus turned, and saw them following, and asked, 'What do you want?' They said to him, 'Master, where are you staying?' [39]He said to them, 'Come and see.' So they went and saw where he was staying [and spent the rest of the day with him: it was the tenth hour]. [40]Now Andrew, the brother of Simon Peter, was one of the two who had heard John speak, and followed him. [41]He first of all found his own brother Simon, and said to him, 'We have found the Messiah,' [42]and he brought him to Jesus. Jesus looked at him and said, 'So you are Simon, the son of John? You will be called Peter.' *Then Peter found Philip and said to him: 'We have found Elijah, who will restore all things.' He brought him to Jesus. [43]Jesus said to him, 'Follow me.' [44]Now Philip, like Andrew and Peter, was from Bethsaida. [45]Philip found Nathanael, and said to him, 'We have found him of whom Moses wrote in the Law [and also the prophets], Jesus of Nazareth, the son of Joseph.' [46]And Nathanael said to him, 'Can anything good come out of Nazareth?' Philip said to him, 'Come and see.' [47]Now Jesus saw Nathanael approaching him, and

[27] Cf. Bultmann, Boismard, Fortna, and especially Martyn, whose reconstruction of 1: 43 (with minor changes) is asterisked in the text. Fortna's later work does not offer a Greek text and differs only in minor respects from *The Gospel of Signs*. At the time of writing I have not had access to U. C. von Wahlde: *The Earliest Version of John's Gospel: Recovering the Gospel of Signs* (Wilmington, Del., 1989).

said of him, 'There truly is an Israelite in whom there is no deceit.'
⁴⁸Nathanael said to him, 'How do you know me?' Jesus answered, 'Before
Philip called you [from under the fig-tree], I saw you.' ⁴⁹Nathanael
answered, 'Master, you are the Son of God! You are the King of Israel!'

(a) Structure and motifs

Although, like the rest of the Gospel, this passage has been seen
differently by different commentators, I believe that even in its
finished form, after a new time-structure has been imposed, it falls
naturally into two distinct but related sections, the first (vv. 19–34)
concerning the witness of John the Baptist (which, following Dodd,
we may call 'the Testament'), the second (vv. 35–51) telling of the
discovery of Jesus by his first disciples (henceforth 'the Discovery').
The third part of the triptych, the marriage-feast at Cana, will be
discussed later. The chapter concludes with a little dialogue between
Jesus and Nathanael, the 'Israelite in whom there is no guile'. The
strange prophetic vision in which the mysterious figure of the Son of
Man appears for the first time in the Gospel seems not to belong to
the source, which is what concerns us here.

The basic structure is simple: (1) John the Baptist renounces all
claim to the three messianic titles that he is invited to assume
(Messiah, Elijah, Prophet); he justifies his baptismal activity by
stating that he has come so that 'one who stands in the midst of you'
may be revealed to Israel. He testifies that he saw the Holy Spirit
coming down upon this man and proclaims him to be the Chosen
One of God. (2) In the second part, after pointing out Jesus to two of
his own disciples ('Behold, the Lamb of God'), John retires from the
stage, in accordance with the principle he will enunciate later: 'He
must grow greater; I must grow less' (3: 30). So he leaves the
disciples to their gradual discovery of Jesus, who is shown, successively, to be Messiah, Elijah, Prophet; and the passage ends with
Nathanael's triumphant acclamation: 'You are the Son of God! You
are the King of Israel!'

The two introductory verses (1: 6 f.), subsequently detached in
order to splice the Testimony with the Prologue,²⁸ had an important
structural function. They contain three ideas that dominate the
three opening sections of the signs source (2: 1–11 must be included

²⁸ The first to suggest that John's narrative source began with 1: 6 was apparently
Spitta (1910).

here): witness, revelation, faith. However, it is to be observed that
these three key concepts (as well as those of mission and coming) are
all referred in the source to the Baptist rather than to Jesus. Whoever
inserted them in the prologue felt it necessary to spell out that the
Baptist was not the light, but although the evangelist took over all
five ideas he totally transformed them by his own special alchemy.
Certainly he did not believe that the Baptist's *witness* was primary
(this is underplayed in ch. 5 and dropped entirely in ch. 8); for him,
the really important *mission* was that of Jesus himself (and secondarily the mission of the Paraclete and that of the disciples); above all, in
the body of the Gospel it is Jesus himself and none other who *reveals*
the truth and leads men to *faith* in him. So we find in embryonic
form a number of terms and concepts that are in one sense
recognizably and obviously 'Johannine', but cannot be said to be
employed in a way characteristic of John's mature theology. If
nevertheless they were present in a rudimentary fashion as the
Johannine group was beginning to form, then it is easier to
understand how in the course of time they could be built into the
great conceptual plan of the finished Gospel.

Even in its truncated form the passage contains a remarkable
series of titles:[29] the first three (Messiah, Elijah, Prophet) constitute a
special case, since they figure in both the Testimony and the
Discovery ('the one of whom Moses wrote' being a clear reference to
the eschatological prophet). Besides these we have the two titles
given to Jesus by John the Baptist, first the Chosen One, secondly the
Lamb of God, and finally the great triumphant acclamation of
Nathanael ('You are the Son of God! You are the King of Israel!') to
which the whole passage has been building up. Taken as a whole it
represents a declaration of faith on the part of the writer and his
readers, but also a challenge to other 'Israelites' of good faith to
show the same open-minded generosity of spirit as Nathanael.[30]

[29] There is only one term with any claim to being a title that is left out in the
reconstruction—ὁ ἐρχόμενος. Wayne Meeks says that it cannot be proved that this was
a messianic title (*Prophet-King*, p. 90), but the Gospel tradition (Matt. 11: 3; John
6: 14; 11: 27) suggests that it was; and in any case it makes little difference whether it
was a regular title: there is no doubt that 'the Coming One', title or not, alluded to the
messianic expectation of the Jews. This series of titles may be compared with those
given to the heavenly being in the *Parables of Enoch*, eventually identified with Enoch
himself.

[30] Nathanael performs much the same function in the Fourth Gospel as Joseph
('the just man') in Matthew. Joseph is contrasted with Herod and is signalled out as
the type of the true descendant of David who is ready to welcome the new king.

Structurally, the title 'Chosen One' has a double function: most importantly, it forms the climax of the first section and so balances out the title 'Son of God' at the end, and is actually replaced by it in many manuscripts. Secondly, it stands over against 'Lamb of God' at the beginning of the Discovery. Of the two titles attributed to Jesus by John the Baptist, one is clearly messianic, the other probably so.

(b) Titles

The *Messiah*, properly speaking, is a man anointed by God and sent by him at the end of time to assist him in establishing his kingly rule. Mowinckel objects to any application of the term outside the sphere of eschatology.[31] But the Messiah first appears as the ideal successor to King David, and, generally speaking, whenever 'Messiah' is used without qualification in the New Testament (i.e. the Greek word Χριστός, for the transliteration Μεσσίας does not appear except in John 1: 41; 4: 25) it is either as a proper name or else in reference to the kingly, Davidic Messiah. According to the tradition, Jesus was at pains to disengage himself from the triumphant political trappings that had understandably come to festoon what he himself, the Gospels would have us believe, thought of as a purely religious figure with a purely religious function. It is hardly surprising to find religious fervour going hand in hand with a strong and often bellicose nationalism, as in the Qumran War Scroll or the Psalms of Solomon: 'See, Lord, and raise up for them their king, the Son of David, at the time you [alone] have knowledge of, so that he may reign over your servant (παῖδά σου) Israel, and gird him with strength, enabling him to smash those that rule without justice' (17: 23 f.). Although idealized, the Davidic Messiah was bound to some extent to be associated with very human hopes for the restoration of the kingdom of Judah.

Elijah did not die like other men, but was taken up to heaven 'by a whirlwind of fire, in a chariot with horses of fire' (Sir. 48: 9). Thence he would be sent forth 'before the great and terrible day of the Lord' (Mal. 3: 18), and his task would be 'to calm the wrath of God before it breaks out in fury, to turn the heart of the father to the son, and to restore the tribes of Jacob' (Sir. 48: 10). According to Malachi (at any rate the final version of this, the last of the canonical prophets),

---

[31] *He that Cometh*, p. 3.

and to Ben Sira too, Elijah's mission was to be one of conciliation, though the Synoptic tradition simply says of him, rather mysteriously, that he would 'restore all things' (Mark 9: 11). But of course he would bring with him the memory of his achievements in his previous existence. A difficulty about this title is that Matthew and Mark assign it unequivocally to John the Baptist: there can be no doubt that in running counter to this tradition the author of this passage intends to assign it to Jesus instead.[32] One reason why this ascription was subsequently blotted out may have been the desire to avoid any suggestion of a double incarnation (for Elijah is the only one of the three figures who was believed to have lived on earth in times gone by). By the same token the identification of Jesus with Elijah could have been one of the sources of the strange concept of pre-existence—later to be associated firmly and unambiguously with the Logos and the Son of Man.

The Prophet, as is universally agreed, is the one foretold by Moses: 'The Lord your God will raise up for you a prophet like me from among you, from your brethren—him you shall heed—just as you desired of the Lord your God. ... And the Lord said to me, "... I will raise up for them a prophet like you from among their brethren; and I will put my words in his mouth, and he shall speak to them all that I command him"' (Deut. 18: 15–18). For the Deuteronomist himself the new Moses was undoubtedly a generic figure—the ideal prophet—but subsequent interpretation lifted him out of this context and gave him a particular identity and a special role. We have already come across him in the *Pseudo-Clementines* and in Stephen's speech in Acts 7. The same passage is also quoted in Acts 3: 22. Wherever he appears in the literature of the period it is as an eschatological figure, one who could be said to be messianic in a broad sense of the term, and in fact even in the Old Testament itself there are two passages in which prophets are said to be anointed (1 Kings 19: 16—the anointing of Elisha by Elijah and Isa. 61: 1–3, an important passage for the Synoptic interpretation of Jesus' miracles).

One question that arises in connection with these three titles is how far they were thought of as distinct one from another and how far they were intended to 'cover all the bases' in much the same manner as religious litanies, both earlier and later, both Christian and non-Christian, were designed to avoid giving offence to saint or

---

[32] Once again I am greatly indebted to J. L. Martyn, and I follow his attempted reconstruction of 1: 43 in *The Gospel of John*, pp. 33–42.

deity by including all possible titles to which he or she might be thought to aspire. On the whole it seems likely that they were thought of as distinct (even though they were to be fused in Jesus), especially since the (or a) prophet appears alongside the twin Messiahs of Aaron in an important passage from Qumran. The members of the community are instructed not to show their hardness of heart by abandoning any of the commandments of the Law, but rather to be guided by the primitive precepts which the community was taught from its inception, 'until there shall come a prophet and the Messiahs of Aaron and Israel' (1QS 9: 10 f.). What is more, these three personages, the prophet, the priest, and the king, may be envisaged in an important collection of texts with a clear messianic bearing: first a reference to the future prophet drawn from a proto-Samaritan version of Exod. 20: 21;[33] next the 'star of Jacob/sceptre of Israel' passage from Numbers (Num. 24: 15–17) and a further passage with a strong liturgical flavour from Deuteronomy (Deut. 33: 8–11). So here once again (4Q 175) come the eschatological priest, prince, and prophet. In the interests of concinnity it would be nice to identify these three with the three named by John's interlocutors, but it is doubtful whether the midrashic view of Elijah as a priest had yet arisen.[34]

The Chosen One (ὁ ἐκλεκτός) is not used as a title of Jesus elsewhere in the New Testament (except Luke 23: 35; cf. 9: 35: ὁ ἐκλελεγμένος), although it seems almost tailor-made for the job, especially in an eschatological setting. Like 'Prophet' it sounds rather vague, but in fact the allusion is quite precise. The earliest form of the signs source may well have included some account of Jesus' baptism, omitted by John to avoid any suggestion that Jesus might be the Baptist's inferior. But in what remains of the source all we have is John's testimony that he saw the Spirit descending upon Jesus, along with his conclusion, 'This is the Chosen One of God'. This is unquestionably a reference to one of Second Isaiah's Servant Songs:

[33] This was thought at first to be from Deut. 18: 18; but it was later shown that the three passages were chosen from three successive biblical books. See P. Skehan, *CBQ* 19 (1957) 435–40.

[34] That this was the view of the rabbis and targumim is shown by A. S. van der Woude, *Die messianischen Vorstellungen*, pp. 60 f. This scholar argues that 'the interpreter of the Law' is to be identified with 'the high priest Elijah'. But all the evidence for the priesthood of Elijah is late. If 'the interpreter of the Law' were to be identified with any of the three messianic figures it would surely be with 'the prophet'. Cf. also Ginzberg, *Legends*, iv. 195–235; vi. 316–42.

Behold my servant (LXX, ὁ παῖς μου) whom I uphold.
my chosen one (MT, בְּחִירִי LXX, ὁ ἐκλεκτός μου) in whom my soul delights:
I have put my spirit upon him,
he will bring forth justice to the nations.   (Isa. 42: 1)

All three Synoptists allude to this verse in their account of Jesus'
baptism (Matt. 3: 17 //), though παῖς becomes υἱός and ἐκλεκτός
becomes ἀγαπητός, literally 'beloved'. But this does not prove that
they wanted to identify Jesus as the Servant. Second Isaiah spurns
convention by calling Cyrus, King of Persia, the 'anointed' of the
Lord (Isa. 45: 1), but messianic expectation in the proper sense is
foreign to the thought of this prophet: what *he* longed for and
foretold was the re-enthronement of Yahweh as king.

Proof that 'the Chosen One' could be used as a messianic title
comes in a near-contemporary Jewish apocryphon: 'And then I will
sound the trumpet out of the air, and I will send my Chosen One,
having in him all my power, a single measure; and he shall summon
my despised people from the nations' (*Apocalypse of Abraham* 31:
1–2). Opposition to 'the Lord and his anointed' in Psalm 2: 1–2
is interpreted at Qumran as directed against 'the elect of Israel'
(בְּחִירֵי יִשְׂרָאֵל) (4Q 174.1: 19), and although the writer has the
whole community in mind here ('elect' is plural), the interpretation
of the Messiah as the chosen ones of Israel lends support to the
suggestion that another fragment from Qumran containing the term
'the Chosen One of God' (בְּחִיר אֱלָהָא) is messianic in intent.[35] At
any rate this personage seems to have been 'chosen' precisely for
the purpose of playing some role in the realisation of the divine
plan.

Lamb of God, a title conferred on Jesus by John the Baptist on
his second appearance, the following day, balances (chiastically?)
'the Chosen One'. It is the title the writer selects to introduce his
account of the Discovery, and in spite of the interest it has excited
among exegetes, who are as fond as anybody else of a knotty puzzle,
I doubt if it has yet been satisfactorily explained. In my view the
phrase 'who takes away the sins of the world' (v. 29) is a later
addition (in line, as Schnackenburg argues, ad loc., with the
theology of 1 John 3: 5), so it is the title itself that presents the first

---

[35] 4 Q243. This is contested by J. A. Fitzmyer, 'The Aramaic "Elect of God"
Text'. But it is hard to deny all relevance to a text that tells of a new-born child of
whom a brilliant future is predicted, within the context of the divine plan, 'because he
is the Chosen One of God'.

problem. C. H. Dodd[36] is clearly attracted by the suggestion that the term alludes to the Suffering Servant, who 'was dumb like a sheep (MT, רָחֵל LXX, ἀμνός) before its shearers' (Isa. 53: 7). If the author of the source had held the two Servant Songs (Isa. 42 and 53) linked in his mind, and consequently intended the two titles (Chosen One and Lamb of God) to have a common reference, then the suggestion may seem a little less whimsical. And given the proximity of the two titles in the source (where they were, I suggest, separated by a single verse, 1: 28), it might be thought to gain slightly more plausibility—but only, surely, the merest whisker, for it still owes more to ingenuity than to sense.

The interpretation Dodd actually favours may appear at first sight even more wildly improbable, for the decidedly ruthless lamb of the Book of Revelation seems to have little in common with the human Jesus pointed to by John.[37] But it must be remembered that *all* the titles in this passage transport us into the world of eschatological speculation. And there is some evidence from pseudepigraphical sources that the messianic leader of the people could be symbolized by a lamb (though not, at least not clearly so, in the most important passage quoted by Dodd, from the *Book of Enoch*).[38] In the *Testament of Joseph*, on the other hand, the lamb shows a fighting spirit it has subsequently lost:

there came forth a lamb (ἀμνός); and on its left all the beasts and all the reptiles attacked, and the lamb overcame and destroyed them (19: 8).

A further text, not quoted by Dodd, which may have been composed at quite an early date, comes in one of the most extraordinary insertions in targumic literature. Its subject is the nature of the four nights of the Passover:

The *fourth night*: When the world reaches its end to be redeemed (למתפרקא: dissolved?) the yokes of iron shall be broken and the genera-

---

[36] *Interpretation*, pp. 235 f. See too the literature cited by K. Wengst, *Bedrängte Gemeinde*, p. 107 n. 339.

[37] What is more, the Greek word (ἀρνίον) is different.

[38] The difficulty here is that the passage (1 *Enoch* 90: 37 f.) has been transmitted in two versions, Ethiopic and Greek, and only the latter contains any reference to a horned lamb. The latest editor of the Ethiopic text, Michael Knibb (Oxford, 1978) translates the passage in such a way as to make the leader a wild-ox. 'Possibly', he says, 'we have in these verses a belief in two messiahs—a priestly leader (the white bull of v. 37) and a military leader (the wild-ox of v. 38)' (p. 216 ad loc.). But he also concedes that the white bull and the wild-ox might be one and the same.

tions of wickedness shall be blotted out; and Moses will go up from the desert and the king Messiah from on high. One will lead at the head of the flock, and the other will lead at the head of the flock, and his Word will lead between the two of them, [and I] and they will proceed together.[39]

Whether or not this fascinating text clinches Dodd's case this derivation seems to me marginally more probable than either of the other two leading candidates, Suffering Servant and Paschal Lamb.

Son of God may be the most important—it is certainly the most misunderstood—of all the titles. Here it is vital to distinguish between the meaning of the source and its interpretation by the evangelist. Schnackenburg fails to do this and consequently stumbles badly in an otherwise smoothly confident article[40] criticizing the one-sided theories of Robinson and van Unnik.

In all probability this title, like the rest, originally indicated messiahship rather than divinity. Mowinckel is suspicious of any suggestion that the Jews ever actually called the Messiah by this name: speaking of *4 Ezra* 7: 28 etc. and *1 Enoch* 105 (Christian?) he remarks that even if these passages 'had originally expressed the idea of the Messiah as the Son of God ... the Jews would understand the term in accordance with Old Testament ideas of the *adopted* son of Yahweh as in Ps. 2, i.e. as indicating not a metaphysical sonship from all eternity, but rather a divine election for a specially close and intimate relationship, and a call from Him to be fulfilled in His power.'[41]

In view of the way the king is addressed by God in Psalm 2: 7 ('Thou are my son, this day I have begotten thee'), and of the assurance to David that God would continue to favour his descendants ('I will be his father, and he shall be my son' (2 Sam. 7: 14)),

---

[39] Codex Neofiti 1/2 (ed. Diez-Macho), p. 79. For 'flock' (עָנָא) in this passage some editors read 'cloud' (עֲנָנָא). But according to R. Le Déaut, this reading has no manuscript support (*Sources Chrétiennes*, No. 256, p. 98 n. 49). The phrase 'king Messiah' (מלכא משיחא) is not in Neofiti but has been added by Le Déaut from a fragmentary targum. See too, by the same author, *La Nuit pascale*.

[40] 'Die Messiasfrage'.

[41] *He that Cometh*, p. 294. The origin of the use of the title within the New Testament is unclear. The widespread use of the so-called 'messianic' psalms, 2 and 110, shows that it rapidly gathered a messianic connotation. I suspect that in the earliest traditions of Jesus' activities as an exorcist, the term 'Son of God', along with 'Holy One of God' (Mark 1: 24), indicates an association with the divine beings (holy ones, sons of God, watchers) that occupy such an important place in the heavenly world of the Dead Sea Scrolls as well as that of apocalypses like Daniel and *I Enoch*. At this point, however, we are concerned exclusively with the signs source.

the term 'Son of God' would seem a natural one to use of the Messiah, and indeed the prophecy of Nathan is commented upon and quoted extensively in another fragmentary text from Qumran which goes on to apply the prophecy to 'the scion of David' (צמח דויד) who stands alongside 'the interpreter of the Law' (דרש התורה—an important personage in the Qumran community): 'as it is written, "I will raise up the fallen booth of David" (Amos 9: 11) which will stand erect so as to save Israel' (4Q 174.1: 11–13). What is more, the passage continues by quoting further texts, ending with Psalm 2, although unfortunately it breaks off before reaching the crucial v. 7.

The expression 'son of God' (בר די אל) does actually occur in yet another fragment from Qumran (4Q 246), discussed by J. A. Fitzmyer,[42] whose translation of the emended text I now quote:

[But] shall be great upon the earth, [O king! All (people) shall make peace], and all shall serve [him. He shall be called the son of the G]reat [God], and by his name shall he be named. He shall be hailed (as) the Son of God, and they shall call him the Son of the Most High. As comets (flash) to the sight, so shall be their kingdom. (For some) year[s] they shall rule upon the earth and shall trample everything (under foot); people shall trample upon people, city upon ci[t]y, (*vacat.*) until there arises the people of God, and everyone rests from the sword.

'There is no indication', comments Fitzmyer, 'that the person to whom the titles "Son of God" or "Son of the Most High" are given in this text is a messianic figure; we are still looking for extra-NT instances in which such titles have been applied to an anointed agent of Yahweh.' This may be so, but the passage has a strongly eschatological flavour, and Fitzmyer himself remarks upon the striking parallels with two of the names promised to Jesus by the angel Gabriel at the moment of the Annunciation (Luke 1: 32, 35).

That there is no need to look outside Jewish circles for the origin of the term 'Son of God' is a main contention of a concise and learned study by Martin Hengel, who points out that this Aramaic text 'makes one thing clear, that the title "Son of God" was not completely alien to Palestinian Judaism'.[43] Hengel's little book ranges too widely for us to follow any further at present; but we have more than enough evidence already to suggest that the term 'Son of

---

[42] 'The Aramaic Language and the Study of the New Testament', pp. 14 f.
[43] *Son of God*, p. 45

God' was, *at least in its early Christian usage*, a messianic title. Equally important is the fact that for establishment Judaism the title had no connotation of divinity in the full sense of 'metaphysical sonship'.

King of Israel, the last of the titles, confirms John the Baptist's description of the purpose of his own mission, that Jesus 'should be revealed to Israel', and recognized as Messiah by one who was 'truly an Israelite', neither deceitful nor deceived. There are two negative facts to be taken into consideration here: first that the title 'Son of David', so important to Matthew, is entirely missing from the Fourth Gospel;[44] secondly that, in contrast with the infancy narrative in Matt. 2: 2; (cf. Luke 1: 32), which performs an introductory function similar to John 1, Jesus is called 'King of Israel' in this passage and not 'King of the Jews'. Wayne Meeks comments: 'Quite possibly there lies behind this usage a polemical situation in which Christians, over against Jewish opponents, call themselves "the true Israel".'[45] It is a comment that deserves to be weighed carefully. Although of course Jesus' messianic claims extend to the *whole* of Israel (which must include Judaea), even so the Gospel assumes (7: 41)—and the source at this point concurs—that he, like his earliest disciples (or at least the four that are named here), is a Galilean. Consequently it has to be asked what we can learn from the sources about the relations between the young Christian group and the Jews (or should one say 'Judaeans' at this point?).

(c) Jesus and the Jews

It will be observed that neither οἱ Ἰουδαῖοι (1: 19) nor the Pharisees (1: 24) figure in the reconstructed text, which attributes the deputation sent to interrogate John the Baptist to the sole initiative of 'priests and Levites'. The term οἱ Ἰουδαῖοι, if retained, must refer, as it sometimes does in the Gospel, to the authorities in Jerusalem. We should then have another example of an expression in the source that the evangelist has adopted for his own purposes. But the Greek is somewhat overloaded at this point and it is more likely that the source has been expanded in line with the evangelist's later preoccupations. However that may be, the sudden appearance of '(the) Pharisees' a little later presents a problem that can scarcely be resolved satisfactorily by those who insist upon explaining the

---

[44] Cf. G. Reim, *Studien*, pp. 247 ff.   [45] *Prophet-King*, p. 83.

passage as a unified composition. For either they are to be understood as a separate group altogether (in which case what are we to
suppose has become in the meantime of the priests and Levites?) or
the former group are being *identified* as belonging to the Pharisaic
sect (if so, why, and why so late?) or else, finally, the Pharisees are
being singled out as the real organizers of the original mission—but
in that case why did not the writer bring them in at the start of his
narrative?[46]

We should remember, moreover, that the Pharisees were predominantly a lay organization, and that although at the time of Jesus
they may have included some priests in their ranks, they will
scarcely have had the authority to initiate the kind of official enquiry
that the story implies. Only much later, when the Jewish priesthood
had lost its political role because of the failure of the Jewish revolt,
was the sect in a position to gather the reins of power into its own
hands. It must also be borne in mind that neither priests nor Levites
appear elsewhere in the Fourth Gospel, whereas the conjunction is a
common one not only in the Old Testament but also in the Rule of
the Community at Qumran. The grouping is particularly appropriate
to the context of the Testimony, which centres upon a rite of
purification, and Dodd is surely correct here in his suggestion of 'a
tradition going back to the period, before AD 70, when the twofold
ministry was still functioning at Jerusalem'.[47]

If this is so, then we should be careful not to read into this passage
the overtones of mistrust and hostility that the term οἱ Ἰουδαῖοι
carries almost everywhere in the body of the Gospel. The priests and
Levites in this story were conscientiously discharging a perfectly
proper function, and it would be wrong to assume, from what we
know elsewhere of the attitudes of the Pharisees, that this was done
with any malevolent intent.[48] What is more, the literary form of the

---

[46] On this point, see U. C. von Wahlde, 'The Terms for Religious Authorities'.

[47] *Tradition*, p. 263. In spite of his refusal to enter into the question of a Johannine
signs source, Dodd believes that the Testimony, though not the Discovery, is built
upon a narrative taken over by the evangelist. He distinguished here between
vv. 19–27, in which 'there is little or nothing which seems to derive from the special
views of the evangelist', and vv. 29–34, in which 'there is evidence of traditional
material lying behind the Johannine presentation, but evidence also of some
pragmatic rehandling of the material in the interests of Johannine doctrine' (ibid.,
p. 276).

[48] Cf. C. J. A. Hickling, 'Attitudes to Judaism'. Hickling examines four passages in
chs. 2–4 (2: 13–22; 4: 9, 35–8, 46–54) and finds in them 'a generally affirmative
attitude towards Judaism in material accepted from tradition' (p. 351).

Testimony is very different from the controversy or pronouncement-story familiar to us from the pages of the Synoptic Gospels, in which everything leads up to a punch-line that results in the discomfiture of Jesus' interlocutors (e.g. 'Render therefore to Caesar ...'). If we then ask, as a structuralist critic might, what is the function of the priests and Levites in the narrative itself (prescinding from any consideration of their actual historical role), then we can scarcely fail to see that their questions serve simply to give John the Baptist a suitable opportunity for uttering his testimony—in the first place, the disclaimers that pave the way for the Discovery that is to follow the next day, and, in the second place, the positive assertion that 'this is the Chosen One of God'. In so far as the priests and Levites may be assumed to assist at the testimony (as they will have done in the first version of the story), they are to be credited with a subsidiary function, which is to witness to what they have heard. Consequently, far from being the aggressive questioners prejudice leads us to expect, they serve to authenticate, albeit indirectly, the Baptist's testimony.

Now given the kind of *Sitz-im-Leben* we have already postulated for the source, this should not surprise us. In a missionary tract, designed to promote the new sect among Jewish listeners who may be conceived to be partly sceptical, partly sympathetic, but at any rate not yet convinced, it seems unlikely that much weight will have been put upon the hostile attitude of the religious authorities in Jerusalem. This does not mean that the priests and Levites need to be credited with any intention of deliberately serving the Christian cause. What must have impressed the listeners first of all is the sincerity of the convert preachers, their burning conviction that they, like Andrew, had 'found the Messiah'. But we still have to ask in what, or rather in whom, the listeners were being asked to put their faith.

(d) The picture of Jesus

We have already seen that no other passage in the Fourth Gospel lends more plausibility to the thesis that the Gospel was designed as a missionary tract to draw Jews of the diaspora to the new faith. For here we have a Jesus who is *presented* to the Jews as the one who has come to fulfil all their hopes: he is the promised Messiah, he is Elijah returned to earth, he is the eschatological prophet foretold by Moses, he is the Chosen One, the Son of God, the King of Israel.

In all this he plays a curiously passive role, utterly untypical of the Johannine Christ whose powerful presence dominates the remainder of the Gospel. Here by contrast, apart from the single invitation, 'Follow me!', addressed to Philip, he appears to be content to wait to be discovered. In the first section it is John the Baptist who enjoys the limelight, and even after he has left the stage, having delivered his testimony and pointed out Jesus to two of his disciples, the writer is still anxious to persuade us that Jesus is *there to be found* if only we care to look for him. He is the object of testimony, not the one who testifies. Elsewhere he it is and he alone who leads to the Father and initiates all the action: even in the passion, as we have noticed, he is not only the protagonist but also the director.[49]

Taken together, the Testimony and the Discovery make up a triumphant and delighted description of how the Messiah came to be found by his first disciples. One of these eventually turns to Nathanael, who fulfils the promise of his name by declaring to the one whom God had indeed given, 'You are the Son of God! You are the King of Israel!' Implicit throughout is the suggestion that Jesus' later disciples, now actively proselytizing within the Jewish community, are carrying on the work of Andrew, Peter, and Philip, by inviting all their fellow Israelites, or at least those 'without guile', to 'come and see' for themselves the one of whom Moses spoke.

But a puzzle remains. Are we not dealing with a *signs* source, a document that backs up its belief in Jesus with the irrefutable evidence of his miracles? Yet up to now there is no trace of the miraculous, and the emphasis is all upon the personal testimony of John and his disciples. Jesus is found, and his messianic dignity proclaimed before he has either *said* anything about himself or *done* anything to attract attention. Neither by words nor gesture has he 'manifested his glory'. Perhaps we should not fall into the trap of attaching undue significance to our own slogans. After all, 'signs source' is just a label, and we have no good reason a priori to suppose that it will convey a more accurate idea of the contents than any comparable label stuck upon another package that similarly claims to be full of wonders. Right from the start the writer makes his intentions plain; much later he will make them even plainer:

[49] A good instance of this is in the story of the healing of the cripple in ch. 5. Asked the identity of his healer, the man cannot reply until Jesus finds him in the Temple and enables him to answer.

'these things are written that you may believe that Jesus is the Messiah, the Son of God' (20: 31).

All the same, in that very passage he writes of *signs*. And it is true that, taken in isolation, the twin stories of testimony and discipleship we have been considering are incomplete. In so far as John the Baptist could bear witness he has done so, but the true revelation is yet to begin. Testimony and Discovery are but two panels of a triptych. Two days have passed but the events of the third have yet to be told.

3. THE COMMENCEMENT OF THE SIGNS

Chapter 2 of the Gospel opens with the phrase καὶ τῇ ἡμέρᾳ τῇ τρίτῃ, which can be translated either, as it usually is, 'on the third day' or 'two days later/the next day but one'. In the former case the suggestion must be that after the incidents recorded on the two previous days there is another to be told; if the latter rendering is preferred the reference does not reach back to the first day (the Testimony) but only as far as the second (the Discovery). (I am here assuming my own reconstruction of the preceding sections, for this simple progression has been obscured by subsequent additions.) In either case the story of the 'sign' that follows is to be seen as the completion of the opening triptych.[50] Once this is concluded in 2: 11, the signs source is interrupted by material hewn from a very different quarry.

Tramping the foothills of biblical scholarship, the exegete is often tempted to stray from the beaten track, and nowhere more so than in the course of investigating the marriage-feast of Cana, where one can easily find oneself waist-high in bracken. The episode is crammed with teasing little problems. What was Jesus' mother (never named Mary in the Gospel) doing at the wedding in the first place? Was it because, as one tradition held, she was the groom's aunt? Or had the whole family recently moved house from Nazareth to Cana? Who invited Jesus and his disciples to the wedding? Was it perhaps Nathanael, who, we are told in a later chapter (21: 2) came

---

[50] Given this natural function of the words 'on the third day', there is no need to postulate any far-fetched symbolism according to which the words would point either to the resurrection (Dodd) or, still more cryptically, to the giving of the Old Law recorded as having taken place 'on the third day' in Exod. 19 (Olsson).

from Cana? And at what stage in the celebrations did they turn up?
Maybe towards the end of the week, when the wine might well have
already been finished, unless it had run out—an alternative explanation—because of gatecrashers to the party. Why did Jesus' mother
become involved, and why was she especially concerned by the
shortage of wine? Was only a portion of the water in the jars changed,
or was it all turned into wine to ensure a plentiful supply during the
celebrations; and how many gallons are there in a firkin anyway?
What eventually became of the bride and groom? One medieval
tradition makes the groom forsake his bride on their wedding night,
leaving the marriage unconsummated, in order to follow Jesus: his
name was John, and he was later to write a Gospel![51] And if none of
these questions is easy to answer or indeed seems particularly
relevant, then one can lope off instead on a hunt of parallels: Jesus
goes one better than Moses, who merely turns the water in the stone-
jars of the Egyptians (Exod. 7: 19) into blood! Even Raymond Brown,
who is especially good on this passage, feels free to follow Bernard and
others in indulging in such harmless little *divertissements*.[52] There are,
however, some serious obstacles to a proper understanding of the
passage, this time blocking the main track: they concern the meaning
of Jesus' reply to his mother, τί ἐμοὶ καὶ σοί, γύναι; (v. 4) and of the
following sentence (statement or question?) concerning Jesus' 'hour'.
Above all there is the problem of the *significance* of the miracle, whose
very singularity (there is nothing quite like it elsewhere in the Gospels)
renders interpretation particularly hazardous.[53] The following exegesis presupposes my own attempted reconstruction of the Cana
episode as it stood in the signs source.

Certain points are of particular interest:

[51] This choice morsel is to be found in Loisy's commentary, p. 269. The whole
crazy idea seems to have been sparked off by someone's misunderstanding of a
passage in Jerome's *Adversus Jovinianum* comparing the roles of Peter and John, and
concluding, among other things, that 'exposuit virginitas quod nuptiae scire non
poterant' (i. 26, *PL* xxiii, col. 259)—a virgin (John) expounded what a married man
(Peter) could never have known! See the meditation addressed to the evangelist by *The
Monk of Farne*, ed. Dom Hugh Farmer, OSB (London, 1961, p. 149): 'If I choose to call
you a virgin, the whole church will be able to bear witness to what I say, for it was as
a virgin that you were singled out by our Lord and called away from your wedding.'

[52] And is rebuked for so doing by Ernst Haenchen, who remarks primly: 'There is
nothing wrong with the critical method, but carried to extremes it can become
ridiculous ('Kritik is keine schlechte Sache, aber übertreibt man sie, kann sie
lächerlich werden' (*Johannesevangelium*, p. 193); cf. ET, p. 176.)

[53] For detailed criticism and an attempted reconstruction of this passage see
Excursus II.

(a) *The role of Jesus' mother*

It is to be noted first of all that she was present at the wedding from
the start, unlike Jesus and his disciples, who arrived later, as invited
guests, from the outside. Like the water-jars mentioned later she was
there (the word ἐκεῖ occurs twice, once in v. 1 and a second time in
v. 6). So although, unlike the jars, she is not exactly part of the
furniture, she is more closely identified with the scene of the wedding
itself, and this first impression is confirmed by her opening words:
'They have no wine.' On the other hand, she says 'they' rather than
'we', and this suggests a certain distancing on her part: not a total
but only a partial identification with those responsible for mounting
the wedding and the other guests. The writer, it must be stressed,
says nothing of her *feelings*, nor, apart from the simple fact of the
shortage of wine, of the reason for her intervention.

In his reply to his mother, Jesus registers a strong protest, which
initially highlights his independence. Of course her comment is at
the same time a *request*, a request for decisive action, a request, at
least implicitly, for a *miracle*. And it is this that prompts Jesus'
seemingly harsh rejoinder, which he follows up with a reference to
his 'hour'. In asking ourselves what Jesus' words mean, we must
bear in mind the fact that she herself did not take them as a total
rebuff, for her response is to turn to the servants with the injunction,
'Do exactly as he tells you.' Far from allowing herself to be deterred
by the apparent rebuke, she rejects the negative role she is evidently
being assigned and takes part in the action, disclosing as she does so
a new set of characters, of whom she is in a certain sense the leader.
There is a temptation to allegorize at this point—Mother Church
and her ministers, οἱ διάκονοι—but there is no obvious justification
for doing so.

So the mother of Jesus occupies a mediating position, ranged in
the first place with the hosts and guests, associating herself with
their need, and eliciting, by her plea on their behalf, a sharp retort
that contains a charge of misunderstanding; and in the second place
with the servants, who are waiting to do Jesus' bidding. This mixture
of incomprehension and compliance is surely part of the *meaning* of
the story, emerging as it does from a study of the text itself, without
recourse to allegory or allusion. In the context of an appeal to Jewish
readers and listeners to come forward and declare themselves for
Christ, the significance of Jesus' mother (or part of it at least) is as a

representative of those who do just that, those for whom misunderstanding is not a permanent obstacle to discipleship. This is not an *allegorical* interpretation: one cannot say, 'for "the mother of Jesus" read "Israel"'. It is rather an interpretation deriving directly from what Olsson calls 'text-linguistic analysis';[54] and though slighter it is also a less wayward example of the method than his own.

(b) The reply of Jesus

'What have I to do with you, woman?' Coming so abruptly, the form of address 'woman' is startling and unexpected; and as Bultmann remarks, 'it sets a peculiar distance between Jesus and his mother',[55] a distance already established by Jesus' opening words, τί ἐμοὶ καὶ σοί; The problem with this expression, as with its Hebrew counterpart, מַה לִּי וָלָךְ, is that it is essentially ambiguous: its meaning needs to be determined independently in each instance. Only from the context can it be determined whether the question about the kind of relation that exists between speaker and addressee expects any sort of positive response. Nor is the expected answer necessarily the one that is given. In reply to what is clearly a request for a miracle Jesus puts a question-mark over the relationship between himself and his mother—perhaps as Vanhoye has argued, with the intention of suggesting that it is time for the relationship to be changed.[56] In any case, though the expression may imply a reproach, it certainly does not signify a refusal to have anything more to do with the other person. When the widow of Zarephath uses it in angry indignation to Elijah after the death of her son, he responds by raising the boy to life again (1 Kings 17: 17–24).

The phrase οὔπω ἥκει ἡ ὥρα μου is almost always translated as a statement: 'My hour has not yet come.' Taking it this way, reading it in the context of the Gospel, and knowing what Jesus' 'hour' will mean later, 'it is unthinkable', remarks Barrett, 'that in this verse ἡ ὥρα should have a different meaning, such as "the hour for me to

---

[54] *Structure and Meaning*, pp. 8–13. Olsson muddies the clear and invigorating waters of textual analysis with a strained and complex theory which would make the understanding of the Cana episode dependent upon a detailed reading of Exod. 19 (and one of its targumic expansions). He relies heavily upon the work of A. M. Serra, 'Le tradizione della teofanica sinaitica nel Targum delle Pseudo-Jonathan Es. 19. 24 e in Giov. 1,19–2,12', *Marianum*, 33 (1971), 1–39. Neither is worried by John's general lack of interest in the contrast between the Old Law and the New.

[55] *Gospel*, p. 116. [56] A. Vanhoye, 'Interrogation johannique', p. 165.

supply them with wine!"'[57] But why should the fact that it is not yet Jesus' hour for passing to the Father in suffering and glory prohibit him from performing a miracle at the beginning of his ministry? This difficulty appears to me a further reason for retaining the phrase as part of the original source. On the level of the source, Bultmann understands it to mean that 'the miracle worker is bound to his own law and must listen to another voice';[58] but perhaps the important point is that the phrase shifts the interest for the first time from the spatial to the temporal. Even from the relatively restricted perspective of the source the *timing* of Jesus' first miracle is important.[59] Why? Because of the risk of misunderstanding. The source once again shows a surprising affinity with the Synoptic tradition, which also sees Jesus as repudiating, in quite harsh terms, the claims of natural kinship (Matt. 12: 46–50 //; Luke 2: 48 ff.—the finding in the Temple). So here, it is 'not yet time' for Jesus to perform a miracle, since there is a risk that it will be misunderstood. The outcome of the story shows that the fear is ill-founded: Mary refuses to take no for an answer, and by showing her faith opens the way for the faith of others.[60]

(c) Water into wine

According to the Synoptic tradition, Jesus' public career began with his baptism, and after the forty days' retreat in the desert continued with the call of the first disciples; only then did he embark on his

---

[57] *Gospel*, p. 159.   [58] *Gospel*, p. 117.

[59] For the motif of 'the right time' in rabbinical literature, see R. Bloch, 'Quelques aspects ...' p. 146 and n. 163.

[60] The phrase can be rendered in such a way as to give it almost the opposite meaning: 'Has not my hour already come?' Vanhoye, who favours this punctuation, argues that elsewhere in the New Testament wherever οὔπω is preceded by a question (Matt. 16: 9; Mark 4: 40 *v.l.* πῶς οὐκ; 8: 17) it introduces a further question. Moreover, this is the only example in the Fourth Gospel in which οὔπω, commencing the sentence, is not followed by a connecting particle. But while this rendering beautifully accounts for the reaction of Jesus' mother, it is not very easy to fit it in with what precedes, unless Vanhoye is right in understanding Jesus to be making a deliberate suggestion that his relationship with his mother be changed: up to the present the authority was hers—now it passes to Jesus. This is something of an over-interpretation, and the parallel in 7: 6 (see the next chapter) tells against it. But if it is right we would have a further example of a theme in the source that the evangelist has adapted for his own purpose: from being the hour of Jesus' self-manifestation at the start of his public career, ἡ ὥρα is absorbed into the new theology of glorification and is utterly transformed in the process. It may even be the evangelist himself who was responsible for erasing the original question-mark!

preaching and healing ministry. The Fourth Gospel follows a similar schema with obvious modifications. So before performing his first miracle he has already been recognized as the Jewish Messiah and gathered round him a number of followers. But he has not yet *shown* the significance of his coming: given any sign of it. This he does in the changing of water into wine.

Here, unquestionably, is the centre of the story, the event that counts as a sign and an invitation to faith. The contextual information supplied, above all the wedding, the huge volume of wine, and the fact that the jars were there to comply with the Jewish custom of purification[61] certainly contributes towards the meaning. Moreover the position of the story in the source (as the third panel of a triptych) must also be taken into account. This in itself rules out of court the theory that the key to the story's meaning lies in the prodigious, that Jesus' primary role is that of thaumaturge, and that the content of the disciples' faith is their justified conviction in his power to work miracles. Rather, the whole context, and not simply the use of 'sign', $\sigma\eta\mu\epsilon\hat{\iota}o\nu$, instead of 'act of power', $\delta\dot{\upsilon}\nu\alpha\mu\iota\varsigma$, the word used by the Synoptists to refer to miracles,[62] points to the need of a symbolic interpretation.

According to Mark, who is very interested in Jesus as a teacher but often, like John, finds the lesson in the performance, Jesus used the image of new wine bursting out of old skins when comparing his own message with the customs of the Pharisees (Mark 2: 22). And it may be significant too that making the same point in a different way he had likened himself to a bridegroom: 'Can the wedding guests fast while the bridegroom is with them?' (Mark 2: 19.)

Brown is right too to stress the significance of the wedding-feast, the most natural possible symbol of joy, fulfilment, and the promise of new life. The Book of Revelation actually speaks of 'the marriage of the Lamb' (Rev. 19: 7), and in the Old Testament we have no need to go further than the Song of Songs for proof that the most human of all mysteries could serve as an inspiration for the most divine

---

[61] The phrase $\kappa\alpha\tau\dot{\alpha}\ \tau\dot{o}\nu\ \kappa\alpha\theta\alpha\rho\iota\sigma\mu\dot{o}\nu\ \tau\hat{\omega}\nu\ \text{'}Iov\delta\alpha\dot{\iota}\omega\nu$ (v. 6) fits badly with the following $\kappa\epsilon\acute{\iota}\mu\epsilon\nu\alpha\iota$ and may well be secondary, as Fortna (*Gospel of Signs*, p. 32) argues, and as Wellhausen (p. 13) had already suggested. In that case the introduction of 'the Jews' here would evince the evangelist's determination to contrast the water of the old dispensation with the wine of the new.

[62] James M. Robinson ('Trajectory', p. 235 n. 9) reverts to Faure's original designation of the source as the 'miracle source' (*Wunderquelle*). It will emerge why I think this suggestion is wrong.

(though whether this was originally more than a glorious love-song is harder to determine). Israel's feeling towards God was profoundly coloured by the image of God as husband and lover and a number of Hosea's key ideas are taken up by a much later prophet in a passage that exploits the earlier images to the full:

You shall no more be termed Forsaken, and your land shall no more be termed Desolate: but you shall be called My delight is in her, and your land Married: for the lord delights in you, and your land shall be married. For as a young man marries a virgin, so shall your sons marry you, and as the bridegroom rejoices over the bride, so shall your God rejoice over you. (Isa. 62: 4 f.)

But clearly the heart of the passage remains the transformation of water into wine, another natural symbol of joyful celebration. 'The days are coming', runs the consolatory ending of the book of Amos, 'when the mountains shall drip sweet wine, and all the hills shall flow with it' (9: 13). Brown cites a number of other passages, the most striking of which comes from *2 Baruch*, where we find 'an exuberantly fantastic description: the earth shall yield its fruit ten thousandfold; each vine shall have 1,000 branches; each branch 1,000 clusters; and each grape about 120 gallons of wine' (*2 Bar.* 29: 5). Perhaps it is not too fanciful to see a link between the two images of the wine and the wedding in the beautiful love-song Isaiah imagines God singing to his vineyard (Isa. 5).[63]

All in all, Brown is fully justified in concluding that 'through such symbolism the Cana miracle could have been understood by the disciples as a sign of the messianic times and the new dispensation, much in the same manner that they would have understood Jesus' statement about the new wine in the Synoptic tradition.'[64] Brown goes on to appeal to a verse from the *Psalms of Solomon* (17: 32) that tells how the Messiah will make the glory of God visible to all the earth. But this is to go too far. The transference of the glory from God

---

[63] All such suggestions are rejected by Bultmann: 'the wine of the marriage at Cana does not come from the Old Testament expectation of salvation but from the Dionysus cult in Syria' (p. 120 n. 1). For further arguments in favour of this provenance see Morton Smith, 'On the Wine God'. Certainly the early church, as Bultmann shows (p. 119), had no hesitation in making the connection. But this does not affect the significance the author himself attached to the story as a powerful proof of Jesus' messianic dignity. Cf. M. Rissi, 'Die Hochzeit in Kana'. M. Hengel's 'Interpretation of the Wine Miracle', though remarkably rich in reference, adds little to the understanding of the passage.   [64] p. 105.

to Jesus is too striking a departure from tradition to see it as just another messianic allusion. As the passage from *Ps. Sol.* 17 shows, the Messiah was simply a particular human being chosen by God as his special assistant in the last days. If δόξα belongs to the vocabulary of the source (which I think unlikely) then it can have meant no more than the glory attaching to Jesus' messiahship, and any suggestion of the glory of God's self-revelation will have been hidden and indirect.[65] But this is not necessarily how the evangelist himself understood it.

(d) Conclusion

It seems worth repeating by way of conclusion that the faith of the disciples that follows the first sign is not just one more example of the kind of superstitious awe aroused in any naïvely credulous audience by the tricks of a magician. This miracle, so different from those that were to come, resembles them in the most important point, for it too suggests by its very nature the *kind* of faith it is designed to inspire: a faith of fulfilment and of transformation, of joy and celebration. Linked deliberately to the accounts of the Testimony and the Discovery ('on the third day'), it completes the triptych with a symbolic affirmation that 'the old order changeth, yielding place to new'.

So far, so good: but out of the water-jars of Cana surges a new problem, for the relationship between miracles and messiahship is far from clear, and the significance of the signs recorded in the source is disputed.

4. SIGNS AND WONDERS

This new problem is not obvious upon a cursory or casual reading of the Gospel, where miracles are firmly linked to messianic expectation: 'many of the people believed in him; they said, "When the Messiah appears, will he do more signs than this man has done?"' (7: 31.) But such evidence as there is in Jewish sources of any

---

[65] For the evangelist, the glory that shines out of Jesus' miracles is very definitely the glory of God: Jesus, about to raise Lazarus, says to Martha: 'Did I not tell you that if you would believe you would see the glory of God?' (11: 40.) Though there, it is to be noted, vision *is preceded by* faith.

association between messiahship and the miraculous is very scanty. Schnackenburg declares roundly that 'Miracles played hardly any part in messianic expectation in Judaism.'[66]

In discussing this question, scholars tend to branch off in two different directions: for the sake of convenience these may be summed up as the *divine* and the *prophetic*. Of the two it is the *divine* school that seems to have attracted the largest following—in fact, so common is the application to Jesus of the sobriquet θεῖος ἀνήρ, or 'divine man', that Dwight Moody Smith, writing in 1976, felt able to say: 'The existence of this *theios aner* is presently regarded as well-established, the only question being at what traditional level this Christology is to be found.'[67] So according to this theory what John (or his source) was doing was to compose something like an aretalogy, a compilation of the wonderful achievements of some great man, and specifically of a θεῖος ἀνήρ. Now if we ask (with Mark) who, or rather (with Matthew) what manner of man is this *theios aner*, the answer is, briefly, 'a very remarkable one': 'He is a man with qualities and abilities far beyond the normal, the darling of the gods, and a kind of mediator between the divinity and human beings, at once their counsellor and their κατορθώτης (champion?), to whom they come drawn from afar.'[68] This avowedly crude sketch is all Ludwig Bieler offers by way of a general characterization of the eponymous hero of his scholarly study, which is respectfully cited by most subsequent writers on the topic. 'Superman', in fact, might be a less misleading translation of the term than the usual 'divine man', which could carry for the unwary overtones of ontological divinity it rarely has in the Greek. For the 'divine man' is seldom divine in the strong metaphysical sense.[69] Bieler himself shows more caution than some others in assigning superhuman traits to Jewish and

---

[66] ii, p. 148.

[67] *Johannine Christianity*, p. 167. The first author to propagate the interpretation of the Johannine Jesus as a 'divine man' was G. A. P. Wetter in his influential book *Der Sohn Gottes*.

[68] Bieler, Θεῖος ἀνήρ, i. 20.

[69] As Morton Smith points out, 'it was natural and common [in the Hellenistic World] to describe as "divine" any man who excelled in any desirable capacity—beauty, strength, wisdom, prestige, song, fame, skill in speaking, or success in love': 'Prolegomena', p. 184. The sheer imprecision of the word should have disqualified it from the use to which it has been put by New Testament scholars. Morton Smith does not mention the gift of healing. This too, as we know from cases like Apollonius and Asclepius, was thought of, along with their other qualities of wisdom and goodness, as a divine power.

Christian heroes.[70] In the whole corpus of Jewish-Christian
literature of the period he can cite only one clear instance (Jos. *AJ*
iii: 180) of the use of the term, and he remarks later in an aside that
it is one for which 'there is of course (*natürlich*) no place in the New
Testament'.[71]

What is very puzzling in this affair is how the consensus of which
Smith speaks was reached in the first place: perhaps the explanation
lies in the readiness with which scholars, not being supermen, follow
one another down culs-de-sac, *Sackgassen*, and the blindest of blind
alleys.[72] Writing about the same time as Smith, Robert Fortna asks,
rather confusingly, 'Granted that it is difficult to say whether in any
absolute sense a particular portrait of Jesus *is* (or is not) that of a
divine man; can we see indications that the Signs-Gospel's Jesus is
more nearly a divine man than John's or vice versa? Does John play
down or emphasize the elements that might be so interpreted in the
pre-Johannine christology?'[73] His answer, which is that the evangelist has suppressed certain 'divine man' features present in the
source, whilst exaggerating others, might suggest that the concept is
unhelpful, not to say misleading. And indeed Fortna himself concludes by questioning the value of the category in the study of the
Fourth Gospel: 'We are led to ask whether John or his predecessor
could consciously have conceived of Jesus as divine man. Hellenistic
as their Judaism surely was, they both—more than most other New

[70] Helmut Koester, for instance, in 'One Jesus and Four Primitive Gospels', has a
paragraph headed 'Jesus as the Divine Man (Aretalogies)', in which he states
categorically that in the primitive sources underlying the gospel miracle stories, 'Jesus
appears as a man endowed with divine power who performs miracles to prove his
divine quality and character' (p. 186). In a vain search for any direct New Testament
evidence to back up his contention that Jesus was regarded as a θεῖος ἀνήρ he lights
upon Acts 2: 22: 'a man attested ... by God with mighty works and wonders and
miraculous signs'. 'In Lucan theology', comments Koester, '"by God" emphasized the
subordination of Jesus to God. But this is not necessarily the original intention of the
formula which Luke used in Acts 2: 22–24' (p. 188 n. 103). An excellent example,
surely, of argument by innuendo! Haenchen is another commentator who assumes
without question that the 'Vorlage' was concerned to give miraculous proofs of Jesus'
divine sonship. He does not accept the theory of the signs source as such, but is
prepared, in assigning the story of the nobleman of Capernaum (4: 46–54) to his
'Vorlage', to say that it belongs to a number of passages 'which aim at narrating
Jesus' miracles in order to demonstrate his divine sonship' (*Johannesevangelium*, p. 83).
Yet there is not a word in this passage that so much as hints at divinity.
[71] Θεῖος ἀνήρ, p. 3 n. 7.
[72] Another example is the widespread assumption, only recently abandoned, that
at the time of Jesus there existed a fully operational anti-Roman faction called the
Zealots.   [73] 'Christology in the Fourth Gospel', p. 491.

Testament writers—retain a sense that Jesus is none other than *the* Messiah of Jewish expectation.'[74] Since, then, the θεῖος ἀνήρ is turning out to be little more than a disconsolate chimera, we may leave him to his lament.[75] But the category Fortna selects to replace him is equally unhelpful; he goes on to ask ('perhaps too crudely'): 'Are the miraculous deeds of Jesus consistent with his humanity or do they rather display his divinity?'[76] And in shifting from the superhuman to the divine (now seemingly in the full sense of the word) he is simply laying one inappropriate category aside in order to pick up another. This emerges only too clearly from his conclusion, which is that the miracles of the signs source are 'merely disclosures of the fact of Jesus' divinity'.[77] To say this is to disregard the fact that 'the Messiah of Jewish expectation' was a human figure, not a divine one, and that in the context of contemporary Judaism miracles, however extraordinary, are not *per se* indications of divinity.

A rather different error vitiates another important attempt to delineate the christology of the signs source:

In the term θεῖος ἀνήρ we have hit upon the one and only word capable of throwing light upon the religio-historical presuppositions of the Signs-Source: all the essential theological traits of the miracle stories in the source are also to be found in the hellenistic concept of the θεῖος ἀνήρ. In point of fact there is not much to separate the Jesus of the Signs-Source from this miracle-worker of the ancient world: all one could adduce would be the name of Jesus, his Jewish origin, his annunciation by the Old Testament prophets, and the fact that as Christ he is the Son of God. *That is little enough.*[78]

What impresses Jürgen Becker most about the source is the way in which it pushes the prodigious aspects of the stories 'right up to the limits of what is tolerable'.[79] But tolerable to whom? Is it not worth

---

[74] 'Christology in the Fourth Gospel', p. 493.

[75] The main credit for the exposure of the fallacy must go to Carl H. Holladay, *Theios Aner in Hellenistic Judaism*. In his treatment of Philo he may underrate the extent to which a Platonic view of the divine qualities of the human νοῦς has affected Philo's evaluation of Jewish heroes, especially Moses (cf. *Vit. Mos.* 1: 27). But he certainly succeeds in his main aim. Having established that the role of the θεῖος ἀνήρ concept in Hellenistic Judaism is a crucial middle link for any theory which emphasizes its importance for New Testament christology, he shows that it 'has been repeatedly based upon the same few bits of data, conspicuous not only for their paucity but also for their ambiguity' (p. 44).   [76] 'Christology', p. 495.

[77] Ibid., p. 498.   [78] J. Becker, 'Wunder', p. 141 (my italics).

[79] 'bis nahezu an die Grenzen des Erträglichen', ibid., p. 137.

investigating the possibility that the evangelist was not utterly transforming the character of his source when what *he* emphasized was not the prodigious but the symbolic? True, Becker, unlike Fortna, does not actually believe that the source saw Jesus as divine. But both are equally guilty of neglecting the properly messianic features with which the source abounds.

Or does it? For we are here back with the difficulty with which we prefaced this section, the difficulty that contemporary Jewish sources do not portray the Messiah as a thaumaturge: 'Of course the Messiah is a wondrous warrior and a marvellously wise ruler. But he is not portrayed as one who heals the paralysed, miraculously provides bread and water, restores sight to the blind, or raises the dead.'[80]

Martyn himself answers this difficulty by appealing first to the prophet-like and secondly to the Elijah-like traits in the source's portrayal of Jesus.[81] Not the Messiah himself but the other two quasi-messianic figures with which Jesus is identified in the Gospel, Elijah and (the new) Moses, are in fact credited with miracle-working powers that show certain similarities with those exhibited by the Jesus of the signs source. The first two signs, the miracle at Cana, and the healing of the nobleman's son (4: 46–54) are reminiscent of Elijah's two great deeds of kindness to the widow of Zarephath—first of provision (the jar of meal and the cruse of oil) and then of resurrection (1 Kings 17: 8–24). As for Moses, it is enough to point to the parallelism between the miracle of manna and the miracle of bread (ch. 6).

Martyn suggests as a general solution to the problem that traits associated with Elijah and the Moses-like prophet may have 'rubbed off' on to the Messiah and thus have accounted for the composite christology we find in the Gospel. This is surely right, but there are two further points to be made.

In the first place, it may be that in drawing such a fine distinction between the miracles of Jesus and those associated with figures like the Samaritan and Theudas, Martyn is paying too little regard to the *general* tendency (to which Hellenism must have contributed) to assign wonder-working powers to any important and influential figure of the day. (So why not the Messiah also?) As Geza Vermes has

---

[80] Martyn, *History*[2], p. 96. Cf. de Jonge, *Jesus*, pp. 91 f.

[81] The first of these comparisons is established chiefly in *History*, chs. 5–6, and the second in *Gospel*, ch. 1. For a good discussion of the wonder-working associated with prophets see John Barton, *Oracles*, pp. 99–102.

argued,[82] the remarkable deeds of Jewish charismatics like Honi the Circle-Drawer and Honina ben Dosa are also relevant to the understanding of Jesus, even if these men, did not actually have any messianic pretensions.

In the second place, there is a real possibility that among the tributaries feeding into the signs source was a Synoptic-type tradition linking Jesus' wonder-working activities first with his preaching of the Kingdom and secondly with his own messsianic claims. Martyn points out that the prophecy of eschatological fulfilment in Isaiah 35 does not even mention the Messiah, and so 'is clearly inadmissible as evidence for an expectation of the Messiah as a miracle-worker'.[83] But according to one tradition, when John the Baptist sent messengers to Jesus to ask 'Are you he who is to come, or shall we look for another?' (Matt. 11: 3; Luke 7: 20), it was largely in terms of this prophecy that Jesus replied. At least in Christian circles Jesus' miracles had already come to be regarded as signs of the fullness of time:[84] 'False Messiahs and false prophets will arise and show signs and wonders, to lead astray, if possible, the elect' (Mark 13: 22). As this quotation makes plain Jesus was seen not just as Messiah but as *prophet*; and the idea that a prophet was authenticated by preternatural signs was rooted in the Old Testament and was accepted in rabbinic Judaism. No doubt the signs source shows no more direct interest than does the evangelist in the theme of the kingdom of God. But there survives in his work a firm connection between the miracle tradition and the person of Jesus, a connection confirmed by his explicit denial (10: 41) that John performed any signs. If Jesus' reply to his mother in John 2: 4 is correctly read as a statement ('My hour has come'), this is how it should be understood.

CONCLUSION

The miracles of Jesus then are above all *signs*: they belong to a tradition that associates Jesus' actions, and especially his healing,

---

[82] *Jesus the Jew*, ch. 3.

[83] *History*², p. 97.

[84] It is true that even later on in Jewish-Christian controversy (e.g. Justin) the miracles of Jesus play no part; cf. Schnackenburg, *Gospel*, ii, p. 475 n. 42. But in the Pseudo-Clementine recognitions, they do constitute evidence of Jesus' messianic status: 'He who was expected comes, bringing signs and miracles as his credentials by which he should be made manifest' (ch. 40. 1).

with the fulfilment of prophecy. Perhaps it takes more than just insight to be able to summarize the healing of the halt and the blind, the raising of the dead, as 'I am the way, the truth and the life'; but before John the evangelist has turned the full beam of his religious genius upon Jesus' signs, it is surely obvious that to see him primarily as a Hellenistic wonder-worker is to fall well wide of the mark.

We have seen that the combination of a Synoptic-type tradition and the 'rubbing-off' of which Martyn speaks helps to explain, among other things, the question of the crowd: 'When the Messiah appears, will he do more signs than this man has done?', where the link between miracles and messiahship is taken for granted. But the passage in which this question occurs (ch. 7) reflects a stage in the history of the community in which growing animosity is evinced by the Jews towards the Christian believers in their midst; moreover, the christological reflection of the group has advanced well beyond the simple messianic faith of its beginnings. In the next chapter some suggestions will be offered about the direction in which the thinking of these Christian Jews was moving.

'We have found him of whom Moses wrote in the Law (the Prophet); we have found Elijah, who is to restore all things; we have found the Messiah and the Son of God.' These are the cardinal affirmations of the signs source, the earliest traceable literary production of the Johannine community, whose conclusion was taken over by the evangelist as a fitting end for his own work: 'these [signs] are written that you may believe that Jesus is the Messiah, the Son of God.'

In his great commentary, Bultmann allows the Old Testament to be jostled and frequently elbowed out by huge numbers of other ancient texts. This fits in with his own perspective: by minimizing the influence of the Old Testament, he can highlight the independence and the novelty of the revelation of Jesus. But it also involves a serious misreading of the Gospel, which remains faithful to its source in its insistence that Jesus fulfils in every respect the eschatological expectations of the Jews. For all the mysteriousness and otherness of his person, he is set firmly in the context of a living tradition. He is *not* utterly unintelligible and remote; the area of his intelligibility is limited and defined in the lapidary formula drawn from one of the most ancient of Christian confessions: 'Jesus is the Messiah.'

Excursus II: A Call to Faith

1. General considerations

If one begins by asking what justification there can be for attempting to reconstruct a source in this chapter (or in any other), the answer must be, as always, the presence of aporias, as the awkward transitions have been called since Schwartz, and in this instance the presence too of clear doublets. Yet the passage we are considering is so complex we might react as Schwartz ('Aporien IV', p. 497) says he did to the puzzles of Ch. 7, being tempted 'to lay down [his] critical knife and to leave these sections in the confusion and disorder into which they have fallen through having been worked over so much (*durch die Überarbeitung*)'. In the opinion of the majority of those scholars who have wrestled with the difficulties of the passage the most feasible explanation of the present text is that an original source has been adapted and expanded by a later editor. This does not mean that a thoroughly convincing reconstruction of the original source is actually possible: the reorganization may have been too complex, the omissions too extensive to permit this. But it does mean that a full understanding of the passage depends upon recognizing that it had a prehistory. If the broad outlines of the source are discernible (enough for its general thrust and purpose to be seen) then this is as much as we can expect. Criticizing the theory of Wolfgang Langbrandtner, Raymond Brown remarks that it depends 'on his ability to reconstruct verse-by-verse the *Grundschrift* and the additions of the redactor'. 'No firm theory', he continues, 'can be built on so disputable a base, for every scholar will have a different assignment of verses to the putative *Grundschrift*.'[1] It is a salutary warning, but not one that should frighten us off altogether. As James M. Robinson insists, 'the question of the difficulty of reconstructing a source is not identical with the question of whether the source existed'.[2] Although certain rungs of our ladder may be more rickety than others, it may be possible to climb down to the *Grundschrift* without too heavy a fall. The validity of many arguments will frequently depend upon previous options, but provided

[1] *Community*, p. 181.   [2] *Trajectories*, p. 242.

these are clearly signalled, then it is possible to proceed—though obviously the further we descend the more caution is required.

As an illustration of the hazards of over-elaboration, it is worth considering the commentary of M.-É. Boismard, which embodies one of the most ambitious and fascinating theories of the origins of the Gospel ever conceived, and one that is carried through with great thoroughness and a real attempt at consistency. But how solid is it? In my opinion, about as solid as a soap-bubble. In his earlier article Boismard argued that the present text of vv. 19–36 has been conflated from two versions of the same story, which he labelled X and Y. This argument is quite telling; it is the most satisfactory explanation of the doublets with which the passage is studded. But the commentary puts forward a much more complex theory of a *Grundschrift* (C) and a triple redaction. What I am concerned with here is partly Boismard's reconstruction of C (in ch. 1 only) and partly his description of its character.

1. Like many other commentators, Boismard thinks that the nucleus of 1: 6 f. originally belonged to the story of the witness of John the Baptist. But he now assigns it not to C but to the first Johannine editor (whom he labels Jean II-A). On what grounds? Because of the striking stylistic resemblance between 1: 6 f. and 3: 1 f. Both open with the phrase, 'There was a man—his name was …' (though there are minor differences in the Greek). But since Jean II-A is supposed to have taken over the Document C, why should he not have adopted one of its phrases where it seemed appropriate? In any case the phrase is reminiscent, as Boismard himself, following Bultmann, observes, of an Old Testament formula introducing a story concerning a particular individual (Judges 13: 2; 1 Sam. 1: 1). If the Old Testament model was available to John II-A, it was equally available to the author of C.

2. According to Boismard (p. 16), C originally opened with a notice concerning John the Baptist now found in ch. 3: ἦν [δὲ καὶ] Ἰωάννης βαπτίζων ἐν Αἰνὼν ἐγγὺς τοῦ Σαλείμ … καὶ παρεγίνοντο καὶ ἐβαπτίζοντο … ἐγένετο οὖν ζήτησις ἐκ τῶν μαθητῶν Ἰωάννου μετὰ Ἰουδαίων περὶ καθαρισμοῦ (3: 23 f.); and then continued with a modified form of John 1: 19. The first difficulty here is not the lack of a subject for the plural verbs, but the fact that there is no evidence for the suggestion that this is where the parenthesis originally belonged. Boismard argues (p. 20) from its close resemblance to

Mark 1: 4 f. that it too should be placed at the beginning of the Gospel; and John the Baptist is certainly introduced very abruptly in John 1 (his baptismal activity is presupposed but nowhere stated). But the *place* is not the same and surely belongs to an independent tradition. Boismard seems to think that this constitutes an additional argument for transferring it. How so? The best one can say for this suggestion is that it remains highly speculative.

3. Following Albright, P. Winter, J. A. T. Robinson, F. M. Abel, Boismard identifies the $\Sigma\alpha\lambda\epsilon\iota\mu$ of 3: 23 with the modern village of Salim, close to the ancient Samaritan town of Shechem (present-day Nablus = $N\epsilon\acute{\alpha}\pi\omega\lambda\iota s$). For some commentators (e.g. Lindars) the Samaritan location constitutes an objection to this suggestion. Not so for Boismard, who concludes: 'Jean exerçait donc son activité baptismale en pleine Samarie à quelques kms seulement du puits de Jacob où Jésus va rencontrer la Samaritaine. Ceci nous explique la tonalité 'samaritaine' de la suite du récit du Document C' (p. 89). But since C is not primarily concerned with the activity of the Baptist, but with his testimony to Jesus, why should his baptismal rite in Samaria offer any clue to the understanding of what the document C (if that is where the passage belongs) says about Jesus? There are recognizable connections here, but they are no more *logical* than the quirky associations of the Freudian id.

4. Boismard's original X included all three of the questions addressed to John the Baptist. C only has one: 'Are you the Prophet?': the other two have been ruthlessly excised. On this, Boismard comments: 'nous n'avons ici … aucun argument littéraire pour le prouver; cette hypothèse dépend étroitement des analyses qui seront faites dans la troisième partie du récit' (p. 82). This is undoubtedly the weakest link in Boismard's elaborate chain. His suggestion is (barely) possible. But can he adduce any other example of the triple question so beloved of folklore being built out of a story in which interest focused on one question only? Supposing, however, that he is right, what reason does he offer for the question of the priests and Levites concerning the Prophet, that is, as all agree, the eschatological prophet, the prophet like Moses? 'Parce que Jean-Baptiste exerce son activité en Samarie, et que l'attente d'un tel Prophète revêtait une importance particulière chez les Samaritains' (p. 90). But why should this be of any interest to priests and Levites from Jerusalem? Boismard does not say. Nevertheless one begins to see how the pieces of his home-made jigsaw fit together. He will

subsequently explain the 'Lamb of God' as an allusion to the new
Moses, who is compared to a lamb (תילא) in a targumic expansion of
Exod. 1: 15: 'Puisque, dans le Document C, Jésus est le nouveau
Moïse, il peut être appelé "Agneau de Dieu", c'est-à-dire "Agneau"
envoyé par Dieu' (p. 92). At this point Boismard goes on to remind us
that 'Israel' was originally the name of the Northern Kingdom, and
continued to be used in various Samaritan writings to distinguish
Samaria from Judaea. Reading such texts, some of which he cites, 'ne
serait-on pas tenté', asks Boismard, 'de donner un sens restreint au
terme "Israel" en Jn 1, 31. 47. 49, étant donné l'insistance du récit
sur le thème du Prophète semblable à Moïse (Jn 1, 21. 25. 45), thème
central de l'espérance samaritaine?' (p. 94). By the time this point is
reached one might well have forgotten that it is this section to which
Boismard appeals to support his otherwise arbitrary elimination of
'Messiah' and 'Elijah' from his C document. Once bewitched into
stepping inside Boismard's particularly vicious circle one might well
find it hard to shake off the spell. But why in any case should a
reference to 'the Prophet' indicate a Samaritan context? After all, the
Prophet also figures prominently in a passage towards the end of
ch. 7, one which Boismard (p. 160) calmly assigns to Jean II-B
without raising the possibility of a Samaritan connection.

One cannot but admire the subtlety and ingenuity with which
Boismard weaves his intricate web, but it hangs like gossamer on a
number of infinitely slender threads which, it seems to me, are too
fragile to withstand the slightest brush with critical examination.
There is an old medieval tag which states that 'ab esse ad posse valet
illatio'. Boismard is not the first exegete to reverse this logic: it would
be going too far to say that his hypothesis is impossible, but,
beautifully consistent as it is, how can it be thought to further
knowledge?

It is a hazardous procedure, then, this business of reconstruction,
and the pitfalls are both many and deep. Nevertheless, we cannot
ignore the real difficulties confronted by those who wish to read John
1: 19–51 as a continuous composition.

Since in this matter I largely agree with Robert Fortna, although
taking more note than he does of Boismard's earlier suggestion that
two different versions have been conflated to produce the present
text of John 1: 19–34, some response must be made to the strictures
of Barnabas Lindars upon Fortna's work in *Behind the Fourth Gospel*

(pp. 28–36). Most of Lindars's most effective arguments ignore the careful and laborious sifting undertaken by Fortna in the course of his reconstruction, and aim instead at his general plan. Certainly the weakest parts of Fortna's thesis are (*a*) his conviction that the document was not just a semeia source but a signs *Gospel*; and (*b*) his belief that the story of the miraculous draught of fishes in chapter 21 originally belonged to the source. And Lindars shows how difficult it is (above all in ch. 11) to separate out narrative and dialogue. (Though this argument loses much of its force if, with Bammel, one holds that the source ended with the notice concerning John the Baptist at the end of ch. 10.)[3] Moreover, Lindars is surely right in his contention that there is no possibility of reconstructing anything like the whole of the original source. Fortna does not actually say that there is, but much of his work seems to lean on that assumption. The evangelist is likely to have been much bolder in his adaptation of the source than Fortna (sometimes) allows. Still, in exposing the weaknesses of Fortna's theory, Lindars ignores its strengths—in particular the presence of the aporias from which the whole theory took its rise. Paradoxically, in arguing that the source was a signs *Gospel* that included both a passion and a resurrection narrative, Fortna relinquishes the one argument that the opponents of the signs-source theory have found most difficult to refute—the reference, right at the end of the Gospel, to 'many other signs that are not written in this book' (20: 30). In his later work (1988) he abandons this theory, suggesting instead that the original signs source was combined with a primitive passion narrative, representing, he thinks (p. 215), a theological stage earlier than Mark's, before being incorporated into the work of the fourth evangelist. This makes for a somewhat complex theory which cannot be considered here. I do not know how the signs source continued, but there are good reasons for thinking that this is how it began.

2. *Reconstruction of the signs source of John 1: 19–2: 11*[4]

(1) ʿΗ Μαρτυρία

[6] Ἐγένετο ἄνθρωπος ἀπεσταλμένος παρὰ θεοῦ, ὄνομα αὐτῷ Ἰωάννης·
[7] οὗτος ἦλθεν εἰς μαρτυρίαν, ἵνα ... πάντες πιστεύσωσιν δι' αὐτοῦ.

---

[3] "John did no miracle".

[4] Square brackets are placed around words in the text when reading or provenance appears to me particularly open to question.

¹⁹Καὶ [αὕτη ἐστὶν ἡ μαρτυρία τοῦ Ἰωάννου, ὅτε] ἀπέστειλαν πρὸς αὐτὸν ... ἱερεῖς καὶ Λευῖται ἵνα ἐρωτήσωσιν αὐτόν· Σὺ τίς εἶ; ... ²⁰Καὶ ... οὐκ ἠρνήσατο καὶ ὡμολόγησεν ὅτι Ἐγὼ οὐκ εἰμὶ ὁ Χριστός. ²¹καὶ ἠρώτησαν αὐτόν, Τί οὖν σύ; Ἐλείας εἶ; καὶ λέγει, Οὐκ εἰμί. Ὁ Προφήτης εἶ σύ; καὶ ἀπεκρίθη, Οὔ. ... ²⁵Καὶ ἠρώτησαν αὐτόν καὶ εἶπαν αὐτῷ, Τί οὖν βαπτίζεις, εἰ σὺ οὐκ εἶ ὁ Χριστὸς οὐδὲ Ἐλείας οὐδὲ ὁ Προφήτης; ²⁶ἀπεκρίθη αὐτοῖς ὁ Ἰωάννης λέγων· ... Μέσος ὑμῶν στήκει ὃν ὑμεῖς οὐκ οἴδατε· ... ³¹κἀγὼ οὐκ ᾔδειν αὐτόν, ἀλλ᾽ ἵνα φανερωθῇ τῷ Ἰσραὴλ διὰ τοῦτο ἦλθον ... βαπτίζων. ³²Καὶ ἐμαρτύρησεν Ἰωάννης λέγων ὅτι Τεθέαμαι τὸ Πνεῦμα καταβαῖνων ὡς περιστερὰν ἐξ οὐρανοῦ, καὶ ἔμεινεν ἐπ᾽ αὐτόν· ... ³⁴Οὗτός ἐστιν ὁ Ἐκλεκτὸς τοῦ θεοῦ.

²⁸Ταῦτα ἐν Βηθανίᾳ ἐγένετο πέραν τοῦ Ἰορδάνου, ὅπου ἦν ὁ Ἰωάννης βαπτίζων.

(2) Ἡ Ἀναγνώρισις

³⁵Τῇ ἐπαύριον εἱστήκει ὁ Ἰωάννης καὶ ἐκ τῶν μαθητῶν αὐτοῦ δύο, ³⁶καὶ ἐμβλέψας τῷ Ἰησοῦ περιπατοῦντι λέγει, Ἴδε ὁ Ἀμνὸς τοῦ Θεοῦ. ³⁷καὶ ἤκουσαν οἱ δύο μαθηταὶ αὐτοῦ λαλοῦντος καὶ ἠκολούθησαν τῷ Ἰησοῦ ... ³⁸οἱ δὲ εἶπαν αὐτῷ, Ῥαββί ... ποῦ μένεις; ³⁹λέγει αὐτοῖς, Ἔρχεσθε καὶ ὄψεσθε. ἦλθαν οὖν καὶ εἶδαν ποῦ μένει, καὶ παρ᾽ αὐτῷ ἔμειναν [τὴν ἡμέραν ἐκείνην· ὥρα ἦν ὡς δεκάτη]. ⁴⁰ἦν Ἀνδρέας ὁ ἀδελφὸς Σίμωνος Πέτρου εἷς ἐκ τῶν δύο ἀκουσάντων παρὰ Ἰωάννου καὶ ἀκολουθησάντων αὐτῷ· ⁴¹εὑρίσκει οὗτος [πρῶτος] τὸν ἀδελφὸν τὸν ἴδιον Σίμωνα καὶ λέγει αὐτῷ, Εὑρήκαμεν τὸν Μεσσίαν. ... ἤγαγεν αὐτὸν πρὸς τὸν Ἰησοῦν. ⁴²ἐμβλέψας αὐτῷ ὁ Ἰησοῦς εἶπεν, Σὺ εἶ Σίμων ὁ υἱὸς Ἰωάννου· σὺ κληθήσῃ Κηφᾶς. *καὶ ὁ Πέτρος εὑρίσκει Φίλιππον καὶ λέγει αὐτῷ, Εὑρήκαμεν Ἐλείαν, ὃς ἀποκαταστήσει πάντα· ⁴³καὶ λέγει αὐτῷ ὁ Ἰησοῦς, Ἀκολούθει μοι. ⁴⁴ἦν δὲ ὁ Φίλιππος ἀπὸ Βηθσαϊδά, ἐκ τῆς πόλεως Ἀνδρέου καὶ Πέτρου. ⁴⁵εὑρίσκει Φίλιππος τὸν Ναθαναὴλ καὶ λέγει αὐτῷ, Ὃν ἔγραψεν Μωυσῆς ἐν τῷ νόμῳ ... εὑρήκαμεν, Ἰησοῦν υἱὸν τοῦ Ἰωσὴφ τὸν ἀπὸ Ναζαρέτ. ⁴⁶Καὶ εἶπεν αὐτῷ Ναθαναήλ, Ἐκ Ναζαρὲτ δύναταί τι ἀγαθὸν εἶναι; λέγει αὐτῷ Φίλιππος, Ἔρχου καὶ ἴδε. ⁴⁷εἶδεν ὁ Ἰησοῦς τὸν Ναθαναὴλ ἐρχόμενον πρὸς αὐτὸν καὶ λέγει περὶ αὐτοῦ, Ἴδε ἀληθῶς Ἰσραηλίτης ἐν ᾧ δόλος οὐκ ἔστιν. ⁴⁸λέγει αὐτῷ Ναθαναήλ, Πόθεν με γινώσκεις; ἀπεκρίθη Ἰησοῦς καὶ εἶπεν αὐτῷ, Πρὸ τοῦ σε Φίλιππον φωνῆσαι ὄντα ὑπὸ τὴν συκῆν εἶδόν σε. ⁴⁹ἀπεκρίθη αὐτῷ Ναθαναήλ, Ῥαββί, σὺ εἶ ὁ Υἱὸς τοῦ Θεοῦ, σὺ Βασιλεὺς εἶ τοῦ Ἰσραήλ.

(3) Ἡ Φανέρωσις

¹Καὶ τῇ ἡμέρᾳ τῇ τρίτῃ γάμος ἐγένετο ἐν Κανὰ τῆς Γαλιλαίας, καὶ ἦν ἡ μήτηρ τοῦ Ἰησοῦ ἐκεῖ· ²ἐκλήθη δὲ καὶ ὁ Ἰησοῦς καὶ οἱ μαθηταὶ αὐτοῦ εἰς

τὸν γάμον. ³καὶ ὑστερησάντος οἴνου λέγει ἡ μήτηρ τοῦ Ἰησοῦ πρὸς αὐτόν, Οἶνον οὐκ ἔχουσιν. ⁴καὶ λέγει αὐτῇ ὁ Ἰησοῦς, Τί ἐμοὶ καὶ σοί, γύναι; οὔπω ἥκει ἡ ὥρα μου. ⁵λέγει ἡ μήτηρ αὐτοῦ τοῖς διακόνοις, Ὅ τι ἂν λέγῃ ὑμῖν, ποιήσατε. ⁶ἦσαν δὲ ἐκεῖ λίθιναι ὑδρίαι ἓξ κατὰ τὸν καθαρισμὸν τῶν Ἰουδαίων κείμεναι, χωροῦσαι ἀνὰ μετρητὰς δύο ἢ τρεῖς. ⁷λέγει αὐτοῖς ὁ Ἰησοῦς, Γεμίσατε τὰς ὑδρίας ὕδατος. Καὶ ἐγέμισαν αὐτὰς ἕως ἄνω. ⁸καὶ λέγει αὐτοῖς Ἀντλήσατε νῦν καὶ φέρετε τῷ ἀρχιτρικλίνῳ. οἱ δὲ ἤνεγκαν. ⁹ὡς δὲ ἐγεύσατο ὁ ἀρχιτρίκλινος τὸ ὕδωρ οἶνον γεγενημένον ... φωνεῖ τὸν νυμφίον ... ¹⁰καὶ λέγει αὐτῷ, Πᾶς ἄνθρωπος πρῶτον τὸν καλὸν οἶνον τίθησιν, καὶ ὅταν μεθυσθῶσιν τὸν ἐλάσσω· σὺ τετήρηκας τὸν καλὸν οἶνον ἕως ἄρτι. ¹¹Ταύτην ἐποίησεν ἀρχὴν τῶν σημείων ὁ Ἰησοῦς ἐν Κανὰ τῆς Γαλιλαίας καὶ ἐφανέρωσεν *ἑαυτόν, καὶ ἐπίστευσαν εἰς αὐτὸν οἱ μαθηταὶ αὐτοῦ.

The present text of 1: 19–51 divides naturally into two parts: (1) vv. 19–34 ('Testimony') and (2) vv. 35–51 ('Discovery'). There can be no question but that the evangelist, who may be responsible for the translations of the Hebrew/Aramaic terms Ῥαββί, Μεσσίας, and Κηφᾶς in (2), intended the passage to be read as a continuous story. This is obvious from the temporal indications, which continue in 2: 1. But the question whether the two halves of the passage were held together in the source is more difficult. One must ask first (a) where the beginning of the source is to be located, and (b) how far the Discovery is to be regarded as a vindication and reaffirmation of the Testimony. Bultmann separates the two episodes and thinks that the signs source began at 1: 35. But as Ernst Bammel points out, '1: 35 ff. is scarcely a suitable beginning':[5] the appearance of John the Baptist is altogether too sudden. But how far back should we go? Even v. 19 seems a very abrupt beginning. As it stands, ἡ μαρτυρία clearly points back, and if we omit the opening clause as secondary, John needs to be introduced to the reader. As long ago as 1910, Spitta suggested that the Grundschrift began with 1: 6–7, 9, and pointed to Luke 2: 25 (Simeon) as a parallel. This suggestion has been revived by Boismard (1953) and J. A. T. Robinson (1962), followed by Fortna (1970). Boismard, citing Bultmann, points to Judges 13: 2 (Manoah) and (a decade later) to 1 Sam. 1: 1 (Elkanah) as parallels: the latter text, the opening words of a book, is particularly convincing. (See too Job 1: 1: Ἄνθρωπός τις ἦν ... ᾧ ὄνομα Ἰωβ.) Bammel thinks this suggestion implausible, but if, as I believe,

⁵ '"John did no miracle"', p. 198.

the Prologue hymn was composed *after* the signs source by a member of the community, then one can easily see why he or another (the evangelist?) will have been anxious to bind it to the source (which we may assume already had canonical status): this was done by an effective dovetail splice; v. 15 (repeated in v. 30) will have been composed at the same time for the sake of balance, and the phrase ἵνα μαρτυρήσῃ περὶ τοῦ φωτός inserted in v. 7 as a lapidary summary of the Testament that is to follow. This results in a good workmanlike introduction, containing a number of Johannine themes later to be modified by the evangelist (see Chapter 7). It is also fitting that, having ended his Gospel with the conclusion of the signs source, he should take over its commencement too: ἵνα πάντες πιστεύσωσιν δι' αὐτοῦ.

Having assigned both introduction and Testament to the source, we may go on to ask whether Testament and Discovery were originally composed together—for it is theoretically possible that the Discovery was a subsequent addition. 'The one of whom Moses wrotes' (v. 45) is clearly a reference to the Prophet, just as the Messiah (v. 41) is a reference to ὁ Χριστός. J. L. Martyn, following up hints of Bultmann and others, has argued that the present v. 43 replaces a short episode in which the missing title, Elijah, was attributed to Jesus by Philip, the third of Jesus' series of visitors. No doubt it is theoretically possible even so that the account of the disciples' discovery of Jesus was built upon the Testimony in order to reinforce John's denials by positive affirmations on Jesus' behalf. But if that were the case we should have to postulate an extremely complicated process of redaction in which the Elijah title was first reintroduced and later obliterated.

The next important question that arises concerns the time-scheme. It is clear, I think, that the τῇ ἐπαύριον of v. 29 is out of place, and that of v. 43, like the rest of that verse, suspect. That of v. 35, on the other hand, makes a natural transition. We have also somehow to account for the τῇ ἡμέρᾳ τῇ τρίτῃ of 2: 1, which makes no sense as a redactional addition (unless one is attracted by Dodd's fantastic suggestion that it is a deliberate allusion to the resurrection).[6] Since behind the multiple adaptation of 1: 19–2: 11 there can easily be discerned a triple development, one is tempted to see just two days in chapter 1, so that the three panels of the triptych will

---

[6] Wellhausen (p. 13) comments drily: 'After the next and the next and again the next day, there now follows the third day.'

have (*a*) the Testimony, (*b*) the Discovery (taking place on a single day), and (*c*) the first sign at Cana. The question of how Jesus managed to move from Bethany to Cana overnight seems to have worried the redactor, but need not have concerned the author of the source. In any case, it is possible to take the phrase τῇ ἡμέρᾳ τῇ τρίτῃ to mean 'on the next day but one', which would allow plenty of time for the journey. Moreover, the presence of the disciples at Cana is hard to explain if the story was conceived independently of what precedes. Accordingly, by bracketing all the notations of time except the τῇ ἐπαύριον of v. 35 and the τῇ ἡμέρᾳ τῇ τρίτῃ of 2: 1, we reveal a clear and logical development. The remaining temporal notions will have been added later not, as T. Barrosse has suggested,[7] to emulate the seven days of creation, but to facilitate the transition between various episodes, much in the manner of Mark's ubiquitous εὐθύς.

Turning to the detailed analysis of (1) the Testimony and (2) the Discovery, we can move more rapidly because the ground is so well-trodden. Fortna, in eliminating 'the Jews from Jerusalem' from v. 19, defends the absolute use of ἀποστέλλειν (making the ἱερεῖς καὶ Λευῖται the subject). I have retained this proposal, though it seems to me more likely that ἀπέστειλαν replaced an original ἦλθον. In that case the ἐξ Ἱεροσολύμων should probably be kept also. The phrase ἀπέστειλαν οἱ Ἰουδαῖοι could have been added by the redactor with the purpose of ensuring a proper reference for John 5: 33: ὑμεῖς ἀπεστάλκατε πρὸς Ἰωάννην. I agree with Bultmann, Boismard, and others in finding v. 25 the natural sequel of v. 21 and v. 31 of v. 26: 'En effet la réponse à la question formulée au v. 25 est donnée au v. 31: "Pourquoi baptises-tu?" "Pour cela je suis venu, moi, baptisant." Or, dans le texte actuel de Jn, cette réponse n'est donnée que le lendemain, et devant un auditoire inexistant!' As Boismard argued in his earlier article, the witness of John the Baptist is directed to the priests and Levites (1: 19). But he does not deliver his testimony until the day after they have put their question, by which time 'ils ont disparu de l'horizon'! I see no way of getting round this objection, and I also agree with Boismard that the contrast between two *types* of baptism, water and the Holy Spirit, is likely to be secondary. On the other hand, the vision of the Holy Spirit descending ὡς περιστερά is scarcely likely to have been added subsequently. In one important respect it resembles a fragment of the *Gospel of the*

---

[7] 'The seven days of the new creation in St. John's gospel', *CBQ* 21 (1959), 507–16.

Nazarenes cited by Jerome (*In Isa.* 11: 12: 'descendit fons omnis spiritus sancti et requievit super eum.') John also, unlike the Synoptists, alludes to the prophecy on which Jerome is commenting: that the spirit of Yahweh will rest (ἀναπαύσεται) on the Messiah. As for the debate concerning the correct reading of v. 34 (ὁ ἐκλεκτός or ὁ υἱός), the arguments in favour of ἐκλεκτός are well summarized by Schnackenburg.[8] De Jonge, having pointed out that 'the title "Son of God" is exactly the one we should expect in 1: 34', adds 'and therefore it is likely to be original',[9] an argument which violates one of the most hallowed of the canons of textual criticism: *lectio difficilior potior*. The episode is rounded off by v. 28, which fills this function well (Bultmann compares it to 6: 59; 8: 20; 12: 36), making it unnecessary to search further (in 3: 28 f., for instance: see Boismard and Fortna).

In the Discovery there are two main problems: v. 43 and the conclusion. Subsidiary questions (e.g. who is responsible for the temporal notations in v. 39) do not merit a long discussion. And in an excursus intended for specialists there is no need to reproduce Martyn's admirably detailed defence of his reconstruction of v. 43. I would simply add that this revised version opens the way for a reconsideration of the alternative readings of the third word of v. 41. Most editors recognize that πρωΐ is an attempt to smooth away the problems raised by reading either πρῶτος or πρῶτον. Generally πρῶτον is accepted as correct, but the adverb seems to have little point ('The first thing Andrew did'), and the trouble with reading the word as an adjective ('Simon was the first he found') is that Andrew is not credited with any further finding (unless he reappears as the subject of εὑρίσκει in v. 43, which is impossible, as this would mean attributing to him the decision to move to Galilee, ἠθέλησεν). But if Martyn's solution is right, then the original reading in v. 41 must be πρῶτος. To Andrew goes the credit of the first discovery in a chain: Andrew finds Simon, Simon finds Philip, Philip finds Nathanael. Once the chain has been broken, then πρῶτος is not just redundant but out of place. (If πρῶτον were the original reading, then πρῶτος could be explained as a scribal error, following οὗτος; but the reverse is just as likely—an original nominative altered to agree with τὸν ἀδελφόν).

Lastly, the conclusion. Most who accept a signs source would

[8] *Gospel*, i. 305 f.   [9] 'Jewish Expectations', p. 108 n. 13.

exclude 1: 51. Even Dodd agrees that this high doctrine 'may well be an addition by the evangelist'.[10] Fortna[11] argues against Bultmann[12] that v. 50 should be retained, for two reasons: (1) there is a hiatus between v. 50 and v. 51 disclosed by the sudden shift from singular (ὄψῃ) to plural (ὄψεσθε); (2) the approval of a vision leading to faith conflicts with the explicit theology of 20: 29. But (1) is scarcely an insuperable difficulty: Jesus turns from Nathanael to address a larger audience. As for (2), the 'vision' here is figurative, not physical, unlike that of Thomas, and accordingly μείζω need not be taken to refer to greater *miracles*. Rather it fits in, as Bultmann saw, with the Johannine theology of 5: 20 and 14: 12. Fortna contends that v. 50 makes an effective transition to ch. 2. That is a matter of opinion: to me it seems a lame ending for an otherwise well-told tale. The fig-tree motif (whatever its significance) belongs to the evangelist too, and has been added by him to v. 48 for the sake of continuity.

The interpretative problems of the Cana episode make source-critical analysis even trickier than usual. There are three main problems.

1. Does the initial exchange between Jesus and his mother belong to the original story or is it a later addition of the evangelist? Fortna opts resolutely for the latter solution: 'All attempts to dismiss the inconsistency in 3b–4 are futile; Jesus clearly rejects (v. 4) what is at least an implicit request for a miracle (v. 3bc)—and yet proceeds in what follows to accomplish one.[13] Besides, he adds, both the theme of Jesus' hour and to a lesser extent his disagreement with his family are Johannine, and almost certainly not from the source. But this reasoning is unsound: there are numerous themes in the source that have been taken over and adapted by the evangelist; in any case, the 'family-disagreement' motif may be Johannine, but it is thoroughly traditional as well (e.g. Matt 12: 46–50 //). As for the inconsistency, if such there be, this is even harder to explain on the hypothesis of an editorial insertion. For if the rejection of a demand for a miracle was absolute and represented the evangelist's considered judgement, then he would have had to have abandoned the source at this point in order to compose instead a Gospel made up entirely of discourse and dialogue.

---

[10] *Tradition*, p. 312.   [11] *Gospel of Signs*, p. 187.   [12] *Gospel*, p. 98 n. 5.
[13] *Gospel of Signs*, p. 31.

2. The contrast (in v. 9) between the ignorance of the ἀρχιτρίκλι-νος and the knowledge of the διάκονοι concerning the source of the transmogrified water is an awkward intrusion: it clutters up the sentence unnecessarily and is syntactically very clumsy. But although the question of mysterious origins is not exclusively the preserve of the evangelist himself (in fact it is reminiscent of something John the Baptist says in a phrase generally assigned to the source: 1: 31), it nevertheless represents one of his central concerns.

3. How much of the conclusion of the story (v. 11) is pre-Johannine? At least 'the commencement of the signs' and the disciples' act of faith, which constitutes an inclusion with 1: 7 and rounds off the triptych. To object, as some have done, that there is no place for an act of faith here, because this has already taken place in the previous chapter, is to overlook the importance for the writer of this 'opening' of Jesus' signs. The phrase 'he manifested his glory', is probably an addition, though it cannot surely have been inserted at the same time as the protest in v. 4—a point Fortna ignores. Alternatively, 'his glory', as understood by the source, will have been the *messianic* glory of Jesus, which is only indirectly a manifestation of the glory of God.

I am unconvinced by the arguments of H.-P. Heekerens, who holds that the two Cana miracles (2: 1–12 and 4: 46b–54) derive from the same source and were added to the Gospel by a later redactor.

8

SON OF GOD

Between the simple messianic faith outlined in the previous chapter and the high christology associated with the figure of the Son of Man lies a middle ground. There can be no question of marking this out clearly, still less of railing it off. Nevertheless, one might reasonably expect to be able to detect in the Gospel at least some traces of the passage from the earlier to the later faith. In searching for these one could of course begin from the strong evidence of the finished gospel, with its clearly defined notions of pre-existence, exaltation, revelation, and so on. But the question I want to attempt to answer in this chapter (the most tentative in the book) means taking a rather different approach, one that involves the imposition of certain methodological restraints. The question is this: How far could the Johannine group proceed along what Koester calls 'the Johannine trajectory' on its own steam, without requiring the kind of external boost provided, in Bultmann's theory, by the Gnostic myth?[1]

This is what we are given: (*a*) the sign-source; (*b*) an indefinite number of Synoptic-type traditions; (*c*) the readiness the group shared with all contemporary Jewish sects, orthodox and heterodox alike, to search in the Old Testament for answers to its religious questions; (*d*) the need to respond to the increasingly hostile queries and challenges of the host community. With regard to this last point, we have to assume that the group was no more anxious to alter or develop its faith than any other religious sect, and will have done so only out of the instinct of self-preservation or (less likely in this

---

[1] If we leave aside the Mandaean sources, the *written* text with the strongest claim for inclusion under this category is undoubtedly the collection of poems known as the *Odes of Solomon*. But for all the remarkable resemblances in thought and idiom these bear to the Fourth Gospel, it is more than doubtful if they can be regarded as a source. Many scholars in fact think the Odist was Christian, e.g. Henry Chadwick: 'The consistently Christian character of the Odes is unambiguous' ('Some Reflections', p. 267). Similarly, J. Charlesworth concludes: 'The numerous and pervasive parallels between the Odes and John cannot be explained by literary dependence of the Odist upon John or vice versa' ('Qumran, John and the Odes of Solomon', p. 135).

instance) the urge to make converts abroad. I am deliberately postponing here any consideration of such strong Christian traditions, absent from the signs source, as could lead directly to the high christology familiar to us—the resurrection/exaltation motif, preexistent Wisdom, the Son of Man. Had these been active elements within the group's thinking from the beginning we might have expected a very rapid fermentation and a consequent 'bursting of the bottles' within a very short time.

There are, in fact, reasons for thinking that the Christian Jews lived fairly peaceably for a time alongside the parent community and that the tension between them and the synagogue authorities did not reach snapping-point straight away. Martyn has shown how traumatic the final irrevocable act of excommunication must have been for the new group. Their pain and their anger, so manifest in the text of the Gospel, cannot be explained except on the hypothesis of a gradual disenchantment on the part of the establishment, even if their decision 'that anyone who confessed Jesus to be the Messiah should be expelled from the synagogue' (9: 22) was reached, as Martyn contends, in response to an authoritative decree from the central committee of the Pharisees in Jamnia, the reformulation of the so-called *Birkath ha-Minim*, the Benediction against Heretics.[2] Moreover, this decree is generally (though insecurely) dated around AD 85. If this is right, then some twenty years must have elapsed between the formation of the group of those who proclaimed Jesus as Messiah and their eventual excommunication. And however much this period is curtailed, there must remain an irreducible minimum phase of cohabitation before the divorce of the two parties.

Even so, it must be confessed that the direct evidence for a slow buildup of tension between the two groups is very slight. By and large, John is faithful to the Synoptic tradition according to which the antagonism of the Pharisees towards Jesus was whipped up to murderous proportions almost at the start of his public career. In Mark 3: 6 we are told that after Jesus had cured a man with a withered hand on the sabbath, 'the Pharisees went out, and immediately held counsel with the Herodians how to destroy him'. Form criticism shows that this is the climax of a series of controversies that are slung together in the gospel with only the most perfunctory regard for questions of time and place. This does not

---

[2] *History*[2], pp. 50–62. But see the reservations discussed in ch. 3, n. 102.

necessarily mean that these stories are all inventions of the Christian community eager to defend their own point of view against their Jewish adversaries (as Bultmann, for instance, holds).[3] But it does make things difficult for the historian, who in any case must conclude that the decision to seek Jesus' death was reached much later in his career than the Gospel text, read uncritically, might be thought to imply.

In the Fourth Gospel the situation is even more complex. It is hard to believe that the literary activity of the Christian group ceased altogether after the composition of the signs source, to be resumed years later, following the expulsion from the synagogue. The present text of the Gospel may include certain episodes written down at a much earlier period, when the attitude of the authorities may have been nervous or suspicious rather than positively belligerent. If so, these have been so thoroughly absorbed into the later text that they are very much harder to detect than comparable episodes in the Synoptic Gospels, in which the oral tradition has left much more obvious traces. Eventually the fourth evangelist shows himself prepared to transfer the story of the cleansing of the Temple, which in other Gospels was the ultimate and unforgivable outrage, and to make of it Jesus' very first act upon entering Jerusalem for the first time (John 2: 13–22). What is more, besides accepting the tradition of the Pharisees' immediate and unremitting hostility to Jesus, John is prepared—as can easily be seen—to impose his own characteristic ideas and preoccupations upon his material throughout. So there are two factors to be taken into consideration by anyone attempting to plot the earliest stages of the Johannine trajectory. On the one hand, there is the very high probability that the development of the new christology was slow rather than sudden. It is this probability that justifies the methodological restraints I have already mentioned. On the other hand, there is the presence throughout the Gospel of the controlling hand of the evangelist. This is what makes any reconstruction necessarily tentative.

I. THE SAMARITAN CONNECTION

As before, I propose to conduct this fresh enquiry by starting from a single chapter, in this case chapter 7. But first it is necessary to spend

---

[3] *The History of the Synoptic Tradition* (Oxford, 1968), pp. 39 f.

some time upon a discussion of an alternative theory concerning the theological development of the Johannine group. This theory is the one outlined by Raymond Brown in his book *The Community of the Beloved Disciple*. Brown is very conscious that a major weakness of Martyn's earlier work, *History and Theology in the Fourth Gospel*, is its failure to account for the shift from the primitive faith of Jesus' earliest disciples to the new theology: 'He offers no real explanation for the appearance of a higher christology in the "Middle Period" of pre-Gospel development.'[4] Brown himself attempts to fill this gap by appealing to the fresh impetus given to the Christian Jews by the accession to their ranks of a largish number of converts from Samaritanism. The special interests of this group will, he thinks, have precipitated a new wave of theological reflection eventually resulting in the high Johannine christology we know so well. Moreover, 'the acceptance of the second group by the majority of the first group is probably what brought upon the whole Johannine community the suspicion and hostility of the synagogue leaders. After the conversion of the Samaritans in chap. 4, the Gospel concentrates on the rejection of Jesus by "the Jews".'[5]

Other scholars attach even more importance than Brown to what I have termed 'the Samaritan connection'. G. W. Buchanan actually concludes that the term 'Jew' in the Fourth Gospel meant simply 'non-Samaritan Palestinian' (which is why Jesus himself could be called a Jew), but that 'the author came from another Semitic group, namely the anti-Judean, Samaritan Christian Church'.[6] Even Oscar Cullmann, who is himself in favour of a strong Samaritan connection, admits that this is pushing the evidence too far (though he does not reject Buchanan's theory out of hand) and leans rather towards the alternative proposal (of J. Bowman)[7] that 'the Gospel was written for Samaritans'.[8] A very different suggestion comes from J. D. Purvis, who handles the evidence much more cautiously than either Buchanan or Cullmann. He 'is inclined to think that the author of the Fourth Gospel was involved in a polemic with Samaritan Mosaism, and not only that, but also in a polemic with a heterodox branch of the Samaritan community which was engaged in the promotion of a particular figure as the Mosaic eschatological prophet.'[9] Against this it must be urged that there is no good reason

---

[4] *Community*, p. 36. [5] Ibid., p. 37. [6] 'The Samaritan Origin', p. 163.
[7] 'Samaritan Studies I'. [8] *The Johannine Circle*, p. 51.
[9] 'The Fourth Gospel', p. 190.

for supposing John's demotion of Moses to be directed exclusively against a Samaritan sect, since many Jewish groups, including the leaders of the establishment who are John's main target elsewhere, were ardent champions of the cause of Moses.

Even a brief sketch of all the arguments advanced on behalf of the various hypotheses put forward regarding the Samaritan connection would take us too far away from the subject of this chapter. (In my Excursus II I have attempted a more detailed refutation of the rather outlandish theories of M.-É. Boismard.) But the story of the Samaritan woman in chapter 4 does undoubtedly suggest that at one point, how early we cannot tell, the young Christian community was joined by a number of Samaritan converts.[10] We have seen how the early process of proselytization is mirrored in chapter 1: one disciple of John the Baptist calls a second, who calls a third, and so on. But the missionary activity reflected in chapter 4 is of a different order, for here it is not the disciples, who are amazed to find Jesus talking with a woman, but the woman herself who spreads the good news: 'Come, see a man who told me all that I ever did. Can this be the Messiah?' And as a result, we are told, 'They (i.e. other Samaritans) emerged from the city and began to approach Jesus.' The evangelist distinguishes between this group, who believed in Jesus because of the woman's testimony (διὰ τὸν λόγον τῆς γυναικός μαρτυρούσης) and a larger group who believed on account of Jesus' own word (διὰ τὸν λόγον αὐτοῦ). These told the woman, 'It is no longer because of what you said (διὰ τὴν σὴν λαλίαν) that we believe, for we have heard for ourselves and we know that this is indeed the Saviour of the world' (4: 39–42).

[10] There are two very distinct themes in ch. 4: 1–42. The most prominent is that of the 'living' or 'fresh' water of revelation, contained in a dialogue closely related to the discussion with Nicodemus in ch. 3. The other theme centres upon Jesus' 'prophetic' insight concerning the woman's marital status, her recognition of Jesus as prophet and Messiah, and the subsequent conversion of many of her fellow-countrymen. This second theme no doubt furnished the core of the original story, round which the evangelist later wove his own characteristic theology of revelation. Fortna (*Gospel*, pp. 184–95, 239) attempts a reconstruction of this source, one I believe to be broadly correct. Boismard (*Évangile*, pp. 128–44) cuts the story up into even smaller pieces, since he believes that the original narrative was already sufficiently clearly set in Samaria, and that the specification of the woman as 'Samaritan' was added later, when the evangelist's realignment of the material made it necessary to indicate nationality more precisely. But a cake sliced as thin as this tends to crumble. It is worth noting, however, that even Olsson, who insists on principle that the text must be interpreted integrally, admits that the passsage 'has a prehistory' and that 'the author who gave the narrative its present form had at his disposal different kinds of material, each with its own "history" ' (*Structure and Meaning*, p. 119).

Brown points out that 'immediately after chapter 4 we get the picture of a very high christology and sharp conflict with "the Jews" who charge that Jesus is being deified (5: 16–18)'.[11] This implication of *post hoc ergo propter hoc* is, I believe, an example of disingenuousness that one would find hard to parallel in Brown's exegetical writings. For it would surely be straining credulity too far to suppose that the sequence of events recorded in the Gospel directly reflects the catalytic effect Brown attributes to the accession of a number of Samaritan converts to the original group. It may well be, as he suggests, and the suggestion is a valuable and important one, that 'the presence of the new group (anti-Temple Jews and their Samaritan converts) would make the Johannine community suspect to the Jewish synagogue authorities'. But what was there in their beliefs that could have prompted the charges of ditheism levelled against Jesus in chapter 5? After all, the Samaritans throughout their long history have shown themselves just as firmly and as aggressively monotheistic as orthodox Jewry.[12]

Now the Samaritan concept of Messiah was far from being identical with that of the Jews of Judaea. It certainly excluded both the traditional Davidic Messiah (for the Samaritans detested both Zion and its king) and 'Elijah back on earth' (for in the Samaritan version of the Book of Kings Elijah was regarded as a false prophet and a sorcerer, who died ignominiously by drowning in the Jordan).[13] The one biblical personage (apart from Joseph) who did claim their unquestioning allegiance was Moses, and Brown argues that the Samaritan *Taheb* (either 'he who returns' or 'he who restores')[14] 'was sometimes seen as a Moses-returned figure'. Now Moses was believed to have conversed with God and to have come

---

[11] *Community*, p. 36.

[12] But see the letter addressed to the Sidonians at Shechem in 166 BC in which they declare to Antiochus their readiness to have Zeus worshipped at their sanctuary. Cf. E. Bickerman in *RHR* 115 (1937), 108–21.

[13] These texts are most conveniently cited by their page references in John Macdonald's edition of the Samaritan Chronicle II. Elijah, for the Samaritans, was a false prophet: so far from being credited with the resurrection of the son of the widow of Zarephath, he was actually held responsible for his death; for having wheedled out of the widow the meal and the oil which was all she had left, 'he wolfed the whole lot and ate them, and he went on his way', with the result that the boy starved to death: Macdonald, p. 164 (Hebrew, p. 76). Later (p. 171: Hebrew, p. 80), he is called a sorcerer (כשׁף).

[14] תהבה or תאבה is a participial form from the Aramaic תוב (= Hebrew שׁוב). Which translation one adopts depends on whether one takes it as a transitive or an intransitive form.

down to reveal to the people what God had said. Consequently, continues Brown,

> if Jesus was interpreted against this background, then Johannine preaching would have drawn from such Moses material but corrected it: it was not Moses but Jesus who had seen God and come down to earth to speak of what he had heard above. . . . Thus the term *catalyst* applied to the newcomers in the Johannine community implies that they brought with them categories for interpreting Jesus that launched the Johannine community towards a theology of descent from above and pre-existence.[15]

The trouble is that those Samaritan sources which do appear to identify Moses and the Taheb (notably the fourth-century *Memar Marqah*) are all late. In the Samaritan Pentateuch extra importance is given to the Moses-like prophet of Deuteronomy (who is introduced into the version of Exodus 20 as well), but there are no grounds for thinking that this personage was identified thus early as Moses redivivus.[16] Wayne Meeks, whose study of the Samaritan texts would be hard to fault (and who believes that the advanced Mosaism of the later texts is probably rooted in much older traditions), admits that 'even the earliest sources do not lead directly to a point much earlier than the fourth century AD, when a major literary revival and reconstitution of Samaritan life and thought took place.'[17] Would we not have considerable hesitation before using similarly dated *Christian* sources (the Cappadocian Fathers, for instance) as witnesses of first-century beliefs? Besides, even if we ignore this difficulty and accept Brown's suggestion that it was the Samaritan presence that launched the community towards its high christology, it must be said that there was still a whole ocean of speculation to travel over before it finally arrived.[18]

Meeks thinks that Samaritan and later Jewish beliefs concerning Moses had a common source. He speaks of 'a mutual cultivation of tradition by Jew and Samaritan' and asks in what region it could have taken place. His own suggestion is that Galilee is far and away the best candidate: 'Its geographical contiguity to Samaria, its

---

[15] *Community*, pp. 44 f.

[16] J. D. Purvis even questions whether these texts prove that first-century Samaritanism saw the prophet as an eschatological figure: 'The Fourth Gospel', p. 188.   [17] *The Prophet-King*, p. 219.

[18] One title that cannot be pressed into service, as Brown himself acknowledges, is 'the Saviour of the World' (4: 42), a *hapax legomenon* in John (and indeed in the whole of the New Testament), for it cannot be located among the tenets of the Samaritan religion either.

susceptibility to Hellenistic influence, the ambiguities of its relation-ship to Jerusalem and Judaea would all help to explain the actual incidence of the traditions in question. If Galilee and Samaria were once the center of the growth of these traditions, it would be quite natural that they would persist at the center of Samaritan and certain Hellenistic Jewish literature, while only occasionally and peripherally in "normative" Jewish documents.'[19] This conjecture must be borne in mind as we in our turn move from Samaria to Galilee.

2. MESSIAH AND PROPHET

'Is the Messiah to come from Galilee?' (7: 41); 'The Prophet[20] will not emerge out of Galilee' (7: 52)

For chapter 7[21] I postulate a rather complex process of composition built round two main blocks of material, the first (vv. 14–19a; 25–31) concerned with Jesus' ascent to the Feast of Tabernacles and an ensuing controversy over the twin titles of Prophet and Messiah, the second (vv. 32; 37–52) telling how the chief priests and Pharisees sent the temple proctors to arrest Jesus and how their failure to do so provoked a further controversy, also centred upon the same two titles. But the focus of interest is very different in the two blocks. The first includes a number of far-reaching reflections upon the deeper implications of the two titles. The second (which we are about to consider) is relatively straightforward, and seems to hinge upon a local quarrel between Galileans in general and the Judaean authorities in Jerusalem (not called Ἰουδαῖοι in these stories).

The controversy that arises out of the dispute recorded in v. 41 concerning the identity of Jesus turns upon a simple but fundamen-tal issue: can either (*a*) the Messiah (v. 41) or (*b*) the Prophet (v. 52) come from Galilee? To understand the story properly we must

---

[19] *The Prophet-King*, p. 257.
[20] The relatively recently discovered Bodmer papyrus (π 66) is the only authority to include the article before προφήτης in this verse, but though now widely accepted by scholars and students, it has not yet found its way into published translations and is not adopted by the latest (26th) Nestlé-Aland edition of the Greek text (1979). See W. Meeks, 'Galilee and Judaea', p. 160 n. 4.
[21] For an exegetical defence of this proposal, see Excursus III.

recognize that 'Galilee' is both a geographical region and a value term. Elsewhere in the Gospel Ἰουδαῖοι is more often than not a value term also, though not, of course, a positive one, but it too was partly a geographical designation, signifying primarily 'the inhabitants of Judaea', partly an indication of religion.[22] (See Chapter 4.) And though οἱ Ἰουδαῖοι are not explicitly mentioned in the story under consideration, they are obviously not very far away. For in tacitly accepting Jesus' Galilean origin, the author of the story is aligning the unlettered populace of Jerusalem (the crowd, who are ignorant of the law) with Jesus and his fellow-Galileans against the rulers (οἱ ἄρχοντες) and the Pharisees, who refuse to be impressed. Nicodemus too, who ventures to protest on Jesus' behalf, is disowned by his own people with the sardonic question, 'Surely you are not a Galilean as well?' So it is in this story, I suggest, that we have the first signs of the rift between the Johannine community and the Jewish authorities. The hostility of 'the high priests and Pharisees' towards Jesus does not yet have any particular ideological thrust; their opposition is based on the simple fact, admitted by all, that Jesus came from Galilee.

Martyn points out that the expression 'chief priests and Pharisees' is 'a very strange combination' because it was possible to be both a priest and a Pharisee.[23] He suggests that the reason for this oddity lies in the evangelist's desire to indicate both (a) the historical opposition of the leaders of the Jerusalem Sanhedrin during Jesus' lifetime and (b) his own local situation at the time of writing, when the local Sanhedrin (Gerousia) will have been largely controlled by Pharisees. But if, as I believe may be the case, this story was composed before AD 70, when the chief priests were still the official leaders of the Jewish community in Jerusalem, then the two-level argument, if indeed this hypothesis is correct, will have been not so much temporal in this case as geographical. That is to say the writer may have intended to suggest that the Pharisees of his own city faithfully reflected the attitudes of the chief priests, whose active opposition to Jesus is one of the relatively few secure elements in the whole tradition.

However this may be, the point of the story is to be found in the stark contrast between the simple but conclusive answer of the ὑπηρέται, the temple proctors, stoutly supported by Nicodemus ('No

---

[22] See M. Lowe, 'Who were the ΙΟΥΔΑΙΟΙ?'
[23] *History*[2], p. 84.

one has ever spoken like this man'), and the automatic response of the Pharisees, whose mindless appeal to authority ('Has a single one of the "rulers" or the Pharisees believed in him?') is accompanied by a curt dismissal of those who do not know the law. The effect of this is to set Jerusalem off against Galilee, the sophisticated south against the unlettered north.

Accordingly I think Wayne Meeks is right to detect here 'a historical bone of controversy between the Johannine community and the Jewish group';[24] if so, then we may have in this story a flickering recollection of an emphasis upon the prophetic and messianic claims of Jesus rooted in a richer soil than we could possibly know about from 'orthodox' Jewish sources. All four of Jesus' first-named disciples were Galileans, Nathanael from Cana, the other three from Bethsaida (which the evangelist thought of as in Galilee: 12: 21), and the commencement of Jesus' signs took place there. More important than the subsequent Samaritan connection, then, was a Galilean connection.

Meeks argues that for John Galilee was the place of acceptance, just as Judaea, Jesus' native land ($\pi\alpha\tau\rho\iota$s) was the place of rejection: 'A prophet has no honour in his own country' (4: 44). This proverb not only has a different application in the Fourth Gospel (in the other three Jesus' $\pi\alpha\tau\rho\iota$s is Galilee), but the addition of the adjective $\iota\delta\iota$os ($\dot{\epsilon}\nu$ $\tau\hat{\eta}$ $\iota\delta\iota\alpha$ $\pi\alpha\tau\rho\iota\delta\iota$) points to a link with the bleak affirmation of the Prologue: 'He came to his own [home] ($\tau\dot{\alpha}$ $\iota\delta\iota\alpha$) and his own [people] ($o\dot{\iota}$ $\iota\delta\iota\iota\iota$) received him not' (1: 11), unlike the Galileans, who did welcome him (4: 45). Accordingly, says Meeks, 'the journeys to Jerusalem in John symbolize the coming of the redeemer to "his own" and his rejection by them, while the emphasized movement from Judea to Galilee (especially 4: 43–54) symbolizes the redeemer's acceptance by others, who thereby become truly "children of God", the real Israel. Thus, while "the Jews" symbolize the natural people of God, who, however, reject God's messenger, "the Galileans" symbolize those who are estranged from the natural people of God, but became truly God's people because they receive God's messenger.'[25] More generally, he says, 'the best explanation for the controversy stories in which "Galilean" and "Samaritan" are epithets applied by Jewish opponents to Jesus or his followers is the

[24] 'Galilee and Judaea', p. 160.
[25] Ibid., p. 165. *Contra* R. Brown, *Community*, pp. 39 f. and W. D. Davies, *The Gospel and the Land* (London, 1974), pp. 321–31.

assumption that Christians of the Johannine circle had at some time met just this kind of polemic. The positive appropriation of these epithets, moreover, suggests that there may have been historical reasons why the Johannine community was willing tacitly to accept an identification as "Samaritans" and "Galileans".'[26]

The author of the story at the end of chapter 7 either did not know of or else was uninterested in any claim that Jesus was actually a linear descendant of David, born in Bethlehem and of Jewish, that is to say, Judaean nationality.[27] He is content to leave unanswered the scriptural argument that the Messiah was to come from Bethlehem (v. 42) and that the Prophet was not to come from Galilee (v. 52). He ironically records how the Pharisees shrugged off any possibility that those who made such claims could come up with any convincing proof: 'This bunch of ignoramuses is under a curse' (v. 49).[28] But at this stage there is no counter proof drawn from Scripture. The rabbinic-type argument in which Jesus explicitly engages so frequently elsewhere in the Gospel (including, as we shall see, this very chapter) is missing here. Instead we have the kind of quietly devastating punch-line that is one of the hallmarks of this particular *Gattung* in the Synoptic Gospels: 'This man has spoken like no one before him' (v. 46).

Now this assertion is of crucial importance for our understanding of how the faith of the community developed. It constitutes a major step forward from the simple argument of the signs-source (still observable in this chapter: v. 31) that Jesus' *miracles* were the chief guarantee of his messiahship, and gives us in this relatively early passage what is really the central theme of the whole Gospel, *revelation*. Already proclaimed as Prophet and Messiah, Jesus is beginning to take on the lineaments of the Revealer. Subsequently, in adapting the signs-source, the evangelist will deliberately include Jesus' words as well as his works in the reference, and thereby the sense, of ἔργα.[29] But even at this stage, I suggest, the movement has

---

[26] 'Galilee and Judaea', p. 168.

[27] See Bultmann, *Gospel*, p. 305 n. 6; Meeks, *Prophet-King*, pp. 36–8; 'Galilee and Judaea', pp. 156–9; De Jonge, 'Jesus as Prophet', p. 55.

[28] Scholars are agreed in finding here a reference to the עם הארץ, literally 'the people of the land', a term frequently used in rabbinic literature to refer to people ignorant of the law. Bultmann (*Gospel*, p. 310 n. 5) disputes Strack–Billerbeck's contention that it was a technical term.

[29] As for instance in 14: 12: 'He who believes in me will also do the works that I do, and greater works than these will he do.' These 'works' surely include the preaching and spreading of the message of the Gospel.

begun, and the Jewish Christian group has already had sufficient experience of what will later be called 'the words of eternal life' (6: 68) to make it the single conclusive answer to the charge of 'leading the people astray'. One might add that the new faith could not have survived simply on the strength of a waning memory of Jesus' miraculous deeds, whatever their symbolic force. The vital difference between words and deeds is that words can be repeated and, in the right context, freshly understood so as to become the source of new life. No Christian writer has ever been more keenly aware of this than the fourth evangelist.[30]

In its present context, the amazement of the ὑπηρέται must refer to the extraordinary pronouncement of Jesus on the last day of the feast: 'out of his belly shall flow rivers of living water' (7: 38). It is easy to see in this pronouncement, especially if one remembers the particular quality of the Feast of Tabernacles and its ritual,[31] an implicit claim on Jesus' part to be a new Moses, less easy, perhaps, to read it as a claim to be the Davidic Messiah. Bultmann argues that it is out of place here on the grounds that the ὑπηρέται would have to have waited overnight before reporting back to the priests and Pharisees who had sent them (vv. 32 and 45).[32] He may be right, but the story would be incomplete without some great prophetic declaration. Moreover, the clear conviction that Jesus has spoken with an unparalleled authority, here put into the mouths of the ὑπηρέται, must surely emerge from an *experience of Christian prophecy*. At this point the experience simply serves to reinforce the primitive faith in Jesus as Prophet and Messiah. But it did not stop there, and we may reasonably suppose that prophecy—in the Pauline sense of a god-given gift—will have continued to play an important role in confirming the conviction of the young community that their insights into the true nature of Jesus' messianic claims were based upon an authentic revelation, and that as followers of Jesus they were not, as the opposing party charged, being 'led astray'. Our next task is to attempt, in a modest way, to chart the appearance of some of these new insights, which as could be expected were associated at first with already established beliefs.

---

[30] Pascal, however, came close (in a passage he later struck out in obedience to the censor): 'Les prophéties sont les seuls miracles subsistants qu'on peut faire' (*Pensées*, 760). But if these more enduring miracles are in fact to endure they must be written down—hence the need for a Gospel.

[31] Raymond Brown (326 f.) gives a good summary of the relevant material.

[32] *Gospel*, p. 287.

3. ORIGINS

'When the Messiah comes, no one will know where he is from' (7: 27)

The other two important themes in chapter 7, mission and origins, arise naturally out of questions concerning the Prophet ('on whose authority does he speak?') and the Messiah ('no one knows where he is from'). Johannine theology carries both themes into realms of mystical speculation far removed from the simple and perfectly justifiable request for some guarantee that Jesus was all that he claimed to be. The deuteronomic promise that Moses would have a successor like himself was accompanied by a warning to anyone eager to don prophetic garb not to 'speak a word in my name which I have not commanded him to speak' (Deut. 18: 20; cf. 13: 1–6)—equivalently a warning against false prophets. And the (historically) earlier promise of a successor to the throne of David was soon made more specific than it was in the original prophecy (2 Sam. 7): in particular, the Davidic Messiah came to be associated with Bethlehem (Mic. 5: 1). So it was only to be expected that Jesus should be required to produce his credentials.

Accordingly, questions concerning Jesus' prophetic mission and special messianic claims need not have been inspired in the first place by theological curiosity on the one hand or by suspicion and hostility on the other. There is a tradition that Jesus' teaching prompted the question, 'On what authority are you doing these things, and who gave you this authority?' (Matt. 21: 23)—a natural enough query to put to any teacher bold enough to challenge the received ideas of the religious establishment. As for the question concerning Jesus' origins, it would be surprising if it had not been put to a messianic pretender, especially one whose Galilean connections were common knowledge. We have already seen that there is no attempt at the end of chapter 7 to cover up these connections in the face of the challenging demand, 'Surely the Messiah is not to come from Galilee?' (7: 41).

In fact the implicit invitation to Jesus to engage in a debate over his own origins has been taken up earlier in the chapter, not this time in response to a suggestion that the Messiah is to come from Judaea, but rather in answer to a question arising out of an altogether different tradition, one that insisted upon the obscurity of the Messiah's origins, for when he appears 'no one will know where he is from' (7: 27).

The objection that the Messiah's origins were to be unknown (v. 27) clearly conflicts with the subsequent objection (v. 42), based on Micah 5: 1 ff., that he is to come from Bethlehem. It is, of course, possible to gloss over this difficulty by saying that the two objections come from different voices in a large crowd. But this is to ignore that the stories in which they are embedded, skilfully spliced as they are, fulfil different purposes and make different points. Whether they were linked by the evangelist himself or found by him already joined together in a continuous narrative need not concern us here. What seems clear is that of the two objections only the one concerning the obscurity of the Messiah's origins is elaborated in a fashion fully consonant with the evangelist's developed christology.

The expectation of an 'unknown' Messiah is attested in an important passage in Justin's *Dialogue with Trypho* (second century), where the Jew Trypho is made to say: 'Even if the Messiah is already born and in existence somewhere, he is nevertheless unknown; even he himself does not know about himself, nor does he have any kind of power until Elijah comes and anoints him and reveals him to all' (*Dial.* 8. 4; cf. 110. 1). This tradition was probably familiar to the Johannine group from the start: it is reflected in the words of John the Baptist, 'There stands among you one whom you do not know ... I myself did not know him' (1: 26, 31; cf. 1: 33). In the Johannine version of the baptism story Elijah is replaced by the descent of the Holy Spirit in the form of a dove (1: 33). But although the passage in chapter 7 clearly depends upon the same tradition, it sharply diverges from it in one important respect by insisting, *against* the tradition, that Jesus does know where he comes from, for his origin is precisely 'the one who sent him': παρ' αὐτοῦ εἰμι, κἀκεῖνός με ἀπέστειλεν.

What is more, in the Gospel account ignorance of the Messiah's origins is restricted to those outside the circle of Jesus' disciples. From being universal, even necessary, it has become the mark of the uninitiated. For these Jesus is a Jew (4: 9; 18: 33–5), a man from Nazareth (18: 5, 7; 19: 19) or Galilee (7: 41, 52), 'whose father and mother we know' (6: 42). They are not, of course, totally mistaken in thinking so; when Jesus first appears on the scene (in the signs source) he is identified as 'the son of Joseph, from Nazareth' (1: 45);

and when he says, in the passage under discussion, 'you know me, and you know where I am from' (7: 28), he is being ironical in the Johannine manner, but there is no need to punctuate the sentence as a question, as is done, for instance, in the RSV. As Bultmann says, the irony does not lie in any suggestion that their knowledge is based on faulty information: 'Yet in a paradoxical way this is at the same time a proof of their ignorance. Their knowledge is unknowing; for they use their knowledge, which is perfectly correct, to conceal the very thing which is important to know. Their knowledge serves only to prevent them from recognizing Jesus; he cannot be the Messiah because they know where he comes from!'[33]

Evidently the gulf between Jesus' adherents and his opponents is immeasurably wider here than in the story that follows at the end of the chapter (which we have already discussed). For there the fundamental opposition was between Galileans and Judaeans, and it was possible to pass, as Nicodemus did, from one group to the other. No doubt in a sense that is true here too, but the principle of division is now not external but internal, and the circle of believers has come to be confined to those who have learned from Jesus (once more against the tradition) where he is from: this knowledge is all that really separates them from Jesus' adversaries, and it is to be expected that those outside the privileged circle will from time to time betray their ignorance and their blindness (cf. 9: 29; 19: 9). Otherwise they would be insiders and not outsiders.

Though the tradition concerning the uncertain provenance of the Messiah may well have given rise to questions regarding Jesus' true origins and therefore helped to account for the growing conviction that his real home was in heaven and not on earth, still it may be doubted whether the Christian group would or indeed could have arrived at this answer without some inspiration from an altogether different source. The evangelist insists very powerfully—it is one of the Gospel's most pervasive themes—that Jesus 'came into' the world as an outsider, and that the question πόθεν, whence, cannot be satisfactorily answered by naming any particular location on this earth. For in the last analysis Jesus is not 'of the world' (ἐκ τοῦ κόσμου) at all. He is (or was) in it but not of it.

The expressions 'to be of' (εἶναι ἐκ) and 'to be born of' (γεννηθῆναι ἐκ) usually carry a double meaning in the Fourth Gospel, implying

[33] *Gospel*, pp. 297 f.

both origin and nature.[34] To be of the earth is to be earthly; to be of the world is to be worldly. To be of heaven is to be heavenly, and also to be *of* heaven, from above (ἄνωθεν).[35] And so this double theme of origin and nature establishes a contrast basic to the thought of the evangelist, the contrast between heavenly and earthly, between God and the world, between above and below: 'You are from below; I am from above; you are of this world; I am not of this world' (8: 23).[36]

The majority of commentators, when discussing the passages in the Fourth Gospel in which this opposition is most vividly expressed, are content to draw up a list of parallels, biblical and extra-biblical,[37] and perhaps to underline the differences between ortho-dox and heterodox examples of the opposition. Bultmann filters out the coarse mythical features of what is here a simple, two-storeyed universe by assigning them to the Gnostic source. He then expounds his own interpretation of the pure theology he has thus succeeded in isolating. This coincides, one is not surprised to see, with the views of the evangelist. But this solution, remarkable as it is, remains extremely insecure, with no firmer support than the tenuous hypothesis of a revelation source.

Wayne Meeks, in an article to which allusion has already been made more than once,[38] partially fills in the gap in our understand-ing of the Gospel's developed theology with his suggestion that the community's profound sense of Jesus' alienation from the world is partly at any rate the reflection of its own experience *vis-à-vis* the Jews. His followers, like him, are in the world (17: 11) but not of it (17: 16): 'For if you were of the world, the world would love its own;

[34] See Ch. 6, p. 207. Bultmann comments on the meaning of εἶναι ἐκ in a series of brilliant notes: *Gospel*, pp. 135 n. 4; 138 n. 1; 162 n. 3; cf. p. 655 n. 7.

[35] In ch. 3, where the entire series of oppositions is displayed, there is also, exceptionally, the contrast between πνεῦμα and σάρξ (v. 6).

[36] Here, almost for the first time in considering the christology of the Fourth Gospel, one is forced to pay some attention to a possible apocalyptic background, not only because, as we shall see in the next chapter, the opposition between the two realms, heaven above and earth beneath, is firmly associated with the (originally) apocalyptic figure of the Son of Man, but also because it is independently attested in contemporary writings: 'Those who dwell upon the earth can understand only what is on the earth, and he who is above the heavens can understand what is above the height of the heavens (*4 Ezra* 4: 21); cf. John 3: 12; Wisd. 9: 16 and other passages cited in Meeks, 'Man from heaven', pp. 168 f. nn. 36–7.

[37] See Str.–B. ii. 424 f.

[38] 'The Man from Heaven'. Meeks pays much attention to the 'Son of Man' theme in this article, but consideration of this topic will be deferred until the next chapter.

but because you are not of the world, but I chose you out of the world, therefore the world hates you' (15: 19).

The fourth evangelist's insistence that Jesus enters the world as a stranger and is never truly at home there runs counter to the whole Synoptic tradition, where Jesus' evident distress at being rejected by his people is accentuated by a persistent awareness that they are *his* people, as they were of the prophets who preceded him: 'O Jerusalem, Jerusalem, killing the prophets and stoning those who are sent to you!' (Luke 13: 34.) The perfectly natural curiosity concerning Jesus' origins cannot of itself have precipitated the whole of this remarkable theology of alienation, nor could it have been carried through without a conscious reversal of the tradition that the Messiah himself would be as much in ignorance of his own origins as those on whose behalf he came. According to John's conception one essential element in Jesus' message was a steady affirmation that his real origins were divine, that his first and only true home was in heaven. Such a formal contradiction of the traditions concerning Jesus himself as well as of those concerning the Messiah he claimed to be is hardly conceivable without some appeal to an equally powerful tradition, one that so far has eluded us.

4. MISSION:[39]

Part of the answer to this puzzle is to be found in the very passage we have just been considering. After his ironic admission that the crowd is not ignorant of his origins, Jesus continues: 'and I have not come on my own initiative, but the one who sent me, whom you do not know, is a true sender:[40] *I* know him because I am from him, and he commissioned me' (7: 28 f.). So Jesus associates the question of his origins with the seemingly very different question of his mission. It is important to realize that these two motifs, however readily yoked, are not in fact natural twins. The mission-motif is primarily associated in the Bible with the title and function of prophet, not that of Messiah, whose origins may have been mysterious, but whose role

---

[39] For the themes and arguments of this and the following section, see J. P. Miranda, *Die Sendung Jesu*. This study covers much of the same ground as the longer work of J.-A. Bühner, *Gesandte*.

[40] The word here is ἀληθινός, which *pace* Bultmann and others, means not 'truthful' but 'genuine', 'authentic'—'true' in the sense that Jesus is the true vine (15: 1) and that God is the true God (17: 3).

as the harbinger of a new era of divine justice was, within certain limits, reasonably assured. Conversely it might appear that although the particular role and function of each individual prophet was unique, there was no mystery about the origins of any of them. True, their commission was in general the consequence of a divine summons, but they were for the most part sent from where they stood, like Moses, the archetypal prophet, who was both called and sent from the holy ground on which he had ventured in order to get a better view of the burning bush (Exod. 3: 2 f.).

No doubt there remain in the Old Testament distinct traces of a mythical concept of prophecy, according to which the prophet is sent directly from the heavenly council-chamber. God is pictured as presiding over his council (סוֹד), which consists of 'the holy ones', 'the sons of God', or 'the gods', and giving instructions to his legates. A striking instance is the strange story of Micaiah (1 Kings 22: 19–23), who explains how it was that a lying spirit came to be sent out and placed in the mouths of the four hundred prophets advising the king of Israel. Jeremiah picks up the same idea in the course of his invective against the false prophets of his own day, of whom he asks, 'Who among them has stood in the council of Yahweh to perceive and hear his word?' (Jer. 23: 18.)

Speaking with the voice of God, he declares: 'I did not send the prophets, yet they ran; I did not speak to them, yet they prophesied. But if they had stood in my council, then they would have proclaimed my words to my people' (23: 21 f.). As James F. Ross asserts, this implies that the prophets' authority is ultimately derived from the divine council itself.[41] Again, Second Isaiah, in some respects the prophet *par excellence* (since his whole identity is absorbed into his prophetic role), also seems to have received his commission as one of a group sent out directly from the heavenly council.[42] There is no doubt that the eschatological prophet foretold by Moses, whether thought of as a type or as an individual, was conceived along the same lines: 'I will put my words in his mouth, and he shall speak to them all that I command him' (Deut. 18: 18). The sense of mission exemplified in Moses himself is shared by all the prophets. Malachi, the last in the canon, sums up in his name ('My angel/messenger') the overwhelming sense of *vocation* (that is both a calling and a sending) held equally by his predecessors.

[41] Cf. 'The Prophet as Yahweh's Messenger'.
[42] Cf. Frank M. Cross, Jr., 'The Council of Yahweh', *JNES* 12 (1953), 174–7.

But even if this ancient myth could be shown to have influenced the evangelist, it still does not adequately account for the theology of the Fourth Gospel, according to which Jesus' home is in heaven. None of the prophets was thought of as anything other than a human being invested with a special authority from on high. The ambiguity in the name of Malachi, suggesting a possible identification of the prophet with an angel-messenger, certainly offers further scope for investigation;[43] but the orthodox tradition at least does not see the prophet as in any sense divine. Moreover, we should remember that in the Fourth Gospel itself John the Baptist also was commissioned (ἀπεσταλμένος) by God (1: 6; 3: 28), whom he could speak of as 'the one who sent me' (ὁ πέμψας με, 1: 33). And since there was never any question that *his* true home was in heaven we must conclude that there is no *necessary* connection, even for the fourth evangelist, between the idea of a heavenly mission or commission and the idea of being 'from God' in the strong sense, even though the two ideas are usually connected in practice in the self-revelation of Jesus.

More promising, because directly attested in the Gospel, is the *juridical* tie between Jesus and God, that is to say, the authority with which he is invested as God's special messenger. We have seen that for Jeremiah the final proof of the untrustworthiness of the false prophets was that God had neither *sent* them nor *addressed* them (Jer. 23: 21). Conversely, Jesus' insistence that he has been sent or commissioned by God is primarily and most importantly a vindication of his claim to be a (or the) prophet. For the question spontaneously arising in the mind of a Jew confronted with someone making this claim is not, as it might have been in the case of a messianic pretender: Where does he come from? Rather, the first questions would be: What are his credentials? On whose authority does he speak?

Not only are these questions the ones that any self-styled prophet might expect to be called upon to answer, but in the deuteronomic tradition, which shows signs of a very profound reflection upon the prophetic calling, they are positively demanded. For alongside the promise of the eschatological prophet ('I will put my words in his mouth, and he shall speak to them all that I command him, Deut.

---

[43] Neither Hebrew (מלאך) nor Greek (ἄγγελος) distinguishes verbally between the messenger and the angel, and we shall see in the next chapter that behind the verbal confusion lies a conceptual confusion also.

18: 18) is placed the warning against a pseudo-prophet, one 'who presumes to speak a word in my name which I have not commanded him to speak' (Deut. 18: 20).

Following T. F. Glasson,[44] Wayne Meeks has argued that the passage in Deuteronomy, taken in conjunction with another passage that concerns the seductions of wonder-workers (ch. 13: 2–6) is what explains the puzzle of John 7: 14–19, where Jesus' repeated assurances that his teaching is from God rather than from himself (ἀφ' ἑαυτοῦ) are directly followed by a reference to the Jews' intention to have him put to death. Meeks considers that the abrupt question, 'Why do you seek to kill me' (7: 19), is to be explained from the threat of execution Deuteronomy holds out against the false prophets.[45] But the strong reaction of the crowd to this question ('You have a demon! Who is seeking to kill you?') certainly conflicts with the other question that is put a few verses further on: 'Is not this the man whom they seek to kill?' *This* is the question that follows on most naturally upon Jesus' claims to speak on God's behalf: if these are unwarranted then he truly deserves to die for his presumption—he is a false prophet and the attempts to get him sentenced are fully understandable. Besides, after the introduction to the whole story in 7: 1, according to which Jesus was avoiding Judaea precisely because of the mortal hostility of its inhabitants, one would expect the people of Jerusalem to evince some awareness of this hostility. So it is not the first question but the second ('Is not this the man whom they seek to kill?') that fits best into the context.[46]

In any case a further link is provided, as Meeks points out, by an interpretative halakah in the Mishnah: '"The false prophet"—he that prophesies what he has not heard and what has not been told him, his death is at the hands of men' (*m. Sanh.* 11: 5). In the first passage from Deuteronomy the death-penalty is prescribed for any prophet or dreamer of dreams who utters 'falsehood about [or 'apostasy against'] (סרה על) Yahweh your God, to make you stray (להדיחך; LXX, πλανῆσαί σε)' (Deut. 13: 6). Lastly there is a famous *baraitha* (allusion to and citation of an ancient tradition) from the Babylonian Talmud which recounts the hanging of 'Yeshu'

---

[44] *Moses in the Fourth Gospel*, p. 30.   [45] *Prophet-King*, pp. 45 ff.

[46] That is why 7: 19b–24 must be regarded as a later insertion. The question in v. 25 follows naturally upon v. 19a and fits equally well into the context of a defence of Jesus' prophetic claims. See Excursus III, where the matter is discussed in more detail.

(יֵשׁוּעַ) on the eve of the Passover, at the end of a period of 40 days during which 'a herald went forth and cried "He is going forth to be stoned because he has practised sorcery and enticed and led Israel astray [the last of these three verbs is נדח, as in Deut. 13: 6]"' (*b. Sanh.* 43a). I am not totally convinced by Martyn's contention that the leading astray in this passage is necessarily to be construed as the incitement to worship false gods, nor that there is an earlier allusion to it in the Gospel, in ch. 5;[47] but it seems certain at least that the charge of leading astray was directed primarily against a false prophet.

So if, as I believe, the affirmations of Jesus recorded in 7: 14–19a do belong in their present context, then they must refer to the charge of false prophecy, as Meeks and Glasson have argued. They mark an important stage in the growing hostility between the Jewish-Christians of the Johannine community and the synagogue. The critical attention to which the claims of the former are being subjected requires a positive response. Thus a platform is provided for the Johannine prophet, and whilst directly defending Jesus' claim to be a true prophet, he was no doubt indirectly defending his own.

5. AGENCY

Commenting on the text from Deuteronomy we have just been considering, Philo wrote: 'The prophet will serve simply as the channel for another's insistent prompting.'[48] According to this conception the prophet is the mouthpiece of God, with no voice of his own. This corresponds closely to the view of Moses' role we find in the early tannaitic commentaries (*Mekilta, Sifra,* and *Sifre*) on the last four books of the Pentateuch. For instance: 'Anyone who claims that even the slightest fraction of the Torah comes from Moses' own

[47] Martyn's discussion (*History*[2], pp. 73–81) fails to take account of some important differences between ch. 5 and ch. 7. In ch. 5, after the plain statement that the Jews sought Jesus' death because he made himself equal with God (v. 18), there is no further debate. The remainder of the chapter is given over to one of the most profound of the Gospel's 'revelation' discourses. There is no room for further argument since there is no common ground between Jesus and the Jews. In ch. 7, on the other hand, the debate is still ongoing and urgent.

[48] ὅσα δ'ἐνηχεῖται, διελεύσεται καθάπερ ὑποβάλλοντος ἑτέρου (*De spec. leg.* i. 65). Philo is, of course, thinking here of the phenomenon of ecstatic prophecy. But in insisting that nothing of the prophet's message will be truly his own (λέγων μὲν οἰκεῖον οὐδέν), he is also faithfully following the tradition.

mouth rather than that of God has thereby shown contempt for the word of God.'[49] Or again, Moses asserts that he speaks 'not on my own authority but out of the mouth of God'.[50]

Sayings such as these are clearly religious applications of the Jewish law of agency, according to which, in the simple formulation of the Mekilta, 'an agent is like the one who sent him'.[51] Ever since Peder Borgen, following up suggestions of Théo Preiss and others, stressed the importance of this idea for understanding the theology of the Fourth Gospel,[52] its centrality has been increasingly recognized, not least because the use Christian thinkers made of the principle can be shown to go back to Jesus himself, or at least to be firmly established in the Synoptic tradition: 'Whoever receives one such child in my name receives me; and whoever receives me receives not me but him who commissioned me ($\tau \grave{o} \nu \ \dot{a} \pi o \sigma \tau \epsilon \acute{\iota} \lambda a \nu \tau \acute{a} \ \mu \epsilon$) (Mark 9: 37; cf. Luke 9: 48). That Jesus should see himself as God's agent is not particularly astonishing in view of the widespread, one could say universal, Jewish conviction concerning the prophets' role as divine emissaries; that he should make 'little children' his own representatives gives the principle such an unusual but (for him) characteristic twist that it is hard to see this as anything but an authentic saying—one of the many instances of Jesus' extraordinary imaginative freedom in his dealings with all social groups whose human dignity for whatever reason was not properly recognized by his contemporaries—not only the religious authorities but sometimes, as here, his own disciples.

Besides the saying just quoted there is a more general application of the principle found, appropriately, towards the end of the missionary discourse in Matthew's Gospel: 'He who receives you', Jesus says to his twelve disciples, 'receives me, and he who receives me receives him who commissioned me' (Matt. 10: 40), a saying which is given its negative complement in Luke: 'He who hears you hears me, and he who rejects ($\dot{a} \theta \epsilon \tau \epsilon \hat{\iota}$) you rejects me,

---

[49] **כל התורה אמר מפי הקדש ודבר משה מפי עצמו אמרו** (*Sif. Num.* 112 on 15: 31).

[50] **לא מצמי אני אומר לכם אלא מפי הק״בה אומר לכם** (*Sif. Deut.* 12 on 5: 9). Both of these texts, it is worth noting, are reproduced in Schlatter's early (1902) commentary in reference to John 7: 17. See *Sprache und Heimat*, p. 106.

[51] Borgen, 'God's Agent', p. 76 n. 5, cites a number of other rabbinical texts as well. This text is from *Mek.* on Exod. 12: 3 (**שלוחו של אדם כמותו**) (Lauterbach, i. 25).

[52] Ibid.

and he who rejects me rejects him who commissioned me' (Luke 10: 16).[53]

The importance of this tradition in the development of the Johannine theology of mission can easily be overlooked. Here for the first time we appear to have an authentic tradition capable under the right conditions of generating the high christology according to which the man who has listened to the words of Jesus has heard the voice of God and, more strikingly, in Jesus' own words to Philip, 'He who has seen me has seen the Father' (John 14: 9; cf. 12: 45). Here is the deepest source of the constantly recurring 'as ... so' ($\kappa\alpha\theta\grave{\omega}s$ ... $o\ddot{v}\tau\omega s$)[54] which, with its double perspective (back to God, forward to the disciples) is one of the most salient characteristics of Johannine theology. What Wayne Meeks nicely calls 'harmonic reinforcement' is not just a natural consequence of universal social forces operating within a cognitive minority, but comes into play as a result of a profound reflection upon the theological principle of the law of agency, a reflection which was evidently initiated by Jesus himself.

The deepest roots of this law are to be found in a _diplomatic_ convention shared by many pre-industrial societies according to which an emissary is to be treated with all the respect and courtesy due to the monarch who sent him. It is natural, too, especially in societies where travel was always subject to delay and often to danger, that the ambassador should often be a plenipotentiary. Otherwise communications between two kingdoms might easily break down altogether. King David, it will be remembered, even did his wooing of Abigail by proxy, after her husband Nabal, who had insulted David's messenger, had been struck down by God (1 Sam. 25: 38–42; cf. 2 Sam. 10—the story of Hanun and the Ammonites).

The transition from _mission_, regularly associated in the Old Testament with prophecy, to _agency_, which need not have any religious overtones at all,[55] is easily disregarded. It is a theological truism that God's dealing with mankind can only be conceptualized _analogically_, for human language is the only language we have. So it is not surprising that in searching for a conceptual framework that would enable them to talk intelligibly of such dealings, Jewish

---

[53] The verb $\dot{\alpha}\theta\epsilon\tau\epsilon\hat{\iota}\nu$ is also found (a _hapax legomenon_) in John 12: 48, which makes it likely that the passage in which it occurs was built upon an inherited logion, or possibly more than one. Cf. P. Borgen, 'The Use of Tradition'.

[54] 5: 30; 8: 28; 12: 50; 14: 31.

[55] J.-A. Bühner rightly insists on this point (pp. 181 ff.).

writers turned to their own legal tradition. This happened very early. In the Book of Numbers God is portrayed as angered by the opposition of Miriam and Aaron to their brother Moses, so much greater than all other prophets because 'I have entrusted him with all my house: with him I speak mouth to mouth' (Num. 12: 7 f.). Reflecting on this passage, a tannaitic writer makes the point clearly: 'With what is the matter to be compared? With a king of flesh and blood who has a consul (agent) in the country. The inhabitants spoke before him. Then said the king to them, you have not spoken concerning my servant but concerning me.'[56] The law of agency is simply a natural development of, or offshoot from, this diplomatic convention,[57] and given the religious application of the latter it was to be expected that the more precise formulations composed to accommodate the complex business dealings of a small but highly structured society should also influence religious thinking, especially in a case where the claims to represent the voice of God were as strong in fact and in tradition as those of Jesus. But always behind the dry and often dreary niceties of the civil law the grand traditions of Judah's imperial history and Israel's prophetic heritage continued to make themselves felt. The convention according to which the agent was fully representative of his master was more than a legal fiction: it illustrated and exemplified *a way of thinking*. Nor does the legal precision in any way diminish the significance of the religious analogies drawn by Jesus himself (as we are about to see) and after him by the early Christians. For John above all but also for the tradition upon which he drew, Théo Preiss's term *mystique juridique* is singularly apt.[58]

One such tradition, with strong claims to authenticity, is the saying in John 13: 16, 'Amen, amen I say to you, the servant ($\delta o\hat{\upsilon}\lambda o\varsigma$) is not greater than his master ($\kappa\acute{\upsilon}\rho\iota o\varsigma$), nor is an agent ($\mathring{a}\pi\acute{o}\sigma\tau o\lambda o\varsigma$) greater than the one who sent him.' Not just the use of the traditional $\mathring{a}\mu\eta\nu$ $\mathring{a}\mu\eta\nu$ but also the technical opposition between $\delta o\hat{\upsilon}\lambda o\varsigma$ and $\kappa\acute{\upsilon}\rho\iota o\varsigma$ and most of all the unique occurrence of the word $\mathring{a}\pi\acute{o}\sigma\tau o\lambda o\varsigma$ make it probable that this belonged to the store of logia inherited by the evangelist.[59] He or an intervening writer makes this saying the

---

[56] *Sif. Num.* 104 on 12: 9, quoted by Borgen, 'God's Agent', p. 68.

[57] In fact the regular word for 'agent' (שלוח) means literally 'one who is sent' ($\mathring{a}\pi\acute{o}\sigma\tau o\lambda o\varsigma$). Cf. John 9: 7.

[58] 'Juridical mysticism', 'Justification', p. 25.

[59] Cf. K. Berger, *Die Amen-Worte Jesu*, pp. 95–9.

corner-stone of the enacted parable of the washing of the feet: the disciples are not to be prouder than their master. But as always in this Gospel the comparison points in two directions—backwards to Jesus' own divine commission as well as forwards to that of his own disciples as the conclusion of the story—itself another traditional logion—makes plain: 'Amen, amen, I say to you, he who receives one whom I send receives me and he who receives me receives him who sent me' (13: 20; cf. Matt. 10: 40).

If now we think of Jesus himself as the servant who is not greater than his master, God, we may find that this is contradicted by the general tenor of the teaching of the Gospel, for according to this Jesus claims equality with God–divine status. This contradiction can only be resolved by bearing in mind that Jesus' relationship with God continues throughout to be conceived on the analogy of the prophetic mission and the law of agency. The paradox of the parity between the sender and the sent cannot be maintained at its proper point of equilibrium unless both its terms are kept in sight. *In fact* the king is greater than his emissary; *in law* the emissary is the king's equal. The pendulum swings gently between these two apparently contradictory propositions, with the result that one is sometimes stressed at the expense of the other.[60] So Jesus can say not only 'I and the Father are one' (10: 30) and 'I am in the Father and the Father is in me' (10: 38; 14: 10) and (perhaps most significantly) 'the Father who dwells in me does his works' (14: 10), but also, very frequently, and most notably in this same context of Jesus' response to Philip (14: 10), 'the words that I say to you I do not speak on my own authority'.[61] In rejecting the hypothesis that Jesus' relationship to God is cast in the prophetic mould, Bultmann points out that no prophet is ever given divine status. But this is only partly true.

[60] The paradoxes of subsequent Trinitarian theory, itself heavily dependent upon a rather literalistic interpretation of Johannine theology, have to be reconciled by a similar capacity for looking at two seemingly opposing propositions at the same time. Käsemann comes quite close to this insight: 'If the formulae of his commission through the Father and his unity with the Father are isolated from each other, the result will be subordinationism or ditheism' (*Testament*, p. 11).

[61] ἀπ' ἐμαυτοῦ οὐ λαλῶ. Cf. 5: 19, 30; 7: 16 ff., 28; 8: 28 f., 42; 16: 13. In the case of John 7: 18a Bühner is even prepared to argue that ὁ ἀφ' ἑαυτοῦ λαλῶν should be translated 'whoever attempts to conceal the fact that he has been commissioned' (*wer seinen Auftrag verschweigt*), and the sequel, τὴν δόξαν τὴν ἰδίαν ζητεῖ, by 'is seeking his own advantage' (*der sucht den eigenen Vorteil*) (*Gesandte*, p. 249; cf. pp. 237 ff.). This suggestion, which follows a discussion of two special clauses in the Jewish law of agency (what Bühner calls 'die Ausweisklausel' and 'die Vorteilsklausel') seems to me to move too far from the Greek text.

Provided that one does not lose sight of the reservations contained in Jesus' insistence that he neither says nor does anything on his own authority, this aspect of John's christology, whose ontological implications are given none of the heavy emphasis they were to receive over two centuries later in the debate against Arius, could be explained as arising from a deeply religious reflection upon the prophetic mission of Jesus within the conceptual framework of the Jewish law of agency.[62] In a sense the parity with God asserted by and for Jesus is a natural inference from the prophetic schema.

Such an inference might seem at first sight to conflict too strongly with the ingrained Jewish belief in the absolute primacy of God to be easily or rapidly drawn. Of course the Johannine group saw the message of Jesus, that is their own message *about* Jesus, as proceeding directly from God, and in rejecting it the religious authorities were rejecting the word of God. But this was classically true of every prophet. Is there anything more to Christian belief which may help to explain why no other Jewish group before the advent of true Gnosticism made such extravagant claims on behalf of its leader?

Perhaps this is the point to appeal once again (see Chapter 4) to the religious discontent of dissident Jewish groups who continued to think of Yahweh as *their own* God, not fully identified with the more remote creator God, El Elyon or El Shaddai. But this alone would not explain how the Jesus people came to claim for their own leader a virtual parity with the 'far' God. For such an explanation we must look beyond the Jewish law of agency.

6. SONSHIP

Part, at any rate, of the answer to this question must lie in the belief that Jesus was, in a quite unique sense, the Son of God. As a messianic title, this expression originally held no connotations of divinity. This we have seen in the previous chapter. But there were stronger claims made on Jesus' behalf which derived in the first instance from a quite separate tradition. We must begin by

---

[62] Many of the 'I am' sayings, as J.-A. Bühner has argued (*Gesandte*, pp. 166–80), may have had their origin in the same broad general context of Near Eastern diplomatic conventions according to which the emissary might preface his message with a statement of intent ('I have come to ...') or of self-introduction ('I am ...'). See Ch. 5.

distinguishing between the plain title 'Son' and the originally
messianic 'Son of God'.[63] It is the former, frequently associated very
closely in the Fourth Gospel with affirmations concerning Jesus'
mission, that must occupy us now. Essentially John saw Jesus'
relationship with God in two clearly distinguishable ways, *sonship*,
and *mission*; and the two names Jesus has for God ('Father' and 'the
one who sent me') though often united in practice ('the Father who
sent me')[64] should not be assumed without further proof or argument to have been linked together in the traditions upon which John
drew. In chapter 7 the term 'Father' is not used: nowhere in this
chapter is there the slightest hint that Jesus regarded himself as the
Son of God.

C. H. Dodd is so impressed by the influence of the prophetic
tradition upon John's christology that he asserts: 'John has deliberately moulded the idea of the Son of God in the first instance upon
the prophetic model.'[65] But sons, first of all begotten by their fathers,
generally loved, frequently educated and sometimes chastised by
them, are rarely *sent*, unless they happen to be princes royal,
venturing abroad to execute some mission at the behest of a kingly
parent. There is no natural association between the idea of sonship
and the idea of mission; and one of the most intriguing challenges set
by the Fourth Gospel is to locate the source of the tradition according
to which the Son was 'sent into the world'. Or is the frequent
conjunction of the two ideas in the Fourth Gospel to be ascribed to
the work of the evangelist, fusing two different traditions into a now
indissoluble whole?

In the opinion of Eduard Schweizer there is evidence in the New
Testament of a tradition according to which God sent his Son into
the world for the specific purpose of bringing salvation. Twice in
Paul (Rom. 8: 3 f., Gal. 4: 4 f.), twice in the Johannine literature
(John 3: 16 f.; 1 John 4: 9), there occurs what Schweizer takes to be
a traditional formula, known presumably to both authors indepen-

---

[63] Cf. F. Hahn, *Titles*, p. 307. Hahn is surely right, against B. M. F. van Iersel, *Der
Sohn*, and I. Howard Marshall, *Origins*, pp. 111–23, to insist upon observing this
distinction.

[64] ὁ πατηρ ὁ πέμψας με—5: 37; 6: 44; 8: 16, 18; 12: 49; 14: 24; αὐτόν with the
same meaning 5: 23. What is more, ὁ πατήρ is regularly the subject of the verb
ἀποστέλλειν: 5: 36; 6: 57; 10: 36; 20: 21; cf. 5: 38. The idea recurs in Jesus' prayer to
the Father (11: 42) and especially in the so-called Sacerdotal Prayer (ch. 17), where it
is found 6 times (vv. 3, 8, 18, 21, 23, 25).

[65] *Interpretation*, p. 255.

dently of each other.[66] Schweizer traces this so-called formula back to the Jewish wisdom tradition, citing in particular the passage in which Solomon is portrayed as beseeching God to grant him the gift of wisdom: 'dispatch (ἐξαπόστειλον) wisdom from the holy heavens and send (πέμψον) her forth from thy throne of glory' (Wisd. 9: 10). But is this a true parallel? The unforced metaphorical language employed in this prayer scarcely offers a convincing analogue to the mission of the Son in Paul and John. There is nothing here to suggest the strong kind of hypostasization of wisdom that would be necessary to establish the parallel Schweizer requires, even though the figure of wisdom is personified in a traditional manner elsewhere in the book. The phrase εἰς τὸν κόσμον is not found in Paul (which reduces the alleged 'formula' to a single word, or pair of words); and the Galatians passage continues by saying that 'God has sent the Spirit of his Son into our hearts' (v. 6). The same word, ἐξαποστέλλειν, is employed, a fact which suggests that the term is in both instances a perfectly simple and natural metaphor which it would be a mistake to overinterpret. Certainly there is no need to postulate, as Schweizer does, that the notion of pre-existence is actively present. If there is indeed a primitive formula underlying both the Pauline and the Johannine usages then it seems a priori quite unlikely that this very sophisticated notion had any part to play in it. Interesting as they are, Schweizer's researches are surely inconclusive.

In the course of his article, however, Schweizer drops one hint that is worth following up. It is an allusion to the parable of the wicked husbandmen (Mark 12: 1–11), in which, after the savage ill-treatment, even murder, of many of his servants, the owner of the vineyard eventually sends 'his beloved son, saying "They will respect my son".' The reaction of the farmer tenants is the opposite of what the owner expects: 'they said to one another, "This is the heir, come let us kill him, and the inheritance will be ours".' This parable—or maybe one should rather speak of allegory here— presents many puzzles. In the context of the Gospel, it is plain that the servants (δοῦλοι) are the prophets and Jesus is the son. The majority of modern commentators have assumed that the Christian

---

[66] 'Zum religionsgeschichtlichen Hintergrund'; cf. *ThDNT* viii. 374–6, s.v. υἱός. However, as J. Ziesler points out, 'that God *sent* Christ (Gal. 4: 4 f.; Rom. 8: 3) as the Son does not in itself mean his pre-existence, for the prophets are also sent (Isa 6: 8; Jer. 1: 6; Ezek. 2: 3) and so are Moses, Aaron, and Miriam (Mic. 6: 4)' (*Pauline Christianity* (Oxford, 1985), p. 41).

meaning of the parable is so strong that it cannot be authentic; but recently certain scholars have marshalled a number of arguments intended to show that the parable, apart from the conclusion, could actually have been told by Jesus.[67] There is no need to take sides on this question. What interests us above all in this parable is the *imaginative space* it occupies: God as a wealthy landowner (who could easily be a king), the prophets as his servants, Jesus as his son—the heir to his land, sent out after the servants on a mission that would end in his rejection and death. There can be no question of pre-existence here, since the actual mission of the son is not conceived any differently as a *sending* from that of the servants who preceded him. Important are (1) the special status of the son within the owner's household; and (2) the general circumstances which would make his mission—as a son, indeed, an only son[68]—not just an adventitious conjunction, but a natural consequence of his privileged position.

J. D. Derrett brings this out very clearly in a careful discussion of the legal aspects of the kind of case presupposed by the parable: 'Formal protest must be made before witnesses, warning the tenants that legal action would commence against them. Slaves, however, could not make this protest, nor could slaves adjure witnesses—a serious handicap in so involved a matter. By that period it had not yet become possible to plead one's cause *through* an agent—one must actually transfer one's right to the 'representative'. Therefore the son had to be sent. He is represented in the parable as if he really was the only son of the owner.'[69]

Martin Hengel adduces examples that show just how difficult it was at this period for an absent landowner to obtain redress from recalcitrant lessees, and how reluctant the local authorities were to

---

[67] B. M. F. van Iersel, '*Der Sohn*', pp. 124–45; X. Léon-Dufour, 'Parabole'; 'Parable'; M. Hengel, 'Gleichnis'.

[68] In the LXX the word ἀγαπητός (literally 'beloved') is regularly used to translate the Hebrew יחיד (literally 'only child')—even in Gen. 22: 2, where the Greek consequently becomes awkwardly overloaded: τὸν υἱόν σου τὸν ἀγαπητόν, ὃν ἠγάπησας. Specially noteworthy is the fact that virtually all the passages in which this relatively rare word occurs concern not just an only child but one that is *doomed to death*—as Isaac was (Gen. 22) and, particularly strikingly, the daughter of Jephtha (Judges 11: 34); cf. Jer. 6: 26; Amos 8: 10; Zech. 12: 10. Many commentators, e.g. Hengel, think that the ἀγαπητόν was added by Mark to his source, but in view of the doom-laden connotations of the word it is a perfectly fitting term for the son of the parable, and the obvious rendering if the Hebrew (or Aramaic) יחיד was used in the source.

[69] 'Parable', pp. 302 f.

intervene—understandably, because they had to take their taxes from the lessees, not the landowner. He also quotes a parable from a tannaitic source which has some important parallels with the Gospel story: 'Like a king owning a field which he had entrusted to tenant farmers, who began to rob and steal. So he took the field from them and entrusted it to their children, but these began to behave even worse than their parents. Then a son was born to the king, and he told them, "Vacate my property; you may not stay any longer."'[70] Hengel also quotes a rather more recent story about a king who wished to journey to a remote province; accordingly he instructed a tenant to look after his garden and to enjoy its produce until his own (the King's son) should come of age.[71]

Hengel is concerned to show that the parable could in all essential respects have been told by Jesus. There is no need, he argues, to suppose that the son was introduced into the parable at a later date in order to make a peculiarly Christian point, since even in the original parable he is *qua* son the only fully accredited representative of the owner.

This interpretation of the parable of the vinedressers depends on certain contemporary laws and customs without which it would be virtually impossible to comprehend why the owner's son should be sent out as a trouble-shooter in a highly delicate and dangerous situation. The New Testament itself provides many examples of the convention that the (eldest) son was his father's natural heir (e.g. Heb. 1: 2: ὃν ἔθηκεν κληρονόμον πάντων); and the Fourth Gospel has its share of these. In particular, the phrase διδόναι ἐν τῇ χειρί (= נתן ביד), 'to give into the hand (of)'[72] is a formal expression signifying the transmission of authority—authority in the first place over the owner's (in this case the father's) property. A good example of this convention is found in an early midrash in which once again a king is selected as the natural metaphorical analogue of the divinity:

Another interpretation of THIS MONTH SHALL BE UNTO YOU. God was like a king who possessed treasure-houses filled with gold and silver, precious stones and pearls, and who had one son (בן אחד = μονογενής). As long as the son was small his father guarded them all, but when the son grew up

---

[70] *Sif. Deut.* 312 on 32: 9, quoted by Hengel, 'Gleichnis', p. 28 n. 92.

[71] *Midr. Tanhuma* B בשלח 29a § 7 (Buber, pp. 56 f.).

[72] 'The Father loves the Son and has given everything into his hand' (3: 35); 'Jesus, knowing that the Father had given everything into his hands ...' (13: 3). Cf. 10: 18; 17: 2.

and reached manhood, his father said to him: 'As long as you were small, I guarded them all; but now that you have reached manhood, everything is handed over to you (הכל מסר לך = πάντα δίδοταί σοι). So God guarded everything, as it says, And let them be for signs and for seasons (Gen. 1: 14); but as soon as Israel was grown up, he entrusted the Israelites with all of these, for it says: THIS MONTH SHALL BE UNTO YOU.[73]

In virtually all the rabbinic parables in which a king (or wealthy landowner) has dealings with his son, the son in question is Israel.[74] But the legal background, the way of thinking, is the same as in the parable of the wicked husbandmen, and does much to explain the ease with which, once Jesus' sonship was assured, he came to be thought of as the natural recipient of the authority of God.

One way in which this relationship was expressed in Jewish law was the pair of reciprocal expressions, בעל בית (literally, 'lord or master of the house') and בן בית (literally 'son of the house'). As J. A. Bühner sees, some awareness of the quasi-juridical role of the latter helps us to understand one of the most extraordinary passages in the Fourth Gospel, that in which Jesus claims to have been given, as God's Son, the twin powers traditionally reserved to God alone, the power of judgement and the power of bestowing life (5: 22, 27):

This formally gives him an authority to be surpassed by none: he is to be honoured in the same way as the Father who sent him. In this connection we must bear in mind the בן בית , the 'son of the house' in Jewish law and custom. In Aramaic court language the בר ביתא referred to the freemen attached to a royal household and in particular the royal princes with the right of inheritance. The בית is the household ('familia') as the fundamental juridical and sociological group, and the בר/בן [respectively Hebrew and Aramaic words for 'son'] denotes the way in which the 'son' belongs. Jewish tradition frequently presupposes this usage, which was by no means confined to the court. 'Son' (בן בית) refers to the members of the household, and denotes a position that guarantees a stable relationship of

---

[73] *Exod. R.* 15: 30 on 12: 12, quoted by Bühner, *Gesandte*, p. 197 n. 17.

[74] e.g. 'To what may this be compared? To a king who took on a large number of workers, among them one who worked with him for several days. The workers came to receive their wages, this man among them. The king said to him, My son, I will have regard for you. All these workers put little effort into their work, and I will give them but little wages. But for you I have reckoned a considerable sum. In the same way the Israelites in this world asked God for their wages; and the nations of the world also asked for their wages before God. And God said to Israel, My sons I will have regard for you' (*Sifra* 111a on Lev. 26: 9). Cf. *Sif. Num.* 105 on 12: 10: 'Here is a parable. A king said to the tutor of his son: "Chastise my son, but not until I have departed, for a father is full of pity for his son." '

particular intimacy. Just such a particular intimacy is implied in the passage in the Mishnah (Taanith 3: 8) where Honi the Circle-drawer is said to know how to gain access to God in the manner that a son of the house has access to his father.

The term בן בית , then, connotes the fact of belonging to a household: but in connection with the teaching on authority it has also acquired a specific juridical meaning. Of fundamental importance here is Mishnah Shebuoth 7: 8, with the interpretation given in the Babylonian Talmud, b48b. The mishnah names those who have been granted the authority to dispose of the property of the בעל הבית ; if they come under the suspicion of misappropriation, even in the most general and unspecified way, they must swear to their innocence: 'An oath may be imposed on these, although no claim is lodged against them: jointholders, tenants, trustees, a wife that manages the affairs of the house, and the son of the house (בן בית)'. Who is this בן בית ? From the association with the wife one may infer that what is meant here is the true or natural son, who can be given the same responsibilities and authority as the master's wife... . The Baraitha (b48b) sheds some light on the matter: 'A Tanna taught: The son of the house who was mentioned does not mean that he walks in and walks out, but he brings in labourers and takes out labourers, brings in produce and takes out produce.'

The expression 'to walk in and out' refers to the normal relationship between the בן בית and his family, whereas the Baraitha derives an important juridical consequence from the position of authority stressed in the Mishnah. Accordingly the בן בית in this case is an administrator with total responsibility. With regard to the question concerning the natural sonship of the בן בית it must be borne in mind that what counts in the Jewish and oriental understanding of the son/father relationship is the *legal* position. The natural son too has to be assigned to his position, as is shown by the law of the first-born. Consequently the term taken as a functional concept may also include the idea of natural sonship, as is evident from the Mishnah; but the converse is not true—natural sonship does not necessarily imply the position of a plenipotentiary agent. So the בן בית is not the κληρονόμος νήπιος (Gal. 4: 1) [for νήπιος is used of a minor] but the υἱός who has already been given full authority over the estate of the בעל הבית .[75]

To consider the christology of the Fourth Gospel in the light of these juridical concepts is like being given another eye. Suddenly the whole relationship between the Father and the Son stands out in startlingly fresh perspective. In particular we can see how the moment of *mission* (sending) is conceived primarily as a *commission* (the bestowal of authority of plenipotentiary powers), much as in the

[75] *Gesandte*, pp. 195–8.

parable of the wicked husbandmen. Naturally the prophetic tradition has played some part here also; but the concept of the household of God over which Jesus, as Son, has been given full control is one to which the prophetic tradition as such made no contribution.[76]

The way in which the often virtually interchangeable functions of fatherhood on the one hand and mission on the other mutually support and reinforce one another[77] cannot be explained by recourse to the Old Testament alone, but this very characteristic feature of Johannine theology becomes fully intelligible when one considers the quite precise juridical conventions to which Bühner has drawn attention. For the Johannine conception of Jesus' sonship comes out of a conceptual world in which the agent appointed by the landowner to look after his estates is thought of as a son (the בן בית), and conversely one in which the first-born son attains his majority at the very moment he receives his appointment.

The relationship between God and Jesus is nowhere more fully articulated than in the dialogue and discourse in John 5: 19–30. This is universally acknowledged, but C. H. Dodd[78] and P. Gaechter[79] in particular have argued independently that behind the high christology in this passage lies a simple *parable of apprenticeship*—a son learning a trade from his father, the only person fully competent to invest him with all his own professional expertise: 'For the [a] Father loves the [his] Son; and shows him all that he himself is doing' (5: 20).[80] This may be right—it is certainly a brilliant suggestion—but the force of Jesus' claim here depends upon the tacit assumption that besides the *skill* he also has the *authority* to perform the quintessentially divine functions of bestowing life and passing judgement. Behind the parable (if parable there be) must

---

[76] Cf. Hebrews 3: 5–6, where Moses the servant of God (πιστὸς ἐν ὅλῳ τῷ οἴκῳ αὐτοῦ ὡς θεράπων) is contrasted with Christ the Son, obviously seen here as בן בית (ὡς υἱὸς ἐπὶ τὸν οἶκον αὐτοῦ).

[77] Not, though, as we have seen, in ch. 7, where the absence of any mention of God as Father may indicate the use of an independent (and possibly earlier) tradition.

[78] 'A hidden parable'.

[79] 'Zur Form von Joh 5, 19–30'.

[80] This interpretation presupposes an Aramaic original—the point being that Aramaic uses the definite article in contexts where Greek (and English) would use the indefinite article, especially when referring generally to a *type*. So where Greek would more naturally speak of '*a* son' and '*a* father', Aramaic would say '*the* son' and '*the* father'. The best known example of a Greek mistranslation of an Aramaic expression is ὁ υἱὸς τοῦ ἀνθρώπου (the Son of Man). The Aramaic בר אנש often means 'a man', 'mankind', or simply 'one'.

stand the overarching juridical conceptions we have already discussed. And here it is impossible to mistake the consequences of using this particular conceptual system as the vehicle of Jesus' message of self-revelation. God's estate or domain is not confined to earth; but on earth his authority is manifest above all in two ways: for he alone has the power to quicken (in the Old English sense) and to judge. So in taking over these two functions Jesus is exercising an authority (ἐξουσία, v. 27) which God alone could have given him. And the conclusion (of the first part of the discourse) is expressed in the now familiar terminology of the law of agency: 'I can do nothing on my own authority (ἀπ' ἐμαυτοῦ = מעצמי); as I hear, I judge; and my judgement is just because I seek not my will but the will of him who sent me (τὸ θέλημα τοῦ πέμψαντός με = דעת המשלחי)' (5: 30; cf. 6: 38, 40).

Illuminating as Bühner's suggestions are, it may still be asked whether the dependence he has argued of Johannine expressions and thought-patterns upon Jewish legal concepts sufficiently accounts for the high christology of John 5 and other such passages. It could do so only if Jewish law were conceived as a *source*; but this seems in the highest degree unlikely. Bühner himself repeatedly stresses that neither the law of agency nor the more general concept of the role of the emissary in the Ancient Near East is confined to the religious sphere. On the contrary, the fourth evangelist, like many another religious writer, has seized upon a conceptual system he found ready to hand in order to put the ineffable into words. The exceptional character of Jesus' relationship with God cannot be *explained* by the law of agency, although it may be partly expressed in a terminology originally elaborated to deal with more mundane matters. True, the prophetic mission of Jesus has a real affinity with that of the human agent on behalf of a human owner, and no doubt the Jewish law of agency was constructed with the prophetic model in mind. But the audacious nature of Jesus' claims cannot be read into or out of any formulation of Jewish law. One of the advantages of Bultmann's postulated revelation-discourse source is that its Emissary is already a divine or semi-divine figure whose lineaments, modified and softened, can easily be transferred to Jesus. And it is this transference, more than an analogy, more than an inference, that justifies Bultmann's claim to have explained the genesis of the Gospel's picture of Christ. The Jewish legal system may furnish a plausible *background* for this christology; it may, seen as an exegetical tool, help us to understand what the evangelist is saying. But it cannot in my opinion be seriously proposed as an alternative *source*; for it leaves unexplained the transition from the idea of a human agent as envisaged by the law (and one must include here the implications of the term 'son of the house') to that of a divine agent to whom God has entrusted his own powers and his own authority. Such a transition is far from being the smooth and uncomplicated adjustment Bühner's argument appears at times to suppose.

I shall be considering a number of other possible influences in the next chapter. But no discussion of the theme of Jesus' divine sonship would be complete without taking some stock of the Synoptic-type traditions that must have helped to form the thought of the fourth evangelist. In spite of the interpenetration of the concepts of mission and sonship (because of the fruitful ambiguity of the term בן בית) the intimacy with God claimed by Jesus is not to be explained simply as the product of Christian reflection upon a law or a legal system. Such reflection can only twine around or rather stem out of an early belief in some kind of special relationship between Jesus and God already expressed in terms of sonship. Obviously the close and exclusive knowledge of God claimed by the Jesus of the Fourth Gospel is very different from anything found in the Synoptic tradition, with the possible exception of the so-called Johannine logion (Matt. 11: 25–7; Luke 10: 21 f.). Nevertheless the original seed of this fine flowering must be sought somewhere, and where more plausibly than in Jesus' own sense of the fatherhood of God?

In fact there is plenty of evidence that this was exceptionally deep and strong. On the personal side there is the tradition of Jesus' continual communication with God in prayer, which was clearly both intimate and unassuming. No doubt his use of the familiar Aramaic address 'Abba' (can this possibly, though, have had overtones resembling those of 'Daddy', 'Papa', or 'Vati'?) is not as telling a proof of an exclusive sense of sonship as Joachim Jeremias would have us believe:[81] certainly if the early Christians had thought of it in this way they would scarcely have adopted it, as they did, in their own prayer.[82] All the same, that Jesus did think of and address God as his father is beyond question.

[81] *Theology*, pp. 61–8. See J. Barr, 'Abba isn't 'Daddy'' '.

[82] Rom. 8: 15; Gal. 4: 6. There is no evidence in pre-Christian Palestinian Judaism that God was addressed as *abba* by an individual Jew in prayer. Jeremias adduces two instances in the Babylonian Talmud from stories told of sages who lived in the first century BC (*The Prayers of Jesus* (London, 1967), p. 59); but G. Schelbert has shown these attributions to be insecure: 'Sprachgeschichtliches zu "Abba" '.

Equally clear, and more significant for our purposes, is the impact of this tradition upon the Fourth Gospel, which had Jesus praying to God on three separate occasions: before the tomb of Lazarus (11: 41 f.), at his final entry into Jerusalem (12: 27 f.), and in the extended prayer of chapter 17. On each occasion he uses the simple vocative πάτερ, which corresponds closely to the more stilted ὁ πατήρ (an Aramaism) found, for instance, in Mark's account of the Agony (14: 36). John clearly experienced some difficulty, even embarrassment, in adapting this particular prayer to fit his own conviction of Jesus' absolute control over his own destiny: Jesus openly wonders whether he should pray in the way that tradition demanded, and then decides that he should not: 'And what shall I say? "Father save me from this hour"? No, for this purpose I have come to this hour' (12: 27). And in concluding his prayer at the tomb of Lazarus he is made to assure his listeners: 'I have said this on account of the people standing by' (11: 42)—because he did not actually need to pray on his own account.

It is not part of my purpose to establish that the historical Jesus knew God as Father in a way that no one else has ever done in fact or could ever do in principle. Such an extreme claim can neither be verified nor disproved.[83] All I wish to insist upon is (*a*) that there is reason to believe that Jesus really did have an unusually deep awareness of God's transcendent majesty and of his all-embracing regard for mankind, and (*b*) that this awareness is at the root of a tradition whose most colourful bloom is the high christology of the Fourth Gospel.

Lastly we must consider briefly the passage in the Synoptic Gospels in which the Father/Son relationship is most strikingly expressed. This is the 'thunderbolt from the Johannine sky', Matt. 11: 25-7/Luke 10: 21 f. Here is Luke's version: 'I thank thee, Father, Lord of heaven and earth, that thou hast hidden these things from the wise and understanding and revealed them to babes; yea, Father, for such was thy gracious will. All things have been delivered to me by my Father; and no one knows who the Son is except the Father, or who the Father is except the Son and anyone to whom the Son chooses to reveal him.'

[83] For a more optimistic view of the possibility of knowing Jesus' inner consciousness of God, cf. J. D. G. Dunn, *Jesus and the Spirit* (London, 1975), esp. pp. 11–40. See too J. Jeremias, *Prayers* (cf. n. 82), pp. 56–61; M. J. Suggs, *Wisdom Christology and Law in Matthew's Gospel* (Cambridge, 1970), pp. 71–97.

Because of their very singularity these two passages in Matthew and Luke, which obviously have a common root, are hard to handle and to assess.[84] Most commentators are reluctant to admit that John may have used the logion as a direct source, in any of its forms, but the fact is that it is as close if not closer to the spirit of his theology than any parallel that has been adduced outside the New Testament.[85] And even if no direct link can be established, and it is hard to know what could count as proof in this respect, there is at least evidence of theological reflection being carried on outside the Johannine circle but along parallel lines. Schnackenburg argues that there are some important differences: 'The mutual knowledge is not so much, as in John 10: 15, an expression of intimacy and unity of the Son with the Father, but forms part of the idea of the fullness of power conferred on the Son by the Father (πάντα παρεδόθη μοι κτλ.). The Father's "knowing" the Son is in the Old Testament and Judaic tradition of election, while knowing on the son's part means acknowledgement: the Son accepts the Father's revelation and his will, which enables him to communicate his revelation to others (ᾧ ἐὰν βούληται κτλ.).'[86] That there are differences is clear, though they do not seem to me as great as Schnackenburg says. The Father's bestowal of authority on the Son is just as important a theme in the Fourth Gospel—as we have seen at length—as that of their mutual knowledge.

CONCLUSION

It must be confessed that this chapter must end somewhat inconclusively. The most valuable result has been the discovery of a thought-world that makes sense of the evangelist's picture of Jesus as the Son of God entrusted by him with a message for the world. As 'the son of

[84] They are all but ignored in C. F. D. Moule's book, *The Origin of Christology* (Cambridge, 1977).

[85] Jeremias (*Prayers*, pp. 56–61) has actually suggested that the Synoptic saying may have originated in a simple comparison to a father–son relationship, in which the natural intimacy of father and son is used to illustrate how Jesus was empowered by his Father to reveal him. His argument follows the lines of the articles of Dodd and Gaechter cited earlier (nn. 78 and 79) and may be thought to receive further support if not complete confirmation from the findings of Bühner we have already considered.

[86] *Gospel*, ii. 179. Schnackenburg rules out altogether the possibility of any direct influence. Aside from this, his Excursus 9, ' "The Son" as Jesus' Self-Designation in the Gospel of John' (ibid., pp. 172–86) is interesting and informative.

the house', he would gradually come to be thought of as emerging from that house (cf. 14: 2, ἡ οἰκία τοῦ Πατρός μου); and even if there were no other influences nudging the evangelist towards a cosmological dualism one can understand how the contrast between heaven and earth, heaven naturally thought of as the home of God and earth the home of men, fits in with the vision of a two-storey universe, and even makes it possible to think that this Emissary occupied a place (μονή) in his real home before embarking upon his mission to earth. Various strands then of the complex pattern of the Gospel's finished theology can be seen to invite this particular weave.

Even so, the themes I have discussed in this chapter, origins, mission, agency, sonship, do not, even in combination, account for the whole of the Gospel's high christology or explain how it was actually generated. Perhaps the investigation of other themes, other strands of the pattern, will enable us to see the full design more clearly. One of these, the Son of Man, will occupy much of our attention in the following chapter.

Excursus III: The Composition of John 7

No chapter in the Gospel poses more problems of analysis than this one, and the continuing disagreement is not surprising.[1] What follows is an attempt to give some exegetical justification to the answers given to these problems in chapter 7.

The core of the chapter is to be found in two sets of material:[2] (*a*) a controversy over the person of Jesus centring upon the twin themes of *mission*, which alludes to the claim that Jesus is the prophet, and *origins*, which is associated with the title of Messiah; (*b*) the story of Jesus' attempted arrest, which itself concludes with a controversy story of a different kind involving the same two titles: a strong and reasonably homogeneous armature, then, over which further material has been laid. Besides this unity of theme, after the introduction there is also a unity of time (the Feast of Tabernacles) and place (the Temple).

The controversy material (*a*) is found in two blocks: vv. 11–31 (excluding vv. 19b–24) and vv. 37–44 (excluding v. 39, which is certainly a later gloss from the hand of the evangelist). The arrest material (*b*) begins at v. 32 and continues in the last paragraph of the chapter, vv. 45–52.

The two sets of material (*a*) and (*b*) overlap in the famous passage that includes the prophecy about 'rivers of living water' (vv. 37–44), the high point of the chapter. In view of its strong emphasis upon the symbolic significance of the Feast of Tabernacles, this may have belonged (in a more primitive form?) to the introductory story (cf. v. 2).

It is here (vv. 1–10) that the earliest material is to be found. This opening narrative probably started life as the introduction to a miracle-story[3] which was subsequently modified and extended (by

---

[1] Apart from the commentators (of whom the most penetrating at this point are Bultmann and Lindars) see J. Schneider, 'Zur Komposition von Joh 7'; C. Dekker, 'Grundschrift'; J. Becker, 'Wunder'; U. C. von Wahlde, 'The Terms for Religious Authorities'; H. W. Attridge, 'Thematic Development'.

[2] Lindars, pp. 277 ff., who takes careful account of all the material but gives a slightly different analysis.

[3] Cf. Bultmann, pp. 288 f., followed by Becker. *Contra* Fortna, *Gospel of Signs*, pp. 186 f.

the addition of vv. 11–13) to serve as the preface to the controversy material (*a*). This is how I suggest the passage originally ran:[4]

(1) Περιεπάτει ὁ Ἰησοῦς ἐν τῇ Γαλιλαίᾳ ... (2) ἦν δὲ ἐγγὺς ἡ ἑορτὴ τῶν Ἰουδαίων ἡ σκηνοπηγία. (3) εἶπον οὖν πρὸς αὐτὸν οἱ ἀδελφοὶ αὐτοῦ, Μετάβηθι ἐντεῦθεν καὶ ὕπαγε εἰς τὴν Ἰουδαίαν, [ἵνα καὶ οἱ μαθηταί σου][5] θεωρήσουσιν τὰ ἔργα σου ἃ ποιεῖς· (4) οὐδεὶς γάρ τι ἐν κρυπτῷ ποιεῖ καὶ ζητεῖ παρρησίᾳ εἶναι [φανέρωσον σεαυτὸν τῷ κόσμῳ][6] ... (6) λέγει οὖν αὐτοῖς ὁ Ἰησοῦς[7] ... (8) ὑμεῖς ἀνάβητε εἰς τὴν ἑορτήν· ἐγὼ οὐκ ἀναβαίνω εἰς τὴν ἑορτὴν ταύτην, ὅτι ὁ ἐμὸς καιρὸς οὔπω πεπλήρωται. (9) ταῦτα δὲ εἰπὼν αὐτοῖς ἔμεινεν ἐν τῇ Γαλιλαίᾳ. (10) ὡς δὲ ἀνέβησαν οἱ ἀδελφοὶ αὐτοῦ εἰς τὴν ἑορτήν, τότε καὶ αὐτὸς ἀνέβη, [οὐ φανερῶς ἀλλ' ὡς ἐν κρυπτῷ].[8]

Like Bultmann, though with certain minor differences, I believe that this passage could have come from the original signs source. Three points may be noted. In the first place, the story closely resembles certain features of the Cana episode.[9] In both cases there is a demand for a sign on the part of Jesus' family (his mother in Cana, his brothers here). In both cases Jesus begins by refusing the request ('my time is not yet come'), and ends by complying with it. The precise nature of this compliance is not recounted here, but the conclusion of the story may well have included a reference to the Feast of Tabernacles; indeed, Jesus' prophetic words, easily seen as a

---

[4] Words and phrases which only doubtfully belonged to the source are put in brackets.

[5] Boismard (p. 210) may be right in thinking these words a later addition, prompted by passages like 2: 23 and 4: 44: 'Le texte primitif avait probablement un pluriel impersonnel.' Fortna (*Gospel of Signs*, p. 196) argues that the mention of disciples implies a previous sojourn in Judaea. But it seems to me more likely that, if the phrase did belong to the source, the emphasis will have been placed on the contrast between what the disciples had already seen in Galilee, thought of as ἐν κρυπτῷ, and what they wished to see παρρησίᾳ in Judaea. Perhaps the original read καὶ ἐκεῖ οἱ μαθηταί σου ... or something similar. In any case, v. 3 implies that no *miracles* have yet been performed in Judaea. Note the indicative mood of θεωρήσουσιν, most unusual after ἵνα, and highly uncharacteristic of the style of the evangelist.

[6] This phrase is not necessarily a later addition (especially if it is correct to excise the words καὶ οἱ μαθηταί σου from the previous verse). It is typical of the evangelist to build his own theology upon the simple tradition he has inherited. In the source, as I have suggested, the 'manifestation to the world' might have been simply a counterpoise to the more private manifestation of Cana.

[7] The phrase ὁ καιρὸς ὁ ἐμός (v. 6) is echoed by ὁ ἐμὸς καιρός (v. 8), an unnecessary duplication which suggests that the text has been tampered with. The simpler form in v. 8 is likely to be that of the source (q.v. 2: 4, οὔπω ἥκει ἡ ὥρα μου). Bultmann (p. 292 n. 2) reckons that v. 7 certainly, and possibly also the antithesis in v. 6, is from the revelation-discourse source.

[8] This phrase looks like an attempt to explain away the apparent contradiction.

[9] Cf. Bultmann, *Gospel*, pp. 121 n. 4; 289 n. 1.

claim to be a second Moses, the eschatological prophet, were probably part of the original conclusion.

A second point of interest is the implication in v. 3 that Jesus had not yet performed any miracles in Judaea.[10] Evidently the initial manifestation of glory in Galilee was to be matched by a similar manifestation in Judaea. Once again the parallel with the Cana episode is very striking. This must put a question-mark over the original placing (in the signs source) of the story of the healing of the cripple at the pool of Bethzatha (ch. 5).

A final point worthy of notice is that the word used in v. 3 to refer to Jesus' works is not σημεῖα but ἔργα. This is the only place in the Gospel where this term is used by anyone other than Jesus himself. When the evangelist takes over the word, he makes it into what is virtually a technical term, whose reference is identical with that of σημεῖα, but whose sense is very different. Boismard thinks that in view of the interest shown by his Document C in seeing Jesus as the new Moses, there is an allusion to Num. 16: 28, where the LXX reads: ἐν τούτῳ γνώσεσθε ὅτι κύριος ἀπέστειλέν με ποιῆσαι πάντα τὰ ἔργα ταῦτα, ὅτι οὐκ ἀπ᾽ ἐμαυτοῦ.[11] It is hard to be sure about this suggestion. If Boismard is right about the relevance of the passage, what should be stressed is probably the concluding phrase, ὅτι οὐκ ἀπ᾽ ἐμαυτοῦ, and its relevance to the controversy story that follows.

The question concerning the original placing of vv. 14–24 divides scholars more than any other. Some, e.g. Dodd, retain the passage on principle in its present position; others (Glasson, Meeks) argue that properly understood, the whole passage can be seen to fit into the context perfectly well; others (Spitta, Hirsch)[12] cut the section into two: 14–18 and 19–24—certainly it is hard to deny a direct allusion to chapter 5 in Jesus' question in v. 23: ἐμοὶ χολᾶτε ὅτι ὅλον ἄνθρωπον ὑγιῆ ἐποίησα ἐν σαββάτῳ; (the ἐν ἔργον mentioned in v. 21). This seems to be the best solution, though I am undecided where precisely to draw the line. The pivotal verse must be v. 19, for the mention of Moses is explicable both as a reference back to the prophetic claims of vv. 14–18 and as a reference forward to the law against healing on the sabbath (vv. 22 f.). At least the question, τίς

---

[10] Cf. n. 5.

[11] 'Jésus est le nouveau Moïse,' comments Boismard, 'et les "œuvres" qu'il "fait", c'est-à-dire les miracles, sont la preuve qu'il fut bien envoyé par Dieu; elles le "manifestent" au monde' (p. 213).   [12] Cf. Bultmann, p. 238 n. 3.

σε ζητεῖ ἀποκτεῖναι; (v. 20) must be assigned to the extraneous material because it contradicts the question that follows in v. 25: οὐκ οὗτός ἐστιν ὃν ζητοῦσιν ἀποκτεῖναι; On the whole I am inclined to draw the line in the middle of v. 19, after Jesus' challenge: οὐ Μωϋσῆς δέδωκεν ὑμῖν τὸν νόμον; In the original composition, 'the law' will have alluded to the passages in Deuteronomy (13: 1–6 and 18: 18–22), which predict the advent of a Moses-like figure and also of false pretenders. This would have furnished an excellent point of insertion for the remainder of the material, where 'the law' now comes to refer to the ban against working on the sabbath. But there can be no certainty on this point, and Bultmann may well be right to see in the whole of vv. 19–24 (though not, I think, vv. 15–18) the original conclusion of the source on which the evangelist based his account of the healing of the cripple in chapter 5.

Looking then at vv. 14–31 (minus 19b–24) as a whole, we see that Jesus is making two claims; first to be a prophet (vv. 14–19a), for he has the mark of a prophet, speaking on God's authority rather than on his own; secondly, to be the Messiah (vv. 25–31), whose true origins are hidden from his listeners. Hovering over the dialogue in each case is the suspicion on the part of some of his hearers that he is a false prophet and a false Messiah.

When the extract from the signs source (roughly as reconstructed above) was adapted to serve as an introduction to this controversy narrative, it was accordingly expanded in two ways. In the first place the controversy was to be seen to take place against the background of the relentless hostility of οἱ Ἰουδαῖοι. In the second place the way was to be prepared for the controversy by an allusion to Jesus' two claims. Hence the addition of (a) v. 1b: οὐ γὰρ ἤθελεν ἐν τῇ Ἰουδαίᾳ περιπατεῖν, ὅτι ἐζήτουν αὐτὸν οἱ Ἰουδαῖοι ἀποκτεῖναι and (b) vv. 11–13: οἱ οὖν Ἰουδαῖοι ἐζήτουν αὐτὸν ἐν τῇ ἑορτῇ καὶ ἔλεγον· ποῦ ἐστιν ἐκεῖνος; (12) καὶ γογγυσμὸς περὶ αὐτὸν ἦν πολὺς ἐν τοῖς ὄχλοις· οἱ μὲν ἔλεγον ὅτι ἀγαθός ἐστιν, ἄλλοι δὲ ἔλεγον· οὔ, ἀλλὰ πλανᾷ τὸν ὄχλον. (13) οὐδεὶς μέντοι παρρησίᾳ ἐλάλει περὶ αὐτοῦ διὰ τὸν φόβον τῶν Ἰουδαίων.

Thus the introductory paragraph is now neatly contained by an opening and closing reference (vv. 1b and 13) to the dangerous threat emanating from the Jews. (οἱ Ἰουδαῖοι are the Jewish leaders here, to be distinguished from οἱ ὄχλοι.) It is made clear that these disagree among themselves. Some think that Jesus is a good man, others that he is leading the people (ὄχλος) astray. The colourless word ἀγαθός, intentionally inexplicit, will soon be seen to comprise a

double claim—to the titles of (1) prophet and (2) Messiah. Conversely, the charge of 'leading the people astray' will be spelled out in
terms associated with (1) a pseudo-prophet (vv. 14–19a) and (2) a
pseudo-Messiah (vv. 25–31).

At this point (v. 32) another and (I believe) earlier controversy
story, one with a very different feel and purpose, is added on. The
suture here is quite visible, since the crowd is described as γογγύζων
περὶ αὐτοῦ ταῦτα, a phrase which does not refer directly to the
preceding question, uttered by many voices in the crowd (ὁ Χριστὸς
ὅταν ἔλθῃ μὴ πλείονα σημεῖα ποιήσει; [v. 31]), but to the γογγυσμός
mentioned in the introduction to the story (v. 12). In other words,
the reference of ταῦτα is to the *whole* of the preceding controversy
narrative. A new story then begins, with new characters, the chief
priests and Pharisees and their ὑπηρέται, sent out in the first place
not to question Jesus but to arrest him.

The dialogue that follows in vv. 33–6 (not, be it noted, with the
ὑπηρέται, but once more with οἱ Ἰουδαῖοι, as is stated explicitly in
13: 33) is out of place. Conceptually, no doubt, it is easy to pass from
the question whence to the question whither—from origins to
destiny. The two are linked, for instance, in 8: 14. And it is possible
(though odd) that Jesus, confronted with those about to arrest him,
should say, ὅπου εἰμι ἐγὼ ὑμεῖς οὐ δύνασθε ἐλθεῖν. But this passage
must have originated elsewhere—in connection with the material
in chapter 8 (see vv. 14 and 21). Brown observes that 'John can
refer interchangeably to "the Jews" and to the chief priests and
Pharisees'; and he cites 18: 3 and 12; 8: 13 and 22.[13] But in this
case the chief priests and Pharisees are not themselves present at the
scene, and the equation of their ὑπηρέται with the Ἰουδαῖοι seems
intolerably harsh.

If, however, we excise vv. 32–6 from our provisional reconstruction we find that there is a hiatus. The powerful prophecy of
vv. 37 f., introduced with such solemnity, is the high point of the
whole chapter, and as a response to an attempted arrest seems just
as inappropriate as the dialogue on destiny. What is more, as
Bultmann notes, it interrupts the arrest story, 'since the servants
sent out in 7: 32 would hardly return only after three or four days!'
Bultmann himself suggests that 7: 37–44 'probably came after
v. 30, for v. 31 is awkward after v. 30 but fits very well after

---

[13] These two instances (at any rate the former) may seem to throw some doubt on
the principles employed by von Wahlde ('The Terms', cf. n. 1).

v. 44'.[14] This is not quite right, because v. 32a is best explained as a deliberate allusion to the whole of the preceding controversy narrative (vv. 11–31)—as we have seen. But there is undoubtedly some dislocation here, since the ὑπηρέται of v. 32b are obviously the same as those of v. 45. Certainly most of the material in vv. 37–44 makes a natural climax to the controversy material earlier in the chapter; but the original meaning of the prophecy was not what the evangelist's gloss (v. 39) suggests, but rather the strongest possible claim on Jesus' part to be prophet and Messiah.

When this chapter was composed the arrest material was integrated with what I have called the controversy material by the simple expedient of detaching its introductory sentence (v. 32) and placing this before two other small episodes, the dialogue on destiny and the great prophecy, first adapting it so as to furnish a link with the preceding controversy material. The effect of this is to move it a long way from the story to which it originally belonged: in the present form of the text twelve whole verses separate v. 32 from v. 45.

The connections are now quite intricate. There is a further division recorded in vv. 40 f. (ἐκ τοῦ ὄχλου οὖν ἀκούσαντες τῶν λόγων ἔλεγον, οὗτός ἐστιν ἀληθῶς ὁ προφήτης· ἄλλοι ἔλεγον, οὗτός ἐστιν ὁ Χριστός). This fits equally well what precedes (i.e. the earlier controversy, vv. 11–31) and what follows. But the next question (μὴ γὰρ ἐκ τῆς Γαλιλαίας ὁ Χριστὸς ἔρχεται;) clearly belongs with the concluding episode, where the objection is that Galilee cannot be the true home either of the Messiah (vv. 41 f.) or of the Prophet (in v. 52 following p66 in reading the full form, ὁ προφήτης).

In Chapter 7 I have offered an interpretation of the original significance of this final story. But a word should be added here about the role of Nicodemus, whose role here corresponds so closely to that of Gamaliel in Acts 5: 33–40.[15] In the history of the composition of the Gospel this was, I suggest, his first appearance, and this story will have been told before the more acrimonious controversies recorded earlier in chapter 7 (as well as in chapter 5 and chapter 8) had taken place. This sympathetic Jew, still not committed to following Jesus, was a natural choice, somewhat later,

---

[14] *Gospel*, p. 287.
[15] The two are conflated in the *Acts of Pilate*, Hennecke–Schneemelcher, *New Testament Apocrypha*, i (London, 1963), pp. 444–70. Cf. J. L. Martyn, *Gospel of John*, ch. 2, esp. pp. 74–89.

for the interlocutor of Jesus in the story dialogue of chapter 3. By the time *that* story was composed it was no longer possible for a prominent Pharisee to engage in open debate with Jesus—he had to come 'by night' (3: 2). Attitudes had hardened between the situation portrayed in the conclusion of chapter 7 and that presupposed at the beginning of chapter 3. In the final composition of the Gospel the necessary link was easily established by the addition of the words ὁ ἐλθὼν πρὸς αὐτὸν πρότερον (v. 50).

Like all other attempted reconstructions, this one remains hypothetical. But what cannot be denied is the clear evidence that this chapter had a prehistory, and nothing is to be gained by pretending that it did not. It is true that any final reading of the Gospel must take into account the text as we have it, and especially, in this case, the important gloss of v. 39. But if one wishes to understand the growth of the Gospel and of the theological thinking of the Johannine community, some kind of speculation along the lines I have indicated is unavoidable.

9

SON OF MAN

INTRODUCTION

Among the many puzzles presented by the Fourth Gospel one of the most intriguing is the paradoxical contrast between the titles 'Son of God' and 'Son of Man'. 'Son of God', originally at any rate, indicates a human being, the Messiah; whereas 'Son of Man' points to a figure whose true home is in heaven. Divine? Well perhaps not necessarily, or not altogether, but certainly invested by God with an authority no ordinary human being would dare to claim. Why this should be so is a question whose answer revolves upon the interpretation of a single text—the famous vision[1] of Daniel 7:

> I was seeing in the night visions,
>   and behold, with (עִם) the clouds of heaven
>   one like a man was coming (כְּבַר אֱנָשׁ אָתֵה הֲוָה)
> And he approached the Ancient of Days (וְעַד עַתִּיק יוֹמַיָּא מְטָא)
>   and was presented before him
> And to him was given dominion and glory and kingship: (שָׁלְטָן וִיקָר וּמַלְכוּ)
>   With all peoples, nations and tongues serving him;
> His dominion an everlasting dominion, not to pass away
>   And his kingship not to be destroyed. (Dan. 7: 13–14)

Somehow or other a move was made from this figure *like a man* (for the Aramaic term meant no more than this)[2] to *the Son of Man*,

---

[1] It is not altogether clear whether Daniel's experience was a vision or a dream. Possibly an earlier version that speaks of a vision has been *interpreted* as a dream: 'I saw visions *in the night*' (7: 13; cf. v. 2). Cf. P. Weimar, 'Daniel'. In what follows the terms 'vision' and 'dream' are interchangeable.

[2] Or, equally possible, 'a man-like figure'—alternatives separated by the finest of nuances, not conveyed by the Aramaic, but with a whole world of interpretative meaning lying between them. For in the first case the 'one like a man' is *something other than a man*, just as the strange animal-like creatures who precede him are something other than ordinary animals. In the second case the 'man-like figure' is no more than a wraith, floating vapidly through the seer's dream until the interpretation gives it a function and a meaning. Much depends upon whether the figures in the

[*cont. on p. 338*]

which is how the innocent Aramaic phrase (having first shifted from the indefinite 'a' to the definite 'the') emerges in the ponderous, literal translation familiar to us from the Gospels.

Whether Jesus, in sober fact, ever thought of himself or referred to himself as the mysterious personage who appears in Daniel's dream is not a question that need concern us here.[3] That the identification was made by the Synoptists I take to be beyond dispute. The clouds, the power, and the glory in Mark 13: 26 leave no room for doubt.[4] That the term 'Son of Man' as used in the Fourth Gospel also implies some sort of heavenly status also seems obvious to me, but requires elucidation, since many of the passages in which it occurs curiously opaque.

Consequently, although the Greek expression ὁ υἱὸς τοῦ ἀνθρώπου (the Son of Man) is certainly a most misleading rendering of the Aramaic בַּר אֱנָשׁ it would be a mistake to assume that the mysterious figure in Daniel's vision can tell us nothing of the early Christian understanding of Jesus. On the contrary, even from the relatively small number of texts in which the allusion to the apocalyptic Son of Man is underlined we can see clearly that the identification was of great significance; and we must therefore allow for the possibility that he may be hovering in the background in other passages where the association is at best implicit. In the Fourth Gospel, I believe, the identification is even stronger, though for the most part it is not directly supported by apocalyptic props. How John fills in the mostly rather tentative and sketchy suggestions of the Synoptists will be considered in the conclusion of this chapter.

dream, the כְּבַר אֱנָשׁ and the monsters, are thought to be no more than empty signifiers, waiting to be interpreted, or whether they are conceived to have some reality, however shadowy and insubstantial, in the world above. In that case the 'one like a man' is an *angel*; so is the 'one in the likeness of men', כִּדְמוּת בְּנֵי אָדָם (10: 16; cf. 10: 18), and a figure introduced similarly as one 'in the appearance of a man' (*vir*), כְּמַרְאֵה גָּבֶר (8: 15). Some object that the figure in Daniel's dream does not merely *represent* Israel but, according to the interpretation, is actually *identified* with 'the saints of the Most High'. In my view this is to underrate and possibly altogether to ignore the significance of the upper-level action in the apocalyptic vision. But in any case the relevance of the passage for the New Testament lies not in its original meaning, but in the interpretation it was given at the turn of the era.

[3] Few questions in modern New Testament scholarship have been more hotly debated than this one. At the time of writing the latest clash has been between B. Lindars, *Jesus Son of Man* and M. Black, 'Aramaic Barnasha'. For a more recent survey see J. R. Donahue, 'Recent Studies'.

[4] Cf. Matt. 24: 30; 25: 31; 26: 64, etc.

(a) The sayings as a group

If we were to attempt to isolate the passages featuring the titles 'Son' or 'Son of God' and to treat them apart, we should find ourselves handicapped by their sheer number and ubiquity. Do the relatively infrequent occurrences of the term 'Son of Man' (thirteen all told)[5] entitle us to consider them, with one recent writer, as 'a cluster'?[6]

Rudolf Schnackenburg too believes that 'all thirteen texts in John which speak of the Son of Man form a consistent and well-knit whole'.[7] What is more, he is convinced that 'apart from the Son of Man logia themselves, there seems to be no grounds for assuming that the concept of the Son of Man has greatly influenced the Fourth Gospel'.[8]

Against this we may set J. L. Martyn's view that the evangelist employed the Son of Man motif as a complement and corrective to the identification of Jesus as Mosaic prophet-Messiah. The latter title, he observes, is never allowed to occupy the centre of the stage for very long: it is always replaced soon afterwards by another motif: 'Furthermore, this other motif always has to do with the Son of Man, and it usually consists of a direct presentation of Jesus as the Son of Man.'[9] On the other hand, Martyn holds the view that 'the titles Son of Man and Son of God have become interchangeable for John'.[10] But this is a careless, throw-away opinion, quite untypical of

---

[5] 1: 51; 3: 13; 3: 14; 5: 27; 6: 27; 6: 53; 6: 62; 8: 28; 9: 35; 12: 23; 12: 34 (*bis*); 13: 31.   [6] W. R. G. Loader, 'The Central Structure'.

[7] i. 532. Similarly Lindars: 'The Son of Man in John is the agent of the revelation which is disclosed in the cross' (*Jesus*, p. 155)—a straightforward but somewhat over-simplified account. J. Coppens, in one of the most thorough of all disquisitions on this subject, speaks of a distinct literary stratum, suggesting, without pressing the point, that the evangelist may have drawn upon 'a florilegium of logia, presumably the work of an early Christian group that has remained loyal and responsive to a christology centred upon the figure of the Son of Man' ('Le Fils de l'homme', p. 65).

[8] i. 534.

[9] *History*[2], p. 134. Martyn adds (n. 194) that 'the single exception is in the Samaritan episode in John 4. There, appropriately, the movement is from the Mosaic Taheb to the Jewish Messiah as the Savior of the World.'

[10] Ibid., n. 193. This he believes to have been demonstrated by S. Schulz in *Menschensohn-Christologie*. In fact Schulz is concerned with the *Son* theme (not Son of God), which he believes to be rooted in the apocalyptic vision of the Son of Man (pp. 127, 132 f., 136 f., 141 f.). If an alternative derivation is preferred (for which see the previous chapter), then there is no good reason to equate the two titles. E. D. Freed is even more emphatic than Martyn: 'Son of Man is only a variation for at least two other titles, namely the Son of God and the Son .... There is no separate Son of Man christology in the Fourth Gospel' ('Son of Man', p. 403).

Martyn's work as a whole, and he would surely have revised it had he undertaken a proper study of the Son of Man sayings individually and as a group.

Nevertheless it is hard to specify any features common to all thirteen sayings apart from the title itself. At most one can speak of a family resemblance, in Wittgenstein's sense, whereby the reader's attention is continually being directed to one particular aspect of Jesus' self-revelation. The title embodies the theme of Jesus' heavenly origin and destiny, and does so often enough to be significant in terms of his descent and (more frequently) ascent. It therefore adds to Messiahship and Sonship, albeit indirectly, the notion of pre-existence. What it does *not* convey, paradoxically, is either humanity[11] (which mostly rests upon the messianic titles) or any suggestion of sonship (differing in this respect from the title 'Son', which points directly to Jesus' relationship with God). Nor is the Son of Man ever said to be *sent*.

(b) The origin of the sayings

The remote origin of all the sayings is the Danielic Son of Man.[12] How far John drew upon traditions in which this figure had already been reinterpreted is a matter of conjecture. The important group of sayings dominated by the concepts of exaltation and glorification (3: 14; 8: 28; 12: 23, 34; 13: 31) is connected with the Synoptic passion-predictions, and perhaps also with sayings involving the concept of Jesus' exaltation at the right hand of God (cf. Mark 12: 36 //; 14: 62 //; etc.).[13] Given his penchant for adopting Synoptic-type traditions and transforming them to suit his own purposes, there is

[11] *Contra* F. J. Moloney: 'There is a concentration on the human figure of Jesus in the use of "the Son of Man". It is a title which is entirely dependent upon the incarnation. The Son of Man reveals the truth to men because he is man—because of the incarnation' (*The Johannine Son of Man*, p. 213). Moloney's error is to take the christology of the incarnate Logos as a kind of axiom from which everything else derives. Equally misguided is C. H. Dodd's view that 'for John the Son of Man is the ἀληθινὸς ἄνθρωπος, the real or archetypal Man, or the Platonic Idea of Man' (*Interpretation*, p. 244). M. Pamment has a similar view: 'It is misleading to label "Son of man" a "Christological term" since, unlike "Son of God", it does not seek to distinguish Jesus' unique nature or function, but defines the attributes of humanity which all men should exemplify': 'The Son of Man'.

[12] *Contra* Dodd: 'if we single out any one passage in the Old Testament which might be regarded as the scriptural basis for the Johannine idea of the Son of Man, Ps 79 (80) would take precedence over Dan 7' (*Interpretation*, p. 245 n. 1).

[13] Cf. Schnackenburg, i. 535 f.

no need to look any further for the immediate source of this group of sayings, though of course one can still ask how he comes to use the tradition as he does.

With such an obvious source lying close to hand in their own inshore waters, why then have New Testament scholars ventured so much further out to sea, trawling for speculative answers in an uncharted deep? Because some of the Son of Man sayings imply not just an appearance among clouds (well attested in the tradition) but a descent from heaven as well. Moreover, in the Fourth Gospel the ascent cannot be completely detached from the descent: 'No one has ascended into heaven except him who descended from heaven, the Son of Man' (3: 13). And 'what if you should see the Son of Man ascending *where he was before?*' (6: 62.) For this pattern of the descent/ascent of a heavenly messenger, argues Wayne Meeks, 'there is no closer parallel than in the Mandaean writings'; accordingly 'it has been and remains the strongest support for the hypothesis that the Johannine christology is connected with gnostic mythology'.[14] How far Meeks is justified in making this inference is a question that must await further discussion. But it is clear at any rate that we cannot furnish a satisfactory explanation of the Johannine 'Son of Man' sayings by appealing to the Synoptic tradition alone.

It can be shown that the evangelist was influenced by a number of currents in the formation of his concept of the Son of Man, all of them somewhere on the outer margins of the broad band of the Jewish tradition. These are most fruitfully considered in the exegesis of individual logia. In each case one must ask (*a*) what it was in this particular tradition that inspired the evangelist to take it over; (*b*) how and why did he use it in the way he did? It is widely agreed that the Son of Man sayings as a whole contain some of John's most profound and individual reflections on the role and person of Jesus. So the question what he understands by the term—in context— is more important than the identification of the sources he used. Certainly there is little value in trying to distinguish the pre-Johannine from the Johannine in this area[15] unless one is prepared at the same time to assess the point and purpose of the adaptations.

---

[14] *Prophet-King*, p. 297.
[15] As Schulz does, without attempting a re-examination of the theme *in situ*.

I. THE WAY UP AND THE WAY DOWN (1:51)

The Son of Man steps into the pages of the Fourth Gospel in what is surely one of the most unusual sayings to be put in the mouth of Jesus by any of the evangelists:

Amen, amen I say to you, you will see heaven opened and the angels of God ascending and descending upon the Son of Man. (1:51)

By no stretch of the imagination could this saying or anything remotely like it be derived from the Synoptic tradition as we know it.[16] The immediate reference is to Jacob's dream at Bethel 'that there was a ladder set up on the earth, and the top of it reached to heaven; and behold, the angels of God were ascending and descending on it' (Gen. 28:12). Walter Bauer acknowledges this; but then he goes on to quote a passage from the Right Ginza in which a warning is issued against 'the dangerous seductions of Christ', who 'sets up a ladder, throws it up from the ground to the sky, ascends and descends, moving between heaven and earth and says to you, "see how I came from high: I am your lord".'[17]

As a parallel, the Mandaean passage may be close, but it is not close enough to afford any real insight into the meaning of the mysterious promise to Nathanael. For this we may turn first of all to C. F. Burney, who pointed out that the interpretation of Jacob's dream given in the Gospel depends on the Hebrew, where the word translated 'on it' (referring to the ladder) could equally well be translated 'on him' (referring to Jacob).[18] After he had reached this conclusion it occurred to Burney to look up what the rabbis had to say on the passage, in the Genesis Rabbah. There he found to his satisfaction that an argument had taken place on that very point. One rabbi translated, 'ascending and descending upon the ladder', the other, 'ascending and descending upon Jacob'. Of these alternative explanations the commentator, according to Burney, prefers the former. But that does not stop him from offering a reading of the latter also: 'Ascending and descending upon Jacob implies that they

---

[16] *Contra* W. Michaelis, rightly criticized by G. Reim, *Studien*, pp. 102 f.

[17] pp. 40 f. Odeberg, pp. 41 f., quotes two different passages, neither of them any closer than the one cited by Bauer.

[18] 'Since סֻלָּם "ladder" is masculine, the force of בּוֹ is ambiguous. In LXX, ἐπ' αὐτῆς can refer only to κλῖμαξ. It may be added that John's ἀναβαίνοντας καὶ καταβαίνοντας literally represents the Hebrew participial construction עֹלִים וְיֹרְדִים, which is obscured in ἀνέβαινον καὶ κατέβαινον of LXX' (*Aramaic Origins*, pp. 115 f.).

were taking up and bringing down upon him.[19] They were leaping and skipping over him and rallying him ...'.

The interpretation now takes a sharp turn in a different direction: 'as it is said "You, O Israel [*Jacob's other name*] in whom I glory[20] (Isa. 49: 3), you are he whose εἰκών [portrait, image][21] is engraved on high." They were ascending on high and looking at his εἰκών, and then descending below and finding him sleeping.' The dreamer is now seen to be in two places at once, the real man sleeping on earth, while his portrait is fixed in heaven. This is an important element in the midrash, according to one of which God has to protect the sleeping Jacob from the hostility of the angels.

The following verse (Gen. 28: 13) is the occasion of a similar divergence of interpretation, since the word עליו can refer (as even the RSV recognizes) either to Jacob or to the ladder. The Rabbi Lakish takes the phrase literally: 'the Lord stood upon Jacob (נצב עליו)'. He adduces two further passages: 'And God went up from upon (מעל) Abraham' (Gen. 17: 22); 'And God went up from upon him (מעליו)' (Gen. 35: 13). These show, he says, that the patriarchs constitute the Merkavah, the divine chariot (האבות הן הן מרכבה). Here there is a hint of the sort of mediating role that Jesus plays in the Gospel—an occasion or vehicle of a heavenly vision.

A further interpretative element comes from the Jerusalem targumim (Onkelos is of no help here), where we learn that Jacob's portrait or image is fixed or engraved (קביע) upon the throne of glory:

the angels who had accompanied him from the house of his father ascended to inform the angels from on high, saying, 'Come and see the just man whose image (איקונין) is engraved on the throne of glory and whom you

---

[19] This is a literal rendering of the Hebrew מעלים ומורדים בו which is simply a Hifil (causative) form of the Qal verbs of the biblical text. Burney comments upon the obscurity of this phrase, made especially difficult by the retention of the בו. His own suggestion is that the angels acted as carriers between earth and heaven. Perhaps it is not too far-fetched to see them clambering up on Jacob's body in order to transport his εἰκών up to heaven. Other versions ignore the difficulty. J. Z. Smith ('Prayer of Joseph', p. 58) reproduces Freedman's translation, 'they praised him and slandered him', but suggests the possibility of a more literal translation: 'they raised him up and put him down' (ibid., n. 85). In an otherwise useful study of the targumic parallels to John 1: 51 C. Rowland fails to mention *The Prayer of Joseph* and I am left unconvinced by his suggestion 'that ἐπὶ τὸν υἱὸν τοῦ ἀνθρώπου should be taken only with καταβαίνοντας and not ἀναβαίνοντας': 'John 1. 51'.

[20] Or rather, 'in whom I will be glorified' (ישראל אשר בו אתפאר). Cf. John 13: 31.

[21] The loan-word איקונין is used.

were longing to see.' And so the angels of the presence of the Lord were ascending and descending and gazing on him.[22]

The third piece of evidence, not used in the earlier commentaries, is an extraordinary fragment of the Prayer of Joseph, preserved by Origen[23] and analysed at length and in depth by J. Z. Smith:

Jacob, at any rate, says: 'I, Jacob, who am speaking to you, am also Israel, an angel of God and a ruling spirit. Abraham and Isaac were created before any work. But I, whom men call Jacob but whose name is Israel, am he whom God called Israel, i.e., a man seeing God, because I am the first born of every living thing to whom God gives life.' And he continues: 'And when I was coming up from Syrian Mesopotamia, Uriel, the angel of God, came out and said that I descended to earth and I had tabernacled among men and that I had been called by the name of Jacob (ὅτι κατέβην ἐπὶ τὴν γῆν καὶ κατεσκήνωσα ἐν ἀνθρώποις, καὶ ὅτι ἐκλήθην ὀνόματι Ἰακωβ). He envied me and fought with me and wrestled with me, saying that his name and the name of him that is before every angel was to be above mine. I told him his name and what rank he held among the sons of God: "Are you not Uriel, the eighth after me, and I Israel, the archangel of the power of the Lord and the chief captain among the sons of God? Am I not Israel, the first minister before the face of God?" And I called upon my God by the inextinguishable name ...'.[24]

What this fragment adds to the foregoing is summed up by Smith in the phrase 'descent myth'. He quotes M. R. James: 'The leading idea of the principal fragment is that angels can become incarnate in human bodies, live on earth in the likeness of men, and be unconscious of their original state. Israel does so apparently that he may become the father of the chosen people.'[25] Smith goes on to point out that the language of the descent myth in the quotation 'clearly derives from the Jewish-Wisdom-Shekinah theology that has been the preoccupation of many students of the Prologue since the pioneering researches of J. Rendel Harris'— 'That I had descended to earth, etc.'

Although these words have a docetic ring, it is doubtful if the writer intends to question the full humanity of Jacob. True, both passages imply a double role, one in heaven, which has at least a

[22] Codex Neofiti; similarly Ps. Jon. The crucial word 'engraved', though included in the Paris MS, is omitted by the Codex Vaticanus of the Fragmentary Targum—which is the version quoted by J. Z. Smith. Cf. F. L. Lentzen-Deis, *Die Taufe Jesu nach den Synoptikern* (Frankfurt, 1970), p. 221.   [23] *Comm. in Joann.*, ii. 31.

[24] 'Prayer of Joseph'. See too the suggestive remarks of Margaret Barker on this text, *The Older Testament*, p. 111 f.

[25] *The Testament of Abraham* (Cambridge, 1892), p. 30.

priority in time, and one on earth. But the question of *ontological* priority is harder to answer. Is the 'real' Jacob the heavenly one, who descends to earth for a particular purpose only to reascend after his work there is done? At first sight it would appear so;[26] but I suspect that to put the question in this way may be to presuppose a dichotomy not envisaged by the writer, who is more concerned to establish the identity of the two figures than to arbitrate between them. We are dealing here with *myth* and myth, like gossamer, cannot be weighed in our clumsy scales.

How much of this speculation upon the Jacob story is relevant to the interpretation of John 1: 51? Are we entitled to use the targum and the Prayer of Joseph in our reading, when their mythological content so far outstrips both the Gospel passage itself and the part of the midrash it most closely resembles?

These imaginative extrapolations should teach us first, I suggest, that speculative exegesis of this kind belongs squarely within the Jewish tradition. In the light of these late developments the Johannine passage, so utterly unlike any of the Son of Man passages in the Synoptic Gospels, seems less surprising. Like other Jewish writers the fourth evangelist sees in the Jacob story a suggestion of a truth he himself was anxious to proclaim. So we need to ask what it was in the story that fired his own imagination and inspired him to construct his own myth.

Unlike the author of the Prayer of Joseph, John sees no link, apparently, between the Jewish legend and the wisdom myth. If he had, this might have been an appropriate place in the Gospel to introduce the notion of incarnation or 'tabernacling on earth', something he signally fails to do.[27] Neither incarnation as such nor tabernacling is in his thoughts at this juncture.

There are four elements requiring discussion: the open heaven, the ladder between heaven and earth, the ascent-descent motif, and the 'greater things'. But what should be emphasized first, perhaps, is

[26] This is the view of Odeberg, pp. 35 f. Cf. Dodd, *Interpretation*, pp. 245 f. The midrash goes on to compare the heavenly Jacob with a king in judgement and the earthly Jacob with a king in sleep. Odeberg concludes from this simile 'that the celestial appearance is meant to be conveyed as the real man'. But the opposite view is urged by Morton Smith, as cited by J. Z. Smith, p. 59 n. 92. This debate seems to me academic in both senses of the word.

[27] This is all the more surprising in view of the brilliant exploitation of these very traditions in the Prologue. The difference between the two passages is an additional proof that the Prologue was not added to the Gospel text until a comparatively late stage of its development.

that, unlike all the Jewish midrashim, John substitutes for 'Jacob' a name of his own, 'Son of Man', assuming that his readers are sufficiently familar with this term to make the required identification (with Jesus) for themselves. In making this move he is doing two things. First of all he is arrogating for Jesus the special place assigned to Jacob in the Jewish tradition; secondly he is associating the various themes that are peculiar to the passage with a particular title which had at best only an indirect link with the messianic claims prominent in the earlier part of the chapter.[28] The move implies, then, that these claims do not exhaust the truth about Jesus; what is more, it already involves a considerable reinterpretation of the role and function of the figure of the Son of Man. Why the evangelist attached his ascent/descent christology to this title and no other will, I hope, become plain in the course of this chapter.

We may begin by reminding ourselves of the way the evangelist highlights this title at the end of chapter 1. In its original form the story of Jesus' Discovery by the disciples constituted, as we saw in Chapter 7, the second panel of a triptych in which the most important of the titles assigned to Jesus matched those that had been repudiated by John the Baptist in the first panel, the Testimony. The climax of the series was initially the one bestowed by the wise and guileless Nathanael: 'You are the Son of God! You are the King of Israel' (1: 49). The evangelist is dissatisfied with these purely messianic titles, which do not, he realizes, adequately impart the real mystery of Jesus. So he replaces the original climax with a mythical κλîμαξ (ladder) of his own, one which is no longer earth-bound but reaches up to heaven. The superiority of the new title is established very firmly by the introductory verse, 'You shall see greater things than these,' because the primary reference of the 'greater things' is the 'open heaven': there is no doubt an allusion here to the Testimony scene—John's vision of the Spirit descending like a dove from heaven (1: 32). But in this version, unlike those of the Synoptists, the heavens are not said to have opened (or 'split' in the case of Mark 1: 10) to allow the dove to descend. Not until the end of John's first chapter are we permitted an anticipatory glimpse of an open heaven; and this is in connection with the title 'Son of Man'.

---

[28] Since the identification between these two traditions is made in the Parables section of *1 Enoch* and *4 Ezra* 13 (both writings roughly contemporary with the Fourth Gospel) some caution is required here. See U. B. Müller, *Messias und Menschensohn*; W. Horbury, 'Messianic Associations'.

(In conformity with Synoptic usage, this title, unlike the preceding ones—all of which are 'discovered' and proclaimed by the disciples—is reserved for the lips of Jesus.)

One of the difficulties of interpreting the saying satisfactorily is that the imagination, for once, is of no avail. Confronted with the bizarre spectacle of the angels clambering up and down on the strange new figure of the Son of Man, it seizes and stalls. This is a common experience of twentieth-century Westerners: as they look at myth, they feel compelled, somehow, to demythologize. But why should a demythologized myth be any more use than dehydrated water? The medium is the message—it does not contain it or hold it imprisoned like a genie in a bottle, waiting to be released. Somehow, then, we have to allow the picture of the ladder, base on earth and top in the clouds, to fuse with that of the Son of Man, and at the same time to allow the busily climbing angels, some going up and others going down, to convey the message with which the evangelist has charged them. But what is this message? It lies in *the picture*: it is simply that there is no other *route* between heaven and earth than the Son of Man—an interpretation which leads us back to the intended function of the Babylonian ziggurat, which is no doubt what prompted Jacob's dream in the first place. What is being suggested to the reader in this striking but perplexing image is not very different from the claim Jesus makes much later in the Gospel: in reply to Thomas's question, 'How can we know the way?' Jesus said to him, 'I am the way ...' (14: 5 f.).

Is that all? Not quite. For in this tiny midrash the evangelist has introduced us to a motif which resonates, as Wayne Meeks has argued,[29] through much of the 'Son of Man' material in the Gospel, namely the ascent/descent motif. If Jesus appears later simply as the way, here he is the way up and the way down. It would be far too simple to say that he now appears as 'the divine man' whose true home is in heaven. Oddly, perhaps, the first of the two verbs here, as in the next passage in which the Son of Man appears, is not 'descend' but 'ascend'. True, it is not yet being stated of the Son of Man himself that he is ascending or descending. But it is he who establishes

---

[29] 'Man from Heaven'. Although I disagree with some of its conclusions, this remains, in my view, the most significant single essay on the Fourth Gospel published since Bultmann. In the present chapter in particular my debt to Meeks's work is very great indeed. I am also indebted to an unpublished paper by John McDade, which shows more insight into the problems raised by this title than most of the other books and articles I have read.

communication between earth and a heaven which is now (permanently) open. We should remember that nowhere in the Gospel is the 'Son of Man' theme directly associated with the mission theme discussed in the previous chapter. If the Son of Man were indeed *sent* then he would have to be thought of as sent from heaven. But this point is not made. The Son of Man is first of all not an emissary but an intermediary.

Schwartz argued[30] that coming as it does so early in the Gospel, in a position that clearly indicates its importance to the evangelist, this prophecy might reasonably be expected to be fulfilled somewhere in the course of the remaining chapters. But where? After this brief appearance angels vanish from the Gospel and play no further role. But to look for an angelophany, as Hans Windisch did,[31] with no success, is to mistake the purpose of the prophecy. Nathanael is being tacitly equated with Jacob here; but this means that his promised vision has the character of a *dream*. And the fulfilment of a dream is not, whatever else it is, another dream. Jacob's interpretation of *his* dream, on awakening, is sobriety itself: '"Surely the Lord is in this place and I did not know it." And he was afraid, and said: "How awesome is this place! This is none other than the house of God, and this is the gate of heaven"' (Gen. 28: 17). What Jacob concluded about a *place*, Bethel, is transferred by the evangelist to a *person* who, as Son of Man, is the locus of revelation. These are the 'greater things' which *you* (plural) will see (ὄψεσθε); by jumping from singular to plural in what looks like a grammatical solecism, the evangelist is deliberately extending the promise made to the individual Nathanael (ὄψῃ) to a larger audience—not just the other disciples present at the scene, but the readers of the Gospel.

2. ASCENT AND DESCENT (3: 13)

The ascent/descent motif recurs in the next passage (3: 11–13), which has caused commentators almost as much trouble as the first. The three verses in question, along with the following two (3: 14–15), have been appended to the discussion with Nicodemus concerning a new kind of birth.[32] They read as follows:

[30] 'Aporien' (1908), p. 517.   [31] 'Angelophanien', pp. 226 f.
[32] The wider context of the whole of ch. 3 is discussed in Excursus IV.

Amen, amen I say to you (σοι, singular), that we (plural) speak of what we know and testify to what we have seen, and you do not accept (λαμβάνετε, plural) our testimony. If I told you (ὑμῖν, plural) of the things of earth (τὰ ἐπίγεια) and you do not believe, then if I tell you of the things of heaven (τὰ ἐπουράνια) how will you believe? The fact is[33] that no one has ascended into heaven except the one who descended from heaven, the Son of Man.

The abrupt transition from singular to plural in v. 11 suggests that an originally plural saying has been adapted to fit on to the dialogue with Nicodemus, a single individual.[34] The evangelist is borrowing from a source here, and it is particularly important to bear in mind that the reference of τὰ ἐπίγεια *may have been different in the source from what it is in the finished Gospel.*[35] The exceptional difficulty of giving any acceptable reference to the phrase in its present context is another indication that it has been lifted from a very different setting. It is the *original* reference of τὰ ἐπίγεια that sheds most light on the meaning of the following verse.

The main difficulty of the passage is in v. 13. How are we to explain the apparent implication that the Son of Man has already ascended into heaven, when he has, so to speak, just arrived on earth?

One way of evading this difficulty is to argue that the Greek need not imply any earlier ascension on the part of the Son of Man: 'No one has ever ascended into heaven [and thus equipped himself to reveal the secrets of God]: the Son of Man alone, who has come down from heaven [is in a position to do so]';[36] or, more simply, 'No one has ever ascended into heaven, but one has descended, the Son

---

[33] To translate the initial καί in this way is to begin to interpret this passage, making a very strong connection between vv. 12 and 13. (The initial καί of v. 14 has a very different force.) The RSV ignores the καί of v. 13; Brown, p. 129, renders it 'Now', a mild adversative. Schnackenburg inserts vv. 31–6 *between* vv. 12 and 13. J.-A. Bühner, though he does not discuss the καί, understands the passage as I do: *Gesandte*, p. 380.

[34] This is different from the change of number in 1: 51.

[35] As may be guessed from the perplexity of the commentators, e.g. Bultmann, pp. 147 f. The sense or *meaning* of the term—things of earth—poses no problem: there are plenty of examples in Jewish and other sources (cf. Bultmann, p. 147 n. 1; Schnackenburg, i. 378, etc.). What is puzzling is the *reference* or denotation in the present context. Bultmann's exegetical bravura at this point is quite dazzling, but not altogether persuasive. For some further suggestions (none of them convincing) see Blank, *Krisis*, p. 61 n. 39. I suspect that the root of the problem lies in the fact that in the text as it stands ἐπίγεια and ἐπουράνια can only refer to the *same* truths concerning the person of Jesus, who, as the previous logion implies, unites earth and heaven in his own person.

[36] This is the solution of E. Ruckstuhl, 'Abstieg und Niedergang'.

of Man.'[37] But this solution places an unbearable strain on the Greek.

We are therefore left with the task of explaining what this ascension could be.

In his truncated commentary of 1929 Odeberg laid the foundations of a solution by showing that the passage has a polemical intent: 'The wording οὐδεὶς ἀναβέβηκεν [no one has ascended], etc., immediately suggests that there is a refutation here of some current notions of ascent into heaven.'[38] The insistence that no one *apart from* the Son of Man ever ascended into heaven is made in the teeth of rival claims of prophets or patriarchs (above all Moses, though Odeberg does not mention him) to have gone up to heaven to receive revelations from God.

There are innumerable examples of such heavenly journeys in all branches of Jewish tradition,[39] ranging from pseudepigraphical apocalyptic texts to the insatiable curiosity of 'orthodox' rabbinism about mystical matters in general and the Merkavah or 'heavenly chariot' tradition in particular, according to which a seer is transported to heaven to receive revelations that far transcend anything vouchsafed to his earthbound contemporaries. The feature all these stories have in common with the passage in John 3: 11–13 is that they involve not just an ascent or assumption into heaven at the end of an individual's earthly life (Enoch and Elijah are the prime examples here) but a descent to earth following upon the heavenly vision. The existence of such a visionary belief throughout all branches of Jewish tradition furnishes us with an important clue to the understanding of this puzzling saying.

For the elucidation of the idea of the ascent of the Johannine Son of Man we are indebted to two important articles which illustrate the ascent/descent motif by highlighting two complementary series of texts. Published about the same time, the two articles are remarkably and interestingly dissimilar.

Charles H. Talbert[40] is eager to shatter the assumption of indebtedness to Gnostic sources.[41] He has gathered together a large

---

[37] Cf. F. M. Sidebottom, *The Christ of the Fourth Gospel*, p. 120. The 'parallel' in Rev. 21: 27 to which he and, following him, Moloney (*Son of Man*, p. 55) appeal actually tells against them. Borgen ('Some Jewish Exegetical Traditions', p. 249) rightly compares John 6: 46; 17: 12.   [38] p. 72.

[39] Out of the huge array of secondary literature see especially G. Scholem, *Major Trends*; I. Gruenwald, *Apocalyptic*; C. Rowland, *The Open Heaven*.   [40] 'Myth'.

[41] One of his main targets is Wayne Meeks (*Prophet-King*, cf. n. 13 above), whom he cites at the beginning of his article (p. 419 and n. 3).

number of bits and pieces flung from the obscure dark of the rich streams that feed into what he calls 'Mediterranean Antiquity'. Many of the texts he packs into his great big blunderbuss of an article miss their target by a wide margin.[42] These range from Ovid and Tacitus to the so-called *Apostolic Constitutions*. His Latin examples alone, he claims, prove 'that a Greco-Roman mythology of descending-ascending gods who appear on earth for redemptive purposes both existed early enough to be available for Christian appropriation and had, by the beginning of our era, already been used to interpret the lives of historical figures'.[43] He stops short, no doubt, of asserting that Ovid and Tacitus, Vergil and Horace, were actually the source of the Jewish myth. But it must be said that his treatment of the Jewish wisdom literature is itself curiously wide of the mark: the personified wisdom-figure (who is in any case usually closer to metaphor than to myth) is nowhere portrayed as ascending and descending *in human shape*.

When he turns to Jewish angelology he certainly gets closer to the heart of the matter, with the observation that the angel/messenger (מלאך) is often virtually identified with the Yahweh of the Old Testament.[44] But for clear evidence of traditions directly relevant to Johannine theology we have to move outside the Hebrew canon altogether.[45]

The most important section, for our purposes, of Talbert's article comes under the heading 'archangels', where he discusses (all too briefly) six major texts[46] and a seventh.[47] Central to each of these is

[42] As Douglas Templeton remarks, 'A well-written book is like a rifle, but a scatter-gun may bring down a pheasant', *Re-exploring Paul's Imagination* (Eilsbrunn, 1988), § 21. 7.

[43] p. 420.

[44] 'Myth', p. 422. Talbert shows how frequently the focus is blurred, sometimes in quite early texts, e.g. Judg. 6: 11 ff., so that God and his angel are confused. This confusion no doubt helped to pave the way for the subsequent identification of Yahweh, originally the Great Angel, with the Most High God. Cf. M. Barker, *The Older Testament, passim*.

[45] This is not to say that there are not to be found embedded in the Hebrew Bible large numbers of allusions whose 'heterodox' elements have for the most part been deliberately concealed.

[46] The Book of Tobit, *Joseph and Aseneth*, the *Testament of Job*, the *Apocalypse of Moses*, the *Testament of Abraham*, and the *Prayer of Joseph* (this last already commented upon in the previous section).

[47] The Melchizedek fragment in *2 Enoch* (chs. 71–3 in F. E. Andersen's translation in *OTPs*, pp. 204–13), briefly considered by Talbert, p. 426 n. 1. It is noteworthy that Talbert does *not* discuss ch. 39 of the longer recension (J) of this document, where

[*cont. on p. 352*]

the descent of an angelic figure with a particular task to perform on earth. This may be healing (Tobit), mystical initiation (Joseph and Aseneth), salvation (Job), guiding into Paradise (Moses), revelation and intercession (Abraham). His mission accomplished, the angel returns to heaven.[48] Not all these texts are pre-Christian but all, in the relevant passages, appear free from Christian influences (the Melchizedek fragment in 2 *Enoch* being a possible exception). 'The conclusion', says Talbert, 'seems irresistable [*sic*!]: in certain circles of ancient Jewish angelology, both B.C.E. and in the first and second centuries C.E. there existed a mythology with a descent-ascent pattern, in which the redeemer figure descends, takes human form, and then ascends back to heaven after or in connection with a saving activity.'[49] To call all these angels 'redeemer figures' without qualification is perhaps to read more into their role than some at least of these texts warrant. Nevertheless, the common mythological pattern is plain enough, and it is one shared by the Johannine Son of Man.[50]

These parallels appear at first sight, then, to provide a useful key to the descent/ascent pattern of the Fourth Gospel. Jesus too is said to have descended from heaven, to have acted out his role as saviour/revealer, and then to have returned whence he came. But if we actually try this key we find that it fails to make a complete turn in the lock. All Talbert's instances involve the descent of superhuman beings—angels—from their proper home in heaven. The starting-point of the fourth evangelist is with the human Jesus of the

Enoch, 'a human being created just like yourselves' (as the text repeatedly insists) is sent from heaven (cf. 38: 1) with a divine admonition for his children. Nor does he mention the passage where Enoch is transported to heaven without dying and then, after 60 days, returns to earth to visit his son: 'And he remained on earth for 30 days, talking with them. And then he was taken up to heaven again' (68: 2). It is significant also that what interests Talbert in the *Testament of Abraham* is Isaac's vision, in which he saw 'a luminous man descending from heaven', who then 'went back up (ἀνῆλθεν) to the heavens from which he had come' (ch. 7). He does not refer to the later passage in which Abraham is transported up to heaven by the archangel Michael, where he sees 'a wondrous man, bright as the sun, like a son of God (ὅμοιος υἱῷ θεοῦ)'. This is the judge of all mankind—who turns out to be Adam's son Abel (chs. 12–13).

[48] James Dunn ('Let John be John, p. 329 n. 75) objects to Talbert's list of angels that they are all 'only short-term visitors'. But so, as the evangelist sees the matter, is Jesus!

[49] p. 426.

[50] Talbert devotes the concluding pages of his article to the Fourth Gospel, but his treatment is summary and unsatisfactory, especially of the Son of Man sayings.

Synoptic tradition.[51] What he is combating—or measuring himself against—in the text under discussion is not the idea of a heavenly figure descending to earth, but the idea of a human being—other than Jesus—mounting up to heaven. This was clearly perceived by Odeberg.

So Peder Borgen, in discussing the background of this passage, is right to turn to the strong Jewish exegetical tradition according to which Moses, after climbing Mount Sinai to receive the tablets of the law, actually went on as far as heaven itself.[52] This tradition must have arisen quite early, since along with the even older and better-attested story of the assumption of Elijah it is evidently felt as undesirable and pernicious by the author of the *Mekilta de-Rabbi Ishmael*: 'Moses and Elijah did not ascend on high; nor did the glory descend down below.'[53] The yawning gap between heaven and earth is to be acknowledged and respected; not even the two most revered of Israel's prophets can be allowed to have transcended their earth-bound condition nor the divine glory to have (con)descended to men in a way that otherwise and elsewhere caused no problem to Jewish readers.

The belligerent assertion that no one has ascended to heaven except Jesus finds a satisfactory *Sitz-im-Leben*, then, in a polemic

---

[51] It is wrong to assume that the perspective of the Prologue, which does of course have its starting-point in heaven, is shared by the rest of the Gospel. This mistake vitiates both Dunn's article, 'Let John be John' and F. J. Moloney's otherwise useful study, *The Johannine Son of Man*. In asking, 'Why has John chosen to speak of the incarnate Logos in terms of the Son of Man?' (p. 214), the latter is begging one question by putting another. Problematic as it may be, 'Son of Man' is a traditional title; not so 'Logos', still less 'incarnate Logos', a coinage of a later age. The real question to be asked about the Johannine Christ is not how an incarnate divine being came to be thought of as Son of Man, but how a human being came to be given a title properly belonging to a heavenly being.

[52] 'Some Jewish Exegetical Traditions'. Borgen lists Philo, *Vita Mos.* i. 158 f.; Josephus, *AJ* iii. 96; Ps.-Philo, *Ant. Bib.* 12: 1; and Rev. 4: 1, and adds a number of rabbinical examples. He alludes to the Enoch tradition, but not to the passage where Enoch ascends and is identified as the Son of Man (*1 Enoch* 71: 14). He might also have mentioned the *Exodus* of the Jewish tragedian Ezekiel, where Moses has a vision in which he is invited by a royal figure with a diadem and sceptre to sit on a great throne and be crowned (*Exagoge*, ed. H. Jacobson, p. 54).

[53] *Mek.* on Exod. 19: 20 (Lauterbach, ii. 224): לא עלה משה ואליהו למעלה (= ἄνω) and לא ירד הכבוד למטה (= κάτω), quoted by Schlatter, p. 93, followed by Borgen, 'Some Jewish Exegetical Traditions', p. 244. Compare Josephus' careful assertion concerning Moses that 'He has written of himself in the sacred books that he died, for fear lest they should venture to say that by reason of his surpassing virtue he had gone back to the divinity' (*AJ* iv. 326)—as apparently some people had done (*AJ* iii. 96).

against counter-claims of unique privilege made on behalf of Moses by more 'orthodox' or conservative groups within the synagogue: 'You are his disciples, but we are disciples of Moses' (9: 28). At this point, however, two further questions arise: (1) why was the claim necessary? (2) why was it made of Jesus *as Son of Man*? Could it not have been asserted, quite simply: 'No one else apart from Jesus—he who descended from heaven in the first place—has ascended to heaven'?

The answer to the first question is contained or suggested in the text: only Jesus can tell about 'heavenly things', because only he has been up to heaven (to learn the secret mysteries he is now dispensing)—and descended to earth to bring the revelation to mankind.

At this point one must resist the temptation to jump back to the Gospel narrative. These verses have been slotted into their present position quite awkwardly, and this prompts a question concerning their original meaning. Bultmann, who discusses vv. 12 and 13 separately, asserts of the latter that it 'cannot ... bear the meaning which is normally attributed to it, that "no one has ever ascended into heaven, in order, that is, to bring back knowledge of the ἐπουράνια, except the one who descended from heaven". For Jesus did not first ascend into heaven to bring such knowledge back to earth again. Rather he first came down from heaven with the message entrusted to him by the Father and then he ascended again into heaven.'[54] Bultmann may conceivably be right to impose this reading upon the verse in its present context, and in doing so to avoid the idea (not otherwise attested in the tradition)[55] that Jesus made a mystical ascent into heaven during his lifetime.[56] But it has to be said that if we extract the passage from its present setting and consider it apart, then the obvious interpretation is the one Bult-mann rejects. Borgen has furnished convincing evidence of a resilient Jewish tradition to the effect that Moses had made such a journey in *his* lifetime. And in view of the strong strain of Moses typology in the Gospel (so well analysed by Meeks in his *Prophet-King*) it seems highly probable that in these two verses from chapter 3 we have traces of a struggle between two rival groups in the synagogue—one sticking to the tradition that the only recipient of

---

[54] pp. 150 f.   [55] Though the transfiguration scene comes close.
[56] As Enoch did. See Gen. 5: 22–4 and *I Enoch* 14. Cf. J. C. VanderKam, *Enoch and the Growth of an Apocalyptic Tradition* (Washington, 1984), p. 131.

the heavenly secrets that were later imparted to Israel was Moses himself, the first and greatest of the prophets; the other, the Johannine group, making the same claims on behalf of Jesus.

There is, however, one puzzle remaining: the wording of the Gospel makes it quite clear that in the case of Jesus *the descent preceded the ascent*, a reversal of the natural pattern whereby the human seer must first mount up to heaven before he can return to inform others of all he has seen and heard. So what we have in the Gospel is *a fusion of two mythological patterns*, one angelic, starting in heaven (stressed by Talbert), the other mystical, starting from earth (stressed by Borgen). How great a conceptual leap is involved in this fusion may be gauged from the fact that in at least one document, *The Testament of Abraham*, the two patterns lie virtually side by side,[57] without the least suggestion that the archangel Michael, who illustrates the first pattern, could ever be confused with Abraham, who illustrates the second. The blinding realization that in Jesus angel and seer are one and the same marks one of the most significant advances in the whole history of Christian thought: its ramifications are endless. Although both elements are abundantly attested in the Jewish tradition their fusion has consequences which Judaism could not contain. Taken separately neither pattern presented any threat: the blending of the two meant a new religion. The conviction that the heavenly being was human and the human being heavenly was the conceptual hub round which the huge wheel of Christian theology would revolve for centuries to come. Meeks's term, 'man from heaven', accurate though it is, fails to convey the tremendous significance of a breakthrough signalled almost unobtrusively by a single verse: 'No one has ascended into heaven except him who descended from heaven, the Son of Man.'

If this is right, then our second question (why was this claim, of ascent-descent, predicated of Jesus *as Son of Man?*) really answers itself. It looks as if the tradition that provided the catalyst for the fusion we have been considering was none other than the tradition that Jesus was not just Son, Emissary, and Messiah, but also *Son of Man*. What was it then about this title which made it such a suitable vehicle for this particular message? This question, I believe, has two complementary answers, one going back

[57] Also possibly in *2 Enoch*. Nor should one overlook the curious fact that two articles by contemporary scholars, written about the same time and on more or less the same topic, *fail to intersect at any point.*

to the Old Testament, the other rooted in the Synoptic tradition. These answers will be discussed separately in the next two sections of the present chapter.

As for the timing of the ascent, we must once again be careful not to confuse the purpose of the source with that of the evangelist. In considering the latter it is probably best to follow Bultmann in his refusal to regard the ascent mentioned in 3: 13 as different from the final ascension referred to in 20: 17: 'go to my brethren and tell them "I am ascending to my Father and your Father, to my God and your God".'[58] In the source there are no such constraints, and here the only difficulty is to decide upon the nature of the ascent. Borgen speaks of a 'pre-existent ascent', whatever that might mean; but against this it must be urged once again that as it stands the passage quite clearly implies that the descent *preceded* the ascent.[59] None the less Borgen's suggestion that the ascent represented a kind of 'installation in office' is an attractive one and fits in well with Jewish ideas concerning Moses.

By the time chapter 6 came to be composed for the second edition of the Gospel the revolutionary new ideas adumbrated in chapter 3 had already been fully assimilated: some notion of pre-existence was by now an accepted element in the community's thinking about Jesus. So when Jesus tells the dissident group of disciples, 'What if you were to see the Son of Man ascending where he was before?' (6: 62), he (or the prophet speaking in his name) is presuming as a shared basis of argument their continuing belief in the ascent/descent pattern now particularly associated with the Son of Man.[60] Just what the bone of contention was between him and his disciples in this passage ('This is a hard saying, who can listen to it?') cannot be resolved here.[61]

[58] So too Barrett, Brown, and Schnackenburg.

[59] It is methodologically improper to argue, as Borgen does, that 'the parallel statement in John 6: 46 ... suggests that the ascent of the Son of Man expressed in 3: 13 refers to an event which is prior to the descent and serves as its pre-condition' ('Some Jewish Exegetical Traditions', p. 249). His additional arguments (pp. 250 ff.) are equally tendentious.

[60] Lindars's conclusion (in his earlier article) that 'descent is not part of the Johannine Son of Man myth, though it is an essential feature of his christology' ('Son of Man', p. 48 n. 16) is the reverse of the truth.

[61] Nor do I wish to take issue here on another question over which scholars continue to wrangle. When Jesus asks, 'What if you were to see the Son of Man ascending where he was before?', is the implication positive ('would you then be encouraged to believe?') or negative ('would you be even more scandalized?')?

3. THE HEAVENLY JUDGE (5: 27)

For as the Father has life in himself, so he has granted to the Son also to have life in himself, and has given him authority (ἐξουσία) to execute judgement, because he is Son of Man.

This saying is unique in two respects: (1) it is the only one in which 'Son' and 'Son of Man' are found side by side; (2) it is the only occurrence in the Gospels of the anarthrous form υἱὸς ἀνθρώπου (which here replaces the cumbersome ὁ υἱὸς τοῦ ἀνθρώπου). Even without this phrase there is an obvious allusion to Dan. 7: 13. The present chapter began with a rendering of the Aramaic text. What follows is a translation of the two Greek versions, the Septuagint and that ascribed to Theodotion, which in the case of Daniel is certainly earlier than the date in the second century AD often assigned to it:[62]

Theodotion	LXX
I was watching in a vision of the night, and behold	
with (μετά) the clouds of heaven	on (ἐπί) the clouds of heaven
one like a son of man (ὡς υἱὸς ἀνθρώπου)	
coming	was coming
and he reached the Ancient of Days	and drew near an Ancient of Days
and approached him	and the bystanders presented him
and to him was given (καί ἐδόθη αὐτῷ)	
rule and honour and kingdom (ἡ ἀρχὴ καὶ ἡ τιμὴ καὶ ἡ βασιλεία)	authority (ἐξουσία)
and all the peoples, tribes, tongues will serve him;	and all the nations of the earth race by race (κατὰ γένη) and all glory, at his service;
his authority (ἐξουσία) is an eternal authority	
which will not pass away	which will never be removed
and his kingdom will not be destroyed.	and his kingdom which will never perish.

[62] These translations, which are based on the edition of Joseph Ziegler (Göttingen, 1954), pp. 169 f., take no account of the many variants. For a recent discussion of the two text-forms, see the Anchor Bible edition of L. F. Hartman and A. A. di Lella (New York, 1978), with copious references to earlier studies. J. A. Montgomery had already shown that the so-called Theodotion Daniel is cited in many passages in the New Testament, especially Hebrews and Revelation. Cf. *Daniel* (Edinburgh, 1927), p. 49. Accordingly, the 2nd-century date proposed for Theodotion by J. Barthélemy, *Les Devanciers d'Aquila*, SuppVT 10 (1963) is too late for this book. It now seems that 'Theodotion-Daniel is not in the same textual tradition as Proto-Theodotion (*kaige*) "Theodotion" existing in the other books of the Old Testament' (Hartman and di Lella, p. 81). Fortunately the exegesis of Daniel 7 in the original need not detain us. The manifold aporias in the text of this chapter suggest that it was not composed as an

[cont. on p. 358]

As early as the Septuagint the literal (and inaccurate) translation of the Aramaic כְּבַר אֱנָשׁ had paved the way for further (fruitful) misunderstanding; and in this passage the form and content of the Johannine logion establish the link beyond all doubt. In each case authority (ἐξουσία) is conferred by God; in the Daniel passage, however, it is not clear that this authority, though everlasting, is precisely 'the authority to execute judgement' mentioned in the Fourth Gospel. Obviously some extraneous influence has been at work here. This may well have been the Synoptic tradition, in which the Son of Man figures quite plainly as the eschatological judge. Alternatively, perhaps additionally, we might think of the tendency in contemporary Jewish thought to assimilate Son of Man and Messiah and to allow their roles to merge.

The texts in question, *1 Enoch*, *4 Ezra*, and *2 Baruch*, are extremely complex; and the first especially has been endlessly debated. The Son of Man features in a section of the work (the Parables or Similitudes, chs. 37–71) of which, unlike the rest of the book, no surviving fragments have been found at Qumran. What is more, Christian interference has been suspected. Few scholars nowadays accept this theory; but difficulties abound—and these are scarcely to be resolved by anyone ignorant of Ethiopic, the only language in which this part of the book has come down to us. It is not even agreed whether Enoch has progressed beyond Daniel to the extent of using the term 'son of man' as a title instead of as an idiomatic way, common to many Semitic languages, of referring to a man.[63]

---

integrated whole; the analysis of its prehistory is as complex and uncertain as anything in the Bible. To take but one example, U. B. Müller holds that the version of the man-like figure, vv. 13 f., was composed *after* the account of the victory of the Saints. Its function was to append a positive conclusion, one that would conform with the writer's view of the role of the Saints (Israel), *on to the vision*. So it was not a case, in Müller's view, of the vision preceding its interpretation; rather, what now stands as the interpretation actually generated the vision—or at least that part of it in which the human-seeming figure appears (cf. *Messias und Menschensohn*, pp. 23–6). For a slightly different view, see P. Weimar, 'Daniel 7', with references to earlier literature. Other scholars, e.g. M. Casey (*Son of Man*), continue to defend the integrity of the chapter.

[63] The Ethiopic version was not translated directly from the Semitic original (Aramaic or Hebrew), but from a Greek translation of this. So there are real problems about finding our way into the heart of this Chinese box. What was the Greek lying behind the 'this' in the Ethiopic term 'this man'? If it was simply the definite article
[*cont. on p. 359*]

Nevertheless, three points may be made: first, Enoch goes beyond Daniel at least in so far as he speaks of '*the* Man', as opposed to the vague 'figure like a man' of Daniel's dream; in the second place, he identifies this man with a messianic redeemer, called initially 'the Righteous One' (38: 2–3) and then 'the Chosen One' (40: 5 and *passim*) or 'my Chosen One' (45: 3, 4; cf. Isa. 42: 1, etc.). The first clear reference to Daniel's vision is in chapter 46, where along with the 'Head of Days' the visionary saw another (being) 'whose face had the appearance of a man' (46: 1). On questioning his accompanying angel about 'that (son of) man', he is told, 'this is the (son of) man who has righteousness, and with whom righteousness dwells' (46: 3). Subsequently this Righteous One, Chosen One, (son of) man is openly called the Messiah of the Lord of Spirits (48: 10; 52: 4).

Thirdly, Enoch recounts in some detail how 'that (son of) man' was *given a name* 'in the presence of the Lord of Spirits ... and before the Head of Days' (48: 2). He is invested with some of the appurtenances of messiahship: he is to 'cast down the kings from their thrones and from their kingdoms' (46: 5), to become a staff for the righteous, a light for the gentiles, a hope for the sick at heart (48: 4). Above all he is the eschatological judge, whose authority extends over 'the holy ones in heaven' (61: 8) and over the mighty on earth (62: 9): 'And he sat on the throne of his glory, and the sum of the judgement was given to the (son of) man, and he will cause

---

(δ υἱὸς τοῦ ἀνθρώπου or even δ ἄνθρωπος) then it looks as though we have to do with a *title* ('the Man'), which in a determinate contextual setting will have contained, or come to contain, a quite precise allusion to a particular role or function. Moreover, since in all human societies except that of the Amazons 'man' is an honourable epithet, it is well suited to carry connotations of authority and power. This is how it is applied to the President of the United States at the White House or to the champion poker-player in *The Cincinnati Kid*. Margaret Barker argues that the Similitudes are simply following a code already established in the indisputably pre-Christian parts of *Enoch*, according to which human beings were represented by animals and angels by human beings, *The Lost Prophet*, pp. 95 f. If, on the other hand, the Greek term translated by Enoch was 'this man' or 'that man' (οὗτος δ υἱὸς τοῦ ἀνθρώπου, say, or ἐκεῖνος δ ἄνθρωπος), then this will simply have been a shorter way of saying 'the man who has just been mentioned' or 'the man we have already encountered in the course of this narrative' (e.g. 46: 2; 48: 2). It is to be noted, however, that even this version presupposes the possibility of distinguishing between *a* man (בר אנש) and *the* man (בר אנשא). The matter is thrashed out in some detail by M. Casey in *JSJ* 7 (1976) (cf. *Son of Man*, p. 100) and M. Black, 'Aramaic Barnasha and the "Son of Man"', who come to different conclusions. In any case the man must be seen as an angel.

sinners to pass away and be destroyed from the face of the earth'
(69: 27).[64]

The conclusion of the Parables, according to which Enoch ascends
to heaven and is identified with the Son of Man (71: 14) is of especial
interest. Collins ('The Heavenly Representative') argues that this
passage was a redactional addition, and suggests that it may have
been 'a reaction to the Christian appropriation of the phrase "son of
man" for another who was believed to have made the transition
from earth to heaven' (p. 126). But the reaction could equally well
have been from the Christian, and specifically the Johannine side.

4 *Ezra* differs from the pseudo-Enoch in presenting what may be
called a Jewish-establishment view of things; but like Enoch he
conjures up for his readers a variant of Daniel's vision, recalling how
in his dream 'something like a figure of a man'[65] rose out of the
heart of the sea and flew with the clouds of heaven (13: 3). This
figure is identified with the Messiah, who has already put in an
appearance earlier in the book—where he is called 'my Son the
Messiah' (7: 29)[66] and portrayed symbolically as a lion (12: 31 f.).

The Messiah in 4 *Ezra* seems in some respects less a man than a
superman, for like the modern fantasy-hero of that name he
renounces human weapons (13: 9) in favour of those associated
with the awesome manifestations of the storm god (13: 10). Nevertheless, he continues to be called a man (13: 3b, 5, 12) and there is
no question here of the term 'Son of Man' being used as a title. And
in the interpretation of the dream given to the seer the Danielic 'man
from the sea' is interpreted allegorically in terms of the tradition of
the hidden Messiah (13: 41–56).

Lastly 2 *Baruch*, much more discreet than the others and even
more opaque. Though he has a vision of redemption in the form of a

---

[64] One title that Enoch denies him is 'king'—which might seem odd in view of the
fact that both the Danielic Son of Man and the Davidic Messiah are kings, one by gift,
the other almost by definition. But Enoch can scarcely be counted a supporter of the
Davidic line, and in any case he ranges *all* human authority-figures among the
wicked. Here, as elsewhere in the book, some things Enoch says are strikingly
reminiscent of the Gospel of Luke: 'This Son of Man whom you have seen is the One
who would remove the kings and the mighty ones from their comfortable seats and
the strong ones from their thrones. He shall loosen the reins of the strong and crush
the teeth of sinners. He shall depose the kings from their thrones and kingdoms'
(46: 4–5, Isaac's translation; cf. Luke 1: 52; also 1 *Enoch* 62: 9, etc.).

[65] Syriac ܐ݇ܢܫܐ ܐܝܟ ܕܡܘܬ (The Latin is defective at this point.)

[66] 'Filius meus Christus'; or possibly, following the Ethiopic, 'my *servant* the
Messiah', suggesting that the Greek here (and elsewhere) was not ὁ υἱός μου but ὁ παῖς
μου, reflecting a Hebrew עַבְדִּי. (Cf. Arab 1 at 13: 32, 52 and Arab 2 at 13: 37, 52.)

flash of lightning (53: 8–11) he avoids all mention of the lightning in his interpretation of the dream (72: 1–6) and introduces his messianic redeemer without warning immediately afterwards, leaving his readers to make what connection they will between the lightning and the one who is destined to usher in an era of joy and rest—but only 'after he has brought down everything which is in the world, and has sat down in eternal peace on the throne of the king' (73: 1; cf. 29: 3). Nevertheless there does seem to have been some contamination, as it were, of this messianic figure by theophanic traits like the lightning—associated elsewhere (cf. Matt. 24: 27) with the Son of Man.

Perhaps the most important evidence of the identification of the two figures is in the Babylonian Talmud, where there is here a direct reference to Daniel 7; what is more, Rabbi Aqiba's idea that David, *qua* Son of Man, should occupy one of the thrones in heaven was seen as blasphemous by at least one of his contemporaries:

One passage says: *His throne was fiery flames* (Dan. 7: 9) and another passage says: Until thrones were placed; and One that was ancient of days did sit (*ibid.*)—there is no contradiction: One (throne) for Him, and one for David: this is the view of R. Aqiba. Said R. Yosi the Galilean to him: Aqiba, how long will you treat the divine presence as profane?[67]

With some caution, then, it may be said that by the end of the first century AD two originally distinct figures, the one like a man in Daniel and the messianic redeemer, had started to coalesce, hesitantly in *2 Baruch*, more perceptibly in *4 Ezra*, and most clearly of all in *1 Enoch*. The identification made by all four evangelists of the one they knew as the Messiah with the Son of Man was perhaps less unprecedented than many have supposed.[68] In any case the fourth evangelist surely inherited a tradition to that effect which had some connection with the various sayings recorded by the other three.

We may now return briefly to the single passage in the Fourth Gospel in which there is an unambiguous allusion to Daniel's vision. For our purposes its most interesting feature is not the blending of

[67] *b. Hag.* 14a. Tr. Epstein; quoted by Segal, *Two Powers*, p. 47, who also refers (n. 21) to *b. Sanh.* 38a, where other rabbis are said to oppose R. Aqiba. What perplexed the rabbis was the apparent contradiction, in the same verse (Segal mistakenly implies that more than one verse was involved), between the singular 'throne' and the plural 'thrones'. Cf. Ch. 4, p. 144.

[68] 4. Horbury. 'Son of Man'.

two different kinds of eschatology[69] but the merging and mutual enrichment of two different traditional titles. The extra-canonical texts we have just been considering combine the motif of the man-like figure in Daniel with that of the Messiah. In John the Messiah has given way to one of the titles this evangelist has made his own, that of 'the Son'. This must be seen against the legal traditions surrounding 'the son of the house' and therefore identified as the one invested by the Father with full authority for his mission on earth. This 'Son' is now identified as 'the Son of Man' (there is no doubt here about the titular use of this term), a heavenly being whose authority is reserved in the first place for a judgement beyond any time or place that can be classed as belonging to this age or this world.

Once the reference to the Danielic Son of Man is accepted and understood we are in a better position to appreciate how admirably this title serves to sum up the extraordinarily bold and novel theology succinctly but enigmatically expressed in John 3: 13. For although, according to the Synoptic tradition, the Son of Man does not pronounce judgement except eschatologically, in a future indefinitely distant and remote, nevertheless that judgement is anticipated by the attitude men adopt to Jesus in his earthly presence.[70] Of all the titles assigned to Jesus in the New Testament, only 'Son of Man' is able to convey the simultaneous existence (we are talking haltingly of myth or mystery here) of a being who, in his solemn reception of authority in heaven, symbolizes a scenario that is actually being played out on earth.

Here we find ourselves at the conceptual origins of two of the most

---

[69] The question whether the discourse in ch. 5 originally included vv. 28–9 continues to divide scholars. Bultmann detects here the futuristic eschatology that so offends him and so assigns the passage to the ecclesiastical redactor; but the very effective combination of the two titles 'Son' and 'Son of Man', with all that each implies, does not have to be seen as a regrettable adulteration of an otherwise pure and particularly full expression of the Johannine theme of judgement. Nor can it be reasonably argued that the exercise of judgement conflicts with the assertion of 3: 17 that God 'sent the Son not to judge the world, but that the world might be saved through him'. For the Son too, not just the Son of Man, is given power to judge (5: 22); whilst the positive aspect of his mission is displayed in the authority to bestow life (in any case a concept much more characteristic of the fourth evangelist than the 'salvation' of 3: 17). But see *supra*, Ch. 6.

[70] e.g. Luke 12: 8: 'Everyone who acknowledges me before man, the Son of Man also will acknowledge before the angels of God; but he who denies me before men will be denied also before the angels of God.' The Matthean parallel (10: 32) reads 'I'. Surely Luke is the one who retains the original text here!

distinctive and pervasive features of the Fourth Gospel, first the sense it conveys of the remoteness and sheer foreignness of its hero, analysed so persuasively by Wayne Meeks in his 'Man from Heaven' article,[71] and secondly what J. L. Martyn calls 'the literary form of the two-level drama', in which 'there are dramas taking place both on the heavenly stage and on the earthly stage'.[72] (These stages will reappear in the next chapter.)

Further confirmation of the association of the title 'Son of Man' with the theme of judgement is furnished by the conclusion of chapter 9,[73] where Jesus, on hearing that the man born blind has been expelled by the Jews, seeks him out and asks him directly, 'Do you believe in the Son of Man?' The use of this term puzzles the man (it is not meant to be immediately perspicuous) and he asks, 'who is he, sir, for me to believe in him?' (9: 35 f.). Though Jesus' reply contains his most explicit claim to the title in any of the Gospels, it retains at the same time a vestige of indirection: 'You have seen him, and it is he who speaks to you' (v. 37). The blind man saw him when he was in the act of establishing his authority—giving sight to the blind and also, incidentally, refuting the Jews' claim to sight. In the Fourth Gospel this is a typical act of *judgement*, as is made explicit in the next verse: 'For judgement I came into this world, that those who do not see may see, and that those who see may become blind' (9: 39).

4. EXALTATION AND GLORY

In the passages we have been considering so far, the Son of Man is a direct descendant of the heavenly man in Daniel 7. The emphasis in these is on the contrast (and on overcoming the contrast) between the heavenly realm and the earthly realm; and the Son of Man, whose 'dominion and glory and kingship' were set, on his first appearance, quite unequivocally in heaven, is seen in the Fourth Gospel, despite his heavenly origins, to exercise judgement here below. But this successful deployment of a double register of meaning (whose reverberations, as we shall see in the third part of

---

[71] It is not altogether surprising, then, that by the time it came to be placed in the bibliography of Meeks's later study, *The First Urban Christians* (New Haven/London, 1983), the Man from Heaven had become 'The Stranger from Heaven'.

[72] *History*², p. 135. [73] Cf. Ch. 5, n. 40.

this book, resound throughout the Gospel) is only one strand in its richly counterpointed theology.

When all is said and done, the Son of Man, heavenly being though he may be, is identified with the figure at the heart of the Christian faith—otherwise there would be no room for him in a Gospel—and that faith is focused first of all not on ascent and descent but upon crucifixion and resurrection. One of the most singular features of Johannine christology is its vision of the crucifixion, that horribly painful and ignominious death, as itself a kind of elevation. Almost equally remarkable, at first sight, is the fact that this vision is associated first and foremost with the title of Son of Man. How was the transition made from the victorious representative of God in a prophet's dream to the tortured figure hanging on the cross in the last act of a barbarous execution?

The complete answer to this question belongs to another book (though a short answer will be attempted in the conclusion to this chapter). By the time of the composition of the Fourth Gospel, the transition had been completed—so effectively that the three great passion predictions in the Synoptic Gospels were all associated with the title 'Son of Man'. Given the strangeness of this association, which for all the explanations that have been offered of it still remains hard to understand, it would be idle, when asking why John made the same connection, to hunt for reasons outside the Synoptic-type traditions we know him to have inherited. John, and the community to which he belonged, will have been aware that on the three separate occasions on which Jesus is said to have foretold his death,[74] he employed terms that linked it inextricably with the figure of the Son of Man.

Corresponding to the three sayings in the Synoptic Gospels are three similar predictions in John: 3: 14; 8: 28; 12: 32–4.[75] Moreover, John shares with the Synoptists that sense of divinely appointed predestination, suggested by the word δεῖ ('it is necessary'), that accompanies the first of the three predictions in each of the Gospels. Where John differs from the Synoptists is chiefly in his

---

[74] Mark 8: 31; 9: 31; 10: 33 f. and parallels. These are the most important of Bultmann's second group of 'Son of Man' sayings, the passion-and-resurrection sayings.

[75] Cf. Brown, p. 146. As he says, 'There is no reason to think that the fourth evangelist is dependent upon the Synoptics for his form of the sayings.' Brown even suggests that the Johannine sayings, being less detailed, 'could be more ancient'. If by this he means 'more authentic', this is surely most improbable.

reluctance to see the crucifixion as demeaning or degrading and in the word he uses to suggest an alternative view. Ὑψοῦν, to 'raise' or 'elevate', does not occur in the LXX version of the story of Moses and the bronze snake that is alluded to in 3: 14;[76] instead of ὑψοῦν the simple verb ἱστάναι is used. (See Num. 21: 9.)

The question how John came to see the raising-up of Jesus on the cross as an exaltation is actually quite misleading, since it tends to obscure the fact that the primary meaning of ὑψοῦν is not to lift up (αἴρειν), still less to crucify (σταυροῦν) but to *exalt*. There is not even any natural ambiguity to exploit, and were it not followed by v. 16[77] it might be possible to insist on the primary significance of the word and to translate it simply by 'exalt'—which is what it means in the other places in the New Testament where it is used: Acts 2: 33; 5: 31; cf. Phil. 2: 9—ὑπερυψοῦν. In all these passages the subject of the verb is God, who concludes the tale of Jesus' sufferings and humiliation by raising him up to heaven. In 8: 28, by contrast, it is actually the Jews who, Jesus foretells, will 'raise him up'.

Accordingly our question is better formulated like this: how does John come to use a term hitherto reserved for elevation into glory for the ignominy of crucifixion? Or rather, why does he suggest that the cross is not merely a decisive moment in the process of Jesus' path to glory, but somehow to be equated with his very entrance into heaven? C. C. Torrey, referring to 12: 34, suggested that the use of the word ὑψοῦν arose from a simple misunderstanding of the Aramaic word אֶסְתַּלַּק , which can mean both 'be lifted up into the heights' and 'depart'.[78] Bultmann waves this suggestion aside with the caustic comment that '12: 34 comes after 8: 29 and was composed by the evangelist, who wrote Greek'.[79] He is equally dismissive of the idea that this sublime theological concept is rooted in the ambiguity, in both Syrian and Palestinian Aramaic, of אִזְדְּקַף ,

---

[76] Since the lesson the evangelist derives from this story is plain enough, there is no pressing need to trace the line of his exegesis, which is also found in *Barn.* 12. 5–7; Justin, *Apol.* i. 60; *Dial.* 91. 94, 112. Odeberg (pp. 100–13) has a fascinating excursus at this point. Some of the Gnostics made the snake itself ascend. Cf. Hippolytus *Ref.* v. 12. 6–13; 16. 4–16 (references in Moloney, *Son of Man*, p. 62 n. 104).

[77] Cf. the evangelist's comment in 12: 33: 'He said this to show by what death he was to die.'

[78] '"When I am lifted up from the earth"'. Torrey's suggestion is repeated by M. McNamara, *Targum and Testament* (Shannon, 1968), p. 143.

[79] p. 354 n. 6.

which can mean both 'to be lifted up' and 'to be crucified'.[80] Were it
not for the fact that contemporary Jewish writings are full of grand
ideas apparently rooted in soil just as shallow, one would be forced
to be just as dismissive as Bultmann. But whatever truth there may
be in suggestions based on Semitic semantics,[81] the real question
must concern the theological insight behind this remarkable shift in
perspective.

A first approach to an answer might be to return to the beginning
of the whole process leading up to the Johannine vision. For what
worried Luke was evidently how to explain and justify the cross in
the first place. His answer, which was to see it as a necessary stage in
Jesus' journey to heaven, cannot be said to exhibit any real
understanding of the need for the cross, though it may be a step
beyond the grudging acquiescence that is the highest response to
undeserved suffering of all but a very few religious believers.

Next, the cross is seen as a voluntary self-emptying, not just
acquiescence but ready acceptance of God's will—'obedience unto
death, even the death of the cross' (Phil. 2: 8). This is a traditional
view, which Paul may well have inherited but which is surely
derived ultimately from the story of the Agony in the Garden. From
here it would be but a step, though a big one, to seeing the cross as
the start of the process of elevation—the first glimpse of glory.[82] And
this, we might infer, is the step taken by John in his account of the
crucifixion, when he substitutes for Mark's cry of desolation a
triumphant τετέλεσται or *consummatum est*.[83] But the final step,
impossible to suggest in any account of the physical crucifixion, is
the one taken in the three passion predictions and implied by the
prayer in chapter 17.

Before continuing this enquiry by pressing even harder the
question concerning the source of the evangelist's novel view of
Jesus' death, we must take into consideration two further passages in which the title 'Son of Man' occurs: 8: 28 and 12: 32–4.

The second of these (12: 32–4) contains a puzzle. What Jesus says
is this: 'And I, when I am lifted up from the earth, will draw all men

---

[80] p. 350 n. 1.

[81] Brown (p. 146) also refers to Hebrew נָשָׂא , 'which can cover both meanings of
death and glorification, as in Gen. 40: 13 and 19'. Other suggestions include the
Aramaic אֲרִים.

[82] For an imaginative but perhaps not totally convincing reconstruction of the
whole process see J. Blank, *Krisis*, pp. 80–90.

[83] How far such an inference is correct will be discussed in Ch. 13, § 2 ('Death').

to myself' (v. 32). To which the response of the crowd is: 'We have heard from the law that the Messiah remains [*or* will abide][84] for ever. How can you say that the Son of Man must be lifted up? Who is this Son of Man?' The nearest mention of 'Son of Man' is in 12: 23, where Jesus states that 'The hour has come for the Son of Man to be glorified.' Bultmann solves the difficulty by making 12: 34 follow immediately upon 8: 28.[85] Others make it follow upon 3: 14. That the present passage does rely upon the reader's memory of one or both of the two earlier predictions is, I think, clear. (It is one of the factors that justify their being considered together.) But reorganization of the text raises as many puzzles as it solves.[86]

Once alerted to the evangelist's wish to expand the messianic faith of the community's beginnings into the fuller, richer, faith implied in the title 'Son of Man', we can see without difficulty that this is part of his intention here. Not surprisingly, the reference to the 'law' has sent the commentators scurrying to their Bibles in search of the passage to which the 'crowd' is alluding in v. 34. But to concentrate on this rather than upon the words of Jesus himself is to perpetuate this error. Indeed, on the lips of the crowd the Law is deprived of its usual authority: in so far as it detracts attention away from the true revelation, such study is not to be applauded but deplored.

The other saying (8: 28) is possibly the most succinct as well as the most enigmatic christological affirmation in the whole Gospel:

When you have lifted up ($\H{o}\tau\alpha\nu$ $\upsilon\psi\acute{\omega}\sigma\eta\tau\epsilon$) the Son of Man, then you will know that I am [he] ($\H{o}\tau\iota$ $\epsilon\gamma\acute{\omega}$ $\epsilon\H{\iota}\mu\iota$). (8: 28)

As Bultmann remarks, the Jews

do not suspect that by 'lifting him up' they themselves make him their judge. The double-meaning of 'lifting up' is obvious. They lift up Jesus by crucifying him; but it is precisely through his crucifixion that he is lifted up to his heavenly glory as the Son of Man. At the very moment when they think they are passing judgement on him, he becomes their judge.[87]

This is surely right. Bultmann also remarks, however, concerning the ambiguity of the saying 'then you will know $\H{o}\tau\iota$ $\epsilon\gamma\acute{\omega}$ $\epsilon\H{\iota}\mu\iota$' that 'it

---

[84] The unaccented Greek of the earliest manuscripts does not distinguish between the present ($\mu\epsilon\nu\epsilon\iota$) and the future tense ($\mu\epsilon\nu\epsilon\hat{\iota}$) of this verb.

[85] pp. 349, 354.

[86] G. H. C. MacGregor, 'A Suggested Rearrangement'; J. G. Gourbillon, 'La parabole du serpent d'airain'. The best solution, in my view, is to see 12: 24–6 as a later gloss. [87] p. 350.

clearly refers back to the unqualified ἐγώ εἰμι in v. 24, while at the same time one must add to the main clause the subordinate clause, "that I am the son of Man". Thus everything that he is can be referred to by the mysterious title "Son of Man"'.[88] But is this enough? Recognized and acknowledged as Son of Man at the moment of exaltation, Jesus also lays claim to an even more prestigious title, the one associated exclusively with Yahweh, the national God of Israel. The irony is profound, for neither at the story level nor at the deeper, spiritual level will Jesus' hearers, the Jews, ever understand who he really is. Later in the same acrimonious debate (8: 56–9) they do come to grasp the full import of the ἐγώ εἰμι. But then, as we have seen (Chapter 4), their response is one of violent rejection.

Of the other instances of 'Son of Man' those in chapter 6 should be understood in the light of what was said about the ascending and descending Son of Man in 3: 13. The two remaining passages (12: 23; 13: 31) do not affect our present discussion and can safely be held over until Chapter 13.

CONCLUSION

Having given some consideration to most of the passages in the Gospel where the term 'Son of Man' occurs, we may turn to the question how far the Johannine conception of the Son of Man can reasonably be thought to have been derived from the Synoptic Gospels. That it goes beyond them in many respects needs no labouring.

Bultmann broaches his solution of the problem of the 'Son of Man' sayings by dividing them into three groups, 'which speak of the Son of Man (1) as coming, (2) as suffering death and rising again, and (3) as now at work. This third group', he says, 'owes its origin to a mere misunderstanding of the translation into Greek. In Aramaic, the son of man in these sayings was not a messianic title at all, but meant "man" or "I". So this group drops out of the present discussion.'[89] This leaves us with the other two groups. Bultmann himself rejected the second group, i.e. those concerning the passion and resurrection,

---

[88] p. 349.
[89] *Theology*, i. 30. With the substitution of the indefinite 'one' for Bultmann's 'I' this may be allowed to stand.

as *vaticinia ex eventu*, and other scholars, in increasing numbers, have denied the authenticity of the first group as well.

What concerns us here is not the very thorny question of the authenticity of the sayings, but the question how the term 'Son of Man' came to be associated with Jesus' passion and resurrection, especially the passion. Here there are two complementary explanations, both of which have a certain appeal. The first is that of Morna Hooker, in her book *The Son of Man in Mark*. Although, she says, the Son of Man in Daniel 7 is predominantly a triumphant figure, a closer exegesis of this text reveals that

the Son of man can—and will—suffer when his rightful position and God's authority are denied: this is the situation in Dan. 7, where the 'beasts' have revolted against God and crushed Israel who, as Son of man, should be ruling the earth with the authority granted by God. Given the situation of the nations' revolt and their rejection of the claims of the one who is intended to exercise authority, it is true to say that the Son of man not only can but must suffer.[90]

The second important contribution comes from John Bowker, in his remarkable book, *The Religious Imagination and the Sense of God*.[91] Bowker agrees that 'the suffering and the vindication are *already* linked in Daniel', and adds that 'It is not in the least improbable that Jesus himself could have made the association as a means of expressing his understanding of his own situation and his trust in the Father.'[92] Then he goes on to point out that, starting from the association of the term with the death-penalty imposed by God on the human race in Gen. 3: 19, many Jewish interpreters of the Bible, up to and including the medieval targumists,

use the phrase 'son of man' so consistently with the association of 'man subject to death', 'man born to die', that they make it clear that to recognize the sense of the phrase, established in the original biblical contexts, is not idiosyncratic. It is clear that the Targum translators recognized that the nuance associated with the phrase 'son of man' in the majority of biblical contexts is 'man born to die', and they therefore used that phrase to translate 'man' in other contexts where man's subjection to death is referred to.[93]

[90] *The Son of Man in Mark* (London, 1967).
[91] pp. 139–69. This chapter is built upon Bowker's article, '"The Son of Man"'.
[92] p. 146. Hooker reaches the same conclusion, but more hesitatingly.
[93] p. 150. It is interesting in this connection that the first known occurrence of the term בר אנש in Aramaic, in an 8th-century inscription from Sefire, concerns human mortality: מה זי מות בר אנש = 'when [*or* in whatever way] someone dies'. The

[*cont. on p. 370*]

There is a nice paradox here, because the 'one like a son of man' in Daniel 7 was anything but a mortal: however hard his struggle to dominate the beasts, it would not result in his death. But in the Synoptic picture, it is fair to say, both elements are included; and they are included, if this interpretation is right, within the passion predictions themselves, where the hope of resurrection must be seen as vindication and ultimate triumph.

In my view it is not easy to establish that Daniel's vision did actually influence not only the 'future' sayings of the Synoptic Gospels but the passion sayings as well. It may be that Bultmann's triple division prejudges the issue by failing to recognize that two at least of the passion sayings occur in contexts in which future sayings are close at hand. So Mark 8: 31 is followed shortly by 8: 38; and hard on the heels of Mark 10: 34 comes the request of the sons of Zebedee 'to sit, one at your right hand, and one at your left, in your glory' (10: 37). However that may be, it is of the essence of an apocalyptic vision to transcribe into celestial symbols a series of events that really belong to human history. Consequently, once Jesus has been identified with the heavenly figure of the Son of Man (as he was without question by the early Church), the way is open to see the events of his life as the fulfilment of those recorded in Daniel's vision: the struggle against the forces of evil that takes place in heaven can be read as Jesus' struggle with those same forces in the course of his passion.

J. L. Martyn, as we have seen, regards apocalyptic as a two-level drama taking place on the heavenly stage and on the earthly stage. God, directing the action of both from behind the scenes, ensures that the same story is enacted on both stages at the same time. Or rather, not quite at the same time, for

events on the heavenly stage not only correspond to events on the earthly stage but also slightly precede them in time, leading them into existence, so to speak. What transpires on the heavenly stage is often called 'things to come'. For that reason events seen on the earthly stage are entirely enigmatic to one who sees only the earthly stage. Stereoptic vision is necessary, and it is precisely stereoptic vision which causes a man to write an apocalypse:

general term here resumes a whole series of people who could conceivably suffer death at the hands of the signatory of the treaty, namely the author himself or members of his family or household. See Gibson, *Textbook of Syrian Semitic Inscriptions*, ii, no. 9. l. 16.

After this I looked, and lo in heaven an *open door*! And the first voice which I had heard ... said, Come hither, and I will show you what must take place after this. (Rev. 4: 1)[94]

But the destiny of Jesus is the reverse of an apocalypse: the unfolding of a divine plan, necessarily originating in heaven, is transcribed in the Gospels in terms of a human life. What Jesus is about to do and to suffer is the revelation of a history that belongs in the first place to God's plan for mankind, fixed mysteriously from all eternity by divine decree and revealed to men for the first time in a totally unexpected way. The nature of this decree, which is exhibited—set forth—in Jesus' life, can be seen by combining the double series of 'Son of man' sayings—those concerning his heavenly destiny, on the one hand, where there is a manifest reluctance on Jesus' part to identify himself too soon or too directly with the celestial judge, and those concerning his earthly destiny, on the other. Whether the Synoptists themselves made this inference does not matter here. What is important is that it is open to their readers and to any who inherited the same tradition to see the concluding events of Jesus' life as the fulfilment on earth of a heavenly battle whose outcome had been foretold long before. Moreover such a fulfilment was necessary, even inevitable, if Jesus was eventually to take on the other role assigned to him of victor and judge.

The tension between the two groups of 'Son of Man' sayings is never fully resolved in the Synoptic Gospels. We can conclude that even if Jesus whilst on earth saw himself as in some sense playing out the same history of triumph through suffering (which is a possible reading of the evidence) he never explicitly identified himself with the heavenly Son of Man. But in the Fourth Gospel, although the paradox is heightened the tension has gone. The mysterious personage who is to be the universal judge at the end of time is now actually on earth; his triumph is no longer reserved for a distant future, it takes place in the here-and-now, or at least is awaited as the immediate and inevitable sequel of an imminent death. Moreover, the sufferings and death are no longer seen as a passage to glory (as they are by Luke and in a more profound way by Paul). The identification between Jesus and the eschatological victor of Daniel 7 is complete. This (and more) is explicitly affirmed in chapter 5: 'And he [God] has given him authority to execute judgement because he is

---

[94] *History*, p. 136. See too 1QS 11: 20–2.

the Son of Man' (5: 27). Which is why J. L. Martyn can say that 'in some respects John 5: 27 appears to be the most "traditional" Son of man saying in the whole of the New Testament'.[95] This identification has various consequences and is expressed in various ways.

In the first place, the Son of Man, according to John, actually walks on earth. His true home is in heaven (still), where Daniel placed him; and so John sees him as having come down, descended, from on high. In other words, the process whereby the role of the Son of Man is drawn back from the futuristic apocalyptic is now carried a stage further. In the Synoptic Gospels there was at most a proleptic identification between Jesus and the heavenly Son of Man, an anticipation of a title which would one day belong to Jesus by right, an identity-in-difference. But in the Fourth Gospel the identification is total and immediate. As long as the Son of Man remained shadowy and insubstantial, his home in the clouds where his triumph would one day be revealed, there was no need to ask questions concerning his origin. For he had as yet no real existence: he was simply a vivid symbol in an apocalyptic dream. At some point, of course, either when the literal Greek translation was misread, or when the suffering-Son of Man sayings were introduced into the Gospel narrative, or when the current tendency to equate the Son of Man with the Messiah had made itself felt in Christian circles—at some point the title was bestowed on the person of Jesus. Just conceivably he may have claimed the title himself. But as long as he was remembered as a real human being the theological implications remained hidden; and there was evidently no temptation to put questions concerning a possible pre-existence: after all, 'Is not this the son of Joseph?', as the people of Nazareth asked when he turned up in the synagogue (Luke 4: 22). Even in the Fourth Gospel the crowd could still ask, 'Is not this Jesus, the son of Joseph, whose father and mother we know?' (John 6: 42.) But by the time these words were written the memory of Jesus as a man, an individual human being, had begun to fade and his distinctive profile to be lost sight of behind the mask of the Son of Man. As long as this was only a *persona* in the classical sense, a mask donned by an actor playing his part, a *role*, then the protagonist of the Gospels could retain his human face: the first act of the drama had been played, the second was still to come. But at some point the actor was identified with the

[95] *History and Theology*[2], p. 139.

mask he wore, the *persona* came to be thought of as a person, the role became a name. And then there is a riddle: 'Is not this Jesus, the son of Joseph, whose father and mother we know? How does he now say, "I have come down from heaven?"' (John 6: 42.) Nor are we surprised to see the question formulated even more sharply: 'Who is this Son of Man?' (John 12: 34.)

In this 'who' is concealed as 'whence', and the 'whence' is effectively a question concerning pre-existence. For in the Synoptic tradition Jesus was seen as a man whose death was followed by resurrection and exaltation at God's right hand, where he would appear on the clouds at the end of time as the divinely appointed judge. But now he is seen as one who had come down to earth from heaven; he would carry out his role as judge while on earth and then return to heaven. John gives no answer to the question *how* Jesus came or how he finally departed. The language of ascent and descent may not be intended to be taken literally: one function of the little midrash in which the Son of Man is introduced, in 1: 51, is to discourage the reader from an over-literal interpretation. But by speaking of descent as well as the traditional ascent (or ascension), John is consciously making an opening for questions concerning Jesus' previous abode, and therefore his previous existence.

Excursus IV: The Structure of John 3

The sequence of thought in John 3 is notoriously hard to follow, and various ways of rearranging the text have been advocated by different scholars. Any understanding of the text must depend upon how one envisages its construction. Before trying to eliminate the aporias it is best to explain how they arose.

The episode really begins with the last 3 verses of chapter 2 (vv. 23–5), which prepare the way for the entry of Nicodemus in chapter 3. The remainder of the material may be divided up into three blocks: 1–21; 22–30; 31–6.

(*a*) 1–21. Most of the difficulties belong to this section, and there is no agreement about where the natural break or breaks, if there are any, should be located. The first eight verses follow on without interruption, and the concluding verses, 16–21, seem to fit together. But what of what lies between? Breaks have been suggested after vv. 8, 9, 10, 12, and 13!

(*b*) 22–30. This section, in which John the Baptist, for once, is given some prominence (if only in a self-deprecating way), is clearly marked out.

(*c*) 31–6. The conclusion is also clearly delineated, and although some scholars ascribe this paragraph to John the Baptist (on the grounds that there is no explicit indication of a change of speaker),[1] most would nowadays assign it either to Jesus or (the vast majority) to the evangelist.

It is easy to see the resemblances between (*c*) and what we may provisionally term the central section of (*a*), vv. 11–15:

—ὁ ὢν ἐκ τῆς γῆς ἐκ τῆς γῆς ἐστιν καὶ ἐκ τῆς γῆς λαλεῖ (31b). This clearly refers back to τὰ ἐπίγεια of v. 12; similarly the next phrase ὁ ἐκ τοῦ οὐρανοῦ ἐρχόμενος ὃ ἑώρακεν καὶ ἤκουσεν τοῦτο μαρτυρεῖ (31c, 32a), points back to τὰ ἐπουράνια in the same verse, whilst the whole section echoes the assertion of v. 11: ὃ οἴδαμεν λαλοῦμεν καὶ ὃ ἑωράκαμεν μαρτυροῦμεν. There are also echoes of vv. 6 and 13b.
—The negative conclusion of v. 32, καὶ τὴν μαρτυρίαν αὐτοῦ οὐδεὶς

---

[1] Most recently David Rensberger, *Overcoming the World*, pp. 52–7. This is one of the least convincing elements in his stimulating exegesis of this chapter.

λαμβάνει, harks back to the ending of v. 11: καὶ τὴν μαρτυρίαν ἡμῶν οὐ λαμβάνετε.

Certain elements of vv. 16–21 also find an echo in the concluding paragraph of the chapter: the notion of the Father's love for the Son (vv. 16 and 35), of mission (vv. 17 and 34), belief (vv. 15 f. and 36), and finally of disbelief (vv. 18 and 36). Thus the end of chapter 3 (*c*) looks like a commentary, part explanation, part justification, of the doctrine contained in the earlier sections.

This does not mean that (*c*) is to be regarded either as preceding v. 13 (so Schnackenburg) or as following on from v. 21 (so Bultmann); for in that case why should an evidently extraneous paragraph (vv. 22–30) have been inserted to interrupt such a natural sequence? Rejecting such solutions, Meeks remarks that 'such rearrangements result from the failure to perceive one of the most striking characteristics of the evangelist's literary procedure: the elucidation of themes by progressive repetition'. But this does not constitute a complete explanation, as Meeks is aware, for he continues: 'in part this procedure was probably forced upon the author by the nature of the traditional material he was using, which had evidently produced, within the Johannine community, a number of stylized didactic units, in the form of the 'revelation discourse' on overlapping themes. Alternative formulations produced by the community did not always perfectly coincide. The variant formulations could be simply juxtaposed ... but characteristically the variants are interspersed with narrative episodes or other kinds of material, with correctives and restatements by the evangelist.'[2] (These passages, along with other variants on the same theme, will be discussed in Chapter 14.)

Meeks has seen more clearly than the commentators how this procedure works, but even he does not allow for the probability that the composition of the present text was a gradual process. The end of chapter 3 (*c*) will have been added after an early form of the Nicodemus episode (*a*), originally regarded as complete, had already been continued by the Baptist episode (*b*). Having this text (vv. 1–30) in front of him, the evangelist (or, less probably, redactor) will have seen how appropriately the Baptist's self-deprecatory remarks could be followed by a paragraph beginning with an assertion that Jesus, being from above, ἄνωθεν, is also above all, ἐπάνω πάντων.

---

[2] 'Man from Heaven', p. 150.

More important, however, than the link between v. 30 and v. 31, is the way in which the phrase ὁ ἄνωθεν ἐρχόμενος (v. 31) is used to interpret the earlier saying of Jesus, ἐὰν μή τις γεννηθῇ ἄνωθεν (v. 3). The evangelist now understands Jesus' dialogue with Nicodemus to have been primarily concerned with his own heavenly origins. (I have further observations to make on the relation between these two passages in Chapter 14.)

This brings us to (a), vv. 1–15, the most complex part of our analysis. Here we may begin by distinguishing the two 'Son of Man' sayings: v. 13 and vv. 14 f. I have already argued that v. 13 was skimmed from the surface of a polemical debate (directed against counter-claims being made on behalf of Moses) before being appended, as it is now, to the dialogue with Nicodemus. The following saying is an entirely different matter; although it now serves to link the dialogue with the short but dense revelatory discourse in vv. 16–21, it probably originated as an adaptation of a Synoptic-type passion prediction. I have already commented extensively on both these sayings.

The dialogue with Nicodemus continues at least as far as v. 10. In v. 11, however, it takes another turn. After speaking to Nicodemus as before, in the singular, σοι, Jesus himself adopts the plural form, οἴδαμεν etc., and continues with the general charge that 'τὴν μαρτυρίαν ἡμῶν οὐ λαμβάνετε'. What up to this point was a private conversation with Nicodemus has now become a public address. We saw that in the concluding verses of chapter 1 there is a similar shift from singular to plural; but in that scene there was already an audience of interested onlookers to whom Jesus could turn. Meeks has provided extensive documentation of the provenance of the wisdom-type saying in v. 12.[3] V. 11, then, marked out as a new and important assertion by the introductory ἀμὴν ἀμήν, is yet another linking verse. The plural ('we speak of what we know') is easy to understand if this saying was drawn from the same polemical context as that in v. 12, where the speaker, as Bultmann suggests, 'was speaking as one of the group of messengers from God'.[4] (The earlier οἴδαμεν of Nicodemus, in v. 2, is more easily explained as a simple gnomic plural.)[5]

---

[3] 'Man from Heaven', p. 148 and nn. 36 and 37.
[4] Cf. Bultmann, p. 134 n. 3.
[5] See the discussion of riddle in Ch. 5; also Leroy, *Rätsel*, p. 136. Rensberger, *Overcoming*, ch. 3, offers a generally persuasive interpretation of the social implications of the Nicodemus episode.

The commencement of the dialogue, vv. 1–10, need not detain us here. Its *Sitz-im-Leben* is not controversy but catechetics, and its purpose will have been to further the consciousness of the Johannine group's sense of superiority to the Jewish establishment within the synagogue. Bultmann suggests that in the phrase 'to see the kingdom of God' (v. 3) the ἰδεῖν reproduces an idiomatic use of ראה ('experience', 'come to know') referring to participation in salvation.[6] In my view the best explanation of the controversial v. 5, attributed by Bultmann to the ecclesiastical redactor, is that of Becker, who suggests that it comes from the same source as v. 3, where the two verses were variants of the same tradition.[7] The evangelist has no problem with the sacramental flavour of v. 5, but it is not what prompts him to pick up the saying, and he exploits it for his own ends.

[6] p. 135 n. 2.   [7] p. 134.

PART III

REVELATION

INTRODUCTION

In the preceding six chapters ('Genesis') we have been searching for an answer to Bultmann's first great puzzle or riddle: what is the place of the Fourth Gospel in the history or development of Christian thought? We have seen that to answer this question it is necessary to devote some attention to contemporary *Jewish* thought, for it is here that the origins of the Gospel are to be found. This first puzzle, although it cannot be solved without careful consideration of the Gospel's major themes, is primarily *historical*: it requires us to survey the background of the Johannine group and to take some cognizance of sectarian movements within the larger Jewish community.

In the remaining chapters ('Revelation') we shall be concentrating primarily upon the answer to Bultmann's second great puzzle. This is not historical but *exegetical*: what is the Gospel's dominating motif or *Grundkonzeption*? The solution to this puzzle, unequivocally and quite straightforwardly, is *revelation*. The modalities of this answer are no doubt both intricate and profound, and to appreciate them fully we must bear in mind the source of the evangelist's main ideas. The object of our enquiry has shifted, formally speaking, from history to exegesis, in so far as we are now asking what is the meaning of the Gospel rather than how it is to be explained. The two questions, though distinguishable, are not entirely separable; it will be necessary to return from time to time to the problem of origins.

One must also retain some awareness of the fact, as I believe it to be, that the Gospel did not emerge fully formed into the world like Athene from the head of Zeus: it grew, it had a history. In what follows I shall be primarily concerned with the Gospel in the form that it has come down to us. Although, for example, the Prologue was composed before being taken over and adapted to form the opening of the Gospel, I shall not hesitate to use it in the concluding chapter to illustrate the evangelist's theology of revelation. Similarly, though inclined to accept Lindars's suggestion that chapter 11 belongs to the second edition of the Gospel and not to the first, I hold it to be the work of John and fully representative of his thinking. About chapters 15–17 I have more doubts, but there is no overpowering reason for ascribing them to another hand. (The only major exception is chapter 21: like most commentators I continue to think of this as an appendix, not written by the evangelist and not added by him to the body of the Gospel.) Broadly speaking, then, an exegete is entitled to take the text in its entirety. Certain caveats, however, are in order. There is no virtue in the kind of pure and unsullied exegesis sponsored by those who used to be known as the New Critics, too high-minded to look outside and behind the text for alternative sources of illumination. In the first place, we cannot exclude a priori the possibility that some passages may not be fully intelligible without a knowledge of their history; from time to time it may be necessary to supplement the broad synchronic approach favoured by many exegetes with rigorous diachronic analysis.

Secondly, the message of the Gospel is conditioned by the environment in which it was composed. It reflects, that is to say, the circumstances of the people for whom it was written and of the Johannine prophet who wrote it. The particular focus given to the uncompromising dualism which makes the Fourth Gospel so different from the other three is best accounted for by the bitterness and fear with which the members of the Johannine group regarded their Jewish neighbours. This means that the direction taken by the evangelist's thought was determined by his experience and that of his community.

INTIMATIONS OF APOCALYPTIC

INTRODUCTION

The word 'apocalyptic' is derived directly from the title of the last book of the Christian Bible:[1] the Greek word for revelation is ἀποκάλυψις, and the Book of Revelation is still referred to in some Christian circles as The Apocalypse. Now since the overriding theme of the Fourth Gospel is, put very succinctly, the revelation of God in Jesus and the way in which it was and should be received, we might conclude directly that a study of Jewish apocalyptic is likely to furnish a useful starting-point. That such a study is helpful and indeed illuminating will be the main contention of this chapter. But it is not straightforwardly so. According to tradition the Book of Revelation shares a common author with the Fourth Gospel: the apostle John; but in language, form, style, and content the two works are utterly different. Furthermore, whereas each of the other three Gospels contains a so-called apocalyptic discourse spoken by Jesus towards the end of his ministry (Matt. 24; Mark 13; Luke 21: 5–36), there is nothing remotely resembling such a discourse in John. The Fourth Gospel has only a few traces of the expectation of an early parousia that is regarded by many as the characteristically Christian form of eschatological hope.

It comes as no surprise, then, to find that in his well-known essay 'The Beginnings of Christian Theology', in which he put forward the controversial thesis that apocalyptic was the mother of all Christian theology, Ernst Käsemann alludes only in passing to the Fourth Gospel. Nevertheless the links are many, various, and important. If they have been neglected in the past, this is largely because until

---

[1] See Morton Smith, *'ΑΠΟΚΑΛΥΠΤΩ and ΑΠΟΚΑΛΥΨΙΣ'*. Smith warns that 'pseudepigraphical apocalypses of the last centuries B.C. and the first A.D. which are commonly listed as evidence of the "apocalyptic movement" owe their apocalyptic titles either to patristic references, or to late MSS, or to modern scholars—and none of these sources is reliable' (p. 19).

relatively recently scholarly interest in apocalyptic was focused exclusively upon the futuristic eschatology often found in apocalyptic writing. Käsemann himself, challenged by Gerhard Ebeling to define what he meant by 'apocalyptic', stated quite bluntly: 'It emerges from the context that almost throughout I speak of primitive Christian apocalyptic to denote the expectation of an imminent Parousia.'[2] Thus Käsemann uses the term 'apocalyptic' in roughly the same way that I used 'eschatology' in Chapter 6. The source of the confusion is not hard to spot. In ordinary speech 'apocalyptic' generally refers to bizarre or paranormal phenomena, heralding some dreadful cataclysm or associated with the kind of nightmarish imagery frequently found in apocalyptic literature. Modern scholarship has objected to the confusion mostly because genuine apocalyptic writing contains much more than eschatology.[3] (I avoided the word in Chapter 6 so as not to lay myself open to the same charge.)

The business of defining the genre of apocalyptic is enormously complex,[4] but for the sake of clarity some definition must be offered. To clear the ground and pave the way for this, I shall first offer some criticisms of an alternative definition by John J. Collins, one of the most highly respected scholars working in this field. 'An apocalypse', he writes,

is defined as a genre of revelatory literature with a narrative framework, in which a revelation is mediated by an otherworldly being to a human recipient, disclosing a transcendent reality which is both temporal, insofar

---

[2] 'On the Subject', p. 109 n. 1.

[3] On this see especially Christopher Rowland, *Open Heaven*, p. 23 ff.

[4] Klaus Koch entitled a preliminary survey of the question *Ratlos vor dem Apokalyptik* (Gütersloh, 1970), a title that evokes the image of someone staring at the whole scene with an expression of baffled bemusement. A few years later James Barr used Koch's work as a starting-point in another, briefer survey: 'Jewish Apocalyptic'. Barr, who favours a kind of Wittgensteinian, family-resemblance approach to the problem, commented that 'the situation is not substantially more difficult than with other definitions of genres and literary forms' (p. 19). His optimism appears to have been misplaced, for a few years later (1979) a group of scholars meeting in Uppsala to discuss the general question of 'apocalypticism' were clearly preoccupied, and understandably so, with stalking this ungainly but elusive beast and tethering it down for closer inspection. The big book that ensued (*Apocalypticism*, 1983) certainly advances the discussion but also evinces a fair measure of disagreement among the dozen or so contributors who were concerned with specifically Jewish apocalyptic. The beast is still at large, and variously described. Among the more recent surveys, that of Michael Knibb, 'Prophecy and the emergence of the Jewish apocalypses', is especially helpful.

as it envisages eschatological salvation, and spatial insofar as it involves another supernatural world.[5]

Although there is no better definition than this available, it is open to several objections:

1. The word 'transcendent' is misleading: it is true that apocalyptic revelations are concerned with 'the eternal secrets which were made in heaven' (*1 Enoch* 9: 6), but these often have to do with astronomy or meteorology and even with such things as jewellery and metalwork and 'the art of making up the eyes and of beautifying the eyelids' (*1 Enoch* 8: 1).[6]

2. Eschatology, though it figures frequently enough, is not a constant or a necessary feature of apocalyptic writing.

3. Prophets too were regarded in early times as messengers from heaven, and their revelations frequently concerned what Collins calls 'eschatological salvation'. Anyone anxious to protect the rather wavy line separating prophecy and apocalyptic[7] must establish some kind of 'exclusion zone'.

4. Nothing is said about the milieu of apocalyptic writing. This is certainly a difficulty, because we know so little of the social and political circumstances in which Jewish apocalyptic arose. What we do know almost always has to be inferred from the writings themselves. The problem is complicated by the fact that some apocalypses, e.g. *1 Enoch* and *Jubilees*, are clearly sectarian works, whereas others, such as *2 Baruch* and of course Daniel, seem to be quite in accord with the religious establishment of the day. We cannot therefore simply label them 'sectarian' or 'conventicle' writings and leave the matter there. *The Epistle of Enoch* (*1 Enoch* 91–108) and *2 Enoch* point to social rather than religious unrest. Yet some specific reference is required if our definition is not to remain uncomfortably loose. Otherwise it would be as if we had to make do with a general description of tragedy that included no reference to the wide differences between Greek, Shakespearian, and French Classical tragedy.

5. As it stands, the definition is too broad: it would include works such as Book Six of the *Aeneid* (as Collins himself admits), Dante's

---

[5] *Apocalyptic Imagination*, p. 4.

[6] On this point see the important study of M. E. Stone, 'Lists of Revealed Things'.

[7] Some may prefer to follow John Barton in blurring the lines. See *Oracles of God*, pp. 9–10; 199–201.

Commedia, and even, provided 'eschatological' is taken in a broad Bultmannian sense, the Fourth Gospel!

From our point of view the last of these objections is of particular interest. Why is it that, although the Fourth Gospel fits Collins' definition so snugly, it is obviously *not* an apocalypse? One answer might be in terms of the shift from the futuristic eschatological hope that is such a notable feature of much apocalyptic writing to the characteristically Johannine understanding of eternal life. By insisting on this difference we would be able to maintain that the Fourth Gospel did not fit Collins' definition after all. But this is not a totally satisfactory answer. We might also wish to say something about the nature of the *imagery* employed, with its crazy, inconsequential, dream-like logic (a feature of apocalyptic which Collins, despite the title of his book, virtually ignores). By this means we should be able to exclude Vergil and Dante, as well as John, from the definition. (Though by the same token it might be necessary to retain William Blake, most of whose Prophetic Books have a genuinely apocalyptic ring and may have been indirectly influenced by Jewish apocalyptic.)

6. Any complete definition must include some reference to the *mode* of apocalyptic revelations: they are invariably bestowed either in a vision or a dream (which then has to be interpreted) or else in a state of ecstasy or rapture—using both these words in the sense in which they are employed in Christian mystical writing. In John 3: 13, as we saw in the last chapter, there is a vestige of an old belief that heavenly secrets were imparted to Jesus after he had ascended into heaven in the manner of an apocalyptic visionary. But the prevailing view of Jesus in the Fourth Gospel is that he himself was the other-worldly visitant, sent to reveal the truth to mankind.

In place of Collins' definition, therefore, I propose the following:

An apocalypse is a narrative, composed in circumstances of political, religious, or social unrest, in the course of which an angelic being discloses heavenly mysteries, otherwise hidden, to a human seer, either indirectly, by interpreting a dream or vision, or directly, in which case the seer may believe that he has been transported to heaven in order to receive a special revelation.

Although according to this revised definition the Fourth Gospel is decidedly *not* an apocalypse, it too is a narrative within which heavenly mysteries are revealed by a messenger sent from heaven. My purpose in this chapter is to map out as best I can the resemblances as well as the differences. I shall be arguing that the Fourth Gospel is profoundly indebted to apocalyptic in all sorts of ways; and I wish to single out four features for closer study. Put schematically, two of these are temporal: two ages (mystery) and two stages (dream or vision); the other two are spatial: insiders/outsiders (riddle) and above/below (correspondence). This grouping is neither hard nor fast; on the contrary, the four features overlap in a way that occasionally confounds analysis. The two stages sometimes merge into two ages and the dream or the vision may function as a riddle. My intention in drawing up these categories is to facilitate understanding: they are not to be regarded either as a model or blueprint or as an armature around which an ideal apocalypse may be constructed. I begin by taking a closer look at a motif which the Fourth Gospel shares with all apocalyptic. We shall see later that the concept of mystery is at the heart of the Gospel genre.

I. MYSTERY: THE TWO AGES

In Chapter 6 it was argued that although John's Gospel is by far the most uninhibitedly dualistic of the four, its dualism falls well short of the metaphysical oppositions of Gnosticism. Some of the writings to which it is affiliated, such as the War Scroll at Qumran, are eschatological in the proper sense, but not apocalyptic, because there is no hint of any heavenly intermediary. But other documents belonging to the Qumran Library (and therefore read, presumably, by at least some members of the community) are full-fledged apocalypses. Four of these have been known since the beginning of the nineteenth century, gathered together, along with one other that was not found at Qumran, and known collectively as *1 Enoch*.[8] An important theme common to these and also to the writings of the sect itself is that of *mystery*: the word רז, also used extensively in the Book of Daniel, occurs dozens of times in the Scrolls, nor is its use confined to any one particular *kind* of writing: it is found in the Community Rule, the War Scroll, the Thanksgiving Hymns, the Habakkuk pesher, and other smaller fragments as well. The idea of a mystery, a secret once hidden and now revealed, is the essence of

---

[8] Or *Ethiopic Enoch*, to distinguish it from *2 (Slavonic)* and *3 (Hebrew) Enoch*. The extensive fragments of these four 'books', all in Aramaic, have been assembled and edited by J. T. Milik: *The Books of Enoch*.

apocalyptic. It is here rather than in eschatology that the true
affinity of Christianity with apocalyptic is to be sought, for the
Christian revelation resembles the revelations communicated to
apocalyptic visionaries in having been previously concealed and
being divulged now for the first time. This is what I mean by two
ages: the age of concealment and the age of disclosure.

This important idea is nowhere more clearly expressed than in the
concluding doxology to Romans: 'Now to him who is able to
strengthen you according to my gospel and the preaching of Jesus
Christ, according to the revelation of the mystery which was kept
secret for long ages (κατὰ ἀποκάλυψιν μυστηρίου χρόνοις αἰωνίοις
σεσιγημένου) but has been disclosed and through the prophetic
writings made known to all nations, according to the command of
the eternal God, to bring about the obedience of faith (φανερωθέντος δὲ
νῦν διὰ γραφῶν προφητικῶν κατ᾽ ἐπιταγὴν τοῦ αἰωνίου θεοῦ ... εἰς πάντα
τὰ ἔθνη γνωρισθέντος)' (Rom. 16: 25 f.; cf 1 Cor. 2: 6–9; Col. 1: 26;
Eph. 3: 4–5, 9). Since knowledge of the mystery is transmitted
through the writings of the prophets—the scriptures—it must have
been somehow contained in these beforehand.

Precisely the same idea is found at Qumran, in a passage from the
Habakkuk pesher elucidating an instruction to the prophet to
transcribe one of his visions (Hab. 2: 2): 'and God told Habakkuk to
write down that which would happen to the final generation, but he
did not make known to him when time would come to an end. And
as for that which he said, *That he who reads may read it speedily*,
interpreted, this concerns the Teacher of Righteousness, to whom
God made known all the mysteries (רזים) of the words of his
servants the prophets' (1QpHab 7: 1–5; cf. CD 1: 11–13; 1QH
9: 24). The position of the Teacher of Righteousness within the
community may not be entirely clear, but the passage makes it plain
that his insight into the old prophecy is one which even its author,
acting as little more than a scribe, did not share. And it is not just
Habakkuk, but the whole prophetic corpus whose mysteries are
revealed, or so the passage appears to imply, for the first time.

This concept originated in apocalyptic. It stands in stark contrast
to what may be called the 'establishment' view of the prophets.
According to this they fully understood their own message. Ben Sira,
for instance, says of Isaiah that he 'revealed what was to occur to the
end of time and the hidden things (τὰ ἀπόκρυφα) before they came to
pass' (Sir. 48: 25). One way in which apocalyptic makes a case for a

very different view is by use of the ingenious device of pseudonymity. It has this device in common with many other writings of the Second Temple period (e.g. the Wisdom of Solomon, the Book of Baruch, the Prayer of Manasseh). In every case it serves to give the writing in question authority and credibility, but a number of the most important apocalypses also use it to emphasize the time that has elapsed between the composition of the work and the recognition of its significance. The prophet or seer was the recipient of certain revelations, but these, it is stressed, were primarily intended for people living in another age, still a long way off at the time that the revelations were first given.

What is probably the oldest of these, *1 Enoch*, opens awkwardly, shifting from the third person to the first in the same sentence: 'And Enoch answered and said: "There was a righteous man whose eyes were opened by the Lord, and he saw a holy vision in the heavens which the angels showed to me. And I heard everything from them, and I understood what I saw, but not for this generation but for a distant generation which will come"' (*1 Enoch* 1: 2). This passage could well have inspired the Teacher of Righteousness to make his own bold claims about the true meaning of Habakkuk and Nahum.

Similar is the explanation of the vision of the ram and the goat given to Daniel by the angel Gabriel: 'The vision of the evenings and the mornings which has been told is true; but seal up the vision, for it pertains to many days hence' (Dan. 8: 26; cf. 8: 17; 12: 4; *4 Ezra* 12: 37 f.; 14: 5 f., 45 ff.; *2 Enoch* 33: 9 f.; 35: 3). Towards the end of the book Daniel is given his valedictory: 'Go your way, Daniel, for the words are shut up and sealed until the time of the end ... None of the wicked shall understand; but those who are wise shall under-stand.' (This introduces a further distinction, which we shall come to in due course.) The understanding of the wise, however, is not in Daniel's own present: it must bide its time, that is *now*, 'the time of the end', when the seal of the book has been broken (12: 4) and the wise are perusing its contents.

4 Ezra, drawing upon the same tradition some two centuries later, towards the end of the first century AD, takes it a step further. This seer is informed that Moses had been instructed to divulge only a part of what had been revealed to him: 'These words you shall publish openly and these you shall keep secret'; Ezra is told to gather a number of trained scribes and spend forty days dictating his revelations. This done, God orders him: 'Make public the twenty-four books that you wrote first and let the worthy and the unworthy read them; but keep the seventy that were written last in order to give them to the wise among your people. For in them is the spring of understanding, the fountain of wisdom, and the river of knowledge' (4 Ezra 14: 45–7). The twenty-four books are what we now know as the Hebrew canon: the rest are apocryphal writings, reserved for the wise.[9]

For a final example we may turn to 2 (i.e. *Slavonic*) *Enoch*, which exhibits essentially the same pattern. In the short recension (B) Enoch is told that the last generation of all will be from his own stock: 'Then in the course of that generation the books you and your fathers have written will be revealed, for the guardians of the earth will show them to men of faith, and they will be explained to that generation and come to be more highly thought of afterwards than they were before' (11: 34).[10]

The resemblance between Romans and 1QpHab on the one hand and the apocalyptic passages on the other conceals an important difference: in the first two passages 'the prophets' are what we now think of as the canonical prophets. There is no *new* revelation, and the task of the Teacher of Righteousness, like that of the Christian preacher, is simply to interpret a mystery whose meaning has hitherto been kept secret. Enoch, on the other hand, was the recipient of a series of visions quite different in content from most of what is found in the canonical prophets. He offers, in other words, an *alternative* revelation.[11] Notwithstanding this difference, it is evident that the idea of the two ages and of the distinction between the hidden mystery and its subsequent disclosure to a later generation was derived from what was basically an apocalyptic convention.

Applied to ancient, revered, and authoritative texts—scriptures—this constitutes an immensely powerful hermeneutical tool, capable of extracting strange new meanings whilst pretending that these were lying there dormant in the first place, only waiting for the right touch before emerging, like Sleeping Beauty, to take their proper place in God's great design. The apocalyptic trick of pseudonymity, another strong hermeneutical tool, is in this respect less

---

[9] See J. Barton, *Oracles*, pp. 64 f.

[10] Thus A. Pennington in Sparks's collection; the translation in Charles (35: 2–3) differs in important respects. According to the longer recension (A), the founder of the race has the task of revealing the books to his descendants; but see 47: 1–3 (only in A), where Enoch instructs his own children to 'take these books of your father's handwriting and read them'.   [11] See I. Gruenwald, *Apocalyptic*, pp. 23–8.

impressive. No doubt the pesher technique, as we may call it (the word simply means interpretation) resembles midrash—the consciously tendentious re-reading of biblical texts that had been widely practised in Israel from very early times (certainly no later than the Book of Deuteronomy, which is largely a rehash of selected passages from Exodus and Numbers). But it distinguishes itself from midrash by insisting that the *whole* meaning of the ancient text has been unavailable until now. Deuteronomy lies comfortably alongside Exodus and Numbers: although it commands, somewhat brazenly, that 'You shall not add to the word which I command you, nor take from it' (4: 2); thus denouncing in advance the numerous midrashim for which it would itself serve as scripture, it contains no mysteries that are hidden from its present readers. On the contrary: 'The secret things (LXX: τὰ κρυπτά) belong to the Lord our God; but the things that are revealed (τὰ φανερά) belong to us and to our children for ever' (29: 29).[12]

It is important to grasp the virtually limitless potential of the pesher method of interpretation; formally speaking it was this innocent-looking device that allowed the Old Testament to be supplanted by the New. Before they could take their place in the canon these modern writings had to present themselves, not as deliberate usurpers, but simply as authoritative readings of what were still regarded as αἱ γραφαί—the Scriptures. Of course this was not the only condition: Christianity is not just a new set of sacred texts. Moreover there seems little likelihood that the Qumran community, employing the same exegetical techniques, would have transformed itself, like Christianity, from a new sect to a new religion. Nevertheless the New Testament may legitimately be regarded, provided that we do not see it *only* in this way, as one gigantic pesher. Certainly this is how the Romans doxology cited at the start of this section appears to function: the Christian gospel is not regarded here as the fulfilment of a prophecy but as the revelation of a mystery.

Far from being the only New Testament writer to appropriate the essentially apocalyptic concept of the two ages of revelation, John is completely typical. Where he differs from all the others except Mark is in how he applies it. This is something that we shall have to examine more closely in the next chapter.

---

[12] For the polemical strain in the deuteronomical writings, see Margaret Barker, *Older Testament*, pp. 142–60.

2. VISIONS AND DREAMS: THE TWO STAGES

And the vision of all this has become to you like the words of a book that is sealed. When men give it to one who can read, saying, 'Read this,' he says, 'I cannot, for it is sealed.' And when they give the book to one who cannot read, saying, 'Read this,' he says, 'I cannot read.' (Isa. 29: 11 f.)

Up to now we have been looking at the common apocalyptic theme of a gap between the composition of a writing and what we may call its publication. That is what the first half of this quotation is about; a sealed book is a closed book: no one can read it until it is opened. The illiterate person, for whom even an open book is effectively closed, *always* stands in need of an interpreter. The convention according to which a revelation comes in two *stages*, one shadowy and obscure, requiring elucidation, the other plain and straightforward, available to all, is not confined to apocalyptic, unlike the convention of the two ages of revelation, which is. The two may overlap, but they should not be confused. Daniel and Ezra, in the passages quoted in the preceding section, assume that 'the wise', those who eventually inherit the books written down by the two seers centuries earlier, will be quite capable of reading them for themselves. The same holds for Enoch: 'But when they write out all my words exactly in their languages, ... everything which I testified about them before, ... [then] I know another mystery, that books will be given to the righteous and the wise ... and they will believe in them and rejoice over them' (*1 Enoch* 104: 11–13). In Romans 16: 25–6, the Gentiles, perhaps a trifle optimistically, are pictured as reading the Scriptures and discovering the message of salvation for themselves. But this was not always the case, and the first Gentile convert we know about, the Ethiopian eunuch, required an interpreter (cf. Acts 8). 1 Peter, in a passage closely resembling the one in Romans, says this:

The prophets who prophesied of the grace that was to be yours searched and enquired about this salvation; they enquired what person or time was indicated by the Spirit of Christ within them when predicting the sufferings of Christ and the subsequent glory. It was revealed ($\dot{\alpha}\pi\epsilon\kappa\alpha\lambda\dot{\upsilon}\phi\theta\eta$) to them that they were serving not themselves but you, in the things which have now been explained to you ($\dot{\alpha}$ $\nu\hat{\upsilon}\nu$ $\dot{\alpha}\nu\eta\gamma\gamma\dot{\epsilon}\lambda\eta$ $\dot{\upsilon}\mu\hat{\imath}\nu$) by those who preached the good news to you through the Holy Spirit, things into which angels long to look. (1 Pet. 1: 10–12)

According to this passage the prophets themselves were granted some inner enlightenment concerning the meaning of their message, but in what looks like a deliberate repudiation of the angelic element in the tradition Peter envisages the angels peering into the Christian mysteries in some frustration: the role assigned in apocalyptic literature to the *angelus interpres* is now assigned to the preachers of the gospel (οἱ εὐαγγελισαμένοι ὑμᾶς).

The origin of the idea of a revelation requiring subsequent elucidation is the dream. Not all dreams require interpretation. In the Old Testament those that do are generally experienced by non-Israelites: the dreamer awakes troubled, because no one can interpret his dream.[13] The role played by Joseph at the court of Pharaoh *vis-à-vis* the butler and the baker (Gen. 40) and Pharaoh himself (Gen. 41) is subsequently assumed by Daniel at the court of Nebuchadnezzar—and so passes into apocalyptic.[14] Like Pharaoh, Nebuchadnezzar is troubled, and he summons his own people to interpret his dream. The scene is reminiscent of another episode at the court of Pharaoh, the one in which Moses confutes and confuses Pharaoh's magicians (Exod. 7), proving himself to be superior in the magical arts of which they are the acknowledged experts, because, as they eventually concede, 'the finger of God is here' (Exod. 8: 19). When the magicians prove incompetent, the king sends for Daniel, who promptly asks for an appointment, 'that he might show to the king the interpretation' (2: 16). Very soon, 'the mystery was revealed to Daniel in a vision of the night' (2: 19), i.e. another dream. The fact that a dream (which of its nature requires an immediate interpretation) can so readily be thought of as a mystery (which does not) shows how difficult it is to preserve an absolute distinction between the two ages and the two stages. The Aramaic word for 'mystery' is רז, that for 'interpretation' is פשרא; the Hebrew word פשר, used at Qumran, is borrowed from this. Both of these words are repeated frequently in the course of this chapter: small mysteries and small interpretations, but with large consequences. In the Greek recension of Theodotion,[15] what corresponds to the RSV's clumsy

---

[13] See M. Ottoson, s.v. חלום, *ThDOT* iv. 430.

[14] The book of Daniel appears to fall into two halves, the first half (chs. 1–6) being concerned with *dreams*, very much in the wisdom manner familiar from the Joseph stories in Genesis, the second with *visions*. But as Peter Coxon has pointed out to me, a detailed examination of the Greek terms for dreams and visions in Theodotion and the LXX indicates considerable overlapping in both sections of the book; e.g. Dan. 1: 17, ἐν πάσῃ ὁράσει καὶ ἐνυπνίοις (Th); ἐν πάντι ... ὁράματι καὶ ἐνυπνίοις (LXX); similarly Dan. 5: 2 (4). Naturally both dreams and visions require interpretation.

[15] For the date of Theodotion's recension of Daniel see Ch. 9, p. 357 and n. 62.

rendering, 'show the interpretation,' is the expression τὴν σύγκρισιν ἀναγγέλλειν (Dan. 2: 4, 9, 16, 24). I. de la Potterie has argued that in apocalyptic literature and elsewhere (especially Second Isaiah) the word ἀναγγέλλειν, which we have just encountered in 1 Peter, has the technical sense of 'explain' or 'expound'.[16] In the first half of Daniel (2: 2, 4, 7, 9 (*bis*), 11, 16, 24, 25, 26, 27) the interpreter is Daniel himself, 'showing the interpretation' of Nebuchadnezzar's dreams; in the second half Daniel's own visions require elucidation, either by Gabriel (9: 23) or by some unnamed angelic being (10: 21; 11: 2). Since no angelic intermediary appears in the first half of the book, this may not be called apocalyptic writing in the strict sense; but the wisdom stories merge easily into apocalyptic in the second half, the transition being assisted by the use of the Aramaic language through to chapter 7.

De la Potterie is not slow to point out that 'reveal' or 'unveil' (*dévoiler*) is precisely the meaning of ἀναγγέλλειν in John 16: 13: 'When the Spirit of truth comes, he will guide you into all the truth; for he will not speak on his own authority, but whatever he hears he will speak, and he will explain to you (ἀναγγελεῖ ὑμῖν) the things that are to come.' This observation is of profound significance, for in indicating that the Paraclete takes over the apocalyptic role of the *angelus interpres*, it proves at the same time the extent of John's debt to a tradition to which he has seemed to most commentators (Odeberg is an honourable exception) either indifferent or hostile. In the next chapter I shall have more to say about the function of the Paraclete within the Gospel genre.

3. RIDDLE: INSIDERS AND OUTSIDERS

The distinction between the wise and the foolish is ingrained, obviously and necessarily, in the wisdom tradition. It lies not far

---

[16] *Vérité*, pp. 445–9. He also points to 2 *Bar.*; Hermas, *Vis.* ii. 1. 3; iii. 3. 1 as standing in the same tradition. In addition, he thinks that ἀναγγελῶ should be read instead of the better-attested ἀπαγγελῶ in John 16: 25. Even if he is wrong about this, his main point stands. It receives striking confirmation from a passage in 4 *Ezra* which recounts how the angel Uriel poses three riddles (*similitudines* = παραβολαί) to the seer: 'Three paths I have been sent to show you and three riddles to set you: if you can explain one of these to me (*si mihi renunciaveris unam ex his*) I in turn will show you the way you long to see …' (4: 3–4). Here the unexpected Latin verb *renunciare* is certainly a literal and rather mindless rendering of ἀναγγέλλειν. This is the verb used in Adolf Hilgenfeld's Greek retroversion: *Messias Judaeorum* (Leipzig, 1869).

below the surface in the contrast between the exceptionally gifted young Daniel and the sorcerers at the court of Nebuchadnezzar. It slots smoothly into place in any invective against 'the wicked', who are naturally thought of as foolish, just as 'the good' or 'the just' are usually assumed to be wise.[17] Furthermore, when any sect, that is to say any 'cognitive minority', sets about articulating its conviction of superiority it is likely to do so by expressing contempt for the stupidity of the rest of mankind. There is more than a hint of this tendency, as we have seen, in the Fourth Gospel, especially in the systematic use of the riddling saying or expression. It comes as no surprise to discover that it is a common theme in apocalyptic literature also. Presumably this will have absorbed the distinction quite unreflectingly as part of the legacy of the wisdom tradition. The following example comes from 2 *Enoch* at the point where the patriarch is giving his final instructions to his family:

Take these books, the books written by your father's hand, and read them, and learn from them the Lord's works ... And pass these books on to your children, and [see that your] children [pass them on] to their children, and [to] all your kind and all your generations, to those who have wisdom and fear the Lord; and they will receive them and take more delight in them than in any choice food, and they will read [them] and hold fast to them. But the foolish and those who do not know the Lord will not receive [them], but will repudiate [them], for their yoke will weigh them down. (Recension A: 13: 49–55)[18]

Humanity is divided into two classes, the wise and the foolish, and true understanding is reserved for the former. No extra act of interpretation appears to be required. There is no essential difference between the generation of Enoch's own children and all subsequent generations (cf. 13: 71, 76; *Jub.* 45: 16).

The same distinction—between the wise and the foolish—may also be used to supplement an earlier, very different distinction— that between the two ages of revelation. One could easily conceive of a final revelation open to all, and that is what we do find when the motif is appropriated by Christianity in the Book of Revelation and in the doxology from Romans quoted earlier. In the Jewish apocalypses, however, the division between wise and foolish is commonly reaffirmed when the hidden writings are eventually opened or

---

[17] We have already seen examples of such groupings: cf. Ch. 6, pp. 210–14
[18] Sparks, p. 347.

unsealed. Here is a passage from *4 Ezra*, which comes after the seer has requested and received the interpretation of the eagle vision:

This is the dream that you saw, and this is its interpretation (*interpretatio*). And you alone were worthy to learn this secret (*secretum*) of the Most High. Therefore write all these things that you have seen in a book, and put it in a hidden place; and you shall teach them to the wise among your people, whose hearts you know are able to comprehend and keep these secrets. (12: 35–8)

In Dan. 12: 9–10 (quoted above, p. 389) the word for 'the wise' is cognate with a verb meaning to instruct (הַשְׂכִּיל) that occurs frequently in the Dead Sea Scrolls and in its participial form indicates the leaders of the sect.

Corresponding to the distinction between the wise and the foolish in wisdom and apocalyptic is the distinction between insiders and outsiders which we find associated with the parable theme in Mark 4: 11–12:

To you [i.e. 'those who were about him with the twelve'] has been given the mystery (μυστήριον) of the kingdom of God, but for those outside the entire universe [i.e. the whole of reality: τὰ πάντα][19] comes in riddles;[20] so that they may indeed see but not perceive, and may indeed hear but not understand; lest they should turn again and be forgiven.

Priscilla Patten has argued that there is a significant similarity between the understanding of parables in Mark and in apocalyptic: 'most important, for both, parables are enigmatic and need an interpretation to convey the extended meaning to the select group. The teaching and event could be said to be the revelation, but without the inspired word of interpretation from the divine speaker the significance of the revelation remained obscure.'[21]

Patten fails to observe that the same is true of many other passages in the Old Testament. Having 'propounded his parable', Ezekiel is then required by God 'to explain it' (Ezek. 17: 2, 11; cf. 24: 3, 6). Nevertheless it is reasonable to suppose that the riddling quality of certain *mᵉšālîm* did have some influence on apocalyptic writing. It is hard to be sure, though, whether Mark deliberately

---

[19] For the justification of this rendering of τὰ πάντα see I. de la Potterie, *Vérité*, pp. 162 f.; Ashton, 'Transformation', p. 184 n. 37.

[20] That this is how ἐν παραβολαῖς must be translated is widely recognized. Cf. Vincent Taylor, *The Gospel according to St. Mark*, p. 256; Joachim Jeremias, *The Parables of Jesus* (London, 1963), p. 16.   [21] 'The Form and Function of Parable'.

incorporated this idea into his general theology of the Messianic Secret, as William Wrede thought he did.[22] No doubt some of the sayings referred to by Mark as παραβολαί are figurative expressions requiring elucidation (e.g. 3: 23–7; 7: 14–17). But the elucidation here follows immediately and is not reserved for a post-Easter understanding. Here, as we shall see, it is John who, by establishing a gap between riddling teaching (παροιμίαι) and interpretation, shows himself to be the true heir of the apocalyptic tradition.

Whether or not Wrede was right about the parable theory in Mark, he was certainly right to underline its importance for John. He suggests that a memory (the historical fact that part of Jesus' preaching was delivered in parables) was reinforced by a tradition (that of the incomprehension of the disciples), and that these two strands were woven together to form the conception of Jesus' riddling discourse (*Rätselreden*) that for John was a characteristic feature of all Jesus' earthly sayings. But the resemblance between John and Mark at this point is far from obvious and a number of difficulties arise:

1. Only one of Jesus' sayings is actually called a παροιμία (the Johannine equivalent of the Synoptic παραβολή) in the Fourth Gospel, the one that concerns the Good Shepherd (10: 6). This may be extended to cover the image of the door to the sheepfold in the same context, but apart from these the only other comparable passage is the allegory of the vine (15: 1–10). So if παροιμία means 'allegory', as it appears to do in 10: 6, it can scarcely be said to be typical of Jesus' habitual manner of speaking in this Gospel.

2. Why is the idea that Jesus spoke in riddles so important for John, given that in his Gospel Jesus openly proclaims his true identity and thus appears to empty the Messianic Secret of all its mystery?

3. The relevant passage in Mark (4: 11–12, quoted above) suggests that the disciples have been given a clear view of the secret but that for outsiders it is shrouded in riddling obscurity. So in Mark the contrast is between two groups, respectively insiders and outsiders; in John, on the other hand (16: 25), the riddling discourse (παροιμίαι) is addressed to the disciples.

It is best to tackle these difficulties in order.

1. The evangelist outlines his theory of riddling speech (παροιμίαι)

---

[22] This is disputed by H. Räisänen, 'Messianic Secret'.

in a passage at the end of chapter 16. This represents a later reflection upon the fundamental difference between two stages of revelation, one partial and obscure, taking place during Jesus's lifetime, the other full and clear, taking place after his death. We have already noted that this second stage of revelation is assigned to 'the Spirit of truth', who will 'take what is mine and explain it to you' (16: 14). Applied to the figure of the Shepherd in a saying addressed to a wider audience, the term παροιμία does indeed have the same meaning as παραβολή in the Synoptic Gospels: both words are employed in the LXX to translate the Hebrew מָשָׁל and the evangelists themselves might not have been impressed by Jülicher's careful distinction between parable and allegory. Further research may turn up other hidden parables in the Fourth Gospel, such as the one discovered by Dodd in chapter 5 (the son in his father's workshop)[23] and many of Jesus' own proverbial sayings have just as good a title to the label παραβολή as the challenge hurled at him in the synagogue at Nazareth, 'Physician, heal thyself!' (Luke 4: 23.) It might even be argued that the Johannine miracles (called 'signs') are enacted parables; and Wrede points out that some of Jesus' actions, such as the entry into Jerusalem (12: 16) and the foot-washing (13: 7), are greeted with incomprehension by the disciples: 'These actions *mean* something, and consequently they are on a par with Jesus' words: they too are teaching';[24] Wrede is on the right track here, but by and large it would be a mistake to cull the pages of the Gospel for examples of παροιμίαι.[25] For this evangelist, as Wrede himself remarks, 'Jesus would speak ἐν παροιμ-ίαις even if nothing of the sort existed.'[26] Riddling discourse is one facet of a carefully worked-out theory of the manner of Jesus' revelation.

2. The difficulty concerning the absence of any real Messianic Secret in John may be urged more strongly still. In 16: 25 Jesus promises the disciples that 'the hour is coming when I will no longer speak to you in riddling discourse, but tell you plainly (παρρησία ἀπαγγελῶ) of the Father'. But this contrast between ἐν παροιμίαις and

---

[23] C. H. Dodd, 'A Hidden Parable'.   [24] p. 206; cf. ET, p. 207.
[25] As Lucien Cerfaux does when he suggests that παροιμία for John signifies 'an enigmatic expression, first misunderstood and then explained (*la formule énigmatique, la méprise et l'explication de la formule*)', in other words: a riddle. In point of fact there are only two passages (2: 21 and 12: 16) in which John actually explains his riddles, and neither of them figures in Cerfaux's list: see *Receuil Lucien Cerfaux*, ii (Gembloux, 1954), pp. 17–26.   [26] ET, p. 206.

παρρησίᾳ (openly, frankly) appears to contradict what Jesus says elsewhere. Perhaps the simple announcement that 'Lazarus is dead' (11: 14), resolving the riddle of 'Lazarus has fallen asleep' (11: 11) is scarcely a counter-example, but what of the occasion when some of the people of Jerusalem express their confidence that he is speaking to them παρρησίᾳ (7: 26)? This confidence does not last: 'If you are the Messiah,' cry the exasperated Jews at the feast of the Dedication, 'tell us plainly'; whereupon Jesus replies, 'I told you, and you do not believe' (10: 24 f.). His clearest and most conclusive statement, however, comes at his interrogation by the high priest after his arrest. The questioning focuses on two points only, his disciples and his teaching. Jesus' response is unequivocal: 'I have spoken openly to the world; I have always taught in the synagogues and in the temple, where all Jews come together; I have said nothing secretly (ἐν κρυπτῷ)' (18: 20).

There are so many examples in the Gospel of what looks like straight talking or 'open speech' on Jesus' part that we may well be puzzled by the disciples' reaction to what Jesus tells them in 16: 28: 'I come from the Father,' he says, 'and have come into the world; again I am leaving the world and going to the Father.' At last, the disciples conclude, 'You are speaking plainly and not in riddling discourse' (16: 29). Yet Jesus has said the same sort of thing many times before, once in fact earlier in the same discourse (16: 5). Evidently παρρησίᾳ, like παροιμίαι, has a technical meaning here: it alludes to the second stage of revelation, which must await Jesus' final departure: 'I have many other things to tell you, but you are not yet able to take them in (οὐ δύνασθε βαστάζειν ἄρτι)' (16: 12). 'Only for the eye of faith', comments Bultmann, 'does the veil of παροιμία fall away',[27] summing up confidently the intentions of the evangelist, some of whose most profound reflections upon the nature of the Gospel genre are contained in this passage (16: 12–33); but it has no bearing on the distinction between outsiders and insiders that was of such importance in the first half of the Gospel. What distinction there is between outsiders and insiders in John does not belong to what he says about παροιμίαι: these have a different function, quite close to the one that has to be ascribed to the term παραβολαί in Mark 4: 13, namely a riddling discourse that requires to be interpreted later. Taken in this way, Jesus' reply makes much

[27] p. 588.

more sense as an answer to the disciples' question in v. 10: 'Those who were about him with the twelve asked him concerning the parables. . . . And he said to them, "Do you not understand this parable [i.e. the Sower]? How then will you understand all the parables?"'

3. What are we to make of Wrede's suggestion that John has adopted and adapted the tradition that Jesus spoke in parables? The true origin of the distinction between insiders and outsiders is Mark 4: 11, where Jesus is said, quite literally, to address 'those outside'. But where does this saying come from? It is clearly irreconcilable with the presumably authentic tradition which has Jesus employing parables to proclaim the message of the kingdom, a tradition which roughly corresponds to the ordinary English meaning of 'parable' as a story with a lesson attached. Taylor, commenting on v. 11, thinks it likely that '4: 10–12 is a separate unit of tradition which has been inserted in this context',[28] but he does not speculate on its origin. H. Räisänen[29] suggests that Mark may have taken the saying from a Christian community completely estranged from its neighbour (i.e. a ghetto). If he is right the riddling discourse will have served its regular function of setting apart those 'in the know' from outsiders excluded from any participation in the truth. If such a community existed its experience must have closely resembled that of the Johannine group in its dealings with the synagogue (see Chapter 5); and if in addition the fourth evangelist knew it or of it, then of course he could have been influenced by it. But in that case we should expect him to have picked up the same word rather than inventing one of his own.

Although, to conclude, the distinction between the wise and the foolish is implicit in John's all-important contrast between believers and unbelievers, it is not one for which he is obviously indebted to apocalyptic. There are several possible explanations, not mutually exclusive, of the Johannine riddle: form-critical, traditio-historical, sociological, theological, literary. The most that can be said is that his use of riddling discourse is perfectly consonant with any more general theory that the Fourth Gospel was profoundly influenced by the apocalyptic tradition and shows strong affinities with it.

[28] *The Gospel according to St. Mark*, p. 256
[29] *Das 'Messiasgeheimnis' im Markusevangelium*, p. 54.

4. CORRESPONDENCE: ABOVE AND BELOW

The last feature of apocalyptic writing I wish to consider closely resembles certain ideas of writers like Jakob Boehme and Emanuel Swedenborg, whom it may have indirectly influenced via the Jewish Kabbalah. I call this feature 'correspondence', with a conscious allusion to the latter's *Treatise concerning Heaven and Hell*: 'the whole natural world corresponds to the spiritual world in general, but also in every particular. Therefore, whatever in the natural world comes into existence from the spiritual world is said to be in correspondence with it. It must be known that the natural world comes into existence and continues in existence from the spiritual world, precisely like an effect from its effecting cause.'[30] Just such a correspondence may well have been one of the meanings of the Hebrew מָשָׁל, as is suggested in an illuminating article by D. W. Suter on the so-called Parables or Similitudes of Enoch (1 Enoch 37–71). Enoch's own title is 'Vision of Wisdom' (*rāʾya ṭebab*), but towards the end an alternative title appears to be offered by the compiler, the seer's great-grandson: 'my great-grandfather Enoch gave me the explanation [*v.l.* teaching] of all the secrets in a book and the parables which had been given to him; and he put them together for me in the words of the Book of the Parables' (68: 1). As Suter says, 'The introductory formulas in 37: 5; 38: 1; 45: 1; 57: 3; 58: 1; and 69: 29 suggest that the three sections of the work (chaps. 38–44, 45–57, and 58–69) are, in some way, three *mĕšālîm* and therefore reinforce this designation.'[31] The fact that he is relying upon an Ethiopic translation is neither here nor there; plainly the original was either Hebrew משל or Aramaic מטל. Suter prefers the alternative name, 'Similitudes', because he thinks it conveys more accurately than 'Parables' the sense of the Ethiopic *mesālē* used to designate this section of the book in 68: 1. Closer still, as we shall see, is my own suggestion of 'correspondence'. This has the additional advantage of being equally well suited to the Book of Proverbs מְשָׁלִים, which are mostly correspondences on a reduced scale, and also the parables of Jesus ('the kingdom of heaven is like ...'). One might add that the Greek παραβολή, the usual translation of משל in the LXX, comes closer than 'similitude' to conveying the meaning

[30] *De Caelo et ejus Mirabilibus, et de Inferno ex Auditis et Visis* (London, 1758, § 89; ET London, 1968, p. 44).
[31] '*Māšāl* in the Similitudes of Enoch', p. 193.

favoured by Suter, since it often retains its literal sense of 'juxtaposition' besides that of 'comparison' or 'analogy'.

Each of the three main correspondences consists of one or more prophecies concerning the fate of the wicked and/or the righteous at the end of time, plus a vision or series of visions which Enoch asks the accompanying angel to explain; e.g. 'I asked the angel of peace who went with me and showed me everything which is secret: "Who are these four figures whom I have seen and whose words I have heard and written down?"' (40: 18; cf. 43: 3; 46: 2; 52: 3; 53: 4; 54: 4; 56: 2; 60: 9; 61: 2.) Somewhere in the third correspondence the explanations begin to be given unasked. For this author, apparently, a correspondence somehow encloses its earthly counterpart: in reply to one of the seer's questions ('What are these?') the angel replies: 'Their correspondence [Knibb: 'likeness'] has the Lord of Spirits shown you,' and then goes on to explain: 'these are the names of the righteous' (43: 4). One of the central features of an apocalypse is here—the interpretation of a vision or dream by a heavenly intermediary when the seer himself cannot understand it. If he can speak of what follows, as he does in his introduction, as *rāy'a ṭebab*, a 'vision of wisdom', it is only by hindsight, with the whole of what follows in mind.

Suter argues that the reason the three component discourses of the book can be called 'Similitudes' is 'because of the complex set of comparisons and likenesses that they contain—comparisons and likenesses that reflect topics traditionally associated with the *māšāl*.[32] An important clue comes in 43: 4, where the Ethiopic *mesl* is used to speak of *the likeness of things above existing on the earth*. Here Black translates: 'has shown you a parable pertaining to them (lit.: their parable)' where Knibb has 'their likeness has the Lord of Spirits shown to you'. Suter cites a passage from *The Ascension of Isaiah* to illustrate how the Enochian Parables (which from now on, to underline my point, I shall call 'Correspondences') establish connections between levels of reality: 'As it is above, so is it also on the earth, for the likeness [Ethiopic *'amsāl*] of that which is on the firmament is also on the earth' (7: 10). Perhaps J. M. T. Barton's translation makes the point even more clearly: 'As it is on high, so also is it on earth: what happens in the vault of heaven happens similarly here on earth.'[33] The burden of Suter's argument is that

[32] p. 211.   [33] Sparks, p. 797.

the Book of the Correspondences 'plays with the implications of spatial dualism (the relationship between the heavenly and earthly orders) in order to solve the problems raised by the presence of disorder in society (ethical dualism) and that this pattern of reasoning is in part derived from yet another polarity present in the wisdom tradition—a polarity between man (or society) and nature'.[34] The term 'dualism', borrowed from J. G. Gammie,[35] is unfortunate. The thrust of the argument goes to prove that the persistent ethical dualism between the good and the wicked is *not* matched by a corresponding dualism between heaven and earth. On the contrary, this opposition is asserted only to be denied (transcended or *aufgehoben* in the Hegelian sense of the term). A verse in one of the *Odes of Solomon* puts it even more succinctly: 'The likeness of that which is below is that which is above.'[36] It is because apocalyptic is *anti*-dualistic in this matter that the above/below contrast was excluded from the discussion of dualism in Chapter 6: for Enoch, and for apocalyptic writers generally, there are not two worlds but one; or rather the whole of reality is split into matching pairs (rather like the biological theory of DNA) in which one half, the lower, is the mirror-image (albeit in this case a distorting mirror) of the higher. That is why a revelation of what is above is not just relevant or related to what happens or is about to happen on earth; rather what happens on earth is a re-enactment in earthly terms of what has happened in heaven: a correspondence!

The complexity of reference of the term *māšāl* is such that Suter's thesis cannot be said to have been proved. It is at best only probable.[37] But that scarcely matters. His exceptionally perceptive

[34] p. 203 n. 39. This is the weakest part of Suter's argument. There is no obvious link between the ethical dualism prominent in much apocalyptic writing and the correspondences we have been discussing. These are not confined to apocalyptic; a clear example occurs in what may be the earliest example of Hebrew poetry that we have, the Song of Deborah (Judg. 5: 19–20): 'The kings came, they fought; | then fought the kings of Canaan, | at Taanach, by the waters of Megiddo; | they got no spoils of silver. | From heaven fought the stars, | from their courses they fought against Sisera.' The conflict on earth evidently mirrors that in heaven, but there is no dualism here. Similar correspondences are found in other literatures of the Ancient Near East. [35] 'Spatial and Ethical Dualism'.

[36] *Od. Sol.* 34: 4 (Charlesworth—to be preferred here to Emerton (in Sparks)).

[37] An alternative theory is proposed by Margaret Barker in *The Older Testament*. She thinks that the word is derived from a homonym meaning 'rule' or 'govern', and suggests that 'those who spoke in the *mᵉšālîm* had as a premise some concept of natural and moral order in the universe' (p. 34). She does not, however, offer an alternative translation of the word itself. To suppose that the apocalyptist spoke the same language as the author of the Book of Proverbs is not necessarily to assume his 'linear descent from canonical texts' (p. 33). But see too her earlier discussion, p. 29.

article highlights a central feature of apocalyptic thinking, one that our definition of apocalyptic failed to bring out—the fundamental unity and structural parallelism of the heavenly and the earthly realms.

No one has perceived this truth—and its relevance to the understanding of the Fourth Gospel—more clearly, or expressed it more eloquently, than J. L. Martyn. (It should be observed that in the following passage Martyn's two stages, unlike mine, are not temporal but spatial: he is concerned with correspondences):

John did not create the literary form of the two-level drama. It was at home in the thought-world of Jewish apocalypticism. The dicta most basic to the apocalyptic thinker are these: God created both heaven and earth. There are dramas taking place both on the heavenly stage and on the earthly stage. Yet these dramas are not really two, but rather one drama. For there are corresponding pairs of actors; a beast of a certain description in heaven represents a tyrannical king on earth, etc. Furthermore, the developments in the drama on its heavenly stage determine the developments on the earthly stage. One might say that events on the heavenly stage not only correspond to events on the earthly stage, but also slightly precede them in time, leading them into existence, so to speak. What transpires on the heavenly stage is often called 'things to come'. For that reason events seen on the earthly stage are entirely enigmatic to the man who sees only the earthly stage. Stereoptic vision is necessary, and it is precisely stereoptic vision which causes a man to write an apocalypse.[38]

Part of this passage has already been quoted in the preceding chapter *vis-à-vis* the Son of Man. It is clear that this mysterious figure, who has stepped out of the Book of Daniel (and conceivably also out of the Book of Enoch) to take his place on the lower of Martyn's two stages, is particularly well fitted to transport a heavenly revelation to mankind. Descending to earth, he carries heaven with him. Like Jacob's ladder, he can reach up to heaven as well as down to earth and is the most powerful symbol in the Gospel of the apocalyptic correspondence between the two realms. When he returns, exalted ($\dot{v}\psi\omega\theta\epsilon\dot{\iota}s$), to heaven—this is surely John's most remarkable conceit—he is stretched out on the cross.

In his book Martyn recognizes that both of John's two dramas, the story of Jesus' life and the projection of this into the experience of the community, are enacted on earth. There is no divine plan first disclosed to a seer in a vision and then repeated in earthly terms. The

[38] *History*[1], p. 127.

divine plan itself—the Logos—is incarnate: fully embodied in the person of Jesus; and it is his life that reveals God's grand design of saving the world, a design now being realized, lived out, by the community. During Jesus' lifetime, as we shall see in the next chapter, the significance of his words and deeds remains opaque: they assume the character of a mystery, one whose meaning cannot be grasped until the dawn of a new age, when, in a second stage, it will at last receive its authoritative interpretation. Thus the fourth evangelist conceives his own work as an apocalypse—in reverse, upside down, inside out.

CONCLUSION

The secret of the dynamism of apocalyptic, what makes it so much more than a literary convention, is the urgent conviction of God's active intervention in human history. The heavenly blueprint of his plan for the world will eventually, in his own good time, be revealed, but not communicated in any ordinary way. The seer or prophet who carries it down from the world above is an active agent and his revelation of what he is the first to know helps to accomplish this great design.

Here, I believe, is the reason why the Jesus of the Fourth Gospel, though delivering the substance of his message orally ('the words of eternal life'), also speaks of his 'works'—what the evangelist calls 'signs'—and, most significantly, in two key passages, of accomplishing (τελειοῦν) his 'work' (ἔργον), a comprehensive term that covers the whole task of revelation entrusted to him by his Father.[39] In the first passage he speaks of his work as 'doing the will of him who sent me' (4: 34); in the second this is seen as equivalent to glorifying God on earth (17: 4). Jesus' task, then, is not just to talk about God but to *establish his glory*. The concept of God's glory (כָּבוֹד) comes from the Old Testament theophanies, which were manifestations of God's power and authority to individual human beings and followed in every case by an event of exceptional significance.

In the concluding chapter we shall see that the divine Logos with

---

[39] Cf. 5: 36: τὰ ἔργα ἃ δέδωκέν μοι ὁ πατὴρ ἵνα τελειώσω αὐτά. It is arguable that the plural form ἔργα has the force of the singular in this passage. See A. Vanhoye, 'L'Œuvre du Christ'.

whom Jesus is identified on the first page of the Gospel is more than just a Word. Jesus, as the fourth evangelist sees him, is the *plan* of God, his grand project for humanity (the world) made flesh and his glory made manifest. This is the very essence of apocalyptic.

THE GOSPEL GENRE

I. THE MESSIANIC SECRET

Few works have had such a profound and long-lasting impact upon Gospel studies as William Wrede's *Das Messiasgeheimnis in den Evangelien*, published in 1901. It has been mauled and modified in scores of ways, but Wrede's central insight has stood firm. This was the recognition of an ineradicable tension (Wrede would say contradiction) between the presentation of Jesus as Messiah and Lord in the account of his words and deeds before the resurrection and the persistent awareness that his real identity remained hidden until after his earthly life was over. The details of Wrede's argument, largely based on the Gospel of Mark, need not concern us here.[1] The key to Mark's own understanding of his Gospel, according to Wrede, is the injunction of Jesus to Peter, James, and John on their descent from the mountain of the transfiguration 'to tell no one what they had seen until the Son of man should have risen from the dead. So they kept the matter to themselves, questioning what the rising from the dead meant' (9: 9–10; cf. 8: 30).[2]

Wrede himself thought that Mark had taken the idea of the messianic secret from his sources but failed to carry it through consistently. Underlying his Gospel, nevertheless, is the picture of the incomprehension of Jesus' followers, an incomprehension that persisted until the resurrection, 'when the scales fell from their eyes'. Then and only then do all Jesus' revelations begin to make sense: 'What was once unintelligible now becomes known and the knowledge is and has to be spread abroad. Thus in spite of their blindness the disciples have had from Jesus all the equipment they need if they

---

[1] Wrede did not, however, confine his study to Mark but recognized a profound affinity between Mark and John. This is discussed by James M. Robinson in two articles: 'On the *Gattung* of Mark (and John)'; 'Gnosticism and the New Testament'. I am indebted to these for some of the ideas in this section.

[2] *The Messianic Secret*, p. 67.

are to become his witnesses and apostles. Their status rests upon what they have received from him and preserved as tradition.'[3] Wrede also held that the earliest traditions about Jesus were simple memories with no particular christological content: the secrecy theory was a way of giving them a Christian meaning without altogether distorting them. He was possibly wrong about this, because Jesus might actually have made messianic claims in his lifetime; even if he did not, the traditions both of his words and of his actions could well have been christologically slanted from the very beginning. But as presented in the Gospels these are more than snippets of a biography strung together in some sort of chronological order. Every episode, every saying and story, is intended to be heard or read in the light of the resurrection. Mark's contribution was to gather together a mass of dissimilar material, some of which may have been put together in sizeable units before him, and to give it some measure of shape and consistency.[4] To establish the continuity between the time of the early Christian community and the life of Jesus that preceded it he had to provide his readers with a guiding-thread. He found what he needed in the secrecy theory.

Mark's Gospel ends abruptly, with no clear indication apart from the mute testimony of its own existence how the news of the resurrection would be either promulgated or received. But Mark does not disguise his own faith. The Risen Jesus does not appear; the brief glimpse that we are allowed is tantalizingly indirect. Even so it is enough to illuminate all that has gone before. Those who argue that the resurrection alone is insufficient to account for faith in Jesus' messiahship have a good case. But the recognition that it nevertheless marked a turning-point in the way Jesus was regarded by his followers—that is to say a change of status—is not confined to the Gospels. It belongs among the most ancient of Christian beliefs. Luke draws upon one of these for Peter's Pentecost speech in Acts: 'Let all the house of Israel therefore know assuredly that God has made him both Lord and Christ, this Jesus whom you crucified' (Acts 2: 36). Paul too starts his letter to the Romans by quoting a much older Christian creed which speaks of Jesus as 'designated ($\dot{\delta}\rho\iota\sigma\theta\epsilon\iota\varsigma$) Son of God in power according to the Holy Spirit ($\kappa\alpha\tau\dot{\alpha}$ $\pi\nu\epsilon\hat{\upsilon}\mu\alpha$ $\dot{\alpha}\gamma\iota\omega\sigma\dot{\upsilon}\nu\eta\varsigma$) by his resurrection from the dead' (Rom. 1: 4; cf. Phil. 2: 9–11).

---

[3] p. 113; ET, p. 112.
[4] Cf. H. Conzelmann, 'Present and Future'. Although I have some disagreements with Conzelmann, I owe a lot to this article.

These texts, all of them cited by Wrede, mark the transition between the human earthly Jesus and the divine heavenly Christ; they testify to a discontinuity that no amount of theological juggling can entirely set aside. Yet at the same time they assert continuity: Jesus is Lord. The paradox of a discontinuity (strongly stressed by Bultmann) plus a continuity (underlined by Bultmann's critics) between the historical Jesus and the kerygmatic Christ is at the heart of the Gospels; indeed it is the essence of the genre. A Gospel is a narrative of the public career of Jesus, his passion and death, told in order to affirm or confirm the faith of Christian believers in the Risen Lord:[5] 'If you confess with your lips that Jesus is Lord and believe in your heart that God raised him from the dead, you will be saved' (Rom. 10: 9). 'Jesus is Lord' is the simplest Christian creed as well as one of the earliest. The earliest is probably the one affirmed by Peter in the Gospel of Mark (8: 29) and by Martha in the Gospel of John (11: 27): 'You are the Messiah.'[6] The Gospels put both these into story form.

This identity-in-difference constitutes the basic structure of both creed and Gospel. Studies of the Gospel genre that confine themselves to observing its resemblances to contemporary biographies or quasi-biographies[7] may not be totally misguided, but they miss the essence of the matter, the one thing necessary. Whether or not the first readers of the Gospel of Mark recognized that they were

[5] Norman Perrin, concluding his observations on 'The Literary *Gattung* "Gospel"', *Exp T* 82 (1970), 4–7, remarks that 'a "gospel" is, among other things, a narrative of an event from the past in which the interests and concerns of the past, present and future have flowed together' (p. 7). There is some truth in this, but Perrin is much too vague. What he says holds for Vergil's *Aeneid* just as much as it does for Mark's Gospel. One has to be much more specific not only about the subject of the narrative, but also about the temporal relationships involved. Perrin's student, John R. Donahue, gets it just right: 'The Gospels are the good news of the risen one told in the form of stories about the earthly life of Jesus' ('Recent Studies', p. 498).

[6] See V. H. Neufeld, *The Earliest Christian Confessions*.

[7] For a discussion of attempts to define the Gospel genre cf. R. Guelich, 'The Gospel Genre'. Guelich distinguishes two categories of answer: 'analogical' and 'derivative'. My own view is closest to the writers of the former category who believe that the most fruitful approach is to compare the Gospels with apocalypses (rather than with, say, biographies, aretalogies, encomia, or even tragicomedia). Nevertheless, provided the texts studied have sufficient formal similarities with the Christian Gospels, some interesting findings can be made. Thus, after a study of Iamblichus' *De mysteriis Aegyptiorum*, Apuleius' *Apologia*, and Philostratus' *Vita Apollonii*, J. Z. Smith reaches the conclusion that '*A "gospel" is a narrative of a son of god who appears among men as a riddle inviting misunderstanding*', and he adds: 'I would want to claim the title "gospel" for the *Vitae* attributed to Mark and John as well as for those by Philostratus and Iamblichus' ('Good News is No News', p. 204).

confronted by a new and unprecedented literary genre[8] is of no importance. A Gospel is not a theological treatise, certainly, but it is not a biography either; nor is it, properly speaking, a compromise between the two nor yet an amalgam of both; it is *sui generis*. Luke has Peter declare that God *made* Jesus Lord and Christ at the resurrection, and Paul asserts in Romans that it was then that he was designated Son of God. Put in this way, as an affirmation of a change of status (there is no need to flinch from the shadow of adoptionism here), the identity-in-difference presents no great problem. Nor does it in the creed. Only when it is fleshed out in a story does it seem strangely paradoxical, even though the paradox is implicit in the creed as well. For on the face of it this story is recounting the events of Jesus' earthly life whilst urging on every page that this same Jesus is the object of Christian worship. He is not yet risen: but he is, so the writer implies and expects his readers to believe, our Risen Lord.

The post-resurrection recognition scenes in Luke and John give the evangelists an opportunity to illustrate the identity-in-difference directly and vividly. Recognition is always slow in coming because the Risen Jesus is not *only* the same; he is also different in certain essential respects from the Jesus the disciples knew before. Paul makes the same point in theological language in 1 Corinthians 15. But now the problem is that to place too much weight upon a post-Easter revelation is to run the risk of detaching the good news from its traditional origin in the person and message of Jesus. This is what happened in certain Gnostic circles, which have produced stories of the Risen Christ wherein he reveals esoteric mysteries and responds to the questions of the disciples in dialogue form. Here, for instance, is the opening of the first book of the *Pistis Sophia* (one of the relatively few Gnostic documents already known in Wrede's day):

But it came to pass, after Jesus was risen from the dead, that he spent eleven years discoursing with his disciples, and taught them only as far as the places (τόποι) of the first commandment and as far as the places of the first mystery (μυστήριον).[9]

---

[8] M. Hengel, *Studies in Mark*, pp. 32 f. Hengel is right to deny that Mark's Gospel is theology, but disingenuous to suggest that it is consequently better considered as a sort of biography. Aware that the Gospels are *proclamations*, he should acknowledge that this distinguishes them just as sharply from biographies as from theological treatises.

[9] Hennecke, *New Testament Apocrypha*, i. 252. Wrede quotes a passage from Clement of Alexandria according to which 'the Lord delivered the γνῶσις to James the Just, Peter and John after the resurrection; and these delivered it to the other apostles,

[*cont. on p. 411*]

Even this comparatively inferior grade of teaching was higher, according to the Gnostic text, than anything that had preceded it during Jesus' lifetime. The real mysteries, we are left to infer, had nothing to do with his earthly career.[10]

The alternative solution, it might seem, is to locate the central revelation *before* the resurrection. The Gnostic gospel exaggerates the discontinuity, widening the gap between earth and heaven so that it cannot, even in principle, be bridged. (Interestingly, Bultmann's uncompromising refusal to admit the identity of the earthly Jesus and the kerygmatic Christ has much the same effect.[11]) But the opposite course has its dangers too. No Christian teacher would wish to assert or imply that the resurrection left the basic message of the gospel unaffected. Hence the dilemma: a pre-Easter revelation ignores the most distinctive element of Christianity; a post-Easter revelation devalues the greater part of its traditions—and is well on the way to Gnosticism.

As Wrede saw the matter, the device of the messianic secret was a way of getting round this dilemma. The continuity between Jesus of Nazareth and the Risen Christ, paradoxical as it is, must be maintained. One way of doing this, the way adopted by Mark, is the secrecy theory; and it is the role and function of this theory within Mark's Gospel that justifies Hans Conzelmann's dictum that 'the secrecy theory is the hermeneutical presupposition of the genre "gospel"'.[12]

Strictly speaking this is not correct. John, as we have seen, makes only limited use of the secrecy theory—at least in its Marcan form. He ensures the continuity between Jesus and Lord by operating on two levels of understanding. This hermeneutical device, which we shall have reason to examine closely later in this chapter, can be

and these in turn to the 70, including Barnabas.' This comes from Eusebius, *HE* ii. 1: 3–4. The *Gospel of Thomas* purports to be a record of 'the secret sayings which the living Jesus spoke and which Didymos Judas Thomas wrote down' (1: 1). See too C. Schmidt's edition of the so-called *Epistula Apostolorum, Gespräche Jesu,* also in Hennecke, i. 189–227.

[10] An analogous move is made in a totally Jewish setting by the *Book of Jubilees.* See I. Gruenwald, *Apocalyptic,* pp. 23–5.

[11] The last of Bultmann's recorded thoughts on this subject were published in German in 1960 and translated as 'The Primitive Christian Kerygma and the Historical Jesus'. Whilst admitting a continuity between the kerygma itself (a historical phenomenon) and the Jesus of history, Bultmann insists that 'the Christ of the kerygma is not a historical figure which could enjoy continuity with the historical Jesus' (p. 18).   [12] Conzelmann, 'Present and Future', p. 43.

aligned with the secrecy theory only at the price of some strain and distortion. The close resemblance between John and Mark, superficially so dissimilar, was well spotted by Wrede, and in the course of his book he makes some penetrating observations on John as well as on Mark. But he realized that the crucial similarity does not lie in the secrecy theory as such but in the profound awareness common to both of the need to establish the identity of Jesus of Nazareth with the Risen Lord.

Reflecting on the Gospel genre and comparing it with the apocalyptic patterns studied in the previous chapter, one can hardly fail to be struck by the formal resemblances. Of its very nature the Christian gospel falls into two stages, the first inchoate and opaque, the second clear and unconfined. In the Gospels the two ages of apocalyptic, where the crucial distinction is between the hidden mystery and the revealed truth, coalesce with the two stages, which focus rather upon the difference between an initial revelation of an essentially puzzling character and one in which the puzzle is finally resolved.

2. TWO LEVELS OF UNDERSTANDING

Towards the end of the previous chapter I discussed the spatial aspect of J. L. Martyn's theory of the two-level drama. Martyn is aware that his metaphor of two stages has a temporal aspect also and he is prepared to exploit the ambiguity to good effect. Here he is commenting upon one of the ways in which John diverges from his apocalyptic model:

The initial stage is not the scene of 'things to come' in heaven. It is the scene of Jesus' life and teaching. Its extension into the contemporary level 'speaks to' current events not by portraying the immediate future but by narrating a story which, on the face of it, is about the past, a story about Jesus of Nazareth. ... John's two stages are past and present, not future and present.[13]

One might be tempted to say that John is simply making use of a device familiar from the Old Testament, whereby past and present are telescoped into a single vision designed to teach the readers

[13] *History*[2], pp. 136 f.

lessons of immediate relevance to their own day.[14] But is this right? And if not, what is the difference? Is not the remarkable literary device Martyn discerns in the Fourth Gospel very similar to, say, Second Isaiah's portrayal of the imminent return from Babylon as a second exodus? Does not the exilic prophet exhibit a similar skill in holding past and present together in a comparative vision that shows the past to foreshadow a more prestigious future, a future that is rapidly approaching? No doubt there is some structural analogy here; but there is a difference too. John, unlike Second Isaiah, is ostensibly writing about the past; the significance of his work for his readers' present is not declared, but suggested. One cannot imagine John exhorting his readers, as the prophet does—however equivocally—to 'remember not the former things, nor consider the things of old' (Isa. 43: 18). A more obvious example might be the chronicler's re-reading of the history of the early monarchy in terms that invite his readers to see the Second Temple and its cult as a direct return to the First, picturing David and Solomon as no less concerned with the constitution and administration of the Temple than his own heroes, Ezra and Nehemiah. The differences between the Fourth Gospel and the other three, all recounting what is basically the same story, are perhaps no less striking than the differences between Chronicles and the books of Samuel and Kings, composed centuries earlier.

Nevertheless, present-day readers of the Fourth Gospel, accepting the story at face-value and lacking the information that would have made it easy for John's contemporaries to pick up the carefully placed allusions, are unlikely to agree without protest to the suggestion that the evangelist is deliberately distorting the Jesus-traditions in order to make them meaningful to the members of his own community—even though they may give notional assent to the general view of the evangelists as creative theologians in their own right. It is scarcely surprising that it has taken a scholar of Martyn's perspicacity, drawing upon contemporary sociological insights, to see that John was not writing a theological treatise for posterity but a work speaking directly to the hopes and fears of his own first readers. Yet at the same time he *is* writing about the past. He telescopes past and present together by operating upon two

[14] Cf. D. S. Russell, *Method and Message*, p. 135.

levels of understanding.[15] There is one passage in the Gospel which furnishes John's readers with a very obvious clue to his intentions.

Unknown to Martyn, the temple episode was singled out, some twenty years earlier, by the French scholar Xavier Léon-Dufour, who subjected it to a penetrating exegesis.[16] In the Synoptic Gospels the episode immediately precedes the passion narrative and may in fact, as E. P. Sanders has argued,[17] have sealed the determination of the Jewish authorities to have Jesus silenced once and for all. In the Fourth Gospel as we have it it is the raising of Lazarus that provokes the murderous decision of the chief priests and Pharisees; the temple episode comes right at the beginning of Jesus' public career.[18] It is the first of his confrontations with the Jews and the first time that he addresses an audience beyond the immediate circle of his friends and disciples. One likely reason for the transposition is the need to alert the readers of the Gospel as early as possible to the way in which they have to interpret the subsequent revelations. Jesus' enigmatic remark to his mother at the wedding-feast is too obscure to be understood straight away as a reference to his passion; in his version of the temple episode the evangelist intervenes directly to suggest that the whole of Jesus' public career will be lived out under the shadow of the cross:

Jesus answered them, 'Destroy this temple ($\tau\grave{o}\nu$ $\nu\alpha\acute{o}\nu$), and in three days I will raise it up ($\dot{\epsilon}\gamma\epsilon\rho\hat{\omega}$ $\alpha\dot{\upsilon}\tau\acute{o}\nu$).' The Jews said, 'It has taken forty-six years to build this temple, and will you raise it up in three days?' But he spoke of the

---

[15] What Martyn proposes may be regarded as a more refined and developed analysis of a feature of the Gospel that others had observed before him. See for instance Oscar Cullmann, *Early Christian Worship* (London, 1953): 'The Gospel of John indicates in so many places the necessity of a double meaning, that enquiry into the deeper unexpressed sense is to be raised, in this gospel, to the status of a principle of interpretation' (p. 57) and C. H. Dodd's approving comment in his review of this book in *J. Eccl. Hist.* 3 (1952), 218–21: 'The events he [the fourth evangelist] records must be apprehended on two levels, as occurrences in the past, and as livingly affecting his readers in the present. The events are "remembered" in the pregnant sense, and such remembrance is prompted by the Holy Spirit in the Church' (p. 218); see too D. W. Wead, *Literary Devices*.

[16] 'Le Signe du temple'; see too, by the same author, 'Symbolic Reading'.

[17] *Jesus and Judaism*, pp. 61–76.

[18] It has already been argued (Excursus I) in favour of Lindars's theory that the raising of Lazarus did not figure in the first edition and that it displaced the temple episode in subsequent editions. In any case the story existed before the evangelist gave it a new twist by reading 'temple' in the way we have discussed. See Bultmann, p. 126 and nn. 1 and 2.

temple of his body. When therefore he was raised from the dead, his disciples remembered (ἐμνήσθησαν) that he had said this; and they believed the scripture and the word which Jesus had spoken. (2: 19–22)

Thus the evangelist transforms a prophecy into a riddle. The precise relationship with the Synoptic versions of the story (cf. also Acts 6: 14) is complex, but requires no discussion here; John alone, reflecting no doubt on the phrase 'three days', finds an allusion to the passion and resurrection.

In Chapter 5 the function of the riddle was considered from a wider form-critical perspective, and there is no need to repeat what was said there. But this particular riddle differs from all others in the Gospel in three important respects: (1) it is the only one provided with a key; (2) the distinction it envisages and effects is first of all between two stages of revelation (and therefore two levels of understanding) and only secondarily between insiders and outsiders; (3) it is the only riddling saying that the disciples are explicitly stated to have *remembered* after the resurrection.

The central feature of all the riddles, what constitutes them as riddles, is that they have two meanings, the plain and the esoteric. Thus ἄνωθεν in chapter 3 means both 'again' and 'from above'; the living water in chapter 4 means both 'fresh (i.e. spring) water' and 'revelation'. And so on. The term ναός, 'temple', in chapter 2 may seem to be an exception, for we are explicitly told by the evangelist that Jesus was referring to his body, and for the Christian reader this is clearly the sense that counts. One may compare the understanding of the temple found at Qumran, where the new, eschatological temple is the community itself: 'And he [Yahweh] has commanded that a sanctuary of men (מקדש אדם) be built for him, that there they might offer before him, like the smoke of incense, the works of the law' (4Q174, 1: 6–7). But it must be stressed that Jesus' identification of the temple as his body was not available to his first hearers. Durand's remark that the temple is a standard image of the human body is beside the point; the desperate suggestion that Jesus was pointing to himself as he spoke even more so. (In the introductory story the word for 'temple', not distinguished in the English translation, is ἱερός (2: 14).) The term ναός here is not a metaphor but a riddle, and its ambiguity is not removed but reinforced when it is made the object of the verb ἐγείρειν. Naturally the Christian reader will associate this term with resurrection, but it is also a perfectly ordinary word to use of the erection of a building.

The importance of this observation lies in the clear distinction it imposes between the first level of meaning, the only one that could conceivably be picked up by *Jesus' hearers*, the Jews, and the second level, exclusively reserved, as the passage itself implies, for *John's readers*.

Incisively and unobtrusively John is combining here three of the elements of apocalyptic discussed in the preceding chapter. In the first place, the distinction between the wise and the foolish appears in a new setting. The evangelist has no need to inform his readers, as they survey the scene from their privileged vantage-point, of the extent of the gulf that separates them from their own contemporaries in the synagogue. This gulf reaches back to the very beginning of Jesus' career. Part of the lesson, then, which does not require to be spelled out, is that the incomprehension of the Jews in the story is shared by their successors. Secondly, there is the distinction between the two ages, where everything preceding the resurrection of Jesus is relegated, so to speak, to the first age, that of the mystery undisclosed. Finally, we have the distinction between two stages of revelation, where the first, obscure revelation, stands in need of an interpreter. In this instance, as we shall see, the interpreter is the Paraclete.

The new insight into the real meaning of Jesus' words depends, we are told, upon a recollection of 'the scripture' (2: 22); this is reminiscent of the Qumran pesher, where the Scriptures are scanned for hidden references to the life of the community and its history. In this respect the Qumran sect is closer to traditional ways of thought than, say, *1 Enoch* or *4 Ezra*, both of whom appeal to revelations above and beyond the Law and the Prophets. The importance that the Scriptures hold for the evangelist is confirmed by an aside embedded in the resurrection narrative, where a knowledge of 'the scripture that he must rise from the dead' is seen to be conditional upon the experience of the resurrection: 'for as yet they did not know the scripture, that he must rise from the dead' (20: 9). This interpretation is confirmed by what Jesus says to Peter about the washing of the feet: 'What I am doing you do not know now (οὐκ οἶδας ἄρτι) but afterwards you will come to know (γνώσῃ)' (13: 7).[19]

---

[19] In this verse, for once, the classical distinction between εἰδέναι (know) and γινώσκειν (come to know) is observed. Cf. I. de la Potterie, 'Οἶδα et γινώσκω'. In general, however, de la Potterie makes too much of this distinction. Brown translates γινώσκειν here as 'understand'. Recognition and understanding are twins.

In 2: 22 John takes an additional step, one with momentous implications. For it is not only 'the scripture' that the disciples are said to have remembered, but also 'the word which Jesus had spoken', which is thus implicitly associated with Scripture as a source of revelation. For John a single saying of Jesus can have the status of a verse of Scripture (18: 9). Even more startlingly, Jesus himself can become the object of midrash (5: 39).

In a later episode towards the end of Jesus' public career the evangelist once again quotes a prophetic saying whose significance remained hidden. On the occasion of his final entry into Jerusalem

Jesus found a young ass and sat upon it; as it is written, 'Fear not, daughter of Zion; behold thy king is coming, sitting on an ass's colt!' His disciples did not understand (οὐκ ἔγνωσαν) this at first; but when Jesus was glorified, then they remembered that this had been written of him and had been done to him. (12: 14–16)

In this case it is not something that Jesus said but something he did that had to be remembered in order to give the prophecy its proper meaning. Jesus' deeds as well as his words remain obscure until after the resurrection, when they are recollected by the believing community.

On the basis of the evangelist's comment in 2: 22 we are entitled to assume, I think, that all the other riddling sayings where the audience catches the straightforward meaning but misses the esoteric are likewise intended to be read on two levels. The additional comment in 12: 16 reinforces this assumption and invites us to look for further examples of events in Jesus' life that acquire their full meaning later. If Martyn fails to use these episodes to buttress his own thesis, this is no doubt because it does not appear to have a special and immediate relevance to the Johannine community. Even so it is reasonable to suppose, as Martyn does, that the principle of two levels of understanding is also to be applied in cases where the esoteric meaning is better concealed (at least from a modern reader) and the more obvious reference remains anchored to the story *qua* story. The ὑπηρέται (servants), for instance, who appear in chapters 7 and 9 are straightforwardly the Levitical temple proctors at the beck and call of the Sanhedrin. Beneath this surface reference, suggests Martyn, they are 'the beadles of a local court, among whose functions may have been that of summoning litigants for trial before

a local Gerousia'.[20] Thus the same word does service for two distinct
sets of people, and the shift of meaning involves a dramatic change
of time, place, and circumstance. This ingenious suggestion may be
hard to verify but it accords well with the declared intentions of the
evangelist in the passages we have been examining.

How far are we justified in using the asides in 2: 22 and 12: 16 as
a key to unlock the secrets of the Gospel as a whole? We have seen
that the key fits Martyn's hypothesis, even though he appears not to
need it; moreover the dialogues in chapters 3 (Nicodemus) and 4
(the Samaritan woman) as well as the discourse in chapter 6 (the
Bread of Life) contain ambiguous expressions that pervade entire
episodes. The same fruitful ambiguity is exploited in the story of
Lazarus in chapter 11 and I shall argue in the next chapter that it is
also applicable to the farewell discourse, which can be read as a
testament and commission either of Jesus himself or of the Johannine
prophet. Much of the first half of the Gospel is dominated, as we have
seen, by the debate, in the manner of a trial, between Jesus and 'the
Jews', and there is abundant evidence that in speaking of 'the Jews'
the writer has in mind the recalcitrant leaders of his own local
synagogue as well as the temple establishment of Jesus' day. The key
turns surprisingly well in the Gospel wherever we insert it. Future
commentators on the Gospel may well find further applications,
large and small.

This technique, it may be observed, is frequently employed both in
literature and in art to draw analogies between the past and the
present and by bestowing a new significance upon a distant episode
or event to illustrate its relevance to the circumstances of the people
to whom the work is addressed.

One reason for adopting this procedure may be to evade censor-
ship. Verdi, for instance, composing the opera *Nabucco*, took a leaf
out of the Book of Daniel by suggesting resemblances between the
fate of the Hebrew slaves under Nebuchadnezzar (the eponymous
Nabucco) and the politically oppressed Italians of his own day, still
suffering in 1842 under the yoke of Austria. Sartre, in *Les Mouches*
and (more questionably) Anouilh in *Antigone* could get their message across during the German occupation of Paris by writing plays
that were ostensibly concerned, like those of their great seventeenth-
century predecessors, with ancient Greek myths. Closer in spirit than

---

[20] *History and Theology*[2], p. 88.

either of these to the Fourth Gospel is Arthur Miller's *The Crucible*, since the witch-hunting of the Massachusetts Puritans actually helped to shape the prejudices and principles of a country that had recently spawned the equally sinister sanctimoniousness of McCarthyism.

The most illuminating comparison, however, comes from the bold use of historical parallelism in Renaissance art. One of the Raphael Stanze in the Vatican furnishes an excellent example. The ostensible subject of the painting is the meeting of Pope Leo I and Attila at the gates of Rome, where Saints Peter and Paul, putting in a miraculous appearance at the last possible moment, succeeded in averting a catastrophe from the city. The Pope is given the features of Leo X, who was reigning at the time the fresco was painted (1513). Thus Raphael appears to be pointing to a contemporary event. What event? Surely, suggests Rudolf Witt-kower, the victory, that very year, of the papal armies over the French at Novara. 'In expressing one event through the other,' he remarks, '*and meaning both*, the painting becomes the symbol of an exalted mystery—the miraculous power of the Church, which remains the same throughout the ages, whether we are in the year 452 or 1513.[21]

Had Martyn noticed the evangelist's careful explanations of the necessary gap between hearing and seeing on the first level of understanding and full comprehension on the second, he would surely have revised his opinion that John was not 'analytic-ally conscious' of his own procedure. On the contrary, he gave

---

[21] *Allegory and the Migration of Symbols* (London, 1977), p. 180. In fact Wittkower was wrong on this point, because in the early sketches of the fresco Leo X appeared with the features of the previous Pope, Julius II, recognizable by his long beard. Cf. L. Pastor, *History of the Popes*, viii (London, 1908), pp. 282 f. But the point is none the less valid, since Julius, too, clearly wished to identify himself with his great predecessor. Attila himself would have appreciated the symbolism: Gibbon recounts how a few months before he was turned away from the gates of Rome, having just taken possession of the royal palace of Milan, Attila 'was surprised and offended at the sight of a picture which represented the Caesars seated on their throne, and the princes of Scythia prostrate at their feet. The revenge which Attila inflicted on this monument of Roman vanity was harmless and ingenious. He commanded a painter to reverse the figures and the attitudes; and the emperors were delineated on the same canvas approaching in a suppliant posture to empty their bags of tributary gold before the throne of the Scythian monarch' (*Decline and Fall*, ch. 35 (The Folio Society, iv; London, 1986, p. 233)). This story, which he got from the *Suda*, reminded Gibbon of the anecdote of the painted lion's retort to the man: 'Leo respondit, humana hoc pictum manu: videres hominem dejectum, si pingere leones scirent.'

considerable thought to the theological implications of the Gospel
genre. But first we must take up one more important point arising
directly out of the two passages (2: 19–22; 12: 14–16) that we have
been considering.

It was remarked earlier that the temple saying differs from all
other riddles in the Gospel in three respects. The first two we have
already discussed—the fact that it is the only one for which the
evangelist himself furnishes the key and the fact that it is primarily
directed to establishing the principle of the two stages of revelation.
It is also the only riddling saying that the disciples are explicitly said
to *remember*. Now neither here nor in the other allusion in the first
half of the Gospel to post-Easter remembrance is there any hint that
the disciples will only remember when they are reminded. Reminding is one of the functions, arguably the most important, of the
Paraclete.

3. THE ROLE OF THE SPIRIT

The Paraclete occupies such a prominent position in the farewell
discourse that with the exception of the saying in 7: 39, which we
will come to in due course, most commentators have rather
neglected the earlier references to the Spirit.[22] It has often been
remarked that the Paraclete shares many of Jesus' functions,
especially those associated with his role as revealer; it is less often
observed that in the body of the Gospel the Spirit is scarcely ever
mentioned without some specific association with the word. The
only exception, 3: 6, is an example of the Spirit's other great work,
creation, or, in this instance, re-creation. A good instance is the
closing paragraph of chapter 3: 'he whom God has sent utters
the words of God (τὰ ῥήματα τοῦ θεοῦ, for it is not by measure
that he gives the Spirit (οὐ γὰρ ἐκ μέτρου δίδωσιν τὸ πνεῦμα)'

---

[22] Notable exceptions are Felix Porsch, whose *Pneuma und Wort* is an important
contribution to Johannine scholarship and, more recently, Gary M. Burge, *The
Anointed Community*. Porsch's main aim is 'to clarify the relationship of the statements
concerning the Spirit-Paraclete in the farewell discourses to the sayings about the
Spirit in the remainder of the Gospel'. Accordingly, his work is intended 'to answer the
question whether there are two distinct conceptions (*Auffassungen*) of the Spirit in the
Gospel or whether there is at bottom essentially one homogeneous concept (*eine
einheitliche Vorstellung*)' (p. 3). He plumps resoundingly for unity.

(3: 34).[23] This may not be the 'completely unjohannine gloss' that Bultmann[24] takes it to be but rather an illustration of the evangelist's awareness that if the words of God are to be completely effective they must be accompanied by the gift of the Spirit.

Another example is 6: 63: 'It is the Spirit that gives life, the flesh is of no avail; the words that I have spoken to you are Spirit and life (τὰ ῥήματα ἃ ἐγὼ ἐλάληκα ὑμῖν πνεῦμά ἐστιν καὶ ζωή ἐστιν).' We know the life-giving Spirit from Paul as one of his terms for Christ (1 Cor. 15: 45). Since for John life is the reward and consequence of faith; this verse suggestively combines the twin roles of the Spirit in revelation and creation.[25]

Despite the constant association of the Spirit with the proclamation of the word, the πνεῦμα is no λόγος. In the Hebrew Bible what is clear, fixed, and determined about God is his word: the spirit, though her presence is constantly felt, is never seen and never grasped; like the sun, she is a source of light but not to be looked at; like the wind, which in Hebrew is the same word as spirit, she is elusive and impalpable (cf. John 3: 8). There could never be any question of her taking flesh.

The Word became flesh in time for the evangelist, on his own account, to have seen his glory (1: 14). The Son, not other than the Word, entered the world at a particular time. The words of Jesus have a fixed and irrevocable quality: as they come to us in the Gospel they are not only spoken but written. In a sense, then, the Gospel is *logocentric*: it shares in the definiteness and definitiveness of the Word that stands at its head. But the Prologue is not quite the compendium of Johannine theology it is often taken to be; there is a notable absentee. The presence of the Spirit is required if the message of the Gospel is not to be confined to those who first heard it; for the Spirit has the great asset of being unfettered by limitations of time and space.

The evangelist is so profoundly aware of the difference between

---

[23] The textual variants of this verse are of particular interest. The best-attested reading is this: ὃν γὰρ ἀπέστειλεν ὁ θεὸς τὰ ῥήματα τοῦ θεοῦ λαλεῖ, οὐ γὰρ ἐκ μέτρου δίδωσιν τὸ πνεῦμα. The subject of δίδωσιν is probably God but grammatically it could also be 'he whom God sent'. The first hand of B, the Codex Vaticanus, omits τὸ πνεῦμα, which could be a slip. Some MSS, however, including the Codex Bezae (D), the most important MS of the Western tradition, insert an extra ὁ θεός before δίδωσιν. This is strange, because one would have expected the Western tradition to leave open the possibility that it was Christ who was giving the Spirit.   [24] p. 164 n. 1.

[25] Once again Bultmann (p. 446 n. 3) raises the question whether the words πνεῦμά ἐστιν καί may not be an editorial addition.

the two stages of Jesus' revelation that for him one salient characteristic of the first stage is the absence, indeed the non-existence, of the
Spirit:

On the last day of the feast, the great day, Jesus stood up and proclaimed
(ἔκραζεν), 'If any one thirst, let him come to me, and let he who believes in
me drink (ἐάν τις διψᾷ ἐρχέσθω πρός με· καὶ πινέτω ὁ πιστεύων εἰς ἐμέ).[26] As
the scripture has said, "Out of his belly (κοιλία) shall flow rivers of living
water."' Now he said this about the Spirit, which those who believed in him
were to receive; for as yet there was no Spirit (οὔπω γὰρ ἦν πνεῦμα) because
Jesus was not yet glorified. (7: 37–9)

The next words refer to the crowd's response to Jesus' proclamation:
it is clear that 7: 39 is one of the evangelist's interpretative asides.
Taken alone, it is puzzling and obscure. Taken in conjunction with
the Paraclete sayings, its meaning is quite plain.

Raymond Brown has shown very clearly how the functions of the
Paraclete, formally identified as the Holy Spirit (14: 26) and the
Spirit of truth (14: 17; 15: 26; cf. 16: 13), are copied from those of
Jesus himself.[27] When he has departed the Paraclete will teach
(διδάξει) and remind (ὑπομνήσει) the disciples of all that he has said
to them (14: 26). He will also bear witness to Jesus (μαρτυρήσει,
15: 26) and guide the disciples into all truth (ὁδηγήσει ὑμᾶς εἰς τὴν
ἀλήθειαν πᾶσαν). Finally, he will speak what he hears (ὅσα ἀκούει
λαλήσει) and expound the things to come (τὰ ἐρχόμενα ἀναγγελεῖ,
16: 13). Specifically, declares Jesus, 'he will take from what is mine
and expound it to you' (ἐκ τοῦ ἐμοῦ λήμψεται καὶ ἀναγγελεῖ ὑμῖν,
16: 14).

In the first version of the farewell discourse (ch. 14) the revelatory
role of the Spirit is already sufficiently characterized as teaching and
reminding. In the second version (chs. 15–16) his role is the same
but described differently. The notion of 'Spirit of truth' is expanded

---

[26] I have preferred this to the alternative, equally well-attested punctuation, 'If
anyone is thirsty, let him come to me and drink. As the scripture says ... (ἐάν τις διψᾷ
ἐρχέσθω πρός με καὶ πινέτω. ὁ πιστεύων εἰς ἐμέ καθὼς εἶπεν ἡ γραφή ...), because it seems
to me marginally more likely that the source of the living water should be Jesus rather
than the believer. Brown, ad loc., discusses the question very fully and also reviews
the likely sources of the scriptural 'quotation'. It is conceivable that both meanings
are intended here and that the punctuation question should consequently be left
unresolved. Before the advent of the Spirit it is Jesus alone who is the source of
revelation; subsequently any believer, sent by him as he was sent by the Father, can
be the spring from which others may drink the life-giving waters of revelation.

[27] pp. 1141 f.

slightly: the Paraclete will now lead the disciples in or into the truth.[28] De la Potterie (1977) has shown conclusively that Dodd is wrong to think of Johannine truth as Platonic and that Bultmann is wrong to think of it as quasi-Gnostic. When Jesus tells the Jews, 'the truth will set you free', and they reply, uncomprehendingly and mendaciously, 'we have never been in bondage to anyone' (8: 32–3), the lie may surprise John's readers, but not the incomprehension. Nor would they expect Pilate to grasp the significance of Jesus' claim that 'Everyone who is of the truth hears my voice' (18: 37). John's use of irony may be less obviously divisive than his use of riddles, but like all dramatic irony, it only works because the audience, unlike the characters in the play, knows how the story ends. When Pilate asks, 'What is truth?' he shows that the irony of which he is the butt is a hair's breadth away from being a riddle. Like the Gospel's other words for revelation, 'living water' and 'bread of life', 'truth' too has an esoteric meaning reserved for those 'in the know'.

'He will not speak on his own authority (οὐ λαλήσει ἀφ' ἑαυτοῦ) but whatever he hears he will speak' (16: 13). With these words Jesus establishes the Paraclete as his own agent, invested with the same qualifications and the same authority that he himself had received from the Father. He had already promised to *send* the Paraclete (16: 7); now he reveals the nature of this mission more fully. Just as God, instead of speaking on his own behalf, sends his prophets and eventually his Son, to speak for him (see Chapter 8), so Jesus, no longer able to speak for himself, empowers the Paraclete to carry on, or rather complete, the task of revelation. 'He will take what is mine and expound it to you. All that the Father has is mine; that is why I said that he takes what is mine and will expound it to you' (16: 14–15). The emphatic repetition of the verb ἀναγγέλλειν, used in this concluding summary in its technical, apocalyptic sense (see Chapter 10), confirms that his role is that of the *angelus interpres*. He is sent from heaven to clarify what could not be fully comprehended without him; he completes a revelation that was previously partial and obscure. There is no aspect of John's extremely elaborate theory

---

[28] Even if we could be sure whether to read ἐν or εἰς (the MSS disagree) the distinction between the two prepositions has become blurred in Koine Greek. In either case 'the truth' is the same, whether it is thought of as a distant country situated on the far side of what is already known, or as a single region whose riches have yet to be fully explored.

of revelation for which he is more clearly indebted to the apocalyptic tradition than his explanation of the interpretative role of the Paraclete.[29] Whatever the origins and etymology of the term 'Paraclete' (and none of the proposed explanations is totally persuasive), John leaves us in no doubt about his role.

One question remains: if the Paraclete has nothing new to reveal, nothing that he has not heard from Jesus, what is meant by saying that he will expound *what is to come* (τὰ ἐρχόμενα ἀναγγελεῖ) (16: 13)? Scholars disagree on the answer to this question; some are more inclined than others to see in τὰ ἐρχόμενα a reference to eschatological truths as yet unrevealed. In the concluding paragraph, speaking of what the Paraclete hears or receives from him, Jesus twice uses the present tense (ἀκούει, 16: 13; λαμβάνει, 16: 15). The role of the *angelus interpres* is not confined to elucidating dreams and visions already communicated to the seer. The example of Uriel in *4 Ezra* shows that he can take the initiative in disclosing other mysteries besides. Probably those who make the Paraclete a mere mouthpiece of Jesus are being unduly restrictive. Perhaps the principle of two levels of understanding may be brought in yet again: to the listening disciples 'the things to come' may mean nothing more than Jesus' approaching passion and resurrection, to be explained to them in due course. John's readers, unless the expression has a more precise reference that is now lost to us, will have seen in it an assurance that the Paraclete would be at hand to instruct them when necessary in what they needed to know of a future as yet veiled from them.

After the farewell discourse there is no further mention of the Spirit until the scene of Jesus' death. But the word πνεῦμα has now acquired such resonance that on being told that Jesus 'gave up the ghost' (παρέδωκεν τὸ πνεῦμα, 19: 30), the reader will not stop at the obvious meaning but is sure to see an allusion to the gift of the Spirit. Not only the noun but also the verb (παραδιδόναι) is a notable instance of that fruitful ambiguity which makes it possible for two different meanings to be conveyed in a single phrase. In the first half of the Gospel John had used the word ὑψοῦν to suggest that Jesus' exaltation is conditional upon and contained in his death, so that

[29] This is not of course the Paraclete's only role. I have omitted to examine the various forensic functions ascribed to him in the fourth of the five Paraclete sayings: 16: 7–11. The source of these is probably not apocalyptic, but the Synoptic tradition according to which the disciples are promised that when they are arraigned before governors and kings the Holy Spirit will prompt them what to say (Matt. 10: 17–20; Mark 13: 9–11; Luke 12: 11–12; 21: 12–15).

passion and resurrection must be viewed as a single happening. Now the simple expression παραδιδόναι τὸ πνεῦμα allows him to fuse Easter and Pentecost as well, hinting that there is no need to think of the latter as a distinct and separate event.

In strict logic John's theology of the cross makes any resurrection narrative superfluous, and in his account of Jesus' death he has already indicated, symbolically, the sending of the Spirit. But the idea of this mission is important to him, and in any case we must assume that he is working with traditional material. He uses this to make the further point that the sending of the Spirit is a conscious and deliberate act, one that involves yet another mission, that of the disciples: 'As the Father has sent me, even so I send you. And when he had said this, he breathed on them and said to them, "Receive the Holy Spirit"' (20: 21–2). Placed here, just before the appearance to Thomas, this scene fulfils the promise of the farewell discourse, just as the scene of Pentecost, in Acts, fulfils the promise made at the end of Luke's Gospel.

4. FACT AND INTERPRETATION

Most of what has been said in the preceding two sections is presumably uncontentious. Some may find the comparison with the structure of apocalyptic unconvincing; others may be left unpersuaded by Martyn's version of the two levels of understanding. But the theory itself is no more than a reformulation of a principle of interpretation established by the evangelist himself: until Jesus is glorified his message cannot be fully grasped.

A number of questions, however, remain unanswered. How is the theory itself best understood? Can it bear the weight the evangelist puts upon it? How is it related to the Gospel genre as such? What are its theological implications? It is to these questions that I now turn, starting with some reflections upon previous attempts to set the theory in perspective.

We may begin with Hoskyns, the first commentator to construct his work upon a carefully considered treatment of the evangelist's own approach. Referring to his long introduction in Chapter 1, I remarked upon his eagerness to identify his own approach with that of the evangelist. In suggesting that the problem of the Gospel lies in its 'steady refusal to come to rest in any solution which

conservative or radical scholars have propounded',[30] he is really
speaking of his own problem and his own refusal. In associating the
evangelist with his own concern 'to barricade the roads which lead
to a disentangling of history and interpretation',[31] he is obviously
writing with nineteenth-century scholars in mind. Equally obviously, however, as we have just seen, the evangelist does invite us to
read the meaning *into* the story. But it should be observed that by
using the term 'history' Hoskyns implies that the narrative possesses
an irreducible factual content quite apart from the interpretation
which the evangelist puts upon it. At the same time, by refusing to
disentangle fact and interpretation, Hoskyns evades the question
that can be put concerning every single episode in the Gospel: what
historical residue would be left if the interpretation were, so to speak,
steamed off? To Hoskyns this question is illegitimate, for to attempt
to interpret the Gospel otherwise than on its own terms is 'to destroy
it, to make it irrelevant and therefore meaningless'.[32]

Hoskyns did not live to complete his introduction, and it was his
editor, F. N. Davey, who supplied the crucial chapter, 'The Fourth
Gospel and the Problem of the Meaning of History'. Davey pretends
to confront the question, 'Did Lazarus rise from the dead?', 'essentially,' he avers, 'a right question, ... because the conscious purpose
of the fourth Evangelist seems to be to force his readers back upon
the history—the flesh of Jesus, in which, according to his account,
the raising of Lazarus played so vital a part. But for this very reason,'
he adds, 'the answer cannot be either a simple "Yes" or a simple
"No".'[33] Davey, like Hoskyns, is confusing two very different
questions. One is the *historian*'s question: if, as Hoskyns maintains,
'John insists with the whole power of his conviction that what he
records is what actually and really occurred',[34] was he right to do
so? The historian is surely entitled to ask this question, just as he
may ask it of the infancy narrative that follows immediately upon
Luke's claim to recount his story accurately (ἀκριβῶς, 1: 3). The
other question is the *exegete*'s question: in searching for the meaning
of the Gospel, can one separate the story from the interpretation
without distortion? These two questions are not necessarily miles
apart. If the historian reaches the conclusion that Lazarus did not
actually rise from the dead, or even that he is a fictitious personage,
fabricated on the basis of a Lucan parable, then one may ask why,

30 p. 131.   31 p. 132.   32 p. 49.
33 p. 109.   34 p. 119.

when composing a Gospel markedly different from the other three, John was so strikingly unconcerned (*pace* Hoskyns) with factual accuracy. Is there perhaps a sub-text here that should convey to the perspicacious reader a message that actually contradicts the surface story, namely that none of this really matters—it is the interpretation that counts, not the history? If Bultmann, who strenuously denied the relevance of history to faith, had chosen to address the question, he might have come out with a reply more or less along these lines. In my opinion, however, the very use of the term 'history', with all its acquired connotations of a reliable factual account, begs the question. If instead we speak of 'story', or adopt Martyn's imperspicuous term 'einmalig', then we must agree that in the Fourth Gospel *story* and interpretation are inseparably locked together.

Would Hoskyns have admitted this substitution? I doubt it. Ludwig Wittgenstein, speaking of Christianity, declares that it 'is not based on a historical truth; rather it offers us a (historical) narrative and says, now believe! But not, believe this narrative with the belief appropriate to a historical narrative, rather: believe through thick and thin.'[35] That is the view of an interested outsider; Bultmann would agree, but he is not perhaps fully representative of mainstream Christianity. None the less it is a fair assessment of the thrust of the Fourth Gospel, and perhaps of the other three as well. Theologically speaking, one may be justified in allowing the Synoptic Gospels to shoulder the burden of historicity: in that case all that the committed Christian needs to say about the Fourth Gospel is that it is about a historical figure, Jesus of Nazareth. *What* it says of him is not history in any meaningful sense, but story—story plus interpretation.

Suppose, then, that the historian has given his answer to the question whether Lazarus actually rose from the dead, and that the answer is 'No'. Does this mean that the Gospel narrative has no truth and no validity? Only if there is no truth in narrative other than historical truth and no validity without historical verifiability. The story of the raising of Lazarus sums up, vividly and effectively, the whole of Jesus' healing ministry, and at the same time carries its central lesson: 'I have come that they may have life and have it more abundantly.' It is at least arguable that the essential purpose and

[35] *Culture and Value* (Oxford, 1970), p. 32 e.

effect of Jesus' ministry is better conveyed by this short narrative than by any amount of abstract theologizing. Moreover if part of the evangelist's purpose was to emphasize that Jesus' offence to the Jewish establishment lay as much in his healing as in his teaching, then he was right to place this episode in its present, climactic position in the Gospel. Why should he be expected to share the scruples and prejudices displayed by the modern reader in what Keats calls 'the irritable reaching after fact'?

To many people, no doubt, this defence will seem lame and inadequate. Ford Madox Ford included in the dedication to his first book of memoirs *Ancient Lights* the following remark: 'This book is full of inaccuracies as to facts but its accuracy as to impressions is absolute ... I don't really deal in facts; I have for facts a most profound contempt.'[36] To which a reviewer retorted: 'This obviously will not do; an account of actual events must be verified by such historical records as we have of those events, and by any objective test Ford's impressions appear as falsehoods.'[37] But if Ford was deliberately dealing in impressions, why should he be required to measure up to standards of historical objectivity that he professed to despise? What evidently disturbed the reviewer was a confusion of genres: flights of fancy that might be perfectly acceptable in a historical novel are reprehensible in a book of memoirs; this, however fallible the author's memory, should at any rate strive for accuracy. A similar unease is likely to affect modern readers, even in these relatively sophisticated days, as they try to come to terms with the fourth evangelist's frequent disregard of the facts, surely more accessible to him than to us, of Jesus' ministry.

One modern writer who strongly objects to what he regards as the cavalier dismissal by the scholarly establishment of John's claims to objectivity is J. A. T. Robinson, whose book *The Priority of John* (1985) is one of the curiosities of contemporary Johannine studies. Hoskyns, as we have seen, believed that the evangelist deliberately blocked the way to any separation of history and theology; he himself was careful to leave the barricade in place: he even reinforced it. Robinson shows less patience and less prudence. He

---

[36] Compare what Proust's Marcel says about a staircase in Swann's house: 'Mon amour de la vérité était si grand que je n'aurais pas hésité à leur donner ce renseignement même si j'avais su qu'il était faux; car seul il pouvait leur permettre d'avoir pour la dignité de l'escalier des Swann le même respect que moi' (*À la recherche du temps perdu* (Éditions de la Pléiade, 1954), i. 505).   [37] *TLS* 1972, p. 519.

begins by asserting his conviction that 'John does not take us further from the history but leads more deeply into it'.[38] This sounds a bit like Hoskyns, but whereas Hoskyns might use such a remark to justify a refusal to engage in detailed historical probing, Robinson's long book is largely a defence of John's historical accuracy in such matters as his portrayal of the career of John the Baptist and his dating of the temple episode.

Those who take the Gospel on its own terms, whatever their view of its general historicity, will remain unmoved by Robinson's ponderous arguments. The test case, for him as for Hoskyns and Davey, must be, 'Did Lazarus rise from the dead?' On this point Robinson exhibits more caution than usual: 'The tradition that Jesus raised the dead is an inalienable part of the proclamation of the powers of the new age, and what would call for explanation would be if John did not, like the Synoptists, present us with the same picture.'[39] Leaving aside the obvious but trival objection that none of the Synoptists says that Jesus raised Lazarus from the dead (why?), the real difficulty persists: Did he? Are we meant to infer from Robinson's evasive remark about the tradition that Jesus actually did raise the dead to life? He does not say so; but neither does he attempt to dispel the suggestion that the story of Lazarus (whom he certainly regards as a historical personage) is grounded upon factual reminiscences. But does the author of *Honest to God* really believe that Jesus raised an already rotting corpse to life in the way that John describes? And if he does not, then why does he regard the widespread scholarly scepticism concerning John's historical accuracy as 'an unwarranted presumption'?

Early in *The Priority of John*, Robinson singles out for special praise two famous lines from Browning's *A Death in the Desert*, taken from the ageing apostle's long address to his disciples as he prepares for death:

> What first were guessed as points I now knew stars,
> And named them in the Gospel I have writ.

It must be said that throughout his book Robinson shows more interest in the points than in the stars, being apparently blind to the difficulties, both practical and theoretical, of reconstructing points from stars. Besides, as James Dunn pertinently enquires, 'What if

---

[38] p. 33.   [39] Ibid., p. 221.

John's Gospel was *not* intended primarily to serve as a source of *historical* information about Jesus in his ministry on earth? In that case an enquiry which sought to *vindicate* John by demonstrating the historical roots of his traditions would in fact be missing the point, *John's* point.'[40] Certainly there is nothing wrong, *pace* Hoskyns, in sifting through the Gospel in the hope of finding authentic historical traditions. Dodd's second great book on the Gospel (1963) is a more circumspect essay in this direction. But Dodd realizes, as seemingly Robinson does not, that this was not the purpose of the evangelist himself. You can use a table-cloth as a bath-towel, but it won't do the job very well because that is not what it is designed for. In short, though well-informed and even, in an idiosyncratic way, quite informative, Robinson's book, does nothing to advance the *understanding* of the Gospel.

We may turn next to two scholars who have attempted to explain the technique of the Fourth Gospel through the concept of *Horizontverschmelzung* propounded by the Heidelberg philosopher Hans-Georg Gadamer in his highly influential *chef-d'œuvre, Wahrheit und Methode* (1960). This is an exercise in philosophical hermeneutics, a transcendental study in the Kantian sense; that is to say one that enquires into *the conditions of the possibility* of hermeneutical understanding. How is it possible, Gadamer asks, either to understand or to interpret an ancient text or tradition, a legal document, say, or a work of art, without deviation and distortion? The interpreter has a horizon of his own, which he can never wriggle out of or shake off and which cannot but affect and determine his understanding of the past. At the same time he is genuinely trying to understand: he is not setting out to distort, he is anxious to be faithful to the original document or tradition, which Gadamer conceives as having a horizon of its own. There are accordingly *two* horizons, which are welded or fused together (that is what *verschmelzen* means) in the work of the historian or interpreter. The result is a third horizon, a fresh perspective that cannot be identified directly with either of the other two.

Now from one point of view Gadamer may be thought to be giving voice to an insight shared by many of his contemporaries: there are no plain facts lying around like nuggets of gold waiting to be picked up by keen-eyed prospectors: there is no uninterpreted interpret-

---

[40] 'Let John be John', p. 316.

able.[41] If Leopold von Ranke ever seriously held that the only function of history was to record what actually happened, then he was wrong. But Gadamer is actually doing something rather different: he is trying to penetrate the nature and essence of historical understanding.

Two contemporary exegetes, Franz Mussner[42] and Takashi Onuki,[43] have sought to make use of Gadamer's theories to understand the Fourth Gospel. In doing so they are not insisting that any modern reader must acknowledge and accept his own distance from the text of the Gospel. Rather they are suggesting that in applying a double perspective to the traditions he has inherited concerning Jesus' life and teaching, John himself is, as it were, putting Gadamer's theories into practice. Onuki thinks that Mussner really has no right to claim to be using Gadamer. Maintaining as he does that the evangelist was an eyewitness of the scenes that he was later to record, Mussner does not, according to Onuki, allow for the kind of gap between tradition and interpretation that Gadamer's theory presupposes. My own objection to Mussner, which holds for Onuki's work as well, is rather different. Gadamer is interested in the attempt of a modern reader to grasp the *original meaning* of ancient texts and traditions. His point is that such a reader is unable to transport himself back on a magic carpet into the world in which these texts were composed and transmitted. He is tethered by an invisible string to his own 'horizon'. The aspect of Gadamer's work that Mussner and Onuki see as particularly applicable to the Fourth Gospel Gadamer himself would assert to be equally (and necessarily!) applicable to John's contemporaries Tacitus and Josephus, the one attempting to write *sine ira et studio* (without rancour or partiality), the other endeavouring to serve up a version of Jewish history intelligible to Gentile readers. The purpose of the fourth evangelist is very different. Certainly he wants to preserve a valuable tradition

---

[41] This image is borrowed from the journalist Claud Cockburn, who expounds as well as any philosopher the dangers of what he calls 'the factual heresy': 'there are no such facts. Or if there are they are meaningless and entirely ineffective; they might as well not be lying about at all until the prospector—the journalist—puts them into relation with other facts: presents them, in other words. Then they become as much of a pattern presented by him as if he were writing a novel. In that sense all stories are written backwards—they are supposed to begin with the facts and develop from there, but in reality they begin with a journalist's point of view, a conception, and it is the point of view from which the facts are subsequently organised. Journalistically speaking, "in the beginning is the word" ' (*In Time of Trouble* (London, 1956), pp. 232 f.).   [42] *Historical Jesus.*   [43] *Gemeinde.*

and to keep its source in mind; but his main concern is to offer a *new* reading, one that transcends any understanding that was possible in the time of Jesus himself. Consequently the transformation to which John, under the compulsion of his own faith, subjects the Jesus-tradition is much more wide-ranging and of far greater significance than the attempt, say, of a modern historian to understand the Second World War.[44]

Since on the whole Mussner and Onuki understand John quite well (though no better, in my view, than Hoskyns), their misapplication of Gadamer's work may be thought fairly harmless. It does, however, indicate a more serious misconception. Gadamer's point was that historians cannot help writing as they do, for all their earnest endeavours to transmit a faithful record of the past. But the evangelists are not writing history at all. To see this one has only to reflect how absurd it would be to apply the term 'Gospel' to any of the huge number of *Lives of Jesus* studied in Schweitzer's *Quest* or indeed to any recent historical investigation such as E. P. Sanders's *Jesus and Judaism*. It is not just that these modern works of imaginative scholarship are not in any sense canonical and do not carry the imprimatur of the Church. It is because a Gospel is more of a creed than a biography: it is a proclamation of faith. Wittgenstein was right, or nearly so. Of its very nature a Gospel requires a response from its readers that differs *toto caelo* from that demanded by a historical narrative.

Edith Stein recounts in her own autobiography how, left alone by her hosts over the weekend in a country house, she came across and read, with mounting absorption, the *Life* of Teresa of Avila. On finishing it she said to herself—and it was the moment which she afterwards thought of as the time both of her conversion to Christianity and of her vocation to the Carmelite Order—'Dies ist die Wahrheit': 'This is the truth.' That is close, very close, to the kind of truth proclaimed by the Gospels. Though writing of revelations, Saint Teresa certainly did not think of her work as revelatory in the way that the Gospels are. But the central purpose of all four Gospels has a close affinity with the impact that her work had upon Edith Stein. John especially wrote his Gospel, as he says, 'that you may believe'. Unlike the ordinary historian, whose main aim is to write

---

[44] Where he may well find, like Paul Fussell, 'the domination of the Second War by the First', since not only generals but also other less exalted combatants think of the war they are fighting as a kind of re-enactment of the Great War of 1914–18. See *The Great War and Modern Memory* (Oxford, 1975), pp. 317 f.

the truth about the past, the evangelists are chiefly interested in projecting a message of immediate relevance to their own present. I believe this to be true of all four Gospels; it is certainly true of the Fourth. One early commentator who recognized this was Origen. He believed that the evangelists intended 'to give the truth where possible at once spiritually and corporeally (outwardly), but where this was not possible to give preference to the spiritual over the corporeal, the true spiritual meaning being often preserved in what at the corporeal level might be called a falsehood': προέκειτο γὰρ αὐτοῖς, ὅπου μὲν ἐνεχώρει, ἀληθεύειν πνευματικῶς ἅμα καὶ σωματικῶς ὅπου μὴ ἐνδέχετο ἀμφοτέρως προκρίνειν τὸ πνευματικὸν τοῦ σωματικοῦ, σωζομένου πολλάκις τοῦ ἀληθοῦς πνευματικοῦ ἐν τῷ σωματικῷ, ὡς ἂν εἴποι τις, ψεύδει.[45] Like Ford Madox Ford, but unlike Sir Edwyn Hoskyns, Origen is not afraid to speak of falsehood here—though he does soften the expression slightly and probably has in mind a falsehood akin to Plato's famous 'noble lie' (καλὸν ψεῦδος) or Wallace Stevens's 'supreme fiction'. He recognizes that John cannot always succeed in combining spiritual truth with historical accuracy. Interestingly, though, he takes no notice of what to a modern reader is the most fascinating and original feature of John's technique: the device he has invented for straddling a *temporal* gap.

The comparison with Stevens deserves to be pressed because of the extraordinarily far-reaching analogy between Stevens's vision of poetry as the application of the imagination to reality and John's considered view of the Gospel as tradition remembered and interpreted in the light of faith. The poet in Stevens felt inhibited by a too bold and overpowering presence of the real, an inhibition which, paradoxically, furnishes him with the theme of some of his finest poems (e.g. 'Bouquet of Roses in Sunlight', 'The Plain Sense of Things', 'The Motive for Metaphor'). Nevertheless what he calls his 'necessary angel' was, when it counted most, the angel of reality[46]

---

[45] *Comm. in Joh.* 10: 4: Migne, *PG* xiv. 313 C.

[46] 'For nine readers out of ten, the necessary angel will appear to be the angel of the imagination and for nine days out of ten that is true, although it is the tenth day that counts' (*Letters of Wallace Stevens* (London, 1967), ed. H. Stevens, p. 753):

> I am the angel of reality
> Seen for a moment standing at the door ...
> I am the necessary angel of earth,
> Since, in my sight, you see the earth again,
> Cleared of its stiff and stubborn, man-locked set.

(*Collected Poems* pp. 496 f.)

and he was aware that 'to be at the end of fact is not to be at the beginning of imagination but to be at the end of both'.[47] Equally, however, to attempt to extract the fact from the poem is to be at the end of both fact and imagination—at the end of poetry. The absence of any fruitful interaction between the imagination and reality was for him a grim and intolerable poverty of spirit.

Stevens saw imagination as having virtually ousted faith from its throne: imagination was now what he called 'the reigning prince'.[48] In his work the transforming power of the imagination has seized and irradiated reality in such a way as to make it irrecoverable in the form in which the poet found it. Similarly the visionary glow of the Johannine prophet has welded tradition and belief into the shining affirmation of the finished Gospel. If the result appears new and extraordinary this is because his religious genius impelled him to disclose more and more of what he called 'the truth', that is to say the revelation of Jesus. What he saw and what he inherited are now contained in the book he wrote. Attempt to prise them apart and the consequence will be at best what Stevens calls somewhere 'an inert savoir'.

5. THE CONSCIOUSNESS OF GENRE

The purpose of this section is to emphasize, by means of a number of comparisons, the remarkable extent to which the reflections John makes upon his own work, the asides discussed in Section 2, and the Paraclete-sayings considered in Section 3, indicate his artistic self-awareness, his consciousness of genre. It is this above all, I believe, that justifies our comparing John with some of the very greatest artists, painters, and composers as well as poets and novelists, in the history of Western civilization.

Since the advent of Symbolism in the latter half of the nineteenth century Western art has exhibited a degree of self-consciousness that far exceeds anything that preceded it. I shall not be suggesting that John's deep interest in the implications of his own work approximates that of James Joyce or Franz Kafka or, still less, Stéphane Mallarmé, who believed, or said he believed, that the whole world existed 'pour aboutir à un livre' and who describes one of his own

[47] *Opus Posthumous* (London, 1959), p. 175.
[48] *The Necessary Angel* (New York, 1965), p. 171.

poems as 'allégorique de lui-même'. John does not write about writing: he is not a Proust, composing a novel about the making of a novelist, or a Thomas Mann, inventing a character (Doktor Faustus) who would embody all that is dangerous and Dionysiac in the arts.

It must be added that it would certainly be a mistake to attribute to John any close awareness of genre as such. There were of course genres in Hellenistic literature as well as in Ancient Israel. The books of Chronicles were modelled on those of Kings, the Qumran psalms on those of David. Certain conventions persisted in what we call the wisdom literature; and so on. But the imitation of what we can see to be widely differing literary genres does not mean that the imitators were conscious of these *as genres*. Indeed John Barton has argued that the writers of the Second Temple were largely oblivious to the distinctions between, say, prophecy and apocalyptic that modern scholars are so keen to establish.[49] I believe that he overstates his case somewhat; even so Martin Hengel has a cogent point when, in claiming for the Gospels (mistakenly, in my view) some sort of biographical or quasi-biographical status, he argues that no reader of Mark would have been conscious of being confronted by a totally new literary genre.[50] So in suggesting that the Fourth Gospel is not only an instance of the Gospel genre but also a reflection upon it, am I not guilty of an anachronism?

Not entirely. Without entering into the largely sterile dispute concerning the so-called intentionalist fallacy, we can detect in John a very deep understanding of the complexities and paradoxes of what he was attempting, however little he may have been interested in generic distinctions between Gospels and other forms of narrative prose. Bousset was wrong as well as illogical to assert that what he called John's *großer Gedanke* was not the product of deliberate reflection,[51] and Martyn equally wrong to suggest that John was not 'analytically conscious' of the two levels of understanding with which he worked.[52]

The world of European literature offers dozens of examples of conscious indebtedness to and divergence from tradition. Among the most celebrated are *Don Quixote*, which at once satirizes and exemplifies the romances that so enthralled its eponymous hero, curiously similar in this respect to that other literary Don, Byron's *Don Juan*, sardonically pillorying the epic genre of which it is itself

---

[49] *Oracles of God*, pp. 198–202.   [50] *Studies in the Gospel of Mark*, pp. 32 f.
[51] *Kyrios Christos*[6], p. 159.   [52] *History and Theology*[2], p. 77.

such a striking specimen. Another outstanding example is *Lycidas*, in which Milton follows Vergil in 'strictly meditating the thankless Muse', invoking as he does so not only the smooth-sliding Mincius of Vergil's native Mantua but his own equally smooth-sliding Cam. *Lycidas* is one of those especially brilliant works of art that compel the reader to look back upon a whole series of earlier works in the same genre and in doing so force him to reflect also on what is and what is not essential to it. From Theocritus onwards pastoral was a self-conscious and artificial genre, its fields and rivers having something of the stylized quality of the formal gardens of Watteau and Fragonard, its shepherds and shepherdesses already anticipating the whims and fancies that Marie-Antoinette wished to capture, indeed to embalm, in Le Petit Trianon. Without some knowledge of the tradition Milton exploits and adapts, one can have at best a partial and superficial understanding of a poem that stands at the end of this tradition, as the poet bids farewell to it and moves on 'to fresh woods and pastures new'—pastures in which pastoral will have no place.

Even music, unlikely as it may seem, offers analogies to this procedure. Janet Johnson, writing of Rossini's late opera *Il Viaggio a Rheims*, which she had to piece together from a number of scattered manuscripts, concludes that 'like many final works of a genre, *Viaggio* is really an opera about opera'.[53] Richard Strauss's *Capriccio*, Wagner's *Meistersinger*, and even Mozart's *Schauspieldirektor* attempt something similar. Other examples include Bach's B Minor Mass and Beethoven's Diabelli Variations and, at the other end of the musical spectrum, Robert Simpson's comments, themselves in quartet form, upon Beethoven's Rasumovsky Quartets.

Painting, too, offers a number of striking parallels. One example is Manet's *Déjeuner sur l'herbe*, which shockingly exposes the bolder implications of the discreet but suggestive genre of pastoral scenes that it both copies and challenges, thus paving the way for the more 'honest' and 'truthful' works of impressionism. More challenging still, and to a modern eye more obviously revolutionary, is the work of the early Cubists, especially Gris, Picasso, and Braque. Though out to break the conventions of single-perspective portraiture, they remained interested in painting portraits, as well as in opening up and setting down on canvas the hidden ambitions that motivate all

---

[53] In the booklet accompanying the discs, *Deutsche Grammophon*, 1984.

true portrait painters. Like all paintings, portraits are creations or inventions: but the cubist portrait, even when painted from life, offers much more to prospective viewers than they could get by standing in front of the traditional flat canvas. At the same time it underlines the truth that *no* portrait is simply an immediate representation of reality: 'ceci n'est pas une pipe' (Magritte); and 'things as they are—are changed upon the blue guitar' (Stevens). Of course there was already a pressure towards abstraction. Picasso says of his *Girl with a Mandolin* that he allowed Fanny Tellier to pose for him against his better judgement, because her presence prevented him 'from painting what I wanted'.[54] John the Evangelist, who also distrusted direct vision, would have appreciated the force of Picasso's misgivings.

Finally, a particularly brilliant example, there is Rembrandt's *Nightwatch*, whose erroneous and misleading name shows how early its bright beauty must have been overlaid by grime. This is an example of what the Dutch call *schutterstukken*, group pictures of guilds of militiamen that were extremely popular in Amsterdam right up to the middle of the seventeenth century. But in exemplifying the genre, Rembrandt also transcends it, merging portraiture with pageantry so as to bring out the historical significance of the city's militia at a time when their role as defenders of the city had already lost any real importance. At the same time his painting is an effective critique of the ordinariness of the work of some of his contemporaries, including certain pieces painted to hang in the same hall, the *groote sael* of the Kloveniersdoelen where members of Banning Cocq's company used to gather for festive occasions. Rembrandt was familiar with the tradition he had inherited and his masterpiece proves that he had reflected upon it deeply.[55]

These varied examples of artistic self-awareness may help to highlight John's own obvious desire to draw attention to the implications of the Gospel genre and in particular his debt to apocalyptic.

Note on Pseudonymity

In conclusion, a word may be added about one aspect of John's technique that has been widely disregarded. I call this, with some hesitation, the device of pseudonymity.

[54] Quoted and discussed by Christopher Green in *TLS*, 20 Mar. 1980, p. 331.
[55] See E. Haverkamp-Begemann, *Rembrandt: The Nightwatch* (Princeton, 1982).

At first sight the pseudonymity of John's Gospel, like that of Matthew, seems far removed from the audacious pretensions of so many near-contemporary apocalypses to reach far back into history, and in some cases (Adam and Enoch), prehistory. But John, too, insists from the outset that he was living at a time and in a place when great mysteries were being revealed. We shall see in the last chapter that the Prologue is more about revelation than creation. Its name for revelation is ὁ Λόγος, the Word, which 'became flesh, and dwelt amongst us ... and we have seen (ἐθεασάμεθα) his glory' (1: 14). This familiar verse must have made a deep impression upon its first readers. There is a similar effect at the beginning of *Madame Bovary*. By numbering himself among Charles's classmates, Flaubert takes his readers aback in the same way: 'Nous étions à l'école, quand ...'. Although he will take no further part in the action, the writer implicitly asserts his authority to tell the tale that follows by establishing his presence in the room where it began.

The 'we' of John's Prologue is perhaps more open to misunderstanding. Bultmann for one is anxious to dispel any impression that it implies some sort of claim to privileged witness:

Those who speak the ἐθεασάμεθα are believers. The old dispute whether the speakers in *v.* 14 are eye-witnesses or those who see in a spiritual sense, is based on a false alternative, inasmuch as the precise character of 'spiritual' sight is not defined. For on the one side it is clear that the specifically Johannine 'seeing' is not concerned with eye-witnessing in a historical or legal sense. For in this sense the 'Jews' were also eye-witnesses, and yet they saw nothing (9: 39–41). On the other hand such 'seeing' has nothing to do with the 'spiritual' sight found in the Greek contemplation of Ideas or in mysticism. ... This 'seeing' is neither sensory nor spiritual, but is the sight of *faith*.[56]

The 'eye-witnesses' as such are considered not as those who stand guarantee for some later generation for the truth of the revelation, but as those who confront every generation anew with the offence that the δόξα must be seen in the one who became σάρξ. ... The ἐθεασάμεθα, in which the offence is overcome, is renewed again and again.[57]

For all its insight, this interpretation is too dismissive of the obvious reading according to which the evangelist is associating himself with those who saw the glory of the Incarnate Logos while he was actually dwelling 'among us'. That, after all, is how the very first

[56] p. 69.   [57] p. 70.

commentator upon the Prologue, the author of 1 John, understood the passage,[58] and while he is not an infallible guide, his comments must carry a certain weight, representing as they do the views of a prominent group of Johannine Christians.

6. 'THE DISCIPLE AT SECOND HAND'

Blessed are those who have not seen and yet believe.

The Philosophical Fragments, from which the heading of this section is derived, was published in 1844. It contains Kierkegaard's response to what Lessing called his 'ditch' (*der garstige breite Graben*), the assertion that 'Accidental truths of history can never become proof of necessary truths of reason.'[59] The work is concerned, then, with the relationship between Christian faith and philosophical idealism. Lessing distinguished sharply between the eyewitnesses of a historical event, for whom it is a truth of experience, and subsequent generations, for whom it can be no more than an 'accidental truth of history'. There is consequently a great gulf between Christian faith and true philosophy: the claim that the former is somehow concerned with eternally valid truths that have entered history at a particular time and place must be rejected.

Kierkegaard's response to this dichotomy is largely derived from a profound reflection upon the Fourth Gospel. In the last chapter of the *Philosophical Fragments* he concludes that the concept of a disciple at second hand is illusory, in particular that there is no basis for the implication that the first generation of Christian believers, Jesus' own contemporaries, is privileged over all subsequent believers:

There is no disciple at second hand. The first and the last are essentially on the same plane, only that a later generation finds its occasion in the testimony of a contemporary generation, while the contemporary generation finds the occasion in its own immediate contemporaneity, and in so far owes nothing to any other generation. But this immediate contemporaneity is merely an occasion which can scarcely be expressed more emphatically than in the proposition that the disciple, if he understood himself, must wish that the immediate contemporaneity should cease, by the God's leaving the

[58] 'That which was from the beginning, which we have heard, which we have seen with our eyes, which we have looked upon and touched with our hands, concerning the word of life ...' (1 John 1: 1).

[59] Gotthold E. Lessing, *Über den Beweis des Geistes und der Kraft* (1777).

earth. ... This thought, that it is profitable for the disciple that the God [*Guden*, i.e. Christ] should leave the earth, is taken from the New Testament: it is found in the Gospel of John.[60]

As indeed it is: 'It is good for you that I go.' In one respect Kierkegaard agrees with Lessing: Christianity is incompatible with philosophical idealism. Never one to shirk paradox, Kierkegaard takes the opposite path to Lessing, refusing to admit that the truth upon which Christianity is based is merely or simply historical:

If our fact is assumed to be a simple historical fact, contemporaneity is a *desideratum*. ... If the fact is an eternal fact, every age is equally near. ... If the fact in question is an absolute fact, it would be a contradiction to suppose that time had any power to differentiate the fortunes of men with respect to it, that is to say, in any decisive sense.[61]

Kierkegaard's own view is that 'the fact' is neither *simply* historical nor yet eternal (i.e. non-historical) but absolute, and 'the absolute fact is also a historical fact'. Kierkegaard himself, I believe, would claim to have leapt over Lessing's ditch, but it might seem to others that he has really refused the jump. Can one resolve a paradox simply by emphasizing it?

However that may be, Kierkegaard's idea that in Christ ('the God') historical and eternal were somehow indissolubly fused together in what he calls an 'absolute' fact is conceptually very close to the notion of the incarnation of the Logos found in the Johannine Prologue. The pre-existent Word (*Λόγος ἄσαρκος*), God's design for the world from the beginning (*ἐν ἀρχῇ*) can easily be thought of as an eternal truth; the Incarnate Word (*Λόγος ἔνσαρκος*) is ineluctably historical—but not simply historical. Like Wisdom, of whom it is the masculine surrogate, the Word is naturally timeless. But when she became identified with the Law (which had entered the world at a particular time and in a particular place—Mount Sinai) Wisdom acquired a history, and so did the Word when he came to dwell among men. Conversely, whereas the Law was invested with eternity on being identified with Wisdom, Jesus Christ had from the beginning the eternity that belonged to the Word: in chapter 17, the only other point in the Gospel in which the name 'Jesus Christ' occurs, 'the glory as of the Father's only Son' (1: 14) is said to have been given him 'before the foundation of the world' (17: 24).

---

[60] *Philosophical Fragments*, pp. 131 f.   [61] Ibid., pp. 124 f.

Though Kierkegaard was certainly unaware of the remote origins of the fusion of the historical (the Law) with the eternal (Wisdom), they help to explain, over a gap of many centuries, the affinity of his thought with that of the fourth evangelist. John, too, was constantly concerned to emphasize the enduring validity of the Christ-event. After establishing this strongly in the Prologue he takes a very different tack in the body of the Gospel, but without ever relinquishing his central insight. The lesson is driven home in the concluding episode of the Gospel, the story of the appearance of the Risen Jesus to Thomas.

Kierkegaard alludes to this episode and to the beatitude that rounds it off towards the end of his book:

The immediate contemporaneity is so far from being an advantage that the contemporary must precisely desire its cessation, lest he be tempted to devote himself to seeing with his bodily eyes and ears, which is all a waste of effort and a grievous, aye a dangerous toil.[62]

Kierkegaard is surely right to associate the blessing of those who do not see with the benefits arising from Jesus' departure. Having identified himself, on the first page of the Gospel, with those who have beheld the glory of the incarnate Logos, the evangelist concludes by disclaiming any special privilege for these—and even, by implication, for himself. 'These [signs] are written that you may believe' (20: 31). A witness is needed, but to believe on the word of the Gospel-writer is to believe the words of his Gospel, and these are the words of Jesus, recorded by the evangelist with the active assistance of the Paraclete.

Apart from 13: 17, the blessing on those deprived of sight is the only beatitude in this Gospel: it is an admirable epitome of the extraordinary favours reserved, according to John, for later Christian believers. Bultmann disagrees. He asks, 'Does this blessing extol those born later, because they have this precedence over the first disciples, in that they believe without seeing, and precisely on the basis of the disciples' word?' That, he answers, 'can hardly be possible'.[63] Rather he sees Thomas as 'representative of the common attitude of men, who cannot believe without seeing miracles'. But this is more than a cautionary tale. It must be taken in conjunction with the conclusion, which succeeds the blessing without a break and expresses the evangelist's purpose in composing his Gospel. The

[62] Ibid., p. 133.   [63] p. 696.

evangelist is deliberately contrasting the situation of those for whom he writes with that of Jesus' contemporaries, and showing them how mistaken they would be to think of these as somehow privileged over against themselves.[64] Where faith is concerned, physical vision is a handicap rather than an advantage, since there is always a risk of confusing vision with faith and even of preferring it. Thomas is rebuked for insisting on touching as well.

Lessing had dug his ditch by applying a philosophical distinction borrowed from Leibniz to one of the most distinctive features of Christianity, its appeal to history and to historical truth. Much nineteenth-century New Testament scholarship can be seen as an attempt to come to terms with his famous dictum and to cross or bridge his famous ditch.[65] In Chapter 1, in our rapid survey of pre-Bultmannian Johannine scholarship, we saw that most of the solutions can be located quite easily on one or other side of the divide. Hoskyns, whether or not in conscious opposition to Lessing, was one of the few theologians to admit no barrier—or ditch—between history and what he called 'the meaning' of the Fourth Gospel. It is worth remembering that Kierkegaard, taking his inspiration from the Gospel itself, had made a similar move nearly a century earlier, thus proving himself for once a better exegete than Bultmann, who had learned much from him and was in other ways theologically closer to him than to any other philosopher except Heidegger.

[64] We shall see in the next chapter how on a second level of meaning the Johannine prophet is also comforting the community as they prepare to mourn his own imminent death.

[65] See R. Slenczka, *Geschichtlichkeit und Personensein.*

12

DEPARTURE AND RETURN

No one assembling an anthology of religious literature could reasonably ignore the Gospel of John. The compiler's choice might well fall upon the four chapters (14–17) comprising the farewell discourse, whose profound and mysterious beauty cannot but make a strong impression on any responsive reader. Unfortunately its delicate colours and fine contours are easily submerged under the soft silt of scholarship. Subjected to close critical analysis, its glowing mysteries rapidly fade into puzzles. Puzzles there are, unquestionably. What, for example, is the origin of the strange term 'Paraclete', not found in the New Testament outside the Johannire writings, and seldom enough elsewhere?[1] What and where are the μοναί (mansions, rooms, dwellings) which Jesus is to prepare for his followers? How are we to explain the sudden, chilling allusion, at the end of chapter 14, to 'the prince of the world'? The many learned and interesting answers that have been given to these and similar questions are mostly inconclusive. Some of the puzzles, to be sure, have been satisfactorily resolved. The hypothesis of a second edition, adopted in one form or another by many commentators, admirably accounts for the curious doublets in chapter 14, on the one hand, and chapters 15–16, on the other. The precise articulation of the terms 'way' and 'truth', and 'life' in one of Jesus' best-known utterances has been determined beyond reasonable doubt.[2] The central message of the discourse, as the community confronts the bleak prospect of Jesus' imminent departure, comes through strongly and clearly.

The present chapter will touch upon many of these questions but,

---

[1] In my judgement the assessment of C. K. Barrett, made some 40 years ago, still stands: 'in spite of the labours of scholars the background of John's thought about the Paraclete Spirit has not yet been satisfactorily illuminated nor has the source of its language been made clear' ('Holy Spirit', p. 12).
[2] See I. de la Potterie, '"Je suis la voie, la vérité et la vie"'.

apart from the last, only incidentally. Its purpose is neither to offer
new answers to the unresolved puzzles nor to expound old answers
to the remainder. Instead I propose to take a fresh look at the
discourse as a whole, or rather at what most agree to be the first
version of it.[3] One is entitled to choose here, because the two
versions are in certain respects alternatives. In a loose sense my
approach will be form-critical, in that I shall be concerned with the
forms of the discourse; but only in a loose sense, because the forms in
question are literary ones, whose original life-situation is to be
sought in a remote past well beyond the purview of the evangelist.
Genuine form criticism is form *history* (*Formgeschichte*) and its two
key concepts, form (*Gattung*) and life-situation (*Sitz-im-Leben*), are
mutually illuminating correlatives. As soon as the forms have been
incorporated into larger literary structures their life-situations are no
longer of any immediate interest.[4] A scholar who enquires after the
Sitz-im-Leben of the farewell discourse is likely to be using this term
too in a loose sense, detached from its own significance within form
criticism and suggesting instead the situation within the life of the
Johannine community that can best account for the contents of
these chapters and their peculiarly plangent tones. This interesting
question will occupy us in the concluding section, where I shall
argue that this discourse, without parallel in the Synoptic Gospels,
except for a brief passage in Luke, was occasioned by a profound
sense of loss, as the community contemplated a future without their
leader and mentor, the Johannine prophet. In the main body of the
chapter, however, prescinding from this more historical question, I
shall attempt a more straightforward exegesis. Prima facie the
passage concerns the departure of Jesus. How is it to be read, I want

[3] One of the earliest writers to put forward the theory that there were originally
two versions of the discourse was Friedrich Spitta (1893 and 1910), who held that
ch. 14 represents the later of the two. He has had few followers in this view, one of
them being Hermann Sasse ('Paraklet'). The arguments are inconclusive. If it seems
marginally more likely that the complaint, 'none of you asks me, "where are you
going?"' (16: 5) should have been composed before rather than after a passage
containing that very question along with its answers (14: 4–7), then, on the other
hand, the elaborate dialogue beginning, 'A little while and you will see me no more'
(16: 16ff.) looks like an exegesis and partial correction of the 'you will see me' in
14: 19.

[4] 'In its original meaning the *terminus technicus* "sociological setting" (*Sitz-im-
Leben*) is completely opposed to the written nature of the form, so that it cannot be
transferred *a priori* or without methodological reflection to a phenomenon within the
"literary" mode of the traditions' (E. Güttgemanns, *Candid Questions Concerning Gospel
Form Criticism* (Pittsburgh, 1979), p. 239).

to ask, on this first level of understanding? My answer will be that the best approach is to examine how the evangelist took over and adapted certain literary forms.

It may be objected straight away that the farewell discourse has long been acknowledged to be one of the relatively rare instances in the New Testament of the form that gives it its name, otherwise known as a testament.[5] Every modern commentary alludes to this and some give long lists of parallels. Can anything more be done than simply to dredge through what I have called the soft silt of scholarship?

The answer to this objection is threefold. In the first place, it is not true that all the relevant materials have been scrutinized with any care. No doubt both Ethelbert Stauffer and, following him, Raymond Brown have given extensive lists of resemblances between the Johannine discourse and other examples of the form;[6] but such lists do little more than confirm what is obvious even to an untrained eye: that in taking a formal farewell from his disciples before his death, Jesus is preparing them for the future they will have to face without him.

In the second place, what is needed, as in all similar enquiries, is an appreciation not only of the continuity of the form but of what may be called deviations from the norm. The points at which the form is bent or twisted out of its usual shape are those which give some clue to the particular pressures to which it has been subjected. And it is with the particular that we are concerned.[7]

Finally, besides the testament form that is universally acknowledged to lie behind the farewell discourse there is another form, sometimes, but not always contiguous with it, that has escaped notice. This I call the commission form: it too requires investigation.

The exegesis that follows is quite untypical of this book, in that it is the only example of a sustained exegesis of a single, continuous passage from the Gospel. Elsewhere the nature of the enquiry has demanded a more eclectic approach. In the second place, it affords

---

[5] Cf. especially J. Munck, 'Discours d'adieu'; E. Cortès, *Discursos de adiós*; for a fuller bibliography see J. Becker, pp. 440 f.

[6] E. Stauffer, *New Testament Theology*, pp. 344–7; R. Brown, pp. 598–600.

[7] The best known testaments in European literature, *Le Lais* and *Le Testament* of François Villon offer an illuminating comparison. Villon takes over an established form, a spectacularly dull one, and uses his special alchemy to transform it into great poetry.

the clearest possible illustration of the distinction that has controlled the division of this book into two main parts, one offering an 'explanation from without' (the main concern of Part II, but touched briefly in the concluding section of this chapter), the other attempting to understand 'from within' the message addressed by the fourth evangelist to his readers. The bulk of the chapter, then, is a rather old-fashioned *explication de texte*. Thirdly, the farewell discourse itself illustrates particularly well the fruitfulness of the principle of two levels of understanding outlined in the previous chapter. Finally, because of its striking affinity with one particular pseudepigraphon, *The Testament of Moses*, I have chosen to include long extracts from this document in an excursus that itself constitutes, I believe, a powerful vindication of my contention that contemporary Jewish writings continue to provide many important aids, not yet fully recognized, to the interpretation of John.

My first task is to examine a series of different elements in the discourse and to show how in each case, in spite of a clear debt to tradition, the evangelist has gone his own way. It will be seen that it is in the divergences that the most distinctive message of the Gospel is to be found. The inclusion of a section headed 'Return' marks, it may be noted immediately, the most startling of the evangelist's deviations from the norm. In a sense it destroys the whole *raison-d'être* of a farewell discourse, for this is not just a temporary goodbye but the last words of a man facing death—a testament. Behind the notion of return there lies, of course, the peculiarly Christian tradition of the parousia, the Second Coming. As the rightful heir to this tradition John could scarcely ignore it. But we shall see that he modifies it in such a way that the weight of the discourse is placed after all upon the absence; in this respect he is more faithful to the basic structure of the testament form than may appear at first sight.

After a detailed consideration of the components of the form it will be possible to undertake a brief study of the chapter as a whole, to see how Jesus appears for the last time as the new Moses, taking his own farewell and responsible for a new commission.

Some may feel that it would be preferable to follow established exegetical practice by first determining the structure of the passage and then organizing one's remarks in a sequence suggested by the text itself. But a glance at the commentaries will show that there is little or no agreement about the structure of the passage; it ends,

unquestionably, with the words 'Let us be off', but that is all. Even
the beginning is somewhat hazy. One obvious starting-point is after
the departure of Judas in 13: 30, as the evangelist sets the scene
with the simple but pregnant phrase, 'it was night'. But the first
word of 13: 33, τεκνία, 'little children', looks like the opening of a
long address; and so does 14: 1, which follows the interchange with
Peter with a word of warning and encouragement that is clearly
intended to establish the tone as well as at least one of the themes of
what is to come. Within the discourse the difficulties multiply: it is
much easier to detect the presence of a number of different themes
than to decide precisely how they are articulated. One cannot, for
instance, say that after developing the theme of departure the
evangelist then moves on, naturally and logically, to the theme of
return: this is actually heard as early as 14: 3.[8] Nor can we be
confident that we have to do with a continuously composed
discourse. Hans Windisch argued long ago that the Paraclete
passages were taken from an originally independent source;[9] although, as I shall show, they fit in remarkably well into the overall
plan, the discourse would be perfectly coherent without them.[10] One
of the commentator's tasks, then, is to determine the nature and
purpose of certain insertions that have had the effect of modifying
the meaning of an already existing text. But these do not have to be
dealt with straight away.

---

[8] Whether the same *kind* of return is envisaged in v. 18ff. as in v. 3 is another
question, one which will engage our attention later in this chapter. M.-É. Boismard
draws attention to a shift in emphasis amounting to a contradiction between v. 3 and
v. 4: 'What need is there to know the way to the Father if Jesus is going to come and
collect us and accompany us on the way?' ('Evolution', p. 519), and refers to a similar
argument in F. Spitta (1910, pp. 342f.). J. Becker, too, believes that vv. 2–3
constitute a nugget of tradition that serves as a basic text, the body of the chapter
being what he calls a 'polemical exegesis' ('Abschiedsreden', p. 228) of its two main
themes: departure (πορεύομαι, v. 2) and return (πάλιν ἔρχομαι, v. 3). Accordingly, he
divides the chapter into four sections: (1) introduction (vv. 1–3); (2) departure (vv.
4–17); (3) return (vv. 18–26); (4) conclusion (vv. 27–31). This analysis is largely
accepted by D. Bruce Woll (*Johannine Christianity*), except that he terminates the
second main section at v. 24 (before the reintroduction of the Paraclete), a division
recognized by most early commentators. Fernando F. Segovia, on the other hand,
extends the section to include v. 27 and adds a detailed structural breakdown of the
two main sections, the first of which he describes as 'progressive' (p. 482), the second
'cyclic in character' ('Structure' p. 485). In a more extended study than either Woll's
or Segovia's, Johannes Beutler (*Habt keine Angst*) divides the whole chapter into three
sections: (1) vv. 1–14, which he regards in part as a midrash on Ps. 42/43; (2) vv.
15–24, Jesus' triple promise; (3) vv. 25–31, his eschatological gifts.

[9] 'Parakletsprüche'.   [10] Cf. B. Lindars, 'Persecution', p. 63.

I. DEPARTURE

(a) Farewell: 'Where I am going you cannot come' (13: 33)

Why should a death be seen as a departure? Is it not odd that a testament, the definitive legacy of a man or woman who may well be looking forward to many years of life, should be equated with a farewell, the parting words of someone about to embark on a journey—equated to the extent of furnishing alternative names for a single literary form? Most goodbyes, even most long goodbyes, are made in the expectation of a return; perhaps most testaments are drawn up with the thought that there will be other opportunities of changing one's mind and altering one's will. Here, though, we have to do with a definitive testament and a final goodbye. No doubt many cultures interpret death itself as a journey (to "the undiscovered country from whose bourn no traveller returns"); so it is not very surprising to see a discourse delivered on the threshold of death take the form of a farewell address. Nevertheless it is worth stressing that this deeply human response to the business of dying beautifully illustrates the instinctive exercise of one of the most singular and least regarded of human skills—the power to see life as a story, in other words the power to fabricate myths.[11]

Myth or metaphor? One of the earliest examples of the farewell discourse form in the Bible (dating from the tenth century BC) may not actually prove the presence of myth, but it does at least suggest it. The passage is a particularly important one, since it demonstrates very early on in the biblical tradition the association of the farewell or testament and the commission forms: David is not just saying goodbye to Solomon for the last time; he is giving him a specific task to perform. That this task should turn out to be a vendetta may surprise, even disturb us; but from the disinterested perspective of the literary critic the conjunction of the two forms is established with exemplary clarity:

When David's time to die drew near, he charged (וַיְצַו) Solomon, his son, saying, 'I am about to go the way of all the earth (אָנֹכִי הֹלֵךְ בְּדֶרֶךְ כָּל־הָאָרֶץ: ἐγώ εἰμι πορεύομαι ἐν ὁδῷ πάσης τῆς γῆς). Be strong and show yourself a man.[12] ... Moreover you know what Joab the son of Zeruiah did

---

[11] On this see especially Frank Kermode, *The Sense of an Ending* (London, 1968).

[12] The next two verses, 3–4, are commonly and rightly thought to have been inserted by the deuteronomic redactor.

to me. ... Act therefore (וְעָשִׂיתָ) according to your wisdom and[13] do not let his head go down to Sheol in peace. ... Now therefore hold him not guiltless, for you are a wise man; you will know what you ought to do to him, and you shall bring his head down with blood to Sheol. (1 Kings 2: 1–9)

Of the many points of interest in this passage the one that concerns us here is the idea of death as a departure. David does not need to spell out the nature of his journey, nor its goal; 'the way of all the earth' cannot but be in the direction of Sheol. The only difference between his own journey and the one he arranges for Joab lies in the manner of their departures. That of Joab is to be bloody (בְּדָם); his own is to be peaceful (בְּשָׁלוֹם). Their destination is the same.

The phrase 'the way of all the earth' is taken up occasionally later (cf. Josh. 23: 14; *Jub.* 36: 1; 2 *Bar.* 44: 2). But it must be said that in any particular context the notion of death as a departure may be no more than a metaphor. Addressing Judas at the Last Supper, Jesus says to him: 'The Son of Man goes (ὑπάγει) as it is written of him, but woe to him by whom the Son of Man is betrayed' (Mark 14: 21). When John selects the same term (ὑπάγειν) he cleverly exploits its ambiguity. The outcome of the journey of the Son of Man in Mark's Gospel is well known. He goes to his death—and consequently to Sheol, the grave, the realm of the νεκροί—only to rise again on the third day.[14] But it is doubtful if the expression in Mark 14: 21 is intended to imply a return: the phrase 'the Son of Man goes' is used simply to hint at his voluntary compliance with the Scriptures and possibly too his acceptance of Judas' treachery. For John, on the other hand, the term suggests an intentional and deliberate action on the part of Jesus, as he embarks on his journey with an open-eyed awareness of his destination.

We cannot say whether or not John borrowed the word ὑπάγειν from Mark; if he did, then he has transferred it from its original context, Judas' treachery, to the closely following story of Peter's brash assertion of loyalty. In Mark the two are separated by the whole of the institution narrative, in John by three words: ἦν δὲ νύξ,

---

[13] The 'but' of the RSV betrays a total misunderstanding of the link between Solomon's 'wisdom' and the charge that is laid on him. This is clear from the ending (in the form of an inclusion: v. 9 is simply a differently worded version of v. 6; the parallel is even more evident in the Hebrew).

[14] Cf. 1 Cor. 15. It is crucial for Paul that Christ be acknowledged to have risen ἐκ νεκρῶν, i.e. out of Sheol.

'it was night'. This is not the first time, however, that John uses the term to refer to Jesus' approaching death. In 13: 33 Jesus reminds his disciples of an earlier prophecy: 'Little children, yet a little while I am with you. You will seek me; and as I said to the Jews so now I say to you, "Where I am going (ὑπάγω) you cannot come."' In fact there is an important difference between this and the earlier passage: What Jesus said to the Jews was this: 'I shall be with you a little longer, and then I go (ὑπάγω) _to him who sent me_; you will seek me and you will not find me; _where I am_ (ὅπου εἰμί) you cannot come' (7: 33f.; cf. 8: 22). Thus in 7: 33 he states explicitly something that is merely implied in the later passage: that his journey has a goal—he is going to the one who sent him.[15]

We may note that in both cases the saying provokes misunderstanding; but the confusion of the Jews is perhaps more comprehensible than that of Peter. He after all finds himself in a traditional farewell discourse situation for which the expression 'I am going' is fully appropriate. In chapter 7, on the contrary, the Jews, locked as they are in argument, might well be confused: 'Where does this man intend to go (πορεύεσθαι) that we shall not find him? Does he intend to go (πορεύεσθαι) to the Dispersion among the Greeks and teach the Greeks? What does he mean by saying, "You will seek me and you will not find me", and "Where I am you cannot come"?' (7: 35f.) In fact the Jews' version of Jesus' words is inaccurate in two respects: they replace the highly charged term ὑπάγειν with the rather colourless πορεύεσθαι;[16] furthermore, like Jesus himself in his report to the disciples, they omit the crucial phrase πρὸς τὸν πέμψαντά με: 'to the one who sent me'. (Compare 16: 5, 10 with 16: 16–19, 28.)

The next time Jesus uses the term the ensuing misunderstanding is quite crass: 'Again he said to them: "I go away (ὑπάγω) and you will seek me and die in your sin; where I am going you cannot

---

[15] In my view, stated in Excursus III (p. 334), the little dialogue in 7: 33–6 is out of place in its present context in ch. 7. But this is probably because it is a late, rather awkward insertion rather than because it has dropped out of its proper position in the Gospel.

[16] According to E. A. Abbott, 'John ... seems to distinguish this mere going (πορεύομαι) from the 'going home' of a child of God, begotten of God and returning to God' (_Johannine Vocabulary_, p. 146). But there is no clear distinction in meaning in John 13–14: the most one can say is that John does not employ πορεύεσθαι in any context that provokes misunderstanding; in other words it does not belong to his _Sondersprache_. This observation may reinforce the suggestion of Boismard and Becker that 14: 2 is a traditional Johannine saying, correctively reinterpreted in what follows.

come" (cf. 7: 33; 13: 33). Then said the Jews; "Will he kill himself, since he says, 'Where I am going you cannot come'?'" (8: 21f) Nevertheless, in spite of the absurdity of the idea that Jesus is contemplating suicide, the Jews on this occasion have actually grasped an essential feature of John's use of the term—its association with death.

To appreciate what is going on in these bitter little exchanges one has to see that John has appropriated the term ὑπάγειν as an element in what Herbert Leroy calls his *Sondersprache*, the private language of the community that reinforces both its internal cohesiveness and its gratifying sense of superiority to those outside.[17] The two episodes probably follow the period of direct confrontation between the Christian group and the Jewish conservatives within the synagogue. But at this point I simply want to underline the resourcefulness of the fourth evangelist as he weaves the simple metaphor of 'death as departure' into the fabric of his distinctive portrait of the role and nature of Christ.

In the Fourth Gospel the idea of death as a final journey has been transformed into that of *the return from a mission*. This is easily seen from the first occurrence of the term in its special meaning: 'I am going *to the one who sent me*' (7: 33). Simple as it may seem, this move is of crucial significance for John's christology: it takes us to the heart of his singular vision of Christ as a divine emissary who came into the world fully aware that he would soon leave it and return to the Father. It is only to be expected that from time to time Jesus should explicitly acknowledge that he was not at home in the world to which he was sent; so one is not surprised to see the second of the ὑπάγειν passages followed immediately by just such an admission: 'You are from below, I am from above; you are of this world, I am not of this world' (8: 23). Here is a good example of the harmonic reinforcement of the social and the ideological analysed by Wayne Meeks (1972). The context of all these passages is one in which the incomprehension of Jesus' hearers both reflects and enhances the sense of alienation experienced by the Johannine group in an environment that has become hostile and incomprehending.

[17] There are 32 occurrences of the verb ὑπάγειν in the Fourth Gospel. In 15 of these it has the perfectly ordinary sense of 'go away'. Elsewhere, apart from one instance (13: 3), in which it also bears the special sense conferred on it by the community, it is almost always found in a context of misunderstanding. Cf. H. Leroy, *Rätsel*, pp. 51–67.

A point of especial importance here is the effect of this remarkable conception upon the farewell discourse itself, resulting as it does in a complete transformation of the testament form. Death is now not just a departure but a journey, and a journey with a goal. The essentially Jewish idea of death as a voyage down to Sheol has now been replaced by the essentially Christian idea of a voyage up to heaven.

Of possibly even greater significance is the fact that the journey itself, as a path between two points, now takes on a thematic significance within the farewell discourse. The theme in question is that of the *way*, developed in the little interchange between Jesus and Thomas: '"Where I am going—you know the way (ὅπου ὑπάγω οἴδατε τὴν ὁδόν)." Thomas said to him, "Lord, we do not know where you are going; how can we know the way?"' (14: 4f.). The end of the journey is soon made plain, and by a further expansion of the form the departure, now a voyage with a particular goal in view, is transferred from speaker to hearers: 'Where I am going you cannot follow me now; but you shall follow afterwards' (13: 36); 'no one comes to the Father, but by me' (14: 6). The way is no longer 'the way of all the earth' but is now a path to heaven, reserved for the followers of Jesus, since by a final startling shift he *is* the way: 'I am the way, the truth, and the life' (14: 6). 'Stylistically', remarks Meeks, 'this shift recalls the "illogic" of ch. 10, in which Jesus himself is both the good shepherd who comes by means of the door and the door by means of which the sheep go in and out.'[18]

(b) Faith: 'Let not your hearts be troubled: believe in God, believe also in me' (14: 1)[19]

Chapter 14, as Dodd points out, 'is clamped together by the repeated uses of the expression μὴ ταρασσέσθω ἡ καρδία in verses 1 and 27'.[20] Among the other links (not mentioned by Dodd) between the beginning and the end of the chapter, we may note here the reiterated insistence on the need for faith (14: 1, 29).

[18] 'Man from Heaven', p. 158.
[19] This translation follows that of most commentators, from Westcott onwards. Sometimes the first πιστεύετε is read as a statement (so Brown), occasionally as a question (so Bultmann). Beutler, who sees here a deliberate adaptation of LXX Ps. 41: 6, 12; 42: 5 (ἔλπισον ἐπὶ τὸν θεόν: hope in God), naturally prefers the double imperative (*Habt keine Angst*, pp. 28f.); clearly this is also the rendering that fits in best with the interpretation given below. [20] *Tradition*, p. 403.

It may seem natural enough for a man to preface a parting address to his family with some words of comfort and reassurance; so one might expect to find this as a constitutive element in the testament form. Stauffer, in a list of some 26 items he believes to be integral to the category of 'valedictions and farewell speeches', includes one entitled 'comfort and promise'.[21] But on examination it turns out that only two of his references are pertinent. One is from the *Testament of Moses*, though the importance of this text, as we shall see, lies elsewhere. The other is *Jubilees* 22: 23, where Abraham is addressing Jacob; but the injunction 'Have no fear and do not be dismayed' is too untypical to support Stauffer's case. The truth is that the note of reassurance and the summons to faith with which Jesus prefaces his discourse in chapter 14 is not a regular element of the farewell form.[22]

The clue lies in the second half of the verse: 'believe in God'. (The sequel, 'believe in me', gives the saying a typically Johannine twist, which will be discussed later.) The demand for faith in God has a long history: its original *Sitz-im-Leben* is probably to be sought in what Gerhard von Rad has called 'the Holy War', where a war oracle (*Kriegsorakel*) was pronounced on the eve of battle,[23] or perhaps more generally in an oracle of salvation (*Heilsorakel*) sought at the outset of any important undertaking. The very name of Yahweh was revealed in the context of a promise of divine assistance (Exod. 3: 6–12) and the 'I am' contained an implicit assurance of God's active support.[24] The worst that could happen to Israel was the withdrawal or cancellation of the divine revelation: 'Call his name "Not my people" since you are not my people and for you *I am* not' (Hosea 1: 9; cf. Num. 14: 43; Jos. 7: 12; 2 Chron. 25: 7f.).

Even a summary sketch of the Old Testament material would take us too far afield. As before, a single example, this time from the book

---

[21] *Theology*, pp. 344–7. H.-J. Michel under the heading 'Encouragement and Consolation' lists Deut. 31: 6; 1 Sam. 12: 20; *Jub.* 22: 23; *T. Zeb.* 10: 1; *T. Iss.* 1: 8–12; 2 *Bar.* 81: 1–82: 1 (*Abschiedsrede*, p. 50).

[22] Karl Kundsin argues that the opening words of the chapter, though intended in the first place to assuage the disciples' sadness at their imminent loss, also contains an implicit promise of Jesus' comfort and assistance in their own approaching martyrdom: 'Die Wiederkunft Jesu'.

[23] *Der Heilige Krieg im alten Israel* (Zurich, 1951).

[24] Cf. Gen. 26: 3, 24; 28: 15; 31: 3; Exod. 3: 12; Deut. 31: 23; Josh. 1: 9; 3: 7; 7: 12; Judg. 6: 12, 16; 1 Kings 11: 38; Isa. 41: 10; 43: 2, 5; Jer. 1: 8; 30: 11; 42: 11; Hag. 1: 13; Zech. 2: 11.

of Deuteronomy, will suffice to demonstrate the extent both of John's indebtedness to the tradition and of his deviation from it. Immediately before his death Moses utters a song (ch. 32) and a blessing (ch. 33), both of which are fine examples of ancient Hebrew poetry. But before this, in a chapter that belongs to a relatively recent stratum of the book, Moses recounts how he has been told by God that he himself will not be leading his people over the Jordan into the Promised Land; instead he is to commission Joshua to take his place. In the earliest form of the tradition, however, it is not Moses but God who commissions Joshua:

And the Lord said to Moses: 'Behold the days aproach when you must die; call Joshua, and present yourselves in the tent of meeting that I may commission him (וַאֲצַוֶּנּוּ).' And Moses and Joshua went and presented themselves in the tent of meeting, and the Lord appeared in the pillar of cloud; and the pillar of cloud stood by the door of the tent. ... And he commissioned (וַיְצַו) Joshua the son of Nun and said, 'Be strong and of good courage (חֲזַק וֶאֱמָץ) for you shall bring the children of Israel into the land which I swore to give them: I will be with you (וְאָנֹכִי אֶהְיֶה עִמָּךְ).' (Deut. 31: 14–15, 23; cf. 3: 28; Josh. 1: 1–9)

There are a number of points to be made about this passage:

1. The deuteronomic editor has taken these verses over (from JE?) and inserted a passage (vv. 16–22) which is in fact a comment on the song (cf. v. 22) that follows in the next chapter. In the Hebrew text there is no indication of the shift of subject from Moses to Yahweh between verses 22 and 23. The awkward hiatus is glossed over in the RSV.

2. The form—an oracle of salvation—has its _Sitz-im-Leben_ in the cult. The tent of meeting is what its name suggests: unlike the ark it is a symbol not of God's abiding presence but of his occasional interventions in the affairs of his people. But this is a special kind of oracle of salvation. The concluding promise is characteristic of the form; the exhortation to 'be strong' and the technical use of the verb 'to commission' (Piel of צוה) show that the oracle of salvation and the commission (originally independent forms) have been combined: compare this episode with David's commission of Solomon, quoted earlier in this chapter.

3. The passage clearly lends itself to adaptation as a testament. If Moses himself, instructed by Yahweh, were to perform the commissioning ceremony, then we would have a testament in the proper

sense, since the time (Moses' approaching death) is also right. And this is in fact what we do have in Deuteronomy 31: 7–8:[25]

> Then Moses summoned Joshua and said to him in the sight of all Israel, 'Be strong and of good courage; for you shall go with this people into the land which the Lord has sworn to their fathers to give them; and you shall put them in possession of it. It is the Lord who goes before you; he will be with you, he will not fail you or forsake you; do not fear or be dismayed (μὴ φοβοῦ μηδὲ δειλία).'

What, it may be asked, has this to do with the farewell discourse in John? The answer lies in the nature of the exhortation. The assurance of divine assistance is not an integral element either of the testament or of the commission form. It is not present in David's commission of Solomon, nor in the equally gruesome commission Absalom lays on his followers in 2 Samuel 13: 28, although he does urge them to 'be courageous and be valiant'. But wherever the charge is made by God himself or with his backing and approval, then his presence is always guaranteed. This guarantee both reinforces and justifies the command to be strong or valiant. As often in the Bible, the essence of the form is given meditative expressions in one of the Psalms:

> The Lord is my light and my salvation;
> whom shall I fear?
> The Lord is the stronghold of my life;
> of whom shall I be afraid (ἀπὸ τίνος δειλιάσω)?
>
> . . . .
>
> Wait for the Lord;
> be strong, and let your heart take courage (κραταιούσθω ἡ καρδία σου);
> yea, wait for the Lord.
>
> (LXX Ps. 26: 1, 14)

Now in the important charge Jesus is about to lay upon his disciples in John 14 we should naturally expect *both* an exhortation to be strong *and* an assurance of divine protection. The former is found in the opening words: 'Let not your hearts be troubled' (μὴ ταρασσέσθω ὑμῶν ἡ καρδία, 14: 1) and in the conclusion: 'neither let

---

[25] But not in the midrash in Pseudo-Philo, *Ant. Bib.* 19–20, where it is God who commissions Joshua after Moses' death (as in the Book of Joshua itself). In Josephus' version (*A. J.* iv. 315), Moses exhorts (παρορμᾶν) Joshua to lead a campaign against the Canaanites. Josephus thus conflates Deut. 31: 7–8 with 1–6, another indirect commission, this time addressed to all Israel. In this passage, the phrase הַמִּצְוָה אֲשֶׁר צִוִּיתִי אֶתְכֶם should be translated, 'the charge which I laid upon you' (*contra* RSV). This is a commission not a commandment.

them be afraid' (μὴ ταρασσέσθω ὑμῶν ἡ καρδία μηδὲ δειλιάτω, 14: 27).[26] The latter presents some difficulty. For Jesus does not merely act *on behalf* of God, as Moses does when he commissions Joshua: besides speaking with God's authority (14: 10) he *represents* God in the fullest possible sense (14: 9f.). It is as if the two forms of the commissioning of Joshua in Deuteronomy 31, one by Moses, the other by Yahweh, were to be fused. But for Jesus to say explicitly, 'I am with you' (as he does at the close of Matthew's Gospel—an alternative version of the commission form) would be too paradoxical in a discourse whose very *raison d'être* is his own imminent departure. What he can—and does—say is, 'Believe in God,' adding, 'believe in me.'

The reader of the Gospel, accustomed to hearing Jesus' demand for faith in his own person, may all too easily miss the great import of this conjunction. In the context of a formal commission any demand for faith can be justified only on the basis of an assurance that God will be of active assistance in the carrying-out of the task. And if God, then Jesus also. It follows that if the disciples' faith is to be securely grounded, his departure must be succeeded by some kind of presence-in-absence. This of course is what we do find: indeed it may be said to be *the* subject of the discourse.

Needless to say, the profound insights of the farewell discourse, especially those contained in the exchange with Philip (14: 8ff.), are not to be explained simply as the logical working-out of the implications of the farewell and commission forms. Rather it is the case that the novel awareness that 'he who has seen me has seen the father' impels a radical reworking of Old Testament models. These, as I have endeavoured to show, are still recognizable, if barely. Nevertheless our appreciation of the magnitude of John's literary achievement is greatly enhanced by observing the extent of his indebtedness to these models as well as his deviations from them.

(c) Commission: 'If you love me, you will keep my commandments'
(14: 15)[27]

The main reason why the testament and commission forms are readily combined, and indeed often confused, is that an essential

---

[26] For this use of the verb δειλιᾶν, a *hapax* in the New Testament, compare Deut. 31: 8 and LXX Ps. 26: 1, quoted above; also Deut. 1: 21; 31: 6; Josh. 1: 9; 8: 1; 10: 25—all deuteronomistic texts.

[27] The MSS are fairly evenly divided between the future (τηρήσετε), the aorist

[*cont. on p. 457*]

element in each of them is an exhortation or command addressed to the hearer or hearers. In the commission form the command concerns some task of special urgency or importance, in the later, more stylized type of testament such as we find in *The Testaments of the Twelve Patriarchs*, the command usually focuses on a more generalized kind of behaviour. This may be either a virtue, perhaps one that the dying man has himself exemplified during his lifetime, or a vice that he is anxious to warn against, or possibly both.

The commission in this generalized sense is important enough to be regarded as the central, indeed the constitutive element of the form. Accordingly, in Marinus de Jonge's edition of the *Testaments* (1978) most of the subtitles point to the vice or virtue that the patriarch in question is most concerned about, e.g. Judah, 'About courage, and love of money and fornication'; Issachar, 'About simplicity'; Zebulon, 'About compassion and mercy'; Dan, 'About anger and falsehood'.

Now it may be thought that the prominent place occupied in the farewell discourse by the new commandment—of fraternal love—proves that it fits quite easily into this pattern. Love, moreover, although not a dominant theme in the *Twelve Testaments* does occur from time to time.[28] One may, like de Jonge, hold that the all-pervasiveness of Christian ingredients in this document makes it unsafe to appeal to it as evidence of pre-Christian influences upon the New Testament, since the influence may well be the other way round. But there is at least one indisputably early source in which the duty of fraternal love is strongly commended, the *Book of Jubilees*, where Isaac, having summoned Esau and Jacob to his death-bed, tells them in the course of a longish speech: 'this command I lay upon you, my sons, ... love one another, my sons, as a man loves his own soul' (30: 3f.; cf. 20: 2).

In spite of the close thematic resemblance between this text and the farewell discourse in John, there are good reasons to reject any easy inference of influence or indebtedness, at any rate as regards chapter 14. For although at first sight the ἐντολαί of chapter 14 look as if they hark back to the ἐντολὴ καινή of 13: 34, it is unlikely that

imperative (τηρήσατε), and the aorist subjunctive (τηρήσητε). The future is probably to be preferred; but if this verse, as I shall suggest, contains a deliberate allusion to Deuteronomy, this future could be a Semitism. In legal contexts the yiqtol form, frequently translated by a future, is often preferred. The Ten Commandments are a case in point.

[28] Cf. *Sim.* 4: 7; *Iss.* 7: 6–7; *Zeb.* 8: 5; *Gad.* 4: 2; 6: 1; *Jos.* 17: 2–3.

the original version of the discourse contained any hint of a new commandment, or indeed of any additional obligation on the part of the disciples beyond their duty to remain faithful to the word of Jesus as this is invoked in the injunction to 'Keep my word/words' (τὸν λόγον/τοὺς λόγους μου τηρεῖν) in 14: 23, 24. The majority of commentators rightly regard this phrase and the 'commandments' of 14: 15, 21 as alternative ways of referring to the demand for faith that pervades the whole Gospel.[29]

In the text of the Gospel as we have it chapter 14 is bracketed by a summary statement of the new commandment in 13: 34, on the one hand, and a developed reflection in 15: 12–17, on the other. So it is easy to conclude, as for instance Lindars does, that 'there is probably an intentional allusion [in 14: 15] to 13. 34f. The plural *commandments* thus refers to the manifold application of the one commandment to love one another'. But apart from the difficulty of the shift from singular to plural (any moral or legal precept, whether couched in the singular or not, necessarily has 'manifold applications'), this exegesis ignores the fact that the new commandment is a late and particularly glaring insertion into Jesus' dialogue with Peter at the end of chapter 13. Peter's question in 13: 36, 'Lord, where are you going?' is obviously a response to Jesus' assertion in 13: 33, 'Where I am going you cannot come', as only those indissolubly wedded to the principle of integral or synchronic exegesis could refuse to admit.[30] In fact if one accepts, as Lindars does, that chapter 15, originally a quite separate homily, has been tacked on to it later, perhaps by the evangelist himself, perhaps by a subsequent redactor, then it is easy to see that the love commandment in 13: 34 has the same provenance as chapter 15 and belongs to the same level of redaction.

Accordingly, it makes more sense to consider chapter 14, provisionally at any rate, on its own; but we are still not out of the wood. One can well understand why Jesus, on the eve of his death, should insist upon the need to 'keep my word'—to continue to respond in faith to his message. But why sum this injunction up as 'my commandments', surely an unnecessarily roundabout and even a clumsy and obscure way of emphasizing the need for faith?

There are two alternative, possibly complementary, answers to this question. The first harks back once again to Deuteronomy. The

[29] e.g. Bultmann, Schnackenburg, Becker.
[30] Bultmann's solution is to insert chs. 15–16 enbloc between 13: 35 and 13: 36. But this conceals the problem instead of resolving it.

first half of the Gospel contains many allusions to Jesus as the new Moses: here too there may be a suggestion that the message of Jesus has replaced the Mosaic Law considered not only as the quintessence of divine *revelation* (λόγος) but also as the definitive summation of God's *commands* (ἐντολαί) to his people. The easy correspondence in John 14 between the two terms ἐντολαί and λόγος/λόγοι strongly recalls Deuteronomic usage.[31] (See too especially Ps. 119.)

The other answer involves a form-critical approach, in this case to the combination of the two forms, testament and commission. In each of these the commission or instruction is regularly expressed by a particular verb, the Piel of צוה in Hebrew, ἐντέλλεσθαι in Greek, with their corresponding nouns מצוה and ἐντολή.[32]

Whether John and his readers regarded 'the commandments' of Jesus as a new law, a radical alternative to the commandments mediated by Moses, or simply as a commission, the final instructions given to his disciples by their departing Lord, *what* he requires of them is fully in accord with the tenor of the whole Gospel. He asks only that they should 'keep his word'. To do this they must literally keep a record of his *words*, which means in practice keeping a copy of the Gospel. The actual composition of the Gospel is part, and an essential part at that, of the carrying-out of Jesus' last commission to his disciples. Thus the farewell discourse effectively reinforces, as it is surely intended to do, the authority of the evangelist and his book.

2. RETURN

In the farewell discourse, as we have had occasion to observe, the testament and commission forms are subjected to various stresses

---

[31] This explanation helps to account for the otherwise puzzling use of the plural, ἐντολαί, in 14: 15, 21. In Deuteronomy the singular מצוה is commonly used to designate the whole Law: 5: 31; 6: 25; 8: 1; 11: 8, 22; 15: 5; 17: 20; 19: 9; 27: 1; 30: 11. But with a single exception (30: 11) the LXX translates all these by the plural, ἐντολαί. The suggestion that ἐντολαί in John 14 may be a deliberate allusion to the Law of Moses, thus implying that the word of Jesus has supplanted this, is reinforced by the fact that both the singular and the plural of דבר (word) are also used to refer to the whole Law (singular: Deut. 4: 2; 30: 14; 32: 47; plural: Deut. 4: 10, 13, 36; 5: 22 (19); 10: 2, 4). The Ten Commandments are also frequently called 'the words' of God or 'the words' of the Law. For a detailed discussion of the relevant material cf. S. Pancaro, *Law*, pp. 403–51.

[32] For the commission see 2 Sam. 13: 28; 1 Kings 2: 1; Deut. 30: 8; 31: 5; 1 Chron. 22: 6; 2 Chron. 19: 9; also *Jub.* 7: 20, 38; 35: 1. For the testament, see Gen. 49: 33; 1 Kings 2: 1 (?); *T. Naphtali* 1: 1, 2, 3, 5, 9; 7: 1 (Hebrew); *T. Rub.* 1: 1–5; 4: 5; 7: 1; *T. Sim.* 7: 3; 8: 1; *T. Lev.* 10: 1; 13: 1; 19: 4; *T. Jud.* 13: 1; *T. Zeb.* 10: 2; *T. Naph.* 9: 1, 3 (Greek); also *Jub.* 21: 1; 36: 3, 5, 17. See too the discussion in Cortès, *Discursos de Adiós*, pp. 57–9.

and strains. When he pictures Jesus summoning his disciples, warning them of his approaching death and urging them to carry on his work after his departure, the evangelist is no doubt following a recognizable pattern. But by including in the farewell a promise to return he may seem to break the mould altogether. In one sense he does; the tradition of the Second Coming is irreconcilable with any final goodbye. If this innovation fails to surprise us this is partly because, like John's original audience, we are familiar with the traditional expectation of the parousia, partly because the testament form slides easily and naturally into a farewell, where there is nothing at all remarkable in a promise to return. Nevertheless the mode of the return—or one of its modes, for there are several—is itself a kind of commission. So the general pattern of the testament/commission form remains precariously intact.

Perhaps the most difficult question posed by the farewell discourse concerns the timing of Jesus' promised return. The latter half of the first discourse appears to relate to the experience of the disciples after the resurrection; and this is what we should expect. The whole Gospel, after all, is permeated by an awareness of what is available to the believer here and now. But such an awareness necessarily reduces the significance of any physical return, even one expected in the proximate future. Hence the majority of modern commentators, headed by Bultmann, ascribe to the fourth evangelist what is commonly called a 'realized eschatology', in which all future hopes are anticipated in the present, although they give differing explanations of the many passages in the Gospel that stubbornly resist being categorized in this way. Undoubtedly one of the most intriguing of these is the one to which we must now turn:

In my father's house there are many rooms (μοναί); if it were not so, would I have told you that I go to prepare a place for you? And when I go to prepare a place for you, I will come again (πάλιν ἔρχομαι) and will take you to myself, that where I am you may be also. (14: 2–3)

Bultmann, recognizing that this passage is couched in the language of myth, understandably ascribes it to his hypothetical revelation source. Dodd noticed here 'the closest approach to the traditional language of the Church's eschatology',[33] particularly to 1 Thessalonians 4: 17; 'we that are alive, who are left, shall be caught up ... in the clouds to meet the Lord in the air; and so we

[33] *Interpretation*, p. 404.

shall be with the Lord.' Bultmann counters this by asserting that the eschatology that lies at the base of the promise in 14: 3 'is the individualistic eschatology of the Gnostic myth'.[34] Now it is true that the coming of Christ was thought of in terms of a public manifestation of power and glory, manifest to all left on earth. That is why Judas is puzzled enough to ask, 'Lord, how is it that you will manifest yourself to us, and not to the world?' (14: 22.) But all Christian eschatology, including that of Paul, is individualistic up to a point. Paul's purpose in 1 Thessalonians is precisely to reassure those individuals in the community who are concerned for the fate of their dead friends and relatives that they too will enjoy the benefits of the parousia. The idea that heaven is the home or 'house' of God is widespread in Jewish sources; throughout the Bible God is conceived as occupying heaven as home. Qohelet, for instance, after speaking of the Temple as the house of God, goes on nevertheless to warn his readers that 'God is in heaven, and you upon earth' (Qoh. 5: 1).[35]

If we reject Bultmann's suggestion of a Gnostic source, yet continue to read 14: 2 as it stands, without recourse to the re-interpretations that occur later (both in chapter 14 and in chapter 16), then Dodd's observation may be given full weight. Jürgen Becker, after remarking how uneasily the conclusion of 14: 2 fits in the context, making the whole sentence syntactically very difficult, suggests that this is a 'stylistically unsuccesful commentary of the evangelist upon an earlier tradition, intended to emphasize its consolatory tone'.[36] He points out how unusual the terminology is: 'many mansions', the Father's 'house', 'prepared', 'take you to myself'. In the latter half of the chapter Jesus does, it is true, promise to 'come' to his disciples, not however with the idea of transporting them back to heaven by his side but rather in order to dwell with and in them on earth. Taken on its own the second half of chapter 14 can only refer to the experience of the disciples 'down below'; yet 14: 2f. is set in heaven, and the real differences must be accepted and explained. Clearly the evangelist himself cannot have regarded the two utterances as contradictory; otherwise he would hardly have left them side by side. But Schnackenburg's attempt to harmonize the

---

[34] p. 602 n. 1.

[35] For further evidence see Fischer, 'Wohnungen', pp. 137–78 and Beutler, *Habt keine Angst*, pp. 33–41. James McCaffrey (*House with Many Rooms*) defends, with an array of learned and ingenious arguments, the thesis that on the first level of understanding the οἰκία in 14: 2 refers to the Jerusalem Temple. This suggestion is surely too far-fetched to gain wide acceptance.   [36] p. 466.

two passages by pretending that 14: 2f. does *not* refer to the parousia[37] results in an impoverishment of this very rich text.

One scholar has set the 'return' theme of John 14 in an imaginatively trinitarian mould.[38] And it must be admitted that the fourth-century Fathers were able to extract from the farewell discourse as a whole most of the material they needed to give an authentically biblical flavour to their elaborate theological confections. There are indeed three distinct ways in which the disciples were promised consolation for the physical absence of their Lord, all depending upon their obedience to his commandments. Yet these are unevenly balanced, the promise of the Paraclete standing apart from the other two in exhibiting, as we shall see, an especially fruitful modification of the commission form. Quite possibly too it represents an afterthought, inserted in an already composed text.[39] The other two, which I propose to treat first, mutually reinforce one another, the coming of the Son hardly separable from the indwelling of Father and Son that succeeds it.

(a) The coming of the Son

'I will not leave you bereft (ὀρφανοί), I will come to you' (14: 18). Here the ἔρχομαι echoes the πάλιν ἔρχομαι of v. 3, an echo of which the author himself must have been aware. Even the manner of the coming, a kind of self-display, seems to point to the parousia. The word ἐμφανίζειν, not found elsewhere in John, suggests a public spectacle rather than a private appearance, and as I have remarked presents a problem to Judas (Jude): 'Lord, how is it that you will manifest yourself to us, and not to the world?' (14: 22.) The universal Christian expectation of the return of Jesus on the clouds of heaven to announce the end of the present age is, it would seem, being consciously modified in its two dimensions, spatial as well as temporal, for this reappearance is to take place on earth. Yet the evangelist has not altogether abandoned the traditional expectation; otherwise, as we have seen, he would not have included the explicit promise in 14: 2f., still less drawn attention to it by repeating the promise to return.

The evocation of the theme of the Second Coming in this passage is strong enough to have persuaded the Latin Fathers that it simply

<hr />

[37] iii. 62.   [38] M.-É. Boismard, 'Evolution', p. 519.
[39] Cf. n. 10.

repeats and re-emphasizes the promise of 14: 2f. Yet the passage undoubtedly operates on another level as well. Given the setting of the whole discourse, as Jesus prepares his disciples to face up to their imminent loss, the promise that in 'a little while' his disciples will see him again cannot but remind the Christian reader (and also of course the Johannine prophet's original audience) of the appearances to the disciples 'on the first day of the week' (20: 1) and again 'eight days later' (20: 26). Here too we are concerned with private rather than public manifestations: unless those to whom Jesus appeared after his death could respond with faith, the term 'resurrection' would have no meaning and the Christian proclamation no content.

Ambiguity is perhaps too weak a word to convey the art with which the evangelist allows both these traditional themes to continue to resonate in the inner ear whilst at the same time subjecting them to a fresh and quite radical reworking. For the fleeting resurrection-appearances are now mere presages of a permanent presence, while the indefinite hope of a Second Coming has been both realized and transformed—internalized into a manifestation that can dispense with the need of a physical appearance and into a vision that can exist without sight. Jesus' followers continue to bask in the afterglow of the resurrection and to enjoy the new life that he has passed on to them: 'because I live, you will live also' (14: 19).

The evangelist, or whoever was responsible for the second edition of his work, is fully aware of the ambiguity of the phrase 'a little while'; he actually underlines and spells it out in the first and, one might say, the most authoritative exegesis of this passage that we have:

'A little while, and you will see me no more; again a little while, and you will see me.' Some of his disciples said to one another, 'What is this that he says to us, "A little while, and you will not see me, and again a little while, and you will see me"; and, "because I go to the Father"?' They said, 'What does he mean by "a little while"? We do not know what he means.' Jesus knew that they wanted to ask him; so he said to them, 'Is this what you are asking yourselves, what I mean by saying, "A little while, and you will not see me, and again a little while and you will see me"?' (16: 16–19)

The paragraph continues with the famous image of the woman in travail and her subsequent joy at giving birth to a child. Similarly, says Jesus, 'You have sorrow now, but I will see you again and your hearts will rejoice' (16: 22). 'In that day', he adds, 'you will ask me no questions' (16: 23). But has he actually solved the original puzzle? Evidently not. When, a little further on, the disciples express their satisfaction ('now we do not need to question you'—16: 30), they are responding to the answer to a different question. Barrett is right here to speak of 'a studied ambiguity'; 'The sayings about going and coming can be interpreted throughout of the departure and return of Jesus in his death and resurrection; but they can equally well be interpreted of the departure to the Father at the ascension and his return at the *parousia*.'[40] All agree that there is a reference to the resurrection; but our attention is also directed to the signs of an imminent end, partly by the image itself, the woman in travail, partly by the use of the significant term θλῖψις (anguish, tribulation) in 16: 21.[41] So Barrett rightly dismisses Bultmann's suggestion that 'Easter and the Parousia are interpreted as one and the same event.'[42] The original question is evaded, the tension is left unresolved, and we are entitled to ask why.

The best answer is in terms of the two levels of understanding. On the first, the story level, we must put ourselves in the position of Jesus' disciples as they listen with dismay to the news of his imminent departure. To them the 'little while' is simply the interval between passion and resurrection. However unusual the language, on this level the saying is a form of passion-and-resurrection prediction. What is said in 14: 29 also holds for the more elaborate version in chapter 16: 'And now I have told you before it takes place, so that when it does take place, you may believe.'

On the second or spiritual level of understanding we must adopt the perspective of John's hearers or the readers of his Gospel, who know that the resurrection has already happened. Heirs to the promise, enjoying as they read or listen the life that Jesus came to bring, they have nevertheless retained (as many modern Christians have) some belief in his eventual return. This may not be a *literal*

---

[40] *Gospel*[2], p. 491.

[41] Two passages from Isaiah are regularly cited in this connection, but neither stands up to close inspection. In Isa. 26: 18 the people turn out to have experienced a phantom pregnancy and in Isa. 66: 7 the birth is achieved without labour. 1 QH 3: 8–12 is closer, with a marvellous birth, perhaps messianic, following heavy pains. The term ὠδῖνες (labour-pangs) is not in John but occurs elsewhere, notably Mark 13: 8, in an eschatological sense. (Cf. G. Bertram, *TDNT* ix, s.v. ὠδίν.) Mark uses θλῖψις with an identical reference (13: 19, 24); cf. Dan. 12: 1 (Theodotion); Zeph. 1: 15; Rom. 2: 9.   [42] p. 586.

belief; it may be experienced, as David Aune has argued, as a cultic anticipation of a distant dream. But the future hope, though drawn back somehow into the present, is not *ipso facto* utterly absorbed. In selecting the term ζωὴ αἰώνιος the evangelist guarantees, as we have seen,[43] a reference to the future life. Here, however, he does more than this: in both versions of the farewell discourse he invites his readers, even as they are concentrating upon their present good fortune, to maintain some awareness of the future.

(b) The indwelling of Father and Son

In the section of the speech that provokes Judas' interjection ('how is it that you will manifest yourself to us and not to the world?'—14: 22) the idea of the coming of Jesus is both echoed and transformed. This we have just seen. In the reply to Judas the additional motif of the heavenly dwellings (14: 2) is taken up and turned inside out. The word μονή does not occur in the New Testament outside these two verses (14: 2, 23). Whereas the original promise remained fully enclosed within the conventional expectation of the parousia, the movement is now in the other direction.[44] The ascent to heaven in an indefinite future is overshadowed (though not replaced) by the movement down from heaven, not just of the Son but of the Father also. Together they will make their home (μονή) with the faithful disciple.

Earlier in the Gospel the Samaritan woman had been told: 'The hour is coming and now is, when true worshippers will worship the Father in spirit and truth, for such the Father seeks to worship him' (4: 23). The interiorization of the cult implied in this saying is now stated formally and explicitly. How else are we to interpret the assertion that Jesus and his Father would come and take up their abode with the faithful Christian believer (πρὸς αὐτὸν ἐλευσόμεθα καὶ μονὴν παρ' αὐτῷ ποιησόμεθα, 14: 23)? Hoskyns comments: 'The sanctuary and home of God, which is in heaven, and was but incompletely revealed in the temple of Jerusalem, will descend upon each Christian believer';[45] and he suggests that this constitutes the fulfilment of the Old Testament promise: 'Let them make me a sanctuary, that I may dwell in their midst' (Exod. 25: 8; cf. Exod. 29: 45;

---

[43] Cf. *supra*. ch. 6, pp. 214–20.   [44] cf. Bultmann, p. 624.
[45] p. 460.

Lev. 26: 11f.; Ezek. 37: 26f.; Zech. 2: 10; cf. *Jub.* 1: 17).[46] This suggestion is plausible and attractive. If Hoskyns is right, then the μοναί (AV 'mansions') of 14: 2, individual rooms or apartments in the house of God, are reinterpreted in 14: 23 as places on earth, localized in the community, where not only Jesus but God himself, coming in a cultic or mystical manner, can find a welcome. Aune goes so far as to propose that the term οἰκία (house) in 14: 2 (and also in 8: 35) probably 'reflects the self-designation of the Johannine community'[47] and this enables him to interpret μονή in the singular in 14: 23 'as the individual believer who is the locus for the pneumatic indwelling of the Father and the Son.'[48]

However this may be, the coming in question is neither the resurrection nor the parousia, nor is it to be confused with the mission of the Paraclete. It presages a mystical union of awesome intimacy, one that indicates the profoundly contemplative character of the Johannine community. To baulk at the term 'mysticism', as many Protestant writers do, is to close one's eyes to the obvious meaning of the passage for the sake of what are ultimately more esoteric and less plausible explanations.

(c) The gift of the Spirit

In John 16 two clearly distinct Paraclete sayings (16: 7–11, 12–15) are placed side by side; in John 14, where there are also two sayings (14: 16f., 26f.), the distinction is emphasized by their being held apart. From a literary point of view the two sayings serve quite different functions; that the leading figure in both sayings should be the same is, formally speaking, one of John's most remarkable innovations. What I mean by this will emerge in due course.

For the present let us confine our attention to the first of the sayings:

---

[46] For a full discussion of these and other texts see Beutler (*Habt keine Angst*), pp. 73–7. Barrett (p. 457) points to the Neofiti targum of Exod. 33: 14; 'The glory of my Shekinah will pass among you and I will prepare you a resting-place.' Note too that in Hebrews the rest (κατάπαυσις) that Israel is to enjoy in Canaan (LXX Ps. 94: 11) is reinterpreted of heaven (Heb. 4: 5). The word μονή possibly reflects Hebrew מעון, used in the Old Testament both for the Temple as the earthly dwelling of God (Ps. 26: 8; 2 Chron. 36: 15) and for God's dwelling in heaven (Deut. 26: 15; 2 Chron. 30: 27). A similar usage is found at Qumran, especially in the Songs of the Sabbath Sacrifice, as is pointed out by the editor of the Songs, Carol Newsom, p. 39. 4 *Ezra* uses 'habitationes' in 7: 80 and 'habitaculum/a' in 7: 85, 101.

[47] *Cultic Setting*, p. 130.   [48] Ibid., p. 131.

And I will give you another Paraclete to be with you for ever, even the Spirit of truth, whom the world cannot receive, because it neither sees him nor knows him; you know him, for he dwells with you, and will be in you. (14: 16–17)

Though I have left it to the last, this is in fact the first of the three promises of presence-in-absence made to the disciples by the departing Jesus. It has obvious parallels with the second, for like Jesus (14: 20) the Paraclete is expected to come and stay—to be 'in' the disciples (14: 17). If we venture outside the framework of the farewell discourse we find additional parallels: like Jesus (3: 16) the Paraclete will be *given* by the Father (14: 16); the world which fails to recognize the light (1: 10) cannot receive the Paraclete either (14: 17). The Jews do not receive the light (1: 11) nor *know* Jesus (8: 19); similarly the world does not *know* the Paraclete (14: 17).[49] It is clear then that although this is 'another' Paraclete, not simply to be identified with Jesus, he nevertheless re-presents Jesus and has no independent existence of his own. His mode of being is different, that is all. As Hans Windisch remarked,[50] he is Jesus' *Doppelgänger* or double, his *alter ego*.

The differences (for we must not confine our attention to the resemblances) are brought out by the language John employs. What is particularly noticeable is that the disciples are nowhere said to *see* the spirit, any more than they see the wind (for which John employs the same word, πνεῦμα, in 3: 8). Though *known* to the disciples (14: 17), he does not, unlike Jesus (14: 21) *manifest* himself to them. As the light of the world Jesus is fully and properly visible; but it would be a sheer solecism to apply the language of vision to the spirit.

Provided that one acknowledges that the first Paraclete saying has been set alongside the promise of the coming of Jesus for a purpose, then both the resemblances and the differences are easy to spot. Less obvious, but equally important, are the results yielded by a form-critical analysis. These emerge quite strikingly from a comparison with one final example of the commission form, this time from the prophet Haggai:

---

[49] See the detailed analysis with which Brown follows up his summary comment: 'Virtually everything that has been said about the Paraclete has been said about Jesus' (p. 1140).

[50] 'Parakletsprüche', p. 129.

Yet now take courage, O Joshua, son of Jehozadak, the high priest; take courage all you people of the land, says the Lord; work, for I am with you, says the Lord of hosts, according to the promise that I made you when you came out of Egypt. My Spirit abides among you; fear not. (Hag. 2: 4–5)

Before proceeding any further it may be helpful here to point out the three key elements in the commission form.[51] The first two of these are (1) the *encouragement*, which regularly occurs as an injunction, 'Fear not', or 'Be strong'; and (2) the *commission*. The regular Hebrew verb for 'commission' is, as we have seen, the Piel of צוה. When, as in this example, the charge is conferred directly, it may take the form of a particular command (e.g. 'you shall bring the children of Israel into the land' (Deut. 31: 23)) or be expressed, as here, simply and unspecifically by the verb עשה ('work' or 'act'); cf. 1 Kings 2: 6. The third element (3) is the *promise of divine assistance*. Although this is not an integral element of the form, since it is missing from some examples (e.g. 2 Sam. 13: 28; 1 Kings 2: 1–9), nevertheless it always accompanies a commission that has divine backing and approval. Sometimes it is put in the form of a prayer: 'The Lord be with you' (1 Chron. 22: 16; cf. 2 Chron. 19: 11); more often as a statement or promise (Deut. 31: 23; Josh. 1: 9). The ultimate origin of this convention is to be found, presumably, in the promise to Moses on the occasion of his call and commission. Accordingly, the promise of divine assistance (Exod. 3: 12) was apparently associated quite early with a commission (Exod. 3: 10–15).

The first two of the three elements have been discussed earlier under the headings of 'Faith' and 'Commission'. It remains to consider the third. In the passage from Haggai quoted above, the traditional formula 'I am with you' is, quite exceptionally, expanded and explained by the promise of the enduring presence of the spirit. So at least from post-exilic times the divine assistance could be envisaged under a new mode. This was a natural development, rooted in a remarkable series of theological reflections that sprang up round the theme of the new covenant. One of these is the prayer of the *Miserere*: 'Create in me a clean heart, O God, and put a new and right spirit within me. Cast me not away from thy presence, and take not thy holy spirit from me' (Ps. 51: 12–13). According to *Jubilees*,

---

[51] On this form see N. Lohfink, 'Die deuteronomistische Darstellung des Übergangs der Führung Israels von Mose auf Josue', *Scholastik*, 37 (1962), 32–44.

Moses employs this very prayer to intercede for his people, and God responds positively in terms that recall other elements of the new covenant as well (*Jub.* 1: 20–25).

Now it is neither possible nor necessary to demonstrate that the Johannine prophet had the Haggai text in mind as he formulated his own message of encouragement. But the passage enables us to see how easy it was for him to adapt the traditional formula, 'I am with you'. The circumstances of the farewell discourse preclude any direct use of this formula, even though Jesus is speaking with God's authority and on his behalf. The promise of the abiding presence of the spirit is, however, a satisfactory equivalent. Here is a favourite image of divine action in the world. Moreover the fourth evangelist is convinced that the spirit of God is actually released into the world by the death of Jesus; indeed, until then, as he remarks in an editorial aside, 'there was as yet no Spirit (οὔπω γὰρ ἦν πνεῦμα) because Jesus was not yet glorified' (7: 39). A later version of the promise of the Spirit faithfully reflects the same conviction: 'It is to your advantage that I go away, for if I do not go away the Paraclete will not come to you' (16: 7). After Jesus' departure, however, the permanent abiding of the Spirit guarantees that his assistance will continue in a new mode, one in which his presence will be discernible, certainly, but irreducible to any crudely physical manifestation.

The situation of the farewell discourse, then, and the evangelist's particular conception of Jesus' role, compel him to make changes in the commission form. Like the other elements, the promise of divine assistance is distorted, though not beyond recognition. But the combination of the two forms, testament and commission, enables John to give the Paraclete not just one function, as a guarantor of the abiding presence of Jesus and therefore of the Father also, but two. For he does not only re-present Jesus, he succeeds him. From the perspective we have adopted so far the Paraclete is simply Jesus himself in another guise, unfettered by the spatial and temporal limitations that beset any individual human life. But from another perspective he has to carry on—and carry out—Jesus' work of teaching and instruction. Expressing this in form-critical terms, and confining ourselves to the commission form, we may say that the Paraclete figures not only in the third element, the promise of assistance, but in the second also, the actual commission. Viewed in this light the form is not so much expanded as compressed, with an artistry that may be appreciated first of all on the sheerly literary level, but whose theological ramifications, as the history of Christian doctrinal development would prove, are virtually endless. Even so, the distinction between the two elements of the form, and equally between the two roles John assigns to the spirit, remain visible in the otherwise puzzling bifurcation of the Paraclete sayings in this chapter. In the first saying (14: 16f.) the presence of the Spirit is both the proof of divine assistance and one of the three modes of Jesus' abiding presence. In the second (14: 25f.) he is not so much Jesus' double, *Christus praesens*, as his successor, *vicarius Christi*—'the vicar of Christ', as Tertullian calls him (*De praescriptione haereticorum*, 28: 6);[52] so it is perhaps wise to follow the evangelist in maintaining a real distinction between these.

The second of the two roles, exhibiting what Raymond Brown has called the tandem relationship between Jesus and the Paraclete, cannot, however, be treated adequately without reinforcing the concept of commission by that of testament. This is the subject of the following section.

3. A SECOND MOSES

We have already seen how the 'commandments' in 14: 15 may be an intentional allusion to the moral exhortation characteristic of the developed testament form. In some respects the disciples represent the 'family' of Jesus, his heirs and successors: they are to keep his commandments after his death and 'He who believes in me will also do the works that I do, and greater works than these will he do, because I go to the father' (14: 12)—greater, presumably, in so far as they are not hampered, as Jesus was in his lifetime, by constrictions of space and time.[53] But the relation between the farewell discourse in John and the newer kind of testament as found, say, in the *Testaments of the Twelve Patriarchs* is in fact rather tenuous, as even E. Cortès acknowledges. From the perspective of form criticism the true literary antecedent of John 14 is the combined testament/commission form that appeared in Hebrew literature as early as the tenth century (1 Kings 2: 1–9) and was taken over by the

---

[52] Having called the Spirit Jesus' *Doppelgänger* in one article ('Die fünf Parakletsprüche', p. 129), Windisch calls him his 'caliph' or 'successor' in another ('Jesus und der Geist', p. 311), thus neatly reinforcing the distinction between the two passages.

[53] Bultmann makes the point about the removal of temporal limitations but denies the relevance of the great geographical expansion of early Christianity (p. 610).

deuteronomist (Deut. 31: 1–6; 7–8; 14–15, 23; Josh. 1: 1–9). Some of these texts have occupied our attention earlier in this chapter.

Now it is no coincidence that of the three paired figures whose relationship, so it has been suggested by Bornkamm[54] and Brown,[55] may have influenced John's conception of the Paraclete, by far the most impressive is the Moses/Joshua duo. Bornkamm's proposal that the Paraclete may be modelled upon Jesus' own relationship with John the Baptist founders on the simple fact that Jesus, though succeeding the Baptist in time, precedes him in rank.[56] As for Elisha, though he asks for a double share of Elijah's spirit and inherits his mantle, he does not appear to have been commissioned by him or to have taken over a task that Elijah left uncompleted. Joshua, on the contrary, is specifically enjoined by God—or by Moses speaking on God's behalf—to carry out tasks that were originally to have been performed by Moses.

There are two main reasons for believing that John's indebtedness to the deuteronomical tradition is not just a matter of background and that we are justified in speaking of a real influence here.[57] In the first place, the numerous references in the Gospel to Moses and to the 'prophet' who was to succeed him show that Jesus was regarded by the community as somehow supplanting Moses and taking his place.[58] Secondly, an analysis of the testament and commission form, separately but more particularly in conjunction, forces one back repeatedly to a study of the concluding chapters of Deuteronomy. A third reason, of less weight than the other two but still not to be ignored, is the number of rewritings of parts of Deuteronomy

---

[54] 'Paraklet' (1949 and 1968). [55] pp. 1135–43.

[56] As Bornkamm himself recognizes (1968, p. 87) without apparently realizing the significance of the concession.

[57] Further reasons are given by A. Lacomara, 'Farewell Discourse'. Among other resemblances Lacomara notes the following: (*a*) the mediating authority of Jesus and Moses respectively is established in both writings by recalling their intimate knowledge of the divine will; (*b*) they share an emphasis on the closeness, indeed the abiding presence, of God among his people; (*c*) both see love as a *commandment* and the basis of all obedience to God; (*d*) both express 'the concern that the words and works of God be conserved and handed on to future generations that they may remain a living memory and constant influence in the lives of the people' (p. 81). Like Beutler, Lacomara believes that the theme of the new covenant is discernible throughout the farewell discourse. He goes beyond Beutler in concluding that 'in the chapters of the farewell discourse we have an extended commentary on the words in the institution of the Eucharist, "of the new covenant"' (p. 84).

[58] See Meeks, *Prophet-King, passim*. Note that for Ben Sira (46: 1–6) Joshua was 'the successor of Moses in prophesying'.

within the Second Temple period: *Jubilees* 1, Pseudo-Philo (*Ant. Bib.* 19), the Words of Moses (1Q22), and above all the *Testament* or *Assumption of Moses*.[59]

The book of Deuteronomy, itself in large measure the reworking of older traditions, is really one gigantic testament, with its natural time-sequence deliberately foreshortened to allow the whole action to be encompassed within a single day. The day in question, specified in Deuteronomy 1: 3, is the first of the eleventh month in the fortieth year after the Exodus. Towards the close of the book, on 'that very day' (Deut. 32: 48), God summons Moses to ascend Mount Nebo (the top of Pisgah) so as to gaze over the Jordan just once before his death: 'For you shall see the land before you; but you shall not go there, into the land which I give to the people of Israel' (Deut. 32: 52). This careful inclusion, as Joseph Blenkinsopp observes, 'redefines the book as a valedictory rather than a law book'.[60] Not only the retrospective view of the wanderings of Israel in the desert (chapters 1–4) but also the complex and detailed legislation of chapters 5–28 may be seen as the official constitution of an emergent nation, which has yet to settle in its destined home. Israel's exodus, like that of Jesus, was simply an overture to yet greater works.

The concluding chapters, 31–34, are of particular importance, containing as they do Moses' final dispositions on the eve of his death. Within them is found the fusion of the testament and commission forms on which I have insisted. They are also the basis of what is for our purposes unquestionably the most significant of all deuteronomic rewritings, the *Testament of Moses*.[61] The best way of illustrating this is to quote from it extensively, and so I have appended a translation of lengthy excerpts (restricted, for practical purposes, to the beginning and the end of the document), plus a number of notes. These will be found in Excursus V.

The remainder of this section will be devoted to a consideration of three major topics that arise from a comparison of the farewell discourse with the Moses tradition.

1. The first concerns Moses himself—the man and the myth. The life of Moses furnishes an ample reservoir of legends from which Jewish writers of all persuasions could draw when searching for fresh models, symbols, or arguments to encourage and inspire their

---

[59] See too Philo, *Life of Moses*; Josephus, *AJ* iv. 302–6.
[60] *Prophecy and Covenant* (Notre Dame, 1977), p. 83.
[61] See D. J. Harrington, 'Interpreting Israel's History'.

own contemporaries. The narrative passages of the book of Deuteronomy give a fresh twist to various episodes in Numbers and Exodus; and as if anticipating the need for further adaptation the author foretells the advent of yet another Moses-like figure who will exhibit all the qualities of a true prophet. Since the Exodus story is, among other things, a foundation myth, the frequency with which other writers turn to it should not surprise us. What may cause surprise is the variety of guises in which Moses appears, not just as a leader and legislator, but as an inventor and engineer (Artapanus), a prophet (Josephus), and a sage in an allegorical country where the wise man is king (Philo). For the author of the *Testament of Moses*, as for Pseudo-Philo, he seems to have been above all the shepherd of his people, and it is possible that a similar tradition helped to shape the picture of Jesus as the Good Shepherd. Moses figures in Attic-style drama (Ezekiel the Tragedian), allegory (Philo), and historical romance (Artapanus), as well as in history (Josephus) and in the testament genre that we have just been examining.

Other writers of the Second Temple period turned elsewhere for inspiration, Enoch to a shadowy figure from prehistory, Baruch to the amanuensis of a great prophet, 4 Ezra, with singular irony in view of his subject, to the founder of the Second Temple. Yet although they were proposing new revelations they were not repudiating the old. Where the fourth evangelist differs from all of these, as well as from those who exploited the Moses tradition, is in his conscious substitution of this tradition by the story of Jesus: 'You search the scriptures,' Jesus tells the Jews, 'and I am the one to which they bear witness' (5: 39). The deliberate replacement of one founder-figure by another (the same step would be taken six centuries later on behalf of Mohammed) is effectively the proclamation of a new religion. We may compare John with Matthew here, for whom Jesus is a second Moses, refining and purifying the law, but not replacing it (5: 17). John, by contrast, puts the law aside, offering instead, in the name of Jesus Christ, 'grace and truth' (1: 17). Similarly the Temple, the second pillar of contemporary Judaism, was for Matthew a place where Jesus' disciples continued to offer their gifts; whereas for John the locus of Christian worship has shifted to a place of 'spirit and truth' (4: 23).

The many echoes of Deuteronomy in the farewell discourse support the inference that here too John sees Jesus as having taken the place of Moses in the new dispensation.

2. Next there is the question of the future, part of the *raison-d'être* of all testaments. According to Deuteronomy, Moses was invited to go up to the top of Pisgah and cast his eyes 'westward and northward and southward and eastward' (3: 27) whereupon God pointed out to him in particular 'the whole land of Judah as far as the Western Sea, the Negeb and the Plain' (34: 1–4)—the Promised Land. Thus he stood on the very frontier, in time as well as in space, that marked the division between God's promise and its fulfilment.

At the close of his life the seer Baruch was granted a more comprehensive vision from the top of a mountain, one that embraced 'all the regions of the land and the figure of the inhabited world' (*2 Bar.* 76: 3); whilst the Enoch of the Animal Apocalypse was given a view of the course of history: everything that was to befall 'these elephants and camels and asses, and the stars, and all the bulls' (*1 Enoch*, 87: 4).

What is there in the farewell discourse to correspond to this tradition? Well, Jesus too stands on the frontier that marks the boundary between the past and the future. In his case, however, the past is his own past, his life on earth, and the future belongs to the community that will have to manage without his bodily presence. In one sense he will be unable to lead them beyond the limits of his own death. In a more important sense, however, he will come and take up his abode ($\mu o\nu\dot{\eta}$) with them, an abode which is a true abiding ($\mu\acute{\epsilon}\nu\epsilon\iota\nu$).

3. We have already seen how successfully the Paraclete tradition has been grafted on to a testament that might be considered complete without it. The recipients of the commission to 'keep my commandments' are Jesus' disciples, who will carry out this command simply by keeping his *word*, a charge that may have been thought to have been partly fulfilled by their preservation of the very Gospel which has been composed to promote faith in Jesus' words among its readers.

Certainly the idea of the preservation of the book, though not present explicitly in the text of Deuteronomy, reflects a real concern of the author of the *Testament of Moses*, which includes precise directions about how the books Moses passes on to Joshua are to be anointed with cedar oil and deposited in earthen vessels in a place made by God 'from the beginning of the world' (1: 16f., cf. 10: 11; 11: 1). There may even be a hint that the *Testament* is actually reproducing the text of Deuteronomy.[62] However this may be, the concern for the preservation of the book or books is certainly shared by other contemporary writers, notably 4 Ezra.[63]

The book of Deuteronomy has a variety of different expressions for the words which it enshrines: like the Fourth Gospel it is very much a book of words, and of words capable of being indefinitely repeated without losing their value. As time went on, however, these words would themselves require explanation, something that the Qumran author of the so-called 'Words of Moses' (1Q22) understood when in his version of the testament he portrayed Moses as making provision for instructors 'whose work it shall be to expound all these works of the law'.

In the Fourth Gospel, clearly, this is the job of the Paraclete. Along with Lindars[64] I think it likely that the evangelist drew upon an already existing tradition at this point. If so, it was one which fitted remarkably well into the testament/commission form, allowing the Paraclete to assume, as many scholars have noticed, the function assigned to Joshua in the conclusion of Deuteronomy as Moses' heir and successor.

The holy spirit in the *Testament of Moses*, like the Johannine Paraclete, is a 'lord of the word ... the most consummate teacher in the world' (11: 16). But whereas in John the role of Joshua is taken over by the Paraclete, in the *Testament of Moses* the spirit is identified

---

[62] In 1: 5, a verse omitted by Charles, there is a reference to 'the prophecy made by Moses in the book of Deuteronomy'. This can only be what Moses says in his final testament, and this in turn appears to refer to all that follows. Cf. E.-M. Lapperrousaz, *Testament*, p. 114 n. 5.

[63] Ulrich Müller ('Parakletenvorstellung') lays great weight on this theme. Besides the present passage, he detects it in *Jub.* 45: 16; *2 Enoch* 33: 5ff.; 36: 1; 47: 1–3; 54: 66: 7 (?); *2 Bar.* 77ff.; 84.f.; and above all in *4 Ezra* 14, which he scrutinizes closely. Only in *Test. Mos.*, however, is this important theme clearly integrated into the testament form. Ezra, for instance, is told by God to make public some of his writings and to entrust others to the wise, but this is a divine instruction, not a testament. In fact Müller admits that he includes in his purview other texts besides formal farewell discourses—so that, he says, 'the problematic of the farewell situation in John may be reflected against the broadest possible background of similar situations' (p. 52). Thus at this crucial point he diverges from the strictly form-critical approach upon whose necessity he had insisted at the beginning of his article. Whilst in the present chapter I have not permitted myself a similar liberty, I agree with Müller on the importance of these texts; in particular, as we have seen in Ch. 10, the distinction between public and esoteric writings bears directly upon the question of the gospel genre. But besides this the proposal that the Paraclete, like Joshua here, is in some sense 'the guardian of the book' deserves careful consideration.

[64] Cf. nn. 9 and 10.

with Moses and will be considered, at any rate by the kings of the Amorites, to have departed with him (ibid.).

Joshua's office, of course, was not that of a teacher but of a leader and guide, what the *Testament of Moses* calls the people's 'guide on the way' (11: 10), a phrase that recalls the Paraclete's task of guiding the community into the truth (16: 13). We are now in a position to see that what Jesus surveyed on the eve of his death was a domain which, in the eyes of the evangelist, held out more promise than the land of Canaan did to the Israelites: it was 'the truth', a territory whose boundaries were already clearly defined as the revelation of Jesus, but the extent of whose riches had yet to be discovered—under the guidance of the Paraclete.

CONCLUSION

In many parts of the Gospel, the passion narrative for instance, questions concerning the circumstances and immediate interests of the community would seem odd, even out of place. In others, such as the episode of the healing of the blind man, only the acumen of individual scholars, in this case J. L. Martyn, has alerted us to the complex way in which the text is operating and suggested how its signals must be read if its full message is to be understood. But there are other passages, above all the farewell discourse and prayer, in which the Gospel itself specifically enjoins its readers to attend to the circumstances of the Christian community after the death and departure of the one whose words and deeds it purports to record. In such instances questions regarding the situation of the community, far from seeming intrusive or imperceptive, are perfectly appropriate.

We should expect, therefore, all commentators on these chapters, before as well as after the exegetical revolution that swung the beam of critical enquiry on to the situation of the earliest readers of the Gospel, to have some comment to offer upon what has come to be called the Johannine community. Similarly, a straightforward form-critical study of the farewell discourse of the kind I have attempted here might be expected to yield some direct insight into the immediate preoccupations of the teacher of the community whom we have called the Johannine prophet.

Very often questions directed towards these areas take the form of an enquiry into the tasks or functions of the Paraclete. The *name*

'Paraclete', in spite of dozens of energetic attempts to elucidate it, remains imperspicuous. Nevertheless—a point well made by Barnabas Lindars—the evangelist gives his readers the necessary information. He 'feels the need to add explanatory phrases each time he uses the Paraclete material'.[65] Since then he is so evidently identified *by* his role he may be said to be identified *with* it. Answers to further questions regarding his identity (e.g. the beloved disciple or 'the teacher of the community') are all wide of the mark. Besides, were he to be identified in any crude or simplistic way with an individual human figure then this person too would eventually have to be replaced on his departure by 'another' Paraclete, presumably with a role indistinguishable from his own.

The very absurdity of this supposition, however, prompts a further question. If the task of the Paraclete extends beyond the lifetime of any individual, so that the work of the Johannine teacher or prophet does not cease with his death, then perhaps this very endurance, more than mere longevity, is part of what is being affirmed at this point. And indeed it is: the word for it—a verb rather than a noun—is μένειν. Part of the very essence of the Paraclete's role is that he should remain or abide.

Since this is so it is not just Jesus' own disciples who are being assured that he will not leave them bereft; subtly and indirectly the members of the community are being told that the prophetic and teaching functions so vital for its survival will not cease abruptly after the death of its present leader. For this discourse to be fully understood it must be read on two levels: what was true of Jesus is also true of the Johannine prophet: his death is a departure but his 'spirit' will live on.

Although this reading emerges naturally and without strain from a careful study of the text, it goes beyond the standard commentaries in its recognition that the interpretative principle I have called 'the two levels of understanding' is fully operational at this point. The Jesus of the farewell discourse is certainly the Jesus of the story but in and through his words may be heard the voice of the Johannine prophet. Hence the urgency of the message, the sense it conveys of a grief surmounted and accepted only with great difficulty. This is more than a profound theological reflection upon the post-Easter situation of the followers of Jesus; it is that, certainly, but it is also

---

[65] 'Persecution', p. 63.

the final valedictory of the Johannine prophet, employing the traditional testament and commission form to console the community in advance for their approaching loss and to assure them of the abiding presence of 'the spirit of truth'.[66]

[66] A recent commentator on John 14, Fernando F. Segovia, distinguishes four types of interpretation. According to the third of these, adopted by the majority of modern scholars, 'the discourse addresses directly the fact of Jesus' departure from the world and from his own' (p. 473); according to the fourth, accepted by Segovia himself, it is 'primarily polemical in tone' ('Structure', p. 474). He thus joins the ranks of those who pretend to detect a polemical tone in ch. 14: these include Becker and Woll. Such a claim is ill-founded: unlike the dialogues in the first half of the Gospel, the farewell discourse is addressed specifically to the *disciples* and its tone is not polemical but consolatory. But Segovia's main mistake lies in his failure to recognize the two levels of understanding. The view that the discourse is concerned with Jesus' departure does not have to be abandoned once it is seen that the evangelist is also thinking of his own situation and that of his hearers. The two readings are complementary—not mutually exclusive alternatives.

Excursus V: *The Testament of Moses*[1]

1 (6) Moses called to him Joshua,[2] the son of Nun, a man who
had won the approval of the Lord, (7) to be the minister[3] of
the people and of the Tent of Witness, with all its sacred objects;
also (8) to lead the people into the land given to their fathers,
(9) that it might be given to them in accordance with the covenant
and the oath that he swore in the Tent to give it them through
Joshua. This is what he said to Joshua: (10) 'Be strong and

These notes are confined (*a*) to points relevant to the preceding discussion; (*b*) to the
elucidation of obscurities arising from the single, garbled manuscript upon which we
depend for our knowledge of a Hebrew or Aramaic work (probably the former) first
translated into Greek and then into very indifferent Latin. A completely literal
translation would be unreadable and virtually unintelligible, but any significant
divergences from the Latin will be pointed out.

[1] For the various editions and translations of this text, assessments concerning its
date and provenance, and accompanying English translations see now *The Old
Testament Pseudepigrapha*, i. 919–34 (J. Priest) and *The Apocryphal Old Testament*,
pp. 601–16 (J. P. M. Sweet). I have consulted both of these as well as the earlier
edition of R. H. Charles (London, 1897), published under the title of *The Assumption of
Moses*, and Charles's revised translation and notes in *APOT* ii (Oxford, 1913),
pp. 414–24. The edition of E.-M. Laperrousaz, *Le Testament de Moïse*, is particularly
useful. Another henceforth indispensable study is Schalit's *Untersuchungen*. This 208-
page book is a detailed commentary, not just line by line but word by word, upon the
first chapter (18 verses) of the Testament—creeping exegesis indeed, but creeping to
some purpose, for its ultimate aim was to have been a reconstruction both of the
Greek translation and of the Hebrew (as it is argued) *Vorlage*. (The chapter and verse
numberings of my own translation are those of Charles's 'Emended and Revised
Text'.)

[2] *Test. Mos.* follows Deut. 31: 7–8, according to which Moses actually appoints his
successor. It should be remembered that the calling or summoning is a constitutive
element of the later, developed testament form.

[3] Here and in 10: 15 the Latin has *successor*. Charles argues that this is a
mistranslation of διάδοκος (= מְשָׁרֵת), 'minister', which does indeed fit this context
better. In 10: 15, however, as Laperrousaz points out, *successor* is more appropriate,
and in any case the author certainly regarded Joshua as Moses' successor. Schalit too
retains *successor*, surmising that it renders κληρονόμος or an equivalent term (= יורש).
He insists that Joshua is Moses' heir—but on behalf of his people: 'the author', he
believes, 'wants to say that Joshua has been appointed by Moses not only as his
successor but also as the heir of his charisma' (p. 89). The purpose of his inheritance
(*Vererbung*) is to ensure 'the continuity of the life of Israel', not just for the sake of the
people but for the sake of the sanctuary (p. 90). Analogies with John 14 are easy to
spot.

courageous:[4] do your best to fulfil what you have been commissioned to do[5] in a way fully acceptable to God. (11) So says the Lord of the world; (12) for he created the world on behalf of his people. (13) But he did not intend[6] to disclose the plan of creation from the origin of the world, in order that the Gentiles might be convicted and to their own shame convict one another by their arguments.[7] (14) That is why he thought me up and invented me: from the origin of the world[8] I have been prepared to be the mediator of his covenant.[9] (15) And now I reveal to you that the span of my life has been completed and I am departing in the presence of the whole people to sleep with my fathers.[10] (16) As for you, take this writing and give thought how to preserve the books that I will pass on to you;[11] (17)

[4] The Latin here has *verbum hoc et promitte*; but in 10: 15, where the context requires the same introduction, *itaque tu jesu naue forma te*. In both instances Charles suggests *confortare et firma te*—'Be strong and courageous', corresponding to Deut. 31: 6, 7, 23; Josh. 1: 6, 7, 9, 18. Here Laperrousaz follows Charles. Priest renders *promitte*, somewhat oddly, by 'Go forward'. Since *Test. Mos.* is following Deuteronomy quite faithfully at both these points one would expect a word of encouragement; and though Charles's argument is very speculative, the *forma te* (surely *firma te!*) in 10: 15 gives it some solid basis. According to Schalit, *et promitte* goes back to the Hebrew ואמר , a corruption, he suggests, of ושמר , i.e. 'and observe'. This is equally speculative.

[5] *Quae mandate sunt ut facias*. The Hebrew will have employed צוות at this point, the standard term, as we have seen, for the commissioning.

[6] *Non coepit* = οὐκ ἤρξατο = לא הואיל (Charles). Charles argues that the Greek translator chose the wrong meaning of הואיל (undertake?), instead of the ordinary meaning (decide).

[7] Compare the role assigned to the Paraclete in John 16: 8–11.

[8] *ab initio orbis terrarum praeparatus sum*. The Greek of this phrase has been preserved in the Acts of the Council of Nicaea (AD 325) in a citation from a document referred to there as *The Assumption of Moses*: καὶ προεθεάσατό με ὁ Θεὸς πρὸ καταβολῆς κόσμου εἶναί με τῆς Διαθήκης αὐτοῦ μεσίτην (Migne, PG ii. 18. 1265). Charles and Laperrousaz agree that the reference is to our *Test. Mos.* But the Greek is in the middle voice, not the passive, and the verb ('foresee' rather than 'prepare') does not necessarily imply pre-existence. (Schalit thinks that the Greek here may have been ἑτοιμασμένος εἰμί, a genuine passive.) The Greek phrase πρὸ καταβολῆς κόσμου exactly corresponds to the one employed by Jesus in his prayer to the Father, when he asks to be glorified 'with the glory which I had with thee *before the world was made*' (John 17: 24); cf. also Mark 10: 6; 13: 19—ἀπ' ἀρχῆς κτίσεως.

[9] *arbiter testamenti illius*. Thus *Test. Mos.* refers explicitly to Moses' role as mediator of the covenant. Cf. Gal. 3: 19; Heb. 8: 6.

[10] *Transio in dormitionem patrum meorum*. Moses does not actually say this in Deuteronomy, but is told by God: 'Behold you are about to sleep with your fathers' (Deut. 31: 16). *Transio* might be a rendering of πορεύομαι, or even of ὑπάγω, but the Greek verb is more probably διαβαίνειν (= ערב). Whatever the term, the departure theme is quite explicit.

[11] *ad recognoscendam tutationem librorum quos tibi tradam*. Tutatio suggests τηρεῖν rather than φυλάσσειν. In Deuteronomy Moses is not actually said to hand any books over to Joshua, though he did 'write the words of the law in a book' (Deut. 31: 24),

[cont. on p. 481]

you are to put them in order and anoint them with cedar oil and deposit them in earthen vessels in a place which he made from the beginning of the world (18) so that his name might be invoked until the day of repentance; in view of this the Lord will watch over them at the time of the consummation of the end of the days.[12]

2 (1) ... Through you they will enter into the land which he decreed and promised to give to their fathers.[13]

10 (11) 'As for you, Joshua, son of Nun, guard these words and this book.'[14] (12) For from my death, my reception,[15] up to his coming there will be 250 times. (13) And this is the course they will follow until they are finished. (14) As for me, I shall go to share the sleep of my fathers.[16] (15) Wherefore Joshua, son of Nun, be strong and of good courage;[17] for God has chosen you to be my successor[18] in the same covenant.'

one that in fact constitutes the bulk of Deuteronomy itself. There is no explicit mention of a book in John 14, but the idea of a written record is not far off (cf. John 20: 31; 21: 24 f.). Schalit argues convincingly here that Moses wishes to protect his book from all possible future falsifications. He shows that *recognoscere* is a technical term for ensuring that a copy tallies perfectly with the original. His Greek retroversion of this passage reads: καὶ ἐναντίον παντὸς τοῦ λαοῦ τούτου δέξαι τὴν γραφὴν ταύτην εἰς τὴν ἀσφάλισιν τῆς ἀναγνώσεως τῶν βιβλίων (pp. 173–8).

[12] A similar futuristic eschatology, absent from Deuteronomy, is implied in John 14: 3, as we have seen, but reinterpreted in John 14: 18.

[13] At this point I move to the conclusion of the document, since the intervening material (2: 7–10: 10) is not relevant to my argument. Note that the ending of *Test. Mos.* repeats many of the themes of the opening.

[14] *custodi verba haec et hunc librum. Custodire* = φυλάσσειν. Note that here we have 'book' rather than 'books' as in 1: 16. In 1Q22 Moses instructs the Israelites to appoint people whose 'work it shall be to expound all the words of the law'. This badly mutilated text allows us to see that the author shares the concern of the author of *Test. Mos.* but ensures continuity in a different way, by providing for teachers. Vermes hazards 'wise men' (*Dead Sea Scrolls*[2], p. 226).

[15] *a morte receptione[m]*. The first editor of *Test. Mos.*, Ceriani, signalled his uncertainty about the *m* by printing it in italics. Charles reads *a morte—receptione—m(ea)*. The original text, he believes, was a *testament*, and alluded simply to Moses' death. The word *receptione* will have been added by a later editor who combined this testament with an *assumption*. But Laperoussaz points out that *receptio* does not necessarily imply an assumption *into heaven*; it could simply anticipate Joshua's question, a little later, 'What place will receive you?', *Quis locus recipiet te?* (11: 5) and be a reference to Moses' burial. This is accepted by Priest, though Sweet remains uncertain. Laperoussaz's suggestion throws into question the long-held belief that *Test. Mos.* is not a *testament* but a truncated *assumption*. He himself argues in favour of the testament hypothesis (pp. 29–62).

[16] *Ego autem ad dormitionem patrum meorum eram* (for *eram* read *eam*).

[17] See n. 4 above.   [18] *successor*. See n. 3 above.

11 (1) And when Joshua heard the words of Moses as written in his writing, all that they had foretold,[19] he rent his garments and cast himself at Moses' feet. (2) And Moses comforted[20] him and wept with him. (3) And Joshua replied: (4) 'Why do you console me, lord Moses, and however shall I be consoled[21] for the bitter word that has proceeded from your mouth, a word full of tears and lamentation in that you are leaving this people behind. (5) What place will receive you? (6) and what monument will mark your tomb, (7) and who will dare to move your body from one place to another? (8) For all who die of old age are buried in their own lands; but your burial-place is from the rising to the setting, and from the south to the bounds of the north:[22] the whole world is your sepulchre. (9) Lord, you are departing:[23] who will feed this people? (10) Who will have compassion on them or be their guide on the way?[24] (11) Who will pray for them, not omitting a single day,[25] so that I may lead them into the land of their forefathers? (12) How can I be to this people like a father to his only son or a wife to her virgin daughter who is being prepared to be handed over to her husband? (She will be anxious for her and shield her body from the sun and take care that her feet are not unshod for running over the ground.) (13) And how shall I provide them with all the food and drink they desire? (14) For there will be [6]00,000 of them: so greatly have their numbers increased in response to your prayers, lord Moses. (15) And what wisdom or understanding have I that I should pronounce judgement

---

[19] *et cum audisset jesus verba moysi tam scripta in sua scriptura omnia quae praedixerant.* Yet another jumble. Charles (1897) inserts *quam* before *omnia* and emends *praedixerant* to *praedixerat*: 'When Joshua had heard the words of Moses, both those written down in his writing and all he had said previously.' This makes little sense; in his later version he retains the second emendation only: 'that were so written in his writing all that he had before said'; similarly Priest.

[20] *hortatus est cum.* Read *eum* (= παρεκάλησεν αὐτόν).

[21] Accepting Charles's emendations: *solaris* for *celares* and *solabor* for *celabor*. Moses' attempt at consolation is a natural human touch, much weaker, of course, than Jesus' οὐκ ἀφήσω ὑμᾶς ὀρφανούς ('I will not leave you bereft') in John 14: 18.

[22] These words are borrowed from Deut. 3: 27, where Moses is told to ascend Pisgah and lift up his eyes to the four points of the compass. Implicitly, therefore, *Test. Mos.* pictures Moses as surveying his burial-place—the whole earth.

[23] *domine ab his*: read *domine abis*.

[24] *quis est qui miserebitur illis et quis eis dux erit in via* = ὁδηγὸς [ἡγεμὼν] ἐν τῇ ὁδῷ. By a nice irony Joshua speaks of tasks that he will have to perform himself: cf. 11: 11, *ut inducam illos in terram*. The parallel with the Paraclete is evident: he will lead them (ὁδηγήσει) into all truth (John 16: 13).

[25] *patiens.* Charles thinks that the translator has picked the wrong meaning of παριείς: 'permit' instead of 'omit'.

or give answer in the house of the Lord?[26] (16) Moreover the kings of the Amorites will then dare to attack us, in the belief that "there is no longer among them the holy spirit, worthy of the Lord, manifold and incomprehensible, the lord of the word, faithful in all things, the divine prophet for the entire earth, the most consummate teacher in the world: so let us proceed against them".[27] (17) If the enemy have acted impiously towards God a single time, then they have no advocate[28] to offer prayers on their behalf to the Lord, as Moses, the great messenger,[29] did, who remained kneeling on the ground every hour, day and night, looking to the Almighty who governs the world in mercy with an oath. (18) So they will say: "He is not with them; so let us proceed against them and blot them off the face of the earth." (19) What will then become of this people, lord Moses?'

12 (1) When he had finished speaking Joshua threw himself once more at Moses' feet. (2) But Moses took his hand and raised him on to the seat in front of him, and answered and said to him: (3) 'Joshua, do not underrate yourself, nor be anxious,[30] but listen to my words. (4) God has created all the nations on earth, just as he has us; he has foreseen them and us from the beginning of the creation of the earth up to the end of age, and nothing, not the least thing, has been neglected by him; but he has foreseen all things and been the prime mover of all. (5) The Lord has foreseen everything that would occur on earth; and this is how it happens ... (6) The Lord has commissioned me[31] ... for them and their sins ... to (?) for them, (7) not for any strength or weakness of mine; but—something more modest—his mercy and patience have fallen to my lot. (8) For I tell you, Joshua: it is not for the sake of the people's piety that you will root out the Gentiles. (9) All the foundations of the globe have been made and approved by God and are under the signet ring of his right hand. (10) Those who fully carry out the commandments of

[26] *sapientia et intellectus.* Cf. the regular biblical conjunction of חכמה with בינה or תבונה : Isa. 29: 14; Job 28: 28; Prov. 3: 13, 19; 4: 5, 7, etc.

[27] By a bold stroke Moses is *identified* with the Holy Spirit here. As in the Fourth Gospel, the spirit is closely associated with the word: he is to prophesy and teach—he is even called 'lord of the Word'. Perhaps John knew this tradition and was influenced by it to see the Spirit assuming the roles elsewhere assigned to Jesus.

[28] *defensor*, not *advocatus*. Intercession is a regular prophetic function.

[29] *nuntius* = ἄγγελος = מלאך .

[30] *praebe te securum*: the characteristic reassurance of the commission form when accompanied by a divine injunction; it is based on the conviction of divine providence.

[31] Apparently *me constituit* (the text is corrupt), presumably reflecting Hebrew צִוַּנִי .

God will increase and go the good way. (11) But those who sin and flout the commandments will be deprived of these promised blessings and will suffer torments at the hands of the nations. (12) But it will prove impossible to root them out and destroy them. (13) For God will intervene, he who has foreseen all things for ever, and his covenant has been established and the oath ...' [*Here the MS breaks off.*]

13

PASSION AND RESURRECTION

I. PASSION

The passion and resurrection of Christ lie at the heart of Christianity. They belong, and belong integrally, to the Gospels. In a famous phrase (which he himself regarded as 'somewhat provocative') Martin Kähler suggested that the Gospels might be called 'passion narratives with extended introductions';[1] however true of the other three this is certainly not true of the Fourth. No one who had given the matter any thought would claim that the first seventeen chapters of the Gospel, or even the first ten, are nothing more than an introduction or overture to what follows. Where John is concerned the problem is the other way round: Ernst Käsemann has gone so far as to say that the passion narrative was more an embarrassment to the evangelist than the natural conclusion of his work: it is an appendix or postscript tacked on to the body of the Gospel—less a coda properly so-called than a reverberation that continues to resound after the work itself has come to an end.[2] We shall see that Käsemann's arguments have a certain force; a similar case, to my mind even more persuasive, can be made for the superfluousness of the resurrection stories in chapter 20.

The problem of the passion in John is primarily an external one. The evangelist makes his meaning quite clear. The trouble is that his readers, from Ignatius of Antioch in the second century up to the present day, are expecting something very different and often inject their pre-understanding into the Gospel text. The temptation to bring John into line with Paul, to harmonize, is very strong. Such resemblances as there are, say, to the Philippians hymn (the triple

---

[1] *Historical Jesus*, p. 80 n. 11. The first German edition was published in 1892.

[2] 'Fast möchte man sagen, sie klappe nach, weil Johannes sie unmöglich übergehen, die überlieferte Gestalt jedoch auch nicht organisch seinem Werk einfügen konnte' (*Jesu Letzter Wille*[3], p. 23). The English translation ('a mere postscript': p. 7) does not quite do justice to the original German, which hints at reverberations that continue to resound after the music has stopped.

movement of descent, death, and exaltation) are superficial: for John
the incarnation is not a self-emptying but a manifestation of divine
glory, and the cross itself an instrument of exaltation.

One might expect the Christian reader who comes to 'the Passion
according to St John' with the other three accounts in mind to be
perplexed and disturbed by the differences. But in fact such a reader
is likely to see the four blending harmlessly together and so to miss
the singularity of John's vision. No modern exegete has shown
himself more keenly aware of this than Käsemann, and he has
highlighted it more than any other theologian.

Taking our cue from him we turn now to the passion narrative.
After the immensely impressive theology of revelation that has been
elaborated in the first half of the Gospel and confirmed in the next
four chapters, what does this add to John's general message?

The conservative-minded Christian may well be taken aback, as
Käsemann clearly intends him to be, by his suggestion that it is a
mere postscript, part of an argument which brazenly concludes that
the Church's acceptance of the Fourth Gospel into its canon was
really a mistake. Even the liberal-minded Günther Bornkamm is
offended by it, as he shows in his extended review of *Testament of
Jesus*. He adduces the numerous allusions to the 'hour' of Jesus, from
Cana onwards (2: 4; 7: 30; 8: 20), culminating in 12: 23 ff. and
13: 1 and the teaching of the farewell discourse (13: 31; 17: 1), the
sayings concerning the ascent of the Son of Man (3: 12–15; 6: 61 ff.;
8: 28; 12: 32 f.), and much else besides.[3] But how far does
Bornkamm's rather perfunctory list constitute a convincing refutation of Käsemann's arguments? Käsemann himself is unimpressed:

Bornkamm's statistics might seem rather to support me than to tell against
me. Obviously no Gospel can entirely ignore Jesus' death. But the question is
not how often reference is made to it and its attendant circumstances.
Rather we have to ask how it is interpreted. 7: 30 and 8: 20 ['my hour is not
yet come'] testify primarily to the exaltation of the earthly Jesus, and also
predict his subsequent arrest. In 12: 1 ff., 23 ff., 32 and 13: 1 death is
understood as the path to glory. The same is true of 2: 19 ff. and 3: 14,
which (like 10: 11) make use of traditional material. For the formula 'give
his life' refers to the external act of love. None of this goes anywhere towards
a theology of the cross. It simply shows that John uses previous ideas about
Jesus' death as a starting-point for his own interpretation. The only
exceptions are 1: 26 [?], 29 ['Behold the Lamb of God, who takes away the

[3] See 'Interpretation', pp. 79–96.

sins of the world'] and it is no accident that these are put in the mouth of the Baptist and thereby marked out as traditional sayings of the community.[4]

Käsemann's case is a strong one, and we shall see that it can be made even stronger. We may begin, however, by challenging it, observing in particular that since the passion narrative is clearly the work of the same writer, occupied by the same concerns, his charge that it is a mere postscript cannot be sustained. Some of the connections are straightforward, traditional, and relatively insignificant. The references to the denial of Peter (13: 38; 18: 17) and the treachery of Judas (13: 2; 18: 2) are of this order. John alone, however, speaks of the prophecy of Caiaphas (11: 51; 18: 14) and establishes a link between the actual arrest of Jesus and earlier attempts to apprehend him in Jerusalem: the same officials (ὑπηρέ-ται) under orders from the same authorities, the chief priests and Pharisees (7: 32; 18: 3). More interestingly, Jesus' challenge to those come to arrest him, 'Whom do you seek?' (18: 4) recalls his earlier response to the same group: 'You will seek me but you will not find me' (7: 34). This link is perhaps coincidental, like his admission, 'I am [he]: ἐγώ εἰμι' (18: 4, 8). We cannot be sure that this reply is intended to carry all the connotations it has accumulated in the book of signs. Nor is it certain that Jesus' address to his mother, 'Woman' (19: 26) is a deliberate echo of the scene at Cana (2: 4).

Some allusions, however, must have been planned. Jesus' acceptance of 'the cup which the Father has given me' (18: 11) reminds us of his refusal to plead to be saved 'from this hour' (12: 27); in the same breath these sayings both recall and reject the Gethsemane tradition. Next there is the evangelist's comment upon Jesus' request to leave his disciples free, which was 'to fulfil the word which he had spoken "Of those whom thou gavest me, I lost not one"' (18: 9). It may be difficult to put one's finger on the precise passage to which John is alluding here (suggestions include 6: 39; 10: 28; and 17: 12); but the main point stands: Jesus' pastoral concern, stated earlier as a promise and prediction, is exhibited from the very moment of his arrest.

Another comment of the evangelist concerns the Jews' assertion that they have no legal right to impose or to carry out the death penalty: 'This was to fulfil the word which Jesus had spoken to show

---

[4] *Jesu Letzter Wille*[3], pp. 96–7.

by what death he was to die' (18: 32). The term 'crucifixion' has not been used up to this point: it does not figure in the saying to which 18: 32 evidently alludes: 'I, when I am lifted up (ἐὰν ὑψωθῶ) from the earth, will draw all men to myself' (12: 32). The evangelist's interjected explanation in 12: 33 is repeated virtually word-for-word in 18: 32, a fact which has led some commentators, e.g. Schnackenburg, to suspect that a glossator has been at work. However that may be, the indirect allusion to crucifixion in both passages is characteristic of the evangelist's style and is a strong indication of his desire to show that the manner of Jesus' death was divinely determined, fulfilling as it did not just the scripture (something which would be stressed later: 19: 24, 28, 29, 36, 37), but also Jesus' own words.

We may appropriately conclude this argument with Jesus' last word on the cross. According to Matthew (27: 50) and Mark (15: 37), Jesus expired with a wordless cry. Luke (23: 46) turns this into a prayer: 'Father, into thy hands I commend my spirit.' John envisages Jesus as fully conscious of the significance of the occasion: εἰδὼς ὅτι ἤδη πάντα τετέλεσται, 'knowing that all was now accomplished' (19: 28), in his final utterance he gives voice to this knowledge, not in a prayer or a wordless cry, but in the single word, τετέλεσται: 'it is accomplished' (19: 30)—the goal, τέλος (cf. 13: 1, the only occurrence of this term in the Gospel), has been achieved. One could ask for no more conclusive proof of the evangelist's *commitment* to his narrative; had he been less interested or involved he would have followed his source more faithfully. Had the passion narrative been a mere postscript it would have ended differently.

There is abundant evidence, then, that John's passion narrative has been deliberately and skilfully integrated with the book of signs. But this is by no means a satisfactory refutation of Käsemann's case. On the level of technical exegesis he is easy to fault. But the essence of his argument is not so much exegetical as theological.[5] He is really suggesting that the evangelist's presentation of Jesus is such as to make a passion narrative superfluous if not altogether meaningless: 'In John the glory of Jesus determines his whole presentation so thoroughly from the very outset that the incorporation and position of the passion narrative of necessity becomes problematical.' When he denies that John was able to fit the passion 'organically' into his

---

[5] We should not allow ourselves to be misled by Käsemann's assertion (*Testament*, p. 3) that he is more interested in historical than in theological questions.

work, this amounts to an assertion that a *true* passion narrative, retaining the shock and the horror, would be out of place in a Gospel that places so much emphasis on Jesus' glory: 'His solution was to imprint the features of the victory of Christ upon the passion story.'[6]

This point is worth stressing, for the extent to which John suppresses the painful and especially the shameful elements of the passion story is truly remarkable. Here a single example must suffice. Compare John's laconic allusion to the scourging and the crown of thorns with, say, Matthew 27: 29–31. John allows the soldiers to strike Jesus but not to strip him or spit upon him, and their mockery, while perhaps suggested, is never explicitly stated: 'His death, to be sure, takes place on the cross, as tradition demands. But this cross is no longer the pillory, the tree of shame, on which hangs the one who had become the companion of thieves. His death is rather the manifestation of divine self-giving love and his victorious return from the alien realm below to the Father who had sent him.'[7]

Of John's omissions the most striking are the cry of desolation on the cross and the agony in the garden. We have just observed the significance to be attached to Jesus' final $\tau\epsilon\tau\epsilon\lambda\epsilon\sigma\tau\alpha\iota$. But by replacing the anguished appeal recorded by Mark and Matthew with a shout of triumph John transforms the cross into a throne. As for Jesus' despairing plea to be rid of the chalice of suffering he sees ahead of him, John actually portrays Jesus in the act of considering whether he should make this prayer or not and then deciding not to (12: 27; cf. 18: 11). The divine promise of glorification that follows 'has come for your sake', Jesus tells the crowd, 'not for mine' (12: 30). 'As the Revealer does not need to express a petition in prayer,' comments Bultmann, 'so he does not need a special divine word of consolation.'[8]

In the case of the Fourth Gospel 'passion' is a misnomer; Jesus controls and orchestrates the whole performance. From the moment of his calm greeting to the soldiers who have come to arrest him, who then start back in fear, to the moment of his death he remains in command. Even his 'giving-up the ghost' can be read as a peaceful handing-over of the Spirit. Confronted by Pilate it is he who is the real judge; such power as Pilate has comes to him from on high, and in acceding to the demand that Jesus be crucified he is unconsciously complying with a divine decree, following the directions and

---

[6] *Testament*, p. 7.   [7] Ibid., p. 10.   [8] p. 430.

speaking the words assigned to him in the text. Bultmann points out[9] that at the end of the farewell discourse (14: 31) what Jesus says is not οὕτως δεῖ γενέσθαι ('it is necessary that it should happen thus'), but οὕτως ποιῶ ('I act thus'). If God is the author of this passion play, Jesus is the protagonist—but also the producer and director!

All in all, then, Käsemann has a powerful case; and it is not to be countered simply by totting up the numbers of references to the passion that are found in the first dozen chapters, nor even by illustrating the evangelist's deliberate attempts to integrate the Christ of the passion narrative with the Christ of the book of signs. It is true that this effort at coherence proves that the evangelist himself did not regard the passion narrative as a mere postscript or appendix. But that does nothing to answer Käsemann's *theological* objections. If, as he correctly maintains against Bornkamm and others, the fourth evangelist has no theology of the cross, what does Jesus' passion mean to him? What significance can it have beyond the triumph of divine folly over human wisdom and of divine weakness over human strength (1 Cor. 1)?

The answer lies in the evangelist's vocabulary of death.[10]

2. DEATH

For Käsemann, as is well known, Jesus' death represents 'his victorious return from the alien realm below to the Father who had sent him'. Yet in the very same sentence he also describes it as 'the manifestation of divine self-giving love'.[11] We shall see that the evangelist's choice of words when speaking of Jesus' death largely vindicates Käsemann's first phrase, the one upon which he lays the most stress. But the issue is a complex one and, as so often, Käsemann skates over any evidence that points away from his own conclusions. We should first enquire in what respects if any the Gospel can be said to suggest what we may call a sacrificial interpretation of Jesus' death.

What at first sight looks like the strongest evidence comes in the allegory of the Good Shepherd. In a gesture that would have little beneficial effect if the flock were really threatened by thieves or wolves, he lays down his life for his sheep: τὴν ψυχὴν αὐτοῦ τίθησιν

---

[9] p. 633.   [10] See on this esp. Ulrich Müller, 'Bedeutung'.
[11] *Testament*, p. 10.

ὑπὲρ τῶν προβάτων (10: 11; cf. 10: 15, 17, 18; 13: 37 f. (Peter); 15: 13; 1 John 3: 16).[12] Next there is Caiaphas' prophecy, highlighted by the evangelist in one of his emphatic asides, 'that it is expedient for you that one man should die for the people and that the whole nation should not perish' (11: 50–2; cf. 18: 14). We should probably not attach too much significance to the title of Lamb of God. In the signs source it is unlikely to have been associated with the passion; moreover, the explanatory phrase, 'who takes away the sins of the world' (1: 29, 36) is quite possibly a redactional addition designed to bring the Gospel into line with the theology of the First Letter.[13] The 'eucharistic' passage, 6: 51c–58, may be similarly accounted for. As for the paschal lamb (19: 36), despite its appearance in 1 Cor. 5: 7, its purpose was not sacrificial but apotropaic. More weight should perhaps be placed upon the saying concerning the grain of corn (12: 24–6), but this too is arguably an editorial insertion.[14] Jesus' determination to consecrate himself on behalf of his disciples (17: 19), unquestionably an allusion to his approaching death, belongs to a second edition of the Gospel. Lastly there is a washing of the feet, widely, and I think rightly, interpreted as a sacrificial gesture.[15]

Although much of this evidence is open to the suspicion of having been included in the Gospel at a fairly late stage, there is surely enough to justify our taking it seriously. Bultmann's judgement that 'the thought of Jesus' death as atonement for sin has no place in John'[16] is far too sweeping. But if it is going too far to speak of it as 'a foreign element' in the Gospel (Bultmann again) it cannot be said to be in any way central. To get to the heart of the evangelist's thinking we must turn to what I have called John's vocabulary of death.

This may be divided into three groups, each marked out by a dominant verb and each linked to one of the titles studied in the last three chapters of Part II: (*a*) the crucifixion of the Messiah, (*b*) the departure of the Son of God, (*c*) the exaltation of the Son of Man.

---

[12] In 10: 11, Bultmann argues, the meaning must be 'to stake one's life, to risk it, to be prepared to lay it down' (p. 370 n. 5), but elsewhere (except 13: 37 f.) the more generally accepted 'lay down one's life' must be the right rendering.

[13] Cf. Becker, p. 92.

[14] Cf. Becker, p. 382. Becker also ascribes the Good Shepherd passage (10: 1–18) to a redactor (pp. 311 f.): it certainly interrupts the sequence, but there is no good reason for thinking that the insertion was not made by the evangelist himself.

[15] In this scene one interpretation is overlaid by another. Here I follow Johannes Beutler ('Heilsbedeutung'), who gives a concise summary of all the evidence and argues that what he calls the 'christologisch-soteriologisch' interpretation is the earlier of the two.   [16] *Theology*, ii. 54.

(a) The crucifixion of the Messiah (σταυροῦν)

The traditional symbolic image of Jesus' death, the crucifix, is a vividly precise representation of what Paul regarded as the essence of his Gospel, which he summed up as 'Christ crucified'. The fact that John does not use the word of Jesus' death outside the passion narrative is of no great significance, for neither do the other evangelists. But the fact that he does use it in the passion narrative is not significant either, since it would be impossible to *tell the story* of Jesus' dying on the cross without it. This means that there could be no Gospel without it either, and in the concluding chapter I shall be reflecting on the importance of this truth. 'Was crucified under Pontius Pilate' is arguably the only genuinely historical element in the Christian creed, the remaining articles being dogmatic additions beyond the reach of the historian's investigations. But just as the title 'Messiah', though received and accepted by John, does not seize his theological imagination and is not invested by him with any additional meaning of his own, so he fails to exploit the notion of crucifixion in a Pauline or Marcan fashion, lighting instead, as we shall see, upon the one feature of this barbarous punishment that allows it to be seen as a glory rather than a disgrace.

(b) The departure of the Son of God (ὑπάγειν)[17]

The theme of departure, extensively explored in the preceding chapter, is the culmination of a theology of mission which, when combined with the concept of Jesus' divine sonship, results in the two characteristically Johannine terms for God, Father and Sender. Jesus enters the world with a mission from the Father and leaves it when his mission is completed. By an extraordinary involution his mission is simply to reveal to mankind his origin and his destiny, his entry and his departure. From this perspective the true significance of his death has nothing to do with the manner of it. No doubt one could say of him that 'nothing in his life became him like the leaving of it', but this is only because it satisfactorily rounds off his mission, allowing him to say, for the first and only time: 'It is accomplished.'

We have already thoroughly investigated the connotations of the

---

[17] Allied words are μεταβαίνειν (13: 1); πορεύεσθαι (14: 2 etc.); ἀπέρχεσθαι (16: 7); ἔρχεσθαι (17: 11, 13).

term ὑπάγειν, part of the private vocabulary of the community. Whenever it is employed in this special sense, the notion of death is always present; nevertheless the pain and the shame of Jesus' actual death have been filtered out of the term itself—much as in the English vulgarism 'pass away'. Jesus has not gone 'the way of all flesh' in the traditional Jewish understanding of the term: there is no trace in the Fourth Gospel of any 'descent into hell'.

(c) The exaltation of the Son of Man (ὑψοῦσθαι)[18]

If the Son of God is sent into the world and departs from it, the Son of Man descends and ascends. The theme of exaltation, implying ascent into heaven, is nowhere associated with the Son of God, just as the theme of mission is nowhere associated with the Son of Man. Because the term ὑψοῦν figures prominently in what have the appearance of passion predictions, we may be tempted to see it as a deliberate evocation of the actual act of crucifixion; but as with ὑπάγειν the evangelist has selected a term whose first meaning has nothing to do with death. It means 'to lift up', 'to raise', 'to exalt' and would be easier to understand of the resurrection than of the crucifixion. Consequently it is misleading, if not altogether wrong, to speak of the sayings in which it occurs as passion predictions. I have already discussed these sayings in connection with the title 'Son of Man' (Chapter 9), but stopped short at the point where exaltation modulates into glorification.

In the first of the sayings that mentions the lifting-up or exaltation of the Son of Man (3: 14) the nature of the elevation is suggested by a comparison with Moses' bronze serpent, which he raised or set up on a pole in the desert. (In LXX Numbers 21: 9 the word used is ἰστάναι, not ὑψοῦν.) In the second, which comes in a debate concerning Jesus' departure from the world, the subject of the verb is 'the Jews': 'When you have lifted up the Son of Man, then you will know ...' (8: 28). The allusion to crucifixion, however indirect, can scarcely be missed, even though it was Romans, not Jews, who actually lifted Jesus up on the cross. In the third saying the allusion is yet clearer, though here too the word 'crucifixion' is avoided (in fact, as we have seen, it is not used outside the passion narrative itself): '"I, when I am lifted

---

[18] Also ἀναβαίνειν: 3: 13; 6: 62; cf. 1: 51. In 20: 17 there is no reference to the Son of Man and the context indicates the use of an old ascension tradition.

up from the earth, will draw all men to myself." He said this to show by what death he was to die' (12: 32 f.).[19]

(d) Glory and glorification (δοξάζειν)

The theology of the fourth evangelist is so singular and strange that it is easy to miss the significance of his final reinterpretation of Jesus' death. One can see why he can think of it as a departure or an ascension, but surely the word 'glory' is out of place? Yet at two points, one of them the passage in which the third prediction occurs, 12: 20–36, 'glory', or rather the verb, δοξάζειν, is the term that is employed to supplement and eventually supplant that of exaltation. The third prediction belongs to the *narrative* conclusion to the book of signs, which perhaps replaces an earlier ending, 10: 42.[20] (The remainder of chapter 12, as Dodd points out, is an epilogue in two parts, the second of which, to be discussed in the next chapter, is a revelation summary.) In what follows, 12: 24–6 will be left out of consideration. These verses interrupt the sequence of thought and are probably a late insertion, whether or not, as Dodd argues,[21] they stem from old, authentic tradition.

In 12: 23 Jesus declares: 'The hour has come for the Son of Man to be glorified.' The remainder of the passage tells the reader what this means and what it implies. In fact the word δοξάζειν has been used a few verses earlier: 'when Jesus was glorified ... then they remembered' (12: 16). This comment of the evangelist is close to 2: 22: 'when he was raised from the dead, his disciples remembered', and proves that the *first* association of glorification is with resurrection. There is therefore an important sense in which Jesus *was not yet glorified* whilst on earth (cf. 7: 39).

[19] Schnackenburg regards the explanatory comment as a gloss. To excise it would be to preserve the indirectness of the other sayings. I am inclined to favour this view but it is impossible to be sure.

[20] From a form-critical point of view it resembles the opening of ch. 3, with which it has much in common both materially and stylistically. Both are dialogues with uncomprehending but not totally unsympathetic interlocutors, pronouncement stories but not controversies. Just as Nicodemus gives way to a larger, unspecified audience, so 'the Greeks', having enlisted the assistance of Philip and Andrew (12: 21 f.), yield to 'the crowd standing by' (12: 29, 34). It is significant that 'the Jews' play no part here. The incomprehension of the crowd serves as an occasion for Jesus' final pronouncement on the need to 'walk in the light'. Before disappearing from public view he ends his preaching as he began it, with a demand for faith.

[21] *Tradition*, pp. 366–9; 338–43; 352 f.

In the comment on the agony tradition that follows (12: 27) it emerges that as used here the word δοξάζειν is associated with Jesus' approaching death. Jesus' prayer to the Father, 'glorify thy name' is met with the response: 'I have glorified it, and I will glorify it again' (12: 28). There is only one feasible interpretation: the first act of glorification of the Father's name must be understood of Jesus' life up to the present (one of service to the Father) and the second act (his 'hour') of his passion and resurrection.[22] Throughout his life the divine emissary had sought the glory of the one who sent him (7: 18). But the ultimate revelation of that glory was yet to come.

Although the object of the glorification in 12: 28 is clearly intended to be the Father's name, the actual object is left unexpressed by the voice from heaven: καὶ ἐδόξασα καὶ πάλιν δοξάσω. From this omission Bultmann infers an intentional ambiguity: 'The δόξα of the Father and the δόξα of the Son are bound to each other.'[23] But is this right? It would certainly be pedantic to dissociate the two completely; nevertheless the glory that concerns the evangelist in this passage (also an epiphany, a moment of *revelation*) occurs at Easter, and is something altogether special. A little further on Jesus is asked by the crowd: 'How can you say that the Son of Man must be lifted up?' (12: 34.) What Jesus had actually said was that the Son of Man was to be *glorified* (12: 23).[24] So 'lifting-up' and 'glorification' are alternative and complementary ways of speaking of the same event.[25]

Bultmann concludes his discussion of this passage by quoting

---

[22] There is really nothing to be said for the very different view held by W. Thüsing, *Erhöhung*, namely that the two stages of Jesus' glorification are first his death and secondly his exaltation. Cf. J. Blank, *Krisis*, p. 268 n. 11.   [23] p. 429.

[24] Bultmann argues that in the verses immediately preceding 12: 34 'there is no mention whatsoever of the Son of Man' (p. 313) and concludes that 12: 34–6 should be placed after 8: 29. This enables him to assert that 12: 34 picks up the saying in 8: 28 (p. 354). But there is no justification for this displacement.

[25] The two verbs occur together in the introduction to the Suffering Servant prophecy of Second Isaiah, where the LXX reads: ἰδοὺ συνήσει ὁ παῖς μου καὶ ὑψωθήσεται καὶ δοξασθήσεται σφόδρα: 'Behold my servant shall understand and shall be raised up and exceedingly glorified' (Isa. 52: 13). Both of these verbs are applied to the Son of Man in the Fourth Gospel, always in contexts where there is a clear allusion to the crucifixion, and it is tempting to conclude that the evangelist must have had this passage in mind, especially because he actually quotes another verse from the same poem (Isa. 53: 1) a little further on (12: 38). But since he never uses the two verbs conjointly it is inadvisable to speak too confidently about the direct influence of a particular text. (The LXX use of συνιέναι in Isa. 52: 13 represents a wrong choice from two alternative meanings of the Hebrew הַשְׂכִּיל: 'understand' and 'prosper'.)

Kierkegaard: 'Humiliation belongs to him just as essentially as exaltation.' This helps us to understand his affirmation that 'It is precisely to humiliation that the divine φωνή [voice] gives the glory and dignity of the δόξα, and in so doing it gives it eternity.'[26] This is a curious reading, however, of a passage in which all the emphasis is upon exaltation and glorification, with not a whisper of humiliation. It is not, as Bultmann affirms, that the glory is to be found in the humiliation, but rather that what the world sees as a defeat is really a triumph, and what the world sees as the end of Jesus' hopes and aspirations is really the beginning of his ascent into glory. The Johannine paradox, remarks Blank, is not that 'the hour of the δοξασθῆναι is the hour of the passion, but the reverse: the hour of the passion is already the hour of the δοξασθῆναι'.[27] But even this interpretation gives the passion a greater prominence than the evidence warrants. The Christian believer is not expected to see the crucifixion as a kind of exaltation or glorification but to *see past* the physical reality of Jesus' death to its true significance: the reascent of the Son of Man to his true home in heaven.[28]

So much for what I have called the narrative conclusion to the book of signs. In the following chapter, which introduces what Dodd calls the book of glory, the passion is imminent: 'Now has the Son of Man been endowed with glory and God has revealed his glory in him; if God has revealed his glory in him God will also endow him with his own glory, and that straight away' (13: 31 f.).[29] The term ὑψοῦν has dropped out; such allusions to Jesus' death as it ever carried have been transferred to δοξάζειν. It is as if the evangelist is gradually eliminating all the more painful and shameful associations of the death of Jesus. The grandeur of this solemn introduction to the farewell discourse is not to be diminished by any suggestion of sorrow or humiliation. What pain and shame there is in the chapters that follow is reserved for the disciples. Jesus' farewell and departure are tranquil and assured.

When the theme of glorification is resumed, at the beginning of

---

[26] p. 433. [27] *Krisis*, p. 269 n. 12.

[28] Cf. U. B. Müller, 'Bedeutung', p. 61.

[29] For this translation cf. G. B. Caird, 'Glory of God'. Caird interprets the Son of Man along the lines adumbrated by Dodd, as a figure representing and almost containing in himself the whole people of God. Though this is certainly true of the figure in Daniel, I do not find it a plausible view of the Son of Man in the Fourth Gospel. Unfortunately, Caird offers no translation of 13: 32, which presents us with the problem of the meaning of the second (or possibly third) ἐν αὐτῷ.

Jesus' great prayer to the Father, it is with a direct reference to
13: 31 f.: 'Father, the hour has come; endow thy Son with glory
that he may reveal thy glory' (17: 1). As this passage stands it
must be regarded as a citation that brackets out the preceding
discourse and furnishes an alternative introduction to the passion
narrative. Much more than the farewell discourse itself (a testament
and commission, as we have seen), it marks the conclusion of Jesus'
mission. As Wayne Meeks puts it: 'Chapter 17 as a whole is only
intelligible within the descent/ascent framework, for it is the
summary "de-briefing" of the messenger who ... has accomplished
his work in the lower regions:'[30] 'I glorified thee on earth, having
accomplished the work which thou gavest me to do' (17: 4); 'And
now I am no more in the world ... and I am coming to thee'
(17: 11; cf. v. 13). Used as it was earlier (12: 23, 28) in close
connection with $ὑψοῦν$, the verb $δοξάζειν$ may continue to suggest,
however obliquely, the death that Jesus is to die. But by now the
suggestion is at best very tenuous and all the emphasis is laid upon
the bright, epiphanic conclusion to Jesus' mission: 'Father, the hour
has come; endow thy Son with glory that he may reveal thy glory,
since thou hast given him power ($ἐξουσία$) over all flesh; to give
eternal life to those whom thou hast given him' (17: 1–2).

(e) Revelation

At this point we are close to the heart of the message of the Gospel
and it is necessary to anticipate some of the conclusions of the final
chapter. John's theology of glory is first and foremost a theology of
revelation. Brown remarks concerning the term $δόξα$ in his first
appendix that glory in the Fourth Gospel involves a *visible* manifestation of God's majesty in *acts of power*, and this is right. But the
English word that springs most insistently to mind in connection
with John's theology of glory is 'revelation'. In the Old Testament the
concepts of glory and revelation are very close, and כָּבוֹד is
frequently found associated with descriptions of a theophany. The
glory of God is not something he possesses in himself independently
of the world he created and from which he receives praise. The word
expresses the impression he makes on humankind when he mani-
fests his power to them; his glory, like his justice, may be said to

---

[30] 'Man from Heaven', p. 159.

imply a relationship; in this case the relationship with those to whom he reveals himself.

When Käsemann takes from John 17 the fundamental orientation (*Basis und Richtung*)[31] of his study of the Gospel, he is not entirely misguided. No doubt this chapter is scarcely the epitome of Johannine theology that he takes it to be (it probably did not figure in the first edition), but it undoubtedly represents the culmination of the evangelist's reflections upon the significance of Jesus' death. But if this is primarily a revelatory event, initiated and implemented by God himself, what does it reveal?

Barnabas Lindars points to an important difference between Jesus' earlier works and his subsequent passion. The former, he says, 'were works of divine power, so that they not only revealed God, and Jesus' own position in relation to God, through the quality of obedience to the Father's will which was inherent in them, but also had the quality of revelatory acts through the sheer display of divine power. … But in the case of the passion there is no display of divine power at all. It is a revelatory act only because it is an expression of the perfect moral union between Jesus and the Father.'[32] He adds that it is 'distinctive, not only as the ultimate test, but also as the one act in which there is no way of discovering its true meaning except by discernment of its moral quality'.[33] The essential union between Jesus and the Father ('he who has seen me has seen the Father') is, for John, displayed above all at the moment of his death. But in the most profound and original thought of the evangelist the moment of death is not distinguished from the moment of exaltation, and he insists that in what we may call, taking its two aspects together, the Easter event, Jesus is truly seen as what he is, God's glory being finally and definitively revealed: '… and now, Father, glorify thou me in thy own presence with the glory which I had with thee before the world was made' (17: 5).

Yet the glorified Christ is the *same* Christ, paradoxically a Christ whose glory had already shone out during his lifetime. In particular John sees Jesus' departure from the world as the mirror image of his entry. Incarnation and Easter are in certain respects the same mystery, taking place between the whence and the whither. Not that either, properly speaking, is an *event*. Like Easter, which in John's

---

[31] *Jesu Letzter Wille*[3], p. 14; ET: 'John 17 serves as the basis and guidepost of my lectures' (*Testament*, p. 3).
[32] 'Passion', p. 80.   [33] Ibid., p. 85 n. 24.

mature thinking is resumed in discourse, the incarnation cannot be seen. If told as a story, as it is by Matthew and Luke, the story is—can only be—myth. Accordingly, the affirmation of the Prologue that the Logos became flesh belongs in a confession of faith. It is in the next clause that the full paradox is displayed: 'we have seen his glory'. Käsemann was not totally wrong to emphasize this half of the verse (1: 14): even if the evangelist cannot be credited with its composition it certainly expresses an important part of his message. If the second pole of the glory motif is a way of insisting upon the centrality of the resurrection the first pole emphasizes the other face of the Gospel paradox—that *the earthly Jesus* is the Risen Lord.[34]

The motif is taken up again in the conclusion to the marriage-feast of Cana, the first of the Gospel's signs, where Jesus 'manifested his glory (ἐφανέρωσεν τὴν δόξαν αὐτοῦ) and his disciples believed in him' (2: 11). So Jesus performs a miracle—more than a miracle, a sign—and it is in this miracle, symbolically foreshadowing something strange, new, and marvellous, that Jesus' glory is seen for the first time. Had it not been seen there would have been no glory; δόξα is a relationship word—it implies *revelation*. This revelation comes not by hearing (one reason why we cannot say, with Käsemann, that the term δόξα is an adequate summary of the message of the whole Gospel), but by sight. Moreover it comes through the performance of a sign—the first of what the Jesus of this Gospel calls ἔργα, 'works'. After the Prologue, the first occurrence of πιστεύειν ('believe') is in Jesus' sardonic question to Nathanael, 'Because I said to you, "I saw you under the fig-tree," do you believe?' (1: 50.) The next is at Cana. In the first instance faith follows an enigmatic saying, in the second an open manifestation of power. This is the kind of faith that interests Käsemann and which he regards, wrongly I think, as paradigmatic of Johannine theology. Nevertheless no serious commentator on the Gospel should evade the question which Käsemann has made peculiarly his own: How is it that a human being can be the vehicle of divine glory? This question throbs insistently through *The Testament of Jesus*, but Käsemann's own answer is too impatient and perfunctory to be satisfactory, dominated as it is by the charge of docetism. Bornkamm is surely right to detect a real anachronism here. This is why no direct answer can be anything but misleading. (It is also why those who attempt to carve

[34] Käsemann fails to distinguish properly between the twin poles of the glory motif, Incarnation and Easter.

the Gospel up into docetic bits and anti-docetic bits get themselves into a hopeless tangle.) The Prologue, starting in heaven, affirms that God's revelatory plan for the world, called the Logos, was embodied in a particular man, Jesus Christ. The remainder of the Gospel, taking its starting-point on earth, claims that a particular man, Jesus of Nazareth, was, in a quite special sense, the Son of God, so intimately associated with God as to represent God to those fortunate enough to have seen him. Extraordinary as these claims are, they do not involve any intentional denial of humanity. On the contrary, the tradition of Jesus' human life is presupposed and assumed throughout. *But it is not what the Gospel is about.* Käsemann is right in what he affirms but wrong in what he denies.

Above all he fails to appreciate the evangelist's dilemma. Glory, in its incarnational mode, is one way in which the evangelist's own faith, his belief that Jesus is Lord, comes to expression. Mark, confronted by the same dilemma, tackled it in a variety of different ways, bundled together by Wrede in a bag labelled 'The Messianic secret'. John's solution (or one of them, for he has many), though actually no more paradoxical than Mark's, is more obviously so. The Jesus of his Gospel is already the Risen Lord!

Even here John's innovation is perhaps smaller than is widely assumed. There is one scene, common to the other three Gospels, in which what John calls Jesus' glory is manifested to a chosen few disciples in his lifetime. This is the scene on the mountain where Jesus 'was transfigured before them, and his garments became glistening intensely white, as no fuller on earth could bleach them' (Mark 9: 2–3). The Fourth Gospel, of course, has no room for a transfiguration, for the Johannine Jesus is transfigured, so to speak, from the outset. Perhaps there is an echo of the tradition in the scene in which Jesus acknowledges before God the purpose of his mission: '"for this purpose I have come to this hour. Father, glorify thy name." Then a voice came from heaven, "I have glorified it and I will glorify it again."' (12: 27 f.) Bultmann, who mentions this, adds as a further possibility 'that the evangelist knew of the story of the Transfiguration in its original sense as a resurrection narrative'.[35] One can see the attractiveness of this suggestion. The transfiguration, logically and theologically, seems out of place in the middle of Jesus' public life. Its presence in Mark is not only inconsistent with

---

[35] p. 428 n. 1; *contra* C. H. Dodd, 'The Appearances of the Risen Christ'.

his general picture of Jesus but it exposes him—and the other Synoptists—to the same kind of objection that Käsemann levels against John. The transfigured Jesus is a heavenly being and it is hard for the modern mind to accept that he can be both heavenly and human at the same time.

Be that as it may, there is no room for a transfiguration scene in the Fourth Gospel. The Johannine Jesus carries his glory with him and his garments are always 'glistening intensely white'. If, however, the Synoptists have imported the lesson of the resurrection, however fleetingly, into their accounts of the earthly life of Jesus, they have in so doing exhibited the essential Gospel paradox *in a typically Johannine way*.

Käsemann himself once argued against Bultmann that John is more than a theologian: he is an evangelist.[36] He will not be properly understood unless he is seen to be wrestling with the problems and paradoxes inherent in his chosen genre.

3. RESURRECTION

When we turn to the resurrection narratives the problems multiply. In composing his passion narrative the evangelist was following a long-established tradition and working, as all are agreed, from a source in which most of the episodes were already present, the main lines of the story having been already laid down. In their resurrection narratives each of John's three predecessors went his own way. Mark's sketchy and enigmatic account did not satisfy the other two, who elaborated upon it in their own distinctive fashion. John too had his sources, certainly for the first half of chapter 20 and probably for the second half as well. Even so we have to ask ourselves why he felt it necessary to conclude his work as he did.

Not, evidently, in order to highlight Jesus' glory. This may be part of Matthew's intention, but John has no need to do this, just as he has no need of a transfiguration story. Jesus' glory was visible from the outset (1: 14). To Käsemann, for whom Jesus is in any case 'a god striding over the earth', the resurrection stories present little theoretical difficulty; his problem is with the passion narrative and a Risen Jesus who is able to appear and vanish at will could neither

---

[36] 'Blind Alleys', pp. 40–1. See the conclusion of Ch. 14.

shock nor surprise him. He might find these stories superfluous, but they are not inconsistent with what he regards as the evangelist's personal perspective. What troubles him, as we have just seen, is the passion narrative; for whatever else gods may do they do not die.

Bultmann, on the other hand, for whom the passion is relatively unproblematic, finds the resurrection stories hard to swallow. He gets round the difficulty partly by assigning some of the most intractable material (e.g. the commission in 20: 23 f.) to the evangelist's source, partly by detecting in the evangelist the same critical attitude towards the stories that he is inclined to adopt himself. Commenting, for instance, upon Jesus' rebuke to Mary, he cuts across the grain of the text by declaring that the 'not yet' of 'I have not yet ascended' (20: 17) refers first and foremost to Mary and not to Jesus: 'She *cannot yet* enter into fellowship with him until she has recognised him as the Lord who is with the Father, and so removed from earthly conditions.'[37] Whatever the evangelist's view on this matter, there is no room in Bultmann's conception of the incarnation for manifestations of Jesus' glory after his earthly life is over: the glory is contained in his humanity; the resurrection is not another *event* that transforms his nature, but a form of thinking that permits Christian faith to find expression. Accordingly, 'there is something peculiarly ambiguous and contradictory attaching to the Easter narratives. For in truth, if contact with physical hands is denied, how can seeing with physical eyes be permitted? Is not the latter also a worldly mode of perception, and on this basis can the Risen Jesus be thought other than an object of perception within the mundane sphere?'[38] This observation is surely not without force.

Nowhere, it has to be said, does the evangelist move further from *history* than in these four episodes. They are not accounts of what actually happened, but moral tales that allow John to drive home a series of important lessons. But is Bultmann right to maintain that 'the Evangelist assumes a critical attitude to the Easter stories'?[39] This is far from obvious.

Confronted by such an intractable puzzle one is tempted to take a leaf out of the bible of deconstruction. When seemingly contradictory passages of the Gospel are allowed to collide the result is an implosion. Why not let the readers of the Gospel pick their way through the resulting debris and draw their own conclusions? There

---

[37] p. 687, my italics. [38] p. 688. [39] p. 688 n. 3.

are indeed serious conceptual ambiguities here. But the evangelist is apparently unworried by the likelihood of quite crude misreadings of his resurrection stories. Before asking why this is so I propose to take a brief look at the stories themselves with a view to ascertaining the particular lessons that are to be derived from each.

The four stories are all very different. The first two cleverly adapt existing traditions. The third also may partly derive from a source. The fourth (Doubting Thomas), which is used to underline the central message of the Gospel, is peculiar to John; it clearly presupposes the preceding scene (the appearance to the disciples) and partially corrects it. But each of the other three has to be considered independently. To attempt to make sense of 20: 1–23 as a continuous narrative as, for instance, Dodd does, is to enter an Alice-in-Wonderland world where one event succeeds another with the crazy logic of a dream. In such a world one is not surprised to find Mary Magdalene, last seen running off in search of the disciples, standing once again by the tomb. Had she seen the two disciples enter the tomb? We are not told. But when she does enter she finds, not the burial clothes, but 'two angels sitting where the body of Jesus had lain, one at the head and one at the foot' (20: 12). Had they just arrived or had they been hiding quietly in a corner until Mary's arrival, their business being with her and not with Peter and 'the other disciple'? These, it may be said, are not very sensible questions to ask. Indeed not; their unanswerability is a very good reason for taking each of the two stories independently.

We embroil ourselves in similar absurdities if we try to read the third episode, the appearance to the disciples, as if it followed upon the second. After informing Mary that he was about to ascend to the Father, did Jesus go up and spend an hour or two in heaven, only to redescend that very same evening for a visit to the disciples? And why, if Mary had informed them of what Jesus had said to her (20: 18), do they betray no knowledge of this?

What then of the last transition, between the third and the fourth episodes? There is not so much as a hint in the third story that one of the disciples was missing. The final scene was certainly composed in the light of the third, but how are we to link it with the second? What strange transformation has Jesus undergone in heaven which made it legitimate for Thomas to place his hands in his side when only a week earlier Mary had been rebuked for touching (or clinging to) him?

This last series of questions, then, is no better focused than the first two. It would not be difficult to lengthen the list of questions so as to induce in the reader the kind of nervous bewilderment normally associated with nightmares. The incoherence that ensues as soon as these four episodes are read in a continuous narrative is perhaps the strongest argument for treating them apart. Such an approach neatly sidesteps the artificial problems that cramp the understanding whenever inappropriate questions are addressed to the text. What is more, it enables us to appreciate a feature of these four episodes which has not been noticed by the commentators: *each of them, taken on its own, constitutes an effective ending to the Gospel.* I hesitate to suggest that they were composed as alternative endings, and it is extremely unlikely that they figured in successive editions. But they all round off the gospel story and round it off differently.

There are broadly speaking four types of Easter traditions. Two of these (recognition and mission scenes) involve the presence of the Risen Jesus. The other two (empty-tomb and angelic-message stories) require his absence. Mark confines himself to the latter pair; Matthew adds a mission scene; both the other evangelists have them all. In the wording of John's stories there are a number of intriguing resemblances, variously explained, to the Synoptic accounts. These will not be discussed here, but it may be remarked that there are also many awkwardnesses in John's own stories, which go to prove that traditions close to, if not identical with, those underlying the Synoptic accounts have at some stage been carved and reshaped to present alternative readings. My concern here is with these new readings, which may be construed as comments upon, or interpretations of, already existing conclusions to the gospel story.

(a) Faith (20: 1–10)

In the Synoptic Gospels the empty-tomb and the angelic-message traditions are found together. John prises them apart. In this first episode he substitutes for the angelic message a source he appears to have shared with Luke and uses this as a basis for a story of his own. This is Luke's version (missing from the Western family of manuscripts): 'But Peter rose and ran to the tomb; stooping and looking in, he saw the linen-cloths (ὀθόνια) by themselves; he went home wondering what had happened' (Luke 24: 12). John, having reduced the holy women to the solitary figure of Mary Magdalene, now adds an extra actor, 'the other disciple', who 'outran Peter and reached the tomb first'. What most interests John is the act of faith of this other disciple, identified (v. 2) as 'the one whom Jesus loved', who, having entered the tomb after Peter, 'saw and believed'.

The part of this story that has attracted most attention is the one concerning the burial-clothes (ὀθόνια), with the napkin or head-cloth (σουδάριον) being rolled or wrapped (ἐντετυλιγμένον) on its own. Not surprisingly this intriguingly precise description has provoked widely differing readings, some interpreters seeking a symbolic meaning, others taking the account literally and looking for a scientific explanation. E. G. Auer, Brown tells us,[40] 'devotes a whole book, illustrated by sketches, to propound the thesis that the bindings, impregnated with the aromatic oil of 19: 40, had remained stiffly erect after the body had passed through them, almost as if one were to slide a corpse out of its mummy wrappings and have the wrappings preserve the form. Moreover the *soudarion* (= *sindōn*), a large cloth that had been around the whole body *inside* the bindings, was now carefully folded in the corner on the left-hand side of the tomb.' Brown is clearly amused by what he regards as Auer's wasted labours[41] and points out that his approach, and others like it, depends for its validity upon the literal acceptance of the power of the risen Jesus to pass through solid objects (cf. 20: 19).

The meaning of this episode, as of so many others, lies in the *story*. The precise significance of the grave-clothes, the way they are folded and their position inside the tomb, may elude us. But something may be said. John is the only evangelist to write an empty-tomb story without adding an explanation. This tradition is widely thought to have originated as a Christian reply to charges that the resurrection never happened. But at least according to the Synoptic accounts belief in the resurrection is a response not to the sight of an empty tomb but to the message of the angel. They all agree too on the content of the message: 'he is not here; he has risen' (ἠγέρθη— or possibly 'he has been raised'). Now angels (a category which may be allowed to cover Luke's two men (24: 4) and Mark's 'young-ish young man' (νεανίσκος, 16: 5)) are divine messengers, whose

---

[40] p. 1008.

[41] Has he the right to be, I wonder, when he himself believes 'that John was no more sophisticated than the other evangelists who accepted the tangibility of the risen Christ' (p. 1081)? The speculative problems involved here will be discussed briefly in the conclusion to this chapter.

veracity and reliability may be taken for granted. There is no room here for faith in the full sense, an act of personal commitment to an unverifiable truth.

By leaving the angels out of this story John opens the door to faith. He is able to record the response the beloved disciple makes, not to the voice of an intermediary, but to a vision of emptiness. The head-band and the grave-clothes are themselves signs of absence, mute witnesses to the truth of one half of the angelic witness: he is not here. The other half has to be supplied by the disciples themselves. Peter, it seems, failed to make the necessary leap of faith[42] (this is supplied in the appendix, 21: 7); the other disciple 'saw and believed'.

The tomb, however, was not quite empty: it contained reminders of Jesus' presence, or rather of the presence of his dead body. So in some sense faith here is still dependent upon sight: the head-cloth and the burial-clothes may be read as *signs*. Perhaps this accounts for the apparent reservation of the following verse: 'for as yet they did not understand (literally *know*: οὐδέπω γὰρ ᾔδεισαν) the scripture, that he must rise from the dead' (20: 9). If they had done, we are presumably meant to infer, this understanding alone would have sufficed to prompt an act of faith without the assistance of the pathetic remnants they had just observed. Whatever the explanation of this difficult verse,[43] the general thrust of the story is reasonably clear. One essential element in Christian belief is faith in the resurrection, something which cannot, obviously, be *narrated* within an account of the words Jesus spoke and the deeds he performed during his lifetime. By including an empty-tomb story and modifying the tradition as he did, the evangelist is able to offer his own considered reflections concerning the significance of the tradition and at the same time an alternative ending to the whole gospel story, one less challenging and disturbing than that of Mark, but equally impressive in its quiet reticence: 'Then the disciples went back to their homes' (20: 10).

(b) Recognition (20: 1, 11–18)

Although, as we have just seen, John omits the angelic-message tradition from his account of the empty tomb, he does not abandon

[42] Bultmann argues that Peter did believe. This is unlikely.

[43] Bultmann attributes it to the ecclesiastical redactor. This may be right. Lindars's attempt to reconcile the verse with what precedes is unconvincing, and I am not sure that my own explanation is any better.

the angels altogether: he simply transports them from the first episode to the second. Yet even here they play only a minor role, being rapidly and effectively upstaged by Jesus himself. In John's account they have no portentous message to deliver; the single line assigned to them is a question: 'Why are you weeping?' The very same question is repeated in the next verse by Jesus, who at this point assumes the central role. In spite of the mysterious promise of 1: 51 this evangelist has no room for any heavenly intermediaries except the Son of Man.

Of John's four resurrection stories this is by far the most problematic. Dodd is unable to categorize it; Bultmann employs a particularly tortuous exegesis in order to make it palatable. As so often, he perceives the difficulty more acutely than any other commentator: 'If the wording [of v. 17] were pressed, it would follow that when he had gone to the Father he would have subsequently presented himself to his followers for fellowship and for physical contact. ... But that can hardly be right. ... First and foremost οὔπω refers to Mary rather than to Jesus; she cannot yet enter into fellowship with him until she has recognised him as the Lord who is with the Father, and so moved from earthly conditions.'[44] Since, however, this is not what John says it seems improbable that it is what he meant! But what other interpretation can be offered?

John does two things here. First he offers his own version, an especially abbreviated one, of the traditional recognition scene; secondly he appends a dialogue of his own composition with obvious affinities to the ascension story in Acts. Now this procedure means combining two ideas of resurrection that are conceptually very difficult to reconcile, one temporal (before/after) the other spatial (below/above). The first of these informs all the recognition scenes. Normally (Matthew 28: 9 is an exception) recognition follows an initial period of some perplexity on the part of the disciples: Jesus has altered; he is not immediately recognizable. Then by a word or a gesture he causes the scales to fall from their eyes and they acknowledge that the man whom they know to have died and been buried is standing before them. (In the Emmaus story recognition is delayed, but the principle is the same.) I have argued in Chapter 11 that this 'identity-in-difference' encapsulates the very essence of the Gospel genre. That the fourth evangelist should have incorporated a

---

[44] p. 687.

scene which so admirably illustrates one of his own central ideas should perhaps not surprise us.

Resurrection, however, is only one of the two traditional ways of envisaging Jesus' change of status. The other is exaltation.[45] The idea of Jesus' ascent into heaven, generally associated in this Gospel with the figure of the Son of Man, is familiar to John's readers as a theme in discourse. 'Ascend' ($\dot{a}\nu a\beta a\acute{\iota}\nu\epsilon\iota\nu$), as we saw in the preceding section ('Death'), is one of the four terms, the others being 'exalt' ($\dot{v}\psi o\hat{v}\nu$), 'depart' ($\dot{v}\pi\acute{a}\gamma\epsilon\iota\nu$), and 'glorify' ($\delta o\xi\acute{a}\zeta\epsilon\iota\nu$), employed by John to signify the climax of the Easter happening. But by introducing this idea into a narrative that forces his readers to see resurrection and ascension in a temporal sequence, John presents them with conceptual puzzles that are impossible to resolve. Even if we detach this episode from what follows and thus relieve ourselves of the need to imagine Jesus redescending after his ascent before once more going up into heaven, the crucial difficulty remains.

To appreciate the gravity of the problem we have only to compare this story with the much fuller account of the Ascension in Acts, which shows us Jesus being hoisted up into the clouds before the astonished gaze of the apostles. This lively description certainly accentuates the difficulty: how far did he ascend, where did he stop, in what part of the physical universe is he now residing? But John's shorter and soberer version poses exactly the same theoretical problem. The idea of exaltation, acceptable enough in a confession or a creed, cannot be put into story form without assuming the contours of a myth. We shall have to return to this difficulty in the conclusion to this chapter.

Here we must be satisfied with a straightforward exegesis of this, the second ending of the gospel story. The fourth evangelist, wrestling throughout his work with the paradox of the genre, has renounced the solution widely attributed to Mark and known as the Messianic Secret. The Christ of the early part of his narrative has been given from the outset the lineaments of divinity. This means that John, unlike Mark, is unable to hint at any reservations on the

---

[45] See E. Schweizer, 'Two New Testament Creeds'. The creeds in question are 1 Cor. 15: 3–5, which speaks of resurrection, and 1 Tim. 3: 16, which speaks of assumption ($\dot{a}\nu a\lambda a\mu\beta\acute{a}\nu\epsilon\iota\nu$). Schweizer points out that the first involves temporal categories (before/after), the second spatial (below/above). The difference lies not in the object of belief but in the expression of it. To treat the two as if they referred to distinct *events*, as Luke does in his account of the ascension, is to plunge into insoluble paradoxes.

part of Jesus himself: the before/after is continually stressed, but its Johannine application, the two levels of understanding, concerns not Jesus himself but Jesus' contemporaries on the one hand, including the disciples, and the readers of the Gospel on the other. There is no split or uncertainty in Jesus' own consciousness. A divine nimbus surrounds him even while he is still on earth, and at his death he simply passes to another mode of glorification. The transformation this entails is of the subtlest and easy to miss. In a sense, then, John—unlike Mark—may be thought to require a recognition scene in order to establish the identity-in-difference between the earthly and the risen Jesus. That he should choose to underline the change of status this implies by Jesus' admonition to Mary may perhaps be taken as a confirmation of this reading: the Christian's true communion is not with the earthly Jesus but with the Risen Lord.

This episode, however, is not quite over yet. It ends with a summary statement of one of the most regular features of the resurrection narratives: the mission tradition. This is implicit in the message Mary is given to pass on to Jesus' 'brothers' and in her fulfilment of this commission: 'she went and said to the disciples, "I have seen the Lord"; and she told them that he had said these things to her' (20: 18). Here we have the quintessence of the early Christian mission: a proclamation, by a witness, that Jesus is risen. Nothing further is required: John could have ended his Gospel here.

(c) Mission (20: 19–23)

The third episode has no connection with the second. The disciples gathered together behind locked doors 'for fear of the Jews' show no knowledge of what they have supposedly just been told, or indeed of the empty tomb. Nor is there any link with the final story. Taken by itself the story of the appearance to the disciples betrays no awareness of the absence of one of their number.[46] In this episode, even more obviously self-sufficient than the first two, we have a third possible ending to the Gospel.

In the preceding episode the main emphasis is upon recognition. The mission theme is handled with such compression that it could easily pass unnoticed. In this story the emphasis is reversed. The identity between the one who hung on the cross and the Risen Lord

---

[46] Cf. Becker, p. 620.

is established by Jesus himself when he shows his followers his hands and his side.[47] Recognition is assumed but not stated. The real interest lies elsewhere, in the fulfilment of promise and in the final mission.

Certain of the elements which go to make up this story have parallels elsewhere: Jesus' actual appearance and salutation (v. 19; cf. Luke 24: 36), the self-display (v. 20; cf. Luke 24: 40), the mission (v. 21; cf. Matt. 28: 19), the bestowal of the Spirit (v. 22; cf. Luke 24: 49; also Acts 1: 4: 'the promise of my Father'), forgiveness of sins (v. 23; cf. Luke 24: 47; Matt. 28: 19 (?)). Nevertheless the most interesting and important allusions here are those that relate this episode to various promises in the farewell discourse.

There are many of these: peace, joy, mission, the bestowal of the Spirit. Read in conjunction with the farewell discourse the episode may be clearly seen as the articulation, in narrative form, of themes that had hitherto been reserved for discourse.[48] Just as in the body of the Gospel the great confrontational scenes between Jesus and his adversaries are the narrative version of the judgement motif, so here, towards the end of his book, the evangelist recapitulates the chief elements of the promise of return that is the main burden of the farewell discourse. Here is prophecy fulfilled.

Central among these elements of promise is mission: 'As thou didst send me into the world, so I have sent them into the world' (17: 18). This remarkable projection, at the heart of Jesus' final prayer, is carried through almost to the letter in the scene we are considering. The implications are momentous. The role of the community is plainly the same as that of Jesus himself. Here, if only we can see it, is all the justification we need for following Martyn's insight that the experience of Jesus recorded in the Gospel embodies lessons for the immediate present of its readers.

[47] Cf. Bultmann, p. 691.
[48] This may not, however, have been the order in which the two were composed. The second version of the farewell discourse (chs. 15–16) and the final prayer (ch. 17) belong in all likelihood to the second edition of the Gospel and so will have been composed *after* ch. 20. This might conceivably be true of ch. 14 also. If so, then the Johannine prophet's understanding of Jesus' promise to return may have been inspired by this scene. In that case a simple greeting ('Peace be with you') was seen to be the fulfilment of a promise of peace, an abiding state of well-being (*shalom*). Similarly the joyous reaction of the disciples to Jesus' appearance in their midst was seen as the proper attitude of Christians secure in the knowledge of Christ's permanent presence among them. The boldest stroke of all is the idea that the breath of the Risen Jesus was to be identified with the Spirit of God.

Recognition and mission are the two sides of a door that opens out from the closed world of the Gospel to that of Christian believers. Janus-like, the first side looks back to the earthly life of Jesus, the second side forward to the life of the community. In the body of the Gospel the evangelist presents a stereoscopic view. In the resurrection stories he allows the twin elements of the Gospel paradox, earthly Jesus and risen Lord, to be seen to succeed one another in a temporal progression. Yet in doing so he is quick to underline the correctness of his earlier perspective. The Crucified One is rightly recognized as the Risen Lord; in pursuing its mission the community re-enacts the experience of Jesus himself.

CONCLUSION

In returning to the problem posed for the interpreter by the resurrection stories, we must first of all be clear about what *kind* of problem we are dealing with. It is not a matter of sifting fact from fantasy or of piercing through the allegorical overlay to get at the bedrock of historical truth beneath. Neither the resurrection itself nor the stories told to illustrate its significance are historical in any meaningful sense of the word. Anyone who disagrees with this statement has a lot of puzzles to wrestle with, puzzles for which, I am convinced, no solutions are available.

One may of course ask whether the evangelist himself believed these stories to be factually true. The answer to this question is not easy either, and may be beyond the reach of exegesis. Some particularly fastidious commentators, afraid of falling prey to the intentionalist fallacy, may regard this question as illegitimate and so refrain from asking it. It is none the less an interesting question, and I shall return to it, but it cannot be answered straight away.

The central question is surely not historical but literary, and concerns the evangelist's *sensibility*. Only a reader whose own imaginative responses have been blunted by familiarity or credulity will be left undisturbed by the shift from the elegance and finesse of, say, the farewell discourses to the fairy-tale atmosphere of the resurrection stories. It is like finding Hans Christian Andersen hand in hand with Søren Kierkegaard. Even if, as I have suggested, we consider each of these stories independently and so avoid the wildest excesses of Wonderland, there are still some very odd images left: a corpse that, apparently unaided, slips out of its burial-wrappings, angels who ask a single question and disappear without waiting for an answer, a man whom Mary now knows to be Jesus rejecting physical contact because he is about to ascend into heaven. And so on.

If the evangelist had contented himself with taking over his traditions more or less as he received them, then it might be argued that he did so half-heartedly, *par acquit de conscience*, his real interest and commitment lying elsewhere, in the subtle and sophisticated theology of glorification that precedes. This after all is roughly how he operates in the body of the Gospel when he takes over stories like the healing of the cripple or the blind man and the feeding of the five thousand. He does not repudiate these, certainly, but the way he exploits them for his own purposes leaves the reader in no doubt where his interests lie. It might be said that the resurrection stories too are made to serve theological ends. True, but the difficulty persists that some of the most troubling features of these stories appear to have been the work of the evangelist himself. The last story of all, which I have omitted from this discussion, is a good example. When Jesus invites Thomas, however ironically, to feel for himself the tangible proof of his real presence, the lesson that is then drawn only partially justifies the crudity of the images that have been evoked.

Two radically contrasting possibilities immediately present themselves. The first is that John is being extraordinarily subtle, implicitly inviting his readers to demythologize these stories for themselves. This is the kind of solution that one expects from Bultmann, and in fact he comments disapprovingly on the views of exegetes such as Dodd, who 'doubt or contest the idea that the evangelist assumes a critical attitude to these stories'.[49] Dodd does indeed say that 'The resurrection is *prima facie* a reality on the spiritual plane, and the evangelist is concerned to show that it is also an event on the temporal, historical plane.'[50] But even he baulks at the suggestion that Jesus went up bodily into heaven: 'It is at all events clear that for John the ἀνάβασις is not a movement in space [*why not, if the resurrection is an event in time?*], but a change in the conditions under which Christ is apprehended as the glorified and exalted Lord.'[51] How difficult it is not to see John as the kind of thinker one would like him to be!

But what is the alternative? Must we then conclude that John is

[49] p. 688 n. 3.   [50] *Interpretation*, p. 442.   [51] Ibid., p. 443 n. 3.

not after all the profound religious genius that we have up to this point taken him to be, but a relatively unsophisticated Christian believer, no more philosophically acute or theologically aware than the vast majority of his contemporaries?

If neither of these alternatives commends itself three other possible courses are open to us. The first, well-tried and familiar, is to absolve John the evangelist from all responsibility for the distasteful elements in his work, either by assigning the bulk of these stories, even where they diverge from tradition, to a pre-Johannine writer from within the community,[52] or by once again hauling in that uncomplaining old scapegoat, the ecclesiastical redactor, who has already been saddled with most of the passages in the Gospel that for one reason or another modern interpreters find theologically reprehensible, and is about to be asked to assume the biggest burden of all, the long appendix of chapter 21.

Now I have nothing in principle against this solution. It is possible, and indeed not uncommon, for biblical exegetes to employ the hypothesis of several levels of redaction as a way of evading difficulties instead of answering them. But this is not to say that it should never be employed at all. The trouble is that here as elsewhere (e.g. the differing 'eschatologies' in chapters 5 and 11) it is virtually impossible to isolate one level from another without arbitrariness. The arguments are simply too weak.

The second course is that of the deconstructionalists. They assume that what we have to interpret is not an author but a text. The Fourth Gospel, so full of paradoxes and puzzles, is especially vulnerable to their ingenious tricks and diabolical devices and one can easily imagine them causing it to self-destruct (another word for deconstruct) by exposing its inner contradictions.

This course too, however tempting, is to be avoided. Even more obviously than the first it is a non-solution, an evasion rather than an answer. Why after all should the exegete abdicate his honourable throne in favour of a court jester?

Nevertheless the deconstructionalists may have something to teach us after all. (One should not be afraid of learning from the devil.) Their readiness to recognize and manipulate contradictions in the text is not entirely to be deplored. But what if we transfer this idea from text to author? The suggestion that the evangelist believed

---

[52] This is Jürgen Becker's solution.

two contradictory things at the same time is in fact quite a simple one. The modern mind finds it difficult to accept only because it cannot rest content with simple stories carrying simple meanings but insists upon probing into the inner recesses of such stories with impertinent and inappropriate questions. Take for example the episode of the appearance before the disciples. Bultmann grasps the main point quite easily: 'The Risen Jesus authenticates himself and proves his identity with the man crucified two days earlier.'[53] So far so good. The lesson is that of identity-in-difference, and there is no need to push behind it. In the following scene the evangelist actually spells the lesson out for us: 'be not faithless, but believing'. Jesus' invitation to Thomas is a rebuke, a way of driving the same point home. Go one step further and we plunge into a morass: 'According to the Jewish idea of bodily resurrection presupposed by John, Jesus is touchable, and perfectly able to invite Thomas to handle him.'[54] If John invented this story, as there is every reason to believe, it was not, surely, to stimulate his readers to reflect upon the tangibility of risen bodies, but to impress upon them the need for faith.

Did John then believe these stories to be factually true? It is hard to be sure. One could invoke Plato here, for the sublime ease with which he temporarily abandons his abstruse philosophizing in order to encapsulate the essence of his argument in a myth. But then Plato surely did not believe in the factual truth of his myths. Whether John did I do not know, though I suspect that he may well have done. Children, after all, who are not without intelligence, believe that their Christmas presents come from Santa Claus even though they know perfectly well that they are given by their parents.[55] Only when they start uneasily picking at the myth (how does he squeeze into the chimney?) are they forced to acknowledge the contradictions and settle for the less colourful world of commonplace fact. The commentator's first task is to get at the meaning of the text. The central lessons of the chapter under discussion, faith, recognition, mission, are plain enough to anyone prepared to search primarily for what Origen calls the 'spiritual' meaning and Browning calls stars. Grubbing around the Gospel in a hunt for corporeal points can only lead to confusion.

[53] p. 691.   [54] Lindars, p. 607.
[55] Cf. Paul Veyne, *Les Grecs ont-ils cru à leurs mythes?* The other example he gives in his preface to this book is that of the Ethiopian tribe of the Dorze who, knowing that the leopard is a Christian animal, believe that, like all good Christians, he fasts on Wednesdays and Fridays. Despite this belief they are just as anxious to protect their herds from his maraudings on these as on other days.

14

THE MEDIUM AND THE MESSAGE

INTRODUCTION

Nobody has ever undertaken a comprehensive study of the concept of revelation in the Fourth Gospel,[1] unless one counts Bultmann's great commentary or the long section on John in his *Theology of the New Testament*. Why is that, given that revelation is unquestionably the dominant theme of the Gospel? The first reason is that despite James Barr's devastating criticisms (in chapter 8 of his *Semantics of Biblical Language*) of the principles underlying Kittel's famous *Wörterbuch*, most scholars, both budding and full-blown, still find it easier to study a word than a concept.[2] Neither the verb ἀποκαλύπτειν nor the noun ἀποκάλυψις occurs in the Gospel, and the nearest synonyms, φανεροῦν,[3] γνωρίζειν, perhaps ἀναγγέλλειν, are not sufficiently prominent and do not carry sufficient weight to merit an extended treatment. To include the various *symbolic* equivalents of revelation would make the task very much more difficult.

The second reason why the concept has never been thoroughly studied is its sheer ubiquity. *Every major motif in the Gospel is directly linked to the concept of revelation.* To start with, there are at least three

---

[1] Edward Malatesta's cumulative and classified bibliography (1920–65) of books and periodical literature on the Fourth Gospel (Rome, 1967) does in fact include 3 entries (out of 3120) under 'revelation', two articles and a relatively short doctoral thesis of 150 pages. Gilbert van Belle's compilation, *Johannine Bibliography 1966–1985: A Cumulative and Classified Bibliography on the Fourth Gospel* (Leiden, 1987) has 7 entries under 'revelation' out of a total of 6300, and one of these relates to the Johannine Apocalypse. Gail O'Day's *Revelation in the Fourth Gospel*, which will be discussed later in the chapter, contains some useful insights, but is uneven and one-sided. The gap remains.

[2] A particularly clear example of the difference between words and concepts is to be found in an article by Quentin Skinner in *The State of the Language*, ed. L. Michaels and C. Ricks (London, 1980), pp. 562–78. Skinner points out that although Milton never used the *word* 'originality' (it had not yet entered the language), the *concept* meant a great deal to him.

[3] There are 9 occurrences of the word φανεροῦν in the Gospel (3 of them in ch. 21) and 8 in 1 John. Like ἐμφανίζειν (14: 21, 22), it suggests vision rather than hearing.

terms which could often (not always) be *translated* 'revelation' without serious distortion: Λόγος (the Word), δόξα (glory), ἀλήθεια (truth); others refer to the vehicle of revelation: λόγος (word), λόγοι and ῥήματα (words), σημεῖα (signs), μαρτυρία (witness); still others indicate the revealing act itself: μαρτυρεῖν (testify), λαλεῖν (speak), λέγειν (say), κράζειν (proclaim), διδάσκειν (teach), ὑπομιμνήσκειν (remind), ἀναγγέλλειν (expound). The key word πιστεύειν (believe) suggests the proper response to revelation, as does ἀκούειν (listen, hear), and occasionally the words meaning 'know' (εἰδέναι, γινώσκειν) do so too. The central symbol of the Gospel, life, sums up what the evangelist sees as the reward and consequence of faith; while the three most important of the subsidiary symbols, light, water, bread, all suggest particular facets of the same concept. The disciples of Jesus are those who believe; those who do not believe ('the Jews', the world) bring judgement or condemnation (κρίσις) upon themselves. Moreover, this is just a list of words, and an incomplete one at that. No doubt each or all of them can provide a useful entry into the conceptual world of the Fourth Gospel, as many excellent studies have shown. But they cannot take us the whole way. At the very least we should have to add the three main titles of Jesus in the Gospel; two of these are specifically said to be the object of faith (20: 31), while the third ('Son of Man') is the very personification of revelation.

The third reason for the reluctance of scholars to embark upon a full study is the extraordinary difficulty, despite the apparent frankness with which the evangelist states his purpose at the conclusion of the Gospel, of seizing upon the *content* of revelation. Bultmann's answer is well known. The Jesus of John's Gospel has but a single truth to reveal, the simple fact that he is the revealer. There is no *what*, only a *that*: *ein bloßes Daß*, a naked 'that'. Bultmann is perfectly well aware that the Gospel itself states the object of faith in propositional form: 'these things are written …' (20: 31; cf. Martha's confession in 11: 27). But he pays no attention to this in his commentary: for the evangelist, he says, 'the faith of "Christians" is not a conviction that is present once for all, but it must perpetually make sure of itself anew, and therefore must continually hear the word anew.'[4] Simply to underline what the Gospel itself appears to state will not do: John himself is at pains to expose the inadequacy of

---

[4] pp. 698 f.

the title 'Messiah',[5] and the special relationship with the Father implied by the title 'Son of God', once divested of its mythological trappings, is slender and insubstantial. One may seek to counter Bultmann's arguments by injecting some content into his empty 'that'. *What* Jesus reveals, it might be said, is his origin ($\pi \acute{o} \theta \epsilon \nu$) and his destiny ($\pi o \hat{v}$), the fact that he has been sent by God and that God is his Father. By the end of the Gospel these ideas have been assumed into the originally messianic title, 'Son of God', and now form part of its meaning. And it is true too that patristic commentators have succeeded in weaving the material of the Gospel into elaborate christological and trinitarian patterns. But in its untreated form the material is flimsy stuff. By coarsening John's delicate suggestions into dogmas one can preserve a superficial fidelity at the price of a deeper betrayal. However suspicious one may be of Bultmann's existential interpretation of John, he shows considerably more insight than most of his critics. John is not a dogmatist but an evangelist; what he writes is not doctrine but gospel.

In Chapters 10 and 11 some answers have been given to fundamental questions concerning the *form* of the Gospel by show-ing its affinity with apocalyptic. It has also been explained how the *mode* of revelation is conditioned by the paradoxical nature of the credal affirmation which it expands and justifies. This chapter focuses upon the *content* of revelation, allowing from the outset that it may not be possible to separate this from the very special way in which it is conveyed. The shadow of Bultmann looms throughout this book, and in discussing the content of revelation I am very much aware of his uncompromising opposition. His own view is nowhere more fully expressed than in his *Theology of the New Testament*:

Jesus as the Revealer of God reveals nothing but that he is the Revealer. And that amounts to saying that it is he for whom the world is waiting, he who brings in his own person that for which all the longing of man yearns; life and truth as the reality out of which man can exist, light as the complete transparence of existence in which questions and riddles are at an end. But how is he that and how does he bring it? In no other way than that he says that he is it and says that he brings it—he a man with his human word, which, without legitimation, demands faith, John, that is, in his Gospel presents only the fact (*das Daß*) of the Revelation without describing its content (*ihr Was*).[6]

---

[5] See M. de Jonge, 'Jesus as Prophet, p. 50 f.   [6] p. 66.

I. WORDS AND CONCEPTS

This is the first of two main parts in this chapter. It treats of a number of key words. Though the ideas suggested by these words are different, they are all related to the concept of revelation and may be said to indicate various facets of it. It is convenient to treat these separately, but they are so intimately and intricately related to one another that some overlap is unavoidable. The second main part is an exegesis of a number of important passages in the Gospel that exemplify what I call 'the revelation form'. One passage that has some claim to be treated under this heading is the Prologue, but I have chosen to discuss it instead in the first part, under 'Logos'.

(a) Signs and works

Beneath the imperative demands for faith that crowd the pages of the Fourth Gospel run a number of powerful and at times conflicting currents of tradition. The first is the all-seeing and all-encompassing providence of God, who through his Wisdom/Word (Λόγος) directs the course of human history: πάντα δι' αὐτοῦ ἐγένετο (1: 3). This universal mastery is exhibited in a special way summed up as *life*: ἐν αὐτῷ ζωὴ ἦν (1: 4). The life is also a *light* that shines in the world and offers mankind the chance to accept God in his creative and revealing work.[7] The bold identification of the Word and the Light conceals a puzzle which, far from being resolved, is emphasized and expanded in the body of the Gospel: a light is seen; a word is heard; how can they be held together?

Various currents of tradition go to make up the revelation motif in Judaism. Of these the most important is undoubtedly the gift of the Law to Moses on Mount Sinai. One element in this story is the assertion that what is *not* given is the vision of God.[8] The essence of this revelation lies in words, some inscribed on tablets of stone,

[7] No one has given a better explanation of the important distinction between 'through him' and 'in him' in this passage than Paul Lamarche ('The Prologue', pp. 47 f.).

[8] This, of course, is the official, establishment line. There is so much evidence to the contrary—records of visions by patriarchs and prophets—that we may be surprised at the success of the deuteronomists in maintaining it. 'The later apocalypses', remarks Margaret Barker, 'have their deepest roots in the early cult exemplified in the theophany [of Exod. 24: 9–11] *which later writers sought to contradict, e.g. Deut. 4: 12*' (*The Older Testament*, p. 123 n. 18; cf. pp. 146 ff.).

others, according to a later tradition, spoken privately to Moses: the written Torah and the oral Torah.

Embedded in the written Torah, which is far more than a series of law codes, is the story of God's active intervention in history on behalf of his own people, from Abraham through to Moses. These interventions often involve demonstrations of power, from the conception of a child by a very old woman to the parting of the waters of the sea. Because events like these are not immediately intelligible they were accompanied by explanations: in the case of the sea-crossing a story (Exod. 14) *and* a song (Exod. 15). God made it clear to Moses and the Patriarchs what he was doing and why he was doing it, the action and the intention being part of the same revelation.

The idea that God both acts and explains his actions is fundamental to both Judaism and Christianity and may indeed be a necessary feature of any religion that sees God as intervening directly in human history.[9] Conversely, a false god—an idol—is one that can neither act nor speak: 'if someone cries to it, it does not answer or save him from his trouble' (Isa. 46: 7).

The Pentateuch may be regarded as the story of the birth of the people of Israel. God continued to speak to his people through the prophets, who were conceived as messengers (angels?) sent from heaven. We have seen in Chapter 8 how the notion of the divine emissary occupies a central place in John's conception of Jesus and his role: one of Jesus' two names for God is ὁ πέμψας με: he who sent me. The existence of prophets proves the ease of communications between heaven and earth. The prophet speaks with the voice of God: 'Thus says the Lord'. The words of some of the prophets were recorded, and these came to be part of the written record of God's dealings with his people. Joshua and Judges, Samuel and Kings, are numbered among the prophets in the Hebrew Bible: so we have *the Law and the Prophets*. By this time the pattern of revelation was clearly established: God had acted and he had spoken.

Such were the marvels that God had wrought on behalf of his people during the Exodus that they might have been expected to respond with enthusiasm and total commitment. We know, however, that they did not. Their lack of faith is always portrayed as

[9] It must not be assumed that the idea is *exclusive* to Judaism and Christianity: cf. B. Albrektson, *History and the Gods* (Lund, 1967).

disobedience—a failure in hearing. What God required of them above all else was to *listen*: 'Hear, O Israel'. Yet the very people who are urged to hear are also said to have *seen*: 'Your eyes have seen' (Deut. 4: 3, 9; 10: 21; 11: 7). Included in what they saw were the signs and great prodigies (τὰ σημεῖα καὶ τὰ τέρατα τὰ μέγαλα) 'that the Lord your God did to Pharaoh and to all Egypt' (Deut. 7: 18 f.; cf. Exod. 7: 3; John 4: 48: σημεῖα καὶ τέρατα). It is possible, however, to witness such prodigies without *really* seeing: more important than the eyes of the body are the eyes of the soul: 'You have seen all that the Lord did before your eyes in the land of Egypt, to Pharaoh and to all his servants and to all his land, the great trials which your [Hebrew singular] eyes saw, the signs and those great wonders; but to this day the Lord has not given you a mind to understand, or eyes to see, or ears to hear' (Deut. 29: 2–4; *Hebrew*, 1–3).

Although the Fourth Gospel preserves the traditional connection between seeing and hearing—so well, in fact, that faith is often described in terms of vision—there is nevertheless a perceptible tension between the two, a tension that comes to full expression in the concluding beatitude. In spite of this, John regards his Gospel as a record of some of the signs that Jesus performed in the sight of his disciples (ἐνώπιον τῶν μαθητῶν)—and the purpose of this record was 'that you may believe' (20: 30–1). The faith of all subsequent generations of Christian believers depends upon the signs witnessed by Jesus' first disciples. Yet it is hard not to see in this conclusion one last spark of the familiar Johannine irony, as the reader reflects how much more the fourth evangelist offers than a plain account of Jesus' deeds and how little such an account would do to elicit the kind of faith that interests him.

Filtered through the evangelist's special understanding and processed, as it were, by his faith, the story of Jesus' life emerges as a Gospel. The word he uses here (20: 30) is 'signs'—signs which, properly regarded, can be seen to point the way to a true faith and are therefore revelatory in the full sense. If, as is probable, he has taken over the word from the signs source, he will certainly have infused it with a new, deeper meaning. Whatever its origins he has made it his own. John's readers, as he knows, cannot see the signs: they can only read what he has written about them. 'Unless you see signs and wonders,' Jesus had said, 'you will not believe' (4: 48), employing the plural form of address whilst ostensibly speaking to the official from Capernaum whose son was on the point of death. But to read about signs is one thing; to see them, and perhaps be dazzled by the prodigy whilst failing to grasp its import, is quite another.

A sign is a miracle, a marvellous happening with a special significance. But in the dialogues and discourses of the Gospel Jesus never uses the word σημεῖον in this sense. In the two instances where it occurs on his lips (4: 48; 6: 26) it has a negative ring. His own term for what he does is ἔργα, 'deeds' or 'works'. The question arises, then, are these words coterminous? Do they have the same reference? And since, obviously, they do not have the same *sense*, what is the difference between them? One possible interpretation would be this: ἔργα signifies the works as Jesus alone can see them, that is to say as tasks given to him by the Father to be performed in the sight of men; whereas σημεῖα signifies Jesus' miracles as they are seen by men; viewed rightly they are signs of Jesus' relationship to the Father, whose emissary he is and whose revelation he embodies— signs, in other words, of his glory. If part of the notion of a sign is that it is intended somehow to lead to faith, it would clearly be inappropriate for Jesus to think or speak of his own works as signs for himself. Broadly speaking, this distinction is correct.[10] But it leaves a lot of questions unanswered, especially the crucial question of the relationship between Jesus' words and his works, a question which brings us back to the sight/hearing antithesis with which we began.

Unlike σημεῖα, ἔργα can be qualified: 'the works of the world' (7: 7); 'the works of God' (9: 4); 'the works of my Father' (10: 37). Works are characterized, then, by their origin or source. 'The works of the world' is a phrase which sums up all worldly transactions —which are evil; 'the works of God' similarly sums up the dealings of God with mankind. But since, for John, it is Jesus who is commissioned to perform these works on God's behalf, acting as his agent, it is only a small step to concluding that in the Fourth Gospel the term refers to God's self-revelation in Jesus. In one passage, 6: 29, we are told that the work of God is faith in Jesus, the one whom God has sent. Bultmann contends that 'the "works which Jesus does at his Father's behest" (5: 20, 36; 9: 4; 10: 25, 32, 37; 14: 12; 15: 24) are

---

[10] In 7: 21 and 10: 33 the singular, ἔργον, is simply one work out of many. Elsewhere, 4: 34, 17: 4, and perhaps 6: 29, it embraces the whole of Jesus' mission, as does the plural in 5: 36. Cf. A. Vanhoye, 'L'Œuvre du Christ'.

ultimately one single work. At the beginning of his ministry we read: "My food is to do the will of him who sent me, and to accomplish his work" (4: 34) and in retrospect we are told a very similar thing at the end of it: "I glorified thee on earth, having accomplished the work which thou gavest me to do" (17: 4).[11] What Bultmann is anxious to establish is that Jesus' single work is that of revelation; if that is right, all works can be reduced to words. He finds the evidence he is looking for in 14: 10 f.: 'The words that I say to you I do not speak on my own authority; but the Father who dwells in me does his works. Believe me that I am in the Father and the Father in me; or else believe me for the sake of the works themselves.' These two verses, says Bultmann, if taken together, 'indicate that the "works" of v. 11 are neither more nor less than the "words" of v. 10. When Jesus thus points away from himself to his working, that can only mean that he is rejecting an authoritarian faith which will meekly accept what is said *about* Jesus. In its place, he is demanding a faith that understands Jesus' words as *personal address* aimed at the believer—i.e. as Jesus "working" upon him. This is the sense in which Jesus refuses the demand of "the Jews" that he openly says whether or not he is the Messiah (10: 24 f.). The answer to that they ought to gather from his works—or workings—which bear witness to him.'[12] But this is Bultmann, not John, for whom Jesus' works, as many other passages show, are often also thought of as signs.

If we resist the temptation to allow our understanding of the Gospel to be determined by one or two of our favourite verses, we can see that John succeeds in preserving the balance—as well as the tension—between words and works. For those who receive the message of Jesus' disciples, as for the readers of the Gospel, *the works have been transformed into words*, spoken in the one case, written in the other. With Jesus' passing the chance of witnessing his signs has gone forever. This is not a matter of regret: 'It is good for you that I go.' There is no longer any risk of wrongly assessing the function of signs, of following Thomas in confusing sight with faith. But whatever our final verdict upon the truth of the story told in the Gospel it cannot be preserved if the events of that story are swallowed up and cancelled by a proclamation that has no room for them.

---

[11] *Theology*, ii. 52.
[12] Ibid., ii. 60 f.

(b) Witness

Signs are not the evangelist's favourite way of communicating
revealed truth—or perhaps it would be better to say that they are
not *his* way. They are part of the story, certainly, but once he has
compiled a selection of signs and transcribed them for posterity their
impact is necessarily indirect: they are now contained in a book. And
a book is not a sign but a testimony: the author of the appendix,
surely someone other than the evangelist himself, asserts of the
person 'who has written these things' that 'we know that his
testimony is true' (21: 24). Thus the evangelist is a witness, the last
of the witnesses of which his Gospel speaks.

A witness is someone who has seen and/or heard something and
then testifies to this to others in order to persuade them of its truth.
When the testimony is a confession of faith in difficult circumstances, the witness may also be a martyr. There is a natural link
between the two concepts and in Greek the same word ($\mu\acute{\alpha}\rho\tau\upsilon s$) does
service for both.[13]

In his article on $\mu\acute{\alpha}\rho\tau\upsilon s$ and its cognates in Kittel's Dictionary,
H. Strathmann singles out for special attention two passages from
Second Isaiah: 43: 9–13 and 44: 7–11. This prophet is especially
concerned with Israel's testimony to the pagan nations regarding
the supremacy of Yahweh. Having experienced Yahweh's saving
power, Israel alone, of all the nations of the world, is able to testify
on his behalf—testify that he is God and that there is no other. This
truth, we may infer, is not accessible to those who have not
experienced it for themselves except through a testimony that Israel
alone is qualified to give.

There are many witnesses in the Fourth Gospel but the truth to
which they testify is always the same: the person of Jesus. This, after
all, is the only truth with which the Gospel is concerned. There is
one apparent exception to this: 'Amen, amen, I say to you, we speak
of what we know, and bear witness to what we have seen; but you
do not receive our testimony. If I have told you earthly things and
you do not believe, how can you believe if I tell you heavenly
things?' (3: 11–12). We have already remarked (in Chapter 9) upon
the exceptional difficulty of giving any satisfactory account of what
these things ($\tau\grave{\alpha}$ $\dot{\epsilon}\pi\acute{\iota}\gamma\epsilon\iota\alpha$ and $\tau\grave{\alpha}$ $\dot{\epsilon}\pi o\upsilon\rho\acute{\alpha}\nu\iota\alpha$) may be. Odeberg has
plausibly suggested that lying behind this claim of Jesus is a tradition

---

[13] Cf. Bultmann, p. 50 n. 5.

of Jesus' ascent into heaven to be the recipient of heavenly secrets. But in the present context these secrets cannot be anything other than the significance, concealed not only from Nathanael but also from every other actor in the story, of Jesus' earthly career. The real irony is that the heavenly truths are to be found—as John's readers will know—in the earthly reality of Jesus' presence. In this case τὰ ἐπίγεια and τὰ ἐπουράνια are the same. What looks like an exception turns out to conform to the general pattern of the Johannine μαρτυρία.

In an earlier chapter (5) it was argued that the characteristically Johannine understanding of witness was hammered out in confrontation with the Pharisees as they challenged the new Christian group to produce evidence that Jesus was what they claimed him to be. It was then that they were forced to reflect on their own faith and eventually to discard the simple idea of direct testimony that they had inherited in the signs source. Whether or not I am right in supposing that this began with the words now found in the Prologue: 'There was a man sent from God, whose name was John' (1: 6), the first three statements about John are all concerned to emphasize his role as witness: 1: 6–8, 15, 19. Having seen the Spirit descend upon Jesus in the form of a dove, he is able to assert: 'I have seen and have borne witness that this is the Son of God' (1: 34). And the Gospel records that on two occasions he pointed to Jesus and said to those who were with him, 'Behold, the Lamb of God' (1: 29, 36). Much of his testimony is indirect: by disowning the titles put to him by a delegation of priests and Levites he prepares the way for them to be conferred on Jesus.[14]

When the first challenge comes to Jesus' authority, in chapter 5, he is still prepared to appeal to the testimony of John: 'You sent to John and he has borne witness to the truth' (5: 33). But John's testimony is discounted in favour of a greater:

For the works which the Father has granted me to accomplish, these very works which I am doing, bear me witness that the Father has sent me. And the Father who sent me has himself borne witness to me ... You search the scriptures, because you think that in them you have eternal life; but they actually bear witness to *me*. (5: 36–9)

---

[14] A. E. Harvey (*Jesus on Trial*) has a good section on John the Baptist in a chapter entitled, 'The Witnesses in the Case'. But 'the other witnesses' turn out to be not those named by the evangelist, but the disciples, notably Nathanael and Peter. Harvey ignores the *theological* aspects of Jesus' trial.

These three, the works, the Father, and the scriptures, are not like three independent witnesses who have all seen the same event and when questioned separately corroborate one another's stories. The Father's form is not seen—but it can be discerned in the works of Jesus; his voice is not heard—but it is echoed in the scriptures.

Bultmann says of the works: 'Even if an allusion to the σημεῖα may be in view [because the occasion of this discourse is the healing of the cripple] it is clear from 5: 19 ff. that the real ἔργα are the κρίνειν and the ζωοποεῖν [Jesus' exercise of his God-given power to judge and to bestow life]. To be more precise, Jesus' words and deeds are μαρτυρία, in that they are the κρίνειν and ζωοποεῖν; i.e. they are not μαρτυρία as visible demonstrative acts, but only taken together with what they effect.'[15] This is partly right: it is obvious too that there is no effective testimony in the scriptures except for those who are attuned to the voice of God. But Bultmann is too anxious to remove Jesus' miracles (which are what the term ἔργα generally refers to) from the sphere of his revelation.

The next main passage, 8: 13–20, opens with the Pharisees' challenge to the validity of Jesus' self-testimony. Had he been concerned simply to meet this challenge by appealing to people who would vouch for him he might well have produced John the Baptist here, or even some of his own disciples who had spoken of him to one another before his ministry had begun. But this would serve no purpose. John claims to have seen quite a lot; but he has seen nothing of the truth which Jesus now wishes to convey. There are now only two credible witnesses: himself and the Father. Ultimately, as I argued in Chapter 5, all truth is self-authenticating. There is nothing *outside* Jesus' revelation which he can call upon for support.

There is one passage which, as we shall see, represents the evangelist's final thoughts on the subject of revelation: 3: 31–6. Of him 'who comes from above' John writes: 'he bears witness to what he has seen and heard, yet no one receives his testimony: he who receives his testimony sets his seal to this, that God is true.' The apparent contradiction is characteristic: reception of Jesus' message is the exception rather than the rule. Josef Blank remarks perceptively on this passage that its difficulty 'lies in the fact that the content of this testimony is not something that can be expressed or grasped above and beyond the actual act of giving witness. This

---

[15] pp. 265 f.

means that the testimony receives its entire material and formal significance from the person who gives it. The witness and his testimony belong indissolubly together.'[16] Bultmann too recognizes the peculiar force of the passage:

Since the μαρτυρία of the Revealer is identical with what it attests, and not complementary to it, it finds confirmation paradoxically not by appealing from the word which bears witness to the truth of that to which it bears witness, but in its acceptance by faith. It is only in faith in the word of witness that man can see what it is to which the word is bearing witness, and consequently can recognize the legitimacy of the witness himself.

Moreover:

God himself speaks in the words of the God-sent Revealer. Now we can see more clearly why the word of witness and that to which the word bears witness are identical, for what God *says*, simply because it is said by *God*, can be nothing else than God's *action*. Inasmuch as he reveals himself, he is the λόγος. If in Jesus the λόγος became flesh, then God's action is carried out in Jesus' words.[17]

Observations of this kind help one to understand why Bultmann is widely regarded as the greatest of all commentators on the Fourth Gospel.

One final passage must be taken into consideration:

When the Paraclete comes, whom I shall send to you from the Father, even the Spirit of truth, he will bear witness to me; and you also are witnesses, because you have been with me from the beginning. (15: 26–7)

The witness of the Paraclete and the disciples is placed firmly on the second level—the spiritual level—of understanding. But how does it relate to Jesus' own witness, and that of the Father? Bultmann reckons that in this passage the word μαρτυρεῖν 'retains its forensic significance, because ... this proclamation has its place within the great lawsuit between God and the world'.[18] But it is as 'the Spirit of truth' that the Paraclete gives witness, and the object of his testimony is once again the person of Jesus. We are surely meant to understand that the testimony of the disciples is Spirit-inspired, just as that of Jesus himself is God-given. Furthermore, John insists that the task of bearing witness is entrusted in the first place to those who have been with Jesus 'from the beginning', i.e. from the commence-

[16] *Krisis*, p. 68. Blank refers to E. Petersen, 'Zeuge der Wahrheit', *Theologische Traktate* (Munich, 1951), pp. 165–224.   [17] p. 163.   [18] p. 553 n. 5.

ment of his ministry (cf. Luke 1: 2; Acts 1: 21 f.). The continuity appears to be important to him.

(c) Logos[19]

'In the beginning was the Word': nothing before—and nothing after. The Prologue offers a vision of eternity, stretching back to before the creation of the world and forward until after its end. The mysterious and decidedly feminine figure whom Jewish tradition calls Wisdom, God's 'darling and delight' (Prov. 8: 30, NEB), who assists him at the creation of the world, 'playing in his presence continually', appears in the opening of John's Gospel as the masculine Logos, equally mysterious but more severe. The way to this transformation had been prepared in another remarkable hymn to Wisdom by the writer known as Ben Sira (Ecclesiasticus), highly regarded in Judaism even though his work was never placed in the Hebrew canon. By an amazing leap of theological imagination he had identified Wisdom, who had 'come forth from the mouth of the Most High and covered the earth like a mist' (Sir. 24: 3)[20] with 'the book of the covenant of the Most High God, the law which Moses commanded us' (24: 23). Earlier in the hymn it is Wisdom herself who speaks, as she describes how she roamed all over the earth, through every people and nation: 'Among all these I sought a resting place (ἀνάπαυσις); I sought in whose territory I might lodge' (24: 7). 'Then', she continues, 'the one who created me assigned a place for my tent. And he said "Make your dwelling in Jacob and in Israel receive your inheritance": ὁ κτίσας με κατέπαυσεν τὴν σκηνήν μου καὶ εἶπεν Ἐν Ἰακὼβ κατασκήνωσον καὶ ἐν Ἰσραὴλ κατακληρονομήθητι' (24: 8). In the eyes of the author of the Prologue, of course, Wisdom is identified not with the Law but with the Logos, who fails to find a home in Israel ('his own received him not') and is eventually lodged 'among us' (ἐσκήνωσεν ἐν ἡμῖν)—the members of the writer's own community. The Wisdom of Solomon envisages Wisdom as remote and timeless, seated by God's throne (9: 4). When she enters the world as the Law, God's special gift to Israel, she acquires a history, but as the Bible tells it this story is largely one of incomprehension

---

[19] See Ashton, 'Transformation'.

[20] ἐγὼ ἀπὸ στόματος ὑψίστου ἐξῆλθον καὶ ὡς ὁμίχλη κατεκάλυψα γῆν; the NEB translates the first clause as 'I am the word which was spoken by the Most High'; one wonders if the translators had the Prologue in mind.

and rejection. Ben Sira puts the conclusion of his hymn, like the beginning, into the mouth of Wisdom: 'I will again pour out teaching like prophecy' (24: 33), and Luke records another of her sayings: 'I will send them prophets and apostles, some of whom they will kill and persecute' (11: 49; cf. Matt. 23: 34). The story of the Logos (now his story, not hers) is the same, but the home he finds is different. The end of the Prologue puts him back in heaven: the story that is about to be told is already over.

Once aware of the true background of the Prologue, one can see why it is a mistake to regard it simply as a hymn about creation, culminating in incarnation. Creation is indeed one of its themes, but it would be closer to the mark to say that it is a hymn about *revelation* that culminates in incarnation—the incarnation of the revealing Logos. The two motifs combine in the concept of the all-controlling providence of God, directing the affairs of men (the κόσμος) from beginning to end, or rather right up to the triumphant moment in which his design (the Λόγος) comes to fruition by descending to earth in human form and finding a home in the small community which was all there was to welcome him. His work has two aspects, life and light, and these correspond to the two facets of God's work: creation and revelation. They are both resumed in a single lapidary phrase: 'the life was light'. The evangelist is interested in both; he expands on the former in chapters 5 and 11, on the latter especially in chapter 9. But his primary concern, like that of the author of the hymn on which he modelled his Prologue, is revelation. The light continues to shine in the darkness (φαίνει, v. 5), which never succeeds in extinguishing it. The human beings for whom this light is intended, mankind in general and Israel in particular, who has a special place in the divine plan, have continually turned their eyes away from it, doing their best to frustrate God's intentions. The most marvellous insight of this extraordinary passage is that divine revelation, hitherto manifested intermittently in the lives of God's messengers, the prophets, and in a Law that has not been kept, has now actually taken flesh and dwelt among men—indeed in a community of which the writer is himself a member: 'we have seen his glory', glory being yet another term for revelation. The general mood of the Prologue is sombre, for the incarnation of God's design was ill received; but a subsidiary insight has found a place in the text: 'to those who did receive him he gave the power to become children of God' (1: 12). Finally, in a movement of ascent that fleetingly mirrors the downward path traced in the opening, the Prologue concludes with a picture of the Logos nestling in the Father's lap (εἰς τὸν κόλπον τοῦ πατρός). The very last word emphasizes yet again the revelatory role of the Logos: ἐξηγήσατο. It is the word which gives us 'exegesis': the only authentic account or 'exegesis' of God, the only valid 'theology' (λόγος τοῦ θεοῦ) is to be found in the Gospel that follows—which may be why the orthodox tradition accords this evangelist, alone among the four, the title of Theologian.

(d) Truth

Of the many revelation-linked words in the Fourth Gospel the one that gets closest to the heart of the matter is ἀλήθεια, 'truth'. This is so, whatever view we may take of the Gospel's origins, for the truth with which it deals is evidently not any old truth but a divine truth offered to mankind for the first time by the one who proclaims it in this book. This is what Bultmann says:

In Hellenism ἀλήθεια received over and above the formal meaning of truth, reality (and truthfulness) the meaning of 'divine reality', with the connotation that this divine reality *reveals* itself. Johannine usage is based on this.[21]

In the subsequent opposition between truth and falsehood he detects Gnostic influences, and in his discussion of 8: 30–40 he asserts that:

the question regarding ἀλήθεια is oriented on the question regarding the ζωή [life] as the authentic being of the man who is concerned about his life, to whom this question is proposed because he is a creature. God's ἀλήθεια is thus God's reality, which alone is reality because it is life and gives life, whereas the seeming reality which belongs to the world is ψεῦδος [falsehood], because it is a reality contrived in opposition to God, and as such is futile and brings death. The promise of knowledge of the ἀλήθεια therefore is actually identical with the promise of ζωή.[22]

Dodd will have no truck with Gnosticism and appeals instead to Platonism. He concludes that ἀλήθεια 'means the eternal reality as revealed to men—either the reality itself or the revelation of it.'[23] This is nearly right: Dodd does not veer away from his sources, as Bultmann does, into speculation about man's authentic being. But

[21] p. 74 n. 2.   [22] p. 434.   [23] *Interpretation*, p. 177.

we gain a much greater insight into Johannine usage by turning to Jewish traditions, as has been conclusively and exhaustively demonstrated by Ignace de la Potterie in his two-volume study, *La Vérité dans Saint Jean*. The ethical dualism that Bultmann attributes to the influence of Gnosticism is already present in the Book of Wisdom, which restricts the understanding of truth to those who trust in God (3: 9), and de la Potterie[24] suggests that this truth is identical with God's plan for the wise (Wisd. 4: 17).

The idea of a divine plan comes out much more strongly in certain passages in the Dead Sea Scrolls, where the knowledge of the truth is seen to depend upon the revelation of divine mysteries:

I [thank thee, O Lord] for thou has enlightened me through thy truth. In thy marvellous mysteries, and in thy lovingkindness to a man [of vanity, and] in the greatness of Thy mercy to a perverse heart Thou hast granted me knowledge. (1QH 7: 26–7)[25]

'At Qumran', concludes de la Potterie, '[the term "truth"] comes to denote the ensemble of the religious ideas of the sons of the Covenant.'[26] The covenanters saw this truth as a privileged possession bestowed on them by God (1QM 13: 12), something not lightly to be divulged to others, recommending instead 'faithful concealment of the mysteries of truth' (1QS 4: 6), a well-known passage that pits the spirit of light against the spirit of darkness and falsehood and claims for the community the title of 'sons of truth in this world' (cf. 1QS 2: 24, 'the community of truth').

The truth of the Gospel may appear less *exclusive* than the jealously guarded secrets of the Qumran community. Jesus, after all, is 'the light of the world' and his message is available to all prepared to listen. But the esoteric side of Johannine Christianity should not be lost sight of either. 'Truth' is such a generous, open-sounding word that all commentators without exception have failed to recognize that like the alternative terms for revelation 'living water' and 'bread of life' it too belongs to what Herbert Leroy calls John's *Sondersprache* —his private language. 'He who is of the truth hears my voice' (18: 37). But what of those who are not of the truth, such as Pilate, to whom these words are spoken, and the Jews, who react with angry incomprehension when told that the truth will set them free (8: 32)? The only question in the Gospel that actually takes the *form*

[24] *Vérité*, p. 135.   [25] Vermes, *Dead Sea Scrolls*[3], p. 186.
[26] 'The Truth in St. John', p. 55.

of a riddle is Pilate's 'What is truth?' And, as we know, he would not stay for an answer.

2. THE REVELATION FORM

Of the five passages that I have selected for discussion under this heading the first four can be treated for practical purposes as two groups: (a) 3: 16–21, 31–6; (b) 7: 33–6; 8: 21–7. The fifth is what, following Dodd, I call the Epilogue: 12: 44–50.

(a) 3: 16–21, 31–6

For God so loved the world that he gave his only Son, that whoever believes in him should not perish but have eternal life. For God sent the Son into the world, not to condemn the world, but that the world might be saved through him. He who believes in him is not condemned: he who does not believe is condemned already, because he has not believed in the name of the only Son of God. And this is the judgement, that the light has come into the world, and men loved darkness rather than light, because their deeds were evil. For everyone who does evil hates the light, and does not come to the light, lest his deeds should be exposed. But he who does what is true comes to the light, that it may be clearly seen that his deeds have been wrought in God. (3: 16–21)

The first of these two remarkable passages is also the first of a series of extended reflections that crop up sporadically in the book of signs. Coming where it does it is particularly surprising to anyone operating simply on the story level of understanding. Nicodemus, Jesus' interlocutor in the early part of the chapter, has thus far shown little aptitude for profound theological discussion. From v. 12 on, of course, Jesus has begun to address his audience in the plural. But this hardly removes the difficulty.

What is there in the early part of the Gospel that could have prepared John's first readers for what confronts them in 3: 16–21? The immediate transition comes in the preceding verse: ἵνα πᾶς ὁ πιστεύων ἐν αὐτῷ (v.l. εἰς αὐτόν) ἔχῃ ζωὴν αἰώνιον—'so that everyone believing in him may have the life of the new age'. Life is a prominent theme in the Prologue, and looking back at this we may wish to equate the life of the new age with the ἐξουσία τέκνα θεοῦ γένεσθαι, the power, or right, to become children of God (1: 12). Coming as it does hard on the heels of a discussion on the conditions of being born from on high (understood by Nicodemus as rebirth, but by Jesus as birth, ἐκ τοῦ πνεύματος: 3: 5, 6, 8), we may surmise that the evangelist too has made this connection. This is strongly argued by Dodd,[27] who points out that ἐκ τοῦ πνεύματος γεννᾶσθαι echoes the expression ἐξ θεοῦ γεννᾶσθαι which is found in 1: 13. Yet reading chapter 3 with the Prologue in mind, one cannot but be struck by the differences. The idea that someone who believes in Jesus should enjoy the life of the new age may fit in well enough with 1: 12–13, but in the Prologue the world is inimical, threatening, possibly evil, and certainly incapable of recognizing the presence of the enlightening Logos. So what can be meant by the saying that 'God loved the world'? Those who have already read on will know of the evangelist's rather ambivalent attitude to the world; in this passage the tone is entirely positive; in v. 19 it is *mankind*, οἱ ἄνθρωποι, not the world, that rejects the light. Here is something new.

Jesus has already spoken of himself in this chapter as 'the Son of Man', so the detached tone of what follows is less startling. Yet only somebody already familar with the Gospel and its message will read what is said about the giving and sending of the only-begotten Son without surprise. In making Jesus allude to himself in the third person as 'the Son of Man', John is conforming to a convention common to all the Gospels. When Jesus speaks at a distance, so to speak, of God's salvific plan and of the part his Son is to play in it, we are left unpuzzled only because we unconsciously import into our reading of the Gospel a broad acquaintance with developed Christian doctrine. No doubt it makes little difference whether we see what follows after 3: 15 as spoken by Jesus or as interjected by the evangelist. For if the latter is putting his own thoughts into the mouth of Jesus he is not thereby investing them with any additional authority. The difficulty, if it is felt to be such, is even more acute in the second passage, 3: 31–6, for this, on the face of it, is uttered by John the Baptist. But what may cause some uneasiness to a modern reader posed no problem to the evangelist.

This passage has another feature which marks it off from anything that has gone before. Although the opposition of 'the Jews' to Jesus' teaching is foreshadowed in the temple episode in chapter 2, the opposition between believers and unbelievers is couched here in much more general terms. The man 'who does evil' (3: 20) is contrasted with the man 'who does the truth' (3: 21): it is much later in the gospel story that the typical evil-doer, who 'hates the

---

[27] *Interpretation*, p. 305.

light and does not come to the light' is replaced by 'the Jews' as the symbol of wilful human blindness. The great trial sequence does not begin until chapter 5; the evangelist does not choose to tell his readers the real reference of τὰ ἴδια, 'his own [country]' and οἱ ἴδιοι, 'his own [people]' until he uses the word again in the proverbial saying, 'a prophet has no honour in his own country (ἐν τῇ ἰδίᾳ πατρίδι)' (4: 44)—a saying which barely hints at the extraordinary explosion of hostility that erupts in the next chapter.

More important is the observation that in the descent of the Son of Man and the mission of the Son of God two originally distinct christological developments stand side by side. Some suggestions have already been offered about each of these; they are mentioned here simply to reinforce the observation that the teaching of 3: 16–21 presupposes a considerable amount of theological reflection. This passage is probably inserted at this point because it follows on so easily from the preceding verse: '... that whoever believes in him may have the life of the new age' (3: 15). Either that, or else 3: 15 is added expressly in order to smooth the way for this very comprehensive statement of Johannine theology. It may well be that the evangelist wished to place this as early as possible in his narrative.

We now turn to the *content* of 3: 16–21. Most of its motifs are discussed at length elsewhere in this book. The only serious difficulty comes in the last couple of verses (20–1). These seem to propound a doctrine of divine predestination, which is hard to reconcile with the plain statement, much more characteristic of Johannine theology, that precedes: 'He who believes in him is not condemned; he who does not believe is condemned already, because he has not believed in the name of the only Son of God' (3: 18). The problem posed by 3: 19–20 is real ('men loved darkness rather than the light because their deeds were evil'): if we were to read these verses in isolation, knowing nothing of the rest of the Gospel, we should undoubtedly conclude that what determines how any individual will receive the Son on his entry into the world is his or her previous moral behaviour. Such an interpretation, if correct, would rob John's very sophisticated concept of judgement of all its force.[28]

[28] Not all commentators recognize this difficulty. Those that do, extricate themselves in various ways. Here it is enough to remark that we should not expect of the evangelist the philosophical subtlety required to unravel a particularly knotty theological puzzle, one that was to engage the attention of Christian theologians many times in subsequent centuries. Augustine, Calvin, Molina, Jansenius are some of the names that spring to mind.

We must acknowledge, then, that this passage is both surprisingly placed and surprisingly rich in typically Johannine motifs. Many of these (not all) are also to be found in the Prologue, but they are articulated much more clearly here. (How many doctrinal propositions could be or have been derived from these half-dozen verses?) Yet we should be wrong to attempt to evade the Bultmannian challenge: does *what* is revealed here go beyond a *that*? For the evangelist, says Bultmann, 'judgement is nothing more or less than the fact that the "light", the Revealer, has come to the world'.[29] Perhaps we may go as far as to assert of the Revealer *that he has come into the world*, given or 'sent' by God. But if so we can go no further. We are back with Bultmann's naked 'that', and the elaborate ramifications of Christian theology are precariously suspended from the metaphors (gift, mission) employed to establish this single affirmation.

I now turn to the second of the two passages under consideration:

He who comes from above is above all; he who is of the earth belongs to the earth, and of the earth he speaks; he who comes from heaven is above all. He bears witness to what he has seen and heard, yet no one receives his testimony; he who receives his testimony sets his seal to this, that God is true. For he whom God has sent utters the words of God, for it is not by measure that he gives the Spirit; the Father loves the Son and has given all things into his hand. He who believes in the Son has eternal life; he who does not obey the Son shall not see life, but the wrath of God rests upon him. (3: 31–6)

This passage is so closely connected with the first that some commentators have reorganized the whole of chapter 3 in order to permit them to lie side by side.[30] We should not conclude too hastily, however, that all the problematic features of the chapter can be satisfactorily resolved simply by redistributing the material in what looks to us like a more logical sequence. Wayne Meeks has argued that the section concerning John the Baptist is given extra point and purpose by being bracketed between two revelatory discourses. 'Rearrangement hypotheses', he says, 'result from failure to perceive one of the most striking characteristics of the evangelist's literary procedure: the elucidation of themes by progressive repetition.'[31] And this observation is followed by some interesting reflections on 3: 31–6.

---

[29] p. 157.
[31] 'Man from Heaven', p. 150.

[30] Cf. Lindars, pp. 146–8.

The opening of the passage is clearly designed to establish links with the first part of the chapter (vv. 1–15). Emphasis was laid there on the need to be born from above in order to be able to enter the kingdom of God. But now 'the one coming from above' (ὁ ἄνωθεν ἐρχόμενος) is Jesus himself—nobody else. Two themes that were originally distinct, new birth and the heavenly man, have been welded together; and the term ἄνωθεν, sloughing off its riddle, now means, quite unambiguously, 'from above'. Building upon the proverbial saying in 3: 12,[32] the evangelist has now introduced a new but quite characteristic distinction: from v. 31 it appears that Jesus' heavenly origin precludes him from saying anything at all about 'things of earth' (τὰ ἐπίγεια): it is only ὁ ὢν ἐκ τῆς γῆς (a purely abstract earthly being, introduced here simply to furnish a contrast with ὁ ἄνωθεν ἐρχόμενος) who speaks ἐκ τῆς γῆς.

In the next verse (32) the term μαρτυρεῖν, previously associated with John the Baptist, is taken over from 3: 11, where it is used for the first time in a properly juristic sense to mean testifying to something which one knows from personal experience. Not surprisingly, Bultmann finds confirmation in this text for his own views on revelation: 'Everything remains shrouded in mystery; for the word of God which he speaks is nothing more nor less than the witness *that* he is the Revealer, *that* he speaks God's word!'[33] And indeed if we ask just what it is that 'the one coming from above' can reveal about 'what he has seen and heard' it is impossible to add to what has already been said about Jesus' entry into the world, his mission and its divisive effect.

In the opening of this passage, then, the evangelist is clearly reflecting and commenting upon 3: 1–21, tightening links in what was originally a rather loose, because adventitious, sequence of ideas. What follows next, concerning the Spirit, looks more like a correction than a comment, redirecting the reader's thinking on the Spirit along more favoured and familiar lines than those suggested in the beginning of the chapter. Of the Spirit's two roles, in creation and in revelation, the evangelist is much more interested in the latter. In the conversation with Nicodemus the theme was rebirth; here it is the mission of the Son.

The ending comes as something of a shock: 'He who believes in

---

[32] For abundant parallels see Meeks, ibid., p. 148 and nn. 36 f.
[33] pp. 160–1.

the Son has eternal life; he who does not obey the Son shall not see life, but the wrath of God rests upon him' (3: 36). The present possession of life is still assured to the believer, and in this context disobedience may be interpreted as the withholding of belief; but the wrath of God smacks of the old, traditional, futuristic eschatology. Jürgen Becker[34] is probably right to see 3: 35 f. as an old community saying (*Gemeindespruch*) that allows a glimpse into an early stage of Johannine theology; he thinks that it was *taken over* by the ecclesiastical redactor, but it is at least conceivable that the evangelist was his own redactor at this point. As Bultmann recognizes, the futuristic language does not affect the general thrust of the whole passage, in which 'the full weight of the eschatological event is found in Jesus' coming'.[35]

A last point of interest in this passage is its unobtrusive combination of two motifs that have different origins and are generally found apart. These are first the ascent/descent motif associated with the Son of Man and secondly the mission motif associated with the Son of God. There could be no clearer indication of the redactional character of this passage than its readiness to hold these two motifs together and the ease with which it does so.

How, to conclude, do these two passages fit into the whole context? In spite of many close and obviously intended resemblances they function very differently. The first is a free-floating prophetic saying loosely attached to what precedes. Its purpose is to establish or confirm the community's sense of privilege in being the chosen recipients of revelation: this revelation is essentially divisive and they are on the right side of the divide. Nowhere in the Gospel does John's language get so close to the bigoted sectarianism of *1 Enoch*, *The Psalms of Solomon*, or the War Scroll. There is no longer any need to specify the community's adversaries: anyone who does not belong is a villain, ὁ φαῦλα πράσσων; anyone who does belong is a hero, ὁ ποιῶν τὴν ἀλήθειαν. Whatever is meant by 'doing the truth', it is clear that 'the truth' belongs to the members of the community and to them alone.

The second passage is quite different, the work not of a prophet but of a writer; it is secondary and reflexive. Its purpose is to tie up some loose ends, which it does subtly and effectively, but without the succinct urgency that distinguishes the earlier passage.

---

[34] pp. 157–8.   [35] p. 167.

(b) 7: 33–6; 8: 21–7

Jesus then said, 'I shall be with you a little longer, and then I go to him who sent me; you will seek me and you will not find me; where I am you cannot come.' The Jews said to one another, 'Where does this man intend to go that we shall not find him? Does he intend to go to the Diaspora among the Greeks and teach the Greeks? What does he mean by saying, "you will seek me and you will not find me", and, "Where I am you cannot come"?' (7: 33–6)

Again he said to them, 'I go away, and you will seek me and die in your sin; where I am going, you cannot come.' Then said the Jews, 'Will he kill himself, since he says "Where I am going, you cannot come"?' He said to them, 'You are from below, I am from above; you are of this world, I am not of this world. I told you that you would die in your sins, for you will die in your sins unless you believe that I am he.' They said to him, 'Who are you?' Jesus said to them, 'Even what I have told you from the beginning. I have much to say about you and much to judge; but he who sent me is true, and I declare to the world what I have heard from him.' They did not understand that he spoke to them of the Father. (8: 21–7)

So close are the parallels between these two passages that it is best to treat them together. I have argued (Excursus III) that the first is out of place in its present context, where it interrupts the story of the attempted arrest of Jesus by the temple police (7: 32, 45–52). Although these are the people to whom Jesus appears to address the words, 'where I am going you cannot come' (7: 34), it is 'the Jews' who question this assertion, as they do in 8: 22. Moreover, when Jesus alludes to it in the introduction to the farewell discourse (13: 33), he says that it was spoken to 'the Jews'. The temple police do not reappear until 7: 45.[36]

One might expect an utterance of such high christological import to be greeted with the same indignant fury that is aroused by the claims to divine status I discussed in Chapter 4 (5: 17–18; 8: 58–9; 10: 34–6). It is not. When Jesus states, a little further on, 'you will die in your sins unless you believe that I am [he], ὅτι ἐγώ εἰμι' (8: 24) he provokes perplexity rather than hostility. Bultmann concludes

---

[36] They play no further part in this little story. Suggesting as it does that the community has virtually abandoned hope of making further converts from within the synagogue and is on the point of turning to 'the Greeks', the episode was presumably inserted during the last stages of the composition of the Gospel. The saying has been used in support of the view that the Gospel as a whole was written with a Gentile audience in mind. Such an argument will only work if one clings to the mistaken assumption of a single edition of the Gospel, put together in a relatively short time.

that this cannot be a deliberate use of the divine name; otherwise the
Jews would have reacted very differently.[37] He may be right, but I
am inclined to think that the true explanation lies further back. The
form-critical background of this saying is the development of the
Johannine *Sondersprache*, of which ὑπάγειν ('depart') is an important
item. By the time that the motif of Jesus' departure was being
developed the ἐγώ εἰμι may have already been added to an increasing store of such fruitfully ambiguous terms. As employed in 8: 24,
28, the ἐγώ εἰμι may have been intended to resume and encapsulate
the other 'I am' sayings, themselves, as I have argued earlier
(Chapter 5), especially concise summaries of the gospel message.[38]

Why was the passage concerning Jesus' mysterious departure
inserted in its present context in chapter 7? Because origin and
destiny are conceptual correlatives. The question, 'Where do you
come from?' is naturally followed by 'Where are you going?' The two
ideas are neatly joined in 8: 14: 'I know whence I have come and
where I am going (ποῦ ὑπάγω); but you do not know whence I come
and where I am going.' (In 3: 8 the motif is associated with those
born of the spirit and has not yet been particularized.) But the
question of origin probably arose in the first place, as was suggested
in Chapter 8, out of speculation concerning the Messiah. The
question of destiny presupposes a christological development of an
altogether different order. We can see from the conclusion of the
second passage that the title with which it is naturally associated is
not 'Messiah' but 'Son of God', though by an additional modulation,
as the sequel shows, it can also be connected with 'Son of Man'. Even
Bultmann confesses himself baffled by the link passage, 8: 25–7. But
that there *is* a connection, and a deliberate one, seems certain:
'When you have lifted up the Son of man, then you will know that I
am [he], ὅτι ἐγώ εἰμι' (8: 28). This is Jesus' answer to the question,
'Who are you?' (8: 25), and it shows, as Bultmann says, 'that
everything that he has claimed for himself is gathered up in the title
"Son of Man"'.[39]

Why should this be so? The answer to this question is interesting,
for it discloses the relationship between the wisdom christology of

---

[37] p. 349 n. 3. Barrett agrees: 'It is simply intolerable that Jesus should be made to
say, "I am God, the Supreme God of the Old Testament, and being God I do as I am
told"' ('Christocentric or Theocentric?', p. 12). Yet perhaps the Johannine prophet,
speaking in Jesus' name, was effectively asserting his identity with Yahweh, the 'near'
God of Israel.   [38] Cf. Becker, p. 208.   [39] p. 349.

the Prologue and that of the remainder of the Gospel, otherwise remarkably free of direct allusions to the wisdom tradition.

'You will seek me and you will not find me; where I am [then] you cannot come' (7: 34, 36; 8: 22; 13: 33). As in the Prologue, the wisdom motif implied in this saying belongs to the old tradition of remote, or inaccessible wisdom. Indeed it is at the heart of this tradition. Wisdom addresses the scoffers: 'They will call upon me, but I will not answer; they will seek me diligently but will not find me' (Prov. 1: 28). The same tradition is reflected in the farewell discourse, where, as we have seen, the ambiguity of the term ὑπάγειν is exploited to rather different effect. But it stems, I believe, from the same fundamental insight that provides the driving-force of the Prologue: the earthly career of Jesus exemplifies and incarnates the fate of divine wisdom—to descend to earth and be rejected by men. The Prologue is concerned with the *entry* of Wisdom—the Logos —into the world of men; the present saying is concerned with her—or his—*departure*, back into the remote and inaccessible region from which she sprang. The first occurrence of the saying makes this plain: it is preceded by the explicit statement, 'I shall be with you a little longer, and then I go to him who sent me: ὑπάγω πρὸς τὸν πέμψαντά με' (7: 33). Death is now envisaged as *a return from a mission*.

The closest conceptual parallel to the Johannine schema is to be found in 1 *Enoch* 42, where Wisdom is said to have left heaven seeking for a home. According to Enoch she found no home, so she 'returned to her place and took her seat in the midst of the angels'. No such journey is recorded in the Book of Proverbs, which contents itself with asserting (though not unequivocally) the inaccessibility of wisdom. In quoting Proverbs, John associates the remoteness and inaccessibility of wisdom with the departure theme that reached him by another route. Although the wording is different here (there is no hint of the Logos), the conceptual background is the same.

At what point the wisdom speculation was married to the mission and agency theology embedded in the phrase 'to him who sent me' is impossible to say. The conjunction may seem unsurprising, but it cannot have been made until the evangelist's thinking concerning Jesus' mission had moved well outside the sphere of its inception in the simple ideas of prophecy and agency. Alternatively we may think that it was the picture of divine wisdom returning to her heavenly home that allowed the Johannine prophet to think of Jesus' mission as something qualitatively different from that of the prophets who had come to Israel as heavenly envoys, bearing but not embodying a message from on high. Certainly the above and below language employed in the second passage (8: 23) to explain and justify Jesus' account of his departure shows that by the time these revelatory discourses had become part of the special Johannine tradition there was already an interplay between two immensely powerful ideas whose origins probably lay far apart.

In spite of this easy conjunction the vocabulary of departure is nowhere confused with that of ascent. The two ideas seem so close as to be virtually indistinguishable, but the evidence suggests that they originated in different conceptual spheres. The connecting link in this case is explicit: it is furnished by the above/below contrast that indicates both origin and essence. In 8: 21–7 this paves the way for the second prophecy of the exaltation of the Son of Man. This, exceptionally, leads on to a statement concerning Jesus' mission, a further indication that this passage, like most of those singled out for discussion in this chapter, represents the final stage of the evangelist's theological reflection, when all the various strands of his thinking have been woven together:

When you have lifted up the Son of man, then you will know that I am [he], and that I do nothing on my own authority, but speak thus as my Father taught me. And he who sent me is with me; he has not left me alone, for I always do what is pleasing to him. (8: 28 f.)

What do these passages contribute to the *content* of the revelatory message? An explicit allusion to Jesus' death? We know by this time of the Jews' determination to track him down and kill him (ch. 5). His disciples received a guarded intimation of this at Cana, in the as yet mysterious reference to his hour (2: 4); in Jerusalem there was another hint, but not one that could be understood at the time (2: 19). Jesus' promise to give his flesh for the life of the world (6: 51) is similarly cryptic, and completely misconstrued. Not even in the forecast concerning the Son of Man that follows the discussion with Nicodemus is there any direct reference to the passion; the full significance of ὑψοῦν is still obscure (and will not be fully clarified until 12: 23–5). In 8: 28 the switch to the active voice, with 'the Jews' as subject (ὅταν ὑψώσητε), is puzzling. Must we infer that the verb ὑψοῦν has come to connote crucifixion? If not, and it is intended to carry its ordinary meaning, 'to exalt', then the Jews are the active agents of Jesus' exaltation. This is difficult, but may well be within the range of Johannine irony. In any case there is certainly an allusion to Jesus' return to heaven.

As revelatory statements the two passages are more loosely constructed than those in chapter 3; none the less they may be said to have injected into Jesus' teaching the new theme of the completion of his mission and his return to the one who sent him. Thus the pattern of the Prologue, where the Logos begins at the side of God and ends nestling in his embrace, is now echoed in the message Jesus passes on to the world: his origin and destiny, beyond the comprehension of those who do not accept him, are what he has to reveal to those who do. Is this 'what the Father taught him' (8: 28)? No doubt it is part of the lesson, but with the addition of an extra nuance—the unity of Father and Son, who speaks *only* what he has heard and is never abandoned by 'the one who sent him'. (This theme, taken over from passages such as 4: 34; 8: 18, 28, is more strongly emphasized in 12: 44–5, a passage yet to be discussed.) Yet we cannot rid ourselves of the question that has haunted us throughout this chapter: what is the real content of the mysteries that Jesus has learned from God?

(c) Epilogue (12: 44–50)

And Jesus cried out and said, 'He who believes in me, believes not in me but in him who sent me. And he who sees me sees him who sent me. I have come as light into the world, that whoever believes in me may not remain in darkness. If anyone hears my sayings and does not keep them, I do not judge him; for I did not come to judge the world but to save the world. He who rejects me and does not receive my sayings has a judge; the word that I have spoken will be his judge on the last day. For I have not spoken on my own authority; the Father who sent me has himself given me commandment what to say and what to speak. And I know that his commandment is eternal life. What I say, therefore, I say as the Father has bidden me.' (12: 44–50)

Misled by his assumption that the Fourth Gospel was composed as a single unified work that could in principle be pieced together again in the proper order, Bultmann thought it necessary to remove the concluding paragraph of the book of signs from its present place. For once it is Dodd who shows the greater insight: this is an epilogue in the proper sense, rounding off and summing up the preceding revelation.

In spite of the striking introduction, in which Jesus proclaims or shouts (κράζειν), it is a carefully constructed piece, belonging, like the passages discussed in the preceding section, to the last stage of the composition of the Gospel. It is set out here in such a way as to highlight the connections.

44b   Ὁ πιστεύων εἰς ἐμὲ
　　　　οὐ πιστεύει εἰς ἐμὲ
　　　　　　ἀλλὰ εἰς τὸν πέμψαντά με.

45　　καὶ ὁ θεωρῶν ἐμὲ
　　　　θεωρεῖ
　　　　　　τὸν πέμψαντά με.

46a　ἐγὼ φῶς εἰς τὸν κόσμον ἐλήλυθα,
　b　　ἵνα πᾶς ὁ πιστεύων εἰς ἐμὲ ἐν τῇ σκοτίᾳ μὴ μείνῃ.

47a　　　καὶ ἐάν τίς μου ἀκούσῃ τῶν ῥημάτων καὶ μὴ φυλάξῃ,
　　　　　ἐγὼ οὐ κρίνω αὐτόν,

　b　οὐ γὰρ ἦλθον
　　　　ἵνα κρίνω τὸν κόσμον
　　　　ἀλλ' ἵνα σώσω τὸν κόσμον.

48a　ὁ ἀθετῶν ἐμὲ καὶ μὴ λαμβάνων τὰ ῥήματά μου
　　　　　ἔχει τὸν κρίνοντα αὐτόν·

　b　　ὁ λόγος ὃν ἐλάλησα ἐκεῖνος κρινεῖ αὐτὸν ἐν τῇ ἐσχάτῃ ἡμέρᾳ·

49a　ὅτι ἐγὼ ἐξ ἐμαυτοῦ οὐκ ἐλάλησα,
　b　　ἀλλ' ὁ πέμψας με πατὴρ αὐτός μοι ἐντολὴν δέδωκεν
　　　　　τί εἴπω καὶ τί λαλήσω.

50a　καὶ οἶδα ὅτι ἡ ἐντολὴ αὐτοῦ ζωὴ αἰώνιός ἐστιν.
　b　　　ἃ οὖν ἐγὼ λαλῶ
　　　　καθὼς εἴρηκέν μοι ὁ πατήρ,
　　　　οὕτως λαλῶ.[40]

---

[40] A full literary analysis of the passage cannot be attempted here. It is constituted of two chiastically structured sections, 44b–48a and 49–50, with an intervening line, 48b, which points backwards to the first section (κρινεῖ) and forwards to the second (ὁ λόγος ὃν ἐλάλησα). The passage begins and ends with the mission/agency motif. This is carried in the first place by the term ὁ πέμψας με (44b, 45), one of the two names for God found in John. When this is picked up in 49b it is accompanied by the second name, πατήρ, which is repeated (alone) in the concluding line, 50b. Both the key words, κρίνειν and λαλεῖν, occur in the intervening line, 48b. Internal resonances are set up by the terms πιστεύειν (44b, 46b), κόσμος (46a, 47b), ῥήματα (47a, 48a), and ἐντολή (49b, 50a). In my view, detailed literary analyses of this kind have only a limited value, since the most they can prove is that the passage in question *can* be read as a tightly structured whole. It is idle to pretend that this method is more objective than any other. None the less it does serve to direct attention to certain features of the text which might otherwise be disregarded.

There is really no room for yet another appearance of Jesus before an unnamed audience. In the *story* of the Gospel he had already gone into hiding (ἐκρύβη, 12: 36), not to be seen again in public before the onset of the passion. The first act of the great trial sequence is over; we are now in the interval, behind the scenes. The evangelist divides his epilogue, as Dodd sees, into two parts. The first (12: 37–43) comments ruefully on the blindness of Israel in a verse from Isaiah (6: 10) drawn from the common stock of the gospel tradition. The second summarizes the *content* of what has been revealed so far. Dodd ingeniously suggests[41] that 'the words Ἰησοῦς δὲ ἔκραξεν do not mean that on a particular occasion Jesus spoke the words following. They mean rather, "This is the content of the κήρυγμα."' Whether or not Dodd is right about this, they are certainly intended (as in 7: 37) to draw the reader's attention to the particular importance of what follows.[42]

Peder Borgen has argued[43] that the passage quotes and adapts a traditional Jesus-saying found in various forms in all four Gospels (Matt. 10: 40; Mark 9: 37; Luke 9: 48; 10: 16; John 5: 23; 8: 19; 13: 20; 14: 7, 9; 15: 23). Those with the firmest place in the gospel tradition, as Borgen points out, involve a chain of two agencies. Single agency sayings, however, are well attested in Judaism and are preferred by John. (John 13: 20, closer to the Synoptic tradition, is an exception.)[44]

I have no wish to contest Borgen's findings. But we must also recognize that the most significant of the traditions from which this passage is compiled come from within the Gospel's own fund of revelation sayings. Borgen points out the formal resemblance between 12: 45 and Synoptic sayings such as Matthew 10: 40: 'he who receives me receives him who sent me' (cf. John 13: 20).[45] But John uses the term θεωρεῖν, 'see', whose closest conceptual parallel, apart from 14: 9 (ὁρᾶν) is in 8: 19 (εἰδέναι, 'know'). The obvious reason for the use of 'see' here, however, is the desire to link this

---

[41] *Interpretation*, p. 382.

[42] J.-A. Bühner, taking v. 36 and v. 44 together, calls this a 'cry out of hiddenness' (*Schrei aus dem Verborgenen*) ('Denkstrukturen', p. 230).

[43] 'The Use of Tradition'.

[44] In fact 13: 16–20, with its unusual vocabulary (ἀπόστολος etc.) draws upon synoptic or synoptic-type traditions more extensively and more obviously than 12: 44–50.

[45] The converse saying, in 12: 48, is much closer to Luke 10: 16, with which, as Brown points out, it shares the verb ἀθετεῖν ('reject'), not found elsewhere in John.

verse up with the blindness motif that precedes and the light motif that follows. (No such link-up was felt to be necessary to the case of 8: 19, although the light saying of 8: 12 is not very far away.) In the present context the light motif has gathered an extra resonance from its proximity to the brilliant sequence of the healing of the blind man in chapter 9. This concludes with a judgement saying (9: 39); and since we were told that the miracle took place at the pool of Siloam ('which means Sent', 9: 7) the opening of the epilogue looks like a compressed reminder of that whole episode, with which it shares the themes of faith, mission, sight, light, darkness, and judgement.

The passage echoes many earlier revelation sayings also, especially those in chapter 3: 'for I did not come to judge the world but to save the world' (cf. 3: 17).[46] In the farewell discourse that follows, 'the world' replaces 'the Jews' as the general term for Jesus' adversaries. Here, though, the connotations are precisely those of 3: 16–21 —Jesus has come into the world in order to save it. As in 3: 31–6 there is a strong hint of futuristic eschatology: 'He who rejects me and does not receive my sayings has a judge; the word that I have spoken will be his judge on the last day' (12: 48). Bultmann naturally assigns this saying to the ecclesiastical redactor, but one may surmise that the author of the Epilogue (who may well be the Johannine prophet himself) is more interested in completeness than consistency.

The main motif of the latter half of the passage is another familiar theme, Jesus' dependence on the Father. This harks back to the opening; for to say that 'He who believes in me believes not in me but in him who sent me' is to imply that 'What I say I say as the Father has bidden me.' The sender and the Father, the two names for God that lie at the heart of Jesus' revelation, neatly bracket the whole passage.

'The fact that 12: 46–8 is very much like 3: 16–19,' comments Brown, 'makes it quite plausible that, in part, 12: 44–50 is a variant of material found elsewhere in John but preserved by a different disciple.'[47] Of course one cannot altogether discount this possibility; but in view of its position, the craft with which it is composed, and the deliberate allusion to all the salient themes of revelation, Dodd's

---

[46] Brown (pp. 147, 490) stresses how closely 12: 46–8 resembles 3: 16–19. The ἐλήλυθα of 12: 46 is the first-person equivalent of a mission-saying; it is a hair's breadth away, as Bühner has shown (*Gesandte*, pp. 138–52), from an 'I am' saying (in this case from 8: 12).   [47] p. 490.

view is to be preferred; the piece was designed as a coping-stone to crown all that has gone before—and perhaps with just a glimpse of what lies ahead.

CONCLUSION

The passages analysed above are the ones singled out by the evangelist himself as representative of his views. To see this there is no need to go to the lengths of excluding all but the handful of passages ascribed by Bultmann to the hand of the evangelist or to his hypothetical revelation source. Virtually all substantial works of literature contain lines or verses to which the discerning critic can point as especially instructive or illuminating. This selection represents an attempt to follow the evangelist's own directions. The conclusion of chapter 12 is particularly significant, constituting as it does a coda to the whole book of signs. Certainly it would be possible to isolate each of the motifs found in these verses and to pursue them through the Gospel. The first part of this chapter is an admittedly sketchy attempt in this direction. But we should then still be left with the question, why these motifs and why not others? This is surely the first question that must be answered, and it is one that partly justifies Bultmann's apparently arbitrary conclusions.

What we have in these passages is a series of vignettes that encapsulate a view of *the gospel as revelation*. They say almost nothing of the content of this revelation; it is to be delivered by a divine envoy, charged with the task of carrying it to the world, the object of God's salvific love. The effect of this revelation will be dramatically divisive. Those who reject it *ipso facto* pronounce judgement upon themselves. Those who accept it are granted a new life—the life of the new age. Having fulfilled his mission, the purpose of his entry into the world, the Son will return to the Father who sent him.

If this is not gnosis it is remarkably close. Where the Fourth Gospel diverges from Gnosticism is in its insistence upon the salvific will of God. There is only one God and only one world, the object of his love. The message is not inconsistent with Christian belief; Paul's teaching on the cross, for example. But it is not tied to this, or only by the slightest and slenderest of threads. In fact there is no mention of the cross in any of these passages: death is conceived as departure (ὑπάγειν), exaltation (ὑψοῦν), or ascent (ἀναβαίνειν). Such descriptions as the Gospel contains of what may be thought of loosely as historical episodes have no place in these summaries. It is as if the gospel story has been filtered through a fine mesh; all that is left is a lingering essence of revelatory discourse, exuding nothing more tangible than a persistent and quite distinctive aroma.

Of the names of Jesus only that of Son (of God) could be deduced with any assurance. There is no trace of 'Messiah'; 'Son of Man' occurs in one passage (8: 28) but not in the epilogue. This is consistent with the main lines of the Gospel narrative and consequently could be superimposed upon this without having to be stretched or trimmed, but by no amount of ingenuity could the Gospel story be derived from the blueprint. To appreciate how easily the narrative fits upon any of these sketches one would have to know it well already.

This knowledge is presupposed, of course, in the reader of the Gospel. It is to ensure that the reader connects the revelatory schema with the history that the evangelist punctuates his narrative with a number of examples of it, modifying these slightly to suit the context. Further to guard against misunderstanding he also inserts at intervals certain helpful hints and pointers (e.g. 2: 22; 7: 39). Nevertheless there are some surprising omissions from the revelatory schema: the name of Jesus, the title Messiah, the cross and the passion—even the resurrection.

From this perspective the attraction of Bultmann's general solution to the puzzles of the Gospel is manifest. For him the revelatory schema is not something the evangelist invented for himself: he found it in his source. This accounts for all the gaps; it is not that he actually cut anything out, since themes and motifs whose omission would otherwise be almost impossible to explain were not present in the first place. My own solution is that the various elements of the schema emerged after prolonged and sometimes painful reflection in the course of a struggle with the establishment party in the synagogue. Traces of this struggle remain in the Gospel text; the witness motif, for example, mentioned only once in a purely revelatory passage (3: 32), was forged in the course of controversies with the Pharisees. Other elements, e.g. the positive use of the light motif, are more probably the fruit of the prophetic activity of the evangelist and his community.

Though this solution is not as neat as Bultmann's, it is less arbitrary, more in accord with the admittedly scanty evidence furnished by the Gospel itself. And at the same time it confronts squarely the problems that Bultmann, alone of the commentators on the Gospel, refuses to shirk.

Why then are the cross and resurrection omitted from these summaries? Faithful to the tradition, the evangelist concludes his narrative much on the same lines as his predecessors, but distils from the two sets of stories lessons of immediate relevance to his community. Cross and resurrection have a double significance for John. On the first level of understanding they signify, together, Jesus' passage from this world to the world above—his return to the Father who sent him. When thinking of the cross in this connection the evangelist uses the term ὑψοῦν; the equivalent term for resurrection is ἀναβαίνειν; ὑπάγειν they share: it straddles the divide between the two halves of the Gospel, but its full meaning does not emerge until the extended reflection of the farewell discourse draws out the implications of Jesus' physical absence for the life of the community. Though not explicitly mentioned in the final summary (12: 44–50), the departure motif certainly belongs to the revelatory schema and does not require to be underlined.

For John the sentence passed on Jesus is above all the final act in the long, sad story of Jesus' rejection by his own people, the Jews. The rejection is experienced in its own way by the Christian community also. Far more than a personal rebuff, it implies a turning away from the light, a culpable blindness for which the Gospel's word is κρίσις, the self-condemnation of those who prefer darkness to light. In a situation where the true believers know themselves to be surrounded by an alien and uncomprehending world the pain of the cross is above all the pain of being repulsed and eventually expelled by one's own people. The trial of Jesus ended in crucifixion, but this was only the culmination of a judgement that began as soon as Jesus started to proclaim his message. It is now being lived out by his disciples.

The spiritual lesson of the resurrection, spelled out in the Lazarus story, is summed up in the term ζωὴ αἰώνιος, the life of the new age, John's version of the preaching of the kingdom. This has been discussed at some length in Chapter 6 and it is unnecessary to say more here. What is picked out by the evangelist for his revelatory schema is not the *event* of resurrection but its enduring significance in the experience of the community.

It may fairly be said, then, that despite appearances the Johannine revelatory schema does include all the basic elements of the Christian kerygma. All Christian preachers instinctively adapt these to the situation of those whom they are addressing. It should occasion no surprise to find John the Evangelist doing the same.

This answer, however, is far from solving all the difficulties. Even if the revelatory schema was not simply taken over from a Gnostic source, as Bultmann maintained, but somehow distilled from the Christian kerygma, it remains curiously devoid of any factual content, utterly unlike, in this respect, the so-called kerygmatic discourses found in the first half of the Book of Acts. We have encountered this difficulty at every stage. 'He who comes from above', we are told, 'bears witness to what he has seen and heard' (3: 31 f.) He declares to the world what he has heard from the one who sent him (8: 26), who has himself instructed him what to say (12: 49). This repeated insistence upon Jesus' revelatory role is like a promise continually reiterated but never fulfilled. Meeks speaks in this context, quite justifiably, of an empty 'revelation form'.[48]

The challenge that has haunted the whole of this chapter must now be tackled head-on. What is revealed in the Fourth Gospel apart from the mere fact of revelation?

We may start by dismissing two untenable answers. The first is the naïve assumption that whatever is stated in propositional form must be taken as literally true, and therefore a proper object of theological reflection and speculation. This will not work, if only because many of the statements in the Gospel are formally contradictory ('My Father who sent me': 'I and the Father are one') and therefore have to be *interpreted* before they are properly understood. And as soon as one abandons a literal understanding one is confronted by the kind of disagreement that muddies up the clear waters of revelation and effectively disables the whole concept.

The second answer is that of Oscar Cullmann. In his book *Salvation in History* he argues that 'the important thing for the [fourth] evangelist is that God's self-communication, its saving activity, has its mid-point in the historical life of the man Jesus of Nazareth ... All revelation, all God's acting, is disclosed from this mid-point.'[49] But John is not interested in salvation-history; it might be true to say that he sees 'the historical life of the man Jesus' (whom

---

[48] 'Man from Heaven', p. 150.   [49] p. 270.

he identifies as the Logos) as the culmination of God's revelation to mankind, but this is a very partial summary of what he is saying, and the concept of a mid-point is Cullmann's, not John's.

Both of these answers labour under the disadvantage of placing the locus of revelation outside the Gospel itself, treating this as a source of sacred truths or even, at worst, as a kind of pond in which to fish for proof-texts. Bultmann's answer, remaining well within the Gospel, is very different: in fact it suffers from the opposite defect, a refined fastidiousness which cuts out much that is integral to the Gospel narrative under the pretext of demythologization.

In an attempt to avoid the dilemma of Bultmann's 'empty that' Gail O'Day has argued that instead of searching for the content of revelation we should rather concern ourselves with its mode: the 'how' rather than the 'what'. She rightly sees that the Bultmannian dichotomy between the bare fact of Jesus as revealer and the content of his revelation, 'allows almost no middle ground, middle ground that should be occupied by the Fourth Gospel text'.[50] Accordingly, she proposes to 'approach the question of revelation by examining the interrelationship of narrative mode and theological claim in the Fourth Gospel';[51] for 'without full attention to the revelatory dynamic of the Fourth Gospel Text,' as she points out, 'we are not in the world of the Fourth Gospel'.[52]

In principle this project is a good one, but it is badly executed because O'Day has failed to ask the first, obvious question: 'What is a Gospel?'[53] The most cogent criticism of Bultmann's position comes,

---

[50] *Revelation*, p. 44.   [51] Ibid., p. 2.   [52] Ibid., p. 45.

[53] Such a question might have led her to the true solution to the problem, but unfortunately she is side-tracked into an examination of the nature of irony. This she regards as the literary form which has provided John 'with the appropriate vehicle for his theology of revelation' (p. 3). In many places, such as in her discussion of the two levels of meaning in irony, her enquiry runs parallel to my own analysis of the Gospel genre. But irony is not a genre or literary form but a trope or technique. It provides at best a partial answer to the question she sets out to solve. Moreover, her interesting discussion of irony fails to issue in a definition and she does not make it quite clear how the key fits. My impression is that it wobbles in the lock. Another writer to make use of the same concept, Paul D. Duke (*Irony*), fares no better. Irony, as Terence Cave has shown (*Recognitions* (Oxford, 1988)), is a relative latecomer in the history of European poetics, dominated for so long by the more flexible and conceptually more powerful model of recognition. This concept, hitherto ignored in Johannine scholarship, plays a significant role in the architecture of the Gospel. The high point of the Prologue is the recognition of the identity of the Logos, God's plan for the world, with the person of Christ, just as the high point of the concluding paragraph is a cry of faith following upon a belated recognition. The second half of ch. 1 consists of a series of

[*cont. on p. 550*]

somewhat surprisingly, from his pupil Ernst Käsemann, who speaks of 'the inclusion of both the history of Jesus and that of the Christian kerygma under the comprehensive concept "Gospel"' and points out that John deliberately chose to couch his message in this particular form. 'It seems to me,' he concludes, 'that if one has absolutely no interest in the historical Jesus, then one does not write a Gospel, but, on the contrary, finds the Gospel form inadequate.'[54]

Käsemann's position is one-sided too, of course. John has no interest in the historical Jesus as such. In Browning's terminology, he is writing about stars, not about points. But it is true that he has chosen to write a Gospel rather than letters or a collection of sayings, and it is instructive to reflect what his Gospel would look like if transferred to another medium, a homily, say, like the Letter to the Hebrews, or a revelatory discourse of the kind found quite frequently in the Gnostic texts from Nag Hammadi (e.g. the Trimorphic Protennoia or the Thunder, Perfect Mind), and in the *Odes of Solomon*.

There is in fact much in the *Odes*, both in style and in content, to remind us of the Fourth Gospel: the dualism, including the symbolism of light and darkness and the opposition of life and death, the sense of persecution and rejection, the unity of the congregation of the saved, who owe their salvation to the intercession of 'the Son of God'. The symbolism is richer and the language more extravagant, as is the case throughout the *Odes*, but it would be easy to prune away the more extreme conceits to leave something with an even closer resemblance to one of the Johannine discourses. Certain of these, especially the allegories of the good shepherd and the vine, are already quite close to some of the *Odes*. But—and this is the point—inserted into a narrative that tells of the life of Jesus on earth, they are part of a story; unlike the *Odes* they are not spoken from on high by a Christ already enthroned by the side of God; they repeatedly affirm, at least implicitly, the identity of the earthly Jesus and the Risen Lord.

confessions, in a section I have labelled ἀναγνώρισις, of Jesus' messianic status, culminating in Nathanael's vision. There follows a series of recognitions—the Samaritan woman, Peter, the blind man, Martha, mostly focused upon a particular title: Saviour, Holy One, Messiah, Son of God, Son of Man. We should perhaps add to this list Pilate's plea for recognition, in a dramatic gesture: 'Behold the Man.' Finally, whilst all these take place, so to speak, on stage, the audience (readers) are experiencing a recognition of their own. This too Cave has shown to be an application of the Aristotelian model.

[54] 'Blind Alleys', p. 41.

In the Letter to the Hebrews, to take our other example, this identity *is* affirmed. What is more, the earthly Jesus is portrayed as a man beset by human weakness, uttering the kind of prayer that the Johannine Jesus explicitly renounced: 'In the days of his flesh, Jesus offered up prayers and supplications with loud cries and tears, to him who was able to save him from death' (Heb. 5: 7; contrast John 12: 27). Hebrews shares with the Fourth Gospel a conviction of the overriding importance of faith in the Christian life, though admittedly it has rather a different conception of the nature of faith. It would not be difficult to extract the lessons of John 4 and 6 from the narratives in which they are embedded and to combine them in a midrash on the story of Exodus. The result would resemble the paraenetic passage in Hebrews 3–4. Then the ideas of the revelation discourses could be woven together into a meditative reflection of the kind found in the central section of Hebrews. Even as it is the Gospel frequently hints at the passion and resurrection before it embarks upon a full account of these in the last few chapters. Such a document could include virtually all that Bultmann says about the Fourth Gospel in the chapters he devotes to it in his *Theology of the New Testament*. But there would be no healing miracles or other signs, no altercations with the Jews, no conversations with the disciples.

What we should miss above all else in such a homily would be Jesus' voice, the voice not of a divine being remote from human concerns, but of one who has taken up residence on earth. He is unique, certainly, a man from above, a stranger from heaven. But he addresses his friends as one who has endured persecution and rejection and won through. His voice is raised from time to time, in emphasis or in anger. But it remains equable, serene, assured. There is no other voice like it in literature.

We are left, then, with a Gospel, and with good reasons for enquiring about the significance of that very fact. It was observed earlier that the frequent references to revelation in the revelatory schema resemble a promise that is continually reiterated but never fulfilled. But the promise is left unfulfilled only because it is unfulfillable, since there are no heavenly mysteries revealed to Jesus by God except those disclosed in his own life and death.

Meeks counters Bultmann's familiar paradox that Jesus reveals only that he is the revealer with a paradox of his own. Not quite, he says: 'He reveals rather that he is an enigma.'[55] But the point is surely that if we seek for answers only in what Jesus *says* we are bound to be disappointed. Neither in the revelatory schema nor in any other of Jesus' discourses will we find the kind of detailed description of heavenly mysteries so frequent in apocalyptic. 'Heavenly things', by yet another paradox, are not to be sought in heaven.

Nor are they disclosed in words alone. In Chapter 11 we saw that the fourth evangelist was keenly aware of the nature and implications of the Gospel genre. He accepted quite as whole-heartedly as Mark the fundamental paradox of the Christian belief in the lordship of Jesus and the complexities of embodying it in a story. Bultmann's conception of the Johannine theology of revelation, for all its brilliance, has a fundamental flaw. He is too anxious to discard the narrative husk of the Gospel in order to get at the kernel of revelation inside. The evangelist's own insight into the meaning of the gospel message is not borrowed from an alien religion, nor is it detachable from his story. He knows that the meaning is a mystery, and a heavenly mystery at that: it is a truth from God, entrusted to a single messenger. Hence a further paradox: there is no extra revelation above and beyond the tradition concerning Jesus that the evangelist has inherited and is anxious to transmit to others. His own understanding of the tradition was acquired gradually and painfully from a profound reflection upon his faith.

At the heart of these paradoxes stands the enigmatic figure of the Son of Man. 'The story of Jesus', Meeks points out, 'is all played out on earth, despite the frequent indications that he really belongs elsewhere.'[56] The *heavenly* persona of Jesus, if one may put it this way, is neither the Messiah nor the divine agent, since traditionally both of these have a job to do on earth. On the other hand, the ascent/descent motif associated with the Son of Man is always accompanied by the assertion that his true home is in heaven. The title of M. de Jonge's book, *Stranger from Heaven*, is an accurate summary of the Jesus of the Fourth Gospel; it is accurate because the ideas associated with 'Son of Man' have been allowed to infiltrate the whole Gospel. Thus the fundamental paradox consists in the identification of a man, Jesus, with a heavenly being whose message has nothing to do with the things of earth. The form is apocalyptic but, to repeat what was said in the conclusion to Chapters 9 and 10, the

---

[55] 'Man from Heaven', p. 151.   [56] Ibid., p. 145.

destiny of Jesus is the reverse of an apocalypse. This, not some esoteric mystery disclosed to a seer or dreamer, is the true revelation. It is indeed God's plan for the world, but in so far as the plan is transcribed in terms of a human life it is not to be understood from words but from deeds. No wonder, then, that any attempt to separate out the message from the life results in an 'empty' revelation form. Not the least of the Gospel's ironies is the emphasis upon dialogue and discourse at the expense of action, the stress upon words as opposed to works, so that Bultmann can actually argue that Jesus' works must be thought of exclusively as words. The truth is that the two must be held together; no understanding of the book is possible if one loses sight of the simple fact that it is not a theological tract but a Gospel. What the divine agent 'heard' from God is disclosed not in his words but in his life; the 'what' is displayed in the 'how'. The matter of the Gospel, its true content, is indistinguishable from its form: the medium is the message.

BIBLIOGRAPHY

This bibliography is restricted to books and articles cited in the text or notes. Fuller, classified bibliographies may be found in the works cited in Chapter 14, n. 1, and in the commentaries of Brown, Becker, Haenchen, and Beasley-Murray.

Commentaries are referred to in the notes by the name of the commentator alone.

Dates in square brackets refer to earlier editions; to the first, unless otherwise indicated.

COMMENTARIES

BARRETT, C. K., *The Gospel according to St. John*[2] (London, 1978 [1955]).

BAUER, W., *Das Johannesevangelium erklärt*[3] (Tübingen, 1933 [1912, 1925]).

BEASLEY-MURRAY, G. R., *John* (Waco, Texas, 1987).

BECKER, J., *Das Evangelium des Johannes*, 2 vols. (Gütersloh, 1979/81).

BERNARD, J. H., *The Gospel according to St. John*, 2 vols., ed. A. H. McNeile (Edinburgh, 1928).

BOISMARD, M.-É., and LAMOUILLE, A., *Synopse des quatre évangiles en français*, iii. *L'Évangile de Jean* (Paris, 1977).

BROWN, R. E., *The Gospel according to John*, 2 vols. (New York, 1966/70).

BULTMANN, R., *The Gospel of John* (Oxford, 1971) [= *Das Evangelium des Johannes* (Göttingen, 1941), with the Supplement of 1966].

ELLIS, P. F., *The Genius of John: A Composition–Critical Commentary on the Fourth Gospel* (Collegeville, 1984).

HAENCHEN, E., *Das Johannesevangelium*, ed. U. Busse (Tübingen, 1980) [= *A commentary on the Gospel of John*, 2 vols. (Philadelphia, 1984)].

HIRSCH, E., *Das vierte Evangelium in seiner ursprünglichen Gestalt verdeutscht und erklärt* (Tübingen, 1936).

HOSKYNS, E. C., *The Fourth Gospel*[2], ed. F. N. Davey (London, 1947 [1940]).

LAGRANGE, M.-J., *Évangile selon Saint Jean* (Paris, 1925).

LIGHTFOOT, R. H., *St. John's Gospel: A Commentary* (Oxford, 1956).

LINDARS, B., *The Gospel of John* (London, 1972).

LOISY, A., *Le Quatrième Évangile* (Paris, 1903).

ODEBERG, H., *The Fourth Gospel: Interpreted in its relation to contemporaneous religious currents in Palestine and the Hellenistic-Oriental world* (Uppsala, 1929).

SCHLATTER, A., *Der Evangelist Johannes: Wie er spricht, denkt und glaubt: Ein Kommentar*[4] (Stuttgart, 1975 [1930]).

SCHNACKENBURG, R., *The Gospel according to St. John*, 3 vols. (London, 1968/80/82).

SCHULZ, S., *Das Evangelium nach Johannes* (Göttingen, 1972).

WELLHAUSEN, J., *Das Evangelium Johannis* (Berlin, 1908).

WESTCOTT, B. F., *The Gospel according to St. John*[2] (London, 1882 [1880]).

BOOKS AND ARTICLES

ABBOTT, E. A., *Johannine Vocabulary: A Comparison of the Words of the Fourth Gospel with those of the Three* (London, 1905).

ABERLE, M. VON, 'Über den Zweck des Johannesevangelium', *Theologische Quartalschrift*, 42 (1861), 37–94.

ABRAMS, M. H., *The Mirror and the Lamp* (Oxford, 1953).

ACKERMANN, J. S., 'The Rabbinical Interpretation of Ps 82 and the Gospel of John: John 10: 34 and the Prologue', *HTR* 59 (1966), 186–91.

ALEXANDER, P. S., 'Rabbinic Judaism and the New Testament', *ZNW* 74 (1983), 237–46.

ASHTON, J., 'The Identity and Function of the Ἰουδαῖοι in the Fourth Gospel', *NT* 27 (1985), 40–75.

—— 'The Transformation of Wisdom: A Study of the Prologue of John's Gospel', *NTS* 32 (1986), 161–86.

—— (ed.), *The Interpretation of John* (London, 1986).

ATTRIDGE, H. W., 'Thematic Development and Source Elaboration in John 7: 1–36', *CBQ* 42 (1980), 160–70.

AUNE, D., *The Cultic Setting of Realized Eschatology in Early Christianity* (Leiden, 1972).

—— *Prophecy in Early Christianity and the Ancient Mediterranean World* (Michigan, 1983).

BACON, B. W., *The Fourth Gospel in Research and Debate* (New Haven, 1918 [1910]).

BAILEY, J. A., *The Traditions Common to the Gospels of Luke and John* (Leiden, 1963).

BALDENSPERGER, W., *Der Prolog des vierten Evangeliums: Sein polemisch-apologetischer Zweck* (Freiburg im Breisgau, 1898).

BAMMEL, E., '"John did no miracle": John 10: 41', *Miracles: Cambridge Studies in their Philosophy and History*, ed. C. F. D. Moule (London, 1965), 175–202.

BARKER, M., *The Lost Prophet: The Book of Enoch and its Influence on Christianity* (London, 1988).

—— *The Older Testament: The Survival of Themes from the Ancient Royal Cult in Sectarian Judaism and Early Christianity* (London, 1987).

BARNETT, A. E., *Paul Becomes a Literary Influence* (Chicago, 1941).

BARR, J., "'Abba isn't "Daddy"'", *JTS* 39 (1988), 28–47.

—— 'Jewish Apocalyptic in Recent Scholarly Study', *BJRL* 58 (1975), 9–35.

—— *The Semantics of Biblical Language* (Oxford, 1961).

BARRETT, C. K., 'Christocentric or Theocentric? Observations on the Theological Method of the Fourth Gospel', *Essays on John* (London, 1982), 1–18.

—— *The Gospel of John and Judaism* (London, 1975).

—— 'The Holy Spirit in the Fourth Gospel', *JTS* 1 (1950), 1–15.

—— 'John and the Synoptic Gospels', *ExpT* 85 (1973/4), 228–33.

—— *The Prologue of St. John's Gospel* (London, 1971).

BARTON, J., *Oracles of God: Perceptions of Ancient Prophecy in Israel after the Exile* (London, 1986).

BAUMGARTEN, A. J., 'The Name of the Pharisees', *JBL* 102 (1983), 411–38.

BAUR, F. C., 'Die Einleitung in das neue Testament als theologische Wissenschaft: Ihr Begriff und ihre Aufgabe, ihr Entwicklungsgang und ihr innerer Organismus', *Theologische Jahrbücher*, 9 (1850), 463–566; 10 (1851), 70–94; 222–53; 291–329.

—— *Kritische Untersuchungen über die kanonischen Evangelien: Ihr Verhältniß zu einander, ihren Charakter und Ursprung* (Tübingen, 1847).

BECKER, H., *Die Reden des Johannesevangeliums und der Stil der gnostischen Offenbarungsreden* (Göttingen, 1956).

BECKER, J., 'Aus der Literatur zum Johannesevangelium (1978–1980)', *TRu* 47 (1982), 279–301; 305–47.

—— 'Beobachtungen zum Dualismus im Johannesevangelium', *ZNW* 65 (1974), 71–87.

—— 'Das Johannesevangelium im Streit der Methoden (1980–1984)', *TRu* 51 (1986), 1–78.

—— 'Wunder und Christologie', *NTS* 16 (1970), 130–48.

BERGER, K., *Die Amen-Worte Jesu* (Berlin, 1970).

BERGER, P., *A Rumour of Angels* (Harmondsworth, 1970).

BERGMEIER, R., 'Zur Frühdatierung samaritanischer Theologumena', *JSJ* 5 (1974), 121–53.

BEUTLER, J., *Habt keine Angst: Die erste johanneische Abschiedsrede (Joh 14)* (Stuttgart, 1984).

—— 'Die Heilsbedeutung des Todes Jesu im Johannesevangelium nach Joh 13, 1–20', *Der Tod Jesu: Deutungen im Neuen Testament*, ed. K. Kertelge (Freiburg im Breisgau/Basle/Vienna, 1976), 188–204.

—— *Martyria: Traditionsgeschichtliche Untersuchungen zum Zeugnisthema bei Johannes* (Frankfurt, 1972).

BIELER, L., Θεῖος ἀνήρ, *das Bild des 'göttlichen Menschen' in Spätantike und Frühchristentum*, 2 vols. (Vienna, 1935/6).

BLACK, M., 'Aramaic Barnasha and the "Son of Man"', *ExpT* 95 (1984), 200–6.

BLANK, J., *Krisis: Untersuchungen zur johanneischen Christologie und Eschatologie* (Freiburg im Breisgau, 1964).

BLINZLER, J., *Johannes und die Synoptiker: Ein Forschungsbericht* (Stuttgart, 1965).

BLOCH, R., 'Quelques aspects de la figure de Moïse dans la tradition rabbinique', *Moïse, l'homme de l'alliance*, ed. H. Cazelles *et al.* (Paris, 1955), 93–167.

BÖCHER, O., *Der johanneische Dualismus im Zusammenhang des nachbiblischen Judentums* (Gütersloh, 1965).

BOISMARD, M.-É., 'L'Évolution du thème eschatologique dans les traditions johanniques', *RB* 68 (1961), 507–24.

—— 'Saint Luc et la rédaction du quatrième évangile (Jn 4: 46–54)', *RB* 69 (1962), 185–211.

—— *et al.*, *L'Évangile de Jean: Études et problèmes* (Louvain, 1958).

BORGEN, P., *Bread from Heaven: An Exegetical Study of the Concept of Manna in the Gospel of John and the Writings of Philo* (Leiden, 1965).

—— 'God's Agent in the Fourth Gospel', *The Interpretation of John*, ed. J. Ashton, 67–78 [= *Religions in Antiquity*, ed. J. Neusner (Leiden, 1968), 137–48].

—— 'Some Jewish Exegetical Traditions as Background for Son of Man Sayings in John's Gospel (Jn 3, 13–14 and context)', *L'Évangile de Jean*, ed. M. de Jonge, 243–58.

—— 'The Use of Tradition in John 3: 13–14', *NTS* 23 (1976), 18–35.

BORING, M. E., 'The Influence of Christian Prophecy on the Johannine Portrayal of the Paraclete and Jesus', *NTS* 25 (1978/9), 113–23.

BORNHÄUSER, K., *Das Johannesevangelium: Eine Missionsschrift für Israel* (Gütersloh, 1928).

BORNKAMM, G., 'Der Paraklet im Johannesevangelium', *Festschrift für R. Bultmann* (Stuttgart, 1949), 12–35 [Reworked in *Geschichte und Glaube*, i (Munich, 1968), 68–89].

—— 'Towards the Interpretation of John's Gospel: A Discussion of *The Testament of Jesus* by Ernst Käsemann', *The Interpretation of John*, ed. J. Ashton, 79–96 [= 'Zur Interpretation des Johannes-Evangeliums', *EvT* 28 (1968), 8–25].

BOUSSET, W., 'Ist das vierte Evangelium eine literarische Einheit?', *TrU* 12 (1909), 1–12; 39–64.

—— 'Johannesevangelium', *RGG*[1], iii (Tübingen, 1912), cols. 608–36.

—— *Kyrios Christos: Geschichte des Christusglaubens von den Anfängen des Christentums bis Irenaeus*[6] (Göttingen, 1964 [1913]).

—— 'Der Verfasser des Johannesevangeliums', *TrU* 8 (1905), 225–44; 277–95.

BOWKER, J., *The Religious Imagination and the Sense of God* (Oxford, 1978).

—— '"The Son of Man"', *JTS* 28 (1977), 1–30.

BOWMAN, J., 'Samaritan Studies I: The Fourth Gospel and the Samaritans', *BJRL* 40 (1957/8), 298–327.

Box, G. H., 'The Jewish Environment of Early Christianity', *Expositor*, 12 (1916), 1–25.

BRAUN, H., *Qumran und das Neue Testament* (Tübingen, 1966).

BRETSCHNEIDER, K. G., *Probabilia de evangelii et epistularum Joannis, apostoli, indole et origine* (Leipzig, 1820).

BROSHI, M., 'The Population of Western Palestine in the Roman-Byzantine Period', *BASOR* 236 (1979), 1–10.

BROWN, R. E., *The Community of the Beloved Disciple: The Life, Loves and Hates of an Individual Church in New Testament Times* (New York/London, 1979).

—— 'Johannine Ecclesiology—The Community's Origins', *Int* 31 (1977), 379–93.

—— '"Other Sheep Not of this Fold": The Johannine Perspective on Christian Diversity in the Late First Century', *JBL* 97 (1978), 5–22.

—— 'The Qumran Scrolls and the Johannine Gospel and Epistles', *CBQ* 17 (1955), 403–19; 559–74.

BROWN, S., 'From Burney to Black: The Fourth Gospel and the Aramaic Question', *CBQ* 26 (1964), 323–39.

BROWNSON, J., 'The Odes of Solomon and the Johannine Tradition, *JSP* 2 (1988), 49–69.

BUBER, S. (ed.), *Midrash Tanhuma on the five books of the Torah* (Wilna, 1883).

BUCHANAN, G. W., 'The Samaritan Origin of the Gospel of John', *Religions in Antiquity: Essays in Memory of Erwin Ramsdell Goodenough*, ed. J. Neusner (Leiden, 1968), 149–75.

BÜHNER, J.-A., 'Denkstrukturen im Johannesevangelium', *Theologische Beiträge*, 13 (Wuppertal, 1982), 224–31.

—— *Der Gesandte und sein Weg im vierten Evangelium: Die kultur- und religionsgeschichtliche Grundlagen der johanneischen Sendungschristologie sowie ihre traditionsgeschichtliche Entwicklung* (Tübingen, 1977).

BULTMANN, R., 'Die Bedeutung der neuerschlossenen mandäischen und manichäischen Quellen für das Verständnis des Johannesevangeliums', *Exegetica*, 55–104 [=ZNW 24 (1925), 100–46].

—— 'The Eschatology of the Gospel of John', *Faith and Understanding*, 165–83.

—— *Exegetica*, ed. E. Dinkler (Tübingen, 1967).

—— *Faith and Understanding: Collected Essays* (London, 1969).

—— *Gesammelte Aufsätze* (East Berlin, 1973).

—— 'Hirsch's Auslegung des Johannes-Evangeliums', *EvT* 4 (1937), 115–42.

—— *History and Eschatology* (New York, 1957).

—— *Jesus Christ and Mythology* (New York, 1958).

—— 'Johanneische Schriften und Gnosis', *Orientalische Literaturzeitung*, 43 (1940), 150–75.

—— 'Johannesevangelium', *RGG*[3], iii (Tübingen, 1959), cols. 840–50.

—— 'The Primitive Christian Kerygma and the Historical Jesus', *The Historical Jesus and the Kerygmatic Christ*, ed. C. E. Braaten and R. A. Harrisville (Nashville, 1964), 15–42 [= 'Das Verhältnis der urchristlichen Christusbotschaft zum historischen Jesus', *Exegetica*, 445–69].

—— *Primitive Christianity in its Contemporary Setting* (London, 1960).

—— 'Das Problem einer theologischen Exegese des Neuen Testaments', *Zwischen den Zeiten*, 3 (1925), 334–57 [= *Gesammelte Aufsätze*, 353–78].

—— 'Der religionsgeschichtliche Hintergrund des Prologs zum Johannesevangelium', *EYXAPIΣTHPION, Festschrift für H. Gunkel*, ii (Göttingen, 1925), 3–26. A slightly abbreviated version of this article may be found in *The Interpretation of John*, ed. J. Ashton, 18–35.

—— *Theology of the New Testament*, ii (London, 1952).

BURGE, G. M., *The Anointed Community* (Grand Rapids, 1986).

BURKITT, F. C., *The Gospel History and its Transmission* (Edinburgh, 1906).

BURNEY, C. F., *The Aramaic Origin of the Fourth Gospel* (Oxford, 1922).

BUTTRICK, D. G. (ed.), *Jesus and Man's Hope*, i (Pittsburgh, 1970).

CAIRD, G. B., 'The Glory of God in the Fourth Gospel: An Exercise in Biblical Semantics', *NTS* 15 (1968/9), 265–77.

CARROLL, K. L., 'The Fourth Gospel and the Exclusion of Christians from Synagogues', *BJRL* 40 (1957/8), 19–32.

CASEY, M., *Son of Man: The Interpretation and Influence of Daniel 7* (London, 1979).

—— 'The Use of the Term "son of man" in the Similitudes of Enoch', *JSJ* 7 (1976), 167–80.

CHADWICK, H., 'Some Reflections on the Character and Theology of the Odes of Solomon', *Kyriakon: Festschrift Johannes Quasten*, ed. P. Granfield and J. A. Jungmann (Münster, 1970), i. 266–70.

CHARLES, R. H. (ed.), *The Apocrypha and Pseudepigrapha of the Old Testament in English*, ii. *The Pseudepigrapha* (Oxford, 1913).

—— (ed.), *The Assumption of Moses* (London, 1897).

CHARLESWORTH, J. H., 'A Critical Comparison of the Dualism in 1QS 3: 13–4: 26 and the "Dualism" Contained in the Gospel of John', *John and Qumran*, 76–106.

—— 'Qumran, John and the Odes of Solomon', *John and Qumran*, 107–36.

—— (ed.), *John and Qumran* (London, 1972).

—— (ed.), *The Old Testament Pseudepigrapha*, 2 vols. (London, 1983/5).

CHILTON, B. (ed.), *The Kingdom of God in the Teaching of Jesus* (London, 1984).

COGGINS, R. J., *Samaritans and Jews* (Oxford, 1975).

COHEN, S. J. D., *From the Maccabees to the Mishnah* (Philadelphia, 1987).

COLLINGWOOD, R. H., *The Idea of History* (Oxford, 1946).

COLLINS, J. J., 'Apocalyptic Eschatology as the Transcendence of Death', *CBQ* 36 (1974), 21–43.

—— *The Apocalyptic Imagination* (New York, 1984).

COLLINS, J. J., 'The Heavenly Representative: The "Son of Man" in the Similitudes of Enoch', *Ideal Figures in Ancient Judaism: Profiles and Paradigms*, ed. J. J. Collins and G. W. E. Nickelsburg (Chico, California, 1980), 111–33.

COLWELL, E. C., *John Defends the Gospel* (Chicago, 1936).

CONZELMANN, H., 'Present and Future in the Synoptic Tradition', *Journal for Theology and the Church*, 5, ed. R. Funk (Tübingen/New York, 1968), 26–44.

COPPENS, J., 'Le Fils de l'homme dans l'évangile johannique', *ETL* 52 (1976), 28–81.

CORTÈS, E., *Los Discursos de adiós de Gn 49 a Jn 13–17: Pistas para la historia de un género literario en la antigua literatura judía* (Barcelona, 1976).

COWLEY, A. (ed.), *Aramaic Papyri of the 5th Century B.C.* (Oxford, 1923).

CROSS, F. M., Jr., 'The Council of Yahweh', *JNES* 12 (1953), 174–7.

CULLMANN, O., *Christology of the New Testament* (London, 1959).

—— *The Johannine Circle: Its place in Judaism, among the disciples of Jesus and in early Christianity: A study in the origin of the Gospel of John* (London, 1976).

—— *Salvation in History* (London, 1967).

CULPEPPER, R. A., *The Anatomy of the Fourth Gospel: A Study in Literary Design* (Philadelphia, 1983).

—— *The Johannine School: An Evaluation of the Johannine-School Hypothesis Based on an Investigation of the Nature of Ancient Schools* (Missoula, 1975).

DAHL, N. A., 'Eschatology and History in the Light of the Dead Sea Scrolls', *The Future of our Religious Past*, ed. J. M. Robinson, 9–28.

—— 'The Johannine Church and History', *The Interpretation of John*, ed. J. Ashton, 122–40 [= *Current Issues in New Testament Interpretation*, ed. W. Klassen and G. F. Snyder (New York, Evanson, and London, 1962), 124–42].

DALMAN, G. H., *Die Worte Jesu mit Berücksichtigung des nachkanonischen jüdischen Schriftums und der aramäischen Sprache*, i (Leipzig, 1898).

DAVIES, W. D., *The Gospel and the Land* (London, 1974).

DEKKER, C., 'Grundschrift und Redaktion im Johannesevangelium', *NTS* 13 (1966/7), 66–80.

DELLING, G., 'Die Bezeichnung "Söhne Gottes" in der jüdischen Literatur der hellenisch-römischen Zeit', *God's Christ and His People, Festschrift N. A. Dahl*, ed. J. Jervell and W. A. Meeks (Oslo/Bergen/Tromsø, 1977), 18–28.

DERRETT, J. D. M., 'The Parable of the Wicked Vinedressers', *Law in the New Testament* (London, 1970), 286–312.

DIBELIUS, M., 'The Christology of Primitive Christianity', *Twentieth Century Theology in the Making, ii. The Theological Dialogue: Issues and Resources*, ed. J. Pelikan (London, 1970), 62–90 [= 'Christologie', *RGG*² i (Tübingen, 1927), cols. 1592–607].

DODD, C. H., 'The Appearances of the Risen Christ: An Essay in Form-Criticism of the Gospels', *More NT Studies*, 102–33.

—— 'A Hidden Parable in the Fourth Gospel', *More NT Studies*, 30–40.

—— *Historical Tradition in the Fourth Gospel* (Cambridge, 1963).

—— *The Interpretation of the Fourth Gospel* (Cambridge, 1953).

—— *More New Testament Studies* (Manchester, 1968).

DONAHUE, J. R., 'Recent Studies on the Origin of "Son of Man" in the Gospels', *CBQ* 48 (1986), 484–98.

DUKE, P. D., *Irony in the Fourth Gospel* (Atlanta, 1985).

DUNN, J. D. G., *Jesus and the Spirit* (London, 1975).

—— 'Let John be John: A Gospel for its Time', *Das Evangelium und die Evangelien*, ed. P. Stuhlmacher, 309–39.

—— 'Prophetic "I"-sayings and the Jesus Tradition: The Importance of testing Prophetic Utterances within Early Christianity', *NTS* 24 (1977/8), 175–98.

DUPONT, J., *Essais sur la christologie de Saint Jean* (Bruges, 1951).

EMERTON, J. A., 'Melchizedek and the Gods: Fresh Evidence for the Jewish Background of John 10: 34–36', *JTS* 17 (1966), 399–401.

—— 'Some New Testament Notes, I. The Interpretation of Psalm 82 and John 10', *JTS* 11 (1960), 329–32.

EVANSON, E., *The Dissonance of the four generally received evangelists and the Evidence of their respective authority examined* (Ipswich, 1792).

FAURE, A., 'Die alttestamentlichen Zitate im vierten Evangelium und die Quellenscheidungshypothese', *ZNW* 21 (1922), 99–121.

FELDMAN, L. H., 'Hengel's Judaism and Hellenism in Retrospect', *JBL* 96 (1977), 371–82.

FISCHER, G., *Die himmlische Wohnungen: Untersuchungen zu Joh 14: 2 f.* (Berne/Frankfurt, 1975).

FITZMYER, J. A., 'The Aramaic "Elect of God" Text from Qumran Cave IV', *CBQ* 27 (1965), 348–72.

—— 'The Aramaic Language and the Study of the New Testament', *JBL* 99 (1980), 5–21.

—— 'Further Light on Melchizedek from Qumran Cave 11', *JBL* 86 (1967), 25–41.

FORTNA, R. T., 'Christology in the Fourth Gospel: Redaction-Critical Perspectives', *NTS* 21 (1974/5), 489–504.

—— *The Fourth Gospel and its Predecessor: From Narrative Source to Present Gospel* (Edinburgh, 1988).

—— *The Gospel of Signs: A Reconstruction of the Narrative Source Underlying the Fourth Gospel* (Cambridge, 1970).

—— 'Source and Redaction in the Fourth Gospel's Portrayal of Jesus' Signs', *JBL* 89 (1970), 151–66.

FREED, E. D., *Old Testament Quotations in the Gospel of John* (Leiden, 1965).

—— 'The Son of Man in the Fourth Gospel', *JBL* 86 (1967), 402–9.

FREEDMAN, H., and SIMON, M. (ed.), *Midrash Rabbah* (London, 1939).

FULLER, R. H., *The Foundations of New Testament Christology* (London, 1965).

GADAMER, H.-G., *Truth and Method* (London, 1975).

GAECHTER, P., 'Zur Form von Joh 5, 19–30', *Neutestamentliche Aufsätze, Festschrift H. Schmid*, ed. J. Blinzler, O. Kuss, F. Mussner (Regensburg, 1963), 65–8.

GAMMIE, J. G., 'Spatial and Ethical Dualism in Jewish Wisdom and Apocalyptic Literature', *JBL* 93 (1974), 356–85.

GARDNER-SMITH, P., *Saint John and the Synoptic Gospels* (Cambridge, 1938).

GIBSON, J. C. L., *Textbook of Syrian Semitic Inscriptions*, ii (Oxford, 1975).

GINZBERG, L., *The Legends of the Jews, translated from the German Manuscript by H. Szold and others*, 7 vols. (Philadelphia, 1909/59).

GLASSON, T. F., *Moses in the Fourth Gospel* (London, 1963).

GOGUEL, M., *Introduction au nouveau Testament*, ii. *Le Quatrième Évangile* (Paris, 1924).

GOLDMANN, L., 'Structuralisme génétique et création littéraire', *Sciences humaines et philosophiques* (Paris, 1966), 151–65.

GOLDSTEIN, J., 'Jewish Acceptance and Rejection of Hellenism', *Jewish and Christian Self-Definition*, ii, ed. E. P. Sanders *et al.*, 64–87.

GOURBILLON, J. G., 'La Parabole du serpent d'airain et la "lacune" du ch. III de l'Évangile selon S. Jean', *Vivre et penser*, 2 (1942), 213–26.

GRUENWALD, I., *Apocalyptic and Merkavah Mysticism* (Leiden, 1980).

GUELICH, R., 'The Gospel Genre', *Das Evangelium und die Evangelien*, ed. P. Stuhlmacher, 182–219.

HAACKER, K., *Die Stiftung des Heils: Untersuchungen zur Struktur der johanneischen Christologie* (Stuttgart, 1972).

HAHN, F., *The Titles of Jesus in Christology: Their History in Early Christianity* (London, 1969).

HARNACK, A. VON, *History of Dogma*, i (New York, 1958) [First German ed. 1886].

HARNER, P. B., *The 'I Am' of the Fourth Gospel: A Study in Johannine Usage and Thought* (Philadelphia, 1970).

HARRINGTON, D. J., 'Interpreting Israel's History: The Testament of Moses as a Rewriting of Deut 31–34', *Studies in the Testament of Moses*, ed. G. W. Nickelsburg (Cambridge, Mass., 1973), 59–70.

HARTMAN, L., 'Johannine Jesus-Belief and Monotheism', *Aspects on the Johannine Literature: Papers presented at a Conference of Scandinavian New Testament Scholars at Uppsala, June 16–19, 1986*, ed. L. Hartman and B. Olsson (Uppsala, 1987).

—— *Prophecy Interpreted: The Formation of some Jewish Apocalyptic Texts and of the Eschatological Discourse Mark 13 par.* (Lund, 1966).

HARVEY, A. E., *Jesus on Trial: A Study in the Fourth Gospel* (London, 1976).

HEEKERENS, H.-P., *Die Zeichen-Quelle der johanneischen Redaktion: Ein Beitrag zur Entstehungsgeschichte des vierten Evangeliums* (Stuttgart, 1984).

HENGEL, M., 'Das Gleichnis von den Weingärtnern Mc 12, 1–12 im Licht der Zenonpapyri und der rabbinischen Gleichnisse', *ZNW* 59 (1968), 1–39.

—— 'The Interpretation of the Wine Miracle at Cana: John 2: 1–11', *The Glory of Christ in the New Testament: Studies in Christology in Memory of G. B. Caird*, ed. L. D. Hurst and N. T. Wright (Oxford, 1987), 83–112.

—— *The Johannine Question* (London, 1989).

—— *Judentum und Hellenismus: Studien zu ihrer Begegnung unter besonderer Berücksichtigung Palästinas bis zur Mitte des 2. Jh. v. Chr.* (Tübingen, 1968).

—— *The Son of God* (London, 1976).

—— *Studies in Mark* (London, 1985).

HENNECKE, E., *New Testament Apocrypha*, 2 vols. (London, 1973/4).

HICKLING, C. J. A., 'Attitudes to Judaism in the Fourth Gospel', *L'Évangile de Jean*, ed. M. de Jonge, 347–54.

HILGENFELD, A., *Das Evangelium und die Briefe Johannes nach ihre Lehrbegriff dargestellt* (Halle, 1849).

HILL, D., 'Dikaioi as a Quasi-Technical Term', *NTS* 11 (1964/5), 296–302.

—— 'Jesus and Josephus' "Messianic Prophets"', *Text and Interpretation: Studies Presented to M. Black*, ed. E. Best and R. McL. Wilson (Cambridge, 1980), 143–54.

—— *New Testament Prophecy* (London, 1979).

HOARE, F. R., *The Original Order and Chapters of St. John's Gospel* (London, 1944).

HOFFMANN, G., *Das Johannesevangelium ein Alterswerk: Eine psychologische Studie* (Gütersloh, 1933).

HOLLADAY, C., *Theios Aner in Hellenistic Judaism: A Critique of the Use of This Category in New Testament Christology* (Missoula, 1977).

HOLTZMANN, H. J., *Evangelium, Briefe und Offenbarung des Johannes*[3], ed. W. Bauer (Tübingen, 1908).

HOOKER, M., *The Son of Man in Mark* (London, 1967).

HORBURY, W., 'The Benediction of the *Minim* and Early Jewish-Christian Controversy', *JTS* 33 (1982), 19–61.

—— 'The Messianic Associations of "The Son of Man"', *JTS* 36 (1985), 34–55.

HORSLEY, R. A., '"Like One of the Prophets of Old": Two Types of Popular Prophets at the Time of Jesus', *CBQ* 47 (1985), 435–63.

—— 'Popular Messianic Movements around the Time of Jesus', *CBQ* 46 (1984), 471–95.

HOWARD, W. F., *The Fourth Gospel in Recent Criticism and Interpretation* (London, 1931).

HÜGEL, F. VON, 'Gospel of St. John', *The Encyclopaedia Britannica*[11], xv (Cambridge, 1911), cols. 453–8.

IERSEL, B. M. F. VAN, *'Der Sohn' in den synoptischen Jesusworten: Christusbezeichnung der Gemeinde oder Selbstbezeichnung Jesu?* (Leiden, 1961).

ISAACS, M. E., 'The Prophetic Spirit in the Fourth Gospel', *HeyJ* 24 (1983), 391–407.

JACKSON, H. LATIMER, *The Problem of the Fourth Gospel* (Cambridge, 1918).

JACOBSON, H. (ed.), *The* Exagoge *of Ezekiel* (Cambridge, 1983).

JEREMIAS, J., *New Testament Theology*, i. *The Proclamation of Jesus* (London, 1971).

JOHNSTON, G., *The Spirit-Paraclete in the Gospel of John* (Cambridge, 1970).

JONGE, M. DE, 'Jesus as Prophet and King in the Fourth Gospel', *Jesus: Stranger from Heaven*, 49–76.

—— *Jesus: Stranger from Heaven and Son of God* (Missoula, 1977).

—— 'Jewish Expectations about the "Messiah" in the Fourth Gospel', *Jesus: Stranger from Heaven*, 77–117.

—— 'The Son of God and the Children of God', *Jesus: Stranger from Heaven*, 141–68.

—— 'The Use of the Word "Anointed" in the Time of Jesus', *NT* 8 (1966), 132–48.

—— (ed.), *L'Évangile de Jean: Sources, rédaction, théologie* (Louvain, 1977).

—— (ed.), *The Testaments of the Twelve Patriarchs: A Critical Edition of the Greek Text* (Leiden, 1978).

—— and VAN DER WOUDE, A. S., '11Q Melchizedek and the New Testament', *NTS* 12 (1965/6), 301–26.

JONSON, P. J., 'The Names Israel and Jew in Ancient Judaism and the New Testament', *Bijdragen, tijdschrift voor filosofie en theologie*, 47 (1986), 120–40; 266–89.

KÄHLER, M., *The So-Called Historical Jesus and the Historic Biblical Christ* (Philadelphia, 1964).

KÄSEMANN, E., 'The Beginnings of Christian Theology', *NT Questions of Today*, 82–107.

—— 'Blind Alleys in the "Jesus of History" Controversy', *NT Questions of Today*, 23–65.

—— *New Testament Questions of Today* (London, 1969).

—— 'On the Subject of Primitive Christian Apocalyptic', *NT Questions of Today*, 108–37.

—— 'The Problem of the Historical Jesus', *Essays on NT Themes* (London, 1964), 15–47.

—— 'Rudolf Bultmann, Das Evangelium des Johannes', *Verkündigung und Forschung, Theologischer Jahresbericht* (1942–6), 182–201.

—— 'The Structure and Purpose of the Prologue to John's Gospel', *NT Questions of Today*, 138–67.

—— *The Testament of Jesus: A Study of the Gospel of John in the Light of Chapter 17* (London, 1968) [= *Jesu Letzter Wille nach Johannes* 17[1] (Tübingen, 1966; [3] 1971)].

KEE, H. C., 'Myth and Miracle: Isis, Wisdom and the Logos of John', *Myth, Symbol and Reality*, ed. A. M. Olson (London, 1980) 145–64.

KEMPER, F., 'Zur literarischen Gestalt des Johannesevangeliums', *TZ* 43 (1987), 247–64.

KIERKEGAARD, S., *The Philosophical Fragments*, ed. N. Thulstrup (Princeton, 1962).

KITTEL, G. (ed.), *Theological Dictionary of the New Testament*, i–x (Grand Rapids, 1964/76).

KNIBB, M., 'Prophecy and the Emergence of the Jewish Apocalypses', *Israel's Prophetic Tradition: Essays in Honour of Peter R. Ackroyd*, ed. R. Coggins *et al.* (Cambridge, 1982), 155–80.

KOESTER, H., 'One Jesus and Four Primitive Gospels', *Trajectories through Early Christianity*, ed. J. M. Robinson and H. Koester, 158–204.

—— 'The Structure and Criteria of Early Christian Beliefs', *Trajectories*, 205–31.

KUHN, H.-W., *Enderwartung und gegenwärtiges Heil: Untersuchungen zu den Gemeindeliedern von Qumran, mit einen Anhang über Eschatologie und Gegenwart in der Verkündigung Jesu* (Göttingen, 1966).

KUHN, K. G., 'Die in Palästina gefundenen hebräischen Texte und das neue Testament', *ZTK* 47 (1950), 192–211.

—— 'Die Sektenschrift und die iranische Religion', *ZTK* 49 (1952), 296–316.

KÜMMEL, W. G., *Introduction to the New Testament*, revised edn. (London, 1975).

—— 'The New Testament: The History of the Investigation of its Problems* (London, 1973).

—— *The Theology of the New Testament* (London, 1974).

KUNDSIN, K., 'Die Wiederkunft Jesu in den Abschiedsreden des Johannesevangeliums', *ZNW* 33 (1934), 210–15.

KYSAR, R., *The Fourth Evangelist and His Gospel* (Minneapolis, 1975).

—— 'The Fourth Gospel: A Report on Recent Research', *ANRW*, ii, 25. 3 (Berlin/New York, 1985), 2391–480.

LACOMARA, A., 'Deuteronomy and the Farewell Discourse (Jn 13: 31–16: 13)', *CBQ* 36 (1974), 65–84.

LAMARCHE, P., 'La Déclaration de Jésus devant le Sanhédrin', *Christ Vivant* (Paris, 1966), 147–63.

—— 'The Prologue of John', *The Interpretation of John*, ed. J. Ashton, 36–52.

LANGBRANDTNER, W., *Weltferner Gott oder Gott der Liebe: Der Ketzerstreit in der johanneischen Kirche. Eine exegetisch-religionsgeschichtliche Berücksichtigung der koptisch-gnostischen Texte aus Nag-Hammadi* (Frankfurt, 1977).

LAPERROUSAZ, E.-M. (ed.), *Le Testament de Moïse, généralement appelé 'Assomption de Moïse'* (*Semitica*, 19; Paris, 1970).

LAUTERBACH, J. Z. (ed.), *Mekilta de Rabbi Ishmael. A Critical Edition on the Basis of the Manuscripts and Early Editions with an English Translation, Introduction and Notes*, 3 vols. (Philadelphia, 1933/5).

LE DÉAUT, R., *La Nuit pascale: Essai sur la signification de la Pâque juive à partir du Targum d'Exode XII 42* (Rome, 1963).

LEE, E. K., 'St. Mark and the Fourth Gospel', *NTS* 3 (1956/7), 50–8.

LÉON-DUFOUR, X., 'La Parabole des Vignerons Homicides', *Études d'Évangile* (Paris, 1965), 303–44.

—— 'Le Signe du Temple selon Saint Jean', *RScR* 39 (1951/2), 155–75.

—— 'Towards a Symbolic Reading of the Fourth Gospel', *NTS* 27 (1981), 439–56.

LEROY, H., *Rätsel und Missverständnis: Ein Beitrag zur Formgeschichte des Johannesevangeliums* (Bonn, 1968).

LICHT, J., 'The Doctrine of the Thanksgiving Scroll', *Israel Exploration Journal*, 6 (1956), 1–15; 89–101.

LINDARS, B., *Behind the Fourth Gospel* (London, 1971).

—— 'Discourse and Tradition: The Use of the Sayings of Jesus in the Discourses of the Fourth Gospel', *JSNT* 13 (1981), 89–97.

—— *Jesus Son of Man* (London, 1983).

—— 'John and the Synoptic Gospels: A Test Case', *NTS* 27 (1980/1), 287–92.

—— 'The Passion in the Fourth Gospel', *God's Christ and His People: Studies in Honour of Nils Astrup Dahl* (Oslo/Bergen/Tromsø, 1977), 71–86.

—— 'The Persecution of Christians in John 15: 18–16: 4a', *Suffering and Martyrdom in the New Testament: Studies presented to G. M. Styler by the Cambridge NT Seminar*, ed. W. Horbury and B. McNeil (Cambridge, 1981), 48–69.

—— 'The Son of Man in the Johannine Christology', *Christ and Spirit in the New Testament: Studies in honour of C. F. D. Moule*, ed. B. Lindars and S. S. Smalley (Cambridge, 1973), 43–60.

LOADER, W. R. G., 'The Central Structure of Johannine Christology', *NTS* 30 (1984), 188–216.

LONA, H. E., *Abraham in Johannes 8: Ein Beitrag zur Methodenfrage* (Berne/Frankfurt, 1976).

LOWE, M., 'Who Were the IOYΔAIOI?', *NT* 18 (1976), 101–30.

MCCAFFREY, J., *The House with Many Rooms: The Temple Theme of Jn. 14, 2–3* (Rome, 1988).

MACGREGOR, G. H. C., 'A Suggested Rearrangement of the Johannine Text (Joh 3, 14–36; 12, 30–36)', *ExpT* 35 (1923/4), 476–7.

MACRAE, G., 'The *Ego*-Proclamation in Gnostic Sources', *The Trial of Jesus: Cambridge Studies in Honour of C. F. D. Moule*, ed. E. Bammel (Cambridge, 1970), 122–34.

—— 'The Fourth Gospel and *Religionsgeschichte*', *CBQ* 32 (1970), 13–24.

MARSHALL, I. H., *The Origins of New Testament Christology* (Downers Grove, 1976).

—— 'Palestinian and Hellenistic Christianity: Some Critical Comments', *NTS* 19 (1972/3), 271–87.

MARTYN, J. L., *The Gospel of John in Christian History* (New York, 1979).

—— *History and Theology in the Fourth Gospel*[1] (New York, 1968); [2] (Nashville, 1979).

—— 'Source Criticism and *Religionsgeschichte* in the Fourth Gospel', *The Interpretation of John*, ed. J. Ashton, 99–121.

MEEKS, W. A., '"Am I a Jew?" Johannine Christianity and Judaism', *Christianity, Judaism and Other Greco-Roman Cults: Studies for Morton Smith at Sixty*, ed. J. Neusner (Leiden, 1975), 163–86.

—— 'The Divine Agent and his Counterfeit in Philo and the Fourth Gospel', *Aspects of Religious Propaganda in Judaism and early Christianity*, ed. E. S. Fiorenza (Notre Dame, 1976).

—— 'Galilee and Judaea in the Fourth Gospel', *JBL* 85 (1966), 159–69.

—— 'The Man from Heaven in Johannine Sectarianism', *The Interpretation of John*, ed. J. Ashton, 141–73 [=*JBL* 91 (1972), 44–72].

—— *The Prophet-King: Moses Traditions and the Johannine Christology* (Leiden, 1967).

MENDNER, S., 'Zum Problem "Johannes und die Synoptiker"', *NTS* 4 (1957/8), 282–307.

MEYER, A., 'Johanneische Literatur', *TRu* 5 (1902), 316–33.

MICHEL, H.-J., *Die Abschiedsrede des Paulus an die Kirche: Apg 20: 17–38: Motivgeschichte und theologische Bedeutung* (Munich, 1973).

MILIK, J. T., *The Books of Enoch: Aramaic Fragments of Qumrân Cave 4* (Oxford, 1976).

MINEAR, P. S., 'The Original Function of John 21', *JBL* 102 (1983), 85–98.

MIRANDA, J. P., *Die Sendung Jesu im vierten Evangelium: Religions- und theologiegeschichtliche Untersuchungen zu den Sendungsformeln* (Stuttgart, 1977).

MLAKUZHYIL, G., *The Christocentric Literary Structure of the Fourth Gospel* (Rome, 1987).

MOFFAT, J., *An Introduction to the Literature of the New Testament* (Edinburgh, 1927 [1911]).

MOLONEY, F. J., *The Johannine Son of Man* (Rome, 1976).

MOORE, G. F., *Judaism in the First Centuries of the Christian Era*, 3 vols. (Cambridge, Mass., 1927–30).

MORGAN, R. (ed.), *The Nature of New Testament Theology* (London, 1973).

MORTON, A. Q., and McLEMAN, J., *The Genesis of John* (Edinburgh, 1980).

MOULE, C. F. D., 'The Intention of the Evangelists', *New Testament Essays: Studies in Memory of Thomas Walter Manson, 1893–1958*, ed. A. J. B. Higgins (Manchester, 1959), 165–79.

—— *The Origin of Christology* (Cambridge, 1977).

MOWINCKEL, S., *He that Cometh* (Oxford, 1956).

MÜLLER, U. B., 'Die Bedeutung des Kreuzestodes Jesu im Johannesevangelium: Erwägungen zur Kreuzestheologie im neuen Testament', *KuD* 21 (1975), 49–71.

—— *Messias und Menschensohn in jüdischen Apokalypsen und in der Offenbarung des Johannes* (Gütersloh, 1972).

—— 'Die Parakletenvorstellung im Johannesevangelium', *ZTK* 71 (1974), 31–77.

MUNCK, J., 'Discours d'adieu dans le NT et dans la littérature biblique', *Aux sources de la tradition chrétienne: Mélanges M. Goguel* (Neuchâtel, 1950), 155–70.

MURRAY, R., '"Disaffected Judaism" and Early Christianity', *'To See Ourselves as Others See Us': Christians, Jews and 'Others' in Late Antiquity*, ed. J. Neusner and E. Frerichs (Chico, California, 1985), 263–89.

—— 'Jews, Hebrews and Christian', *NT* 24 (1982), 194–208.

—— *Symbols of Church and Kingdom* (Cambridge, 1975).

MUSSNER, F., *Die johanneische Sehweise und die Frage nach dem historischen Jesus* (Freiburg im Breisgau/Basle/Vienna) [= *The Historical Jesus in the Gospel of John* (London, 1967)].

NEIRYNCK, F., 'John and the Synoptics', *L'Évangile de Jean*, ed. M. de Jonge, 73–106.

NEUFELD, V. H., *The Earliest Christian Confessions* (Leiden, 1963).

NEUSNER, J., *et al.* (ed.), *Judaisms and their Messiahs at the Turn of the Christian Era* (Cambridge, 1987).

NEWSOM, C., *Songs of the Sabbath Sacrifice: A Critical Edition* (Atlanta, 1985).

NICHOLSON, G. C., *Death as Departure* (Chico, California, 1983).

NICKELSBURG, G. W. E., *Jewish Literature between the Bible and the Midrash: A Historical and Literary Introduction* (London, 1981).

—— *Resurrection, Immortality and Eternal Life in Intertestamental Judaism* (Cambridge, Mass., 1972).

NORDEN, E., *Agnostos Theos: Untersuchungen zur Formgeschichte religiöser Rede* (Leipzig/Berlin, 1913).

O'DAY, G. M., *Revelation in the Fourth Gospel* (Philadelphia, 1986).

OEHLER, W., *Das Johannesevangelium: Eine Missionsschrift für die Welt, der Gemeinde ausgelegt* (Gütersloh, 1936).

—— *Zum Missionscharakter des Johannesevangelium* (Gütersloh, 1941).

OLSSON, B., *Structure and Meaning in the Fourth Gospel: A Text-Linguistic Analysis of John 2: 1–11 and 4: 1–42* (Lund, 1974).

ONUKI, T., *Gemeinde und Welt im Johannesevangelium: Ein Beitrag zur Frage nach der theologischen und pragmatischen Funktion des johanneischen 'Dualismus'* (Neukirchen-Vluyn, 1984).

OTTOSON, M., חָלַם , חֲלוֹם , *Theological Dictionary of the Old Testament*, iv, ed. G. J. Botterweck and H. Ringren (Grand Rapids, 1980), 421–32.

PAMMENT, M., 'The Son of Man in the Fourth Gospel', *JTS* 36 (1985), 56–66.

PANCARO, S., *The Law in the Fourth Gospel: The Torah and the Gospel, Moses and Jesus, Judaism and Christianity according to John* (Leiden, 1975).

PATTEN, P., 'The Form and Function of Parable in Select Apocalyptic Literature and their Significance for Parables in the Gospel of Mark', *NTS* 29 (1983), 246–58.

PERRIN, N., 'The Christology of Mark: A Study in Methodology', *JR* 51 (1971), 173–87.

—— 'The Literary *Gattung* "Gospel"', *ExpT* 82 (1970), 4–7.

PESCH, R., and SCHNACKENBURG, R. (edd.), *Jesus und der Menschensohn: Für Anton Vögtle* (Freiburg im Breisgau/Basle/Vienna, 1975).

PÉTREMENT, S., *Le Dieu séparé: Les Origines du Gnosticisme* (Paris, 1984).

PFLEIDERER, O., *Das Urchristentum, seine Schriften und Lehre, in geschichtlichen Zusammenhang beschrieben* (Berlin, 1902 [1887]).

PLÖGER, O., *Theology and Eschatology* (Oxford, 1968).

PORSCH, F., *Pneuma und Wort: Ein exegetischer Beitrag zur Pneumatologie des Johannesevangeliums* (Frankfurt, 1974).

POTTERIE, I. DE LA, '"Je suis la voie, la vérité et la vie" (Joh 14: 6)', *NRT* 88 (1966), 917–26.

—— '*Οἶδα* et *γινώσκω*, les deux modes de la connaissance dans le quatrième évangile', *Bib* 40 (1959), 709–25.

—— 'The Truth in St. John', *The Interpretation of John*, ed. J. Ashton, 53–66.

—— *La Vérité dans Saint Jean*, i. *Le Christ et la vérité. L'Esprit et la vérité*; ii. *Le croyant et la vérité* (Rome, 1977).

PREISS, TH., 'Justification in Johannine Thought', *Life in Christ* (London, 1954), 9–31.

PUMMER, R., 'The Present State of Samaritan Studies', *JSS* 21 (1976), 39–61; 22 (1977), 27–47.

PURVIS, J. D., 'The Fourth Gospel and the Samaritans', *NT* 17 (1975), 161–98.

QUISPEL, G., 'L'Évangile de Jean et la Gnose', *L'Évangile de Jean*, ed. M.-É. Boismard *et al.*, 197–208.

RÄISÄNEN, H., 'The "Messianic Secret" in Mark's Gospel', *The Messianic Secret*, ed. C. Tuckett, 132–40.

—— *Das 'Messiasgeheimnis' im Markusevangelium* (Helsinki, 1976).

REIM, G., *Studien zum alttestamentlichen Hintergrund des Johannesevangeliums* (Cambridge, 1974).

—— 'Targum und Johannesevangelium', *BZ* 27 (1983), 1–13.

—— 'Zur Lokalisierung der johanneischen Gemeinde', *BZ* 32 (1988), 72–86.

RENAN, E., *Les Origines du Christianisme*², v. *Les Évangiles*; vi. *L'Église chrétienne* (Paris, 1877/9).

RENGSTORF, K. H. (ed.), *Johannes und sein Evangelium* (Darmstadt, 1973).

RENSBERGER, D., *Overcoming the World: Politics and Community in the Gospel of John* (London, 1989).

RICHARD, E., 'Expressions of Double Meaning and their Function in the Gospel of John', *NTS* 31 (1985), 96–112.

RICHTER, G., 'Die Fleischwerdung des Logos im Johannesevangelium', *NT* 13 (1971), 81–126; 14 (1972), 257–76.

—— *Die Fußwaschung im Johannesevangelium* (Regensburg, 1967).

—— *Studien zum Johannesevangelium*, ed. J. Hainz (Regensburg, 1977).

RICOEUR, P., 'Preface to Bultmann', *Essays on Biblical Interpretation* (London, 1980), 49–70.

Rissi, M., 'Die Hochzeit in Kana (Joh 2: 1–11)' in *Oikonomia: Heilgeschichte als Thema der Theologie. Oscar Cullmann zum 65. Geburtstag gewidmet*, ed. F. Christ (Hamburg/Bergstedt, 1967), 76–92.

Rivkin, E., 'Defining the Pharisees: The Tannaitic Sources', *HUCA* 40/41 (1969/70), 234–8.

Robinson, J. A. T., 'The Destination and Purpose of St. John's Gospel', *New Testament Issues*, ed. R. Batey (London, 1970), 191–209.

—— *The Priority of John* (London, 1985).

—— *Redating the New Testament* (London, 1976).

Robinson, J. M., 'Gnosticism and the New Testament', *Gnosis: Festschrift für Hans Jonas, in Verbindung mit U. Bianchi et al.*, ed. B. Aland (Göttingen, 1978), 125–43.

—— 'The Johannine Trajectory', *Trajectories through Early Christianity*, ed. J. M. Robinson and H. Koester, 232–68.

—— '*Logoi Sophon*: On the *Gattung* of Mark (and John)', *The Future of our Religious Past*, 84–130.

—— (ed.), *The Future of our Religious Past: Essays in Honour of Rudolf Bultmann* (London, 1971).

—— (ed.), *The Nag Hammadi Library in English* (Leiden, 1977).

—— and Koester, H. (edd.), *Trajectories through Early Christianity* (Philadelphia, 1971).

Ross, J. F., 'The Prophet as Yahweh's Messenger', *Essays in Honor of James Muilenberg*, ed. B. W. Anderson and W. Harrelson (London, 1962), 98–107.

Rowland, C., 'John 1. 51, Jewish Apocalyptic and Targumic Tradition', *NTS* 30 (1984), 498–507.

—— *The Open Heaven: A Study of Apocalyptic in Judaism and Early Christianity* (London, 1982).

Rubinkiewicz, R. (ed.), *The Apocalypse of Abraham, OTPs*, i, ed. J. H. Charlesworth, 681–705.

Ruckstuhl, E., 'Abstieg und Niedergang des johanneischen Menschensohnes', *Jesus und der Menschensohn*, ed. R. Pesch and R. Schnackenburg, 314–41.

—— *Die literarische Einheit des vierten Evangeliums: Der gegenwärtige Stand der einschlägigen Erforschung* (Fribourg, 1951).

Rudolph, K., *Gnosis* (Edinburgh, 1983).

Runes, D. D., *The Gospel according to St. John in the Words of the King James Version of the Year 1611: Edited in Conformity with the True Ecumenical Spirit of His Holiness Pope John XXIII* (New York, 1967).

Russell, D. G., *The Method and Message of Jewish Apocalyptic* (London, 1964).

Sanday, W., *The Criticism of the Fourth Gospel* (Oxford, 1905).

Sanders, E. P., *Jesus and Judaism* (London, 1985).

—— *Paul and Palestinian Judaism* (London, 1977).

—— *et al.* (edd.), *Jewish and Christian Self-Definition*, ii. *Aspects of Judaism in the Graeco-Roman Period* (London, 1981).

SANDMEL, S., 'Palestinian and Hellenistic Judaism and Christianity: The Question of the Comfortable Theory', *HUCA* 50 (1979), 137–48.

SASSE, H., 'Der Paraklet im Johannesevangelium', *ZNW* 24 (1925), 260–7.

—— 'Die Wiederkunft Jesu in den Abschiedsreden des Johannesevangeliums', *ZNW* 33 (1934), 210–15.

SCHALIT, A., *Untersuchungen zur Assumptio Mosis*, ed. H. Schreckenberg (Leiden, 1989).

SCHELBERT, G., 'Sprachgeschichtliches zu "Abba"', *Mélanges Dominique Barthélemy* (Freibourg, 1981), 395–447.

SCHENKE, L., 'Der "Dialog Jesu mit den Juden" im Johannesevangelium: Eine Rekonstruktionsversuch', *NTS* 34 (1988), 573–603.

SCHLATTER, A., *Die Sprache und Heimat des vierten Evangelisten* (Gütersloh, 1902), repr. in *Johannes und sein Evangelium*, ed. K. H. Rengstorf, 28–201.

SCHLIER, H., ἀμήν, *ThDNT*, i, ed. G. Kittel, 335–8.

SCHMIDT, C. (ed.), *Gespräche Jesu mit seinen Jüngern nach seiner Auferstehung: Ein katholisch-apostolisch Sendschreiben des 2. Jahrhunderts* (TU 43; Leipzig, 1919).

SCHNACKENBURG, R., 'Die Messiasfrage im Johannesevangelium', *Neutestamentliche Aufsätze, Festschrift J. Schmid* (Regensburg, 1963), 240–64.

—— 'On the Origin of the Fourth Gospel', *Jesus and Man's Hope*, i, ed. D. G. Buttrick, 223–46.

SCHNEIDER, J., 'Zur Komposition von Joh 7', *ZNW* 45 (1954), 108–19.

SCHNELLE, U., *Antidoketische Christologie im Johannesevangelium: Eine Untersuchung zur Stellung des vierten Evangeliums in der johanneischen Schule* (Göttingen, 1987).

SCHOLEM, G., *Major Trends in Jewish Mysticism* (London, 1955).

SCHOTTROFF, L., *Der Glaubende und die feindliche Welt: Beobachtungen zum gnostischen Dualismus* (Neukirchen-Vluyn, 1970).

SCHULZ, S., *Untersuchungen zur Menschensohn-Christologie im Johannesevangelium, zugleich ein Beitrag zur Methodengeschichte der Auslegung des 4. Evangeliums* (Göttingen, 1957).

SCHÜRER, E., *The History of the Jewish People in the Age of Jesus Christ*[2], ed. G. Vermes *et al.*, 3 vols. (Edinburgh, 1973/79/86/87).

—— 'Über den gegenwärtigen Stand der johanneischen Frage', *Johannes und sein Evangelium*, ed. K. H. Rengstorf, 1–27.

SCHWARTZ, E., 'Aporien im vierten Evangelium', *Nachrichten von der Königlichen Gesellschaft der Wissenschaft zu Göttingen: Philologisch-historische Klasse* (1907), 342–72; (1908), 115–48; 149–88; 497–650.

SCHWEITZER, A., *The Mysticism of Paul the Apostle* (London, 1931).

—— *The Quest of the Historical Jesus*[3] (London, 1954 [1910]).

SCHWEIZER, E., *EGO EIMI* (Göttingen, 1965 [1939]).

—— 'Two New Testament Creeds Compared', *Current Issues in New Testament Interpretation: Essays in honor of Otto A. Piper*, ed. W. Klassen and G. W. Snyder (London, 1962), 166–77.

SCHWEIZER, E., 'Zum religionsgeschichtlichen Hintergrund der "Sendungs-formel": Gal. 4, 4 f.; Rm. 8, 3 f.; Joh. 3, 16 f.; 1 Joh 4, 9', *ZNW* 57 (1966), 199–210.

SCOTT, E. G., *The Fourth Gospel, its Purpose and Theology* (Edinburgh, 1906).

SEGAL, A. F., 'Judaism, Christianity and Gnosticism', *Anti-Judaism in Early Christianity*, ii. *Separation and Polemic*, ed. S. G. Wilson (Waterloo, Ontario, 1986), 133–61.

——'Ruler of This World: Attitudes about Mediator Figures and the Importance of Sociology for Self-Definition', *Jewish and Christian Self-Definition*, ii, ed. E. P. Sanders *et al.*, 245–68.

—— *Two Powers in Heaven: Early Rabbinic Reports about Christianity and Gnosticism* (Leiden, 1977).

SEGOVIA, F. F., 'John 15: 18–16: 4a: A First Addition to the Original Fare-well Discourse?', *CBQ* 45 (1983), 210–30.

—— 'The Structure, *Tendenz*, and *Sitz im Leben* of John 13: 31–14: 31', *JBL* 104 (1985), 471–93.

SIDEBOTTOM, F. M., *The Christ of the Fourth Gospel in the Light of First Century Thought* (London, 1961).

SIMON, M., *St. Stephen and the Hellenists in the Primitive Church* (London, 1958).

SLENCZKA, R., *Geschichtlichkeit und Personensein Jesu Christi: Studien zur christologischen Problematik der historischen Jesusfrage* (Göttingen, 1967).

SMALLEY, S. S., 'Keeping up with Recent Studies XII: St. John's Gospel', *ExpT* 97 (1985/6), 102–8.

SMITH, D. MOODY, *The Composition and Order of the Fourth Gospel* (New Haven/London, 1965).

—— *Johannine Christianity: Essays on its Setting, Sources, and Theology* (South Carolina, 1984).

—— 'John and the Synoptics: Some Dimensions of the Problem', *Johannine Christianity*, 145–72.

SMITH, J. Z., 'Good News is No News: Aretalogy and Gospel', *Map is not Territory* (Leiden, 1978), 190–270.

—— 'Prayer of Joseph', *Map is not Territory*, 24–66.

SMITH, M., 'On the History of ΑΠΟΚΑΛΥΠΤΩ and ΑΠΟΚΑΛΥΨΙΣ', *Apocalypticism in the Mediterranean World and the Near East*, ed. D. Hellholm (Tübingen, 1983), 9–20.

—— 'On the Wine God in Palestine (Gen. 18, Jn. 2 and Achilles Tatius)', *S. W. Baron Jubilee Volume*, ii, ed. S. Liebermann *et al.* (Jerusalem, 1974), 815–29.

—— *Palestinian Parties and Politics that Shaped the Old Testament* (London, 1987 [1971]).

—— 'Prolegomena to a Discussion of Aretalogies, Divine Men, the Gospels and Jesus', *JBL* 90 (1971), 174–99.

SOLTAU, G. C. W., *Das vierte Evangelium in seiner Entstehungsgeschichte dargelegt* (Heidelberg, 1916).

Bibliography 573

SPARKS, H. E. D. (ed.), *The Apocryphal Old Testament* (Oxford, 1984).

SPITTA, F., *Das Johannes-Evangelium als Quelle der Geschichte Jesu* (Göttingen, 1910).

—— *Zur Geschichte und Literatur des Urchristentums*, i (Göttingen, 1893).

STALEY, J. L., *The Print's First Kiss: A Rhetorical Investigation of the Implied Reader in the Fourth Gospel* (Atlanta, 1988).

STAUFFER, E., *New Testament* (London, 1955).

STOLZ, F., *Strukturen und Figuren im Kult von Jerusalem: Studien zur altorientalischen, vor- und frühisraelitischen Religion* (Berlin, 1970).

STONE, M. E., 'Lists of Revealed Things in the Apocalyptic Literature', *Magnalia Dei*, ed. F. M. Cross *et al.* (New York, 1976), 414–52.

—— *Scriptures, Sects and Visions: A Profile of Judaism from Ezra to the Jewish Revolts* (Philadelphia, 1980).

STRACK, H. L., and BILLERBECK, P., *Kommentar zum neuen Testament aus Talmud und Midrasch*[7], 6 vols. (Munich, 1978).

STRATHMANN, H., μάρτυς κτλ., *ThDNT*, iv, ed. G. Kittel, 474–514.

STRAUSS, D. F., *Das Leben Jesu für das deutsche Volk bearbeitet* (Leipzig, 1864).

—— *Das Leben Jesu kritisch bearbeitet* (Tübingen, 1835/6) [= *The Life of Jesus Critically Examined* (London, 1973 [1846])].

STRECKER, G., *Das Judenchristentum in den Pseudoklementinen* (Berlin, 1958).

STREETER, B. H., *The Four Gospels: A Study in Origins*[5] (London, 1936 [1924]).

STRUGNELL, J., 'The Angelic Liturgy at Qumran—4Q Serek Sîrôt 'Ôlat Hassabat', *SuppVT* 7 (1960), 308–45.

STUHLMACHER, P. (ed.), *Das Evangelium und die Evangelien* (Tübingen, 1973).

SUGGS, M. J., *Wisdom Christology and Law in Matthew's Gospel* (Cambridge, 1970), 71–97.

SUTER, D. W., '*Māšāl* in the Similitudes of Enoch', *JBL* 100 (1981), 193–212.

TALBERT, C. H., 'The Myth of a Descending-Ascending Redeemer in Mediterranean Antiquity', *NTS* 22 (1975/6), 418–43.

TAYLOR, V., 'The Fourth Gospel and Some Recent Criticism', *Hibbert Journal*, 25 (1926/7), 725–43.

—— *The Gospel according to St. Mark* (London, 1952).

TEEPLE, H. M., 'Qumran and the Origin of the Fourth Gospel', *NT* 4 (1960), 6–25.

THOMPSON, J. M., 'The Structure of the Fourth Gospel', *Expositor*, 10 (1915), 512–26.

THÜSING, W., *Die Erhöhung und Verherrlichung Jesu im Johannesevangelium*[2] (Münster, 1970 [1960]).

THYEN, H., 'Aus der Literatur zum Johannesevangelium': *TRu* 39 (1974), 1–69; 222–52; 289–330; 42 (1977), 211–70; 43 (1978), 328–59; 44 (1979), 97–134.

THYEN, H., 'Entwicklungen innerhalb der johanneischen Theologie und Kirche im Spiegel von Joh 21 und der Lieblingsjüngertexte des Evangeliums', *L'Évangile de Jean*, ed. M. de Jonge, 259–99.

—— '"Das Heil kommt von den Juden"', *Kirche: Festschrift für Günther Bornkamm zum 75. Geburtstag* (Tübingen, 1980), 163–84.

TORREY, C. C., '"When I am lifted up from the earth": John 12: 32', *JBL* 51 (1932), 320–2.

TUCKETT, C. (ed.), *The Messianic Secret* (London, 1983).

UNNIK, W. C. VAN, 'The Purpose of St. John's Gospel', *Studia Evangelica*, i [= *Texte und Untersuchungen*, 73 (Berlin, 1959), 382–411].

VANDERKAM, J. C., *Enoch and the Growth of an Apocalyptic Tradition* (Washington, 1984).

VANHOYE, A., 'Interrogation johannique et exégèse de Cana (Jn 2, 4)', *Bib* 55 (1974), 157–67.

—— 'L'Œuvre du Christ, don du Père (Jn 5, 36 et 17, 4)', *RScR* 48 (1960), 377–419.

VERMES, G., *The Dead Sea Scrolls in English*³ (London, 1987 [1962, 1975]).

—— *Jesus the Jew* (London, 1973).

VEYNE, P., *Les Grecs ont-ils cru à leurs mythes?* (Paris, 1983).

VOUGA, F., *Le Cadre historique et l'intention théologique de Jean* (Paris, 1977).

WAHLDE, U. C. VON, 'The Johannine Jews: A Critical Survey', *NTS* 28 (1982), 33–60.

—— 'The Terms for Religious Authorities in the Fourth Gospel: A Key to Literary-Strata?', *JBL* 98 (1979), 231–53.

WEAD, D. W., *The Literary Devices in the Fourth Gospel* (Basle, 1970).

WEIMER, P., 'Daniel: Eine Textanalyse', *Jesus und der Menschensohn*, ed. R. Pesch and R. Schnackenburg, 11–36.

WEISS, K. P. B., *Lehrbuch der biblischen Theologie des Neuen Testaments* (Berlin, 1868).

WEISSE, C. H., *Die Evangelienfrage in ihrem gegenwärtigen Stadium* (Leipzig, 1856).

—— *Die evangelische Geschichte kritisch und philosophisch bearbeitet* (Leipzig, 1838).

—— *Das Johannesevangelium als einheitliche Werk* (Berlin, 1912).

WEIZSÄCKER, C. VON, *Untersuchungen über die evangelische Geschichte* (Gotha, Stuttgart, 1864).

WELLHAUSEN, J., *Erweiterungen und Änderungen im vierten Evangelium* (Berlin, 1907).

WENGST, K., *Bedrängte Gemeinde und verherrlichter Christus: Der historische Ort des Johannesevangeliums als Schlüssel zu seiner Interpretation* (Neukirchen-Vluyn, 1981).

WETTER, G. A. P., *Der Sohn Gottes: Eine Untersuchung über den Charakter und die Tendenz des Johannes-Evangeliums* (Göttingen, 1916).

WILKENS, W., *Die Entstehungsgeschichte des vierten Evangeliums* (Zollikon, 1958).

WINDISCH, H., 'Angelophanien um den Menschensohn auf Erden: Zu Joh 1, 51', *ZNW* 30 (1931), 215–33.

—— 'Die fünf johanneische Parakletsprüche', *Festgabe für Adolf Jülicher zum 70. Geburtstag* (Tübingen, 1927), 110–37 [= *The Spirit-Paraclete in the Fourth Gospel*, trans. J. W. Cox (Philadelphia, 1968)].

—— 'Jesus und der Geist im Johannes-Evangelium', *Amicitiae Corolla: Essays presented to James Rendel Harris*, ed. H. G. Wood (London, 1933), 303–18.

WOLL, D. B., *Johannine Christianity in Conflict* (Ann Arbor, 1981).

WOUDE, A. S. VAN DER, 'Melchisedek als himmlische Erlösergestalt in den neugefundenen eschatologischen Midrashim aus Qumran Höhle XI', *OTS* 14 (1965), 354–73.

—— *Die messianischen Vorstellungen der Gemeinde von Qumran* (Assen, 1957).

WREDE, W., *Charakter und Tendenz des Johannesevangelium* (Tübingen, 1903).

—— *Das Messiasgeheimnis in den Evangelien* (Göttingen, 1901) [= *The Messianic Secret* (Cambridge/London, 1971)].

—— 'The Task and Methods of "New Testament Theology"', *The Nature of New Testament Theology*, ed. R. Morgan, 68–116.

YAMAUCHI, E., *Pre-Christian Gnosticism* (London, 1973).

INDEX OF REFERENCES

Bold print indicates that the passage in question is discussed in some detail.

Where reference is made to more than one note on the same page the numbers are not given.

Certain Christian writings, such as *The Ascension of Isaiah* are included, as is customary, among the Old Testament Pseudepigrapha.

INDEX OF MODERN AUTHORS